FRAMEWORKS
of POWER

Stewart R. Clegg

FRAMEWORKS
of POWER

2nd Edition

Los Angeles | London | New Delhi
Singapore | Washington DC | Melbourne

Los Angeles | London | New Delhi
Singapore | Washington DC | Melbourne

SAGE Publications Ltd
1 Oliver's Yard
55 City Road
London EC1Y 1SP

SAGE Publications Inc.
2455 Teller Road
Thousand Oaks, California 91320

SAGE Publications India Pvt Ltd
Unit No 323-333, Third Floor, F-Block
International Trade Tower Nehru Place
New Delhi 110 019

SAGE Publications Asia-Pacific Pte Ltd
3 Church Street
#10-04 Samsung Hub
Singapore 049483

Acquisitions Editor: Natalie Aguilera
Editorial Assistant: Daniel Price
Production Editor: Zoheb Khan and Neelu Sahu
Copyeditor: Diana Chambers
Proofreader: Genevieve Friar
Indexer: Avril Ehrlich
Marketing Manager: Ruslana Khatagova
Cover Design: Wendy Scott
Typeset by KnowledgeWorks Global Ltd
Printed in the UK

Library of Congress Control Number: 2022946357

British Library Cataloguing in Publication data

A catalogue record for this book is available from the British Library

ISBN 978-1-5264-5691-5
ISBN 978-1-5264-5692-2 (pbk)

At SAGE we take sustainability seriously. Most of our products are printed in the UK using responsibly sourced papers and boards. When we print overseas we ensure sustainable papers are used as measured by the PREPS grading system. We undertake an annual audit to monitor our sustainability.

DEDICATION

For my family

CONTENTS

Preface to the second edition   x
Acknowledgements   xii

1 Frameworks of Power Revisited   1
Antecedents   1
Paradoxes of power   5
Power theory: legislators and interpreters   8
Power and agency in the 'Community Power Debate'   11
Power and intention   13
Non-decision, mobilization of bias and the two faces of power   14
Power and three dimensions: a radical view   16
Dimensions of power and ordinary language   20
Agency and structure in the analysis of power   23
Dominant ideology and disciplinary power   25
Circuits of power   26
From a history of the past to a history of the present   29
Conclusion   31

2 Power: Traditional Roots, Modern Problems   33
Introduction   33
Hobbes   34
Hobbes' myth   37
Hobbes' choice and its conceptual extension   39
Machiavelli: the contrast with Hobbes   41
Metaphors for moderns: Hobbes and Machiavelli   46
Conclusion   48

3 Political Community, Methodological Procedures and the Agency Model   **51**

Introduction   51

Metaphorical continuities   53

Classical elitism   58

Floyd Hunter and the community power elite   60

Dahl's methodological challenge to contemporary elitism   62

Dahl's critique of the ruling elite model   68

Newton's critique of the pluralist model   71

Conclusion   76

4 The Power of Intention   **77**

Introduction   77

Some stories about power   78

Elaborating stories   80

Russell, Weber and Wrong: the power of intention   83

Bachrach and Baratz: the two faces of power?   86

Is power something actualized or not?   94

Conclusion   94

5 Lukes' Dimensions and Epistemology   **97**

Introduction   97

Lukes' three-dimensional model and the centrality of 'interests'   99

Habermas: real interests in ideal speech situations   103

Benton and the 'paradox of emancipation'   106

Lukes' model of power and structure   109

Power, interests and hegemony: Gaventa and Whitt   114

Interests and epistemology   125

Realism, causal powers and objectives   131

Conclusion   137

6 Giddens' Critique of Parsons and the Duality of Structure   **139**

Introduction   139

Parsons' power   140

Habermas on Parsons on power   143

Giddens on Parsons on power   145

Giddens' duality of structure   148

Conclusion   157

7 Post-structuralism, Sovereign Power and Disciplinary Power   **159**

Introduction   159

Post-structuralism and Foucault   160

Disciplinary power, bio-power and sovereign power   163

Sovereign power and its conceptual overextension into dominant ideology   169

Disciplinary power and the dissolution of the sovereign power conception   176

From structural ideology to post-structuralist hegemony in Laclau and Mouffe   187

Radical conceptions of power compared   191

Conclusion   193

8 Circuits of Power: a Framework for Analysis   **197**

Introduction   197

Power in organizations   199

Mechanisms of power: disciplinary practices of surveillance   200

Organization and agency   203

Strategic agency   208

The reformation of power: the contributions of Callon, Latour and colleagues   212

Power and resistance   216

Rules and power   218

Episodic agency power: the 'normal power' of social science   221

Organizational outflanking of resistance: Mann's contribution   227

Social integration and system integration: dispositional and facilitative power
    respectively   232

Conclusion   247

9 Constituting Circuits of Power in Modernity   **249**

Introduction   249

Urbanism as a feudal nodal point   250

Centralized states and the emergence of 'public' administration   259

Markets and states and power   264

The modern constitutional nation state   272

Conclusion   278

10 A History of the Present   **281**

Introduction   281

Dis/integration and dominant myths   285

From integration by repression to disintegration by reform   287

Integrations' consequences, West and East   289

Solidarities   294

The Covid-19 crisis   297

The climate crisis   307
Becoming reflexive about actants' effects   310
Responsibilities and power   313
In conclusion   318

   Post-modern postscript   319
   References   322
   Index   355

PREFACE TO THE SECOND EDITION

Frameworks of Power was the product of a period in my professional life that was relatively less busy than subsequently proved to be the case. As Professor of Sociology at the University of New England I mostly taught two subjects, on Power and Conflict and Power and the State, largely to students studying by correspondence. Between classes, apart from what in retrospect seems to have been remarkably little administrative load as a Head of Department, considerable time was available for reading, reflection and writing. It was in this mileu that many of the ideas that entered 'Frameworks' were initially developed. Subsequently, life became busier as continents were changed, different jobs taken, diverse research fields entered and different university regimes dealt with, all ensuring that the second edition of this book was a lot longer in the making than I had ever intended. So many other books and papers, revisions and further editions delayed the task, not to mention the increasing commitments attached to being a busy academic.

Then there was the question of what a second edition should be. I envisaged rewriting every chapter, updating them with subsequent debates, a process that began with extensive consultation of papers in the *Journal of Political Power*. A host of other commitments rapidly crowded out the time available, notably collaborations producing various editions of books which, in concert with numerous revisions and resubmissions of journal articles, eclipsed that ambition within a few months of its initial undertaking.[1] Had this not been the case, the labours of my friend, Mark Haugaard (2020a), surveying the scene from his vantage point as the founding editor of the *Journal of Political Power*, would have served to make the exercise somewhat unnecessary. While I had considered summarizing the several empirical papers that I, together with others, had published using the circuits of power framework (e.g., Major et al., 2018; Oliviera and Clegg 2015) or that others had used (e.g., Davenport and Leitch 2005; Hutchinson et al., 2010; Silva and Backhouse 2003; Smith et al., 2010; Vaara et al., 2005), this seemed to be lacking in coherent narrative possibilities.

---

1 The most recent of which are Clegg, Pitelis, Schweitzer and Whittle, 2022; Clegg, Mount and Pitsis, 2021, and Clegg, Skyttermoen and Vaagaasar, 2021.

David Jones, of Northumbria University, unknowingly solved my problem of what the second edition should comprise. He asked me to present an online talk to the Baltic seminar (named after the Baltic Centre in Newcastle, where the talks were held, before COVID-19). I agreed and gave some thought to what I would write about. It was shortly after Russia invaded Ukraine. Russia and Ukraine were matters I had written about previously, in 2014, when Russia seized Crimea (Clegg 2014). A little later, in 2015, I wrote about Russia again, in terms of the collapse of the USSR (Deroy and Clegg 2015). Additionally, I had recently written on COVID-19, with my colleagues Miguel Pina e Cunha and Marco Berti (Cunha et al., 2021a), as well as on climate crisis (Heikkurinen et al., 2021). I drew on these contributions to present my talk and I am indebted to my colleagues for sharing their ideas with me, which I have added and subtracted from to produce the new chapter, 'A History of the Present', for this edition. I should stress that the indefinite article is important in the title of this chapter. Chapter 10 is an account of these recent crises – COVID-19, the climate crisis and the war in Ukraine – seen through the circuits of power framework, the central concept of the first edition.

Generous comments on earlier drafts were provided by David Jones, Mark Haugaard and Daphne Freeder, while Marco Berti provided feedback at the initial proof stage. David advised a restructuring of themes which improved the overall structure; Mark engaged in a critical dialogue with the text, which I incorporated into a penultimate revision; Daphne gracefully offered nuance on some of the events written about in the last chapter, which I accepted as a final revision, glad that she had noted the need for such nuance. Close readers of the first edition may note modifications. Substantively, some examples were updated and the occasional infelicity edited, as were technical errors arising from digital reproduction of the floppy discs of the original text. Redrafting is an ever-present possibility and there comes a time when the computer must be closed, the draft saved, the manuscript submitted. Marco's insights, as ever, were acutely relevant.

Having reached this stage, a final reflection. In the Introduction to the first edition of this book, I remarked that many of the texts to be addressed constituted major circuits of power in the academic marketplace. In writing those words I harboured the aspiration that *Frameworks of Power* might also become such a circuit. I hope that this second edition continues to warrant that aspiration.

Stewart Clegg
Sydney
2 December 2022

ACKNOWLEDGEMENTS (FIRST EDITION)

In this acknowledgement, revised to accommodate life's passing, I acknowledge all who have aided me in writing the first edition of this book. First, some universities, chief among which was the University of New England, which allowed me study leave to be able to work on this, among other projects, and the University of Otago in Dunedin, New Zealand, whose Department of Management invited me to spend some time with them while I was completing the book. The period which I spent there during the latter part of 1988 will long be remembered not only for the warmth and friendship of individuals but also for the stimulation of the intellectual environment. In addition, towards the end of 1988 when I was making late revisions to the manuscript, I was fortunate to be able to use the excellent facilities provided by the Department of Social Policy and Sociology at the University of Leeds. The final revisions were undertaken in Hong Kong during the first few weeks of 1989, when I was a Visiting Professor in the University of Hong Kong, Department of Management Studies. The customary warmth and collegiality of the department, particularly in the form of Gordon Redding, with whom I was at the time collaborating on another project, were, as always, stimulating.

Second, I would like to acknowledge some institutions. The ones I have in mind, like most enjoyable institutions, are really loose networks of people, the most immediate of which are the Australian and Pacific Researchers in Organization Studies (APROS) whose colloquia and seminars over the years provided collegial scholarship and exchange of ideas, even between antagonists. Thanks should also be expressed to the European Group for Organization Studies (EGOS) under whose auspices much of the initial background for this book was acquired, and in whose conferences and publications many subsequent ideas were first elaborated.

Third, I would like to acknowledge some places and people that helped lay foundations for this academic life. I refer to the Grammar School, Elland, Yorkshire; the universities of Bradford and Aston; Griffith University, Brisbane,where I held my first significant appointment as an academic, as well as the International Institute of Management in Berlin, that funded my post-doctoral research prior to taking that appointment. As so much knowledge is institutionally sustained and yet not acknowledged as such, I wish to take this opportunity to place my appreciation on record. Each of these institutions enabled a young man, growing up in a small deindustrializing mill town in West Yorkshire, to broaden his horizons and achieve things he had barely dreamed of attempting.

The people whom I wish to thank as part of the context of the first edition were many. In the decade prior to writing the first edition I had probably spent more time working with Paul Boreham and Geoff Dow than anyone else. They were an enduring source of discussion and issues with which to grapple. The other collaborators with whom I worked chiefly during this period were Winton Higgins and Wai-Fong Chua. John Western[†] was a good friend and colleague for a long time. Some of the issues canvassed in the book arose in the course of our collaboration both as editors and researchers. Another member of the small group of scholars with whom I worked in Brisbane is Mike Emmison. Some of our discussions and collaboration, especially about ethnomethodology, entered this book.

For many years, Zygmunt Bauman, David Hickson and David Silverman were among my correspondents, sources of friendship, and occasional visitors from the UK. It would be hard not to have learned something from them over all the years and I hope that I have not failed in this respect. Sadly, only the latter is still with us. As a Visiting Professor, David is to be found, when pandemics permit, wintering in Coogee for the British Winter between presenting workshops on qualitative research. I profited greatly from friendship and exchange of ideas with Peter Blunt, Barry Hindess, Bob Holton, Jane Marceau, Michael Pusey and Bryan Turner during the years preceding the production of the first edition; sadly Jane and Barry no longer live, except in memory and contributions. In the Department of Sociology at the University of New England, Ellie Vasta and I spent many hours discussing issues connected with feminist and post-structuralist theory. In addition, with respect to aspects of this particular project, former colleagues in the Department of Sociology at the University of New England, with whom I lost contact as a result of subsequent shifts of continent on my part, freely shared time and patience with me. The Department of Sociology at the University of New England proved to be a congenial host for the initial writing of this book in its first edition.

It is appropriate to acknowledge the prior publication of some of the ideas in the first edition of the book in earlier papers. Some use is made in Chapter 7 of arguments that were first advanced in a paper co-authored with Mike Emmison and Paul Boreham. The paper was called 'Against Antinomies: For a Post-Marxist Politics' and was published by *Thesis Eleven* (1987/88, 18: 124–42). Some of Chapter 8 comprises material contained in a paper published in *Organization Studies* (2 (1): 101–19) as 'Radical Revisions: Power, Discipline and Organization'. With these exceptions, the remainder of the book made its first appearance here.

A number of colleagues were kind enough to share their assessment of the manuscript with me in order that I might improve it as a result of their comments. In particular,

Malcolm Lewis and Ralph Stablein, the latter sadly passed, colleagues from the Department of Management at the University of Otago, read and discussed the manuscript with me as it evolved during the time that I spent there. I gained a great deal from our discussions. Others who commented on the drafts of the first edition of the manuscript included David Hickson[†], David Silverman, Zygmunt Bauman[†], Winton Higgins, Lucien Karpik, Richard Hall[†], John Mayer, John Child, Ric Collignon, Tony Spybey, Gary Hamilton and Derek Layder. As with all of the good advice and support that kind people and institutions offered over the years, I am sure that I probably did not heed nearly enough of it; indeed, I know that I did not, particularly as I tried to effect closure on the project of writing. Consequently, the usual clause applies: no one of those mentioned is in any way responsible for what I have written. That responsibility still lies with the notion of the author.

ACKNOWLEDGEMENTS
(SECOND EDITION)

The concept of power is *the* central concept of the social sciences (Clegg and Haugaard 2009) and the central issue in *all* forms of politics and organization, especially when it is not openly acknowledged to be so. Power is ubiquitous. In my earlier treatment of the concept in this first edition of this book, there is very little that I would revise or resile from; consequently, very little has changed, other than in the first chapter and the new concluding chapter.

In many ways, this second edition of *Frameworks of Power* connects to conversations and ideas engaged in with a network of collaborators, from all of whom I have learnt, over many years. These include Mark Haugaard, Miguel Pina e Cunha, Arménio Rego, Marco Berti, Ace Simpson, Luca Giuistiano, Pasi Heikkurinen, Ashly Pinnington and Xavier Deroy as well as, from further back in time, Cynthia Hardy, while even further back, the work that I did with Geoff Dow and Paul Boreham was influential in understanding politics.

I have gained a great deal from collaborations with all these people but there are many others, people whose contributions to the ideas in this book are not as evident but who have been a continuing source of inspiration, collaboration and critique. To all these people, I say "I thank you", echoing David Porter and Isaac Hayes' (1968) sentiment that it is a great experience to share time with people pulling something new out of the bag, new things that one needs to try hard to keep up with. Above all, however, one person deserves thanks: without the support, understanding and love of Caroline Lynne, few of the things accomplished would have been possible.

1
FRAMEWORKS OF POWER REVISITED

ANTECEDENTS

While *Frameworks of Power* was neither the first nor the last book that I wrote about the topic of power, it has undoubtedly been the most influential. I had started working on the concept of power for a PhD at the University of Bradford where colleagues introduced me to Bachrach and Baratz and their critique of the community power debate (1962; 1963; 1970) to add to my reading of Dahl (1957) and other more behavioural theorists who wrote about causal power. My thinking about power was less in terms of the evident positivism of approaches such as Dahl's (1957) stipulations, being more oriented to the social construction of phenomena, sparked by Bachrach and Baratz's contributions to the 'community power debate', read in the context of a general appreciation of interpretative sociology.

To sketch what issues and non-issues might mean in practice, an empirical contribution was required. I spent several months in fieldwork on a construction site, mostly in the project office, using a tape recorder which I would trigger when talk started. The data collected was reported in *Power, Rule and Domination* (1975; 2013) the book produced from the thesis. My understanding, in coming to terms with the discourses of the site, was guided by ethnomethodology's view that everyone is a practical theorist, doing everyday theorizing to make sense of situations and events. Drawing on Wittgenstein (1968), whom ethnomethodology's founder, Garfinkel (1967), briefly refers to in *Studies in Ethnomethodology*, I reasoned that what people said could be considered as a surface structure, the underlying rules of which one could formulate analytically.

One key issue was about what kind of clay was 'normal'. An interaction sequence concerning 'normal clay' only made sense in terms of the inherent indexicality of contractual documents. Their interpretation depended on what party, with what interests, was doing the interpreting. For the project manager the contractual documents' indexicality afforded an opportunity to squeeze more profit from the project through claims for variation orders. The contractual documents could be interpreted opportunistically to constitute issues in certain sorts of ways that the client representative resisted. It was mundane discussions about clay that helped me access an underlying deep structure. It occurs to me now, after all these years, that it was ironical that an insight about the empirical application of the idea of deep structure related, literally, to digging beneath the surface.

I came up with a scheme with three structural levels. First, there was the surface structure – what the members of the project said in the everyday processes of work. Second, underlying this was what I thought of as a deep structure, the ways in which implicit rules formed a coherent mode of rationality underlying speech. These provided grounds and auspices for action that analysis established as contextually coherent even if not explicable as such when being spoken. In an analogy with grammar, speakers did not formulate the rules in use while speaking. Third, there was another level – a deeper structure, which, after Wittgenstein (1968), I termed 'form of life'. The form of life revolved around profit as the icon of capitalism, which proved pivotal in the data analysis as I realized the centrality of the contract and its indexicality to practices on site. Each level corresponded respectively to power, rule and domination.

These ideas about theorizing stayed with me a long time; in fact, they never went away. They resurfaced, quite explicitly, in a much later argument about the nature of theorizing in management and organization studies (Clegg et al., 2022). Different interests (both in terms of 'object of curiosity' and of 'something that brings advantage') are involved in the development of different ways to approach and interpret the subject of power. Different research movements shape their intellectual production not just in relation to formal philosophical reasoning but because of practical social interactions. Theorizing is not merely a question of different intellectual inclinations but represents a political, social, practical stance: in other words, power relations have an impact on how we think about power, (something elaborated further in Clegg et al., (1986/2013) in its conception of political economy). Theories not only strive to represent reality but also performatively shape practices that, in turn, shape, theorizing, which holds for both 'lay' and 'professional' theorizing. Theorizing as a professional practice is more formalized, ritualized and institutionalized than lay theorizing, but it is not essentially different. There are different grammars of theorizing; as McHugh (1970, p. 335) sagely advised: "No canon, no collective, no institution can go outside itself to a world of independent objects for criteria of knowledge, since there is no other way except by its own rules to describe what's being done with regard to knowledge."

Shortly after finishing the Doctoral thesis I dispatched it for production as *Power, Rule and Domination: A Critical and Empirical Understanding of Power in Sociological Theory and Organizational Life*. The book was first published in 1975, after a delay caused, according to my editor at Routledge, Peter Hopkins, by the loss of the proofread manuscript by

British Mail. Visiting Routledge's Dickensian offices, near St. Paul's Cathedral in London, I sought to reconstruct my sense of the proof reading that had been lost from the uncorrected manuscript they held there. While I waited for the book to be produced, Steven Lukes' book on *Power: A Radical View* (1974) was published. Intriguingly, in parallel and unknown to me, Lukes (1974), with exemplary brevity, had developed a tripartite division of power into three dimensions that seemed similar in many respects to the levels of power that I had developed as a model. He was not the only one.

Giddens' books, written in the late 1970s, were always an event to anticipate. Hence, when *New Rules of Sociological Method* (Giddens 1976), arrived in my mailbox, I read it with great interest. It was a very sharp departure from his earlier work on the great three founding fathers of sociology, Marx, Weber and Durkheim. In the book was a table that was similar in several respects to the schema of power, rule and domination that I had devised (Clegg, 1975/2013, p. 78). It seemed evident that Lukes, Giddens and I had been reading some similar material and had drawn similar conclusions. While Giddens had clearly been reading phenomenology and ethnomethodology, as I had also been doing, which I think Lukes had not, Lukes had been reading the 'community power debate', which Giddens did not discuss. Nonetheless, we all ended up with a tripartite and structural analysis of power.

Subsequently, I published *The Theory of Power and Organization* (Clegg 1979/2013), a book that emerged from postdoctoral work in which I sought to take account of Lukes' (1974) three dimensions of power and connect it to broader theoretical debates in sociology. *The Theory of Power and Organization* incorporated debate around Gramscian and Marxist approaches. Prior to Lukes' (1974) book, I had not been familiar with Gramsci. That book added a more structural account to that outlined in the first book, opening routes to more macro thinking. If Marxist analyses resolved all the analytical problems involved in discussing power, the articulation of the concept of 'hegemony' (discussed in detail in Clegg, 1979/2013) would probably be the final analytical move in understanding power's conceptual interpretation. Notions of cultural hegemony (e.g., Connell 1976) have been perennially popular, in the past, as categories of a 'dominant ideology' (Abercrombie et al. 1980). More recently, in a latter-day version of the representative democracy arguments that go back to Schattschneider (1960), the notion of dominant ideology has been repurposed in terms of intersectionality, in which dominant ideas of ethnicity, gender, sexuality, class and embodied ability are seen as sources of cultural hegemony, symbolic and actual violence (Liu 2018) present in legitimations that lack social and demographic representativeness to support them.

In the early 1970s I had read Foucault's *The Archaeology of Knowledge* (1972). Subsequently, I hadn't read much Foucault, until *Discipline and Punish* (1977). What was most notable was that Foucault on power was entirely disconnected from the debates about power that framed the contemporary literature that I was familiar with in political science, sociology and organization studies. Reading Foucault inspired me to return to power as a topic once more. What seemed evident was that the work of Foucault and other 'post-structuralist' texts could not be readily assimilated to a narrative flow whose terminus is another version of Lukes' (1974) hegemonic third dimension – although this has not stopped many scholars from making the effort.

Armed with new insights that drew on Foucault, I produced a short paper that ended up being published as 'Radical Revisions' (Clegg 1989) in *Organization Studies*. It was initially presented to some senior EGOS scholars of the day at a small seminar in Wassenaar, where its reception was so unacknowledged as to constitute what I thought initially was hostile indifference; subsequently, I realized that it might have been a matter of established orthodoxy being confronted with material that seemed paradoxical. Undeterred, indeed, empowered to tell my story, despite indifference, I started work on what became the first edition of this book, *Frameworks of Power*.

One of the starting points for *Frameworks of Power* was a critique of Lukes' third dimension because it assumed a position that grants omnipotent power to a theorist who knows people's real interests better than they did themselves. It ascribes the theorist an extraordinarily privileged position of making visible what is invisible to the benighted. In a realm as interpretative and changing as social theory, this is neither justifiable nor democratic. Perhaps if one were to be in the position of trying to manage the effects of something such as a contagion spreading, by consulting professional epidemiologists, it might be different? Perhaps not: the unfolding of various national and regional politics of the COVID-19 pandemic in relation to different scientific professional judgements suggest otherwise. What is indubitable is that while a virus has no interest other than a proclivity to reproduce and mutate, many different interests come into play in interpreting its nature and limiting its impact on and transmission to human hosts. Science is rarely as disinterested as some of its philosophers represent it as being.

I began *Frameworks of Power* by consulting foundational works in the emergence of modern ideas about power. I read Hobbes ([1651] 1962) and Machiavelli ([1532] 1958) for the first time. Reading *Leviathan*, I saw that, many hundreds of years previously, almost all the ideas framing the behavioural models of much contemporary scholarship seemed to be prefigured there. Power is equivalent to cause, was effectively Hobbes' message. My initial introduction to Machiavelli came through reading Sheldon S. Wolin's (1960) remarkable *Politics and Vision*. After reading *The Prince* (Machiavelli 1958), becoming familiar with Machiavelli observing the strategies, scheming and plotting of courtly life, I could better see how the Machiavellian approach to power had influenced Gramsci, whose reflections on Machiavelli I had read previously. Once I had read Machiavelli, I discerned foundations for an alternative way of thinking about power, much closer to Foucault. Doing this was crucial in resolving a paradox.

PARADOXES OF POWER

There is a tension between Machiavelli and Hobbes' approaches to power. Approached from the standard behaviourally influenced perspectives that stressed power as a causal concept between spatially and temporally related actors, Machiavelli did not easily fit in with modern approaches, while Hobbes' insistence in regarding power as a causal concept did. The contrast between Hobbes and Machiavelli provided grounds for thinking about a conception of power that was more processual and less behavioural, a tradition of research from which Foucault's concept of power did not seem as estranged as might seem if one took Dahl's (1959) work as foundational text.

The paradoxical continuity and discontinuity defining the initial research question of *Frameworks of Power* is inscribed in a trajectory from Hobbes to Lukes, a line linking the doyen of seventeenth-century political theory to late twentieth-century social science. There is an obvious difficulty in fixing a co-ordinate anywhere on this imaginary line, which would be a point of entry for some more recent debates, particularly those sparked by the work of Foucault. The central issue would be how and where to intersect debates about power centred on conceptions of causality and agency with others that call into question the premises of such a narrative. Until these questions became apparent, the debates appeared to have a relatively coherent character. Reference was usually made to a distinct causal conception of power and then arguments were constructed about its theoretical specification: how to conceptualize it, to what it should refer, and how it should apply methodologically to the collection of what types of data. The causal narrative is a central element in the modern understanding of power.

The 'modernism' of the equation of power and causality in mainstream writers such as Dahl (1958) has been challenged. Theorists such as Ball (1975; 1976; 1978) carefully inspected the archaeology of knowledge constituting contemporary political science, which differentiated it from more classical political philosophy. Ball (1975; 1976) correctly points to the continuities stretching from Hobbes to Dahl. Moreover, there was also an underlying tacit and constitutive conception of power formulated after the manner of 'sovereignty': power as a locus of will, as a supreme agency to which other wills would bend, as prohibitive; the classic conception of power as zero-sum; in short, power as negation of the power of others, as Foucault (1981) was to argue. It was models of causality that framed the genealogy connecting Hobbes to Dahl. For Hobbes, these models were best expressed through analogies with clockwork. Subsequently, the adequacy of that conception of causality, fixed by models derived from the 'regularity' principles of David Hume (1902), has been challenged by writers in the philosophy of science, such as Harré and Madden (1975). New questions for the analysis of power but also interesting angles on old debates were posed by these different conceptions of causality. Evident interruptions and discontinuities became discernible that earlier debates about power had not dwelt on.

Lukes (1974) had felt able to characterize 'power' as a concept that had a common essence subject to endless contestation. It was, he suggested, an 'essentially contested concept'. If one accepted these terms, a reasonably coherent narrative could indeed be constructed from Hobbes through Lukes, even into some of the subsequent debates contingent on the latter's work. The terms defining causality were not unproblematic. For one thing, although an agency conception of power had been constituted as central to the debate, some writers had postulated a dispositional conception (Wrong 1979), in which power was equated with a set of capacities, while others had suggested a facilitative conception, following Parsons' (1967) lead, in which power was regarded in terms of its ability to achieve goals, to get things done. This was to stress power as something positive rather than as something negative. Among those who followed this path was Foucault (1977; 1981). None of these conceptions fitted easily into a narrative structure constructed around a single, essentially contested conception of power. Moreover, while the extant debates centred on defining, conceptualizing and measuring power, Foucault's usage was by contrast quite distinctive; indeed, it was almost cavalier by comparison. Power was rarely pinned down or specified in terms related specifically to the debates as one knew them. Instead, it was constantly referred to as a 'practice', as associated with 'discipline', with the 'drilling' of bodies, particularly through notions of discourse: medical discourse, psychiatric discourse, and so on. By contrast to the mainstream of careful debate deriving from Dahl (1957; 1958; 1968), Foucault's influence seemed to be promiscuously metaphorical where one had been schooled to anticipate more clinical precision.

The well-established tradition that virtually equated the exercise of power with a classical conception of causality reached back as far as Hobbes. Thomas Hobbes (1651), in his famous book on state power, *Leviathan*, saw the essence of power as contained in the metaphor of clockwork. Clockwork, as an assembly of cogs, wheels and springs, could be calibrated to create an orderly representation of time passing. What fascinated Hobbes was the set of causal relations so apparent in the uses of clockwork: wind up the mechanism of a clock and a predictable set of relations between cogwheels would produce a predictable result, if a prime mover maintained the clockwork as tightly wound. For this reason, Hobbes argued that cause is equivalent to power.

Dahl's definition of power added the notion of constraint to Hobbes. For Dahl, when an A gets a B to do something that the B would not otherwise do, power is exercised. For power to be exercised, it would be targeted at another and signified by constraining their freedom of action. For Dahl, there could be no power at a distance; the metaphorical clockwork had to be connected. I became more sympathetic to Dahl's position when writing the first edition of this book than had previously been the case. Dahl was trying to frame the concept of power with empirical protocols that did not rely on reputational measures but an empirical reckoning of actions. The reputational methodology in the community power debate (Mills 1959) was not as rigorous as Dahl's focus on decision-making.

Dahl put some empirically observable parameters around power with his notions of scope, domain, and so on.

Extending and questioning the classical causal argument

Many subsequent contributors to debates about power did not seek to replace the classical causal argument. Instead, they sought to repair it. Suitably restyled, the logic of classical causality might be stretched to incorporate whatever absence was problematic. In the literature of power, attempts were commonly made to repair causal argument by recourse to admitting things other than merely observable events might have the status of causes. Most notable among the candidates were 'intentions': what people actually thought and intended to happen, usually expressed in terms of the 'reasons' that people might give for their actions. These, it has been argued, had an explanatory and causal role to play in the analysis of power. I shall return to this point subsequently to explain why, in matters of power, some theorists do not trust what people say about their intentions and interests.

It is possible not only to construct a central tradition to power, incorporating the debates with which writers such as Lukes had dealt. One can explain equally well-grounded but seemingly alternative conceptions of power. An instance would be the contrast between the centrality of notions of causality for Hobbes (1962) and the stress on organization and strategy which could be found in Machiavelli (1958). Machiavelli is a classical writer equally as renowned as Hobbes. Where Hobbes sets out the terms of a debate around a conception of sovereignty and community, Machiavelli initiated a concern with strategy and organization. Machiavelli's concerns with power were quite distinct from those of Hobbes and, to be truthful, far less in keeping with what became the modernist project of power in the twentieth century. Machiavelli's conception of power was imprecise, contingent, strategic and organizational, whereas the central tradition has sought precision usually cast in implicitly individualist terms. Moreover, its core was a conception of necessity through causality rather than a more contingent interpretation. Nonetheless, Machiavelli's work was to have a particular resonance in one country in the late twentieth century. In France, some writers found Machiavelli's approach explicitly congenial in the intellectual climate that prevailed during the 1970s. The climate was one in which a post-'68 suspicion of Marxism combined with a realization of the profoundly contingent and unprincipled nature of power's actual play as it frequently moved unbeholden to the grand scripts of history as interpreted by theorists of whatever political persuasion. Among these writers were Foucault (1981) and Callon (1986). What was implied was a distinctive interpretation of both Machiavelli and the concept of power.

In terms of the subsequent trajectory of mid-twentieth century scholarship and research on power, Hobbes' conception appeared to be the intellectual victor. Coming as it did a century later than Machiavelli, its metaphors accorded with and represented the more modernist spirit of an emerging scientific project, doing so with greater causal clarity than Machiavelli's frequent recourse to military analogies. As the new modernist age of reason developed, the leading exponents, whatever else they thought they might have accomplished, believed that 'militant' or military society was due to be abolished in the future (Spencer 1893).

It was to be the metaphorically mechanical, modernist spirit that was appropriated by some of the most successful mid-twentieth-century writers on power. For these texts, power was to be conceived in positivist terms as something directly observable and measurable. Many who joined the debate on power in the twentieth century were to find a mechanical metaphorical spirit more than congenial. It was, for instance, central to mainstream organization studies accounts of power in which control of some strategic resources, such as uncertainty, became an orthodox pillar for explaining who had power in organizations (Hickson et al. 1971; Hinings et al. 1974; Salancik and Pfeffer 1977). Metaphorically, Hobbes' clockwork was now assumed to be the set of structural relationships between the sub-unit 'cogs, wheels and springs' of an organization. These went out of balance when one sub-unit element controlled a highly strategically contingent uncertainty for the organization. For the personnel controlling this strategic uncertainty, if they were able to position themselves, in the terms of a later parlance, as valuable, rare, inimitable and non-substitutable, it was predicted that, in theory (if not in practice), they *could* have strategic power to strike beneficial bargains over others in the organization.

POWER THEORY: LEGISLATORS AND INTERPRETERS

The difference between Hobbes and Machiavelli can be expressed in simple terms. Where Hobbes and his successors may be said to have endlessly legislated on what power is, Machiavelli and his successors may be said to have interpreted what power does. The distinction between 'legislators' and 'interpreters' is derived from Zygmunt Bauman (1987). It is meant to capture the difference between a knowledge whose origin is wholly implicated with state power and one that is quite divorced from it.

Hobbes, the archetypal early modern theorist of power, was a classic legislator. He provided a rationalized account of the order that state power could produce. In addition, he was a servant of power. Hobbes was a tutor of the influential Cavendish family (Hamilton 1978), as well as of the exiled King Charles II (Malcolm 2002). Hobbes' *Leviathan* was 'a relatively autonomous, self-managing discourse' (Bauman 1987: 2) which generated an explicit model of order. Machiavelli's concerns, by contrast, were of necessity at some remove from the role of legislator. Not only did he fail to serve a strong unified state power, but he was also spurned by the state power in which he resided, imprisoned by the Medici and then isolated on his farm in Fiesole, outside of the centres of power. When Machiavelli lost his position in the Chancery, from which the Medici dismissed him in 1512, he could only interpret from afar rather than seek to legislate, distilling experience interpretatively in *The Prince* (Butters 2010). While *The Prince* is a lively reflection of interpretative musings on the observation of power at work, Machiavelli did not seek to produce a legislator's model of order. In contrast to Hobbes, he wrote only to interpret the strategies of power rather than to fix and serve power, the opportunity to do which was denied him by the Medici return to rule after the end of the Republic. By Bauman's (1987) criteria, he was 'postmodern' before even modernity: an intellectual writing on the state and on power, but, through the politics of his time and place, separated from both power and the state.

Machiavelli presents an alluring model for some significant writers on power. For instance, the Florentine's emphases accorded in some respects with the strategic, local, and practical concerns implicit in Gramsci's invocation of the modern Prince (Hoare and Nowell-Smith, 1971a). Moreover, both were marginal figures, excluded from state power, imprisoned and tortured (Pierpoint, 2008 on Machiavelli and the use of the *strappado*; Hoare and Smith 1971b, on the denial of medical care to Gramsci). Their concerns with strategy as diffuse process rather than the proclamation of a singular event were also attractive for late twentieth-century writers, such as Laclau and Mouffe (1985), as well as Foucault. In Foucault's dissection of discursive practices, one would also reveal a strategic, non-totalizing concern with power. This is not to say that Foucault was in some sense a lineal intellectual descendant of Machiavelli. What an irony that would be, considering Foucault's (1972) strictures on the myth of origins in *The Archaeology of Knowledge*. Rather, it is to acknowledge that both writers confronted a similar problematic. For Machiavelli, this was interpreting the strategy and organization that seemed most likely to secure an ordered totality of power in a scene characterized by a flux, a vortex, of politics. Foucault's concern in his later work was with how ordered totalities, such as existed in institutional form and discursive practice, which secured the 'birth of the clinic' and the power of the 'medical gaze' as well as the 'medical subject', could have been constructed. What strategies and what organization secured these powerful outcomes? The continuity, such as it is, is of a problematic rather than anything else.

Hobbes, by contrast with Machiavelli, sought to legitimate a myth of order premised on sovereignty. Since he was writing over a hundred years after Machiavelli, it is not surprising that the terms in which he did this drew on contemporary intellectual tools for constructing order. For instance, Malcolm (2002) stresses not only Hobbes' growing interest in mathematics but also in physical sciences. Machiavelli, the frustrated schemer, the calculating would-be adviser to a prince of a minor power, was naturally consigned, outside certain European traditions, to a primarily historical role in political theory. His advice came wrapped in aphorisms rather than the discourses of the emerging science. Hence, Machiavelli's work was not really a metaphorical constituent of the modernist project of power. That project was sparked from the complex mechanics of clockwork, connecting cogs, moving hands, keeping time, maintaining temporal order.

Given the context in which these early modern debates were situated and to which they were addressed, when one looks at them contemporaneously it is not difficult to recapture a sense of Machiavelli's project. It represents a full-blown, if somewhat marginalized, way of seeing power, one with perhaps more relevance in these allegedly 'postmodern times' than the victorious modernist project whose ground was sketched by Hobbes. The latter project has been characterized by a narrative sweep orchestrated from that mythical, heroic, modernist law-bringer whose role was so central to Hobbes' *Leviathan*. The apotheosis of these tendencies is the radical perspective of Lukes (1974). Here, power extends even into the other's thoughts and consciousness. No more sovereign sweep could be imagined than is encapsulated by this indebtedness to a Marxian problematic of 'false consciousness'.

Projects more aligned to those of Machiavelli tend to undercut the sense of a total score in favour of more contingent and local interpretation. It is in this sense that Foucault's 'postmodern' world of flux and discontinuity is more closely aligned with the early modern world of Machiavelli's Florence. It shares an analytical focus on and fascination for shifting, unstable alliances, a concern for military strategy and a disinclination to believe in any single origin and decisive centre of power. In addition, it was a world experienced by two men who, for different reasons, observed social realities and history from the margins of normative order; Foucault, discriminated against categorically because of a sexuality held to be deviant for much of his life; Machiavelli, as one discriminated against by the Medici because of his service to the Republic of Florence (Pierpoint 2008). Hence, there is some distance between their perspectives and the mythical world of order that is represented so positively by Hobbes. Hobbes' representations have left their mark on modern theories' insistence on the causal, atomistic, mechanical nature of power relations, views that remain implicit in the insistence on prime movement and first causes in behavioural and one-dimensional views of power.

In the terms of this book, both Hobbes and Marx would represent archetypal modernist thinkers. Both were committed to notions of the necessity of order. Marx, of course, differed in his conception of the likelihood of it ever being achieved under the existing political economy, given the tendencies to disorder that prevailed in his conceptualization of capitalist circuits of production. Many subsequent Marxists have explained the persistence of these circuits in terms of the ruling hegemony that capitalist social and state relations are presumed to have ensured. Of late, these accounts have lost considerable intellectual credence as they came under not only political attack (which, of course, is nothing new) but also a broad front of intellectual attack. Some of these attacks have been concerned with the empirical problems involved in the search for the holy grail of hegemony (Abercrombie et al. 1980; Chamberlain 1982). Other attacks have come from the 'postmodern' world of 'post-Marxism' and 'post-structuralism', a world in which no space has been left for belief in a rational, guiding architectonic of action. No originating source of action inhabits the post-structural world, just an endless series of contingencies. Although this is most evident in the work of Laclau and Mouffe (1985), as Chapter 7 argues, some critics such as Perry Anderson (1983) saw these tendencies as already implicit in Foucault. As has been noted elsewhere, it is in this respect that, having decentred the loci of power, Foucault perhaps may be the last pluralist (Clegg 1987).

POWER AND AGENCY IN THE 'COMMUNITY POWER DEBATE'

The implicit link from Hobbes to contemporary concerns with power is via a common 'agency' model, as Ball (1978) terms it, in which 'ontologically autarchic' individuals held sway. Such individuals were conceived on a classical liberal model as natural entities that were, without doubt, at the centre of analysis. Hence, power was something held by people, rather than, say, organizations. Explicitly, the formal model was developed as a contribution to what has become known as the community power debate. The chief contributor was Dahl (1957; 1958; 1961; 1968) who, in a series of publications, mapped out a behavioural science-oriented response to the much looser methodologies that had been used by the contemporary elite theory of Hunter (1953) and Mills (1956). Elite theory also has linkages with writers who are sometimes termed neo-Machiavellians, such as Pareto (1935). However, their concern with elite rule as a normatively good thing is refracted in the work of writers like Hunter and Mills. For the latter, the existence of elite rule, rather than proving the 'impossibility' of an ideal democracy as the earlier generation of European scholars had suggested, instead served to display a moral concern with the lack of realization of the democratic ideals of the founding fathers of the United States. Hunter (1953: 1) expresses this concern at the outset: 'There appears to be a tenuous line of communication between the governors of our society and the governed.' It is a situation he abhors because it 'does not square with the concept of democracy we have been taught to revere'.

Writers like Dahl regarded the elitists as being methodologically slack. It was against this methodological looseness that Dahl honed his own perspective. Consequently, as explored via some of Dahl's central essays, the concern was very much with methodology. The methodology constructed a particular model of formal power. At the centre of the methodology was a concern with precision. Precision was to be achieved through a methodological focus on the measurement of power. Rather than measure what power was thought to be, power was instead to be measured through 'responses'. Responses were taken as an indicant of the power that stood as the cause of the measured reaction. Just as a billiard ball colliding with another ball could be said to cause the latter's motion or response, so the power of an A could be measured through the response of a B. Implicit in this was a mechanical and behaviourist view of the world. Empirical exactitude was achieved at the expense of closing off precisely those lines of enquiry that would have most fruitfully pointed towards a less 'ontologically autarchic' distribution of power than pluralism was wont to discover – that is, something other than one in which individuals exist in a splendid and celebrated conceptual disorganization from each other. In part, it was the excessive individualism of researchers' conceptions of power as much as aspects of the real structure of American communities that oriented them towards pluralist conclusions. 'Values' were not unimportant either: one has a strong sense of the way in which pluralist models served to license and legitimate post-war American democracy, despite whatever flaws might have been evident in it. In seeing power in America as distributed plurally, then the democratic ideal could be preserved.

Individualist and mechanistic conceptions of power tended to orient their theorists to see instances of pluralistic power rather than more structural conceptions. For many pluralist writers, power was something that a concrete individual had to be seen to be exercising. Power prevented some other equally concrete individual from doing something that he or she would prefer to have done. Power was exercised in order to have those that were its subject falling in line with the individual preferences of the powerful. Indeed, in these formulations power would be the subordination of others' preferences and the extension of one's own to incorporate these others.

Characteristically, pluralists regarded power as most likely to be dispersed among many rather than fewer people; to be visible in instances of concrete decision-making rather than through reputation; to be competitively bargained for rather than structurally pervasive; to be best viewed through relatively formal instances of voting and to be more widely dispersed than narrowly concentrated in communities. Presthus (1964) came closest to articulating what an ideal type of pluralist analysis would be. It is not that pluralists deny the existence of elites: they simply see them as more dispersed, more specialized and less co-ordinated than would elite theorists. Dahl (1963), for instance, employs some explicitly elite notions in his conception of polyarchy, but is by no means an elitist; moreover, as critics have argued, on a number of occasions his analysis of power in New Haven implicitly undermines his own methodological protocols. One writer who makes this claim is Newton (1969), in a thoroughgoing critique of Dahl's (1961) empirical study of New Haven. Much of Newton's strategy in constructing his argument consists of hoisting Dahl (1961) with the petard of his own writing, demonstrating that in fact some of his argument could lead one as readily to 'elitist' as 'pluralist' conclusions, depending upon one's ideological affinities.

With respect to the concept of power, the pluralists certainly made the running. Dahl's formal model of power undoubtedly appears to be far more rigorous and thus more valid than was the attribution of power on a reputational basis, as employed by writers like

Hunter and Mills. However, the rigour is in some respects spurious. While considerable attention is paid to constructing a precise instrument for measuring power in terms of responses to its exercise, many less precise aspects of analysis are to be found in the model's application to the empirical analysis of the community of New Haven (Dahl 1961). In fact, this is to be expected, if for no other reason than that the model itself retains many imprecise and tacit assumptions. One would find it difficult to conceive of a formal model in which complete closure could be achieved, which at the same time retained much empirical utility. Instead, one might see the imprecision and tacit assumptions as indicating 'fault lines', areas of weakness, in the formal model. As such, they are damaging to the terms of closure which the formal model attempts. The argument of the book is not that these sources of damage be repaired, but that they alert us to fundamental flaws in the restrictive assumptions that construct the model.

POWER AND INTENTION

Dahl espoused an intellectual position known as behaviourism. The central tenet of this position is to treat social explanation as no different in principle from the explanation of non-social phenomena. In practice, this comes down to disregarding most of what it is that makes human society possible in favour of a radically constrained conception of behaviour expunged of inherent meaning. Given the behaviourism of Dahl's position, he is disinclined to consider issues of intentionality; from this perspective, one would obviously be suspicious of any concept seemingly quite so mentalist and unmeasurable as an intention. Consequently, some of the considerable criticism that Dahl's approach has engendered has focused on the lack of any criteria for deciding whether an exercise of power was, in fact, intended. Eventually, in Lukes' (1974) work, this generates considerable concern with the question of deciding responsibility for action.

Dahl's model of power deliberately refuses reference to the intentions that an agent might be said to have. Other writers have been more concerned with questions of intentionality, including Weber (1978), Russell (1938) and Wrong (1979). Weber illuminates aspects of the phenomenon of power whose figuration would remain obscured by strict adherence to the formal model of power as Dahl defines it. This is not to say that the notion of intention deployed by these writers is correct. It is not. Indeed, as a useful tool for the analysis of power, the way in which these writers conceptualize the notion of intention will prove to be very limited. The limitations of the concept are revealingly evident in its most sophisticated use in Wrong. In his book, Wrong (1979) uses many examples to advance his argument. Of particular interest is a discussion of sexual etiquette at cocktail parties. It proves to be a discussion that is very restricted in its applicability and value as a guide to practical action in the post-feminist world in which most professors of sociology are obliged to act, perhaps including even Wrong himself. The reason for this lack of utility is the restriction of the concept of power to a notion of intentional agency rather than to a conception of rules of the game.

In this book, I have followed the custom among analysts of power of inventing likely stories to make analytic points. Some of these likely stories are used to address issues of 'power and intention'. These stories are designed to produce apparent instances of power exercised in terms of Dahl's formal model of event causation. At the same time, the stories are pointing away from an account constructed in terms of event causation towards one constructed in terms of what will be called 'social causation'. Where event causation refers to Humean universal causal laws, social causation refers to concepts of rules and games. In using these 'likely stories' one is not simply using a methodological device much favoured by writers on power, including Dahl, but also reproducing a folklore whereby important analytical points are transmitted through homely anecdotes.

The ascendancy of Dahl's pluralist analysis was reached with the publication in 1961 of his empirical study of New Haven, *Who Governs*? The ascendancy was soon under attack, such that it has been the fashion for some time to be highly critical of Dahl's contributions. There is no doubt that much of this criticism is warranted, as the self-denying ordinances associated with Dahl's project rob it of opportunities for insight. However, it should always be remembered that the formal model that Dahl produces for the analysis of power, while it may have been restricted in scope, was nonetheless deliberately so. It effectively questioned those much looser and less precise research programmes associated with the elitist style of analysis which previously had held the centre ground of power research. It produced a much sharper model of power than had previously been seen, even if its actual representations were not as clearly focused.

NON-DECISION, MOBILIZATION OF BIAS AND THE TWO FACES OF POWER

Dahl's work is a landmark in the analysis of power. For some, however, it was less a monument and rather more of a blot on the landscape. Its error was not merely that it obscured an important aspect of the structure of power, that it might merely be an aesthetic shortcoming. The disfigurement was also a political action in the judgement of Bachrach and Baratz (1962), two researchers who made substantial criticisms of Dahl's framework. 'Two faces of power' were identified by these writers. One face was clearly illuminated by Dahl's formal model but at the cost of casting the second face of power into the shade. Lurking in the dark was the structural face of power. Enlightenment could be cast not only by focusing the investigative gaze on concrete acts of decision-making by specific agencies but also by directing it towards a phenomenon which they were to call 'non-decision-making'. By looking only at things that had happened, one forgot, so the critics said, that power might be manifested not only by doing things but also by ensuring that things do not get done. Whether this 'ensuring' was itself a 'doing' or should be considered in more structural and less agency-oriented terms remains a debate that has raged intermittently ever since.

Dahl's interest in definitional precision and formal theoretical models was concerned with epistemic rather than technical or phronetic interests, to use an Aristotelian nomenclature. What is missing from his account of New Haven are contexts, positions and interests that exploded, literally, in 1967 (O'Leary, Stannard and Abdul-Karim 2017), demonstrating that power and its exclusions shapes knowledge about power itself. Riots, burning and looting, pitched battles between residents of the neighbourhoods adjacent to Yale in New Haven ensued after the shooting of a Puerto Rican man by a white restaurant owner during an altercation in which the latter yielded a knife. The exclusion of black voices from New Haven politics was a deliberate act of non-inclusion, of ignoring issues that were exploding in the small community in New Haven from 1967 in relation to this incident, escalating especially after the assassination of Martin Luther King in 1968 (Williams 2001). Bachrach and Baratz (1970) were not blind to these events.

The critique that Bachrach and Baratz offered was not universally accepted. Some doubted that any hidden or obscured phenomenon lurked in the dark, outside the empiricist epistemic gaze. If something such as the second face of power could not be seen, they argued, what proof could there possibly be that it existed? Writers like Wolfinger (1971a; 1971b) accorded as much credence to the idea that there was something unobservable called non-decision-making as they might have done to the notion that there were fairies at the bottom of their garden. Nor were the mediations of diplomats such as Frey (1971) given much shrift by the sceptics. Either things were real and could be clearly seen or they were not real at all, except in what was taken to be the hothouse imagination of left-wing zealots. Such people's political preoccupations clearly seemed to indicate a disturbed mind, in Wolfinger's view. Although this was a representative judgement by a leading member of the United States political science community, it was not one unanimously shared in British sociological circles where Bachrach and Baratz's critiques were to be well received by writers like Lukes (1974/2005), Clegg (1975/2013) and Saunders (1979: 29). Indeed, Saunders was able to offer an extremely clear model of the analytic moves entailed by the critique, a model which is reproduced in Chapter 4 of this book.

In 1970, when Bachrach and Baratz published their long-awaited empirical study of Baltimore politics, as *Power and Poverty*, there were significant retreats from some of the positions initially advanced in the papers from the early sixties. For instance, the notions of non-decision-making and mobilization of bias were diluted. The idea of mobilization of bias had been one of the key terms of debate which had come into the currency of political exchange with its adoption by Bachrach and Baratz (1962). The term had originally been coined by Schattschneider (1960). Reference to a mobilization of bias was meant to indicate that behind any episode of power that occurred in an organized setting, there was an institutional structure that prefigured the concrete exchange. Structure prefigured the exercise of power and was itself always saturated with power rather than being something external, residual, or incidental to power. The contemporary importance of the concept of institutional racism, first articulated by the Black Panthers (Carmichael and Hamilton 1967), is testament to how practical theorizing from lived experience has become a conventional theoretical orthodoxy.

The concept of mobilization of bias was later to be given a novel twist by Newton (1975) who seized and turned it into a weapon aimed straight at the core of the empirical test upon which Dahl (1961) rested his case. The study of New Haven came under renewed scrutiny, not so much in terms of what it included, but in terms of what it did not include. However, the notion of inclusion was specified in quite literal terms such that no empiricist objections could be raised. A tacit assumption of the study of New Haven, or indeed of any other community, was that the formal area of local authority governance coincided with the boundaries of some real community. Newton made a simple but potent observation. The boundaries of administrative entities in the United States are frequently drawn in quite specific and restricted ways. New Haven was no exception to this. Many of the notable members of the New Haven community were not residents of the New Haven political arena as identified by the local authority. Consequently, they had little interest in what went on with taxpayers' money within this area of governance. Nor was it an accident that this was so, he suggested. The drawing of political boundaries in the formal sense is itself always an act of politics, representing a mobilization of bias, particularly where a suburban space can be isolated from an adjacent and problematic urban space. The costs and blight of the latter can be isolated, the charm and serenity of the former maintained. Why would issues of housing or schooling in the urban arena concern notable citizens of the community who neither lived in nor were taxed by that urban area local authority? The limits of accepting that assumption of a political community of interest which Hobbes had located at the beginning of the modernist project of power were now made evident in a strikingly empirical manner. The 'Community Power Debate' was premised on questionable assumptions about what constituted a community. Whereas a structural view of power was systematically occluded by pluralist scholarship, in recent year it has become central to political debate in the United States and elsewhere, as the intersection of socio-economic status, class, gender and ethnicity have come to dominate discussion of social and urban politics (Collins and Bilge 2020).

POWER AND THREE DIMENSIONS: A RADICAL VIEW

The power debate received a major new contribution with the extension of the two faces of power to a model of its three dimensions, with the publication of Lukes' (1974) *Power: A*

Radical View. Although the focus of research and conceptualization of power had hitherto largely occurred within the context of the 'Community Power Debate', the analytic centre of gravity was now changed to a concern with power per se. Lukes (1974) introduced the nomenclature of 'dimensions' into power analysis in a move that successfully usurped discussion of the 'two faces' of power. Henceforth, debate focused on three dimensions rather than two faces, as the latter perspective was rapidly superseded.

Chapter 5 of this book begins by elaborating what the 'three-dimensional' model had to say about power, isolating both its critiques of positions already encountered and the original contribution it had to make. In addition, the chapter also opens up for discussion some of the problematic aspects of the third-dimensional model. At the heart of these problems are certain consequences that flow from epistemological decisions that Lukes implicitly and explicitly makes in constructing his 'radical view'. In Chapter 5, Lukes' effective substitution of a moral philosophy for a sociology of power is spelt out. The central problem with Lukes' (1974) model is his conception of the necessarily morally irreducible nature of any idea of interests. Interests can be conceived from one or other of a liberal, a reformist or a radical perspective in any analysis of power, Lukes suggested. These moral perspectives are ungrounded by Lukes. One has the feeling that such moral decencies and questions are simply not open for debate. Some people will be liberals, some reformists, others will be radicals, it seems. From the three moral positions are generated three distinct dimensional approaches to the analysis of power. The model proposed sits uneasily between a conventionalist epistemological position and one closer to a realist position.

Conventionalism proposes that knowledge is wholly socially constructed; while realism accepts this, it would also add that social constructs change as real structures become better appropriated through knowledge constructs. Lukes' model refracts some elements of a Marxist analysis, such as the concern with real interests, through a humanistic and morally relativistic (rather than theoretically absolutist) lens. As Chapter 5 demonstrates, this is to exchange the empiricist and positivist epistemology of the one-dimensional formal model which Dahl proposes for one that is conventionalist. Discussion of conventionalism and positivism as positions in the philosophy of science is contrasted with a position known as realism. The epistemological discussion frames much of the chapter. It is through an understanding of this epistemological frame that much that is left implicit in Lukes' model can be made more explicit. It also opens up the possibility of a route from the moral impasse into which Lukes leads us via the realist position.

Realism enters the agenda through Benton's (1981) critique of Lukes. This realist critique is discussed in detail in Chapter 5. As a result of the discussion, a dispositional conception of power is sketched in addition to that episodic agency concept already encountered in Dahl and implicit in some aspects of Bachrach and Baratz's criticisms. The chapter concludes by looking at a couple of empirical studies that have used different resolutions of the structure/agency problem as part of their research design to see if these enable us to resolve whether any one view of power is better than another. Whitt (1979; 1982) studied urban transit lobbying in California, comparing a pluralist, elitist and class-dialectic approach. These implicitly correspond with Lukes' (1974) three dimensions. The conclusion that is drawn by this chapter from Whitt's study is that on this occasion the class-hegemonic or three-dimensional model does not, in fact, give a particularly fine-grained account of the data. In this respect, it is less usefully discussed than is the elite model whose advantages over the pluralist model are well established by Whitt. Gaventa's (1980) analysis of an Appalachian coal-mining community explicitly uses the Lukes (1974) approach and in fact improves on the basic model by not making the focus on interests a constitutive feature of it. The 'hegemonic' perspective is persuasively argued by Gaventa in a case constructed primarily through the fine detail of historical analysis.

At their most subtle, hegemonic and three-dimensional approaches unravel into conceptions of power that penetrate into the very thoughts and consciousness of others. A form of supremely sovereign will was thus constituted from which there could seem to be no escape. Those subject to power's sovereignty were literally unable to recognize their own will, captured by the sovereign power of another. Models of ideology and hegemony present such conceptions of power as 'false' consciousness. Thus, one can see how Lukes' (1974) 'third-dimensional' conception of power as something unknowably lodged in one's subjectivity and consciousness as only a further stretching of the extant terms of power's causal, sovereign domain. Hence, it will be argued that Lukes' 'view' is somewhat less 'radical' than it might initially appear to be in its break with the central tradition of power analysis.

There are problems associated with accessing just what the internal mental and intentional well-springs of another's causal actions might be. These problems will necessarily present themselves to any analyst who wants to argue that intentions can function as causes. Other people may well have minds, but how on earth can we know what is in them other than by asking the people to report on their 'state of mind'? For anyone with an interest in power, such questioning is deeply problematic. Some 'three-dimensional' and 'hegemonic' approaches to power would argue that it is 'the supreme exercise of power to get another or others to have the desires you want them to have ... to secure their compliance by controlling their thoughts and desires' (Lukes 1974: 23). If this argument is accepted, then when people say what their consciousness of something is, these accounts cannot be taken at face value, nor can they function as explanations. Consequently, any recourse to the actor's own account as an explanation will be fundamentally flawed. From this perspective, it may be said that people do not know their own minds. It is precisely the belief that they falsely think that they do, which is the locus of what has been called the problem of hegemony wrapped up in the dominant ideology thesis (Abercrombie et al. 1980).

As if three-dimensional structuralism was not sufficient, more recent writers have proposed a four-fold schema. Cynthia Hardy and Leiba-O'Sullivan (1998), as well as Fleming and Spicer (2014), write about a fourth dimension of power incorporating Foucault's perspective within Lukes' dimensional framework (Lukes 1974, 2005). I addressed this tendency as 'super-structuralism' in *Power and Organizations* (Clegg et al., 2006), a critique also shared with Lukes (2005).

There is an exception to this judgement of 'super-structuralism' in the work of Haugaard (2012; 2020a; 2020b), whose version of the fourth dimension is not systemic but ontological and agency oriented. It addresses the dispositions of social subjects, revealed in the type of agency with which they feel ontologically secure. Comparative discussion of the social organization of violence is instructive in respect of discussion of the ontology of agency. What is tolerated and what is stigmatized as violence is highly variable. For instance, the subjective dispositions of the knightly social subject (as theorized by Elias 1983; also see Pine 2022), displays an attitude to combat embedded only in the present moment and the institutional norms of knightly behaviour. Under these circumstances, a challenge must be responded to if honour is to be served. By contrast, the modern bureaucratic social subject plans future action in a linear way, guided by internal restraint regarding legal bureaucratic rules, even in seeking not to be held accountable to them. There is considerable difference in the ways in which the two types of actors act. For instance, a feudal knight is happy to engage in direct combat and kill, despite the blood and gore produced at first hand. Modern bureaucratic subjects are more likely to kill at a distance, using drones, robots or missiles and sanctions that starve the enemy to death. Killing at first hand will be unlikely because such a subject will follow rules for what they do and how they do it that make death procedural in terms of bureaucratic regulation.

Bureaucratic subjects that kill rationally and at a distance inhabit a 'Heart of Darkness' (Clegg et al., 2006, chapter 6). To the modern bureaucratic subject, knightly behaviour, despite its complex codes of honour and chivalry, would be as 'barbarian' as the sledgehammer executioners of the Russian mercenaries comprising the Wagner Group in the contemporary war with Ukraine, killers with no knightly ethic (Faulconbridge 2022). Each has a different subjectivity making different kinds of behaviour conducive to ontological security.[1] Such conduct takes place within the framing of modes of rationality (Clegg 1975/2013) in which violence can be freely perpetrated, whether in Auschwitz, Abu Ghraib, the Ukraine or anywhere in which overarching attempts at instilling universal legal norms of rationality are not followed. Phronetically, there is no universal ethics; in terms of practical theorizing, it depends on the modes of rationality in question in regarding those things considered good or bad (Barnes 1984).

Haugaard (2020) points out how ontological constitution can lead to paradoxes of power, for which he uses the example of parents and children. Parents constrain the freedoms of a child to explore certain phenomena to preserve their safety. Not only that;

writers influenced by Judith Butler (1990) look at the way in which children are brought into adulthood in terms of gender relations by their parents and acquaintances. After Foucault, such authors see the whole process of socialization as a form of power that is shaping identity (fourth dimension) in terms of available scripts. So, while the father who tells his little daughter that she looks very pretty isn't trying to reproduce a woman whose self-reflection is through a male gaze, he may inadvertently be producing this disposition on the parts of the girl in question, such that it becomes the case; likewise, it is the case when the father says to the son, 'Oh, start acting like a man and grow up'.

When a parent warns a child about the dangers of fire, these are not ways of trying to canalize and constrain the freedoms of the person to do as they please, but to keep the child from harm. Are not the freedoms of the person always contextual? It isn't as if there is a *tabula rasa* of options available for us or our freedoms so that, in various ways, exogenous forces somehow come and box us in. We're always boxed; we cannot not be boxed; we are always being constrained by the discourses, the language, available to us to use. Therefore, while power is pervasive, surrounding us; its entanglements inscribing and interpolating existence, it is somewhat totalizing to credit this as a fourth dimension without the qualifications on which Haugaard (2020) insists.

DIMENSIONS OF POWER AND ORDINARY LANGUAGE

Although the debate about the three dimensions of power has been conducted largely in relation to *power over*, it could be extended productively by thinking of how one might use the three-dimensional framing to extend analysis to *power with* and *power to*. If we consider ordinary language differences in the use of *power over, power to* and *power with*, some differences in the ways that power operates become apparent. *Power over* is simple: A exercises power over B by getting B to do something that they would not otherwise do. In this context, an exercise of *power over* others seeks to impose a direction that these others might resist. From a *power to* perspective, actors will strive to use power to make a difference, to achieve something that need not be constraining of another but could be empowering. Actors that explicitly work by sharing *power with* others to achieve a common purpose point out how *power with* and *power over* are antithetical.

The *power to do something* approximates far more closely to the verb use of *to power*, as one might refer to an engine powering a car; the engine has the capacity to move the vehicle. The capacity concept still underlies the notion of power to, expressed in everyday use by reference to the cubic capacity of a conventional carbon-powered engine. However, in the use that Talcott Parsons (1963) made of the concept of 'power to', the capacity was equipped with an accelerator that could increase the velocity of power to do things. Parsons captured this in an analogy between the role of money in the economy and power in the polity. In conventional economic theory, the velocity of circulation of money is the number of units of money circulating in the economy during a given period, measured by dividing GDP by the country's total money supply. The money supply can be boosted by what has come to be called quantitative easing, when the money supply is increased to stimulate economic activity so that more goods and services are bought and sold, generating enhanced economic activity. Like money, Parsons conceived of power as a circulatory medium that could generate political returns in an analogy with economic returns. 'Power to' moved things, made things happen, rather than being a constraint, as was 'power over'. Parsons thought that power to do things was a positive form of power; he broke with any negative conception of power over being a form of constraint. Power could be positive; it could make a difference; it could add value; it could get things done. In its gerund form, it can be empowering. It can also be shared, as in *power with* others, power sharing, as Follett (1987) conceived it to be.

The most effective forms of power sharing are to be found, paradoxically, in collectivist organizations that share a dominant ideology. The paradox is that the dominant ideology both empowers and subordinates them simultaneously. In its name, whether that name be that of a political or religious leader, a philosopher or a science fiction writer, they are free to act as long as they do so within the protocols and beliefs to which they subscribe. Those collectivist organizations that sustain themselves over time are paradoxical in these terms, according to Joyce Rothschild-Whitt's (1979) research on collectivist organizations. They empower their members to have to collaborate and work with each other. In the longer-lived collectives, the members first subordinated their selves to some deeply dominating religious or political imperative, such as Christianity, feminism or socialism. The paradox is that 'power to', empowerment, a collective endeavour, flourished best in a context in which people shared and trusted their sense of the rightness of subordination to an overarching ideal. In these conditions of membership, having first accepted the meaningfulness of an overarching ideological ideal, they could share power with others so inclined. Such collectivist organizations were channelling, even if they did not know it, insights first explicitly articulated by Mary Parker Follett (1987; 1941/2003) about how sharing power with others was democratizing.

Many organizations seek empowerment by insisting, paradoxically, that employees 'speak up' (Cunha et al., 2018), while being inscribed within a structure of domination, in which people are 'empowered' through the delegation of others who maintain structural supremacy. The limits to what and how employees may address issues can easily be breached. Breaches require repair (Garfinkel 1967). Breaches of voice are not evidently deviant until pointed out as such either by some structural authority or those considerate of the risks posed to the breacher by the breach. Breaches reveal the subtle constraints and accommodations that exist in employing organizations terms of tacit assumptions about matters such as power and purpose (Clegg et al., 2021), constituting a key paradox of power. If authoritative agents must exercise coercive power to gain compliance, this is not demonstrating that they 'have power'; it is demonstrating that they do not. Real power resides in the normative rather than the coercive ordering of affairs. When power doesn't have the authority to configure how things are turning out, it intervenes by exercising power forcefully, demonstrating that interventions of power frequently show not so much strength as weakness. The paradoxes of power have been explored in more detail in Cunha et al. (2021a).

When, in a two-dimensional sense, agendas and decision-making are organized in such a way as to create non-issues because they do not make it on to the agenda, then non-decision-making about issues occurs. In van Iterson and Clegg (2008) how issues were attempted to be made non-issues was dealt with. There is also the matter of how issues arise. Goffman's (1974) framing approach suggests ways that new issues can be brought on to the agenda by introducing new participants into decision-making with the power to challenge implicit understandings in crucial decision-making arenas.[2] For instance, Jamal's (2007) analysis of how Arab minorities in Israel use the structures of opportunities available to them through citizenship by mobilizing strategies to improve their status suggests ways that a two-dimensional conception of power can be brought into analysis. By sharing power with others from outside normal fields of practice, fresh issues and participants can enter strategic decision-making. Democratic organizing practices may enable corporations to successfully pursue social and environmental objectives alongside financial ones, through sharing decision-making with green stakeholders, as Shah et al.'s (2022) green governance framework for the oil and gas industries suggests.

From a three-dimensional perspective, when subaltern interests are discursively aligned with those of elites, then the organizational members and civil society participants will view the world in ways that reflect elite interests, rather than their 'real interests'. Essentially, from this perspective, power works to veil specific interests as the public interest. Analysis of media coverage and fossil-fuel industry public relations during the period 2008–19 shows how fossil-fuel hegemony has been maintained and extended, and how corporate discourses aimed at maintaining hegemony are assisted by the state as an ideological promoter, demonstrated in Wright et al. (2021).

Power to is facilitative empowerment, supporting an individual's power to act and enact their will without interference. Power to is generally viewed as a mode of power 'softer' than that of power over, but that sets about achieving objectives in a more benign and subtle manner. The Italian feminism of difference, grounding theory in articulating practices of political and personal transformation through the *partire da sé* (departing from oneself), prepared by the practice of *autocoscienza* (political consciousness-raising), provides a way of conceiving how three-dimensional *power over* can be resisted through *power to*. Muraro phrased this practice as 'a strategy invented to fight against the imposition of starting from what others had established as truthful and right' (Muraro, 1996: 13; cited in Pierazzini et al., 2021). Essentially, the argument is that an agency can, by raising theoretical consciousness about the conditions of another's practical consciousness, transform that consciousness. What was taken for granted can be reimagined as a form of mental bondage from which one can liberate oneself, with the aid of the agency that is the interlocuter. The risk, as is the case with any conversion strategy, is that one may embrace new ways of seeing the world that become so compelling that one can only trace their frame in a new hegemony.

In public administration, the ideas of what Cohen (2009) refers to as 'radical democratic reform, premised on *power with*, have been explored in research on the systematic involvement of relevant and affected actors in the co-creation of innovation and public value in the public sector. As Kornberger (2017) has argued, co-creation processes are interactive and emergent in form, content and outcome. Using deliberative democracy for co-creation, innovative solutions to complex problems have been developed, such as collaborative climate partnerships and interactive political leadership in the field of transport policy, preventive healthcare and work safety, producing value for citizens and commercial enterprises, as well as society at large, suggest Torfing et al. (2021).

AGENCY AND STRUCTURE IN THE ANALYSIS OF POWER

Lukes (1977: 29) defines the key problem of power in terms that have generally been accepted as the definitive specification of the issues involved: 'No social theory merits serious attention that fails to retain an ever-present sense of the dialectics of power and structure.' With this specification, a 'central problem' is located not only by Lukes (1977) but also in the work of Giddens (1979; 1984), another influential British theorist (see Clegg, 1992). Lukes (1974; 1977) opened an evident 'dualism' of agency and structure which Giddens (1976; 1984) attempted to restitch together with a notion of the 'duality' of power and structure. Giddens' influential (1984) conceptualization of power took place within the context of the development of something which Giddens (1984) terms the theory of 'structuration'. In structuration, theory is a view of social structure being produced by and acting back on the knowledgeable agents who are the subjects of that structure they 'instantiate' through its constitution. Many criticisms have been made of structuration theory, notably those of Archer (1982), Barbalet (1987) and Layder (1987), which particularly address the agency/structure issue. With some justice these critiques claim that Giddens' system of structuration theory, once it is stripped down, offers the analysis of power little more than another, albeit complex, subjectivist position.

Giddens' (1984) later work is informed by a facilitative conception of power. Such a conception can be found not only in the work of Foucault's (1977) positive, non-zero-sum conception of power, but also in the work of Talcott Parsons (1967). Parsons' view of power was criticized by Giddens (1968) quite early in his career. Until recently, Parsons' work had not been looked at in any detail by subsequent social theorists. It seemed as if Parsons' concerns were very much a perspective whose time was past. It is doubtful that this view still prevails. There was a posthumous revival of Parsons' 'neo-functionalism' as a burgeoning sociological perspective (Holton and Turner 1986). In part, this is because of the affinities it displays with Foucault's (1977) non-zero-sum and productive conception of power (Kroker 1984) and in part because of the attention that Habermas (1987) directed in its direction. The Parsons/Foucault nexus, as Giddens' work attests, represents a clear convergence on the importance of a facilitative, conception of power.

A facilitative conception of power assumes that actors can do things to make a difference. Elite actors are routinely able to do more things that affect more people than nonelites. Bourdieu's (1977) conceptions of power look at the ways in which power begets power, looks at the way in which control of financial capital begets flows of intellectual capital, of social capital and so on. Consider the way in which the 1 per cent canalize and channel the life chances and probabilities of the 99 per cent or how certain ethnicities outnumber others in powerful arenas, or how these other ethnicities, clustered in less desirable parts of secondary labour markets, rarely see themselves in dominant circuits of power. There is a sense in which, in the trajectory of theorizing, older theoretical debates between pluralists and elites have become forgotten. It's a material fact that there are real elites, not the 'socially constructed' elites that one reads about, those created by populist politicians castigating intellectuals and experts. The 400 or so major multinational corporations that individually orchestrate the vast amount of global economic relations are one major site in which the real elites, not those socially constructed through celebrity, are to be found (van Krieken, 2018).

There are institutional crucibles in which discourse that is recognisably elite discourse emerges spontaneously. These crucibles, elite schools, universities and so forth, are not hermetically sealed. Outsiders' sheer ability, through genetic and environmental good fortune, can funnel others there alongside those arrived through more conventional socially transmitted sources of privilege. It's not a sealed zone, not an entirely homogenous zone. Wealth helps prepare a path as well as pay the fees: the offspring of drug dealers, rock stars and corrupt politicians and their enablers can end up going to Eton, Harrow or Rodean, but they usually become very different people from their parents; that's the point – social capital washing away the stain of a lack of class. The crucial thing is that certain sorts of institutional spaces are characterized by certain modes of rationality. Effectively, to the extent that one doesn't respect these, one's deviance will be, if not acted upon, be remarked upon; one will learn the rules on those occasions that one breaks them. Alternatively, those who, through inherited habitus, carry the predispositions of socialization too strongly, who can't shake them off for reasons of class or identity loyalty, for instance, will find themselves out of place. Yet, for those who change ontological dispositions or who can mimic the right dispositions, or possibly develop a kind of dual social ontology, as described by Scott (2003), absorption into the elites is indeed possible. Elites, that were substantially impermeable, were constantly confronted with the prospect of revolution. Consequently, they had to be highly coercive to maintain power.

Contemporary elites are highly permeable, otherwise new elite formations would be impossible. Old elites, such as the British aristocracy, are a caste whose performativity, rituals and relation to decaying institutions of feudal entitlement is increasingly at odds with the tech-based entrepreneurs, the innovators of Silicon Valley and elsewhere, who certainly do not seek to reproduce any *ancien regime*. New entrants to the elites, such as these, transform the ways in which the elites produce and reproduce themselves. Additionally, there are significant differences between national elites, who they are, the resources they command, the relations that they can access, and the ways that these power relations play out in terms of their command of events (Maclean et al., 2010 provide a well-documented comparison).

DOMINANT IDEOLOGY AND DISCIPLINARY POWER

Much of the debate about power has focused on the ways in which ideology operates through conceptions of hegemony. The concern with the concept of ideology has focused on one or other of two things. First, there has been a suggestion that much of both contemporary Marxism and sociology has been characterized by an unnecessary 'dominant ideology thesis' (Abercrombie et al. 1980). The argument of the proponents of this view is considered and the general 'dominant ideology thesis' is criticized. Having considered this thesis, attention is turned to a second major contemporary emphasis on ideology. This proposes that, rather than thinking of either ideology or hegemony as a state of mind, one would better regard it as a set of practices, primarily of a discursive provenance that seeks to foreclose the indefinite possibilities of signifying elements and their relations in determinate ways (Laclau and Mouffe 1985). The thrust of this second emphasis derives from 'post-structuralist' perspectives, particularly those that have been encouraged by Foucault's work on disciplinary power. Foucault (1977) provides a sophisticated discussion of power that explicitly breaks with any conception of ideology.

Foucault is interesting in at least two ways for such a book as this. First, he provides us with a critique of much of the conventional 'views' on power. The core of this critique is that the conception of power needs to be freed from its 'sovereign' auspices as a prohibitory concept. Such a concern with the facilitative and productive aspects of power relates well to the kind of arguments that have been made most clearly by Parsons (1967). Foucault's emphasis is a useful additional contribution in this regard. Second, Foucault provides us with a detailed history of some of the power practices and techniques that have characterized emergent modernity, doing so in a non-reductive way. Compared with some Marxist accounts of similar events, the discussion is all the better for that. The historical record that Foucault produces stands as a corrective.

In recent years, Foucault has become one of a series of French intellectual fashions as far as many English-speaking writers are concerned. Many of the critics who have 'taken up' Foucault have not been sociologically trained, any more than Foucault himself was. The absence of a sociological framework led Foucault to understate the importance of Max Weber's (1978) contribution to arguments concerning discipline. In addition, Foucault seemed unaware of the 'labour process' debate that had been current in English-speaking sociology since the mid-1970s. Consideration of either of these would have strengthened Foucault's analyses of 'disciplinary power'. The omissions of the master have not always been redressed by some of the disciples. Quite often one finds, among some dedicated followers of this intellectual fashion, evident insights frequently wrapped up in the densest prose imaginable. Since the focus on Foucault in this volume is less on the fashionable French philosopher and more on the administrative historian of modernity, much of Chapter 7 is taken up with a discussion of his conception of 'disciplinary power', both as it has been used by him and illuminated by others.

CIRCUITS OF POWER

Chapter 7 concludes with a critique and partial endorsement of certain positions that have emerged out of a general 'post-structuralist' problematic with which Foucault has frequently (he would have insisted) been erroneously associated. It is in the work of Laclau and Mouffe (1985) that the implications of this become most apparent for the project of power analysis. The compatibility of a realist perspective with the issues raised by more discursive analysis will be mooted. Several researchers in the sociology of science have gone furthest in developing the insights that one might draw from post-structuralism into a workable approach to the sociology of power. (Interestingly, they themselves do not acknowledge that this is what they have done.) In a group that clusters around the work of Michel Callon, Bruno Latour and their various colleagues (for example, Callon 1986), there has developed a highly distinctive sociology of 'translation'. Chapter 8 outlines this contribution before placing it in the context of a general framework for power analysis.

The notion of 'obligatory passage points' was the key concept that I took from Callon. I found a very similar idea in Laclau and Mouffe's (1985) *Hegemony and Socialist Strategy*, when they wrote about necessary nodal points. There is not a hair's breadth of difference between a necessary nodal point and an obligatory passage point. Given my interest in the sociology of organizations, it seemed evident that one way of thinking about those abstractions called 'organizations' was to see their composition in terms of obligatory passage points. What are key to producing these obligatory passage points are the rules and routines formally produced, particularly by HRM departments as well as the many implicit and informal rules of everyday organizational life that sustain and resist these. Organizations are an architectonic device for constructing formal obligatory passage points that shift with the flow of events, often informally. Organizational employees are practical theorists, trying to make sense of their contexts to configure their relations in ways that produce the kinds of effects they desire. They are engaged in what Weick (1995) called 'sensemaking', an idea that seems to relate to his early interest in ethnomethodology (Weick 1969). Organizations try to make the determinism that they privilege possible, always doing so in the face of events and interpretations that they cannot necessarily control.

Inspired by Bhaskar's realism (Bhaskar 1975;1979a; 1979b) I had earlier published a (rarely cited) paper on 'Phenomenology and Formal Organizations: A Realist Critique' (Clegg 1983). Two other books on realism were also influential: Rom Harré and Harry Madden's (1975) *Causal Powers* and Harré's (1985) *Varieties of Realism*. The realist view of science chimes with the notion that we're all practical ethnomethodologists, trying to configure scenes and stable routines to create the kinds of effects that we want, which became instrumental in my thinking about what I subsequently termed 'episodic power'. I also had been reading Actor Network theory, especially Callon (1986), Callon and Latour (1981) and Callon and Law (1982). The scallops of St Brieuc Bay, those mute little creatures that were major and recalcitrant actants in relation to the agency of fishermen and scientists, were intriguing in their power effects, stressing the importance of non-human actors for socially constructed realities. While human realities are socially constructed not all the key actants are meaningfully doing the constructing, even when they affect its constructions in significant ways. Phenomena other than human beings play significant roles in shaping the world that is socially constructed.

Any generally applicable theory of power must also be a theory of organization. Much of the theory of power in organizations has been oriented towards the explanation of how organizational obedience is produced. In the next to the last chapter, this orientation is built on to develop a framework in which both 'obedience' and 'resistance' can be located. In doing so, some radical revisions are made of both more conventional and more critical approaches to the analysis of power in organizations. Essential to my conception of organization is a particular use of a concept of 'agency'. Agency is something that is achieved. It is a concept that has been deliberately stretched to accommodate several different forms within its contours. Agency is something that is achieved by virtue of organization, whether of a human being's dispositional capacities or of a collective nature, in the sense usually reserved for the referent of 'organizations'. Organization is essential to the achievement of effective agency in the terms of this book. It is the stabilizing and fixing factor in circuits of power. The point of using agency in this way is to avoid reductionism to either putative human agents or to certain conceptions of a structure that always determines. In the terms of organization analysis, such matters of determination are always more or less contingent as an effect of organization. An understanding of either 'organization' or 'power' entails a reciprocal conceptualization of both terms.

A theory of power must examine how the field of force in which power is arranged has been fixed, coupled and constituted in such a way that, intentionally or not, certain 'nodal points' of practice are privileged in this unstable and shifting terrain. From this perspective, a radical view of power would consist not in identifying what putative 'real interests' are, so much as the practices by which agents are recruited to views of their interests that align with the discursive field of force that an enrolling agency is able to construct. The view of power is of a far less massive, oppressive and prohibitive apparatus than it is often imagined to be. Certainly, such effects can be secured by power, but nowhere near as easily as some 'dominant ideology', 'hegemonic' or 'third-dimensional' views would suggest. Power is better regarded not as having two faces or being layered into three dimensions, but as a process that may pass through distinct circuits of power and resistance. Hence, I do not see power as a thing or as structurally composed of different dimensions. I see it as essentially a matter of processes and flows, in which actors and actants both have their effects.

The general framework of circuits of power that is proposed in Chapter 8 is developed from the insights of David Lockwood (1964) into the nature of system and social integration. These forms of integration are conceptualized as distinct circuits of facilitative and dispositional power respectively, to be seen in the context of their relationship to the episodic agency circuit of power. A formal model of circuits of power is developed. The circuit of power passing through system integration is conceptualized in terms of techniques of discipline and production, while the circuit of social integration is conceptualized in terms of rules that fix relations of meaning and membership. A conception of rules is essential to an adequate understanding of power. The concern with post-structuralism and Foucault, addressed in the previous chapter, also fed into the conceptualization of the formal model of circuits of power.

The formal model of circuits of power produces some surprising conclusions. One of these concerns the status of conceptions of one-dimensional or episodic and agency views of power. To the extent that power remains purely episodic and does not enter the other circuits of power, it will be argued that analysis can be constructed appropriately in terms of a modified version of the classical framework of an A getting a B to do something that B would not otherwise have done. Contrary to Lukes (1974), the unproblematic reproduction of power through a one-dimensional circuit of power does not restrict power. On the contrary, it maximizes it most effectively and economically. Power which makes only one circuit, which has no need to struggle against relations of meaning and membership, or to institute new disciplinary techniques of production or of force, is an economy of power.

It is power that can efficiently deploy given capacities where resistance, if it too remains in that circuit, will be overwhelmed. Evidently, there is both more difficulty at stake for resistance than for power, and more incentive to switch out of the episodic, taken-for-granted circuit of power. Incentive may provide motivation, but it will rarely be either the mother of invention or the reshaper of meaning.

At the core of the conception of circuits of power is the concept of organization out-lined at the beginning of Chapter 8. This conception is allied to a modified conception of one-dimensional or episodic power. The modifications are significant, however. They are made to a framework derived by Coleman (1977) from the questionable assumptions of the neoclassical economics paradigm. In this text, these assumptions are revised accord-ing to realist precepts. The revisions will be seen to be marked. Coleman's text is a point of departure and reference because of the widespread acceptance of the assumptions of the neoclassical paradigm, however erroneous and unrealistic these may be.

One writer who has made use of a concern with organization in relation to power is Mann (1986), for whom a key concept is that of 'organizational outflanking'. The term is used by him to explain why it is typically the case that the dominated tend to comply rather than to revolt. The answer is simple. Lacking the organizational resources to outmanoeuvre existing networks and alliances of power, subordinated agencies are usually able to achieve effective resistance only based on a collective organization for which they frequently lack capacities for action. With such collective organization, they may be able to exploit fis-sure and division in the ruling ranks. In Chapter 8, it will be argued that pressures towards 'institutional isomorphism' in the circuit of social integration will tend to reproduce dispo-sitionally existing fields of force, while the circuit of system integration will tend to facilitate innovation in this field of force. These are only tendencies, however. Innovation and repro-duction do not necessarily run only through these circuits. System integration, premised on techniques of production and discipline, which are innovated under imperatives of compe-tition and environmental efficiency, will tend to be a potent source of transformation and strain. It will open up opportunities both for resistance under existing rules and for changes in the rules, changes that can create new agencies, new handicaps and advantages, and new pathways through existing fields of force. Before any such changes can take place, however, there must be an effective organization on the part of any agencies that aspire to strategy. It is in conceptualizing this that Mann's conception of organizational outflanking is useful.

FROM A HISTORY OF THE PAST TO A HISTORY OF THE PRESENT

Organizational analysis of a kind also frames the chapter on the history of the past, Chap-ter 9, focused on the state. Here, the concern is with showing how the circuits of power argument can be turned to some central issues in understanding the emergence of the contemporary administrative national state. The chapter deploys an argument that sensitizes one to the issues that the proposed framework for the analysis of power would raise. Thus, the model is used to review major areas of scholarship that address questions that bear directly on any adequate sociology of power. The focus is turned to the constitution of the modern state to show how some of the central ideas of the 'circuits' perspective can be brought to bear in an explanation of the emergence of the classic loci of modern power. To readers who are familiar with much historical sociology of the state, there will be little that is novel in the account offered. While the chapter is no more than an illustrative review, it does serve to give the reader some idea of the way in which the circuits framework can address some classic questions of sociology, modernity and power. While that chapter addresses a history of the past, the new concluding chapter addresses a history of the present, designed to complement the concluding chapter of the original volume, as a history of the past.

One influential way of seeing social science is to conceive of its role as translating histories and other stories in a way that engages publics (Burawoy 2005; 2008). In this way scholars can challenge official memorialization of the past. For instance, some histories become officially institutionally memorialized, as is the case in China, with the Opium Wars (Lovell 2011). Museums commemorate these as potent symbols of the Communist Party in emancipating the country from colonial domination. Elsewhere, others, busy toppling commemorations and memorials, challenge selective memorialization. Sometimes political solvent dissolves what previous generations can remember and forget. As things fade away and are no longer discussed, there is no need to police them socially. Such a fate, no doubt, is what the Communist Party of China hoped for in relation to Tiananmen Square in June 1989. Citizens, asserting their power to protest peacefully, were slaughtered by the state. The state that enacted these events strove to wipe them from the memory of their citizens although outbreaks of civil disobedience in defiance of the lockdowns pursued in China during COVID-19 suggest that memories may be suppressed but not forgotten.

Mills (1959) argues that good social theory, to use a broader term than sociology, should neither obfuscate public issues nor ignore private troubles. That intention, of applying social theory, using the tools created in the first edition of this text, to public issues sparked by the crises of the present, guided the writing of the final chapter. First amongst these was COVID-19. Some of the writing of this second edition occurred in lockdown and social isolation because of the COVID-19 pandemic. Not surprisingly, the pandemic features as a central element of 'A history of the present', the new chapter concluding this edition, which draws upon an earlier article written with Miguel Pina e Cunha and Marco Berti (Cunha et al., 2021b). The way in which nations around the world have reacted to the COVID-19 virus, essentially shows their weakness before nature, before a phenomenon they cannot control, a phenomenon whose mutations are entirely disinterested as it proceeds randomly to replicate. The assumption of draconian powers is not an indication of the *powerfulness* of the state or a government, but of the relative *powerlessness* of the state and government in the face of the virus' random contingency which they sought to counter by creating new dispositional powers. The powers of lockdown would not have been considered within the conditions of possibility of liberal democracies prior to COVID. The state acquired dispositional powers through the social construction of COVID as a state of exception (to the citizen's rights of liberal democracy). In some cases, states were able to contain and constrain the viral infection to a greater extent. The other two crises that are considered, the war in Ukraine and climate change, present different but related aspects of the history of the present, bringing the role of the state to the fore in power relations, somewhere it has been analytically marginalized from for some time.

The more that episodic powers are available to a state, the more able it is to strive to exert power over a populace to 'defeat' the virus, however futile the battle fought might turn out to be. The greatest difficulty is presented by situations in which power is more dispersed, pluralistically distributed, as in more classical democracies; in these situations, considerable moral suasion must accompany powers of intervention. In a city state that is effectively a one party state, such as Singapore, which has not always had friendly neighbours, a collectively inward orientation is not so hard to produce; likewise, in a culturally and ethnically homogenous state such as South Korea, also lacking friendly neighbours, a certain history of compliance is easier to achieve. In addition, as well as their citizens having certain social ontological predispositions towards obedience, unlike citizens accustomed to extreme individualism, these states were better prepared to deal with COVID-19 because they had experienced SARS beforehand.

CONCLUSION

The elites that made the past do not necessarily own or chart our futures. We do not have to live in the pasts that have been made in the futures still to be created. Future-making should be a major concern of the social sciences. In accord with Gergen (2014) we need to stop being obsessed as social scientists only with gaining knowledge that corresponds to the world as it is; of far more importance is to explore what it could be. If we are to change the world we need to change power relations. Before we can change the world then we must understand how that world was made and that requires a substantial engagement with the role that conceptions of power have played in its making. The bulk of this book attempts a modest attempt doing that. Moreover, in this second edition, given the three critical challenges of the contemporary conjuncture that this book concludes with, it also charts a possible path to a more sustainable future.

NOTES

1 Thanks to Mark Haugaard for pointing out the ontological argument.
2 Goffman's (1961) analysis of total institutions as a system of power is something missing from this book; the absence is remedied in part by the discussion of 'The Heart of Darkness' in Clegg et al. (2006).

2
POWER: TRADITIONAL ROOTS, MODERN PROBLEMS

INTRODUCTION

This chapter will consider alternative foundations for the modern analysis of power: the contributions of the seventeenth-century English political theorist, Thomas Hobbes, and the writings of the sixteenth century Florentine Niccolò Machiavelli. These two were the most famous of early modern writers on power. They took an analytical and empirically oriented stance towards power, rather than the primarily religious or ethical stance adopted by their forebears. Although it may be argued that these authors provide two distinct, traditional roots for modern concerns with power, one has been far more fertile for modern developments than the other. Modern problems of power derive their conceptualization primarily from the discursive premises which Hobbes first outlined in detail. Machiavelli has been far less evident as a precursor, although his strategic conception of power, which was played out in the micro-politics of the court, bears a distinctly contemporary cast, as some recent contributors have explicitly recognized.

If modern problems of power seem to display more of an affinity with Hobbes than with Machiavelli, what role has the latter to play? One scenario might cast him not as a precursor of the foundations for contemporary conceptualization of power but as the protagonist of an opposed conception. Such a scenario would entail that the relation between these two contributions is one not only of succession in time but also of discursive tension. The tension was resolved in favour of Hobbes' articulation of modernity rather than that of Machiavelli. Hobbes' work on power and his conception of the problem of order have thus shaped our understanding and experience of the modern world.

In constructing, representing and making sense of a concept like power we can never be free from the matter of words. Specific conceptions of the world in particular formulations bear the power of signification: they define the nature of reality as we experience it. Consequently, definitions and conceptualizations of terms so central to our experience of social reality, as are those of 'power', are themselves enormously powerful. With their guidance we will see distinct realities of power: distinct visions of hierarchy, architectonics, configuration, relief and local colour. The modernist view, from its roots in Hobbes, traces a world of eurhythmic (as in harmoniously ordered and proportioned) power, stretching even to the Marxist critics of domination, as will be argued later. The contrasting view from Machiavelli is of a world far more dissonant and difficult to play upon, which is characterized by strategic manoeuvres made in contingent circumstances, is bereft of any overall harmonic and is without the guidance of any overall conductor. It is a world in which the intellectual cannot 'serve' power, since it cannot be simply located; one can only advise on strategies for its deployment in specific sites.

Later in the book it will be argued that Machiavelli's stress on strategies of power, rather than on power as a causal force, is an important corrective to the 'push-and-shove' mechanical conception of power which is implicit in both Hobbes and some present-day approaches to the analysis of power. In some respects, as authors such as Foucault and Callon have recognized, Machiavelli is much closer to 'post-modern' analyses of power than he is to the 'modernist' current. In turn, this modernist current is much closer to Hobbes' concerns. At the centre of this modernist current is a view of power initiated by human agency, expressed through causal relations and measurable in terms of mechanistic indicators. It is the metaphorical nature of Hobbes' mechanistic, causal and agency view of power that has been transmitted through the 'one-dimensional' models of power into so much present-day work. The transmission is more implicit than explicit. By contrast, the citation of Machiavelli by writers such as Foucault (1981) and Callon (1986) is a much more explicit attempt at signposting their less orthodox conceptions of power. Current debates will occasionally be mentioned in this chapter in anticipation of arguments that will be encountered later in the book.

The function of this chapter is to introduce the reader to some of the different emphases to be found in Hobbes and Machiavelli. Although Machiavelli preceded Hobbes, we shall begin with the latter because the argument of the book is that Hobbes is much closer to what is regarded as the central tradition of enquiry into power.

HOBBES

Why bother to read Hobbes today? In some respects his work might appear to be an unlikely point of departure for any modern consideration of power. He is hardly a present-day theorist, any more than Machiavelli would appear to be. While he did write in English, it was scarcely in a style that is easily or quickly scanned with a present-day sensibility. In that parlance, Hobbes is hardly 'user-friendly' (no matter that his prose is amongst the most rhythmical and elegant that one is likely to encounter in the social sciences). Like the King James edition of the Bible, his prose is many revisions away from modern sense.

Various reasons can and will be adduced as to why one might still want to read Hobbes. Of these, the most important is his constitutive role vis à vis the mainstream modern conception of power. Quite simply, had Hobbes not existed and his texts remained unwritten, it is doubtful whether the predominant view of power as a causal relation would have been so strongly and influentially grounded. This does not make Hobbes unique. On the contrary, many of his arguments were a 'representative' (Dawe 1973) articulation of a common experience of the world as a mechanism, which was shared amongst an elite of educated and scientifically aware people who were Hobbes' contemporaries. In the absence of Hobbes, such views would still have been propounded, although, perhaps, not so clearly.

To justify reading Hobbes today only because of his role as a representative of a context or as a foundational statement of a particularly influential worldview, while obviously important, might still be insufficient reason. Additional support may be found in Connolly (1988):

> World historical figures need not be confined to the context of their thought because, first, thought is itself a creative response to particular conditions irreducible to its preconditions of existence, second, highly creative thinkers transcend and transfigure understandings of their own time, and, third, those in other times and places who use these texts as a prod to their own thought often come to them with questions, interests and anxieties divergent from those which governed the composition of the texts. Thinking is often advanced by lifting theories out of contexts in which they were created. (Connolly 1988: vii-viii)

Connolly's three reasons not only stand as legitimate justifications for reading Hobbes but also offer implicit advice on how not to read him, or indeed any august forebear. Do not read reverentially, as if by doing so one could uncover or retrieve some real and utterly intended meaning from the text. This would be in vain since such authorially authentic interpretations are a chimera. Instead, read as one only ever can: as an active interpreter and interlocutor of meaning mined from the text. One will find, in some respects, what one seeks simply because of the questions one brings to bear on the text. Consequently, reading will take an interrogatory form: posing questions, raising problems, taking issue. How should we do this with Hobbes? A first question might consider the circumstances which enabled him to pose the questions that he did. This does not mean probing for a reductive answer nor does it even necessarily call for a genealogy of ideas (as provided by both Wolin [1960] and Connolly [1988] from the viewpoint of political philosophy).

One might instead pose the issue in terms of those conditions of late seventeenth century England which enabled Hobbes to raise the prospect of a relatively unified state power.

Hobbes advised the monarch of a nation which had recently undergone a civil war. The king was a national figure, an expressive manifestation of that insular 'cultural and linguistic unit, England [which] was virtually complete by about 1600' (Mann 1986: 462). Other actors, presently excluded from the 'imagined community [of] the nation', as Benedict Anderson (1983) has argued, would subsequently struggle for membership, in terms which were frequently mythologized as participation in the rights of a free-born Englishman (Thompson 1968). Hobbes' conceptual system was designed to ensure that all should know that the community of the nation was identical with the benign and expressive will of its monarch.

What made this conception possible was the emergence of a unified and hence novel, state power which had control of a culturally and religiously unified geo-political entity (Mann 1986). It was a state that was relatively safe from competing intra-national loci of power yet it was sufficiently mobilized on a maritime basis, by competing international powers, to require recurrent state-building resources. In the past the mechanism for sequestering resources had been a straightforward, intermittent and painful extraction of agricultural surplus into the bellies and coffers of the courtly elite. These methods were of less value when the monarch had to rule with a modicum of consent, as the state proliferated as an ensemble of office-holders. Consent became increasingly important in producing servants with good practical reason to support monarchical power. It is against this background that Hobbes' innovations should be viewed. The major innovation was the development of a distinctive discourse of sovereignty and an allied conception of power.

Hobbes' conception of sovereignty buttressed practical reasons for loyalty to a monarch with a model of moral reason. The premises of this moral order were founded on the universal claims of science's rational intelligence. As Wolin (1960: 243) remarks, it seemed undeniable to Hobbes that 'armed with the right method, and further armed with opportunity, man could construct a political order as timeless as a Euclidian theorem'. This combination of state power, resources and discursive framework is precisely what Bauman (1982) terms 'modernity', a context in which the role of key intellectuals would be to act as 'legislators' on the correct status of knowledge. Characteristically, this knowledge would be theorized in terms of its place in grand systems or meta-narratives, such as those of 'scientific laws' or the 'great tradition'. An imagined order, constructed as a totality, would be the representational hallmark of the worldview that was constructed. In the sciences, the methods would be those oriented towards the prediction and control of the subject matter of realms of enquiry; in the humanities, it would be the construction of interpretations of a panoply of canonical texts. The important thing would be to achieve a knowledge of that which is signified and to regard the process of signification as itself instrumental. Through such means one can legislate on what is to be regarded as worthwhile or objective knowledge.

The legislators are familiar to us from every stipulative and normative text of how to do science, particularly those written for the social sciences. How it is to be done is through strict attention to rules and the external discipline of being self-regarding in respect of one's conduct according to the rules. One will have the same regard for others who would be one's intellectual peers as they will have for one's self, with respect to following these rules. For those who play other games, one will have nothing but contempt or pity, depending on how one rates their arrogance. It is participation in a hard and difficult game whose rules are, in Durkheim's memorable phrase, 'social facts'. The purpose of following the rules is to achieve a provisionally accurate picture of the accepted states of affairs that one is representing. The means of representation, ideally, will have no instrumentality but will be pure conduits to a true knowledge of things. Means for arriving at this knowledge will be the known-in-common focus for creating a community of scientific legislators. Disagreements occur within the community; they concern the interpretation and application of the rules, not the rules themselves (at least not 'normally', as Kuhn (1962) makes clear). Hobbes' importance is in being one of the first scholars of power to propose an understanding of this key concept in terms which are procedurally legislative; unlike his many forebears in political philosophy, Hobbes tells us not what power ought to be but how we may know what it is.

HOBBES' MYTH

In bequeathing to us a set of precepts for the cognition of power Hobbes produced one of the most persistently cited oppositions in all social science: that between a world in which modernity, civility, sovereignty and rule flourished, and a world without these: one in which

> there is no place for industry; because the fruit thereof is uncertain: and consequently no culture of the earth; no navigation, nor use of the commodities that may be imposed by sea; no commodious building; no instruments of moving, and removing, such things as require much force; no knowledge of the face of the earth; no account of time; no arts; no letters; no society; and which is worst of all, continual fear and danger of violent death; and the life of man, solitary, poor, nasty, brutish, and short. (Hobbes 1962: 143)

There is much that could be and has been said about such a famous passage. Perhaps the most insightful commentary on the text itself is that made by Connolly (1988: 30) when he notes the increasing austerity of the prose as the passage unfolds. Finally it is sculpted down to an extraordinary construction ('and the life of man, solitary, poor, nasty, brutish and, short') which renders more through form than words alone the horror and emptiness of life outside civil society.

It is well known that no anthropological referent existed for this negation of civility, modernity, sovereignty and rule. Its expression has been seen by Macpherson (1962: 18–19) not as a representation of a natural state but as a kind of working hypothesis: what life would be like if it were abandoned to a setting bereft of civility, modernity, etc. Bauman's (1987: 34) view of the matter is somewhat different. For him, 'Hobbes was the victim of an optical illusion'. Illusion led him mistakenly to regard the outriders of capitalist modernity, the competitive, possessive individualists of Macpherson's (1962) account, as 'the living relics of the state of nature'. Others have regarded the 'state of nature' as altogether mythical (Clegg 1979: 30).

A myth may be said to do many things. Some writers have regarded myth as deifying the human and humanizing the divine (Zeraffa 1976: 77). Others have noted how myth theorizes the possible society and states of being of a people as an architectonic creation which 'fixes' the flux of time. Other interpretations abound. For anthropologists such as Bailey (1977), it is advisable that, in interpreting the meaning of myth, one should not stray too far from either the Greek root or the political function that myth has:

> A myth tells what one should desire ... and how to get it; the way people are and how they should be; the reasons why things happen the way they do, especially when they go wrong; in short, myths provide values and meaning and ideas and plans and stratagems and alternative forms of social organization. Only through a myth does one see the 'real' world. A myth is a form of pretence, an oversimplified representation of a more complex reality. (Bailey 1977: 7)

Hobbes' myth, as an 'oversimplified representation' concerned not only the 'state of nature' but also the 'state of order'. Each was equally fanciful but both served a strategic purpose: that of producing legitimation for a political community. Hobbes' means of achieving this was to seek secular order through divine grace. Order was to be constructed in the world through secularizing and generalizing God, 'the first author of *speech*' (Hobbes 1962: 33), into a rational method capable of reconstituting the 'body politic' through '*pacts*' and '*covenants*' premised on the divine act of fiat. There were actually two aspects to these pacts and covenants. One aspect concerned the abandonment of individualistic pretensions by those whom Bauman (1987) terms intellectual legislators. Instead of each person trying to make his or her own peculiar and particular mark, Hobbes proposes that each should knuckle down to work within a clear set of procedural rules concerning the definition of their terms. Central to this definition of terms was a particular conception of power that was to become 'normalized'. It was a conception of power as identical to cause. 'Power and Cause are the same thing,' said Hobbes (1839: 72). Thus, power was expressed in terms of motion.

Hobbes' notion of power was irrevocably bound up with the institution of the monarchy. Hobbes' *Leviathan* necessitated the vesting of architectonic power in the body of the sovereign as the solution to what was seen as the 'state of nature'. Representationally this solution was underscored by the frontispiece which adorned the 1651 edition of *Leviathan*. The sovereign is depicted as a huge figure overlooking an orderly and, by contrast, miniature scene of civil and industrious peace, achieved by virtue of the overwhelming authority of the sovereign.

> Yet there is another feature of the frontispiece worth noting. The sovereign's powerful body is, so to speak, not his own; its outline is completely filled in by the miniature figures of his subjects. He exists, in other words, only through them. Equally important, each subject is clearly discernible in the body of the sovereign. The citizens are not swallowed up in an anonymous mass, nor sacramentally merged into a mystical body. Each remains a discrete individual and each retains his identity in an absolute way. (Wolin 1960: 266)

Consequently, we may say, the organizing principle of the whole system is the identity of each subject with the sovereign power. Their identity is composed within the sovereign body. This is an idea, a motif, which we will find recurring in quite distant echoes of this image. Most clearly it is in Callon and Latour's (1981: 278) reconception of Hobbes' contractual framework in terms of translation; the means whereby an actor translates the 'voice' (Hirschman 1970) of other actors into passive voice, with the privilege of active voice being captured by the translator. Thus the Leviathan, Hobbes' old testament metaphor for the supreme power of the sovereign, 'is the people itself in another state' (Callon and Latour 1981: 278), not in a mystical way but as a result of a symbolic translation of voice: the social contract. What is achieved contractually is a fictive basis for the 'body politic' through the surrender, silencing and translation of each individual's sovereign act of subjectivity – the possession of *their* voice – into the 'loyalty' authorized by the translation: the discursive and practical disharmony of many competing sovereign subjects is rendered into, on the one hand, *sovereign* subjectivity in the shape of the Leviathan, and on the other hand, *subjectivity*, both as subjects and as expressive beings, whose expressivity, in fact, ought not to challenge the translation rights secured by the active voice of Leviathan. The rule of Leviathan thus becomes the process of ensuring that this does not happen.

HOBBES' CHOICE AND ITS CONCEPTUAL EXTENSION

What is progressively built on from Hobbes' choice of metaphors is an acceptance of the idea of a political community in which may be located the mechanical, causal and atomistic concept of power. What are progressively marginalized in the initial concern with sovereignty are issues of how rule is organized. What power is, irrespective of its organizational rule, becomes the predominant question. None the less, such issues of rule were not entirely absent. One way of conceptualizing what Hobbes wanted to make problematic would be to see his method as a means whereby the sovereign subjectivity of individuated bodies could be translated from an active to a passive voice within the body politic: precisely in order to make them individuals whose will is authorized by the Leviathan. In consequence, action initiated by these wills does not step outside such authorizations. In the event that wills do not conform then the 'reserve powers' of the Leviathan are available to make others desist from doing what their unauthorized expressions of will would otherwise have them do. Note the appellation 'reserve powers': these are powers which are literally held in reserve. The first line of power that the Leviathan has is the translator's right to determine passive and active voice: in other words, to authorize. Appetites, passions or interests, however, are deemed to be intrinsically unruly: they cannot be legislated out of existence and they may intrude into the orderly public sphere. In the interests of order they must be rebuked, reprimanded, restricted, ruled (one is tempted to say over-ruled), hence the concept of reserve powers.

It has been argued by Foucault (1980) that the 'reserve' notion of power, originating in the institution of the monarchy in the post-feudal period in Europe, is the central feature of the concept of power in modernity:

> I wonder if this modern conception of power isn't bound up with the institution of monarchy. This developed during the Middle Ages against the backdrop of the previously endemic struggles between feudal power agencies. The monarchy presented itself as a referee, a power capable of putting an end to war, violence and pillage and saying no to these struggles and private feuds. It made itself acceptable by allocating itself a juridical and negative function, albeit one whose limits it naturally began at once to overstep. Sovereign, law and prohibition formed a system of representation of power which was extended during the subsequent era by the theories of right: political theory has never ceased to be obsessed with the person of the sovereign. Such theories still continue today to busy themselves with the problem of sovereignty. What we need, however, is a political philosophy that isn't erected around the problem of sovereignty, nor therefore around the problems of law prohibition. We need to cut off the King's head: in political theory that has still to be done. (Foucault 1980: 121)

Foucault's colourful metaphor of a *coup de grâce* is, as we shall subsequently explore, an apposite, if somewhat flamboyant statement; however, its interpretation should not be too narrow. It is not just those negative, prohibitive connotations which were constituted by Hobbes' foundational statement of power that require execution.

Contemporary western Marxism, with its search for sovereign expressions of capitalism in the cultural and ideological sphere, and its theoretical gravitation in the orbit of hegemony, produces a social order which is equally as fictive as Hobbes' contractual view. In the latter each body was conceptualized potentially as a part of the sovereign order.

In western Marxism each mind was to be conceptualized potentially as a part of the hegemonic order. Hegemony becomes the metaphorical basis for constituting sovereign dominion even in the face of individuals who do not act: in fact, it is reserved precisely to translate inaction into non-action and non-action into prohibited action. Individuals do not act because, paradoxically, they know not to want to act; prohibition runs deep into the consciousness of the possible range of actions that individuals may have. Order, where it has been achieved, is secured by the sovereign power exerting dominion over the very ingredients of individual consciousness: the appetites, passions and especially the *interests* that these individuals have. Thus, the supreme prohibitory concept of power comes to hold sway precisely through constituting individuals in such a way that they are not being actors in particular scenes of power. Power is negative not simply because there are actors who negate but because there are actors who, through no action of their own, can live their lives only as an inauthentic negation of their individual agency. Free to choose they may be, but what they can choose from is already chosen: not specifically by anyone but by default and by virtue of what is discursively available for individuals to use to be or not to be actors in particular scenes.

Discursive unavailability, the ultimate prohibition, becomes in this radical view 'the supreme and most invidious exercise of power' (one is tempted to say, the sovereign power). Lukes (1974) asks rhetorically whether this functions

> to prevent people, to whatever degree, from having grievances by shaping their percep-
> tions, cognitions and preferences in such a way that they accept their role in the existing
> order of things, either because they can see or imagine no alternative to it, or because
> they see it as natural and unchangeable, or because they value it as divinely ordained and
> beneficial? To assume that the absence of grievance equals genuine consensus is simply
> to rule out the possibility of false or manipulated consensus by definitional fiat. (Lukes
> 1974: 24)

'False or manipulated consensus' thus functions as a means of explaining how and why actors behave as they choose and not as a given theoretical observer would expect them to choose, according to theoretical affinities. It is a way of not taking people seriously; of regarding them as having been culturally duped; of preserving, against contra-indications, a view of power as orchestrated by a single sovereign, ruling entity. What makes it seem so may be less the nature of empirical tendencies and more the mythical meta-narratives of a grand and systemic view of the world.

MACHIAVELLI: THE CONTRAST WITH HOBBES

Foucault (1979a) provides a brief overview of the myths that have surrounded Machi-avelli's variable reception from the sixteenth century. Myth is no more lacking in an understanding of Machiavelli than it is in the understanding of Hobbes. Yet there is a significant difference in the role that myth plays for each of these early modern theorists of power. As Bailey (1977) makes clear, there is more than one way to employ myth: not only can it function as part of the constitutive metaphors which frame analysis, as it does in Hobbes, but it can also be seen in its function *in* political discourse, rather than simply *as* political discourse. Bailey (1977: 8) defines politics as 'the art of bringing unacceptable myths into, and preserving one's own myths from, derision'. Such an explicitly political conception of myth (and a conception of politics as discursive) resonates with themes that abound in Machiavelli. Indeed, much of *The Discourses* (Machiavelli 1970) can be read as a sustained attempt to undermine existing myths of honourable conduct and to create instead a model of precepts framed by the myth of strategy: to act expediently with respect to means in order to be honourable to the ends one should serve.

In Machiavelli, by contrast with Hobbes' myth of public order, the concern with strategy leads him to a view of reality not as reflecting the order granted by a beneficent sovereign but as an arena in which such order may be secured by the strategically mindful prince (Machiavelli 1958). The focus is on strategies, deals, negotiation, fraud and conflict in which myths concerning moral action become gameplayers' resources rather than a topic which frames what the game should be.

As an idea, Hobbes' notion of political community could function as myth, when seen from Machiavelli's more cynical, rationalist and realist perception. For the latter, the stress is on interpreting extant games rather than on legislating their form; on following the moves actually made rather than on determining whether the moves belong to the game legislated as 'power'. While the interpretivist thrust operates with a broad, conceptually kaleidoscopic and imprecise conception of power, the legislative imagination stitches up one which is neat, tight and precise. Precision ought to produce a better tool for science although its instrumentality may be severely restricted in interpreting the detail of actual game play. Although it can prescribe what the game should consist of, normatively, if it is to be an occasion for scientifically precise instruments to do their stuff, it can offer no guarantees that reality will adopt the form it requires. It is for this reason that the experiment is the exemplary method of the natural sciences. The experiment, as an artificially constructed and achieved exclusion of unwarranted phenomena, creates an environment of restricted possibilities in which the scientist can manipulate a limited number of variables and can legislate relationships such that an A will always have the same determinate effect on a B, 'experimental error' permitting. Outside of the controlled conditions prevailing in the laboratory (those which enable scientific intervention to fashion pure instrumentality), reality can rarely be guaranteed to effect the form that precise instruments require. In more rough and ready conditions a less pure instrument may be required.

Hobbes offers a relatively pure instrumentality of power in his definition of 'the power of a man' as 'his present means to obtain some future apparent good' (Hobbes 1962: 72).

In Hobbes power is carefully defined and stipulated within a framework in which it is a key term for legislating political community and securing moral order. One would search in vain for similar concerns in Machiavelli's corpus. Machiavelli avoids the ethical issue of constructing ultimate values: he is to be seen not so much as a legislator of what the modern condition should be but as an interpreter of what it actually is, to employ Bauman's (1987) terms. With respect to power this involves not so much stipulating what it should be as interpreting and translating what it is. For Machiavelli power is conceived as pure expediency and strategy rather than as pure instrumentality. While Hobbes would propose to legislate for a social contract, Machiavelli would interpret a strategy; where Hobbes founds a discursive framework for analysis of power as motion, causality, agency and action, Machiavelli instead describes an ethnographic research method for uncovering the rules of the game.

The difference between these two key figures is explicable. Hobbes served the monarch of a nation which had achieved a fair degree of cultural and linguistic unity, as remarked at the outset. The framework in which the legislator's role could be played was thus already constructed (although not, it must be added, with the effectiveness that Bauman [1987: 21–37] identifies for *les philosophes* a century later and a short distance further east). Moreover, Hobbes wrote with that great intellectual confidence which the example of the scientific project provided for those who followed it. However, Hobbes' importance lies not in his scientific claims nor in his practical administrative, organizational or managerial effects, but in his articulation of key conceptual tenets of modernity as power. Henceforward, power was to be constituted primarily as an essentially modern, mechanical concept. Hobbes was legislator not for state power *per se* but for a science in which power was a key concept. In this respect he was, in Bauman's (1987) terms, a legislator of the very role of legislator:

> Whereas sense and memory are but knowledge of fact, which is a thing past and irrevocable; *science* is the knowledge of consequences, and dependence of one fact upon another: by which, out of that we can presently do, we know how to do something else when we will, or the like another time; because when we see how any thing comes about, upon what causes, and by what manner; when the like causes come into our power, we see how to make it produce the like effects. (Hobbes 1962: 45)

Machiavelli had no such options open to him. Cast adrift from state service by the changing nature of political adventurism and division in Medici Florence, he wrote his work not as a trusted legislator, from a position of intellectual, scientific and political certainty, but as an uncertain explorer for a power which refused him employment and which spurned him to a degree far greater than the prudent Hobbes ever encountered at the hands of his monarch, Charles II of England. Moreover, within Florence there was little to encourage musings on settled social contracts so much as on strategic action: 'a pragmatic method of analysis concentrating almost exclusively on questions of power' (Wolin 1960: 199), as Machiavelli's most astute commentator has observed. Against this backdrop of turmoil in Florentine politics Machiavelli forged a new interpretation of power in which one of its most significant aspects 'was that it was unrelated to a systematic philosophy' (Wolin 1960: 211). This interpretation holds, despite, one may note, the many attempts to provide such a philosophy on the part of subsequent observers. (See Crick [1958] for a brief and elegant account of these.)

The characteristics of Machiavelli's new interpretation of power derived their sense from the political world in which he lived and studied: a world of flux, discontinuity, intrigue and illusion, in which 'everyone is equipped to see, few can understand' (cited in Wolin [1960: 212]). Illusion is less to be legislated out of existence by a scientific declaration of 'right method' than to be interpreted as to its effectiveness in the political armoury of strategic actors such as the prince: 'the new science was more in the nature of a body of knowledge adjusted to a world of movement, rather than one aimed at freezing it' (Wolin 1960: 213). Such movement could not be totally controlled because too much of it was contingent. Knowledge alone could not hope to grasp this contingency but the combination of power *and* knowledge might enable some strategic understanding.

Hobbes was the great designer, architectonically legislating on the 'right method' for constituting power. By contrast Machiavelli's 'aim was political mastery not political sculpture' as Wolin (1960: 216) so nicely phrases it. Knowledge of the strategies and techniques of political mastery, of power, was achieved through what Callon and his colleagues have termed a 'thoroughgoing determination to follow the actors wherever they go, to uncover what they might prefer to keep concealed, and to avoid being misled by myths' (Callon et al. 1986: 5). In this interpretation what is of importance is Machiavelli's method and his insistence on studying strategies of power whatever and wherever they might be rather than being restricted by any a priori mechanical or causal conceptions.

In *The Prince* Machiavelli offers a rich descriptive ethnography of power conceived in terms of its strategies. Towards these strategies he takes no moral stance: they are neither good nor bad, their only purpose is their effectiveness. They flow from no principle of sovereignty; they serve no principle of sovereignty; they reproduce no principle of sovereignty. Machiavelli does not serve power: he merely describes its strategies as he sees it at work within the arena of the palace. Power does not belong to anyone nor to any place; it is not something that princes necessarily have; it is no Leviathan. Power is simply the effectiveness of strategies for achieving for oneself a greater scope for action than for others implicated by one's strategies. Power is not any thing nor is it necessarily inherent in any one; it is a tenuously produced and reproduced effect which is contingent upon the strategic competencies and skills of actors who would be powerful.

From the shadows of the palace Machiavelli observes and describes power at play. It is this stress on description, on interpretation, on the translation of power, that signals Machiavelli's distinctiveness. In marked contrast to Hobbes, his focus is on power *in situ*, in the specific arena of the palace with its many locales, rather than power as a generalizing concept for daunting the world or for making it seem awesome. It is in the very prosaic refusal of any grand theory or meta-narrative, above all, that Machiavelli's distinctiveness resides. Power is embedded in many diverse forms of practice within the arena constituted by the palace; such practices may be methodically interpreted as to their strategicality but cannot be assumed to be effective simply by virtue of their author. The strategic concern has two facets, according to Ehnmark (1986, especially 169–209. I am grateful to Winton Higgins for the reference and the translation). One facet is a concern with liberation from tyranny, the strategic concern of *The Prince*, while the concern of *The Discourses* is with freedom and the need to dismantle the counter-power that is required to overwhelm tyranny immediately after it has done its job, in order to prevent it from turning into tyranny itself. In this respect liberation should be considered as an event rather than as a permanent state of affairs to be designed into existence by some grand architectonic.

The subtitle of Wolin's (1960) chapter on Machiavelli is 'politics and the economy of violence'. At the core of Machiavelli's concern with power is 'the primordial fact that the hard core of power is violence and to exercise power is often to bring violence to bear on someone else's person or possessions' (Wolin 1960: 220). Strategy, to be effective, must know when to be cruel and when to withdraw: in other words it must practise an economy of violence, sparingly, appropriately and creatively. An effective economy of violence requires careful consideration of its military forms, knowledge of the means required to translate armed bodies into disciplined organized power. Most especially, it should exercise such power sparingly: wreaking violence as a political strategy which is followed too often or too easily serves to demonstrate the real structural weakness of a power which has to intervene so ferociously. Securing consent may be a more effective form of translating power into strategic action than always having to coerce recalcitrant bodies. Or it may not. On some occasions, at least, violence may be judged more effective.

Where consent may be secured Machiavelli does not believe that it will be generalized, the application of some universal or essential fiat across all spheres of action. Part of the flux of life inheres in its radical discontinuities: different forms of life display their own rationalities rather than the invisible hand of any architectonic reason. (Smith and Marx both admitted of such an essential principle. Of course they differed on what they believed its effects and prime movers to be.) Strategy which was effective as a knowledge of power in one sphere may have no effect at all in another form of life.

METAPHORS FOR MODERNS: HOBBES AND MACHIAVELLI

The intellectual concerns of those substantive fields of politics and sociology that are involved with power have tended to follow tracks laid down in the Hobbesian problematic rather than in Machiavelli's strategic observations. This is so even where the object of analysis has been organizational rather than community power: the pervasive mechanism of concepts derived from Hobbes' metaphors of political community have tended, with some exceptions, to frame the discourse on 'power in organizations' (Clegg 1977). Modernity has tracked the concern with power conceived in mechanical terms. In Machiavelli we find signs of a quite distinct conception which is not amenable to Hobbesian terms. Table 2.1 contrasts Hobbes and Machiavelli in terms of the distinct metaphors that each assembles in his work.

It is in the light of the opposition between the metaphors central to the image of power which each constructs that Hobbes and Machiavelli have been read. The suggestion is that Hobbes' terms have been the dominant mode of representing the concept of power. Consequently, its motif has been a recurrent concern with political order. It has been assumed that it is political community as order whose functioning requires explanation. Most frequently this has been in terms of the metaphorical substitute for the sovereign with which rule is orchestrated. In pluralist theory, this has been the sovereign subjects of the people, arranged in interest groups. For elitist theorists, neither all people nor all interest groups are equally instrumental: sovereignty is displayed through the capture and relatively stable deployment of key resources as instruments for the rule of elite groups – those who control the commanding heights of the economy, polity and society.

Table 2.1   Machiavelli and Hobbes' metaphors for modernity

Hobbes	Machiavelli
Emphasis on 'causality'	Emphasis on 'strategy'
Science and the monarch each constituted as authoritative origins of action as it should be	Pragmatic advice and ethnographic orientation towards forms of action actually encountered
Adoption of the role of 'legislator'	Adoption of the role of 'interpreter'
Emphasis on mechanistic metaphors	Emphasis on military metaphors
Emphasis on a source of 'prime motion' behind action	Emphasis on the contingent nature of action
Problematic of legitimacy lending the account of power an implicitly 'moral' stance, with a stress on the legitimate identification (in terms of science) of the means of power as well as a concern for good order in the ends that power serves	Problematic of strategy lending the account of power an implicitly 'amoral' stance, with a stress on the efficiency of means rather than the goodness of ends
The use of the myth of political community	The use of myths in political organization

For structuralist or class hegemonic theorists, political community is simply translated into ideological reproduction, class hegemony or false consciousness – a false moral order for which sovereignty resides in the ruling class, ruling structures and ruling meanings.

A conception of political order and community unites each position however much its interpretation in each instance distinguishes them. For conservative pluralists, political community is a democracy; for liberal elitists, it is an oligarchy; for radical structuralists, it is ideological hegemony. For each tradition of theory, political order is real: it is taken for granted; it has only to be explained. Hobbes' heirs share their inheritance on this one point only. It is self evident that there is order and that power produces it, however much disagreement there is on either the nature of that power or the authenticity of that order in terms of its expression of people's real interests.

Political community and order might have been sustainable within a *gemeinschaft* world of face-to-face contact and discourse. In such a world, a concept of power modelled on notions of 'direct control' (Simon 1952) between individuals would be most appropriate. Hobbes is, of course, the *locus classicus* of such a notion. Its consequences are evident. One could only think of power as occurring when one powerful individual succeeded in imposing his or her will on another. Such a world of direct control may today be a relatively rare provenance of pockets of social life in a world increasingly dominated by large complex organizations, both in the state and in the economy. Order, where it is achieved, is more likely to be an accomplishment of mechanisms of discipline, which are more mediated, more formalized, and more routinized, than simply 'direct control' someone getting others to do something that they would not otherwise have done. Such power mediated by discipline – 'disciplinary power' – first emerged in monastic orders (as we shall see in chapter seven), before becoming a set of generalized edicts, precepts and practices of honourable behaviour within more explicitly political forms of life. As Bauman (1982) shows, advice and precept-giving slowly changed from being oriented to princes and increasingly came to be addressed to paupers, prisoners, patients, proletarians, pupils and the public in general. While Elias (1982) guides us through the precepts of high society, Bauman (1982) orients us towards the practices of disciplinary power developed for mass rather than merely elite consumption. Consequently, disciplinary power increasingly came to address, from a myriad of discursive sites, those vile bodies arranged outside the political community that were to be politically organized: in armies, prisons, factories, and workhouses. As such, it extended the application of that discrimination organized in courtly society, to use Elias' (1983) phrase. Unevenly, divisively and slowly that discrimination was exteriorized from matters of taste to matters of fact which were legislated through the application of right method. Through matters of fact being made apparent 'real' bases of order could be shown. Initially this extension was achieved through practices of cultural isomorphism; latterly, this was to be achieved through deliberately constructed settings of tutelage whereby great masses of people 'outside' *civil* society were coached, coaxed, and placed, if never entirely subordinated, within the civil strata. Passions were to be subordinated to interests; the base animal to be refined into the human form; the dangerous and unruly to be disciplined into the orderly and predictable; the savage to be civilized; the ignorant to be made enlightened (Bauman 1982 represents an excellent account). This was a project of power that could never be envisaged in the pre-modern state.

Within the master symbols and metaphors which have represented the concept of power since Hobbes, the idea that power may be seen through the notion of a disciplinary apparatus rather than through particular causal incidents of prohibition was not easily registered. Such representations bore so clearly the marks of Hobbes' 'right method' that they were wont to be oriented, above all, to a notion of power that was conceived in terms of Hobbes' discursive orientations towards sovereign subjects exerting their will rather than to mundane practices shaping subjectivity. In short, they were attuned to a concept of power as supreme subjectivity, creating a practical consensus of two or more individual wills, rather than to a concept of power expressed in and through mundane practices of organization.

CONCLUSION

Sovereignty was the core of Hobbes' concern. His elaborate system for conceptualizing power was formally subordinated to the sovereignty concept. Sovereignty, the old theoretical centre of power, as Bauman (1982: 43) suggests, did not hold for long as the practical centre of power. By the nineteenth century and the full flowering of 'tutelary' complexes, the rationalizing project had dispersed power over subjects far from any single sovereign centre. None the less, it will be suggested, in one form or another replays of this central idea of a ruling sovereignty were to be widely produced until at least the late 1970s. Other, newer candidates for sovereign status as an originating and central point of prime motion were to be proposed: most notably the ruling capitalist class and the ruling capitalist state. One might say that this continuity of concern demonstrates that, irrespective of the *practices* of disciplinary power, the formal theoretical concern with what was taken to be power had been fixed by Hobbes in a preoccupation with questions of causality, sovereignty and order. One consequence of this is that a gulf or lacuna exists in moving from consideration of both conventional and radical views of power (e.g. Lukes 1974), which are oriented precisely to concerns of order, responsibility and cause, to the 'disciplinary power' of Foucault. On the one hand there is a predominant concern with legislating the parameters of concepts of power and, on the other, much more concern with power's strategies.

The gulf is not entirely incommensurable but it does require, in a word, *translation*, as has been demonstrated by Callon and Latour (1981) in their 'unscrewing' of the 'big

Leviathan'. The translation is not of equal value in both directions. The questions posed within the 'foundational' tradition of power in its modernity by Hobbes and his heirs, it will be argued, can be understood as so many ritual moves through the rules of a particular language game which has become thoroughly restrictive. It will take us only so far; if we wish to go further we have to move out of the game and into another. In this respect the foundational tradition of power may be said to have framed the major moves in a game of theorizing power. These moves can be traced from attempts to specify more precisely the metaphysical concerns in the 'agency view' of Hobbes, Locke and Hume. They lead to major areas of contest within the game: Is power distributed 'plurally' or held by an 'elite'? Is power intentional or not intentional? Is power confined to decision making or is it evident in non-decision making? Is not making a decision an action or a non-action? Is power a capacity for action or the exercise of action? The questions spin on as if a conceptual arachnid were endlessly weaving a linguistic funnel-web with which to ensnare our understanding.

Part of the problem, this book will argue, is to persist in thinking of conceptions of power in unitary terms to which all issues of theorization must be resolved. Even a writer like Lukes (1974), who has done so much to further our understanding of power through his three-dimensional model, still regards the dimensions as layers of a single conceptual structure built on the slab defined by the foundational tradition. Against such a view this book will argue for three distinct but related conceptions of power, and will construct them accordingly in terms not only of their internal relations but also their relations to each other. In this way the funnel-web of an imaginary unitary power can be avoided.

Central to this revised trinity of conceptions will be the emphasis in Machiavelli on strategies of power, interpreted through a post-structuralist perspective. The central debates in the attempt to prescribe the unitary conception of power have either been internal to an agency perspective, inherited from Hobbes and his successors, or between agency and structural perspectives. Post-structuralism has been largely absent from debate. Within the agency-structure debate, persistent tendencies to reduce the debate to one or other of the terms are evident. It is for this reason that a third way for resolving the debate will be proposed.

The many attempts at legislating a unitary meaning of power have not fulfilled Hobbes' promise: if anything they have left us more 'entangled', more 'belimed' (Hobbes 1962: 37). It is less important to adjudicate the debate by declaring in favour of this or that one true concept of power, once and for all time. Instead, perhaps we should explore the language games for theorizing power, note the political myths, identify the rules and pinpoint a few moves and strategies in them. Maybe it is in these moves, these strategies, these passages constructed through the ensnaring funnel-web that prototypes of power may be seen? Power may consist in the networking of relations, in the way in which moves in the game implicate others as allies or adversaries in one's interpretation of what the game is. The suggestion is that this may be as true for theorizing power as for any other kind of power. In constructing such interpretations one necessarily creates yet more webs of power. There may be no way out of this process. Perhaps we are as much condemned to interpretation as we are to strategies of power? Certainly, without the latter we could never achieve the former in the public realm.

In conclusion, this chapter has explored two distinct foundations of a modernist problematic of power. One of these has been the predominant *leitmotif* of contemporary concerns, while the other has been far less evident. The ascendant conception, as we shall see in the next chapter, was that of Hobbes, while the concerns of Machiavelli have been of far less currency for those central planks of modern scholarship concerned with the concept of power. The chapter has sought to contrast the two conceptions in order to throw into relief the version of enquiry into power which each favours. Later in the book we shall have cause to recover the sense of power as it is found in Machiavelli's strategic conception. Machiavelli's insights are important in that they alert us to a conception of power altogether less mythical and more realistic in its appreciation of strategy, alliances and networks in the analysis of power. Such insights are important in order to develop a less one-sided perspective than those which are inscribed at the core of many present-day power analyses. The major traditions of these derive their terms primarily from Hobbes, usually in a manner which is more implicit than explicit. The derivation is one of domain assumptions which frame and ground the sense of what it is that they do. It is these terms which we shall consider in detail in the next chapter.

3
POLITICAL COMMUNITY, METHODOLOGICAL PROCEDURES AND THE AGENCY MODEL

INTRODUCTION

The most pervasive present-day view of power is closely aligned with that 'agency' model which was prefigured in Hobbes, Locke and Hume (Ball 1978). In this respect it does seem to be the case that what were once philosophers' metaphors can indeed become behavioural scientists' models (Ball 1975: 211). Essentially Ball's argument consists in establishing that the modern representation of power in the work of political scientists like Dahl is every bit as mechanistic, atomistic and classically causal in its arguments as were those of Hobbes or Locke. The vocabulary has changed somewhat, as Ball says, but the metaphors have remained very similar. Metaphorically the focus is on models of causal power. In these models, just as in Hobbes, subjects constituted as individuals with clear preference orders are sovereign. Their sovereignty is exercised either by making others do things that they would otherwise rather not do, or by their resisting the attempts of others to make them do such things as would be against their preferences. Implicitly the model draws on some classical arguments about causality, as Hobbes developed them, coupled with a more rigorous concern with aspects of contemporary hard-edged social science methodology, in an attempt to generate formal models of power. Not only are these models implicitly reflective upon long-dead philosophers' causal metaphors of power, but they also represent some of the same philosophers' normative assumptions about the existence of political community. On the one hand, the notion of community is replete with what Martindale (1960: 52) has termed 'organicism' (that is, the elements of the totality which is termed a community display integral, vital relations); on the other hand, 'political' is a notion summoning up ideas of the artful construction of forms of rule over what might otherwise be unruly. As we have seen, the basis of Hobbes' construction of the myth of an orderly, ruled community of subjects is the assumption of a sovereign subject exercising power: it is the supreme, sovereign subjectivity of the *Leviathan* which is the basis for political community.

When Ball (1976) traced the unravelling of causal metaphors in contemporary political science, the authors that he addressed were, on the whole, participants in the 'Community Power Debate'. This had its origins in the efforts of mostly United States political scientists to study the empirical distribution of power in American communities. (Clark [1972] and Leiff [1972] respectively provided overviews of the debate and the bibliography that it had generated.) The genesis of the community power debate was quite straightforward, developing out of criticisms by one group of scholars of the methodologies, values and findings of another group of scholars; the 'pluralists' critiquing the 'elitists'. Before there was a community power debate, there were studies of political elites in communities. Although these have typically been identified as the more politically left-oriented of the two camps of scholars (the pluralists on the whole being seen as more right-oriented as a result of the predominance of liberal assumptions in their models), elite analysis need not be anticonservative. This is evident and recognized in a work of relevant analysis of *Elitism* by Higley and Field (1976). In fact, in reconstituting elitism as a normative advocacy of the need for elite dominance to secure social order, the latter authors are much closer to the spirit of classical elitism than the radical elitists such as C. Wright Mills (1956).

This chapter will begin with a brief résumé of the argument linking Hobbes' causal conception of power with contemporary causal approaches as exemplified by the work of Robert Dahl. The continuities are evident in terms of the implicit assumptions that underline Hobbes' mechanicalism and Dahl's behaviouralism. The chapter will then turn to a consideration of the context within which Dahl developed his ideas about power: that of explicit opposition to 'elitist' approaches to the study of power and democracy in the United States. The elitism opposed should be differentiated from the classical conception of elitism in political theory. Its generally critical tone and attitude towards the way in which the practice of democracy in America did not appear to be consistent with the ideals generally understood to underlie that democracy, meant that many of the elitists were quite radically oriented scholars. This was not the case for the pluralists. In order to clarify the difference between 'classical elitism' and contemporary elitism, the former will be briefly discussed before moving to a consideration of the latter, and of Dahl's challenge to it. The challenge was constructed in methodological terms and so the focus will be on questions of how to study power rather more than on what results were produced by the many studies that have been made. A decade after Dahl had produced his methodological critique of elitism, a British writer, Kenneth Newton (1969), was to produce an equally powerful challenge to pluralism. In order to clarify the contrast between the two approaches, a table will be used which explicitly compares the pluralist and elitist models. It will be seen that many of Dahl's critical points lose some of their edge when contrasted with a systematic rejoinder such as Newton's.

METAPHORICAL CONTINUITIES

In a number of publications, Terence Ball (1975; 1976; 1978; 1988), an American political theorist, has spelt out an interesting argument about the way in which the modern conception of political science has frequently been implicitly limited to an 'agency' model of power whose roots are clearly discernible in political liberalism, with a tap-root reaching back into Hobbes' concept of power. In fact, the agency model of power, as pertaining when one agent causes another agent to do something that the latter would otherwise not do, is explicitly Hobbesian: it is Hobbes (1839) who introduces the term 'agency' in *De Corpore* in his *English Works*. Such a model is no more than a view of power which 'directs our attention to individual agents who act intentionally', as Ball (1978: 99) expresses it. Ball draws attention not only to the modernist ethos of this notion but also to its roots in modernity which, he plausibly argues, were nourished from the fertile context of Hobbes' writings. 'What is his *Leviathan*', he asks, 'if not an extension and elaboration of metaphors drawn from Galilean mechanics?' (Ball 1975: 214). Without any doubt the powerful accomplishments of Galileo's new mechanical science constituted the framework for Hobbes' thinking (Clegg 1979). Hobbes' thought was characterized by its atomism, mechanicalism and causalism, which, with only minor emendation and change, was to be endorsed by those subsequent figures who were to become intellectual pathways every part as central and strategic as Hobbes. Locke thought of the mechanisms in terms of the motion of billiard balls (or later tennis balls), an imagery picked up by Hume. People were to be thought of as individuals who move around as if they were billiard balls, impelled not by external agency but by wants or preferences. These Hobbes called 'appetites' or 'desires'. They were later to be designated as interests by Adam Smith. Meanwhile, David Hume was to clarify the causal basis implicit in earlier conceptions (see Ball 1975: 213–16). Hume's arguments concerning causality are well known and Ball (1978) elaborates them clearly. A genuinely causal relation will only hold between things or events which are entirely discrete or separate from one another in space and time but which share a contingent or contiguous relationship. Effects must be distinct from causes: they cannot be at all implicated as the same phenomenon but must be rigorously separate in actuality, in conceptual distinction and in logical relation. As far as social reality is concerned, the universe of causal relations takes place between individuals conceived in the manner of 'ontologically autarchic' entities (Ball 1978: 102), bodies discrete, separate and distinct. What makes them so is that they are individually embodied: because each body is a unique space-time conjuncture then so is each individual.

Initially in Hobbes and more recently in critiques of the behaviouralist tendencies of contemporary theorizations of power, the agent was invariably considered as an intentional being. While Hobbes' prioritization of causality may have been retained by the modern behaviourists, the stress on power as an intentional phenomenon was not. The critique of behaviouralism in contemporary political science was made necessary by the adoption in the United States of an explicitly behavioural perspective on politics in the years 1924–26. During this time were held three annual conferences on the 'science of politics', which were reported in the *American Political Science Review* in volumes 18–20. The conferences were based on the views of the leading political scientists of the day: that a behavioural science approach to politics, derived from Watsonian approaches in psychology, was the 'chief hope for the future of the science' in attacking 'problems of technique and method' (Caton 1976: 155, note 1). From that time, the behavioural persuasion began to flourish in the ranks of political science, reaching its zenith during the 1950s, notably with the contributions of Lasswell and Kaplan (1950) and Dahl (1957).

Elsewhere in the discipline of politics, the classical liberal faith in intentionality which Hobbes had manifested had been maintained by writers like Hayek (1944) and Berlin (1969), for whom agency, intentionality and liberty were an indissoluble trinity of concepts. In some respects the evacuation of the classical liberal concern with the specificity of the person left behavioural political science with little other than the shell of the traditional conception. The shell consisted in a certain metaphoricality in which mechanistic, atomistic and, above all, causal images reigned supreme. As already remarked, the tap-root of these conceptions had been nourished from Hobbes. Ball (1978: 100) notes that Hobbes' imagery was once condensed by Watkins (1965) into the simple motto: 'No change without push'. It is a world in which causal power relations occur between individuated and atomistic entities 'whirling through a social void', a world 'comprised of matter in motion, of forces in collision, of bodies pushing... and being pushed'. Today this may seem almost to be second nature as a view of what power is. Once, however, it was a novel conception which was one spawned in the triumph of the mechanical world-view that furnished Hobbes with his striking imagery of clockwork and mechanical engineering as the model for his method of hypothetical dissolution and recomposition:

> For as in a watch, or some small engine, the matter, figure, and motion of the wheels cannot be well known, except it be taken asunder and viewed in parts; so as to make a more curious search into the rights of states and duties of subjects, it is necessary... that they be so considered as if they were dissolved. (Hobbes 1839, *De Cive*: 15, xiv; cited in Ball 1975: 214)

Hobbes was explicit about his use of metaphor but this is not the case, contends Ball, when we come to look at the twentieth-century behavioural echo in political science (Ball 1975; 1976; 1978; also see Clegg 1979: ch. 3).

Locke (1959) may be regarded as largely accepting Hobbes' causal view of power, while adding a dash of rationality to the mechanics bequeathed to him, according to Ball (1978). It is through the representations of sense data that we perceive the idea of power in mechanical movements, a conception which Locke was inclined to render in game terms. He struck a metaphor for conceptualizing power which has persisted to the present day: the cause and motion exhibited by the clash of billiard balls upon the baize. Later he was to note that, although human clashing may appear to be like that of billiard balls, there was the important difference that humans, unlike balls, could have preferences about what or whom they hit or indeed about whether or not they preferred to stay at rest. Rationality concerned the justification of these preferences, such that people may be said to have interests in certain outcomes. The modern concern with power in behavioural science has tended to retain both the causal clashing and the conception of interest as an individual preference – a source of almost insuperable problems as we shall see.

Hume (1902) is rightly regarded as the theorist who did most to fix the causal representation of the world in a fully elaborated ontology of agency. This ontology undergirds the major contribution to debate of so many modern causal theorists of power (see Clegg 1979: ch. 3 for a review of some of this literature). Hume's (1902) innovation was to place the notion of causality upon sound footings. The argument was that 'genuinely causal relations would obtain only between discrete things or events which are both contingent and contiguous. Causal relations may obtain only between distinct things or events; that is, causal relations hold only between individuated entities' (Ball 1978: 101). A cause has to be identified and described in terms absolutely independent of the effect. It was this requirement, composing the outer shell of possible causal practice for present-day political scientists such as Dahl (1957), which made it imperative that intentional phenomena could not be causes. A reason, belief or intention could not function as a cause for one who was adhering to Hume's specifications of what the context of a causal argument could be. This was because it could never be clear that the putative intentional cause and the alleged action effect were in fact separable. The description of an action as a specific type of action and the statement of an intention as the cause of that action would invariably be implicated in each other because the intention-description would be the identification of the action as *that* type of action, rather than another. The cause and the effect would not be logically or conceptually distinct relations between 'things' but would be relations between a described action and the description applied to that action. The description of the action and the description of the intention would be inseparable (see the discussion in Clegg 1979: 48–54). Ball (1978: 102) makes the point clearly. If someone is male and unmarried, this cannot be considered to be the cause of his being a bachelor because the relation is a conceptual and not a contiguous one. Being male and being unmarried means being a bachelor. The description of the action and its cause would be indissolubly linked. Such conceptual linkages undergird a great deal of what we term a causal relationship in the more relaxed world of everyday life, compared to the world of science. Sometimes these conceptual linkages have been advanced scientifically (see MacIntyre's 1962 argument against such advances). For instance, the intentional refraining from action by a B is much used as an instance of the power of an A in some recent accounts of power which have taken issue with the behavioural view (Bachrach and Baratz 1962). The influence of this work in the 1960s and 1970s saw a renewed defence of the intentional elements of action, frequently from a politically left-liberal perspective. By contrast, more behaviourally oriented political science tended to view agents without any assumptions about their having intentionality. Dispensing with questions about whether or not individuals 'intended' to do something or not leaves one free to concentrate on actual doings conceived in mechanistic terms.

There is one interesting side-effect of the stripping down of the classical liberal conception of agency to that of modern causal conceptions derived from behaviouralism. It is that, on the whole, agencies have lost their embodiment. Indeed, it was left to Foucault (1977) to re-discover embodiment at the heart of power and thus recapture a central theme of the liberal tradition. Whereas the agents of liberal theory were people whose uniqueness resided in their distinct embodiment so that the body was the defining characteristic of the individual, modern behavioural conceptions of power in writers like Dahl (1957) have kept the individualism but have abandoned the body. With this abandonment, as Ball (1978: 102) suggests, they have lost another of the foundations for their theory which classical theory had prepared. The reason why theorists from Hobbes to Locke were preoccupied with physical safety, suggests Ball, is because the *raison d'être* of the 'body politic' was the preservation of the individual bodies composing it. (One may add that, where Hobbes was concerned, this was particularly true of the body of the sovereign.) It is for this reason that individuation is not viewed as a problem for classical liberal theory: the individuated, atomistic view of agency was built into the bedrock on which the theory stood. With the abandonment of this humanism, by the modern behavioural fixation on As and Bs who may or may not happen to be individuals, the 'ontological autarchy' of the agency perspective ceases to have secure roots.

The continuities between the classical and modern agency views are in fact largely confined to the assumption of the self-evidence of power as a causal phenomenon in terms which would have been recognizable to the classical theorists. The contributions of any number of writers could be used to support this proposition, as has been argued elsewhere (Ball 1975; 1976; Clegg 1979). On this occasion one can simply cite the ready acceptance by the most influential and important of the behavioural and pluralist theorists of the mechanical metaphors. Dahl (1963) explicitly frames his *Modern Political Analysis* in terms which invoke Galileo's law of inertia. While cautious about the metaphor Dahl (1963: 7) acknowledges that 'our ideas about underlying measures of influence rest on intuitive notions very similar to those on which the idea of force rests in mechanics' (see Ball 1975: 216–20). There is nothing peculiar about this. As Isaac (1987: 19–25) has observed, such tenets form the contemporary hard-core of prevailing beliefs in the philosophy of science. These beliefs promote a view of scientific activity as consisting of 'the documentation and prediction of empirical regularities' (Isaac 1987: 19), a view canonized in authoritative texts such as those of Nagel (1965), in which a standard advocacy of a deductive-nomological view of science may be found. On this view, the appropriate task of science is to discover empirical regularities in the behaviour of things; having done so it should seek to establish the covering law which explains the observed regularities as a set of deductive predictions derivable from the statement of initial conditions contained in the law. In the most sophisticated philosophies of science, these are not statements of timeless truths but are provisional, expressed in a propositional form as hypotheses which are always in principle subject to empirical disconfirmation. They are conjectures which are systematically grounded but which remain open to refutation (Popper 1965). At base these conjectures remain dependent upon that view of causality whose metaphors were first sketched by Hume (1902) because it would be either the establishment of a counterfactual empirical regularity or the demonstration of an irregularity where one was previously not established which would occasion the refutation of a conjecture.

What is the point of constructing an argument which alerts us to these metaphorical continuities? Metaphors and analogies can wreak their own power over our conceptions, says Ball (1975: 217). While they may initially have been intended as a mere secondary device facilitating the primary task of analysis, they often have a tendency to turn back upon and transform the analysis which they were intended to illuminate (Ball [1975: 217–18]), after Black [1962] and Hesse [1960]). Ball suggests that this has happened with the present-day political scientists who have followed Dahl in placing so much emphasis on a particular understanding of what causal metaphors are, as a necessary and constitutive feature of any adequate conception of power. As Isaac (1987: 27) has commented, it is not so much the case that present-day theorists of power 'consciously wished to endorse the Humean view of causality. It is, rather, simply that they failed to challenge it, most likely because they failed to recognize it as an interesting example of the power of a view that is neither asserted nor recognized as such, and that is sustained by virtue of its misrecognition as a simple fact of life.' The reliance, whether explicit or implicit, on a mechanical and observable model of cause and effect, as theorists from Hobbes through Locke to Hume understood the notion, does not enable us to grasp those kinds of cause which are not some types of observable event in the world. To quote Ball (1975: 218), 'For example: an engineer may causally explain a bridge's collapse by citing structural weakness (a standing condition) or, perhaps, excessively rapid rusting of its supports (a process). Similarly a psychologist may explain some behaviour in terms of a person's dispositions or attitudes'. As such examples demonstrate, metaphors of causality which are not classically Humean are regularly and routinely used by scientists. Given that this is so, why should it be the case that the imagination of political and social scientists generally should be held captive by a far more restrictive conception of causality? As we shall see subsequently in chapter five, the expansion of the implicit model of causality away from one focusing only on event-causation to one capable of addressing phenomena such as standing conditions and dispositions has major implications for power analysis.

Ball (1976) has elsewhere attempted to generate an explanation of the disagreements which have characterized the contemporary community power debate in terms of the traces of those classical conceptions of politics which still lurk in the behavioural corpus. These are, on the whole, assumptions about the nature of causality, an individualist rather than structural orientation towards the analysis of power, and a liberal predisposition towards politically conservative interpretations of both the reality and the concept of power. Held in common between modern and classical scholars of a liberal disposition is the conception of causality modelled on Humean assumptions. This is contrasted by Ball with the conception of causality held by their opponents in recent debate. On the one hand the 'pluralists', who tend to be behavioural scientists, have attempted to maintain the Humean view that only 'events' can function as causes. By contrast, he suggests, elite theorists such as Bachrach and Baratz (1962) have regarded reasons as causes. This is indeed correct. However, it should not be thought that elite theory is thus allied to the broader foundations of classical liberalism with their intentional stress. On the contrary, the trajectory of contemporary elitism's critique leads ultimately to Marxism, as we shall see. For a school of analysis which started off under a nomenclature, elitism, which was explicitly anti-Marxian, this is a somewhat surprising terminus.

Having identified some continuities between the metaphorical basis of contemporary pluralist and behavioural approaches to power and those of classical liberalism, it is necessary to explore briefly the roots of classical elitism in order to see how far the concerns of contemporary elitists have shifted from these. Whereas there are some continuities between classical agency views and contemporary behavioural expressions of these, there are few indeed between classical and contemporary elitism.

CLASSICAL ELITISM

The origins of elite analysis can be found in the work of early twentieth century European writers who criticized what they regarded as insuperable political problems associated with the implementation of democracy. Mosca (1939), a leading Italian advocate of elitism, was of the firm opinion that in any society an elite must rule of necessity: rule was not possible on any other basis. He did concede that elite rule could be organized in such a way that it was based on representative institutions but maintained that it was still necessary for elites actually to rule these. The basis of the necessity which Mosca constructed for elite rule was that, in his view, social order required explicit planning and organization. To be effective this required that an elite group actually did the planning and organization and oversaw its implementation. It was their command of this rational apparatus of planning which produced both order and the concentration of power in their hands. Out of power and order, he believed, community might emerge in the same way as a stable basis for moral order might develop around the levers of power. Where Hobbes believed that moral order would precede effective power and legitimate it, Mosca believed that effective power would itself be the mechanism for moral order to emerge.

Organization featured as a key focus in the work of another founder of elite theory: Michels (1949). Famous for his formulation of the 'iron law of oligarchy', Michels argued from the results of empirical research which he had conducted on social democratic unions in Germany. These organizations, even though formally committed to workers' democratic control, could not avoid in their own affairs being subject to elite rule. Michels produced an incipient functionalist argument for bureaucracy and elite rule against ideals of democracy and participatory rule.

Elite views were also propounded by Pareto (1935), whose work was the subject of an extremely influential seminar held at Harvard during the 1930s. Talcott Parsons regularly participated and was later to develop Pareto's views on power. Pareto regarded power as a circulatory medium, carried by the elites. A stable society, he argued, was based upon a 'circulation of elites'. He identified two types of elite: one inherently innovative, the other inherently conservative. The former are the 'foxes' of society: the clever, scheming strategists – the 'Machiavellians', as they might be called. The latter are the lions: the strong, forceful types. While the forceful lion types can produce social stability out of inherently unstable conditions (can produce political community), they are easy prey to depredation by those who can preserve political community through political chicanery, trickery and strategy – the foxes. Hence there is a circulation of foxes into the ranks of the lions, as the lions – the conservatives – have to recruit individuals from outside their ranks in order to maintain their rule. However, they are always liable to be 'out-foxed' and to lose their elite position to the newcomers, who in turn will become the new lions, and so on.

Although neither Pareto nor Mosca used terms which would be procedurally acceptable to contemporary scholars, both of them attended to processes whereby political community was constructed, albeit, in Pareto's case in particular, in somewhat fanciful terms. While Pareto's elite of 'lions and foxes' is extremely allusive, Mosca sounds more modern. He employs terms such as 'ruling elite' and 'ruling class' which do not sound like the basis of such an archaic science as one would find in Pareto. However, when modern scholars have subjected Mosca to closer scrutiny, his terms have been demonstrated to be almost as imprecise as Pareto's theriomorphism. His lack of definition of key terms has proved the problem. In the absence of those functional characteristics which constitute co-ordinated rule (defined by Meisel [1962] as the existence of concerted action to achieve a common group consciousness which displays a coherent purpose), it has been argued that the attribution of rule to an elite cannot be warranted. This demands a reasonably precise specification of what would have to be achieved in order that a ruling elite existed. As we shall see shortly, similar demands were to be made of later elite theorists such as C. Wright Mills (1956).

FLOYD HUNTER AND THE COMMUNITY POWER ELITE

For all their fetishistic attribution of animality to humans and the imprecision of their notions of rule, these early elite theorists were at least attending to the processes whereby political community was constituted. This was not to be the case for mid-twentieth century elite theorists. They were neither articulating an inherently conservative position nor were they concerned with processes of elite rule and circulation. At the focus of their concern was the structure of elite power in local communities.

The most significant of the elite studies was probably the first, which became the reference point for subsequent critical studies. Consequently, the earliest debates invariably referred to Hunter's (1953) study of Atlanta, Georgia. In this empirical study Hunter interviewed people in the community. These were not, as is often the case in social research, a random sample of people. On the contrary they were people who might be expected to have an actual insight into how that community really was politically organized, because it was their business to know how decision-making was accomplished, who made these decisions and who were the most influential people in the community. The people asked were journalists, interest group leaders, business executives and so on. In short, they were people who could be expected to know how to access the elite.

The Atlanta study established the broad methodological outlines for study into elites, although subsequent investigators were to modify it somewhat. The methodology was simple: compare the lists of the people deemed most influential by the people chosen as judges, then tally up the score for each person named to arrive at those thought to be the most powerful. Such a study employs a 'reputational' methodology. Forty key individuals were identified in this way as people who recurred across the different judges' estimates. Hunter termed these people the local community political elite. The group was not composed randomly but was heavily weighted towards business interests. Hunter abhorred this perceived distribution of power on the principle that it did not accord with the democratic communitarianism of the American way of life, as propounded by the founders of federalism in the United States. He characterized power at the local community level as a relationship appropriated and shared between governmental and economic agencies. In his analysis this was representative of a pattern which he regarded as repeated at both the regional and national level (Hunter 1953: 5–6). It would be fair to say, however, that power remains a shorthand and descriptive term in Hunter's study.

The focus of the study was on identifying ruling elites, according to well-placed opinion, who it was assumed would have power by virtue of their visible position. It is never entirely clear what power is in Hunter's study. However, in many respects it seems a reasonable assumption that, if a consistent profile is produced by cross-checking between people whom one would anticipate should be in a position to know who has power, by virtue of their leadership position in many aspects of organization life in the community, the chances are that the picture is accurate. None the less, the elitist depiction of relatively stable ruling elites, and cliques within them, has been widely challenged.

Critics have been quick to pounce on flaws within this reputational approach to power. At the outset we may note that it is somewhat normatively self-fulfilling: to ask people who are the most influential people in a given community assumes at least four things. First, that there are clearly identifiable influential people. Even though a null option may be proffered, presumably the researcher thinks there is such a group, otherwise why bother asking the questions? Second, it assumes that there is a community. An assumption of organic vitality about a place may not be warranted. It may well be the case that not everyone in the place is actually in the community: black people; people whose lives are largely privatized rather than largely public, such as the many women who will not be active in the labour force, who are 'housewives' and mothers; the unemployed; the institutionalized, and so on. By implicitly accepting the assumption of community and place, those people are effectively marginalized. While this may not seem to affect a study of power which is focused on elites, it should alert us to the problem that power may be present not just in the evidently public but also in the evidently private. On this reckoning, not only would power be present in the public gaze, it would also be constituted in the definition of the margins of public power. We might refer to this as the dark side of the dialectic of power and community.

The third assumption that this research makes is that individuals are the social actors who are the agency of power. Now, at one level this would seem appropriate, but note that it does assume that the appropriate question is *who* has power around here, not *what*. In a world of organizations in the form of governments, political parties, churches, unions, and major businesses such as breweries, banks, media outlets, and so on, *what* may be a far more appropriate question than *who*. Communities are shaped by organizations of all kinds, in which the individuals who hold positions responsible for determining what these organizations do may well be relatively invisible to public scrutiny and knowledge. Moreover, if the individuals change, as they do all the time, the organizations' presence still remains. Irrespective of who runs a corporation such as Coca-Cola, which has its headquarters in Atlanta, one might reasonably anticipate that it will be a major presence in Atlanta's life.

The fourth problem is that the reputational approach makes power equivalent to the average of some specifically chosen people's perceptions of it. What these people think power is may not accord with what it 'really' is, assuming that there is a reality to power outside people's perceptions of it. The 'reality' problem can be encountered in another way in reputational studies. There is no guarantee that another, later study of the same place will tap the same perceptions. (In the case of Atlanta one could cite Banfield's [1966] study.) In such a case, would the change be attributable to the structure of perception, to the structure of reality, or to an interactive change in both? Unless these could be parcelled out, the problems of interpretation over time would be difficult.

When Dahl (1958; 1971) contributed his critique of the ruling elite model to the literature, his target was not really Hunter's (1953) work. During the 1950s the most widely discussed example of power research became C. Wright Mills' (1956) study of *The Power Elite*. It was this target which Dahl had in his sights when he made his critique, although, as we shall see, one or two asides were aimed at Hunter (1953). Dahl's (1958) critique was to become a major reference point of the literature on power. While elite theorists may have operated with an imprecise notion of what power is, Dahl, by contrast, operates with one which is very precise. Where the elitists attribute power to highly visible people, Dahl (1957) develops a situational and relational concept of power.

DAHL'S METHODOLOGICAL CHALLENGE TO CONTEMPORARY ELITISM

A famous article in the journal *Behavioural Science* clearly spelt out Dahl's (1957) approach to 'the concept of power'. He begins his article by noting how central power and its synonyms have been for the 'language of civilized peoples'. Almost immediately he qualifies this by observing that something that has seemed so central to so many people in so many times, places and ways, ought in principle to 'exist in a form capable of being studied more or less systematically'. However, this is not the case, he argues, because 'it may actually well be thought by some contemporary observers to be instead a "bottomless swamp"' (Dahl 1957: 201). Whether this is so, he believes, is a judgement on which the evidence must wait, 'as it is only lately that serious attempts have been made to formulate the concept rigorously enough for systematic study' (201). (As we have seen, this is not a view which all commentators accept: see Ball [1978]).

In the vanguard of these recent attempts at rigorous definition is Dahl's (1957) conceptualization, which he is adamant to suggest is not to be mistaken for a 'theory' of power *per se*, nor even to be taken as a single conceptualization for application in every study. The ambition is distinctly modest: 'to essay a formal definition of power that will, I hope, catch something of one's intuitive-notions as to what the Thing is' (202). By a 'formal definition' reference is made to the practical, implementational problems which may be associated with the precise definition to be offered. It may not always be possible to make the kinds of observations which the definition requires if it is to be used appropriately. In striving for a 'formal definition' Dahl (1957: 202) is seeking to explicate the 'primitive notion' of power behind all conceptions of it. By 'primitive' he means the first, the deepest, the most underlying concept. Hence his definition is 'formal': he seeks to capture the essential form of any and every notion of power.

An example serves to illustrate this primitive, formal idea. It is a famous example, much discussed in the literature, and so it is well worth while citing it here.

> What is the intuitive idea we are trying to capture? Suppose I stand on a street corner and say to myself, 'I command all automobile drivers on this street to drive on the right side of the road'; suppose further that all the drivers actually do as I 'command' them to do; still, most people will regard me as mentally ill if I insist that I have enough power over automobile drivers to compel them to use the right side of the road. On the other hand, suppose a policeman is standing in the middle of an intersection at which most traffic ordinarily moves ahead; he orders all traffic to turn right or left; the traffic moves as he orders it to do. Then it accords with what I conceive to be the bedrock idea of power to say that the policeman acting in this particular role evidently has the power to make automobile drivers turn right or left rather than go ahead. My intuitive idea of power, then, is something like this: A has power over B to the extent that he can get B to do something B would not otherwise do. (Dahl 1957: 202–3)

A more detailed discussion of this 'intuitive idea' appears somewhat later in the book, in chapter four. For now, the concern is only to elaborate Dahl's position as clearly as possible. Drawing from the example, he notes, first, that power is a relation between actors who 'may be individuals, groups, roles, offices, governments, nation-states or other human aggregates' (203). Second, he introduces a nomenclature which has become quite conventional in discussions of power: he refers to an instance of a power relation in terms of an A having power over a B (although, confusingly, he does not stick to it himself). Third, he notes that A's power over B will have what he terms a source, domain, or base, conceptualized in terms of resources open to exploitation by A vis à vis B; it will be expressed through means or instruments of power such as love, fear, money, and so on; it will be expressed in an amount of power of A over B which can be rendered in a probabilistic statement and finally, A's power will have a limited range or scope over B; that is, not everything which B might conceivably do will fall within the scope of A's power but only some clearly specified range of things which B might do.

> Evidently what we are willing to regard as a 'greater' or 'lesser' scope of responses will be dictated by the particular piece of research at hand; it seems fruitless to attempt to

devise any single scale. At one extreme we may wish to say that A's scope is greater than B's only if A's scope contains in it every response in B's and at least one more; this would appear to be the narrowest definition. At the other extreme, we may be prepared to treat a broad category of responses as comparable, and A's scope is then said to be greater than B's if the number of comparable responses in his scope is larger than the number in B's. There are other possible definitions. The important point is that the particular definition one chooses will evidently have to emerge from considerations of the substance and objectives of a specific piece of research and not from general theoretical considerations. (Dahl 1957: 207)

The same type of problem confronts comparison of the number of Bs. Unless one works on the assumption that all potential actors are equal, it will be the case that some actors, to borrow a famous phrase from Orwell (1948), will be more equal than others. Dahl's (1957: 207) view of questions of equality between actors is that it too 'can be determined only in view of the nature and aims of the research at hand'. On these criteria, social research begins to look as if it may be decidedly non-cumulative and highly contextually specific where power is concerned.

Probability, Dahl proposes, is inherently less problematic in comparative terms than are the other elements of this formal model. An A whose probability of securing a desired response in a B is higher than that of another A, will, all other things being equal, have greater power than that other A. The 'other things being equal clause' would, Dahl implies, have to include some assumptions not only about sets of respondents but also sets of responses.

In an explicit criticism of Hunter's (1953) research into Atlanta's political community, Dahl makes his point forcefully. Hunter asked his judges to rank putative elites on their reputed implementational ability on decisions in general. In Dahl's terms, this would be an undifferentiated, non-specific and de-contextual concept of scope, which failed to discriminate among different kinds of responses. Specify these, he suggests, in terms of decisions over issues such as local taxes, schools or local industry policy, and would the artifactual finding of *an* elite (an artifact of asking only a general question about a non-specific decision rather than specific decisions) be sustained? Might not different decision-issues evoke different responses? The choice is posed rhetorically:

Are we to conclude that in 'Regional City' there is a small determinate group of leaders whose power significantly exceeds that of all other members of the community on all or nearly all key issues that arise? Or are we to conclude, at the other extreme, that some leaders are relatively powerful on some issues and not on others, and that no leaders are relatively powerful on all issues? We have no way of choosing between these two interpretations or indeed among many others that might be formulated. (Dahl 1957: 208)

The criticism of Hunter is quite damning: given the questions he asked, Dahl suggests, his answers would follow. Ask a better formulated range of questions about what one anticipates key decision-issues might be, and a more empirically sensitive answer might eventuate. This was an argument Dahl (1961) subsequently put to the test in his analysis of power in the local community surrounding Yale University, where he worked. The community was New Haven, the time the late 1950s, and the study *Who Governs?* (Dahl 1961). As is well known, Dahl's conclusion is that no one single elite does govern: different actors (people, in fact) prevail over different issues, producing a 'pluralist' rather than an 'elitist' distribution of power. The methodology, whether designed to or not, produces a pluralist representation of power.

In studying New Haven, Dahl (1961) does not entirely follow the methodological precepts that he outlines in 'the concept of power' (Dahl 1957). For instance, he does not compare New Haven with another community, to contrast responses explicitly in terms of comparable ranges of Bs facing comparable ranges of As in terms of some theoretical criteria. Comparison is of various As with all other potential As constituted as Bs, in terms of a prior list of decision-issues. These were urban redevelopment, public education, and political nominations. It seemed reasonable that these would be key issue-areas because, at that time, the New Haven programme for urban redevelopment was the largest in America, in terms of per capita expenditure, while public education was the 'big ticket' budget item in the city finances. Decisions on these were made by the incumbents of political office.

Dahl actually began with a reputational approach to find out who comprised the 'leadership pool' in New Haven. Then he studied the participation and role of these notable people in the three issue areas, using data collected from newspaper reports, official documents, accounts by participants and observers, as well as through his own participant observation. In this way, 'key decisions' in each 'issue area' could be identified, although, as critics have pointed out, Dahl (1961) did not at the time offer any objective criteria for making the distinction of 'key' issues (Bachrach and Baratz 1962). Subsequent to Dahl's (1961) study, another pluralist investigator did in fact offer four specific criteria for identifying key decisions: the number of people affected by the outcomes; the number of different kinds of community resources which are distributed by the outcomes; the quantity or value of resources ('how much') distributed by the outcomes and finally, how drastically these outcomes alter existing states of affairs in terms of community resource distribution (Polsby 1963: 95–6). Such criteria seem eminently reasonable in terms of Dahl's (1957) notion of the importance of scope.

Consideration of who has power over such key decisions lends itself most readily to formal decision situations in which respondents have to vote either for or against an issue, if they do not choose to abstain. It is, in fact, such contexts of US Senate voting records that Dahl (1957) discussed, looking at Senators' recorded roll-call votes on what are constituted as being historically prior instances of the same issue. A formal set of paired probabilities of N-respondents can thus be produced, in order to 'measure a

Senator's influence by the difference between the probability that the Senate will pass a measure the Senator opposes and the probability that it will pass a measure he supports' (Dahl 1957: 211). (Needless to say, it should be acknowledged that not all Senators are likely to be male.)

Dahl's (1957) *Behavioural Science* paper closes with an imaginary dialogue between a 'conceptual' theoretician (a nit-picking sort of character) and an 'operationalist' (with whose hard-headed resolution of conceptual puzzlement by the operation of measurement we are clearly led to sympathize). In brief, he concludes that the formal properties of his proposed definition are its strength in that they will enable us, in particular studies, to produce better alternative definitions suited for particular contexts of enquiry. The formal definition will function as a Weberian ideal-type, a conceptual measure against which all other deviations from the ideal, primitive type may be compared.

Dahl's ambitions are rigorous. On this basis alone there is much to recommend his approach, which, as he establishes, does offer certain advantages over Hunter's (1953) less careful approach. Moreover, Dahl is adept at second-guessing possible objections to arguments which might 'white-ant' or undercut his methodological grounds. Not all potential criticism is avoided, however. Consider the following critical remarks occasioned by some of his assumptions. In Dahl's 'concept of power' there is no sense of contextual temporality. Foreign affairs issues in the Senate are foreign affairs issues no matter when they occur, or what the surrounding context of debate is. Consequently the two sides to an issue are considered to be the same, irrespective of changing context. An empirical instance of this point would be where there is a quite sudden revision of previous judgements of who are allies, who are adversaries, or of what is sacred and what is profane. Recent United States examples might be the changes occasioned in the Biden White House foreign policy as a result of incursion by China's spy balloons in the skies above US territory, or by Russia's invasion of The Ukraine and subsequent alleged war crimes. In either case the meaning of foreign affairs would be seen quite differently as a result of the policy shifts and revelations. Past votes might not be good guide to future votes if the meaning of the issues have changed markedly in the meantime, even where substantively the events remain the same. The absence of reference to the meaningful context, and how it can be understood, is a pervasive problem with Dahl's work.

Not only is there no consideration of the meaning of surrounding context but also the context of power itself, in Dahl's (1957) article if not in his empirical study of New Haven (Dahl 1961), is structurally a remarkably flat, one-dimensional topography. It shows little relief in terms of the differences which might already be there in most contexts, prior to a formal exercise of power by voting, for instance. Certainly, there is discussion of different resources, but this rapidly gives way to consideration of responses as the instrument best suited to comparison of what resources might be. Resources, as causes, become known only through their effects. The focus is neither on how access to the former may structure the latter, nor on how actors come to have variable membership conditions in the political community in question. In considering already elected members of the political community of the US Senate, such potentially tricky questions of how access to political community is secured and organized, can be neatly avoided. They are, in fact, non-issues, given the circumspect nature of the research problem and political community as they are defined. The political community functions as a tacit assumption owing to the formal membership rules. In the absence of these, who is a member and what is a community become much harder to specify.

Dahl (1968) returned to the formal model of power in an encyclopaedia entry on 'Power' (reprinted in Lukes' [1986] edited book on *Power*). We shall examine the additional insights that can be gleaned from this paper before considering the thrust of his attack on the elitist methodology as C. Wright Mills (1956) used it. With this critique, once more, we will find much that is rigorous and precise compared to the position which he tackles. However, we will also note some drawbacks of the arguments advanced, which can readily be aligned with those already identified in Dahl's (1957) work.

One innovation in Dahl (1968) is to refer to the number of Bs over whom an A may have power as the 'domain of power'. This insight was seen earlier in Polsby's (1963) work. Configurational differences in these in comparative studies can then be the basis for distinct types of power structures (Agger et al. 1964). The concept of resources is also elaborated in some more detail. Resources are defined in terms of the distribution of cash, popularity and control over jobs, and control over information sources (Dahl 1968: 409). Resource utilization is addressed via consideration of the notions of political skill, which some may have more than others motivation to exercise power, which some may also have more of than others and costs, which in terms of the opportunity costs involved in utilizing resources, will also be distributed unevenly.

These resource considerations do much to qualify the earlier specification of 'the concept of power' (Dahl 1957), by noting how resource control which is unequally distributed will already structure the political field prior to any specific relational action occurring. Moreover, the notion of political skill suggests something which will be honed by its exercise and, other things being equal, will be exercised more, the less the opportunity cost of each exercise. The latter will go down as the access to resources increases. Amongst the most important of these will be wealth. All of these are important qualifications of the more restricted view of power presented a decade earlier.

Qualifications are all very well however, but they do nothing to eliminate the fact that:

> Unfortunately, in the analysis of power, existing methods of measurement are rather inadequate, the data are often inescapably crude and limited, a variety of simple alternative explanations fit the data about equally well, and in any case the complexity of the relations requires extraordinarily complex models. (Dahl 1968: 411)

In consideration of this complexity Dahl opts for a model of 'causal inference' (adapted from Blalock 1964) rather than a straightforward causal model. (Indeed, in both the earlier paper and this later one, Dahl [1957; 1968] shies away from too explicit an identity between power and causal relations. However, the identity is implicit in his treatment in both instances.) Power relations are defined as a subset of causal relations, subject to the assumptions which Blalock (1964: 62) specifies for causal modelling: a finite set of explicitly defined variables: certain assumptions about the likely causal direction and assumptions which negate the confounding influence that variables that are not under consideration may have for those which are. On this basis a causal model of 'chains' and 'links' between As and Bs may be constructed in which, somehow or other, on the basis of some assumptions, closure must be achieved. Otherwise the causal chain risks being stretched to a degree which exceeds one's judgement of the explanatory utility involved in doing so. Utility is measured in terms of complexity, conceptual over-extension, and general opportunity costs. There is a limit beyond which the costs of conceptual closure on the causal chain would become prohibitive. Where to effect closure and what to exclude will thus always be practical judgements in which,

> it is important to specify which effects are at the focus of an explanatory theory and which are not. A good deal of confusion, and no little controversy, are produced when different analysts focus on different links in the chain of power and causation without specifying clearly what effects they wish to explain; and a good deal of criticism of dubious relevance is produced by critics who hold that an investigator has focused on the 'wrong' links or did not provide a 'complete' explanation. (Dahl 1961: 412)

Implicitly, although he does not say so, one would anticipate that amongst such critics should be counted Bachrach and Baratz (1962), whom Dahl (1968) goes on to discuss later in the encyclopaedia article. Their contribution to the power debate is equally as important as Dahl's and will be examined later in the book. Dahl concludes his article by considering three types of criteria for measuring power which are classified as game-theoretic, Newtonian, and economic (Dahl 1968: 413–14).

It is clear that there is considerable merit in much of what Dahl (1957; 1968) proposes in these two articles. They have been deservedly influential for the modesty and rigour of analysis which they seek to exemplify. The same sense of purpose was evident in Dahl's (1958; 1971) 'critique of the ruling elite model', in which debate was explicitly joined with Hunter (1953) and Mills (1956).

DAHL'S CRITIQUE OF THE RULING ELITE MODEL

The battle ground is clear: is the ruling elite model of power, which sees American 'communities' and 'society' as dominated by an oligarchy of elite figures, in principle able to be controverted by empirical evidence or are such views immune to such data, securely ensconced within 'metaphysical or polemical doctrine', and hence irrefutable? Dahl (1971: 354–5) proposes that, in order to ensure that the latter is not the case (as he clearly suspects it to be), he will devise a challenge which any proponents of a ruling elite model ought to rise to if they wish their theory to be considered as scientifically serious, at least according to the criteria propounded by Dahl (1971). The challenge involves two components: first, a simple description of what Dahl conceives to be a ruling elite system; second, a 'simple but satisfactory test of any hypothesis asserting that a particular political system is, in fact, a ruling elite system' (Dahl 1971: 355).

As we might anticipate from the articles already considered, Dahl begins with a number of specific limiting assumptions. First, that the scope of responses of Bs be specified in advance. Second, that there be a principle of difference operative such that there are either mutually exclusive or alternative preferences exhibited by As and Bs. There should not be complete consensus at all times between As and Bs because such conditions preclude 'a satisfactory direct test' of the ruling elite hypothesis although they may allow 'indirect and rather unsatisfactory' ones (Dahl 1971: 355). A satisfactory direct test requires differences in preferences between individuals in the system. For the ruling elite hypothesis to be confirmed, there would have to be among these individuals some minority, which was not a pure artifact of democratic rules, whose preferences regularly prevailed, at the very least, in all cases of disagreement over 'key' political issues.

In order to drive home his point about the difference between satisfactory and unsatisfactory direct tests of the ruling elite hypothesis, Dahl (1971) demonstrates what 'some bad tests' might be. First, it would not be adequate to say that a group with a high potential for control, like Mills' (1956) political-military-industrial complex, would be a ruling elite. It would be adequate only if this high potential for control owing to strategic position were in fact turned into action which produced agreement on and implementation of preferences over a key political issue. (This example was later to be picked up by Meisel (1962).) This may well be so but it does not negate the point made by Mills, that certain possibilities for collusion did in fact exist. Establishing whether these are actually used is of course important, but it is also a slightly different issue. Dahl would see it as the more germane issue. Another improper test would be to establish that some individuals have more influence over key decisions than others. Political equality is an ideal more observed in the breach than the practice. The absence of it, suggests Dahl, is no proof of the existence of a ruling elite. In many respects it is difficult to see why this is considered to be an improper or bad test, as it seems very close to the probabilistic procedures for determining Senators' voting power that Dahl (1957) had earlier espoused. One may concur that an ideal democracy is rarely encountered outside of its blueprints yet still recognize that in some democratic systems some people will be more or less influential than others in securing their preferences. The rigour crumbles slightly here.

The issue of scope, which we have seen is central to Dahl's analytic concerns, is the focus for his specification of a third improper test. Unless scope is precisely differentiated, 'sloppy questions' (a dig at Hunter 1953) 'could easily seem to discover that there exists a unified ruling elite' (Dahl 1971: 358). What, then, would be a good and proper test according to Dahl?

The hypothesis of a ruling elite can be strictly tested only if:

1. The hypothetical ruling elite is a well-defined group.
2. There is a fair sample of cases involving key political decisions in which the preferences of the hypothetical ruling elite run counter to those of any other likely group that might be suggested.
3. In such cases, the preferences of the elite regularly prevail.
   (Dahl 1971: 359)

Some possible objections to his argument are anticipated by Dahl. Of these, the most interesting for our purposes is the second objection which proposes that perhaps the test is too strong. In this objection he wants to undercut any claim that a small ruling elite may exist by virtue not so much of its superior power in contests for preference implementation but of the indifference of the ruled to the preferences of any putative ruling elite group. This example is worth noting because, as we shall subsequently see, it is often precisely through reference to some notion of mass indifference that many 'structural' views of power actually operate. Against such views, Dahl (1971: 362) maintains that there must be a situation in which, 'as a necessary although possibly not a sufficient condition', key political issues exist which 'should involve actual disagreement in preferences among two or more groups'.

A further crumbling of the outer ramparts of rigour may be detected in this 'strong test'. Early in the example Dahl presents it in the following terms: 'suppose that the members of the "ruled" group are indifferent as to the outcome of various political alternatives' (360). However, if that is so, and if the ruling elite hypothesis is upheld, then on Dahl's own criteria there must be a plurality of elites in order for there to be a plurality of preferences. Indifference by the majority to the preferences of Electoral College elites may well co-exist with actual disagreement in preferences among voters. In the 2016 presidential election in the United States 2.1% more people voted for Clinton than Trump but the elite votes of the Electoral College prevailed. More people opposed Trump or did not vote than those that supported him. Almost half of the voters did not vote, with the majority perhaps being more interested in other, more trivial pursuits: in beer and skittles, spectacles and scandals, sex and drugs and rock-'n-roll, for instance. Indeed, some structural theorists would point precisely to the existence of these trivial pursuits as indication of mechanisms ensuring ruling reproduction.

Additional breaches of Dahl's barricades may also be detected. As has been remarked elsewhere (Clegg 1975: 24–5), a number of important issues still remain unresolved: closure has not been effected on, for instance, what is 'a fair sample of cases involving key political decisions' (Dahl 1971: 359).

> Members of a community might tell us that they agree with the proposition that a well defined group does exist, and does routinely prevail in getting its preferences adopted. What value do we use for determining what given number of members agreeing with the proposition secures the proposition's factual status? Dahl (1971) 'offers all or nearly all'. How near? Would 99 percent be high enough? Would 60 percent be too low? Would 69 percent be acceptable, but 65 percent not? For what reason? (Clegg 1975: 24)

The problem is that unless one produces such calculable criteria in advance as one of the assumptions that one makes in doing research, they will invariably operate as tacit assumptions in the project. Beneath the rigorous surface, behind the barricades of 'proper tests' and 'explicit assumptions', reside judgements of a necessarily common sense character, of an implicit, tacit, taken-for-granted quality within any theoretical framework, the intricate network of which sustains the sense of what one does when deploying one's 'proper', as opposed to 'improper', theory.

NEWTON'S CRITIQUE OF THE PLURALIST MODEL

One result of Dahl's (1958) critique of the ruling elite model was that neither the theory nor the empirical study of political power was ever quite the same again, as Newton (1969: 209) acknowledged. Somewhat cheekily, perhaps, Newton's homage was delivered in an article titled 'A Critique of the Pluralist Model', published in the journal *Acta Sociologica* eleven years after Dahl's celebrated 'A Critique of the Ruling Elite Model'. In this article Newton regards it as time that the 'new orthodoxy' of the pluralist model 'was questioned'. In fact the new orthodoxy had already been criticized, most notably by Domhoff (1967: 138–56). In the same year that Newton's critique was published, Miliband was also to publish his celebrated elitist study of *The State in Capitalist Society*. In this book he convincingly argued that the background of the leading capitalist nations' ruling elites was remarkably homogeneous, although he did not demonstrate that this background homology translated effortlessly into concerted action. The Miliband/Domhoff axis of enquiry into elites as the 'instruments' of class rule was subsequently to be subjected to criticism from the 'structuralist' left-field: by Poulantzas (1969) in his critique of Miliband (1969), as well as by a number of critics of Domhoff in a special issue of *The Insurgent Sociologist* which he edited in 1976. These structuralist critiques are not central to our purpose here, which is to contrast the ruling elite with the pluralist model.

Newton's critique begins by trying to specify adequately what a pluralist model is. Rather than simply being the diametrical opposite of a monistic system, Newton (1969: 212) more accurately specifies it as one of competing elites in which the elites are necessarily responsive and responsible to non-elites on whose support they are dependent. Many pluralist studies, he observes, fail to look adequately at elite/non-elite relations, counting only the number of plural elites that exist in a community to demonstrate competition and an absence of monism. It is such a model of competitive, responsive, pluralist elites which characterizes Dahl as the 'most able,... most systematic, and altogether the most convincing critic of elitism and exponent of pluralism among contemporary writers' (Newton 1969: 212). To examine his work critically is to focus on the best considered and strongest argued examples of the pluralist model available. The central points of Dahl's pluralist model can be contrasted with Newton's critique of them (Table 3.1).

We will briefly iterate Newton's consideration of each issue before drawing some conclusions. Dahl's arguments for the inclusive nature of American pluralist democracy are countered by Newton's reference to empirical evidence that

> compared with working class people, middle class people are more likely to participate in politics, be better informed about politics, more interested in politics, more likely to join political and other organizations, have a higher sense of political competence, have more

Table 3.1 Pluralism and its critique

Dahl's pluralist model	Newton's critique
1 Modern America is an inclusive pluralist system.	1 Modern American pluralism is not inclusive of all groups.
2 The major actors are the leaders of a wide variety of interest groups which have political resources available to them.	2 Some interests do not gain representation and some groups are politically weaker than others.
3 The resources are not equally distributed but nor are the inequalities cumulative in the structure of the system.	3 Resources are inequitably distributed and political inequalities are cumulative.
4 Most people exercise power through voting.	4 Many people do not vote.
5 The system of leaders and decision-makers is a relatively open process.	5 Some groups are denied access to the decision-making process.
6 While each interest group may be oligarchical, the end result is pluralist, because they are competitive, even if internally oligarchic, interest groups.	6 A set of competing oligarchies does not make a pluralist system.
7 A workable democracy is the outcome, in which compromises between competitive groups produce some general distribution of satisfaction.	7 The political system does not distribute power at all equally; the system does not deliver general satisfaction, but heavily favours some groups or sections against others.

Source: after Newton (1969: 213)

political skills, and are more likely to vote, and are more likely to attempt to influence the course of political events. (Newton 1969: 214)

Subsequent research by Wright (1985), in the most detailed investigation to date of the American class structure, supports this argument and also demonstrates that the working class in the United States is disproportionately black and female. Unlike Dahl's view, it shows that inequalities are cumulatively interactive. Newton (1969: 214) affirms it with what was perhaps unintended force by virtue of the gender used: 'the end result of this process is not necessarily a single power elite within society but it may tend to produce a fairly small number of men who are constantly more powerful than other men.' More recent research has demonstrated the role that private education plays in the reproduction of this elite in New Haven (Soloway 1987).

Unlike Australia, voting is not compulsory in the United States. Even today, two decades after the voter registration drives of the civil rights movement in the 1960s, many disadvantaged Americans are not registered to vote. Notably, Cloward and Fox-Piven (1988) detailed the role of obstacles to voter registration in large parts of the United States, which militate against the poor achieving membership in the formal political community of voters. These obstacles are interpreted as deriving from a presumption on the part of established sources of power that the poor really are not part of the political community. Where voter registration drives occur, they are privately sponsored rather than publicly shaped; consequently the agenda which shapes them is one of private interests with resources available to them. Registration is unnecessarily difficult for the poor to achieve; the process itself, with its bureaucratic stages and assumptions of literacy and fixity of place in those whom it handles, actively discourages the poor to register. Registering the poor through state programmes is actively discouraged by all levels of government, the researchers conclude, even by those elected people who claim to be the 'representatives' of poor, black and welfare constituencies. To the extent that they make a living out of representing the poor, their power is potentially undermined by the extent to which their constituency achieves the possibilities of political voice other than through their representation.

Dahl (1961: 277) acknowledged that 'a large proportion of the adult population of New Haven does not even vote', even amongst those who are registered to do so. Newton (1969: 215) notes that between 1948 and 1952, between 50 percent and 20 percent of adults did not vote in mayoral elections in eighteen large American cities. About 50–60 percent fail to vote as a matter of routine in US Presidential elections. These data add weight to earlier remarks about community: inclusion in a community is assumed as a frame for power, rather than being regarded as an effect of power. These non-voters tend to be the cumulatively disadvantaged whose formal exclusion is rarely if ever countervailed by access of a more direct kind to the political system. Moreover, Newton suggests that Dahl overstates the 'indirect influence' that voters have over leaders by virtue of voting, for four reasons. First, votes are cast for aggregate packages of policies and person-nel. 'Observing the whole range of these factors is difficult, sorting them out is extremely difficult, and weighing them is impossible' (Newton 1969: 215). Indeed, Dahl's rigour deserts him on this aspect of power as he 'never substantiates his argument and it is dif-ficult to see how it could be empirically substantiated' (Newton 1969: 216).

Second, indirect influence via the medium of voting assumes a degree of aggregation of voters' interests, their clear articulation and correct cognition by a selfless representative, that is difficult to sustain empirically. Third, the voting power of some social groups can be effectively ignored, suggests Newton (1969: 216). Finally, the power of elected officials may be severely constrained by permanent officials (see the argument in Clegg: 1983).

Through judicious citation of Dahl's (1961) own work in *Who Governs?*, Newton under-mines the countervailing opportunity of access argument:

> The professionals, of course, have access to extensive political resources which they employ at a high rate with superior efficiency. Consequently, a challenge to the exist-ing norms is bound to be costly to the challenger, for legitimist professionals can quickly shift their skills and resources into the urgent task of doing in the dissenter. As long as the professionals remain substantially legitimist in outlook, therefore, the critic is likely to make little headway. Indeed, the chances are that anyone who advo-cates extensive changes in the prevailing democratic norms is likely to be treated by the professionals, and even by a fair share of the political stratum, as an outsider, possibly even as a crackpot whose views need not be seriously debated. No worse fate can befall the dissenter, for unless he can gain the attention of the political stra-tum, it is difficult for him to gain space in the mass media; if he cannot win space in the mass media, it is difficult for him to win a large following; if he cannot win a large following, it is difficult for him to gain the attention of the political stratum. (Dahl 1961: 320; cited by Newton 1969: 216–17)

The same ploy is used to undercut Dahl's notion of a key decision: these are not just an effect of the local community ecology but are politically constituted and managed (Dahl 1961: 92; 321). Those 'outside' the political system who are blue-collar rather than white-collar workers (45 percent of New Haven was comprised of blue-collar workers), will, Dahl (1961: 229–30) suggests, be handicapped in their access to the political system. On the question of access, research by Stern (1988) makes interesting reading. Money is probably the most important factor in someone becoming and staying elected in the United States. Senators and Congressional members have to raise enormous sums of money not only to be in a position to win office but also to retain it once there. Consequently, newcom-ers in general have a more difficult task ahead of them than do those who are already established, particularly where the former have no access to either personal or sponsoring resources of wealth. Because of this, there is a persistent influence accruing to those who regulate access to political donations. Political contenders who espouse issues detrimental

to the agenda of the major contributors, whether they are corporate or labour organizations, are unlikely to see these issues gain much support nor be articulated into the political process through alternate routes such as the media.

It would be incorrect to say that Dahl was not aware of these issues. Although the
research that has been cited is well-known, this does not mean that the issues at stake
were not recognized, even if their import was not interpreted in the way that critical writers such as Stern (1988) and Cloward and Fox-Piven (1988) suggested. Newton exploits
Dahl's (1961: 337) recognition with an acidic alacrity:

> With a few crisp sentences Dahl seems to have relegated some social groups to live in
> the desert beyond American pluralist democracy – those who are out of favour with the
> prevailing ideology of the political stratum, those who cannot get in to the political stra-
> tum, the vast majority of the working class population who are 'severely handicapped' in
> any attempt to gain direct influence over political affairs, and all 'fringe' groups who have
> the temerity to question the American way of life. (Newton 1969: 217–18)

Dahl is once more hoist with his own petard by Newton (1969: 219–20) on the competitiveness of elite rule: in New Haven, under Mayor Lee it was government by 'executive-
centred coalition' rather than by competitive oligarchies. Newton's conclusions suggest
that Dahl's model of pluralist democracy is not only primarily ideological but also at
some remove from his own literal descriptions of it in New Haven (Dahl 1961). We may
also note that it is at some remove from the formal model of power proposed by Dahl
(1957).

If Dahl's (1958) critique proposes a tough set of criteria for a ruling elite model,
Newton's (1969) critique, rather than pointing to an alternative set of criteria to those
of Dahl's (1961) pluralist model, notes simply that Dahl's findings are much closer to
those of the elite model than he seems to realize. Two points may be added to this.
First, in the context of a rebuttal of charges that he is an 'elitist' Dahl (1966) does in
fact acknowledge some of the criticisms which Newton was later to raise, when, for
instance, he says that

> political apathy, alienation, indifference, lack of confidence, and feelings of inefficacy are
> widespread in the United States among the poor, Negroes, and even many individuals and
> segments in other strata, and that the feelings create obstacles to effective participation
> in political life. (Dahl 1966: 303)

Second, in the light of Dahl's (1961; 1966) subsequent admission of these barriers to
political agency, what is the status of the formal model of power premised on an agency
perspective, which he takes to be a 'proper' rather than an 'improper' approach to power
analysis? It is useful to reconsider some of the tacit assumptions of the formal model of
power. This will be done in the next chapter.

CONCLUSION

Dahl's contribution to models of power has been the central focus of this chapter. In this corpus of work we see an attempt at rigorous closure on the terms that a formal definition of power might construct. However, despite the fact that Dahl proposes an advance on the looser constructions favoured by Hunter (1953) or the imputation of agency implied by Mills (1956) to a conspiracy whose mechanisms of organization are underspecified, it is a closure which renounces rather than resolves some major problems for the analysis of power. Two important aspects remain unresolved in the formal model which Dahl proposes, one implicit and the other explicit.

The assumption of political community is the implicit problem. Against the assumption that a given social space is a community displaying ordered totality, one would want to propose instead that ordered totality is an achievement and resource of power rather than its tacit frame. In fact, it was as both achievement and resource that this assumption entered the discourse of power in Hobbes. The empirical consequences of assuming that there is a community of politics which is equivalent to an urban administrative area were later to be addressed by Newton (1975) in a powerful critique, as we shall see in the next chapter.

The second unresolved problem concerns those persons, nearly 50 percent of New Haven's inhabitants according to Newton's (1969) calculations, who are excluded from the political community because of their non-participation in elections and are thus excluded from access to political agency. They do not enter the calculus of power: their exclusion counts for nothing. They do not exercise power nor is it clear that power is exercised to exclude them. They remain unaccounted and unaccountable. It was precisely this question of 'absence' from the agenda of politics which was to frame the next important round in the development of contemporary approaches to the analysis of power. The next chapter will concentrate on the contribution that Bachrach and Baratz, as well as others concerned with questions relating to 'intentionality', have made to the study of power.

4
THE POWER OF INTENTION

INTRODUCTION

In Dahl's (1957) framework a proper perspective on power is proposed in terms of an 'agency' view but it has a set of inbuilt tacit assumptions concerning causal inference. Revealingly, in an implicit critique of Bachrach and Baratz (1962) in his 'encyclopaedia' article, Dahl (1968) hints at but does not sketch a contrary 'agency' view of power to that which he holds. He does this when he suggests that a second 'improper' test might be one in which indifference on a mass scale becomes an occasion not for voiding power analysis but for extending it. To follow this path, however, would be not so much to resolve problems of power analysis but to introduce a further set of problems; it would also, as we shall see, admit intentionality as a possible basis for causal inference, something Dahl's formal model is reluctant to do. The reluctance derives from an attachment to the tacit assumptions of a 'behavioural science' which constructs its knowledge through practices consciously adapted from models of natural science, particularly as these have been mediated in behavioural psychology's focus on stimulus-response mechanisms. Hence, this explains why Dahl's focus is always on responses as the proper signification of power: they are the effects, registered through Bs, of the cause that can be attributed as A's power.

One problem with such a construction of power is that it leaves the door open for a paradox: if B responds to an A, despite A having done nothing in the way of a concretely episodic action oriented to B prior to B's responses, how can we have responses without causes, responses without stimuli, power without initiation? The answer would be provided via the medium of 'intentionality'. Intentions are absent from the agency model of power which Dahl constructs. They are one aspect of Hobbes' views on power which are not to be found in Dahl's preferred formal model. In this model, access to any attempt at interpretive understanding of As is of far less importance than systematic observation of putative Bs. It is the responses of Bs which can be constituted such that they are in fact in A's field of force, thus, consequently in a relation of power with A.

The formal model which Dahl (1968) constructs explicitly marginalizes any reference to the 'intentions' that an A may or may not have with respect to a B in a relation of power. The analytical consequences of this are worth considering because they lead to some quite peculiar and some quite stilted views of power. To aid consideration, we will use a device to which Dahl and many other writers on power frequently have recourse: imaginative vignettes or hypothetical stories which can be used to introduce analytical points.

SOME STORIES ABOUT POWER

Story one

Two people live in adjacent houses. Without knowing it, they have an inquisitive neighbour in a high-rise apartment across the way. Let us call this person 'behavioural scientist'. The two householders may be termed A and B. Behavioural scientist is such a nosy fellow that he keeps the street where he lives under surveillance. He watches it as often as he can and records his observations of what is happening in the street. After making and repeating observations for many weeks, he begins to see a pattern in some of the events in the street. Some of these are unremarkable in the light of behavioural scientist's own stock of knowledge about people going to work at a certain time, coming home at a certain time, and so on.

Behavioural scientist is actually a community power researcher. When he's not being nosy about the street, he's being nosy about the community of which he knows the street is part. Because behavioural scientist has adopted a formal model of power much influenced by the work of Robert Dahl, he is particularly alert in his investigations to predictable observable relationships between As and Bs, in which some of B's scope for behaviour appears to be limited by some exercise of action by A. Normally behavioural scientist reserves his A-B observations for business hours. However, in his observation of the street, he begins to note not only unremarkable patterns of comings and goings (unremarkable because they fit in with his tacit knowledge of everyday life) but also a remarkable pattern (remarkable because it fits into his explicit knowledge of formal power relations). The remarkable pattern concerns householders A and B who live opposite to behavioural scientist and adjacent to each other. Their houses have open-plan front lawns with only some restrained shrubbery and planting breaking up the verdant green of well-watered grass. Each of them spends considerable time attending to garden maintenance. However, and this is what constitutes the remarkable pattern, whenever B is already working in the garden and A comes out to work in the neighbouring garden, B will immediately dash inside the house. In the absence of A in the adjacent garden, B will work regardless of distraction. When A appears, B disappears. Behavioural scientist notes that, from his observations, it appears as if A has power over B: A can evidently get B to do what B would not otherwise do with respect to gardening; that is, to cease it immediately if it entails doing it at the same time as A. Satisfied with this extension of the formal model to every-day observation (albeit that, in its attention purely to observable responses, it matches the formal model's requirements), behavioural scientist turns in for the night.

(Some months later, at a cocktail party to launch the book produced from the community power study, behavioural scientist meets A, and remarks on the observation of A's power, speculating on what its basis might be. A is stunned: being short-sighted, A had never even been aware of B's presence, dash indoors, and absence, in respect of their gardens.)

Story two

This story concerns a space probe to planet Earth from another world in the far-away reaches of the solar system. The other world has no name in English so, for the purposes of the story we shall call it Xaxos.

Once upon a time, the inhabitants of Xaxos sent a number of space probes out into the far reaches of the solar system to investigate whether any of the planets supported life of an observable nature.

Their brief was specific: the Xaxosians were to observe without being seen and to pro-vide a detailed field report to Xaxos on their safe return. The scouts were, in fact, trained social science observers. They were to observe by hovering above the space of the planet under investigation but outside its time: hence they would not be detectable by any primitive forms of surveillance developed in that time.

Hovering above planet Earth, high above an immense urban area, they began their observations. When they were satisfied that they had understood what was remarkable and important about life on Earth, they filed their report. An extract from this report read as follows:

Life on earth is apparent. It takes the form of variously shaped, sized and coloured earth-lings. What these earthlings have in common are aspects of their appearance and behav-iour. In appearance they all seem to move by virtue of some round mechanisms, of which each earthling usually has four, which maintain contact with well-beaten conduits which they traverse in large, slowmoving groups whose social composition seems to vary as these earthlings move around. We have not yet been able to work out what are the exact relational properties of the group composition and structure (although it will be noted in the appendix that a proposal has been submitted for further funding for this purpose from the Xaxos Economic and Social Research Committee's 'Alien anthropology' project).

Although the elementary forms of structure of group composition are yet to be deduced, we have discovered one matter of great importance concerning power relations on Earth.

These earthlings are clearly deeply religious people whose religious life manifests itself in ritual obeisance to totems of enormous power. These totems are liberally distributed in the earthling community. Descriptively each totem pole is surmounted by three signs which flash in a simple code.

The simple code is a combinatory composed of three colours: red, amber and green. These colours exert great power over earthlings. Our calculations are that, with a probability of 98 percent, the red light alone will cause earthling movement to cease while the green light will, with a similar probability of 96.8 percent, cause the earthlings to move. The amber colour is less clear to us in its causal powers. Our hypothesis is that these causal powers are related to religious functions performed by earthlings as obeisance to these mighty totems...

(The remainder of the report re-iterated the research finding that red causes an absence of movement, and green causes movement.)

Story three

This story, which was first told by Robert Dahl (1957: 202–3) has already been used in the previous chapter. However, it is reiterated briefly here.

Imagine a person called Dahl. He stands on street corners in the USA and tells us that he says things to himself like 'I command all the automobile drivers on this street to drive on the right side of the road'. All the drivers actually do as he 'commands'. However, Dahl maintains that if he really thought that these motorists were driving on the right side of the road because he uttered a command to himself for them to do so, then he would best be regarded as mentally ill. However, Dahl continues, suppose that a policeman stands in the middle of an intersection at which most of the traffic ordinarily moves ahead. The suppositional policeman orders all traffic to turn right or left and the traffic moves as he orders it to do. To quote Dahl (1957) directly,

> it accords with what I conceive to be the bedrock idea of power to say that the policeman acting in this particular role evidently has the power to make automobile drivers turn right or left rather than go ahead. My intuitive idea of power is something like this: A has power over B to the extent that he can get B to do something that B would not otherwise do. (Dahl 1957: 202–3)

ELABORATING STORIES

The point of story one is to construct a scenario in which what looks like power, according to Dahl's formal model of it, may not be what it seems. Although there are consistent

A-B relations with predictable outcomes on a specific scope of B's responses, would we want to think of this relation as a power relation? It looks like one from the outside but, if we were to accept A's account, it should not be regarded as such, since A maintains that it was never intended to cause any response in B. (Of course, A could be a consummate liar, especially to nosy neighbours and behavioural scientists, and so we ought not to rule out this possibility. Further research might establish this, but not easily, especially if A has a strong sense of 'consistency rules'.)

The question posed by story one is: does A have to intend the response which B evidences for the 'relation' to be power? 'Relation' is in inverted commas because it is, of course, not clear that any relation actually exists between A and B. There is no reciprocal regard. Is intentionality vis à vis responses and reciprocity in regard to relations a necessary feature of power as the formal model defines it?

A closely related issue to this is in fact tackled by Dahl (1968: 412–13) when he discusses a Senator who regularly votes the way that he thinks will incur the President's future favour. The President has done nothing to persuade him in any way that this will be so. It is a supposition of the Senator's of which the President is unaware. Here the issue is similar to that in story one: does an A (in this case the President) 'exercise' power unknowingly by virtue of the responses of a B (the Senator)? 'Exercise' is in inverted commas because, again, it is not clear that the President has in fact done anything at all that would secure the 'relation' which the Senator intends. The difference between the two cases is that in story one we have only pure observational data, while the episode of the Senator and the President not only has the observational examples but also intuits what the Senator thinks. This intuition of why B acted in the way B did would have been a necessary next step in the account of story one by anyone other than the most rigorous of behavioural scientists, determined to banish all recourse to mentalism from their discourse.

Intimations of the disturbing role that concepts of intentionality can play in the conceptual closure which Dahl (1968) would construct leads him to introduce the distinction between having and exercising power (attributed to Lasswell and Kaplan [1950] and Oppenheim [1961]). What distinguishes exercising and having power, Dahl (1968: 413) suggests, is 'the presence or absence of a manifest intention'. The exercise of power would require that causal agent A 'manifest an intention to act in some way in the future' contingent upon B's responses. In each such case, A may be said to *have* power even though A does not *exercise* power. It is the evidence of a response together with B's implicit intuition of some intentionality by A that might lead one to think of their being in a power relationship. One consequence of the analytic marginalization of A, in favour of direct interpretation from B's responses, is implicitly to downgrade A's intentionality while simultaneously elevating B's. Where A does not manifest an intention but the respondent B imputes an intention to A, A might be said to have power over B. However,

> carried to the extreme, then, this kind of analysis could lead to the discovery of as many different power structures in a political system as there are individuals who impute different intentions to other individuals, groups or strata in the system. (Dahl 1968: 413)

This might be the case if all of these individuals, groups or strata were as conceptually isolated or ontologically autarchic as agency theory in its formal modelling suggests. That they are not can in fact be seen from stories two and three.

The point of story two is that strict adherence to formal models which require social scientists to deny their known-in-common knowledge can produce ludicrous results. While Xaxosians may not know better, we should. Almost anyone knows that traffic lights have no power in and of themselves. The colours which flash are purely conventional, the meaning relational in terms of the law known as the highway code. The lights have no power over vehicles (earthlings) but the drivers of these vehicles constitute their actions in terms of their understanding of and orientation towards a body of highway-related law. Because it is law it has institutional form and sanction through the instrument of police, courts, fines, prisons and so on. The regularities in response behaviour are not 'caused' by any event. Any attempt to render them as such does not or will not grasp that the individuals constituted as subjects of the law are not autarchic: they are bound by rules whose effectiveness is a matter of individuals' constitutive reproduction of a ruled order through their routine judgements of the advisability or not of running a red light. There are patterned responses but no event cause.

Story three ought to be closely related in its moral to story two, as in this example the semiotics of the traffic light are simply replaced by those of the police uniform and by hand signals. However, Dahl does not take the opportunity to use the example to point to the role of rules as constituting and underlying the exercise of power, and thus to cast light on how one may have power without exercising it, by virtue of rules. Nor does he accept the opportunity offered by another of his suppositional stories, that of the Senator and the President, which we encountered earlier. In explaining why the Senator should vote as he does, Dahl (1968) notes that the

> immediate determinant of his vote is his expectations. If we ask what 'caused' his expectations there are many possible answers. For example, he might have concluded that in American society if favours are extended to C, this makes it more likely that C will be indulgent later on. Or he may have acquired from political lore the understanding that the general rule applies specifically to relations of senators and presidents. Thus, the causal chain recedes into the senator's previous learning – but not necessarily to any specific past act of the incumbent president or any other president. (Dahl 1968: 412)

On this account, expectations, or tacit knowledge, can be granted no ontological status other than as the caused effect of some antecedent event and if past events are to have any credibility they had better be only recently past: the construction of an efficacious causal chain requires connecting *this* event effect with *that* event cause.

A consequence of this extraordinarily stilted and stunted way of viewing the world would be to make games almost inexplicable. In what causal event sequence does one's making *this* move in a game determine *that* move by another? Are not moves in a game explicable by reference to an explicit knowledge of what the game is – what the rules are and the moves that they allow – and to a tacit knowledge of what, within the constitutive rules of the game, preferential moves might be, in view of one's experience, skill and competence as a game-player? Perhaps if interpretation of Locke's views of the billiard table had subsequently been focused not so much on the movement of balls on baize but on the forms of calculation which, for reasons of the game, sought to place them here and not there, and to control their trajectory, velocity, impact and so on, then the metaphors of power might have been more adequate to the games people play. As it is, the recourse to a view of the world in which individual judgements are treated almost as if they were an effect of isolated, asocial beings deploying a great plurality of private languages, is wholly relativistic. It is also profoundly wrong. In no way can it stand as a realistic model of how 'individuals... impute different intentions to other individuals, groups or strata in the system'. To argue that it does is to invoke the 'state of nature' a second time around. This time, however, the invocation is made not so much as myth but as farce.

RUSSELL, WEBER AND WRONG: THE POWER OF INTENTION

'Power may be defined as the production of intended effects' (Russell 1986: 19). It was Bertrand Russell, the great philosopher and public figure, who in a book titled *Power: A New Social Analysis* (1938), promulgated one of the definitive statements that links power and intention. In his view it is easy to say, roughly, that A has more power than B, if A achieves many intended effects and B only a few (Russell 1986: 19). Would that it were so straightforward; as another philosopher, Dorothy Emmet, (1953) observes:

> But is it useful to measure power by the *number* of achieved effects unless we take into consideration the *kind* of effect? A may have wanted to do a lot of little things, and have succeeded in doing them all. B, after a life of frustration, may have at last succeeded in one big thing. Are we to say that A has more power than B? (Emmet 1953: 4)

It is for precisely these reasons that Dahl's focus on responses, in terms of concepts such as 'scope', is important. However, if there are evident limitations to Russell's simple definition, it does occur in a context where some useful points are made. For instance, Russell (1986: 21) distinguishes between 'traditional power' and 'newly acquired power', noting that power sanctioned by tradition tends to be regarded simultaneously as more benign, because it has become part of the rules of the game, and more unjust, because 'where ancient institutions persist, the injustices to which holders of power are always prone have the sanction of immemorial custom'.

The 'sanction of immemorial custom' would be merely a special case of what Max Weber (1978; 1986: 28–36) termed a 'structure of dominancy'. Such a structure would be concerned with the different types of substantive rule which govern various institutional arenas and thus make it probable that action within that arena would be action which was authorized: that is, it would be action which was not only explicable but also reasonably predictable, because of its rule-guided nature. This is not to say that it would be entirely predictable. In some circumstances structures of dominancy may be able to invoke seemingly automatic responses – the liturgical routines of a church service, for instance. However, for much of the time, arenas will rarely be so tightly ruled nor will there be only one 'game' conducted in the arena. (This is not beginning to enter into issues of interpretation of rules and of moves in the game.)

For Weber, domination is a special instance of power. Power he defines as 'the probability that an actor within a social relationship will be in a position to carry out his own will despite resistance, regardless of the basis on which this probability rests' (Weber 1947: 152). Like Russell, Weber defines power in terms of intention. This intention is termed 'will', the realization of which, even against the resistance of another, is to be an exercise of power. However, unlike Russell, this power concept is seen in the context of an explicit concept of domination which specifies the basis on which power rests. Weber (1978: 943–5) distinguishes two bases of power as types of domination (although it is clear that he does not think that these two types are the end of the matter). They are based on domination by virtue of 'constellations of interests', which coalesce in economic possession, and authority. It is well known that he distinguishes three sub-types of authority, which are based respectively on domination ceded legitimacy by virtue of rational legal precept, charismatic appeal on the part of the power holder, and tradition – Russell's 'sanction of immemorial custom'.

A number of more contemporary writers follow the lead of precursors such as Russell and Weber in linking power and intention. For such writers, an action can be considered an act of power only if it is concerned with the achievement of intended effects by A vis à vis B. A good illustrative example would be Dennis Wrong's modification of Russell's (1986) position in which he defines power as 'the capacity of some persons to produce intended and foreseen effects on others' (Wrong 1979: 2). Wrong is actually modifying the simple formula 'A gets B to do something that B would not otherwise do' in a number of complex ways. As well as adding a criterion of intentionality (that A had beforehand resolved what B would do if B were to be subject to A's power) the definition also alerts us to a criterion of effectiveness, namely that what A intended should be what B does if it is to count as an exercise of power. Wrong (1979: 3–5) begins by distinguishing power as a specific concept from a more diffuse concept of 'social control'. The latter he regards as evident in all recurrent or patterned social interaction, in terms of the normative regulation exercised by the group over its members. This should be differentiated from 'direct, intentional efforts by a specific person or group to affect another's conduct. Power is identical with *intended* and effective influence.' This is to distinguish it from unintended influence.

It is interesting to consider in detail the quoted examples of 'unintended influence' because, together with Wrong's concept of social control, they point to important types of power-related phenomena excluded from consideration in Wrong's concept of power.

> I do not see how we can avoid restricting the term power to intentional and effective acts of influence by some persons on other persons. It may be readily acknowledged that intentional effects to influence others often produce unintended as well as intended effects on their behaviour – a dominating and overprotective mother does not intend to feminize the character of her son. But all social interaction produces such unintended effects – a boss does not mean to plunge an employee into despair by greeting him somewhat distractedly in the morning, nor does a woman mean to arouse a man's sexual interest by paying polite attention to his conversation at a cocktail party. (Wrong 1979: 4)

Consider these examples. Each of them trades off an implicit legitimization of explanations couched in terms of 'rules' (as will be elaborated in chapter eight). This should be clearly distinguished from explanations couched in terms of event-causation, as in Dahl. However, Wrong is excluding from power considerations in these examples an untheorized tacit acceptance of the 'rightness' and 'just so' quality of a set of social rules which structure the relational qualities of social actors (into 'feminized' vs. 'masculinized' sons, or into 'bosses' vs. 'employees'). The example of sexual etiquette at a cocktail party is the most interesting. It implies a complex set of conventions which ground and pre-figure power relations: a woman, who out of courtesy pays attention to another person at a party; a man, for whom polite attention paid to him by women is sufficient to cause sexual arousal; cocktail parties as arenas in which this complex game is played out. This complex game glosses a whole practice of sexual politics, of male power and female subordination, which Wrong (1979) does not admit to the discourse of power. Oddly, he chooses examples which could hardly make his point more badly if he had tried: the 'feminized son' example is an instance of the discursive power of some forms of psycho-analytic theory which are capable of constituting notions of 'normal' sexuality and 'explanations' of 'abnormality'; the second example sees no power in the contractual relations between employers and employees, an oversight which is repeated in his discussion later in the same book of the notion of power resources (Wrong 1979: 124–45; see Barbalet 1987: 4). The last example sees no power in the ways in which male-female relations are 'normally' constituted.

One problem with Wrong's (1979) analysis has been identified: the exclusion of pre-existing structures of meaning, gender and production relations from consideration of the intentional actions which are available for subjects to act. If Wrong is too restrictive in this regard one might argue that he is too permissive in another: any foreseen but 'not aimed at' effects of an A on a B will count as power.

Wrong (1979: 5) defines 'foreseen' but 'not aimed at' effects as falling within the ambit of power and on the same page notes that 'When attempts to exercise power over others are unsuccessful, when the intended effects of the aspiring power-wielder are not in fact produced, we are confronted with an absence or failure of power'. This is contradictory. If one intends something, according to Wrong, and achieves something else 'unforeseen' it is not power; however, if it is 'foreseen' but not aimed for, it is. Everything hinges on how things may or may not be foreseen. Surely one's foresight of social affairs is consequent upon one's knowledge of the 'rules' of various social games? So, if 'rules' can enter the picture implicitly, the contradiction hinges on not admitting them explicitly.

One can see that one's attempts at implicating another in one's sexual arousal may offend the other even as one is attempting to entice. Consequently, a snub to one's self, a slap in the face, or a kick in the groin, would, despite such interactions frequently offending the recipient, by Wrong's calculus, be an instance of one's power, even where one had intended a sexual conquest! Apart from reference to the 'rules' of sexual politics and the way in which they might favour one type of actor over another, such a view of power must strike one as perverse. It is an odd kind of power which can be signalled by humiliation and pain to one's self. Given Wrong's own criteria of power 'effectiveness', it is doubly perverse.

Analytically, the problems identified in this section result from a conception of power which is restricted solely to issues of agency, to the detriment of any adequate conception of the linkage between agency and structure. As we shall see in the following chapters, the resolution of this problem is central to conceptualization of power.

BACHRACH AND BARATZ: THE TWO FACES OF POWER?

The writers who were most instrumental in attempting to forge a link between agency and structure were two trenchant critics of the pluralist position in the 'community power debate'. The two scholars were Peter Bachrach and Morton Baratz. While accepting some of the pluralist criticisms of elitist studies which we have earlier discussed, they also made what became an extremely influential criticism of the pluralist approach. Two drawbacks are identified. One of these is that power may often be

exercised by confining the scope of decision-making to relatively 'safe' issues. The other is that the model provides no objective criteria for distinguishing between 'important' and 'unimportant' issues arising in the political arena. (Bachrach and Baratz 1962: 948)

At the crux of Bachrach and Baratz's (1962) critique is the question of whether or not 'a sound concept of power' would be equivalent to one which regards it as 'totally embodied and fully reflected in "concrete decisions" or in activity bearing directly upon their making?' (Bachrach and Baratz 1962: 948). They answer in the negative.

The first criticism leads to the celebrated concept of 'non-decision-making', in which 'an A devotes his energies to creating or reinforcing social and political values and institutional practices that limit the scope of the political process to public consideration of only those issues which are comparatively innocuous to A' (Bachrach and Baratz 1962: 948). In this way, they suggest, B is hindered in raising issues which may be detrimental to A's preferences. As an example, they recount a story familiar in its details to any academic audience, of a professor who opposes a faculty issue, resolves to speak out about it at the next faculty meeting but does not do so. As possible reasons why, Bachrach and Baratz (1962: 949) propose three: first, a fear of being regarded as disloyal; second, a realization by the professor that the opinion held on the issue would not be one shared by any colleagues; third, a belief that his proposals would never see implementation. To underscore the analytic point of the story, Schattschneider is cited to the effect that

> All forms of political organization have a bias in favour of the exploitation of some kinds of conflict and the suppression of others because *organization is the mobilization of bias*. Some issues are organized into politics while others are organized out. (Schattschneider 1960: 71)

This 'organizing in and out' of issues is what they refer to as the 'non-decision-making process', where 'latent' power conflicts do not rise above the public face of power which is confined to 'the dominant values and the political myths, rituals, and institutions which tend to favour the vested interests of one or more groups, relative to others' (Bachrach and Baratz 1962: 950). Consequently, they connect their first critique of 'non-decision-making' to their second criticism concerning 'important' and 'unimportant' issues. An important issue will be one which challenges the 'rules of the game' as reflected in these dominant values, political myths, rituals and institutions: in short, the mobilization of bias.

Non-decision-making may work in three ways. First, the powerful may not attend to, may not listen to, or may not 'hear' demands articulated by the less powerful. If these demands do gain admission to the political agenda they may be effectively sequestered via endless committees, enquiries, or co-optation: negative decision-making, as it is termed by Parry and Morris (1974). The second way in which non-decision-making may operate is through Friedrich's (1937) celebrated 'rule of anticipated reaction': B anticipates A's likely opposition and consequently does not raise an issue. The chairperson of a board or committee never vetoes anything. Are such persons powerless, never prohibiting anything, or are they so well entrenched that their responses, and thus their power, is taken into account in formulating issues? Finally, non-decision-making may occur by means of the mobilization of bias

> which refers to those situations where dominant interests may exert such a degree of control over the way in which a political system operates, and over the values, beliefs and opinions of less powerful groups within it, that they can effectively determine not only whether certain demands come to be expressed and needed, but also whether such demands will even cross people's minds... Crucial issues thus never emerge for public debate, and to study the course of contentious issues (as Dahl did in New Haven) is merely to study what happens to the political crumbs strewn carelessly about by an elite with its hands clasped firmly around the cake. (Saunders 1979: 30–1)

Power can produce a situation in which there is little or no behaviourally admissible evidence of power being exercised but in which, nonetheless, power is pervasively present. The argument has been summarized in the form of a 'non-decision-making filter' by Saunders (Figure 4.1).

It is on the basis of this discrimination of non-decisions from important issues that Bachrach and Baratz charge that two of Dahl's (1961) three 'key political decisions' were not so important after all. It was because of the spatially concentrated nature of the New Haven formal political community that neither public schooling nor political nominations was a matter of much concern to the business elite of 'economic notables'. These people may have made their money in New Haven but they lived in a suburban space outside its political scope. They neither sent their children to its public schools nor were

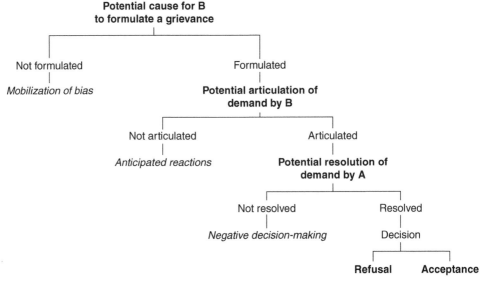

Figure 4.1   The non-decision making filter (Saunders 1979: 29)

they eligible to be, or to nominate, candidates for New Haven political office. Consequently these 'key decisions' were unimportant for them, as a result of the way the political boundaries were drawn. As Newton has commented,

> the drawing of a political boundary is itself a potent political act with all sorts of implications for community decisions, for not infrequently a line is drawn between the city and its suburbs. This is an example of the mobilization of bias, or rather the institutionalization of bias, in so far as the division cuts off middleclass suburbs, with money and few problems, from the inner city, which often has little money and a gigantic set of social problems. (Newton 1975: 18)

In fact, it is harder to think of a better instance of bias than this, which calls into question the very notion of a community. Those who are excluded from a given public sphere may not bother even to attend to its issues, particularly when their own suburban space is so much safer, cleaner, wealthier and more comfortable than the excluded decaying inner city. Such political boundaries are extremely important in the United States in general, and New Haven in particular. A consequence of this is that there is rarely any public policy-making body with overall control of both the urban and suburban spaces. As public squalor in the inner city increases, those with the assets are able to vote with their feet, leaving for the suburbs. The resource base of the urban area shrinks in consequence and the problems, which are now non-issues for those beyond the urban political community boundaries in suburbia, mount accordingly as the resources to tackle them diminish (Newton 1975: 19–20).

Bachrach and Baratz's discussion of mobilization of bias and non-issues with respect to some urban issues seems well supported by the points raised by writers like Newton (1975). Urban redevelopment was an issue addressed by Dahl (1961), who found no strong evidence that the economic notables were interested in it. Consequently, it is suggested by Bachrach and Baratz that this finding may be caused by restrictions in Dahl's model rather than the structure of reality. Looking only at initiation, opposition, vetoing or altering of proposals in formal meetings is likely to miss that 'mobilization of bias' which operates through the 'rule of anticipated reaction' (Friedrich 1937). Issues might not be raised, they suggest, because it could be anticipated that they would not succeed. Potential protagonists remain mute, from the expectation that they would evoke strenuous opposition.

In the following year, Bachrach and Baratz (1963) published a related essay to 'The two faces of power', which fleshed out in more detail the argument about 'decisions and non-decisions'. This later article clarifies their conception of power as relational, involving a conflict of interests or values between two or more agencies, in which one agent actually does as some other agent(s) wishes, where the powerful party can invoke sanctions. Sanctions are a necessary but not sufficient aspect of the concept of power. Where A can sanction B, it will be a case of power over B only where B knows what A expects that B should do; B regards the sanction as a deprivation (of B's powers); B holds the integrity of an intended course of action to be of greater value than the foreseeable sanctioned costs of persisting with that action, even against the power of A, and B is sure that A will not hesitate in actually imposing the sanction. Once more, as in the earlier article, Bachrach and Baratz are mindful of the operation of Friedrich's (1937) 'rule of anticipated reaction': where B regularly obeys A, but A only ever demands what A thinks that B will accept.

A number of distinctions are made between power and related concepts of authority, influence, manipulation and force. Each of these other concepts is defined in terms of some combinatorial presence or absence of the core elements defined as power: that it is relational, based on a demand rationally perceived, where there is a conflict of values, and the threat of severe sanctions. (Such discriminatory lists differentiating between the 'family relations' of power concepts are many and varied in the literature. Wrong [1979] is an excellent guide to the distinctions which can be made.) While their model of power applies to decision-making, they also argue that it can apply to non-decision-making as well, in terms of the impact of the mobilization of bias upon an issue which remains latent because of this pressure.

The repercussions of Bachrach and Baratz's (1962; 1963) contribution were significant and prompted a book from the authors on *Power and Poverty* (1970), in which their framework was argued and applied at greater length. They also responded to the many critics of their earlier articles by withdrawing in part from some aspects of the positions which they had advanced. Baratz (1977: 1168), for instance, was to speak of having 'unwisely retreated' from the forcefulness of their initial criticisms to a position closer to that of a 'modified behaviouralism'. Rather than being a trenchant critique of 'decisionism' as the hallmark of power, their modified position sought to extend the boundaries of a decision from those advocated by writers such as Dahl.

Power and Poverty was to be a controversial book despite the ground which was ceded. It occasioned a spirited counter-attack on the non-decision-making perspective by Wolfinger (1971a) and a rejoinder by Frey (1971). Most significantly, it led Steven Lukes (1974) to extend their 'two faces' of power into a third dimension. While Lukes' (1974) response was that their work was on the right track but did not quite go far enough, Wolfinger (1971a) declared that they had not only gone far enough but, in fact, too far. As Wolfinger put it, 'parts of the neo-elitist research agenda are not practicable… even the feasible aspects do not provide a sensible basis for statements about the distribution of political power' (Wolfinger 1971a: 1064). Furthermore, he suggests, it is only through 'introducing ideological premises specifying how members of the polity should behave' that the critique launched by Bachrach and Baratz could ever be satisfied.

Recall that for Bachrach and Baratz (1962) an important issue would be one which challenged the rules of the game. By the time of their book Bachrach and Baratz (1970) had lowered the stakes somewhat: now a key issue 'involves a genuine challenge to the resources of power or authority of those who currently dominate the process by which policy outputs in the system are determined' (Bachrach and Baratz 1970: 47–8). Two things may be noted. First, as Wolfinger (1971a: 1064) observes, it assumes one knows the answer to the research question, 'who rules?', before one has done the research to determine 'those who currently dominate'. Second, all the nit-picking criticisms of Dahl's (1959) unspecified terms that were made earlier would apply equally here: just what is a 'genuine challenge', for instance? Compared to what? How will we know?

Wolfinger (1971a: 1066) implies that the criteria are only too evident. The judgemental standard is all too clearly ' "false [class] consciousness", a label for popular opinion that does not follow leftist prescriptions and a shorthand way of saying that "the people" don't know what's good for them'. From this point the criticisms become both more specific and more swingeing. Bachrach and Baratz's (1962) view that the mayor of New Haven may rarely have been vetoed or overruled, with respect to the Citizens Action Committee (CAC) and its position on urban renewal, because of the 'rule of anticipated reaction' on the CAC's part, is held up to scorn and empirical ridicule over several pages of carefully documented discussion (Wolfinger 1971a: 1065–70). At the core of Wolfinger's critique of what he terms a 'renunciation' view of non-decisions (where both As and Bs decide not to do something because of what they think is its unacceptability to some potential protagonist) is the view that much of what Bachrach and Baratz would call an effect of political structure is more realistically regarded as unconscious, unreflected routine. It is something which is just so, rather than being political. Routines are a form of unconscious limitation of alternatives which reduce the confusion of a world that would otherwise be composed of too many stimuli. It would be incorrect to assume instead that they were an intentional effect of powerful agents who had a strong self-interest in preserving their power from conscious questioning. Certainly, elites may sometimes cause prudent politicians not to offend what their prudence dictates is an elite interest. However, for Wolfinger, this prudential anticipation is just normal politics, not an insidious form of power.

A second form of non-decision identified by Wolfinger (1971a: 1070–2) is 'abstention', a conscious act of deciding not to be involved in a decision. Whereas renunciation has to be done by some A or B already evidently in the political arena, abstention does not. Anyone might have decided not to have become involved in a particular decision but how do we determine *who* actually did not do something as an *intended* action? Anyone might be an abstainer and for any number of reasons ranging from apathy, laziness, or lack of interest to their realistic assessment, by means of a cogent analysis, of the real structure of power in a given setting.

In a 'comment' on Wolfinger's (1971a) article, Frey (1971: 1092) goes some way to clarifying the non-issue/abstention approach. He defines an instance of a non-issue as an occasion where there is an effective use of power by an A to deter a B from even attempting to exert influence. Non-issues thus have to be the result of an exercise of power by an A over a B. A good reason must be held by a researcher for the view that B might have or could have done something but chose not to because of power exercised by A. Comparative analysis would clearly be an appropriate frame for generating good reasons which would explicitly have to make reference to an *exercise* of power. Loose talk of 'rules of the game' simply will not suffice, says Frey (1971 : 1092–3). Moreover, rules of the game, mobilization of bias and so on will not only prohibit issues but also produce issues: there will be a positive as well as a negative face to them.

The third form of non-decision identified is 'non-participation'. People are unaware of their interests and therefore are not in a position to be able to demand that their 'interests' be satisfied because they do not know that they have them! Interests are invisible, as it were, because of the dominant myths, values, rituals etc., which are assumed to support some unified elite. How one determines that this is so remains unclear other than by reference to an empirical recognition by agents of what their interests are, compared with some theoretical cognition of what their interests ought to be, as some normative model of good practice would have it. Such a model might be, for instance, Marxist, feminist, vegetarian, anti-smoking, animal liberationist, creationist, pro-life and so on.

Wolfinger does not so much want to rule out questions concerning non-participation but does require that some specification be attempted of the generative organization mechanisms which may explain comparative variation in participation. Such an attempt at comparative public policy analysis does not appear to be a part of Bachrach and Baratz's brief. Short of such attempts Wolfinger finds it reasonable to propose that the 'non-decisions' critique is more of an ideological polemic than a serviceable research strategy. Moreover, as a polemic, it is capable of attracting diverse bedfellows from critics of the 'new left' to critics of the 'new right'. They may disagree on almost everything except the capacity of the existing structures of power ('finance capital' or 'new class', as the case may be) to blind people to their fundamental interest in, for instance, 'socialism', 'the market' or some other abstraction. In other words, 'what is a nondecision depends on one's beliefs about how well contemporary political discussion and action match the ultimate political good' (Wolfinger 1971a: 1077). In some cases, such as the example of southern United States 'Negroes' through much of their history, at least according to Wolfinger (1971a: 1077), the non-decisional aspect is indisputable. Such clear-cut cases are rare, he suggests. (In fact, he notes on the next page that, even when discrimination was apparently a non-decision in the 1930s, 'some Negroes were discontented and tried to do something about it'.) If cases of non-decisions are to be identified then a comparative method would undoubtedly be the approach best designed to examine them. Comparison of differences between well-matched concrete cases in the range of decisions may alert us to a rational empirical model of likely areas of non-decision. Other than this, analysis appears to be subject rather more to the theoretical prerogative of ideological stipulation than to the metre of empirical study. As Frey (1971: 1094) puts it, 'one must operate somewhere between a metaphysical disdain for measurement and a paralytically fastidious operationalism'. Explicit empirical comparison is the best way to achieve this, as demonstrated by Crenson's (1971) oft-cited study of *The Un-politics of Air Pollution: A Study of Nondecision Making in the Cities*. In this study, the absence of opposition to air pollution in a city can be seen to be significant when this absence is contrasted with its vocal presence in other cities. If the structural particulars which relate to the 'mobilization of bias' in that city can be seen to differ significantly in terms of the holders of the balance of power, and their organization and resources, one may safely draw conclusions imputing these as the causal mechanism which produces what one might otherwise have had good reason to anticipate, based on knowledge of similar comparative cases.

When inequalities in the distribution of some commonly valued desiderata coexist with little or no attempt by those disadvantaged to challenge them, Frey (1971: 1097) suggests that we look for a non-decision. Although this position might seem plausible it can generate considerable problems. One might reasonably suppose that such criteria would make any search for instances of non-decision-making almost inexhaustible. The proposal that inequality coupled with consent means non-decision-making may well be true. However, the empirical consequences of accepting such a formula are almost boundless in any situation that is marked by more than a modicum of inequalities. For any complex situation of multiple inequalities and variable consent, the argument will not be entirely persuasive; Wolfinger, for one, remained wholly unconvinced of any of Frey's suggestions (Wolfinger 1971b). The objections that he made remained entirely empiricist and boiled down to the argument that one cannot observe things which do not occur. While Wolfinger (1971a; 1971b) takes issue with the concepts of non-decisions and non-issues as Bachrach and Baratz (1962; 1963) raised them, other writers have been more sympathetic to the proposal that power bears two faces, as a Janus-headed concept. Chief amongst these are Ball (1976) and Lukes (1974). As we shall investigate in chapter six, it was the latter who was to re-animate the agency/structure problematic that Bachrach and Baratz's two faces of power model bequeathed for analysis.

For Ball, the second face of power is one whose physiognomy is 'uneventful'. As non-decision theorists, Bachrach and Baratz, unlike pluralists, hold that 'non-events' may have causal status. In particular, they admit 'beliefs' as non-event causes. However, in the concept of causality employed by Ball (1976: 199), 'non-events' such as beliefs are conceptualized to 'closely resemble standing conditions'. A belief on the part of a B that an A would challenge any power attempt by B may well be sufficient reason for B not to try to exercise power against A with respect to some issue. If A knew that B already held this belief or had deliberately inculcated it, then Ball (1976: 202) would agree with Bachrach and Baratz (1962) that A had intentionally exercised power over B, by virtue of either A's knowledge of or A's actions towards B. If A is aware of B's beliefs, whether they are erroneous or not, then, according to

Ball, A has power over B because A has the *power to* do something specific vis à vis B: that is, to get B to renounce a course of action which B might otherwise have anticipated. Not only is there *power over* another actualized in the exercise of power but there may well also be a dispositional power capacity. Exercise and capacity, action and disposition, events and standing conditions took shape from the two faces of power first elaborated by Bachrach and Baratz against the formal behavioural model of pluralism.

IS POWER SOMETHING ACTUALIZED OR NOT?

Dahl (1957; 1968) is quite clear on the answer to this question. Power can only ever be attributed when it has been seen to be exercised. Ball and Wrong, for instance, disagree. Wrong offers a definition of power in which power is a *capacity*. With Dahl (1968) he distinguishes between having and exercising power; unlike Dahl he does not want to see the concept of power restricted only to exercise. Power, when regarded in terms of its capacity, as something that someone may have while not actually exercising it, is called a 'dispositional' concept by Wrong (1979: 6), following Ryle's (1949) discussion in *The Concept of Mind*. In this respect Wrong joins forces with other writers such as Gibson (1971), who refers to the policeman on traffic duty (the subject of story three earlier) to make his case. Power, he says, is a facility to cause something to happen. Policemen can be said to have the power to direct traffic not only while they actually do it but also when no vehicle is in sight. If some traffic were to come along then the policeman would have the power to hold up his hand and thus to make it stop. He can have the power without exercising it.

   Wrong (1979: 6) terms possession of power, a dispositional, as opposed to an episodic, concept of power. Dispositional power is concerned with 'recurrent tendencies of human beings to behave in certain ways'. The distinction between *episodic* and *dispositional* power will subsequently open the way for a consideration of the relation between power in the conventional A-B sense and the earlier discussion of rules and of Weberian domination. Recall that one of the bases of domination which Weber (1978) explicitly addresses is 'possession'. Wrong (1979) identifies possession in its verb form as a dispositional concept. Episodic agency power, the focus of Dahl's concerns, may be seen from this perspective as something which is based on effective utilization of resource control or possession. The latter provides a more or less generalized capacity from which base particular power assaults may be more or less successfully launched.

CONCLUSION

This chapter opened with some contrived stories. The contrivance was meant to suggest that, with respect to B's responses, what may appear from the rubric of a strictly Humean approach to causality to be power cannot necessarily be assumed to be so. An A may not be present or the intentions attributable to A may not be attributable as power even when there appear to be effects registered on Bs. Some writers hold that intentionality is endemic to conceptions of agency and power. On this basis an important conceptual distinction has been made. On the one hand, there is the episodic exercise of power which is initiated by an agency, while, on the other hand, there is the dispositional power which is said to structure that agency's capacity to act. The dispositional concept is distinguishable by reference to a notion of the differential capacities for power which agencies have, irrespective of whether or not they exercise this power. The distinction made is between an *episodic agency* and a *dispositional* conception of power.

The episodic agency concept has been at issue in the community power debate. Attacks on it by writers such as Bachrach and Baratz have sought to extend it in order to encompass a range of concerns which refer to notions of both structural and intentional aspects of power. Some other investigators, such as Wrong or Ball, see these intentional and structurally oriented perspectives as better discussed outside of the framework of the episodic concept of agency power. For them, episodic concepts of power have their limits. The dispositional concept is another matter. They would neither defend the agency view as myopically as some of the true defenders of the behaviouralist faith nor would they write it off totally. Perhaps most importantly, they are not prepared to over-extend the agency view of power as something intermittently exercised to areas of analysis for which the concept is patently unsuited. They do not deny the existence of intentions or structures associated with power. They argue that one will have chosen a poor tool for the purpose if one tries to hone the behaviourist concept for uses beyond the rather limited range of applications for which it was designed. Rather than extend the existing tool to non-decision-making, mobilization of bias and so on, might not these ideas be better served by an alternative, dispositional conception of power?

If episodic power is a limited conception of power, which none the less has considerable analytical leverage when applied carefully, consistently and without imperialist tendencies, how does this concept of power relate to other concepts of power which might be differentiated, such as a dispositional concept of power? What is the relation of power to structure in the light of the 'two faces of power' debate? How do intentions relate to power? How does one connect the metaphysic of a present intention with that of an absent structure in the analysis of power?

Although these issues were raised by Bachrach and Baratz, they were not resolved by them. As has already been intimated, it was left to Steven Lukes (1974), most notably, to address some of the same issues in his book *Power: A Radical View*. While this was not the only book on power to raise these issues, it did so most clearly and effectively. Books which were contemporary with Lukes' *Power* and which also addressed some similar issues, but not as elegantly nor as economically as that distinguished work, were *Power,*

Rule and Domination (Clegg 1975) and *New Rules of Sociological Method* (Giddens 1976). Broadly similar 'trinitarian' conceptions of power were to be found in each of these texts. The serendipitous occurrence of these three books, published within two years of each other, indicated a theoretical convergence. Henceforth the central issues for the agenda of power analysis would concern the theoretical interrelationship of concepts of agency and concepts of structure within a single coherent framework. In the following chapter the focus will be on how aspects of 'moral relativism' in Lukes' work jeopardize the coherence of his framework. In chapter six the focus will be expanded to include not only Lukes' but also Giddens' views on the relationship of agency and structure.

5
LUKES' DIMENSIONS
AND EPISTEMOLOGY

INTRODUCTION

In Dahl's view of power, scientific orthodoxies determine what power is, what it may be and what it cannot be. The orthodoxies are those of classical mechanics allied with classical conceptions of causality. In Dahl these are represented and fused in a singular orthodoxy in which empiricism determines those things that we may have knowledge of while positivism determines the knowledge we may have of those things that we can know. It is this orthodoxy which Bachrach and Baratz run up against when they seek to illuminate the two faces of power. The second face of power, as they define it, cannot be seen from an orthodox perspective.

Lukes (1974) presents a 'radical view' of power which he claims to have constructed by radicalizing Bachrach and Baratz's theorization of power. Does he also radicalize their epistemological underpinnings? By Lukes' (1974) account, these underpinnings are a somewhat rickety extension of Dahl's positivism, shaped so as to allow intentions to function as if they were causes. Each of the three 'views' which Lukes advances is distinguished epistemologically. One of these views is 'radical', so we may ask what would a radicalized epistemology look like? Some clues concerning these issues of epistemology are present in Lukes' three-dimensional model.

In this chapter the initial argument will focus on the 'moral relativism' which, it is proposed, is at the centre of the three-dimensional model. In addition, the epistemological issues which are implicit in attempts to redefine the range and type of causal phenomena that are admitted to power analysis will be discussed. It will be suggested that, while Dahl depends upon a positivist conception of scientific enquiry for which Lukes (1974) roundly condemns him, the status of Lukes' own epistemological position is imprecise. Some elements of his position are 'conventionalist' while others are structured according to implicit 'realist' principles. In fact, his three-dimensional schema vacillates uneasily between the two positions. At the core of the problems with Lukes' framework is the 'moral relativism' of his stance on 'real interests'. Conceptions of what real interests are, he argues, will differ according to whether one is a liberal, a reformist or a radical. Whichever of these one is, he holds to be a result of moral choice. It is thus something which is not only a priori but also beyond the bounds of analytical explanation.

'Real interests' are specified by Lukes (1974) as the major conceptual innovation contributed by the third dimensional viewpoint. The model of 'real interests' is contrasted with notions of individual interests, preferences or grievances which are excluded from the formal agenda of politics. The theorization of interests in Lukes' schema will be considered in detail. It will be argued that the ground of Lukes' third dimensional theorization is an 'uneasy' Kantianism which centres on an ethic of responsibility. Given these Kantian auspices, it will be proposed that a more thoroughgoing Kantianism, such as that adopted by Habermas (1972; 1979), would have been more appropriate, at least in theoretical terms, for Lukes' purposes. However, drawbacks which would have been incorporated in this solution will also be identified.

Lukes explicitly opts for a conventionalist epistemology with respect to the theorization of real interests. Some of his critics, such as Benton (1981), adopt an implicit realism with respect to their conceptualization of power and its related family of concepts. The criticisms which Benton (1981) makes of Lukes' (1974; 1977) schema and his synthesis of power and structure are an important contribution to the literature. According to Benton, a 'paradox of emancipation' inhabits the unstable centre of Lukes' analysis of power and in order to avoid this paradox, one will be obliged to adopt an alternative realist epistemology. This introduces an alternative epistemological position to those options already implicitly encountered, which are threefold. The first option is Dahl's fusion of a positivist stance with an empiricist method. A second alternative is Lukes' conventionalism and moral relativism, while the third alternative is Benton's realism. These three positions will be elaborated in order to clarify the terms of epistemological argument. The terms of the three positions will be briefly discussed and their implications will be specified for the analysis of power.

Neither of the alternatives of conventionalism or realism is easily allied to positivism. Both of these would present problems for one schooled in the rigour of Dahl's epistemology. However, it will be argued that the two contrary positions are not equally useful. The 'conventionalist' epistemological argument will be opposed and an argument in favour of a 'realist' model of 'causal powers' will be mounted, elaborated and justified. This model will serve to underpin a conception of 'circuits of power' which will be elaborated in chapter eight.

LUKES' THREE-DIMENSIONAL MODEL AND THE CENTRALITY OF 'INTERESTS'

At the core of the agency concept of power, as exemplified in Dahl's (1957) formal model, is what philosophers of science call the 'regularity principle', comprising 'the doctrine that the empirical content of a statement of a causal relation is no more than a statement that events, states etc. of the type of the cause are regularly preceded to events, states etc. of the type of effect' (Harré and Madden 1975: 27). According to this principle, it is imperative that whatever is to be constituted as cause and as effect, by virtue of the observed regularity (which may be of the nature of a probability statement), should be a relation between two 'absolutely independent' (Harré and Madden 1975: 27) entities. The principle is founded on a notion of passive equilibrium. Objects at rest, such as inanimate objects on a level table, will remain as they are for as long as they are subject to no extrinsic interference. Extrinsic interference is the source of movement from rest of any inanimate object. The classic case is conceived in terms of billiard balls being on the table. We need only add reference to a conception of the constant inertia or mass of the balls in question to arrive at the basis for a statement couched in the terms of classical mechanics.

Many of the ingredients of Dahl's (1957) formal model are to be found in classical mechanics. Bodies are independent: they are As and Bs. Relations between them have to exist: As exert a cause and Bs register an effect in the same field of force – they are not acting 'at a distance'. Whatever the situation it will remain the same, at rest, unless A's causal attempts succeed in getting B to be the object of an exercise of power. In that case, Bs will do something that they would not otherwise do. They will no longer be 'at rest' (doing whatever it was that they were doing and, more importantly, not doing what they subsequently did) once A, the source of extrinsic motion, interferes in the scene. Moreover, As and Bs have been typically conceived as existing in relation on a more or less level plane. The assumptions of pluralism, countervailing power and equity in access to broadly conceived resources are equivalent to modelling the terrain on which relations of motion occur as being characterized by few depths and heights of social power. The topography, once subject to empirical inspection via a decisionist and episodic conception of power, is seen to be remarkably level, a tableland, without the relief of major features of stratification disturbing the horizon upon which power is mapped.

Some elements of this representation have already been subject to criticism for their lack of verisimilitude. The discussion of Newton's (1969) critique of the pluralist model was such a strategy of attack, as was the 'two faces of power' argument launched by Bachrach and Baratz (1962), or the distinction between 'episodic' and 'dispositional' power which Wrong (1979) made. The criticisms made by Bachrach and Baratz (1962) and by Wrong (1979) both raise issues about the conceptual over-extension of the mechanical metaphors underlying the agency conception of power. These criticisms of mechanicalism alert us to the limits of positivism in the analysis of power (see Clegg 1975: 1–16 for an earlier discussion of some of these issues).

The modernist vector in power analysis has developed to its outer limits in the episodic agency concept of power. Analytical modernism was constituted by a conceptual subordination to classical modernist ideas about mechanics and causality. Among the most significant recent challenges to this concept were those raised by Bachrach and Baratz. Ultimately this challenge was posed by means of a conception which, in Lukes' (1974) judgement, remained within the limits of the modernist project. Other writers, such as Wrong (1979) or Ball (1976), have raised objections to those conceptions of power which rule out, as inadmissible evidence, anything other than a restrictive agency model. Their identification of an alternative 'power to' capacity or dispositional concept of power (as opposed to a 'power over' exercise or episodic agency concept) was centred on a conception of power that was capable of implementing certain enabling and disabling strategies vis à vis protagonists, should the occasion arise. Harré and Madden (1975) provide the most sophisticated epistemological underpinnings of this view.

To differentiate notions of an episodic and dispositional concept of power is to suggest that power is not a unitary concept. We have a situation in which a dominant pattern of usage has extended and developed an episodic and agency concept of power. The explicit roots of this concept are to be found in Lasswell and Kaplan (1950) and in Dahl (1957) although, as we have seen, they can be imaginatively reconstructed to a set of assumptions first espoused by Hobbes (Ball 1975). It would be incorrect, however, to regard the episodic agency concept of power as equivalent to the concept of power *per se*. The mistake would consist in assuming, against the evidence, that there actually is a single authoritative concept of power. Clearly, this is not the case. Only a conflation of the episodic concept might make it appear to be so. However, as the argument of the previous chapter has sought to establish, the episodic concept of power has functioned almost as if it were 'an original exemplar whose authority is acknowledged by all the contestant users of the concept' (Gallie 1955: 100). The episodic concept has become, in fact, an almost obligatory point of passage for discussion of power, if only because a prohibitive, causal conception of power, while not the entirety of power as a phenomenon, is essential to a great deal of the range of phenomena that have normally been classified as power.

In order to avoid the conceptual over-extension of this episodic agency concept, this book will develop an approach based on the framework of circuits of power, in which the episodic circuit is the most evident and apparent. It is only the key role that this episodic conception has played in debate that makes it appropriate to agree with Lukes' (1974) application of Gallie's (1955) notion of an 'essentially contested concept' to the concept of power. The concept does appear to have been both essentially contested and irremediably evaluative. It has not proven capable of formal and rational verification in any way which has decisively settled rather than merely foreclosed debate. However, this is not to propose that the concept is entirely evaluative and relativistic. Many of the points made in the course of debate, particularly by the pluralists against the early elitists, have been widely accepted as being sound, although the subsequent debate around Bachrach and Baratz's objections has been far more hotly contested.

Arguments which developed in the course of this debate were the premise for Lukes' (1974) extension of the 'two faces of power' into a 'three-dimensional' view. The one-dimensional view was associated with Dahl's (1957) formal model of episodes of agency power. It involved 'a focus on *behaviour* in the making of *decisions* on *issues* over which there is an observable *conflict* of (subjective) *interests*, seen as express policy preferences, revealed by political participation' (Lukes 1974: 15). Against this, Bachrach and Baratz developed a 'qualified critique' of the one-dimensional behavioural focus. This approach taps a second dimension of power by virtue of its 'consideration of the ways in which *decisions* are prevented from being taken on *potential issues* over which there is an observable *conflict* of (subjective) *interests*, seen as embodied in express policy preferences and sub-political grievances' (Lukes 1974: 20). The differences between a one- and two-dimensional view of power can be represented in tabular form (table 5.1). However, it was not by its excellent and economical summary of these debates that Lukes' (1974) book achieved its 'radical view'. This distinction was claimed on the basis of expanding the analysis of power into a third dimension (which is added to the comparison of the one- and two-dimensional models in table 5.1).

The table is constructed in a particular way. It is designed to demonstrate visually how Lukes regards the second and third dimension of power as developing out of the underlying causal and episodic notion of one-dimensional power. This conception is as much of a primitive for Lukes as it was for Dahl. Each of the additional dimensions provides further specifications of the significant manner in which As affect Bs. For the two-dimensional view, this comes down to a focus on intentional refraining from action by B because of either something that A has done or some belief held by B that A will do something should B do what B currently projects doing. Considerable argument exists as to whether or not A should know of or assist in formulating or reinforcing B's belief, if A is to be said to have exercised power over B. The more one insists on observable intervention by A then the less qualified will be the behaviouralism of the one-dimensional view. The less one insists on any observable intervention by an A in the formulation of B's preferences and the more one regards these as systemically produced in some way then the closer one is to the three-dimensional view of power.

What characterizes a three-dimensional view of power proper is a focus on 'interests'. Although Lukes (1974: 25) constructs his comparison of the three-dimensional view in terms of different conceptions of 'interests' (the first two dimensions hold a view of interests as subjective, he insists), it is only really with the radical, three-dimensional view that 'interests' come to the fore. From Lukes' radical perspective, 'talk of interests provides

	Three-dimensional view incorporates the first, second and a third dimension		
	Two-dimensional view incorporates the first and a second dimension		
	One-dimensional view incorporates only the first dimension		
Key elements	**First dimension**	**Second dimension**	**Third dimension**
Objects of analysis	Behaviour	Interpretive understanding of intentional action	Evaluative theorization of interests in action
	Concrete decisions	Non-decisions	Political agenda
	Issues	Potential issues	Issues and potential issues
Indicators	Overt conflict	Covert conflict	Latent conflict
Field of analysis	Express policy preferences revealed in political participation	Express policy preferences embodied in sub-political grievances	Relation between express policy preferences and 'real interests'

Figure 5.1   The three-dimensional framework

a licence for the making of normative judgements of a moral and political character' (Lukes 1974: 34). Consequently, he regards conceptions of interests as ineradicably evaluative, such that

> Extremely crudely, one might say that the liberal takes men as they are and applies want-regarding principles to them, relating their interests to what they actually want or prefer, to their policy preferences as manifested by their political participation. The reformist,

seeing and deploring that not all men's wants are given equal weight by the political system, also relates their interests to what they want or prefer, but allows that this may be revealed in more indirect and sub-political ways – in the form of deflected, submerged or concealed wants and preferences. The radical, however, maintains that men's wants may themselves be a product of a system which works against their interests, and in such cases, relates the latter to what they would want and prefer, were they able to make the choice. (Lukes 1974: 34)

The perspective is thus implicitly both radical and humanist (see Burrell and Morgan 1979 on 'radical humanism'). It theorizes and evaluates actual behaviour by reference to a model of what people would do if they knew what their real interests were. The model is never made particularly explicit in Lukes. It derives from Connolly's (1972) account, in which he proposes that interests can be seen in the choices that individuals would make if they could first experience what the consequences of their choices were. The argument could have been considerably stronger had Lukes (1974) made reference to an existing model which claimed to be able to reveal what real interests are, given that a specific set of conditions are met. Habermas (1976) has termed these an 'ideal speech situation': a situation in which individuals are absolutely unconstrained in their ability to participate in any discourse on the conditions of their own existence.

Lukes (1974) did not choose to adopt the 'ideal speech situation' criterion, despite the fact that Connolly's (1972) conception clearly owed a great deal to Habermas' (1972) *Knowledge and Human Interests* (which had been available in translation since 1968 in the United States but was not published in the United Kingdom until 1972). In a later paper Lukes (1982) was to make the implicit linkage with contemporary critical theory more apparent. Clearly, however, he did not embrace it wholeheartedly. This is evidenced by the conscious rejection in this later work both of that earlier conception of 'objective interests' that he had advanced in *Power: A Radical View* and the transcendental view of interests that Habermas (1972) advocated. We shall consider what might have been gained from acceptance of the latter view of interests.

HABERMAS: REAL INTERESTS IN IDEAL SPEECH SITUATIONS

Elements of both Lukes' and Habermas' positions display an affinity with Kantianism, that is, principles deriving from the philosophy of Immanuel Kant. The difference would be that Habermas attempts to develop a position which is not morally relativistic. This is not the case with Lukes, who explicitly endorses moral relativism which almost seems to make the analysis of power a branch of moral philosophy. Rawls (1978: 251), an explicit Kantian, defines moral philosophy as 'the study of the conception and outcome of a suitably defined rational decision'. He argues that this is consistent with Kant's view that a person who acts autonomously is a person who chooses the principles of individual action 'as the most adequate possible expression' of his or her 'nature as a free and equal being'. Autonomous action would not be consistent with adopting those principles which one adopts because of one's 'position or natural endowments, or in view of the particular kind of society' in which one lives, or the preferences that one has. Action on such principles would be heteronomous, according to Rawls (1978: 252).

The desire to specify the conditions under which individuals can autonomously realize their interests is one common Kantian thread in both Lukes and Rawls. Lukes goes further than Rawls in specifying the conditions under which autonomy might be said to prevail. He does this in order to be able to say when heteronomy intervenes. Under such conditions it would not be possible for people to make rational choices. Heteronomy functions rather like the concept of an 'ideal speech situation' in the work of Habermas. Habermas (1972) constructs a model of those conditions under which, he believes, it would be appropriate to say that people can rationally choose. This model is also derived from Kant (1966: 16), as Pusey (1987) elaborates. Had Lukes also adopted this Habermasian position he would have strengthened his stance considerably. It would have provided him with some 'in principle' rational grounds for his discussion of interests. In brief, what would these be?

For Habermas (1979) a transcendent 'judicial reason' exists as a set of conditions under which autonomy is realizable. Following his reworking of the Weberian theory of action, action is seen as fundamentally a matter of communicative competence on the part of any speakers and hearers. All social action, it is argued, implies a reciprocity of perspective and thus implies a dialogue of justification. Why one should have done a particular act will always be open to justification to another who may be witness to it. Language competence carries with it an explanatory and justificatory imperative. Action is the product of speaking, hearing, acting and interlocutive subjects whose subjectivity is expressed through their social action. Social action, in turn, is explicable only through language.

The shared community of language only makes sense, in Habermasian terms, as a normative phenomenon. It is by language that action is justified. Its 'conversation' is the judicial court of reason. Only through the dialogue of language may mutual, shared and uncoerced understanding be achieved. In principle, according to Habermas (1984), it is always possible to settle any difference in agreement if the parties to the disputation are mindful to do so and if the appropriate conditions exist. He argues firstly, that the search for consensus is inherent to community expressed through language, because such a speech-community can be built only on trust, not power. Where power is present, communication is 'systematically distorted' (Habermas 1970; 1972). Power would act as a barrier to the free and unconstrained realization of the human interest in achieving rational truth or enlightenment. Habermas (1970: 372) puts it in these terms: 'the design

of an ideal speech situation', that is, one which is without power and constraint, 'is necessarily implied in the structure of potential speech, since all speech, even of intentional
deception, is oriented towards the idea of truth'. The ideal speech situation is thus the
counter-factual by which real interests may be realized. Consequently, power would consist of placing barriers which constrain others from realizing what their interests are in
the structure of a situation. In an ideal speech situation, the absence of these barriers to
interest realization will be evident in the simultaneous realization of the three types of
social action which Habermas derives from Weber (1978): the co-presence of instrumental, strategic, and communicative action. The co-presence of these is taken to produce a
transparency of language between speakers and hearers. One's strategic and instrumental
action would thus be accountable in the court of communicative reason as action.

As must be evident, were the stakes to be pitched like this, they might well be free of
moral relativism but they would also be almost entirely bereft of empirical application in
a systematically distorted world, that is, one in which real interests cannot be grasped.
Consequently, Lukes, although he could have grounded his radical third dimensional
case more adequately in this way, would at the same time have emptied it of empirical
applicability in all but the most open, communal and committed situations. It is precisely the absence of these conditions which is at issue. Hence, the notion of an 'ideal
speech situation', although it would have been helpful in showing under what circumstances people might know their 'real interests', would be of little value in analyzing how
their apparent interests are formed under non-ideal circumstances. It would also remain
an observer's privilege to formulate whether or not the circumstances which prevail are
ideal. Despite the Kantian affinities, one suspects that it was for these reasons that such a
route was avoided. (There will be further discussion of Habermas, in the subsequent context of his consideration of Parsons' views on power, in the following chapter.)

Some observers have been highly critical of the approach to interests that Lukes actually does adopt. Bradshaw (1976: 121) has suggested that Lukes confuses 'different preferences' with 'real interests'. These 'different preferences' are expressed by individuals under
those conditions of 'relative autonomy' which would prevail under a regime of democratic participation. If individuals who were free to choose under these circumstances
opted for something, then one would have to conclude that it was in their interest to do
so. Thus, real interests can be settled by reference to the conventions that are current in a
community and expressed by individuals. Odd conclusions flow from making individual
expression of communal conventions the arbiter of real interests. As Wall (1975) has
proposed, from this perspective one would be obliged to accept that an addiction (Wall
uses the case of addiction to heroin, but it could equally be to cigarettes or to some other
life-threatening narcotic) is in the interests of an addict if such a person, under conditions
of relative autonomy, maintains that he or she would still want to have become addicted.
It is difficult to accept these conclusions, as Saunders (1979: 38) suggests. Being addicted

to something which threatens one's life can hardly be in one's interests, despite one's choosing to be so addicted. We have encountered what has been termed a 'paradox of emancipation' (Benton 1981).

BENTON AND THE 'PARADOX OF EMANCIPATION'

What cigarette smokers and addicts in general have in common with people who do not recognize the interests that some others would prescribe for them is their stubborn belief that they are the best arbiters of their own interests. Because of this, Benton (1981) identifies a 'paradox of emancipation' as being at the core of Lukes' (1974) radical view of power. He sees it as similar to the 'central problem' with which Marxists have been confronted:

> In its simplest form this is the problem of how to reconcile a conception of socialist practice as a form of collective self-emancipation with a critique of the established order which holds that the consciousness of those from whom collective self-emancipation is to be expected is systematically manipulated, distorted and falsified by essential features of that order. If the autonomy of subordinate groups (classes) is to be respected then emancipation is out of the question; whereas if emancipation is to be brought about, it cannot be self-emancipation. I shall refer to this problem as the 'paradox of emancipation'.
> (Benton 1981: 162)

In short, it deals with the persistent problem in Marxism of its claim to both theoretical and, more seriously, practical primacy in determining what real interests should be, despite what people maintain their interests to be. The historical tragedies arising from such claims to omniscience are too well known to recount here. It also addresses the tension at the centre of Lukes' (1974) analysis between a conception of real interests and the possibility of our knowledge of them. Benton proposes abandoning the relationship between power and interests and modifying Lukes' (1974) conception of three-dimensional power. He calls for a more thoroughgoing 'realist' analysis. We shall shortly see what this entails but first we will consider the paradox of emancipation.

Something akin to the paradox of emancipation arises, suggests Benton (1981: 164–5), at that point in Lukes (1974: 33) where he suggests that it is possible for power to be exercised over an agent against its preferences but in its real interests. The agent would not be able to realize that this was the case because of the non-existence of conditions of relative autonomy and democratic participation. In short, we would have a classic A-B situation, but with an added twist. In the absence of the counterfactual conditions of B's relative autonomy and democratic participation, Benton maintains it must be A who makes the judgement of what B's interests really are or should be, and who then exercises power on the basis of that attribution and judgement. B's interests are thus clearly other-ascribed, and would seem to qualify as a model of objective interests inasmuch as they are not constituted in B's subjectivity but brought to bear in assessing it.

Benton (1981) identifies three distinct ways in which Lukes differentiates preferences from 'real interests'. First, interests are self-ascribed preferences which can be exhibited only under the appropriate counterfactual conditions of relative autonomy and democratic participation. Agents operating under these conditions would be the *ultimate* arbiters of their own interests. While these conditions are absent, they cannot be the *immediate* arbiters because the appropriate standing conditions for conducting arbitration are absent. It is because of the ultimate appeal to the agents' authority that Lukes could claim to avoid Benton's paradox in this formulation. However, Benton (1981: 166–7) is correct in regarding this as an unsuccessful gambit. In the immediate situation it cannot apply. In these cases an outside observer, of necessity, has to judge how the agent would act under the hypothetical counter-factual conditions. Where these conditions may be said to pertain, it still remains an observer's privilege to cede that they do exist. Otherwise, in that situation, Bs may simply be mistaken about their real interests. An additional problem with this position is that any judgement of the relevant counterfactual conditions 'presupposes a value-commitment to one or another conception of human nature and potential' (Benton 1981: 167). Consequently, the paradox of emancipation will once more be apparent. If one is not to endorse covertly a privileged set of value preferences for determining interests then one has to opt for the moral relativism which is Lukes' choice and accept the correlatively weakened force of a merely conventionalist and thus epistemologically pluralist critique.

Irrespective of these problems in assigning the counterfactual, the conditions privileged by the counterfactual are inchoate. To imagine an agent exerting agency outside of the conditions of existence of the existing agency is to imagine another agency altogether. If we are to imagine an agent's identity as the outcome of practices which are quite different from those with which we are familiar with regard to that agent, then it is hard to see how it would be appropriate to speak of the author of the 'new' hypothetical preferences, wants, etc. as the 'same' agent. Certainly, we can imagine the same biological organism, the same body, subjected to these different processes of social constitution. People are capable of sustaining quite different identities at different stages in the career of their body, at different times in the life of the body. The body itself may well change as a result of a heart-transplant or some other type of spare-parts surgery. The person is not a necessarily unitary character nor are specific bodies necessarily unitary any more than is the relationship between the two. Persons are capable of constituting themselves in quite different ways at different times in different contexts, not just as a result of an illness such as schizophrenia but also as normally healthy people. If we can imagine a person undergoing a transformation in the span of a life-time, perhaps as a result of a major historical change or through migration, then this point can certainly be conceded. The question now would be: what are the grounds for privileging the newly acquired identity over the former? Consider instances of those persons who claim to be born-again Christians. Why should any greater moral integrity or credence be given to their claims to be a new person? Why privilege the insights of a born-again Christian over those of that unrepentant sinner who had previously exhibited the same biology as that which now characterizes the changed agent? One could argue that a sinner's insights would be no less realistic than a pietist's. Some might even consider them more so.

The issue is obvious. Are conditions of religious conviction or liberal political participation or communist party membership guaranteed to lift scales from eyes and reveal interests as they are? Only if one happens to believe in the authenticity of the post-conversion state, be it due to the correct reading of new testament, John Stuart Mill or Karl Marx. Ascription of real interests requires some evaluative measure which is itself suspended from evaluation by virtue of a commitment to its tenets as being true. No necessity attaches to these, however, and the act of faith can never be a rationally persuasive mechanism for one who does not believe. Part of the 'logical grammar' of interest attribution, says Benton (1981: 169–70), is some notion of general rules for attribution. Those provided by Lukes lack generality and require cognitive privilege for a moral position.

A second position on interests in Lukes may be suggested in which objective interests correspond to an objective position, the classic Marxist account (see Wright 1978). Bradshaw (1976) has suggested that Lukes (1974) implicitly adopts this position, although Lukes (1976) denies this. Certainly, he does not embrace the further reaches of objectivist, structuralist Marxism in which real interests correspond to class position according to some favoured Marxian model of the class structure. However, in some respects, his position is consistent with a humanist Marxism such as one would find in the 'critical theory' of Habermas (1976) or Marcuse (1964). This leads directly into the debate surrounding the 'dominant ideology thesis' (Abercrombie et al. 1980), which we shall consider subsequently in chapter seven. However, without anticipating that discussion, one may note that this position on interests still requires an ethically transcendent standpoint from which to make its case.

Finally Lukes (1974) attempts to resolve the problem by adopting Gramsci's (1971) distinction between interests expressed in moments of extraordinary action and beliefs normally manifested under the more usual conditions of subordination. However, as Benton (1981: 172–3) elaborates, the cogency of this distinction derives from an explicitly structural and Marxist model of social relations in which action derives from objective location in an inherently contradictory totality. One may not usually grasp the 'real' nature of the contradictory structure. It should be clear, however, that the reality test is conducted according to the Marxist model. Such a model is not specified in Lukes' (1974) text. Once more the concept of objective interests is left anchorless.

The overall conclusion is that the problems of moral relativism scuttle the objectivity of interests in Lukes' radical view. At the centre of the problems with Lukes' 'three-dimensional' model, as we have seen, is the unavoidable moral relativism of its conception of interests. Without sacrificing this moral relativism for the moral absolutism of Marxism, which Lukes (1974) strenuously avoids, it is difficult to see how the power/interests relation can be calibrated in terms which escape either horn of this moral dilemma. For these reasons Benton (1981) proposes abandoning the link between power and interests which Lukes (1974) constructs in an unstable bridge to Marxism. It might be objected that perhaps the problem should be approached from both sides. If the source of tension is the uneasy bridge with Marxism, should one not summon up one's courage and make the crossing into a full-blown Marxist analysis, as Bradshaw (1976) seems to recommend? To do this would take us into the terrain of debates about the nature of ideology. For the moment we will remain with the debate on Lukes.

LUKES' MODEL OF POWER AND STRUCTURE

At the heart of Lukes' (1974) analysis of power is a strong commitment to an ethic of responsible individualism. It is responsible individuals who exercise power. Responsibility is for the effects that individuals either promote or might have hindered. Responsible individuals are the agency exercising choice at the heart of the structures of power. The argument of Lukes' (1974) book remorselessly drives to a conclusion in which the analysis of the relationship between power and structure remains residual to the central conception of agency. Agency, conceptualized in terms of moral responsibility, is the locus of individuals who choose their actions under conditions of more or less relative autonomy, exhibiting, as I have put it elsewhere, 'a space somewhere between fate and freedom, in external and contingent relationship with structures' (Clegg 1979: 63). Their responsibility is to choose whether to act in terms of selfish interests or some conception of the real interests of broad segments of society as a whole (Lukes 1974: 56). The reasons for the foregrounding of the focus on agency and responsibility rather than on structure and determination are evident. What is being avoided is any 'conceptual assimilation of power to structural determination' (Lukes 1974: 55), because, in Lukes' vie structural determination precludes moral responsibility, such that 'within a system characterized by total structural determinism, there would be no place for power' (Lukes 1974: 54–5).

At the back of Lukes' strategy is the celebrated debate between Miliband (1969; 1970) and Poulantzas (1969; also see 1973; 1976) which occurred in the *New Left Review*. Lukes comes down in this debate much closer to Miliband's 'instrumental' view of power than he does to Poulantzian 'superstructural determinism'. For Miliband the state is *in* capitalist society. Power in the state is an instrument whose levers may be controlled by personnel recruited from a different social class background than are the present 'ruling class' occupants. The social background of these occupants is established by Miliband for the major western nations in an exercise of considerable comparative detail. Against this, Poulantzas charges that the nature of the personnel staffing the state apparatus is unimportant. It is because the state functions as the factor which makes capitalism 'cohere' during periods of crisis or when faced with intra-class conflicts between different fractions of capital, that the state in capitalist society will always be a capitalist state. Given the structure of the 'mode of production', according to Poulantzas, this must be the state function. A sophisticated analysis of Poulantzas' changing analyses of the state is to be found in Jessop (1982; also see Jessop 1985). The debates around Marxist state theory have not been entered into in the confines of this book, although they have been discussed elsewhere both by the present author (see Clegg et al. 1983; 1986) and by many others (for a good example see Alford and Friedland [1985]).

For Lukes, power requires agency; the essence of agency is being able to choose. Choice entails responsibility. However, it is not at all clear what the responsibility is to, other than to what Hindess (1982: 502) terms 'the unmoved mover of society and history', the free, creative, responsible human agent serving broad social interests. Perversely, Lukes' (1974) book concludes with an instance of the exercise of power on the part of structural agents but with no conception of power as a structural property. In large part this must surely be a result of his having taken the basic A-B episodic conception of power as the foundational cornerstone for constructing the three-dimensional model, as argued elsewhere (Clegg 1979: ch. 4). Having developed from a conception which bears all too clearly the traces of its classical past restriction to a world composed wholly of mechanical movements, the third dimension does not transcend them, despite Lukes' claims that his dialectical position does so. The focus is still very clearly on As and Bs involved in concrete exercises of social action. The novelty, over and above the more behavioural focus of the one-dimensionalist Dahl's (1957) formal model, is the focus on meaningful social action rather than on simply observable behaviour. The drawback with this is that the loci of meaning become an observer's judgement. Such judgements can either be made under conditions for which a theoretical privilege is claimed or they will not articulate decisive and clear criteria for determining the authenticity or 'realness' of the action observed. There can be no satisfactory solution to this particular conundrum. Either the judgement is that of an observer or that of a subject. If that of an observer, it will be made either according to some standard of 'real interests' or capriciously or inconsistently. If that of the subject (which is where, under ideal conditions, Lukes would locate it), it is impossible to differentiate an authentic, real, articulation of interest, which is made from 'without' power, from an unauthentic, false articulation of interest, which is made as a result of the constraints of power. If subjects cannot know their own minds, how can observers? Moreover, how can observers determine what the conditions must be for subjects to articulate freely their real interests without compromising the freedom of the interests thus articulated?

Despite these conundrums, Lukes explicitly formulates the relation between power and structure on the premise of a notion of power which remains ineradicably tied to human agency:

> power... presupposes human agency. To use the vocabulary of power (and its cognates) in application to social relationships is to speak of human agents separately or together, in groups or organizations, through action or inaction, significantly affecting the thoughts or actions of others. In speaking thus, one assumes that although agents operate within structurally determined limits, they none the less have a relative autonomy and could have acted differently. (Lukes 1977: 6–7)

Power exists when human agents can be shown to have been theoretic actors who could have acted otherwise (see Shwayder 1965). Three intellectual positions militate against being able to establish whether this was the case. First is a voluntarist anti-structural position in which 'the constraints facing choice-making agents are minimal... the only structural constraints are external to the choosing agent; internal constraints are always rational ones and can always be surmounted' (Lukes 1977: 14). As evidenced by Lukes' choice of Sartre (1959) and Popper (1962) as examples, voluntarism ranges over a diverse field. Second is a structuralist position which reduces human agents to the bearers of a structure. Structural Marxism (e.g. Althusser and Balibar, 1970; Poulantzas 1973) is the antagonist here. Third is a relativist position 'which simply holds that there are just different points of view, or levels of analysis, or problematics, and there is no way to decide between them' (Lukes 1977: 17). Of the many writers who could have been chosen to exemplify this tendency, Lukes proposes Laclau (1975). Each of these three positions is a way of denying that there is any problem inherent in the relation of power and structure. 'The first position denies that there are structures (except minimally); the second denies that there are human agents; and the third refuses to relate them to one another' as Lukes (1977: 18) pithily puts it. So, what is to be done to avoid these denials?

Not surprisingly, if extremes are to be avoided, synthetic solutions will be preferred, which is what Lukes (1977) proposes. The centrality of agents' choosing is taken from voluntarist perspectives; the notion of structural constraint which restricts their relative autonomy is taken from structuralism; from relativism it is accepted that 'appeal to evidence and argument' will 'always be indirect and ultimately inconclusive', even if 'more or less plausible' (Lukes 1977: 24). Doubtless the last position rests on the moral relativism which we have seen is so central to Lukes' (1974) position.

Critics have argued both that Lukes (1974; 1977) remains more voluntarist than dialectical (Clegg 1979; Layder 1985; Barbalet 1987) and that the voluntarism is morally overdetermined (Barbalet 1987). There is little doubt that the position is voluntarist rather than the dialectical synthesis that Lukes (1977) claims. Layder (1985: 138), for instance, argues that the distinction which is made between an all-determining structure and structural constraint is incoherent. Structural constraints impose limits on a universe of possibilities, while structural determination abolishes possibility. If structural constraints limit possibilities (in the way that Wright's [1978] model of structural selectivity suggests, perhaps?), what defines the theoretical universe as restricted? Moreover, as Layder suggests, if structure and power are mutually exclusive, then qualifying structure with constraint means merely that, whatever else these constraints are, they cannot be structural, since otherwise they could not allow for power, given the initial supposition of mutual exclusivity. The mutual exclusiveness, plus the centrality of the power/agency tension cedes the practical resolution of this logical quandary on terms determined by power, automatically dissolving the structural components of the explanation.

Structural constraint is not antithetical to structural determination but should instead be considered as one degree of determinism. This determinism might be a variable condition, running from total control to the limitation of opportunities to just two, in which the agent may have a choice as to which to choose, but no choice over whether or not these are the preferred choices. Molotch and Boden's (1985) analysis of the use of questions which demanded a 'yes' or a 'no' answer during the Watergate Congressional hearings demonstrates this situation nicely. Witnesses were obliged by the judicial setting to answer either 'yes' or 'no' to questions. Although they had the power to choose between these terms, the choice situation itself was structurally determined by the legal form of questioning so that only a negative or positive answer was allowable as a sufficient response. There would be choice on the part of an agency and thus power, coexisting with structural determination of that agency, in Lukes' (1974) terms. Power and structure would thus not be the necessarily mutually exclusive phenomena which Lukes (1977) proposes. Lukes does not make it clear 'where structural determinism ends and structural constraint begins' (Layder 1985: 139); consequently the structure-power antinomy cannot be said to be sustained.

Additionally, as Barbalet (1987: 6) reminds us, any definition of power which has developed from one in which As get Bs to do things that they would not otherwise do necessarily implies that power and structural determination are connected. From B's perspective this is precisely how A's power will be experienced. Consequently, it is only when one has power vis à vis another that one can be said to be free of determination; to be the subject of another's power is precisely to have some aspect of the scope of one's action determined in ways that one would not have chosen for oneself.

Barbalet (1987) argues that it is Lukes' moral relativism which explains why he seeks to sustain the general opposition of structure and power. One way in which Lukes (1974) could have stabilized his conception of real interests (the heart of Lukes' third dimensional conception of power) would have been by reference to some criteria drawn from Marxism. Lukes was evidently averse to the absolutism implicit in this. However, Barbalet (1987) suggests that the source of the instability between the key terms of power and structure is less an aversion to Marxist absolutism than a preference for Kantianism which has already been indicated:

> To take responsibility in the Kantian sense involves determining what one ought to do. This requires acquiring relevant knowledge of conditions, opportunities, and consequences, examining motives and principles, and in general acquiring or discovering one's true interest in a situation in which one is removed from the constraints of authority. (Barbalet 1987: 7)

As almost all of Lukes' critics have agreed, however, the morality of interests is of little value in determining their sociological reality or, even more problematically, their sociological unreality (that is, those interests which agents fail to recognize; see Betts 1986: 54–5 for an example of an account which draws out clearly the problematic status of 'interests' in Lukes). Barbalet (1987) goes straight to the consequences of this moral relativism:

> If to be subject to power is to have one's real interests contravened, and if real interests can be identified only outside of a subordination to power, then it is impossible ever to determine whether one is subjected to power, except when it ceases to matter. (Barbalet 1987: 8)

The judgement is harsh but not unfair: 'In this sense the treatment of power in Lukes is sociologically vacuous.' This judgement was prepared in an earlier article (Barbalet 1985: 540) in which the issue of moral relativism was considered in the context of one of Lukes' own examples (Lukes 1974: 52): did cigarette companies exercise power over the public interest (in healthy life) prior to the establishment of a causal link between smoking and cancer? Lukes thinks not, and Barbalet argues that this verdict can be seen as just only in terms of a criterion of moral culpability. In terms of power, what would be relevant would have been the complex of practices whereby cigarette marketing achieved the effect of reproducing new and expanding markets for cigarette consumption even as existing consumers died, for whatever reasons. On these criteria, ignorance would not absolve the cigarette companies from having exercised power which was grounded in what Weber (1978: 943) termed 'domination by virtue of a constellation of interests'. Power would have been evident in constructing a situation in which there was an embodied discipline of smoking in a populace. People may choose to smoke, but it would be foolish to think that their choice absolves cigarette companies of any power in the constitution of these people as more probable loci of cancer than would otherwise have been the case.

It may be adduced that Lukes' (1974) three-dimensional view of power does not succeed in delimiting a space in which a privileged insight into power can be developed.

'Real' interests have not been successfully fixed. Moral relativism has not been avoided. Agency and structure are not dialectically synthesized. Agency remains predominant and structure has been marginalized.

POWER, INTERESTS AND HEGEMONY: GAVENTA AND WHITT

It has been established that Lukes does not achieve a satisfactory resolution of the relationship between power and structure. There are a number of ways one might respond to this impasse. First, one might be tempted to withdraw from the debate altogether and cede the analytical terrain opened up by two-and three-dimensional writers. As we have seen, Wolfinger's strategy is to call for precisely this. Such a strategy would be wrong in that it restricts us to a world modelled only on the assumptions of an empiricism that is disciplined by positivism. Such a narrow and restricted view of the world limits our ability to say almost anything of consequence on the topic of power, beyond limited episodic encounters and interaction. It is an unduly restrictive self-denying ordinance. A second option can demonstrate this.

A number of writers, in particular J. Allen Whitt (1979; 1982) and John Gaventa (1980), have employed a comparative analysis of distinct approaches to power in order to establish whether or not any one of them is of greater empirical value than the others. Implicitly in Whitt's (1979) case and explicitly in Gaventa's (1980), the three models used correspond to Lukes' (1974) three dimensions. While it is not clear that Whitt establishes the superiority of the third dimension, Gaventa does achieve a re-specified model of three-dimensional power which is expunged of notions of 'real interests'. By contrast, Whitt's analysis deduces interests from structure. One way of comparing the explanatory potential of different conceptions of power is to apply them systematically to understanding of the same phenomena. The advantage of discussing Whitt's (1979) study is that it is an economical and well-constructed case which clearly demonstrates both the weaknesses of one-dimensional, pluralist approaches and the problems inherent in a traditional Marxian conception of interests allied to social classes.

As the basic units for analysis, the pluralistic model has interest groups, the elite model has institutional elites, and the class dialectical model has social classes. The essential processes for each are: interest group competition for pluralism, hierarchical dominance by elites for elitism, and the imperatives of social class, domination and conflict for the class dialectical model. The key actions are: interest group competition, hierarchical dominance, and class domination respectively for each model. The resources which are the bases of group power would include: for the pluralistic model, organizational, governmental, economic, social and personal bases; for the elite model, institutional position, common social background and convergent interests; for the class dialectical model, class position and the degree of class consciousness and organization. The distribution of power is dispersed amongst competing groups in the pluralist model; concentrated in relatively hegemonic elites in the elite model; held by dominant classes but potentially available for subordinate classes in the class dialectical model. The limits and the stability of group power for the pluralist model are very weak. Stability is limited by democratic value consensus, by the shifting strength of organized interests, and by cross-cutting allegiances. In the elite model, power is stable because there are no identifiable limits to elite domination. For the class dialectical model stability is a historically contingent situation which is generally strong but limited by class conflict and contradictions within and among social institutions.

For the pluralists, states are 'brokers' which are able to preserve some autonomy by balancing competing interests. For the elites, the states have little if any autonomy and are the captives of elite interests. The class dialectical model has a view of the state serving the interests of the dominant class while, at the same time, having a degree of autonomy from segments of the dominant class in order to act to preserve the basis of class hegemony (a much fuller characterization of the present authors theory of the state may be found in Clegg et al. 1983; 1986) and is developed further in chapter 10.

Let us look at the class dialectical model in more detail. What are some of its assumptions? First, there is an assumption of class intentionality (not individual intentionality, which is difficult enough to establish). As Whitt (1979: 84) puts it, 'there is a mutually reinforcing relationship between social institutions and dominant classes'. Dominant classes act to preserve those institutions which are the basis of their own hegemony. Institutions shape the behaviour of both dominant and subordinate classes. The dominant class often shapes institutions.

What is implied in saying that dominant classes act to preserve those institutions which are the basis of their own hegemony? This assumes, first, that dominant classes know what they are doing, that is, maintaining hegemony; second, that they know how they do what they are doing, that is, which institutions serve to preserve their own hegemony; third, that they can act intentionally to preserve those institutions; fourth, that they do have the organizational capacities to realize this prescient knowledge. Dominant classes presumably know not only what they are doing but also how to act self-consciously in order to further those interests they recognise. One might be a little sceptical about all this. Given the problems involved in showing that individuals can realize their interests, is it going to be that much easier to show that classes can do it?

Dominant classes are defined by Whitt in a fairly conventional way, by their control of the means of production. This is the crucial resource base for class power. Classes rule because they control means of production. In Whitt's (1979: 84) words: 'Capitalist societies are characterized by the presence of the dominant class which controls the means of production. This control is the basic resource for power in society. With it comes the ability to shape the more super-structural institutions of society, including the ability to carry out ideological hegemony.'

The key word is 'hegemony'. A general definition of the concept of hegemony has been offered by Bocock (1986: 63) in a useful introductory text devoted to the concept. Hegemony, he says, occurs 'when the intellectual, moral and philosophical leadership provided by the class or alliance of class and class fractions which is ruling, successfully achieves its objective of providing the fundamental outlook for the whole society'. Behind the rule of consent always stands the force of arms yielded by the state in Gramsci's (1971) original formulations: the power of the state is available in the wings if the spectacle of hegemonic leadership should prove to be insufficiently edifying to maintain popular consent amongst some sections of the people. In contemporary terms these may be climate activists, ethnic minorities trade unionists and so on. (Note that the examples come easiest from a state in which hegemony clearly does not incorporate sizeable specific groups of 'the nation' who may otherwise be formulated as 'the people'.)

It is evidently a much more specific conception of hegemony which Whitt (1979) is working with than this more general framework of analysis. We shall consider this broader framework later. For the present, let us look at the role that hegemony plays in Whitt's (1979) analysis. He sees it as equivalent to business leadership by some enterprises over others. With this hegemony comes an ability generally to manipulate the societal context in which political contests are waged. Other resources for power, he suggests, are the degree of class consciousness and the extent of class political organization. The more traditional notion of hegemony appears when the state functions to serve the interest of the dominant class by preserving the bases of class hegemony. However, power is potentially available to the subordinate classes if they become sufficiently class conscious and politically organized to seize or to challenge the control of the means of production. Thus the power of the dominant classes is not absolute. This is all the more true, he suggests, for two reasons. First, there are not only inter-class but also intra-class conflicts among capitalists. Second, there are contradictions within the economic and class structure which produce disruptions that may limit the ability of the dominant class to act. It is this dialectical conception of power and of the relation between social classes and history that is the most important difference separating the elitist and class dialectical models.

Overall the most salient differences between the three models which Whitt (1979) specifies are as follows. The elitist and class dialectic models use much larger units of analysis than does the pluralist model. The former two models also hold that power is more concentrated than is true in the pluralist model. The pluralist model presents a very unstable pattern of power relations although this produces an orderly outcome. The class dialectical model conceives of power as much more stable than in the pluralist model but somewhat less stable than in the elitist model. Interestingly, says Whitt (1979), differences concerning the role of the state are clearest between the pluralist and elitist models. The pluralist state has autonomy, the elitist state does not. The class dialectic model regarding state autonomy holds that the state serves the interests of the dominant class.

Whitt (1979) tries to derive hypotheses from each position that he will be able to test out on research into a particular arena and set of issues. Plural hypotheses are considered first. If the pluralist model is correct, a study of an important political issue should reveal, he suggests, (a) the active involvement of numerous interest groups, (b) divisions of interest among the groups, (c) a vigorous competitive relationship among the groups, (d) interest and alliances that shift all the time, and (e) political outcomes that consistently favour no particular group more than others. If the power elite model is correct, the study of an important political issue should reveal (a) a high degree of elite involvement, (b) general convergence of interests among elites, (c) elite study and dominance on the issue, (d) stability of the political allegiances, and (e) outcomes that tend to favour elite interest. If the class dialectical model is correct, the study of an important political issue should reveal (a) processes of social institutions that expel what is not beneficial to dominant classes, (b) evidence of latent class conflict, divergent interests, or observable class conflict over the issue, perhaps including intra-class conflicts among the dominant class, accompanied by attempts to achieve class unity and cohesion, (c) political alliance and stability of power relations that are historically contingent, reflecting the need to respond to inter-and intra-class conflicts and structural crises, and (d) outcomes that usually favour dominant class interest but may also reflect the power of opposing classes and the limitations that are imposed by structural contradictions.

Whitt (1979) follows the strictest methodological requirements in doing his empirical work, which he suggests are those of pluralists. This is interesting because, having pitched his analysis methodologically on the pluralist ground, if he can show the greater explanatory power of either of the elitist or class dialectical models, then he clearly has a compelling case.

Whitt (1979) finds in favour of the class dialectical model. This research design works, he maintains, even on its adversaries' terms. Whitt's study explored the issue of public transportation policy in the United States; more explicitly, in California. The importance of any issue under investigation is crucial and transportation could be defended as an important issue on several grounds. The empirical focus was provided by a number of campaigns concerning interrelated transportation decisions affecting California and its major urban areas, which occurred between 1962 and 1974. The campaigns were concerned with various 'propositions' posed as potential new laws subject to electoral referenda. A crucial datum was the amount contributed to the campaigns either for or against by various corporate bodies. Such contributions are publicly recorded in California. Empirically the focus of the study is best shown by going through Whitt's (1979) cases and the discussion of these in terms of his hypotheses.

At a simple level the campaigns appeared to provide partial support for the pluralist model. There was active involvement of several groups in these campaigns. For instance, the pattern of financial support exhibited in the five transit campaigns shows that, within the business world, there were two relatively distinct interest groups, the highway lobby and the downtown transit lobby. These competed to influence public transportation policy. Over time, he suggests, the political outcomes demonstrate that political power would appear to be pluralistic. However, he maintains that this argument, while plausible, does not dig deeply enough beneath the surface of the events. It tends to overlook some crucial aspects of the campaigns. These shortcomings are made clear when the next set of hypotheses is considered.

Most of the groups involved in the five campaigns were actually elite groups. All of the campaigns studied were initiated, organized and supported by business elites, with the exception of one proposition, the so-called proposition 18, which was the sole issue that did not appear to be a business production. All were passed except this. Thus there was a high degree of business elite involvement and dominance in the victorious campaigns. In each of the five campaigns, business contributions were non-competitive. Where changes in funding occurred, they were so complete a reversal that, Whitt suggests, they would appear unlikely to be caused by each company making a totally independent decision. Whitt takes this as evidence of business collusion and so indicative of support of the elite hypothesis. Indeed, Whitt argues that there is evidence of elite cohesiveness, resulting in essentially non-competitive business interest behaviour, achieved particularly through informal networks, ties and clubs. He shows the relationship between the amount of gasoline sold by the largest companies in California and the size of their contributions against the 'anti-business' proposition 18. It is doubtful that such a strong relationship, which came out at nearly 90 percent correlation, would hold in campaigns which were truly spontaneous and uncoordinated, and where each contributor does not know the amount given by others. This is taken as evidence to suggest that the firms were contributing on a proportional basis, dependent upon their market share. An even stronger relationship, a nearly perfect one, was found in the case of bank contributions for one of the 'pro-business' propositions. This does seem to be important evidence to support the elite hypothesis. However, Whitt (1979) maintains that an even greater understanding of these campaigns can be achieved by considering the three-dimensional class dialectic model.

How does this differ from the elite model? First it stresses intra-class conflicts. Second, it stresses the functions of legitimation. Third, it does this within a very high level of the generality and abstractedness that is supplied by some aspects of a neo-Marxian theory. The neo-Marxian theory serves as the broader context which Whitt (1979) believes the class-dialectical model can provide.

He suggests that this broader context allows us to appreciate more fully the political events that are analysed. Now we see more of the motivation behind such campaigns, the contradictions and conflicts manifested therein, as well as the reasons for the pattern of political contributions, which was previously difficult to explain. These political events are to be understood, he suggests (Whitt 1979: 97–8), in the context of the contradictions which the dominant class must face: first, the market economy versus the need for planning; second, the selling of transportation as a private good versus the requirement for public service; third, the competition amongst cities and among capitalists for growth-generating developments versus coherent structure and regulation in urban development; fourth, the need to construct a new urban transit system versus the budget crisis and occasional mass resistance; fifth, the desire for class hegemony versus the requirements of legitimacy and mass persuasion; finally, the desire for class unity versus the divisive tendencies of intra-capitalist class difference and conflicts.

Rather than seeing these political events as simply the classic case of organizing interest groups pursuing their own goals, as the pluralist model would hold, or as the reflection of an elite working its will, Whitt suggests that the situation is more complex than either of these models would lead us to believe. There is both competition and cohesion, and so we should

> understand that the capitalist class must respond to contradictions and crises in the economy, in the cities, and in the polity. Continued class hegemony and the legitimacy of present social institutions require class-based action. Yet, those actions must contend with numerous contradictions. New ones arise as old ones are vanquished. (Whitt 1979: 98)

Class dialectical approaches, as Whitt (1979) calls his neo-Marxian three-dimensional analysis, operate at a very high level of generality indeed. In fact, the level of generality seems quite divorced from the actual detail of the cases considered and is really a statement of the tenets of the functionalist and Marxist model involved. Whitt (1979) has pushed the moral relativism of Lukes' position towards one in which the theorization of real interests could be made absolutely. It therefore ends up being rather reductive and explaining very little because the general theory is not really grounded in the discussion of the data. It does little to illuminate the particularities of the case under consideration, except in the most general of terms.

Whitt's (1979) study is implicitly comparative of the three dimensions. A study by John Gaventa (1980) of *Power and Powerlessness: Quiescence and Rebellion in an Appalachian Valley* explicitly addresses the three dimensions and, in so doing, illuminates three indirect mechanisms of power's third dimension. First, he suggests that Bs who lose a lot give up trying to win against As after a while. Apathy or fatalism can become the norm (Katznelson [1973] is cited as an example of analysis of these processes), as can acceptance and resignation. Second, and relatedly, he notes the literature from political theorists such as Pateman (1970) which observes that participation increases political consciousness: where people are not political participants, for whatever reasons, their level of political consciousness will not be as developed as it would be if they were participating. (Also see Freire 1972.) Third, consciousness may be chronically disorganized as Garson (1973) suggests.

Each of these is a quite concrete and useful illustration of the sorts of processes through which third dimensional power might operate. Gaventa's (1980) book provides an excellent historical case study of these processes. The quality of the study resides particularly in terms of its depiction of the history of power, its embeddedness, and the experience of it in everyday life as a local coherent force against which acts of resistance can be measured. In addition, Gaventa (1980: 21) produces a most useful 'process' model from the three-dimensional schema. It is reproduced here in a simplified form (figure 5.2).

The model is straightforward and requires no elaboration in this context. However, it is worth noting that although it is a three-dimensional model, there is no reference to 'interests' as such. In many ways, this makes it much less problematic, when allied to historical analysis, than the original three-dimensional model which Lukes (1974) produced. Gaventa resolves many of the issues which are problematic in Lukes (1974) through an historical case study in which the data persuasively make his case. The actual processes of myth, persuasion, legitimation, ideologization and so on are given a reality which was clearly not available to Lukes (1974) in the condensed space of his purely analytical study of power.

A/B relations	First dimension	Second dimension	Third dimension
Power of A over B	Prevalence of A over B through A's control of superior bargaining resources	A constructs barriers to the participation of B through non-decision-making and the mobilization of bias	A influences and shapes B's consciousness about the existence of inequalities through the production of myths, information control, ideologies, etc.
Rebellion of B against the benefits held by A relative to B	A defeats B owing to B's lack of resources	B does not participate in the existing political agendas because of real and perceived barriers to entry and owing to anticipation by B that to participate would mean defeat	Susceptibility to myths, legitimation of ideologies; a sense of powerlessness; an uncritical or fragmentary and multiple consciousness about issues on B's part as a result of A's influence, shaping and barriers to entry
Powerlessness of B relative to A	Open conflict between A and B, with each holding competing resources, the conflict occurring over clearly defined issues	Mobilization upon issues and action against barriers	Formulation of issues and strategies

Figure 5.2 Gaventa's three-dimensional model

By contrast to Gaventa, Whitt's (1979) analysis resolves the power/structure problem via the medium of class hegemonic interests. It has been argued that this type of exercise necessarily involves a form of 'reductionism' (e.g. Hindess 1982; 1989) or 'essentialism' (of which Bocock 1986: 112–16 presents a defence). In such perspectives, interests are deduced from structures. An alternative to this deduction of interests from some allegedly essential elements of a structure would clearly have been a reduction to the other axis of the agency/structure terms. To do this would be to reduce phenomena such as interests to the actions of individuals, who would thus be the arbiters of their own interests. This would not get us very far at all in respect of the power/structure debate, since it simply restates the conditions of the problem. Giddens' (1984) position, as we shall see, is a particularly complex version of this theoretical humanism.

An alternative essentialist position to that of theoretical humanism would be to reduce interests to the effects of a structure which is manifested through a form of structural rather than individual causality. This is the traditional conception of class interests in Marxist analysis, which Whitt (1979) exemplifies. Objective interests can be ascribed to classes depending on their relation to the overall mode of production. Classes have an interest either in the reproduction of a given mode of production or in its supersession. Wright's (1985) *Classes* would be the most cogent and sophisticated statement of this. Class interests are located within a discussion of the constraints imposed by assumptions of Marxian analysis: namely, that class structure imposes limits on the formation, consciousness and action of classes. Wright (1985: 28) proposes that the realization of interests is associated with gaining 'access to resources necessary to accomplish various kinds of goals or objectives. People certainly have an "objective interest" in increasing their capacity to act.' These 'objective interests', it is further argued, are determined by class structure. In other words, people's interests are an effect, the cause of which is class structure. Realization of this is class consciousness. (By implication, failure to realize this is class unconsciousness, or false consciousness as it is more often called.) Wright states it unequivocally:

> The argument that the class structure imposes the basic limits on class formation, class consciousness and class struggle is essentially a claim that it constitutes the basic mechanism for distributing access to resources in a society, and thus distributing capacities to act. Class consciousness in these terms is, above all, the conscious understanding of these mechanisms, and thus the realization by subordinate classes that transformations of the class structure are necessary for any basic transformations in people's capacities to act (and by dominant classes that the reproduction of their power depends upon the reproduction of the class structure). Class formation, on the other hand, is the process by which individual capacities are organizationally linked together in order to generate a collective capacity to act, a capacity which can potentially be directed at the class structure itself. Both of these are limited by the class structure. (Wright 1985: 28)

What is objectionable about this? The assumption is that a specific form of given, a priori interests – 'class interests' – necessarily (although not uniquely) constitutes the basis of the mobilization of actors; it is conflict over these interests which 'provides the dynamic for trajectories of social change'. Theoretically, the processes whereby consciousness is constituted are absent from this formulation. Whether actors are aware or unaware of their class location and the class issues at stake is unclear. They 'must be' class actors and they 'must be' in conflict on 'class lines'. Specification of the imperative seems all too clearly to be a theoretician's prerogative. Later in the text these theoretical processes are provided:

> If class structure is understood as a terrain of social relations that determine objective material interests of actors and class struggle is understood as the form of social practice which attempts to realize these interests then class consciousness can be understood as the subjective processes that shape intentional choices with respect to those interests and struggles. (Wright 1985: 246)

The effect of this provision, for Wright (1985: 244), is that consciousness should be investigated as 'those elements of a person's subjectivity which are discursively accessible to the individual's own awareness'. Class consciousness is thus most appropriately operationalized as a variable at the individual level, which, in the context of an avowedly 'structural' enterprise, might seem somewhat contradictory. The subjective processes referred to concern perceived alternatives, theories of consequences, and preferences. Different forms of class consciousness are possible in this interpretation depending on the extent to which the three dimensions 'advance or impede the pursuit of class interests'. Empirically, class consciousness becomes the extent to which individuals have attitudes that are consistent with 'working class' or 'capitalist class' interests. Consciousness is seen as the possession of a particular class and the way becomes open for each class to be granted a coherent, 'structurally correct' consciousness or else an ambiguous, fragmented one, depending on whether they realize what their real interests are ('real' according to Marxist theory, that is). In Wright (1985) the theory is re-specified in terms of 'rational choice' but the theoretical strategy remains constant. First, objective interests provide an explanatory link between action and social structure. This is because interests may be seen to provide a reason for political action which stems directly from the social structure. Individuals are seen to possess objective interests in relation to a collective class position, and so their political behaviour may be expected to be conducted in accordance with these class interests. Second, according to Hindess (1986), objective class interests might be seen to facilitate the patterning of a wide variety of relationships and struggles into a unitary picture. Elsewhere, Hindess (1986: 114) has noted problems facing these interpretations of objective interests. If interests are to be regarded as being objective, then they cannot depend on any subjective awareness on the part of those whose interests they are supposed to be. Consequently, as in Wright (1985), they are usually only imperfectly realized. The problem then becomes one of explaining how miscognition of real interests so routinely occurs. At this stage, as in Lukes' (1974: 47) citation of Gramsci (1971: 327), a notion of ideology or hegemony is usually brought into play to explain how the working class is ideologically incorporated or subordinated by dominant ideology. It need not be the working class which is subordinated, but it usually is: it could be a collectivity that is defined by real interests being attributed to people on the basis of their sharing some particular conditions with members of a category, class, gender, lifestyle, etc. Where this commonality occurs in conditions of a collectively articulated and spatially concentrated community, such as a ghetto of some kind, the attribution may well be appropriate. When it is extended spatially, discursively and temporally from such 'instantiations', the problems become more evident, as Hindess (1982) has argued.

> Interests, in the sense of acknowledged objectives, cannot be regarded as providing a general model or explanation for the ways agents are mobilized in struggles. 'Interests' in this sense clearly depends on the use of particular discursive means of formulating objectives and situating the agent in relation to them. But the forms of discourse available to agents generally allow the formulation of a variety of distinct and often incompatible objectives. So the objectives around which agents do mobilize in any given case cannot themselves suffice to account for the mobilization. For example, racialist and sexist forms of discourse are available to workers in many enterprises which would allow them to formulate objectives that are incompatible with those of worker or union solidarity against management: refusal to work with blacks, restriction of women to certain grades of work, failure to respect picketing by blacks or women, etc. But it would be absurd, because completely circular, to account for the formulation of one set of objectives rather than another in terms of those objectives themselves. (Hindess 1982: 507)

Indeed, why should conditions that are supposed to be common to those of the same gender or the same class entail equally common interests that are 'real', unlike interests pertaining to those conditions not shared? Did the 'Women who want to be Women', an Australian interest group in past Queensland politics, which articulated that women's real interests were in the home, as wives and mothers, have a more correct analysis of what women's interests are than do 'lesbian feminist separatists'? Many women may not recognize their interests in either articulation – are they deluded?

The other basis for commonality of unrecognized interests is the formulation of the conditions under which they would/could be recognized. Lukes (1977), as we have seen, proposes norms of liberal democracy, but why this particular mode of political practice should be privileged over any others is not clear. Different interests may be acknowledged under liberal democracy from those which might be acknowledged under other conditions, but why should one be more real? It is here that the 'ideal speech situation' favoured by Habermas (1982) would have aided Lukes (1974). It would have provided a justification for the conditions of choice which Lukes so clearly favours. In the absence of such justification some interests will necessarily be 'ontologically privileged'.

With characteristic forcefulness, the issue is once more put clearly by Hindess:

> What is at issue in this singling out of certain 'interests' as ontologically privileged is a problematic of domination and, at least implicitly, of emancipation under the guidance of the enlightened few. The problem posed here is: why do the dominated put up with it? For example, in the case of hegemony, why are the popular masses not mobilized around their real interests (the overthrow of capitalist domination); why are they mobilized in ways which fail to pose their real interests as an object of struggle? What has to be explained here is an absence of recognition and, therefore, of action. What is missing is enlightenment, and it is said to be missing because of rule by consent, bourgeois hegemony, three-dimensional power, or whatever, an approach which reduces a complex variety of specific conditions, practices and struggles to yet another of the great simplicities. (Hindess 1982: 508)

Whitt's (1979) 'class dialectical', Lukes' (1974) 'three-dimensional', and indeed my own 'hegemonic domination' framework (Clegg 1979) have in common some notion of the reproduction of agents' preferences against their real interests: Benton's (1981) 'paradox of emancipation'. We are to be emancipated from 'domination' by 'ideology'.

The options appear to reduce to three. First, one can identify interests with people's expressed preferences. The problem with this is that the notion of interests is supposed to be a measuring rod against which preferences can be evaluated. To identify interests with expressed preferences empties the concept of interests of value. Second, one can claim some theoretical privilege in evaluating what real interests are as against expressed preferences. The problem with this is that the claimed position of privilege lapses into either absolutism or incoherence when the grounds for the claim are uncovered or when they are formulated in Habermas' terms as in an 'ideal speech situation'; they will be empirically unavailable. Third, one can bar talk of interests altogether. The problems with such an ordinance have been captured by Benton:

> To deny, or to overlook, the counter-tendencies to the social production of consensual wants and identifications is to deny the possibility of ideological and political struggle which is simultaneously democratic and genuinely radical and emancipatory. It is to remain locked within a strategic perspective which offers only the imposition of 'solutions' on an unwilling population, or acquiescence in the status quo. It is, complementarily, to remain within a theoretical perspective which offers criticism anchored in the shifting sand of a transcendent value-standpoint as its only coherent alternative to the legitimation of prevailing patterns of social distribution of power. (Benton 1981: 182)

To avoid these quandaries, Benton (1981: 180–2) proposes a resolution of the interests problem by virtue of the centrality of conceptions of 'identity' and 'ideological struggles' as 'an internally contradictory process' (181). Without being explicit about it, Benton appears to be calling for a move towards a 'post-structuralist' conception of ideology as the appropriate vehicle for a realist, radical and emancipatory conception of social enquiry. It is, he suggests, in 'patterns of actually or potentially cross-cutting, interlocking or conflicting identifications, loyalties, and locations of interests' that we can locate 'the raw materials in everyday life which provide the essential "purchase" for the whole range of persuasive uses of the concept of interests' (Benton 1981: 181). Ideology can thus be seen as the medium of struggles over identity within which agents strive to 'secure' an identity through those relationships they engender (see Knights and Willmott's [1982] comment on Benton [1981] which, despite their individualistic bias, does suggest such an interpretation). In common with Therborn (1980), one could thus see ideology as a set of practices which constitute the universe within which the dimensions of human subjectivity can find expression, by situating individuals in time and space, by reference to positional, personal and social characteristics. This is a far cry from traditional Marxian conceptions of ideology, as chapter seven will develop.

INTERESTS AND EPISTEMOLOGY

It has been suggested by some writers, such as Saunders (1979: 34–5), that it is useful for an understanding of the concept of interests to locate different conceptions of it in the distinct epistemological frameworks which underlie debate. The criteria of interests used by Lukes and Connolly are conventionalist as opposed to the positivist assumptions of writers like Dahl. Positivism has grounded most of the criticisms made of two-dimensional approaches by one-dimensional theorists. It insists that science can deal only with those observable entities known to experience. The prior restriction of knowledge to such entities and the reliance on observable, concrete phenomena as the only real stuff of science comprises an intellectual position known as 'empiricism' (on which see the discussion in Doyal and Harris 1986: 1–26). Empiricism is an epistemological position which argues for the restriction of indubitable knowledge to that provided by sense data alone. Knowledge ought to correspond to given, observably evident facts if it is to be regarded as reliable (note the moral imperative). The strength of this position is that it enables us to suspend belief in all sorts of fanciful and unobservable notions. It would exclude the occult or other forms of what may well be 'spurious science'. The addition of positivism to empiricism means that one has chosen to operate with the assumption that explanation expressed in terms of law conceived on a regularity principle is the only appropriate form of knowledge for grasping an external world which exists independently of our perceptions of it. The appropriateness of different theorizations can always be settled through testing hypotheses against the observation of direct sense data (Clegg 1975: 3–5).

A conventionalist perspective differs from positivism in the following respects. Unlike positivism, it does not regard observation as an atheoretical and unmediated appropriation of real data via sense data. Observation of things will always be theory-laden: 'whether or not something is warranted to be true or a "fact" is a *conventional* arrangement, with no necessity residing in the world, and this will be a study of conventions for using language in a particular way' (Clegg 1975: 7). A conventionalist analysis, as we have seen in Lukes' (1974: 34–5) discussion of 'power and interests', readily leads to a position in which ungrounded conceptions of moral preferences determine what will and will not count as examples of power and interest. Lukes (1977) calls this position 'moral relativism'. Sometimes it is referred to as 'nihilism' because it annihilates the rational grounds for debate. It would be a position in which nothing is grounded (see Clegg 1975; 1976).

A conventionalist position is capable of attack on at least two fronts. One of these has already been considered in detail in earlier chapters, under the guise of the behaviouralist critiques made of Bachrach and Baratz. Such a critique traces the evident fault-lines separating a conventionalist analysis from one which is grounded in classical empiricism and disciplined by a positivist conception of epistemology. From such auspices an immediate relationship is assumed between a formal representational model of concepts, such as power, and the reality to which the model is taken as corresponding. To achieve isomorphism between model and reality one uses 'operational measures', the idea that any concept means 'nothing more than a set of operations' for measuring it (Bridgman 1927: 5). The meaning of a concept can thus be considered to be equivalent to its method of verification through a finite set of operations for collecting empirical data on what that concept is observed to be (Benton 1977: 50). Such an approach is clearly evident, for instance, in Wolfinger's (1971a) objections to the unmeasurability of non-decision-making. The evident weakness of this position is that it proposes a set of conditions which once might have characterized a very immature and underdeveloped practice of natural science as if they were and ought to be the contemporary limit to adequate scientific knowledge. The irony is that very few contemporary natural scientists accept these limitations on knowledge because, while concepts may well be defined operationally, 'the development of scientific knowledge involves the progressive introduction of new techniques for measuring the properties referred to by existing scientific concepts in a way that is not specifiable in advance' (Benton 1977: 50). Operational method has long outstripped empiricism, so the retention of the latter as a bulwark against irrationalism loses its purpose for an instrumentally sophisticated science. Confirmation of hypotheses will necessarily proceed on the basis of complex measures of putative but unobservable entities. Indeed, in the light of Kuhn's (1962) investigations into the history of science, the verificational or confirmational basis of explanation becomes quite problematic, in as much as such explanations are shown to be theory dependent. One first has to have a theoretical hunch about what one is looking for before one finds it, on a gestalt principle. One's objects of analysis are thus theoretically dependent rather than empirically given.

When scientists are empirically observed at work, even where they have profound disagreements they are usually able to specify what they disagree about, regardless of whether these disagreements can simply be resolved by recourse to some unambiguously empiricist conception of what the data really say (see the argument in Barnes 1981b). Doyal and Harris (1986: 24) observe the matter well when they conclude their consideration of 'the problems of empiricism' with the point that 'Observation in itself can no longer be viewed as the unambiguous arbiter of scientific dispute of whatever kind'. This is not, of course, to license unbridled theoreticism and speculation, but to record that science is more than merely observational. It is also social and conceptual. Despite the fact that observation is not an unmediated experience, it is still important as an empirical component of any science. One should not assume that a disdain for the empirical follows from a disdain for its appropriation through empiricism. 'The social drive for new discovery and the necessity for common empirical reference points in science will ensure the continuing importance of empirical research within scientific enquiry, no matter how much observations are dependent on the social use of concepts for their intelligibility' (Doyal and Harris 1986: 24).

The conventionalist argument is the harbinger of relativism with its realization of 'theory dependence'. In the social sciences this relativism is frequently untempered by sophisticated instrumentalism. The conventionalist position has already been seen at work producing Lukes' relativism on 'interests'. Lacking a sophisticated instrument for measuring these we find ourselves in a position of moral relativism when we try to adjudicate between competing conceptions of what should really be constituted as interests. The only alternative to moral relativism would appear to be recourse to some external observer's standard of what real interests are. One would thus be damned by others who did not share that observer's value-preferences. Alternatively one may trust the subjects' own conception of their interests. The latter course of action would settle nothing which is at issue. The issue is precisely whether, how and in what way people may know what their real interests are. According to the viewpoint of any but the most rank empiricist, what people will tell us may itself simply be an effect of power occluding their conceptions of what their interests are.

At this stage one might be forgiven for wanting to return quickly to the concrete, observable and behavioural world of one-dimensionalism. There at least one can depend on simple but reasonably reliable instruments for simple concepts, rather than unreliable instruments for complex concepts. Resignation would be premature. Earlier it was suggested that the conventionalist position was subject to attack on two fronts. Thus far, only one has been reconnoitred. The other front of attack is known in the literature as a 'realist' perspective.

Realism can best be understood in terms of its opposition to both an empiricist and a conventionalist position, although it shares some tenets with each of them. With empiricism it accepts that there must be an independent reality distinct from our ways of seeing it. From a realist perspective, the distinct dimensional views, if they do depict reality, cannot all be equally valid. Some of the views of power must come nearer to grasping the nature of reality than others. In fact, Lukes (1974) seems to hold this view of the three-dimensional model. Consequently, his position is an uneasy mixture of conventionalism and realism. What would push it into a realist framework would be the substitution of a conception of theoretically critical issues for the empirically actual or potential issues which define the third dimension of the schema. Such a move would resolve a central tension in Lukes (1974). The tension would be between his evaluative theorization of the interests implicit in action and the absence of any coherent theoretical framework by which these interests might be evaluated. (This is resolved in his text by using Crenson's [1972] study as an exemplar of comparative method. As Lukes [1974] notes, however, this study is unusual in its careful construction. Without either an a priori theoretical measure or a comparative difference – which still has to be evaluated as such – the contrast between preferences and real interests is inexplicable.) There are good reasons for this inconsistency in Lukes (1974). They concern his reluctance to accept what was, in fact, the only well-developed alternative position in the analysis of power and interests. That position was Marxist structuralism. We shall return later to the problems inherent in this type of analysis.

Realism is closer to conventionalism in its conception of knowledge than it is to empiricism. Knowledge is to be considered neither as an empiricist reflection nor as an idealist convention. Theoretical discourse has its own internal method of settling what is anomalous and what is not. It is the inability to resolve either internal contradictions in the knowledge produced or the relationship of this knowledge to our experience of 'the ways of acting of things' (Bhaskar 1975: 14) which generates social changes in knowledge. Such change is an open-ended dialogue between existing knowledge, with its own practices and products, and the material conditions which support these. Hence, to coin a phrase, 'theorizing is a twin dialogue' (Clegg 1975: 37). Knowledge may thus be produced only by means of knowledge. Knowledge seeks to produce a theory of the real world: that is, a model with an existential commitment (Bhaskar 1975: 192). Such a theory would be an explanation of the structures that sustain social reality, a reality of structures which are in fact visible in their effects. Theoretical knowledge in the natural sciences would thus be an identification of the nature of things. As such it would be an explanatory dialectic 'between knowledge of what things there are and knowledge of how the things there are behave' (Bhaskar 1975: 211). Knowledge of things also requires knowledge of their constitution, whether one is dealing with a chemical or a social element.

Against positivistic empiricism and with conventionalism, realism holds that 'knowledge is a social product, produced by means of antecedent social products'. In addition, it holds that 'the objects of which, in the social activity of science, knowledge comes to be produced, exist and act quite independently of people' (Bhaskar, 1975: 16–17). In the natural sciences we may refer to these as a transitive and intransitive dimension. The transitive dimension refers to the knowledge domain in which the theoretical object is produced. The intransitive dimension refers to the real object, structure, or mechanism which 'exists' and acts quite 'independently' of people, such as experimentalists, who construct situations in which nature's tendencies can be seen. These conditions enable people to replicate the conditions that provide access to knowledge of the nature in question.

In dealing with a socially constructed reality, a history that people inhabit, albeit not always nor even usually under conditions of their own choosing, we cannot hold that this world would exist without people. Social reality cannot endure other than through its reproduction and, occasionally, transformation. Social reality differs from natural events in that the latter structures are intransitive, while those of the former are not. Social structures exist only in as much as they endure; they endure only in as much as there are social practices which reproduce them. In as much as there are social practices which reproduce them, then these structures exist.

> Because social structures are themselves social products, they are themselves possible objects of transformation and so may be only relatively enduring. And because social activities are interdependent, social structures may be only relatively autonomous. Society may thus be conceived as an articulated ensemble of such relatively independent and enduring structures; that is as a complex totality subject to change both in its components and their interrelations. (Bhaskar 1979a: 122)

One implication to be drawn from this is that social structures, because of their realization in practices, cannot meaningfully be said to exist independently of the conceptions of those agents involved in those practices (Bhaskar 1979b). This does not mean that one should uncritically accept some canon which insists that reality is somehow dependent upon the usage which is conventional in a community. While agents may know they are doing something and may have some idea of what it is they are doing, this does not mean that their knowledge, their self-conceptions, are incorrigible. Furthermore, although agents may be doing something competently, according to public knowledge, they may be unable to formulate the basis in knowledge which produces that competence.

Examples of competence coexisting with technical ignorance abound. The most obvious is the common example of grammatical competence. People may well be able to speak in such a way as to make themselves understood to another speaker of their language who hears them, without explicitly knowing the complex rules of grammar which enable them to do so. Of course, they must know them implicitly, if they are understood, otherwise they would not be comprehensible. Another example might be one in which agents' actions and reasons for acting may have functional consequences of which they are quite unaware. Many different possible reasons of time, space, and understanding could contribute to this lack of knowledge. While agents do understand their actions, social science should not be responsible to these. Any such understanding as agents might have must have social conditions of existence. These are the standing conditions which sustain such understanding and which will consist of relatively enduring relationships and practices. Through these, more or less reified and taken-for-granted frameworks for understanding existence are sustained.

The system in which these standing conditions operate is in principle and practice uncontrollable, owing to its unique instability (the system being the totality of social relations and interdependencies) and unboundedness. In consequence, prediction on a Humean model must remain chimerical. Explanation through explanatory understanding will be appropriate to social science. Necessarily such explanation must always remain incomplete, at the level of hypothetical knowledge as it were, not only because of the ontological openness of social possibilities, both in time and space, but also in as much as reality will not always be open to, or limited to, direct unmediated observation. Reality may possess, as it were, both an apparent surface and a deep structure which cannot immediately be apprehended. The latter is no less real than the apparent, actual, or 'eventual' world of appearance. Indeed, to the extent that the world of appearance is subject to our empirical experience of it, these may often, and sometimes systematically, occlude the real nature of things, precisely because of our conventional ways of seeing. When ancient mariners thought the world they perceived and experienced was flat and feared sailing off the edge of it, its appearance of being flat did not make it so. Its real structure, confirmed by more systematic enquiry and observation as a sphere, remained so even when it was systematically denied in both actual events and empirical experience.

What does realism have to do with the concept of power? Implicitly, it has a great deal to offer, as Benton (1981) recognizes (although it is appropriate to enter the caveat that there are, as in the title of one of Harré's [1985] books, *Varieties of Realism;* not all realists would agree with all aspects of the characterization presented here). The major contribution concerns the re-thinking of the central plank of power analysis, the nature of a causal relation. A realist conception of causality is quite distinct from the more usual positivist conceptions. In addition, it differs from conventionalism in not typically having recourse to actors' reasons as its causal mechanism. One of the central planks of realism in the writings of two of its central exponents, Harré and Madden (1975), has been an argument in support of a concept of 'causal powers' underlying the nature of things. Can 'causal powers' underlie the nature of power phenomena? Benton (1981) suggests so in an argument which seeks to circumvent Lukes' moral relativism by replacing reference to 'interests' with reference to 'objectives'.

REALISM, CAUSAL POWERS AND OBJECTIVES

It is important to understand how the concept of 'causal powers' may function in the natural sciences before spelling out its use in the social sciences. In the sphere of natural explanation, Harré and Madden (1975) have developed a coherent critique of the causal model implicit in regularity theory. They propose replacing it with a conception of causality based on the structure of things and the structure of relations between things. Causality is regarded as being inherent, in the form of causal powers, to the structures of some things. Under certain 'standing conditions', circumstances which enable causal powers to be realized, these causal powers will eventuate. Under certain other standing conditions, which are restrictive rather than enabling, they will not be realized. Whether the tendencies of things to display certain properties, elements, structures or practices will eventuate is contingent on these standing conditions. Causal powers will be manifested to the extent that not only certain structural conditions prevail but also there are no impediments pertaining to the realization of those powers. Power would thus be the freedom to act in such a way as to realize the inherent *dispositions* of either the structure of a thing or its place in a structure of relations. The failure of a causal power to manifest itself, where one would have no reason to expect it not to do so, in terms of the standing conditions, is to be explained either by a substitution of or change in the nature of the phenomenon taken to have causal powers. Alternatively, it will be explained by the failure of that phenomenon to achieve the threshold level at which its power would be realized, owing to either insufficient enabling or sufficient restricting of the standing conditions.

Examples of this conception would be:

> The atmosphere has the power to raise the water (in a suction pump) though it will not produce an effect unless a partial vacuum in the cylinder exists. The earth has the power of attraction which is manifested when the barn collapses, though this effect would not have occurred unless the centre beam had been removed...

> An important aspect of this concept of power is that it catches what might be called the strong sense of potentiality or potency, namely, 'what would happen, as a matter of course, if interfering conditions were absent or taken away'. As long as there is air in the cylinder of the pump the power of the atmosphere to raise the water is frustrated; and as long as the centre beam is intact the attraction between barn roof and earth is kept in check. But as soon as the air is removed, or the beam rots, the operation of these powers, whose constancy in the given set-up is ultimately a product of the basic structural nature of our universe, comes into play. They finally produce the effect which has been held in abeyance by interfering conditions.

> ... efficient causes comprise both the presence of stimuli which activate a quiescent individual and the absence or removal of constraint upon an individual already in a state of activity. (Harré and Madden 1975: 11–12)

At the basis of this conception is the argument that reality displays, in the appropriate conditions, structural tendencies which will eventuate. It is inherent in the disposition of some things to do or be certain things. Some things are 'malleable', 'brittle' or 'conduct' electricity and so on. They display properties of 'malleability', 'brittleness', or 'conductivity' which are inherent to their ontic structure. These powers – to be malleable, to break, to conduct, and so on – persist or endure even when these things are not malleable, not breaking, not conducting. Their capacity to do these things remains. It is intrinsic to their nature rather than an extrinsic effect of the interference to which they are subjected. Extrinsic structuring of the appropriate standing conditions may be necessary to realize these capacities but these capacities remain there, if not realized, in other conditions. Defined formally, this can be rendered thus: 'A has the power to do X' means that 'A can do X, in the appropriate conditions, *in virtue of its intrinsic nature or constitution*' (after Harré and Madden 1975: 86). In this formulation, 'X' would stand for 'getting B to do something that B would not otherwise do'. Consequently, we may say:

> 'A has the power to get B to do what B would not otherwise do', means that A can get B to do what B would not otherwise do, in the appropriate conditions, in virtue of A's intrinsic nature or constitution.

What must be considered further, in order to clarify this episodic but dispositionally based concept of power, are the notions of intrinsic nature or constitution applied to social relations rather than natural phenomena, and of appropriate conditions and the agency of B. The ascription of causal power to an agency is to specify that it can do something in the appropriate conditions. It is not to say that it will do it or must do it. It can do it because of its 'intrinsic nature'.

The notion of having an 'intrinsic nature' is clearly unproblematic if the agency is a natural phenomenon, such as an acid. An acid will dissolve in water, in the appropriate conditions, because it is in the nature of an acid to do that. A stationary billiard ball resting on a level and smooth table, when hit by a moving ball, will itself move. Although the source of motion is extrinsic, it is the intrinsic nature of the body at rest, its mass and inertia, which enables the velocity of the other ball to have an effect on it that the ball does not have on the edge of the table, for instance. Inertia and a specific mass are the enabling conditions for the stimulus condition of velocity to have its effect.

The concepts of intrinsic constitution and appropriate conditions are ineluctably interlinked: it is only in appropriate conditions that an intrinsic nature or constitution will manifest itself. This is the basis of experimental method. Such an interactive relationship is both more marked and less stable – less subject to control – with regard to social phenomena. It is more marked because it is less stable and is thus less subject to control.

The stability of the relationship between the nature of a thing and the appropriate conditions for the realization of that nature is highly problematic for social phenomena, precisely because the causal relationship is mediated by judgement, choice, will (subjectivity) rather than being unmediated by reflection. Of course, the range is variable: in perhaps 90 percent of cases, one may say that drivers in such and such a city, at a specific intersection (observed for a specific period) and at a recurrent time, always stop at a red light. However, it is still knowledge of the highway code which enables them to stop: they know what a red light means and have reasons for almost never running a red light at this particular intersection. At another place, time or period, the percentage may be much lower. The appropriate conditions will include not only reference to the highway code itself but also its policing, the density of traffic, the danger of the intersection, and the skill and competence of the drivers. There are a great many standing conditions, not easily controlled.

Intrinsic constitution in this example clearly refers to the normative stipulations of what being a good and competent driver means at intersections controlled by red and green lights. It is an intrinsic knowledge of and governability by rules, which in this instance have the force of law behind them, with its complex institutional framing and organizational governance. At its ideal, law would be like a dispositional intrinsic nature: one would always, without reflection as it were, do or not do certain things in the appropriate standing conditions. It would be intrinsic to one's nature – 'second nature' as it is called – to do or not do something (see Bauman [1976] for an argument on the role of 'second nature' in framing predominant forms of social scientific discourse). In the social sciences, Humean causality requires 'second nature' to produce its effects: conceptions of 'culture' or ideology invariably fill this role (as chapter seven will discuss). Rarely, if ever, is this the case. Consequently, the law is a more or less imperfect tool, shaping what we conventionally and intrinsically do, but its imperfection is only so in comparison to some absolute ideal. Empirically, it may be relatively more or less efficient. This is because human agency will always be variable: although all may be liable under law, the efficiency and effectiveness of the implementation of particular laws will be variable as well, hence the interactive effects being high. Under certain conditions, human agency may be rendered almost passive. Of course, the more that the range of passivity of another's agency can be extended relative to the agency of some other – the greater the freedom of action with regard to the other – then the greater the power relationship.

The construction of a realist interpretation of power from Harré and Madden's (1975) analysis of causal powers has led to the 'alternative concept of power' which Benton (1981: 173–82) develops. For him, a realist analysis would abolish the definitional links between power and interest and would replace it, with reference to power and objectives, such that 'A has the power to achieve A's objective' means 'A has capabilities and resources such that, if A utilizes these abilities and resources, A will achieve A's objectives'

(Benton 1981: 175). In such a definition, A would be any locus of agency; A's 'objective' would be a purposefully aimed for and intended state of affairs; 'capabilities' will refer to constitutive factors in A's disposition, which will qualify that agency's competence in achieving its objectives; 'resources' are those bases of power derived from the preferential relationships which agency A may enjoy with other things, agents and phenomena generally. A successful exercise of power would entail the following:

> A has capabilities and resources, and B has capabilities and resources, such that if A mobilizes A's capabilities and resources in pursuit of A's objective, and B mobilizes B's capabilities and resources in pursuit of B's objective, then A still achieves A's objective. (Benton 1981: 176)

In this formulation, Harré and Madden's (1975) intrinsic nature or constitution has been rendered as intrinsic 'capabilities', while the concept of 'extrinsic resources' seems to replace their notion of standing conditions.

Benton's (1981) revisions of the sociology of power towards a realist model have not been without criticism, some of which he anticipates himself. First, he notes that it would fail to distinguish a case of genuine consensus between an A and a B from a situation in which A and B have compatible objectives. The solution proposed is to invoke the distinction between 'power to' and 'power over', so that an A may have the power to mobilize resources or exercise capabilities against an objective of a B, but it remains unexercised where B's objectives are compatible with A's. Extending this further, he suggests that 'reference could be made to A's *actual* possession of an objective whose achievement would be incompatible with a *possible* objective of B' (Benton 1981: 177). This would extend the three-dimensional model to include not just issues and potential issues but also theoretically 'critical issues'. In fact, necessarily it would reopen the door once more to ethical absolutism because it would cede theoretical privilege to an observer in determining what the 'real issues' are. Real interests may have been eliminated but their strategic purpose re-enters and re-presents the 'paradox of emancipation' via what may be termed 'critical issues'. Whereas for Lukes, in common with Marxism, the third dimension of power operates through people not knowing their own interests, now it is seen to operate through agents not realizing those issues which are critical for them. Agents are subordinated through not realizing 'that certain wants, beliefs, practices, etc., on the part of a subordinate group are more conducive to the maintenance of control by a dominant group, or of political stability, than are other wants, etc.', where 'the dominant group is able to affect directionally the formation of wants, beliefs, etc., of the subordinate group' (Benton 1981: 179–80). Issues are thus rooted in the constitution of wants, beliefs, etc. A number of other objections are anticipated by Benton, such as the confounding of A-B relations through the existence of other agents in the arena of power and the possibilities for alliances that these present, as well as the plurality of 'objective priorities' that As and Bs may have, which would thus affect their likely degree of mobilization of resources.

Hindess (1982) wants to argue in general against what he terms 'capacity-outcome' conceptions of power, such as Benton (1981) provides, and against conceptions which, in various 'three-dimensional' moves, link conceptions of power to conceptions of interests which remain unrealized because of hegemony. The case against interpreting power in terms of the capacities of agents is premised on arguing that

> First, the means of action of agents are dependent on conditions that are not in their hands. Second, the deployment of these means of action invariably confront obstacles, which often include the opposing practices of others. Success in overcoming these obstacles cannot in general be guaranteed. Power as *capacity* to secure therefore disappears, for outcomes are not 'predictable and unvarying' in the way this conception requires. (Hindess 1982: 501–2)

In fact, the argument is not particularly novel, as Hindess (1982: 505) recognizes. We are back in the familiar territory mapped by Dahl's (1957) formal model: power needs to be conceptualized as having a definite and delimited scope rather than being seen as a generalized capacity. Actually, this point is implicit in any recognition of standing conditions or 'extrinsic resources' (Benton 1981: 175). Any extrinsic resource is not necessarily a constitutive capability of an agency. It may be more or less dependable, compliant or recalcitrant as a resource for A or B. Consequently, in determining the scope of an agent's power, one would, if following the realist model, have to acknowledge that any specific power scope of an agency, A, will depend upon securing some degree of control over the relations fixing and governing the standing conditions of extrinsic resources. Such control will not itself be an evident part of any specific A-B relationship, although it may be a necessary aspect of its accomplishment. In the terms which this book will subsequently develop, it would be a necessary circuit of power for sustaining a specific power scope. However, these circuits may well be bypassed because, where they are tacit and unchallenged in the normal course of affairs, they are no longer necessary to facilitate power. One might say that power can flow more immediately because of a common interpretation of it as normal, as according to rule. In such situations the organization of the standing conditions (the means or, in Benton's terms, the capabilities for mobilizing resources) are such that outcomes *will* reflect capacities because of the stability and fixity of the terms of the power transaction. To that extent, these capacities are not undercut because the circuit of power which might undercut them is not activated. The mobilization of bias will be equivalent to the existence of episodic power relations in which 'capacity-outcome' conjectures are neither refuted nor routed through circuits of power which seek to transform existing standing conditions or to destabilize and reroute those existing relations-defining agents.

Note that the characterization of power provided in the previous paragraph makes no reference to 'interests' nor does it assume that capacities will determine conditions. They might, but only under those specific conditions where the circuit of power remains causally episodic or, as Lukes would term it, one-dimensional. This reverses the calibration of dimensions somewhat: it is the achievement of keeping power within the one-dimensional framework, without recourse to the phenomena which Lukes characterizes as two- and three-dimensional power, which is the supreme achievement of power. For as long as it remains there, capacities may well determine outcomes. If it cannot be contained, if existing relations between agents are no longer routinely reproduced, if some agents are less than wholly competent game players while some others are unusually competent, or if standing conditions are destabilized, then outcomes become altogether more problematic. This argument will be developed at greater length in chapter eight.

Benton's (1981) consideration of criticisms of his position raises the question of how one would decide between the opposing frameworks of power from which different criticisms may be made. Which one of a number of competing theories or frameworks has the greater explanatory power? As should be clear from the discussion in this chapter, this is a question which cannot readily be adjudicated simply by reference to some empirically extra-theoretical reality. Only the most naive of empiricists would actually believe that it could. Theories must always be compared one with another rather than each being compared to some theoretically unmediated reality from whom utterance of the clarion call of 'truth!' can reasonably be expected. None the less, despite the absence of nature's authority, there are some reasonable guidelines as to how we may proceed. Isaac (1987: 68–9) usefully proposes three straightforward criteria for adjudicating inter-theoretical determination which he derives from Sayer (1979). These are criteria of *exhaustiveness, independence* and *consistency*. Exhaustiveness is important because a superior or more adequate theory should be able not only to account for known phenomena but also to anticipate new phenomena by developing a 'research programme': a direction for future research in terms of concepts, topics and their interconnection in projected lines of enquiry. This should be marked by an explanation which is couched in terms of explicit and independent mechanisms, hypothesized to account for the phenomena under consideration. Frequently these will take the form of a structural explanation where a causal mechanism is posited as underlying the production of phenomenal effects, not as an antecedent contingency but as something which is structurally inherent under the appropriate standing conditions. 'What distinguishes realism is its insistence that the aim of social science is to explain causal mechanisms that are not reducible to their empirical effects, which are, so to speak, real but not empirical' (Isaac 1987: 71). The causal mechanisms become the theoretical linchpin of realist epistemologies. Finally, a theory should advance an internally and logically consistent framework, not as a scaffolding of rigid propositions, but at the very least as an aesthetically pleasing ensemble of possibilities which admit of empirical conjecture and theoretical change. It is by criteria such as these that the various frameworks of power should be judged.

CONCLUSION

The three dimensions of power which Lukes (1974) provides do not, unfortunately, align with the three epistemological perspectives considered earlier in this chapter. While the one-dimensional perspective is undoubtedly positivist and the two-dimensional perspective is clearly conventionalist, Lukes' third dimension is quite ambiguous. It is not a 'realist' model, although on occasion it might be taken to be one. For Lukes (1974) reality is structured in accordance with realist precepts: it holds latent, unobservable conflicts and real interest. These are apparent neither to positivist, one-dimensional observers nor are they known to those who are subject to power. They are subjected precisely by virtue of their failing to realize that these interests and conflicts exist. In as much as Lukes generates a framework for theorizing about underlying and unobservable conflicts and interests, he is a prototypical realist. However, this must be set beside the conventionalist elements of his analysis: the moral relativism vis à vis interests. Interests are thus left in a void which remains unresolved in Lukes (1974), somewhere between being 'objective' interests and 'subjective' interests. One resolution of this limbo would have been to follow Marcuse (1964), for instance, back into the world of 'one-dimensional' power and argue that individuals cannot recognize whatever their real interests are for as long as they are subject to distorting dominant ideologies. Such dominant ideologies, it would be claimed, mask true needs with false wants. They would be alleged to do so in order to serve the interests of those who profit from the 'false consciousness' exhibited by people whose interests are suppressed and unrealized. The problematic of 'hegemony' and the 'dominant ideology thesis' develop from this perspective (see Abercrombie et al. 1980). Note that Lukes' (1974: 47) endorsement of Gramsci's (1971: 326) contrast of the difference between the normal intellectual subordination of a group and its rare, extraordinary and embryonic grasp of its 'own conception of the world' comes close to this position, as does his statement that

> A may exercise power over B by getting him to do what he does not want to do, but he also exercises power over him by influencing, shaping or determining his very wants. Indeed, is it not the supreme exercise of power to get another or others to have the desires you want them to have – that is to secure their compliance by controlling their thoughts and desires? (Lukes 1974: 23)

Although Lukes' (1974) endorsement of this position on 'the supreme exercise of power' need not necessarily lead to a Marxist analysis (it could be the basis for a Freudian or radical feminist argument, for instance), the most notable examples of it which do address issues of 'power and interests' are, in fact, of a Marxian provenance. In such formulations, real interests are defined according to the precepts of Marxian analysis, a belief or faith in which must necessarily be a basis for analysis. It is the difference between what people's actual short-term interests are and what Marxist theory requires their fundamental long-term interests to be which is the measure for determining whether or not real interests are realized. Objective interests are determined by a position in an objective structure of class relations. These issues enter debate in terms of Lukes' (1974) resistance to the blandishments of structural Marxism in its attempt to evacuate a conception of agency from consideration of power. Indeed, for most observers of Lukes' (1974) radical view, the perspective remains one in which the tension between conceptions of agency power and structural power have not been adequately resolved.

6

GIDDENS' CRITIQUE OF PARSONS AND THE DUALITY OF STRUCTURE

INTRODUCTION

The ethical focus of Lukes' (1974) book was concerned with 'the complex interrelations between objective coordinates and motivations of conduct of individual actors' within the difficult context of determining 'where structural determination ends and power and responsibility begins' (Lukes 1974: 54; 56). Some commentators, including Knights and Willmott (1982: 580–4) have regarded Lukes' interrelation of these terms as producing an implicit and unresolved 'dualism' between action and structure. In making this charge they are drawing on a notion of the 'duality of structure', a cornerstone of Giddens' (1979) 'structuration theory'. Other writers, notably Callinicos (1985), Layder (1985) and Barbalet (1987), have also addressed this central nexus of power analysis: the relation between conceptions of power, conceptions of structure and conceptions of agency. In doing so they have also focused on Giddens' (1976; 1977; 1979; 1981; 1984) work, as well as that of Lukes (1974; 1977).

The resolution of the agency-structure problem attempted by Lukes was but one of two influential theoretical responses originating in British social science during the mid-1970s. The other theoretical response came from Anthony Giddens, initially in his *New Rules of Sociological Method* (1976) and then in a rapid progression of texts (see especially 1976; 1977; 1979; 1981; 1984). Rather than achieve a 'dialectic' of agency and structure as Lukes had defined it, Giddens instead planned to overcome what he took to be a 'dualism' attaching to these two terms. Against this dualism he proposed that the agency-structure terms of debate should be reconceptualized as a unity rather than as an opposition of terms. The new unity was to be called the 'duality of structure'.

This chapter will briefly consider the development of Giddens' views on power which began with a critique of Parsons' (1967) conception of power (Giddens 1968). In order to do this properly, the views being criticized must first be outlined. Hence the chapter will begin with a consideration of Talcott Parsons' views on power. In his subsequent work, Giddens was to launch his own views of power, rather than merely critique those of others. *New Rules of Sociological Method* (Giddens 1976) marked a significant shift in Giddens' work, which was subsequently emended in a prolific and almost continuous display of writing and publishing on numerous occasions since.

The sociological debate about the relation of power as a concept of individual agency to concepts of structural determination has proved enduring; it seems to be well on the way to acquiring that rhythmical repetition which attends the annual invocation of Marx, Weber and Durkheim in sociological theory finals papers. No doubt, despite my best efforts here, the agency/structure debate will remain an essentially contested target in the lists which social and political scientists are so chronically prone to enter. Perhaps, when it has been re-mounted and re-lanced many more times, we may even have trophies for the most stylish blows struck against it. Presently any such hypothetical cup would have to be shared between Derek Layder (1987) and Jack Barbalet (1987).

Giddens (1968) first focused explicitly on the concept of power in an article on Talcott Parsons. Parsons' work has recently been the object of renewed critical scrutiny, in part because of Habermas' (1987) reconsideration of it, in part because of a general renaissance of functionalism. Parsons' views on power were inherent to, and an intrinsic part of, his developed functionalist system. Consequently, it is important that when one considers Parsons' views on power one should always place them in the context of his broader contribution to systematic sociological theory. Functionalism is not an incidental aspect of Parsons' writings on power but is integral to them.

PARSONS' POWER

At the heart of Parsons' (1967) approach to the analysis of power was an analogy between the concept of money and the concept of power. Just as money functions as a generalized mechanism or means for securing desiderata available within the economic system, he suggests that power functions in a similar manner in the political system. Both money and power, when considered as circulatory media, may be seen to have an effectiveness which is well in excess of their actual resource base in monetary metal or in the available means of coercion, influence, persuasion, determent and so on. Each is able to achieve this because of the legitimacy which is vested in the symbols of the underlying resources. Symbolic legitimacy enables the holders of both power and money to call forth binding obligations from others. It is this symbolic legitimacy which is the orderly background of the context of Parsons' theory as a system, whether he is referring to either money or power (Barnes 1988: 20).

Parsons' conception of the framework of order is couched explicitly in terms of a consideration of the Hobbesian problem of order. Parsons explicitly constitutes his work within the context of a Hobbesian framework. However, his answer to the question of how order is possible differs from that which Hobbes thought appropriate. In *The Structure of Social Action*, Parsons (1937) raises the problem of order as the fundamental question which any social theory has to address. How does a degree of coherence and order in the fabric of institutions emerge when it would be so easy for life to be instead 'solitary, poor, nasty, brutish, and short' in Hobbes' (1962: 143) memorable invocation of the fate which awaits outside civil society? How was civility possible?

Social life, as Parsons saw it, displayed a social context marked by stable, recurrent, patterned and cooperative interaction: society was thus taken to refer to the framework within which orderly, explicable and facilitative uses of power might flourish. This contrasted with the disorderly, mean-spirited and selfish scramble for unconstrained self-advantage which would characterize the conflictual dwellers outside of civil society. Parsons' acceptance of the Hobbesian premises, even if not following the argument through to the same conclusions, did carry the implication that a conflictual conception of power had to be accommodated within an orderly framework. Rather than follow the path of the later pluralist theorists, who saw order as an emergent property of a world in which power was conflictual in its expression but countervailing in its distribution, Parsons chose to expunge the conflict concept of power from the centre of his theoretical frame. Parsons' conception of power was not to be a 'zero-sum' game in which one could only ever win at the expense of another. On the contrary, he sought to show how power contributed to the general accomplishment of order and civility.

First, he argued, if one reasoned purely in the terms of an individualist framework within which As and Bs were constituted without regard to the social context, then an answer to the problem of how order is possible would not be readily intelligible. Durkheim (1964) establishes this clearly with his focus on the role of non-contractual elements in exchange. The self-interest of the parties to the exchange, the basis for order premised by economic liberalism since the days of Adam Smith, was in itself an insufficient answer. It simply presumes that the moral framework within which a particular type of market exchange occurs is something which has the status of a natural order, without recognizing it as a historically particular basis for reciprocity and order.

It is Parsons' view that conceptions of self-interested individuals are an unlikely specification of the raw material upon which social order depends. Rather than seeing people merely as utilitarian self-seekers, Parsons regards them as socialized actors: that is, they are individuals who, in the life-course of socialization, develop into more or less moral agents who have inculcated and can act upon certain binding obligations and are oriented to a *normative* context within which social action occurs. It is precisely because successful social action occurs, social action which is reproduced and reproductive rather than destructive, that the normative order is shaped, structured and transmitted over time.

Power is exercised within this context of norms. The binding obligations which are mobilized by the exercise of power are normatively embedded and thus shared both by the power exerciser and by others. The sanctions which they can threaten are similarly seen by Parsons to be normatively constrained. Norms are at the root not only of all exercise of power but of all social conduct. Power, rather than being a conflictual mechanism which is opposed to social order, is both enabled by and constrained within that social order because of its normative basis.

Recently, writers have referred to Parsons' views of these matters as 'normative determinism' (Barnes 1988: 26), in arguments which question the all-enveloping nature of norms, their ineffable inculcation in individuals' consciousnesses, and the unequivocal spur to unambiguous actions which their enactment entails. It is not just that there are occasional normative deviations: whole categories of authentically social action occur which have not sprung from any over-arching normative framework. One thinks, for instance, of the various tribalisms of youth sub-cultures which would be denied their evident normative coherence and patterning if they were to be assimilated simply to failures of socialization in the dominant culture. There are clearly authentic ways of being a punk, a rasta or a skinhead, which cannot be understood solely in terms of the breakdown of some normative functioning in the central value system and its institutions. One would maintain that there is a social logic to the 'disorderly conduct' of such members: it is not merely random mutation nor a failure somehow to grasp the elaborated and explicit rules of social order. For one thing, such elaborated and explicit rules do not exist as if in so many rule books. For another, certain forms of deviance grasp only too clearly in their attention to style, demeanour and outrage precisely what it is that they oppose. Moreover, they can be contextually quite specific in their instantiation, despite the fact that no inventory of contextualized instructions exists, let alone one which is as de-contextualized as Parsons' framework of order would suggest. There does not appear to be any still, small voice which clearly articulates the normative order in our consciousness prior to our action, any more than there is a normative order *per se*. Instead, as Barnes (1988: 30–1) has argued, in as much as the normative view is useful, it should refer not to individual minds, the private realm of mental action in the psyche, but to the public realm and social context of more or less skilful participants in diverse and complex arenas of social interaction. Internalization is less important, as the basis of whatever normative order there may be held to be, than the knowledgeability and reasoning which occurs between people, individually and in forms of collective agency. Such agents may choose to adopt, propose or impose this norm or that, to rationalize this conduct by reference to that norm or in violation of some other norm. Norms function more as terms which are discursively available than as psychologically internalized by this account.

It is on the basis of this notion of social action that Barnes (1988) argues that the normative order which exists is grounded. Order is a result of agents acting calculatingly in terms of the calculations which they attribute to other agents, where these agents have a reasonable knowledge of the distribution of sanctioning resources, the likely effect of which enters into their own calculations. Consequently, normative order is the emergent effect of their calculations and differential access to, utilization of and effectiveness in sanctioning resources, just as much as is normative disorder. As will be argued in chapter eight, *organization* is required to bring calculations and resources into alignment. Among recent commentators on Parsons, it is only Barnes (1988) and Habermas (1987) who have seen the centrality of organization to any grounding of Parsons' views on power. Having briefly discussed Barnes (1988) in the context of elaborating 'Parsons' power', it is now appropriate to turn to 'Habermas on Parsons on power'.

HABERMAS ON PARSONS ON POWER

Parsons' views on power have not been much discussed in debates about power. Under the impact of writers such as Habermas and Foucault, a renewal of interest in Parsons' work occurred. Kroker (1984), for example, remarked on the Foucault connection in an article which, despite its somewhat effusive and affected style, does have some pertinent comments to make on the connections between these two post-modernist theorizations of power as a regulatory, circulatory and coded medium. Kroker sees the locus of the 'circulatory' metaphor as a common reference to biological analogies. This, in fact, works better as a key to Parsons' conception of power than does the usual comparison with money which Parsons drew himself. In this section it is the Parsons-Habermas interface which is of interest.

Habermas (1987) has revised consideration of Parsons' views on power in the context of a consideration of the 'circulatory media' of power and money. A number of contrasts are noted between the two terms appropriated by Parsons for the circulatory metaphor. What emerges from the comparison most strikingly is the organizational embeddedness of power compared to money. (In terms of biological metaphor, organization is the life-form upon which power depends as both its host and its medium of expression.) Consider the 'rights' that possession of each entails. For money, the right to possession means access to market transactions; for power, the right to its exercise means having a position in a hierarchy of power relations in an organization. Power can be rendered permanent only through organization, Habermas (1987: 270) argues correctly. While property rights do not require some standing organization to channel the flow of binding decisions, this is not the case for power.

The organizational specificity of power signals an important evolutionary distinction between these two circulatory media, according to Habermas. While money may have circulatory effects, even in quite primitive economic conditions, power may not. It requires complex organization to carry it beyond what Giddens would term limited space-time instantiation tied to specific persons and positions. To carry it across space and time it requires, like money, not only means of enforcement and normative legality but also, says Habermas (1987: 270), 'legitimation'. No precise analogy exists for 'legitimation' in the circulation of money, he suggests. (Although he does not touch on this, this is presumably because of the role of a central bank as the sole issuer of bona fide currency. One may lose confidence in a currency, relatively, but even the lowliest peso retains legitimacy for as long as the central bank issues or honours it.)

Habermas (1987) also finds problems with the power-authority relation as Parsons formulates it, but these are of a different order to the objections that Giddens raises. Giddens perceives Parsons as sanctifying power by always seeing it in tandem with legitimate authority. As Sciulli (1987) observes, this misses the point of the conceptual system in Parsons. Habermas' insight is more acute. Confidence in power as a system quality has to be secured on a higher level than confidence in the monetary system. Power implies not only compliance but also obligation when it is tied to authority: that is, it requires a 'duty based on the recognition of normative validity claims' (Habermas 1987: 271).

The implications of this reach back into Habermas' rational criteria of an 'ideal speech situation'. Monetary exchange ordinarily involves a calculation of utility by definition: it is only beyond ordinary transactions that elements of coercion will enter into exchange. Normally, neither party is disadvantaged by the calculation of utility. By contrast, 'a person taking orders is structurally disadvantaged in relation to a person with the power to give them' (Habermas 1987: 271). It is because of organization embeddedness that this is so. An A *can* make a B do things that B might prefer not to do simply by virtue of the continuing conditions of B's membership of an organization under the power of the A in question. Thus, the facilitative aspect of Parsons' definition of power becomes clearer under Habermas' consideration.

Power is facilitative for those who are As rather than Bs, since it is the As who decide what are the collective goals to be facilitated, at least as far as Bs are concerned. Bear in mind, of course, that an A may also be a B in the organizational chain of command. Where Bs cannot enter into the process of goal formation, they can never offset the structural disadvantage that they suffer at the hands of A's ability to coerce their recalcitrance. Recalcitrance to collective objectives may well be ethically sanctionable, according to this formulation, but not where it is resistance to a facilitative power in which one has played no part.

Habermas is arguing that power, although it may be facilitative and may serve collective goals, is somewhat hollow if one's participation in the pursuit of goals is both sanctioned and unsolicited. These are, of course, the conditions of organization membership for most subordinates. Discursive participation in consensual goal formation is not a normal condition for most organization members (Clegg and Higgins 1987). Whereas money is not dependent on processes of consensus formation in language for its effectiveness, power without resistance will be. Money requires its recognition as such: beyond that it is transparent. Power requires more than mere recognition as such if exchange is to proceed. One may well recognize and resist in a way in which resistance to the social fact of a national currency would be inexplicable. It is precisely for this reason, given the conditions of membership of most organizations, that we may find resistance an entirely explicable phenomenon on the part of those excluded from what Habermas terms 'processes of discursive will formation'. To be invariably told, rarely asked, infrequently consulted and be expected not to participate in the formation of collective goals is hardly a secure basis for obtaining commitment to these goals. Hence the *realpolitik* of power and resistance are the normal conditions of membership and meaning for many organization personnel (see, for example, the many 'labour process' studies, such as Knights and Collinson 1985).

The medium of power thus routinely elicits resistance to its deployment or expenditure in a way that is not the case for money. The facilitative nature of power has quite particular organizational conditions of existence. These were to be relatively unexplored by Giddens in his 1968 critique.

GIDDENS ON PARSONS ON POWER

The critique of Parsons (1967) was Giddens' (1968) first foray into the power arena. Giddens begins with a series of quite conventional criticisms which are drawn from the 'conflict' perspective. Where consensus theory typically had been held to be weakest was in its approach to topics such as power. Hence, a functionalist theory of power presented a particularly robust challenge for exponents of a conflict perspective. Parsons' (1967) application of his general analytical framework to the concept of power was a particularly choice target for anyone who wished to score a decisive hit on the corpus of functionalist theory. To hit the conception of power was to hit functionalism where once it had appeared to be weakest. Following Parsons' conceptual extension of his system to this core 'conflict' term, the judgement that functionalism was 'soft' on power could no longer be sustained. Hence, if the leading functionalist perspective could be lanced at what must now seem to be its least vulnerable spot, the victory would indeed be sweet and the defeat decisive. The choice made by Giddens of Parsons' writings on power was thus significant and strategic. It focused on the legitimacy of Parsons' theory by seeking to undercut the capacity of Parsons' (1967) claim that functionalism was able to handle power adequately. To do so thoroughly would have meant not only addressing Parsons' (1967) particular discussions of power and influence but also locating these discussions in a consideration of the general analytical framework for functionalism which Parsons produced.

At the core of Parsons' functionalist theory was a detailed general analytical framework. The framework can perhaps best be understood in terms of specifying the possibility of how social order might be secured on the basis of uncoerced action. It has recently been characterized as an argument 'against nostalgia' (Holton and Turner 1986) and for modernity. From this perspective, nostalgia resides in views common to both Weberian pessimism and 'critical theory'. Nostalgics view the world as increasingly rationalized and enclosed within an iron cage, requiring such an inexorably increasing power of bureaucracy that the space for affective, non-bureaucratic and uncoerced action is marginalized and diminished. Against the specification of these tendencies as the dominant features of modernity, Parsons sought instead to make his representation of the world concordant with the achievements of a democratic society as he regarded them. Parsons demonstrated that all spheres of agency, while they may be characterized in terms of political and economic processes of rationalization, can also be characterized as having spheres of integrative and normative processes. These four processes were referred to as the conceptual and analytical universe of subsystems of adaptive, goal-oriented, integrative and normative processes. The existence of the integrative and normative (or latent tension management) subsystems mediate the rationalizing tendencies of the economic and political subsystems by providing a plurality of moral orders which countervail economic and bureaucratic rationalization.

Moral relativism poses problems for political order in that it fragments possible substantive bases for that order. It is on this basis that models of a 'vicious cycle' of bureaucratization are developed, as bureaucratic responses to moral relativism, based on substantive processes, may serve to escalate the structural gap between expectations and control. Consequently, power is the medium whereby this gap is narrowed. Despite moral and other differences between agents, the consequence of effective goal orientation is facilitated and efficient organization is produced, using sanctions if necessary. However, the widespread recourse to sanction would hardly be the sign of a functionally efficient system.

Power is thus *facilitative* in Parsons' (1967) schema: it produces, or rather facilitates the production of binding obligations within organizational settings. The reality of the power to sanction waits unused but ready, should the outcome desired not be secured by the exercise of symbolic power over the agent whose outcomes are to be affected. It is not so much that 'power over' slips away from Parsons' conceptualization but that he focuses on the more economical, subtle and productive aspects of power rather than on those that automatically produce conflict. There was always something naïve about the celebration of conflict *per se*, as if it were somehow more realist to analyse discord rather than accord. In the analysis of power, the limits of this naïvety are quickly reached. It is a crude power indeed which constantly creates conflict in order to get its way. Moreover, it is probably a relatively weak and a rapidly weakening power which must always make recourse to the intervention of force in order to secure its objectives. How much easier it is to achieve these objectives through concerted action with rather than against others.

Giddens (1968: 260) observes that Parsons' power is 'directly derivative of authority: authority is the institutionalized legitimation which underlies power'. This is correct, but it should be seen in the context of Parsons' analytic framework, in which the concept of power was reserved specifically for goal-oriented organization. Other concepts such as force or influence, for example, stood in for the limited analytic conception of power in situations other than those of effective goal organization; those situations where personnel, goal support and normative commitment have already been secured. Parsons' analytic coupling of power and authority does not lead him to see only consensus, to disregard conflict, to ignore hierarchy, as Giddens (1968: 264) suggests. They are present in the overall analytic schema but are excluded from the facilitative conception of power which Parsons was developing (Savage 1982; also see Sciulli 1987: 16–26).

Giddens' major criticism of Parsons was contained in the following passage:

> What slips away from sight almost completely in the Parsonian analysis is the very fact that power, even as Parsons defines it, is always exercised over someone! By treating power as necessarily (by definition) legitimate and thus *starting* from the assumption of consensus of some kind between power-holders and those subordinate to them, Parsons virtually ignores, quite consciously and deliberately, the necessarily hierarchical character of power, and the divisions of interest which are frequently consequent upon it. However much it is true that power can rest upon 'agreement' to code authority which can be used for collective aims, it is also true that interests of power-holders and those subject to that power often clash. (Giddens 1968: 264)

The latter half of Giddens' criticism, where he refers to interests, is clearly open to all the objections that have been raised already, vis à vis the concept of 'interests' in Lukes, and there is no point in repeating them here. If Giddens does occupy some privileged theoretical or moral space which enables him to identify what interests are, it is never made evident in the article in question. The first half of Giddens' criticism is that Parsons' conception of power is analytically restricted vis à vis 'power over' and 'hierarchy' but, in the context of the explicitly analytic family of concepts to which it belongs, this criticism is not particularly useful. In fact, one can assimilate the criticism of Parsons by Giddens (1968) to that genre noted by Turner (1986a). The conceptual system which Parsons provides is marginalized by focusing on a particular substantive aspect of that system without sustained consideration of the context as a whole.

GIDDENS' DUALITY OF STRUCTURE

Giddens subsequently went on to develop his own views on the analysis of power in such a way that, rather than developing the initial criticisms of Parsons into a non-relativistic and non-absolutist theory of interests, he tacitly embraced some aspects of the approach that he had initially criticized in Parsons. Indeed, the embrace is occasionally explicit, as when Giddens acknowledges that his own critical commentary ignored 'the basic correctives' which Parsons helped to 'introduce into the literature', including the insight that power 'is not necessarily linked with conflict in the sense of either division of interest or active struggle and power is not inherently oppressive' (Giddens 1984: 257; also see 279 n. 57). Accepting these points, Giddens (1984: 257) defines power as 'the capacity to achieve outcomes. Whether or not these are connected to purely sectional interests is not germane to its definition.' Giddens goes on to say that power should not be regarded as an obstacle to freedom or emancipation but is their very medium, although he notes that it would be foolish, of course, to ignore its constraining properties.

The capacity-outcomes definition which is cited was developed by Giddens within the context of what is called 'structuration theory', a key aspect of which focuses on the problem of the relationship between conceptions of structure and of action. It was this relationship which Lukes had identified as the crux of any adequate conceptualization of power. Giddens (1979: 91) has criticized Lukes' own conception of this relationship quite explicitly as one which 'tends to repeat the dualism of agency and structure'. By this he means that the conceptions of power *qua* structure and power *qua* agency remain analytically separate, such that structure is inadequately 'implicated' in power relations while power relations are equally inadequately 'implicated' in structure. While Lukes regards the relationship between power and structure as dialectical, Giddens wants to sever the relationship as being between two distinct things, a dualism, and, instead, reconstitute it as a duality, in which power and structure are interpenetrated. He refers to this as the 'duality of structure'.

In many ways, Giddens (1976; 1977; 1979; 1981; 1984) picks over much of the ground of social theory as it has developed since the simple opposition of 'order' and 'conflict' theories, by writers like Rex (1964) and Cohen (1968), first undercut any putative sociological consensus within which disagreements flourished. Consequently, as well as elements of functionalism, one also finds the clear traces that competing theoretical schools, such as ethnomethodology, structuralism and phenomenology, have deposited in his brilliantly fertile imagination. A constant theme of the attempted synthesis is to overcome the problem of adopting either too voluntaristic or too deterministic a position on social theory. Voluntaristic social theories, such as ethnomethodology or phenomenology, concentrate upon human agency as knowledgeable, creative and constitutive of reality.

By contrast, more deterministic theories, such as structuralism and functionalism, concentrate on what Lukes has termed the 'structural constraints' surrounding social action. Characteristically, the focus of voluntarism is on individuals' sensemaking activities shaping the world, while for determinism the focus is not so much on the production of reality through human agency as on its reproduction through structural forms which themselves shape human agency.

Against dualism Giddens (1976) posits the 'duality of structure' which apparently imbricates both aspects of production and reproduction. Human agency produces structures which simultaneously serve as the conditions for reproduction of human agency in a continuing process. Human agency is ineradicably tied to power: without power there is no human agency.

> To be an agent is to be able to deploy (chronically, in the flow of daily life) a range of causal powers, including that of influencing those deployed by others. Action depends upon the capability of the individual to 'make a difference' to a pre-existing state of affairs or course of events. An agent ceases to be such if he or she loses the capability to 'make a difference', that is to exercise some sort of power. (Giddens 1984: 14)

Power is defined in terms of agency, which is defined in terms of action, which in turn is defined as power. Breaking the circle somewhat, the crux seems to be the definition of power in terms of an unconstrained individual capability.

Given the complexity and sheer volume of work by Giddens on 'structuration theory', it is extremely difficult to move to an appreciation of his analysis of power without first obtaining some grasp of the overall framework. One is aided in this by what is now an extensive secondary literature on Giddens' work. One may consult, for instance, the symposium in which Giddens (1982) responds to questions from Bleicher and Featherstone (1982) and to criticisms from Hirst (1982), Gross (1982), Smith (1982), Ashley (1982) and Urry (1982) in the journal *Theory, Culture and Society* (also see the subsequent 'comment' by McLennan [1984] in the same journal). In addition, a useful exercise of 'periodization' is performed on Giddens' *oeuvre* by Gane (1983) in a review of 'structuration theory'. Few of the reviewers are convinced by the great synthesis which structuration theory attempts. The majority reach the conclusion that the theory is ultimately subjectivist. The complexities of Giddens' syncretism are indeed labyrinthine (as I discovered after briefly reviewing Giddens [1984] in *The Australian and New Zealand Journal of Sociology* [Clegg 1986]) and tracking through them to the conceptual core is no easy matter. On this occasion, as once before, the focus will be restricted to the question of power (Clegg 1979), although readers who are not familiar with Giddens' prodigious output may find some of the above secondary sources useful as navigation aids. In addition, considerations of Giddens on power are contained in two incisive commentaries by Layder (1987) and Barbalet (1987).

The focus of recent power debates around Lukes' work, particularly Lukes (1977), has been the relationship of agency and structure in a single coherent analytic framework. It is this which Giddens' 'duality of structure' promises but does not deliver because, as argued elsewhere (Clegg 1979), it is a duality which remains tightly coupled to the individualist and voluntarist side of the dualism. Consequently, as Layder (1987: 26) states, the case against arguments from the structural perspective, which centres on the 'collectivist and objectivist moments of social reality', is not as compelling as Giddens (1984) would seem to propose nor does it grasp the necessity of some notion of 'objective structure' for a coherent resolution of the agency-structure problem. In short, Giddens' resolution of the problem in his conception of power is one in which the agency perspective is dominant. That this is so is the result of Giddens' (1984) explicit ontology: his conception of what the agents are which exist. Hitherto in this book I have had frequent recourse to a conception of agency; it should be clear that this conception is not restricted to a human agent. None of the discussion thus far precludes reference to forms of collective agency, as, for instance, organizational action. By contrast, Giddens' (1984: xx) conception of agency is far more anthropocentric in its prime focus on 'human being and human doing'.

A humanist ontology serves as a bulwark in Giddens' opposition to any deterministic and mechanical view of social action as something externally caused or conditioned. Behind this opposition is a particular view of the relationship between the natural and social sciences which derives from the hermeneutic principle which Schutz (1970: 11) expressed so clearly with his argument that 'there is an essential difference in the structure of the thought objects or mental constructs formed by the social sciences and those formed by the natural sciences'.

The phenomena studied by the natural sciences have no conception of themselves; atoms, iron filings and magnets have no meaning in and of themselves. On the contrary, the phenomena of social reality have 'a specific meaning and relevance structure for beings living, acting and thinking with it'. Consequently, Schutz (1970: 11–12) argued, 'The thought objects constructed by the social scientist, in order to grasp this social reality, have to be founded upon the thought objects constructed by the commonsense thinking of men, living their daily life within their social world.' Because of this, Schutz believed that the constructs of the social sciences have to be founded on, grounded in, and agreeable with the commonsense experiences of the social world. Schutz's (1962; 1964; 1967) phenomenology developed a radically subjectivist sociology which Bauman (1978) aptly characterized as 'existentialist' because of its insistence on the self as an active being-in-the-world who not only is in the world but also actively constructs the world in which he or she is, as one which has meaning for him or herself. The self is both a social constructor of reality and a socially constructed being, as Berger and Luckmann (1966) were to develop in their elaboration of some of Schutz's ideas.

Giddens (1976; 1984) does not depart far from this ontology, nor does he justify it. While he grants a relative autonomy to second order constructs, which Schutz's (1970) grounding would deny, for Giddens the world is 'constituted or produced by the active doings of subjects' and its 'production and reproduction [as] society thus has to be treated as a skilled performance on the part of its members' (Giddens 1976: 160, italics omitted). It is because of this irreducibly active human agency that the human or social sciences must differ from the natural sciences. The very 'object' of analysis of the human sciences is quite unlike the natural objects of the natural sciences. It is the knowledgeability, skill, reflexivity and recursivity of the human being embodied in language which requires that social analysis must be grounded in interpretive understanding (of a *post-verstehende* kind, that is, of discursive meaning rather than individual subjectivity) rather than in any analysis which takes an external, purely observational stance towards its data, and thus ignores the knowledgeability of human agents. Thus, we may take it that Giddens would be more interested in the highway code and its discursive constitution and reproduction than he would be in correlating the presence or absence of traffic movement with red or green lights. For him the highway code would be equivalent to a structure, conceptualized not 'as simply placing constraints upon human agency, but as enabling'. This corresponds precisely to the 'duality of structure' which is at the heart of structuration theory, intertwining both constraint and enablement and production and reproduction of social action. Structures such as the highway code are constituted by human agency and at the same time are the media of its constitution because they both enable and constrain its expression, such that motoring or crossing the road is something other than 'dicing' with death (Rhinehart 1972). The highway code as a structure is composed of 'rules and resources' which people acting as drivers, pedestrians and so on draw upon in their traffic interactions. It is this structure, the highway code, which underlies the orderly 'discernible pattern of surface particulars' (Giddens 1977: 113) that the correlation of traffic light colours and presence or absence of traffic movement systematically establishes. System thus concerns the regularities of human action, while structure concerns the rules and resources that human agents can draw on to produce and reproduce systematicity. In his inimitable way, Giddens (1984) clarifies how people are able to reproduce structures like the highway code and to live to drive in another place and on another day:

> Structure thus refers, in social analysis, to the structuring properties allowing the 'binding' of time-space in social systems, the properties which make it possible for discernibly similar social practices to exist across varying spans of time and space and which lend them 'systemic' form. To say that structure is a 'virtual order' of transformative relations means that social systems, as reproduced social practices, do not have 'structures' but rather exhibit 'structural properties', and that structure exists, as time-space presence, only in its instantiations in such as practices and as memory traces orienting the conduct of knowledgeable human agents. (Giddens 1984: 18)

In other words, to continue our example, people who know the highway code can use their knowledge of what it allows and restricts to be successful drivers at times and places other than where and when they first read or learned the code. As a consequence, accident rates are fairly predictable in terms of a number of variables such as traffic density, weather conditions, road conditions and so on.

At the core of structuration theory are people doing things because they know things. People are like that because Giddens sees things that way. This 'allows him to say that social reality is coextensive with the active subjects who produce social activity and cannot be understood in any external, objective sense' (Layder 1987: 30). The rejection of objectivism is a result of Giddens' personal ontology. Human agency and interaction comprise the unsecured footings of Giddens' (1984) structuration theory. 'All interaction involves the use of power' (Giddens 1981: 28) because all interaction is concerned with the production and reproduction of structure, drawing on rules and resources. Power relates to those resources which actors draw upon in interaction, in 'making a difference':

> *Power* is an integral element of all social life as are meaning and norms; this is the significance of the claim that structure can be analysed as *rules* and *resources*, resources being drawn upon in the constitution of power relations. All social interaction involves the use of power, as a necessary implication of the logical connection between human action and *transformative capacity*. Power within social systems can be analysed as relations of autonomy and dependence between actors in which these actors draw upon and reproduce structural properties of *domination*. (Giddens 1981: 28–9)

As commentators such as Barbalet (1987: 9) and Layder (1985: 142) have noted, the 'duality' of power and structure is not established in these formulations. As a result of the initial subjectivist ontology, the enablement of power as a transformative capacity is too tightly coupled to agency, at the expense of a more structural conception of power expressed through already existing objective relations of domination and subordination. A notion of structure could have filled this role, but it does not, because of the ontological exclusion of an objectivist conception of structure in preference 'to one in which the reality of structure is a practical accomplishment of the reproduced conduct of situated actions with definite intentions and interests' (Giddens 1976: 127). It is not clear how one knows what these interests are, other than that one would assume that the 'knowledgeable agents' themselves would know. The problems with any such specification should by now be apparent. Agents may know many things but they can never know that they know their interests outside 'ideal speech situations'. Indeed, as Barbalet (1987: 11) observes, 'the evidence suggests that most people most of the time do not know a great deal about the institutions of their society, but they have a limited and partial knowledge that serves to maintain their subservience within it.' A procedural commitment to what 'every competent member of every society knows... about the institutions of that society'

(Giddens 1979: 71) should not impress anyone at all familiar with the community power debate as an adequate basis for piercing through 'mobilization of bias' or grasping 'non-decision-making'. The elevation of ignorance or insufficiency of knowledge to an onto-logical privilege is most peculiar.

Actors, ignorant or not, are at centre stage in Giddens' theory, with structure and system being illusions sustained by their projective powers. Structures are 'rules and resources'. System is 'reproduced and regular social practices'. Actors draw on structures to produce systems. More especially, they draw on resources as the media through which power is exercised to produce systemic regularities. It is through this 'drawing' that structure is reproduced. What resources are remains unclear: with Barbalet (1987: 11–12) and Layder (1987: 34) one agrees that it seems as if the apparent distinction between rules and resources breaks down, since resources as bases for action seem to be understood only in relation to power in as much as they are realized by rules. Rules have a distinct immate-riality which one would not have thought necessarily characteristic of resources. That it should be so seems to be something necessitated by the agency ontology and its view of structure. System as reproduced social relations is no more real than structure. It too is an effect of the 'instantiation' (Giddens 1977: 118), even though it is also supposed to have some reality transcending particular time-space coordinates. In fact, once more this real-ity is lost in the occluding realm of the ontic imagination (Layder 1987: 34–5).

Callinicos (1985: 139) has noticed how Wittgenstein's (1968) argument against the possibility of a private language also seems to undercut the concept of rules which Gid-dens employs. If rules, as criteria of correct usage, are 'provided by the common action of members' (as Callinicos [1985: 139] suggests is the case, and with which ethnomethodol-ogy, the branch of knowledge which has had most to say on rule-use, would agree [McH-oul 1986]), then rules cannot generate social structure. On the contrary, when confronted with a given practice, what was done would formulate the basis for attributing what some practice was. Or, as Callinicos (1985: 139) puts it, 'Rather than generating practices, rules collapse into them' (also see Dallmayr 1982).

The consensus of the critics appears to be that Giddens' (1984) structuration theory is at base premised primarily on the subjective term of his duality of structure. In his opposition to a deterministic sociology Giddens goes too far in identifying any mode of determinism and objectivism with the strong naturalism of functionalist and structuralist sociology. This is as a result of the sociological opposition to these having been mounted principally through anti-naturalist positions drawn from hermeneutic, phenomenologi-cal and interpretive sociologies. If his objection to these deterministic approaches is that they have marginalized human agency, then it must be demonstrated to Giddens that he has equally one-sidedly marginalized objective structure. Indeed, overcoming dualism with duality suggests that one or other marginalization will occur because the monadic unity under which duality will occur must be premised on the dominance of one or other of the antinomies of dualism, which are conceived in sharp contrast to duality (Layder 1987: 32). Given the ontological auspices, it was always clear in principle, even if not always in execution, which term would predominate: subjectivism rules through a 'philosophical invocation' of subjects' capacities rather than through an analysis of the historically variable structural conditions under which subjects may themselves act variably (Callinicos 1985: 140–1). Habermas (1982: 286) hits the nail on the head when he writes of a metaphorical over-extension of action-concepts in structuration theory such that structure becomes secondary to these allegedly 'knowledgeable' human agents who are anthropomorphically constituting it.

Some aspects of Giddens' (1979) conception of structure are indeed well observed, if hardly novel. The idea that structures both restrict and enable action was systematically developed by Shwayder (1965) and applied by Clegg (1975) to the analysis of power. However, the overall context of structuration theory in which they are located in Giddens is such that notions of structural shaping, selectivity and constraint end up being too facile in their relation to power. The 'duality' of a structure subject for its reality on the instantiation of its subjects makes vacuous the notion of structure as constraint. Layder (1985) has argued that:

> Without some explicit reference to the fact that the structural contexts of action (which can refer to both wider and more immediate contexts) are *durable* in time and space, to varying degrees, the instantiation thesis could be taken to imply (as indeed it does seem to) that the 'structures' and, systems' concerned are inchoate and evanescent, appearing and disappearing at the behest of specific individuals in specific encounters. (Layder 1985: 143)

Additionally, it empties the notion of reproduction of content: if some reproduced relation exists only as it is produced and reproduced, then surely reproduction requires something extant to be re-made. This is the sense in which a reproduction is always a further representation and re-presentation of an already existing portrait or photograph. The produced object is the existing phenomenon which makes the reproduction possible. Reproduction must reproduce something which has materiality already as the result of a now past production. Structure would thus have a reality which was independent and objective rather than being dependent on a subjectivity constituting it for an instant and then, what? Nothingness? A memory trace? Whatever the limbo is to which structure is cast, outside of its constitution by subjects, it is clearly neither ontologically real nor separate from the constitutive role of agency. With Callinicos (1986: 155) one would want to argue that, instead of this empty conception of structure, one can accept an agency conception of power but see it as 'to a large extent structurally determined'. What agents can or cannot do depends very much on their position in relations of production and, one would want to add (without repeating arguments elaborated at length elsewhere

[Clegg et al. 1986]), in other forms of social relations in the state and civil society as well as the economy.

Structure's absence markedly weakens the conception of power. Power is defined as a transformative capacity in outcome terms. To employ the sociological argot adopted here, it is an episodic and agency conception. Power is exercised through the medium of resources. These resources appear to be structurally derived but the appearance is sundered from any objective conception of structure by virtue of the ontological supremacy of the 'instantiation principle'. Although those over whom power is exercised are supposedly constrained by the structure of domination, this constraint seems to be dependent upon the practical accomplishment of that same structure's enabling capacities by those in power. Dominance is an effect of instantiation. Enablement is the basis of the transformative capacity which is power, the freedom to 'make a difference', but it is an empty freedom because the other term of freedom's necessary dialectic is absent. Freedom always involves some freedom from some constraint as well as some freedom to do some things. As Layder (1987: 37) has correctly observed, 'freedom cannot mean freedom from itself. There has to be some limiting other to give substance to the notion.'

As remarked in an earlier appraisal of Giddens' (1976) approach, 'the key to the "duality of structures" must be the acting individual "drawing" from, and "reproducing", "that order of domination"' (Clegg 1979: 73–4). The key unlocks an empty room, however. Its only furnishings, its only resources, appear only as an effect of actors' instantiations and the illusion vanishes with the distanciation of the actors. This is an unfortunate idealism. The resources on which power draws must have some real existence prior to their enablement of some action that constrains some other's action. Distributions of power relations are logically and ontologically prior and external to instances of situated social activity (Layder 1987: 38). Otherwise, the notion of power *and* structure dissolves. Structures which exist only in conditions where individuals instantiate them are not structures at all: they do not display any enduring relations. The criterion of structure is not that there are individuals constituting it through their instantiations but that relations between individuals and other forms of collective agency are constituted in relatively enduring ways which routinely constrain and enable differential opportunities for action and inaction on the part of those agencies. One would refer to sociologists such as Weber (1978) and their analyses of formal structures of dominancy and the role that these play in defining the choices available to a person, particularly as these analyses have been developed at the juncture of organization and class analysis (for example, Clegg and Dunkerley 1980; Clegg et al. 1986, and the papers collected in Clegg 1989). The importance of this juncture is that it does deal with the structural intersection shaping the primary reality of economic life: one's job as a member of a specific organization in a specific position under specific contractual relations in an overall labour market structure which transcends and shapes the immediate correlates of the position one is thus in. (Chapter eight will address the issue of 'organization' in some more detail.)

The locus of Giddens' difficulties with seeing structural enablement and constraint as a constitutive framework, within which episodic power unfolds, rather than as somehow being only co-terminous with those episodes, concerns his opposition to the regularity principle as a feature of social enquiry: it is, he writes, a 'vain enterprise' to 'see in structural constraint a source of causation more or less equivalent to the operation of impersonal causal forces in nature' (Giddens 1984: 174). One can agree with this without necessarily opposing a conception of naturalism *per se*. One can still accept a model of objective causation and not be a Humean; not to be a Humean in social explanation does not necessarily entail the embrace of subjectivist positions in which individual motives and reasons attain an essential, irreducible privilege. This is so if only because 'motives' and 'reasons' cannot be understood as other than structural, as enduring relational terms which are routinely employed to constitute data on observed behaviour as social action, through reference to 'rules'. Mills' (1940) 'vocabulary of motives' is the appropriate point of departure for such an approach. This would be in marked contrast to the subjectivism which Giddens expounds in making constraints the effects of motives rather than motives the effects of constraints, a position exemplified in Taylor's (1972) analysis of the contextual nature of the motivational accounts available for use in specific situations and stages of their sentencing career by sex offenders. These situations, as structural arenas, constrain the representational possibilities for sex offenders to display varying types of human agency. Moreover, the accounts available to them are overwhelmingly discursively provided through what Foucault (1977) terms 'disciplinary power'. Reflective instantiation of one's own actions cannot escape power: it is not subjects who are the authors of their own motives but the disciplines which are structurally available to account with. The psychiatric, medical, social work, therapeutic and pharmacological discourses and encounters are more likely the sites of motive. Nor are sex offenders peculiar in being subject to such constraint on their agency. Agency can only ever be represented by actors and others in terms of structurally available, relevant and appropriate accounts within which the bounds of normalcy are routinely negotiated. As Foucault's (1984) work suggests, this may well be one fruitful area of investigation for the study of power and structure.

Giddens (1984) equates structural constraint in social explanation with the regularity principle of Humean explanation. It is a case of mistaken identity on his part. It need not be the case. Certainly, this is true of positivism, as we have seen in the development of a 'one-dimensional' view of power, which explicitly excluded reference to subjective phenomena in order to construct a realm of data amenable to probabilistic versions of the regularity principle. However, the choice is not simply between excluding either subjectivism (positivism) or objectivism (versions of idealism, such as hermeneutics, phenomenology, and structuration theory). The other option is to accept that there may well be relatively intransitive structural constraints which have a more tendential than necessary expression in the appropriate standing conditions. Such a notion of structural constraint is not only distinct from the naturalism which Giddens (1984) opposes but also distinct from the idealism which he proposes.

Structural constraint and enablement need to be conceptualized as determining the differential relations of autonomy and dependence between agents, and as constituting their causal powers which, under appropriate standing conditions, will reproduce (or even transform) the structural properties of domination within which these facilities are grounded. Giddens, like Lukes (albeit in a quite distinct way), subsumes structure to power, constraint to agency. In Giddens we have, as has been remarked on another occasion, 'dialectics without any specific determination' (Clegg 1979: 74) because, at the centre of the project, is the illusory freedom of the constituting subject. Despite claims to the contrary, in Giddens' structuration theory the sovereign subject whom Hobbes first installed at the centre of power remains there, albeit in a less than transparent manner.

CONCLUSION

At the focus of most recent debate about the concept of power has been a concern to provide an analytical specification of the relation between 'agency' and 'structure'. Both Lukes and Giddens have agreed that this is the central question. Equally, they are united on what would be an appropriate resolution: power and structure have to be grasped within a coherent framework. For Lukes, this framework would be one of a dialectic of power and structure; for Giddens, it would be one of a duality of power and structure.

Neither Lukes nor Giddens satisfactorily resolves the agency/structure nexus in the study of power. For each of them the agency perspective remains predominant over and against the concern with structure. In Lukes, as we saw in the previous chapter, agency predominates as a result of moral relativism. In Giddens, the preponderance is a result of an ontological assumption in favour of agency and instantiation over and against a concern with structure. A number of well-developed criticisms by writers such as Benton (1981), Hindess (1982), Knights and Willmott (1982), Layder (1985; 1987) Callinicos (1985) and Barbalet (1985; 1987) establish these points. Barbalet (1987), in particular, with his reconsideration of Lockwood's (1964) conceptualization of social integration and system integration, indicates the lines which an alternative conception should develop.

The next chapter will argue that the notion of social integration will require consideration through a perspective very different from traditional conceptions of ideology. An appreciation of post-structuralism and its concern with a distinctive conception of ideology will be developed. It will be argued that this move is necessary in order to grasp the nature of social integration from beyond the 'shifting sand' of a 'transcendental value standpoint'. Such standpoints, it will be argued, do not capture the reality of that 'ideologically contradictory process' which Benton (1981) identifies. In recent times it has been the development of post-structuralism which has most thoroughly opposed transcendental value standpoints. Poststructuralism and its relation with power will thus be the focus of the next chapter. In this way the ground will be prepared for chapter eight, in which backward linkage to a realist model, linking agency, social and system integration, will be developed in tandem with insights derived from post-structuralism.

7

POST-STRUCTURALISM, SOVEREIGN POWER AND DISCIPLINARY POWER

INTRODUCTION

Power is about politics, not just in the formal sense but more broadly, about the politics of everyday life. Although this book has necessarily been concerned with quite academic debates, power in the politics of everyday life has not been absent: it is most obvious in issues of interpretation of what some quite mundane examples might mean in terms of power. Do cigarette smokers or the working class know their own interests? If they do not, who does and how do they know? Do traffic lights 'have' causal power? Does a woman at a cocktail party paying polite attention to a man mean to arouse his sexual interest?

The last example was taken from Dennis Wrong's (1979) book on power. Here I want to explore some of its implications, in a way in which Wrong does not. For Wrong, the cocktail party incident would not be an example of power because the woman in question intended no desire to be elicited from the man in question. For feminists, this would be regarded as a naive response on Wrong's part; the issue would be that individual men and women can be seen only within the context of the 'patriarchal' structuring of social relations. Within this context, male/female relations are necessarily subject to a surplus of meaning over and above whatever interpretations particular participants might put on an instance of them. The fundamental reality of social relations would be their patriarchal character as far as feminists are concerned:

> The term 'patriarchal' refers to power relations in which women's interests are subordinated to the interests of men... Patriarchal power rests on the social meanings given to biological sexual difference. In patriarchal discourse the nature and social role of women are defined in relation to a norm which is male... To say that patriarchal relations are

structural is to suggest that they exist in the institutions and social practices of our society and cannot be explained by the intentions, good or bad, of individual women and men. (Weedon 1987: 2, 3)

The point should be clear. Not only would the cocktail party interaction between a man and a woman, which Wrong describes, be an instance of power from this perspective, but so also would Wrong's (1979) denial of power's presence. Both the interaction and the author's orientation towards it would be seen as evidently patriarchal in their constitution. For Weedon (1987) the existence of patriarchal structures requires

a theory which can explain how and why people oppress each other, a theory of subjectivity, of conscious and unconscious thoughts and emotions, which can account for the relationship between the individual and the social. (Weedon 1987: 3)

Such a theory, as she argues convincingly, would not have to be grounded in the constitutive experience of individuals. The reasons for this are evident and have been the central focus of the previous two chapters. A person's experience and the subjective content of the expression of that experience can never be an adequate basis for an explanation of power implicated in that experience. Where idealism is transcendent, in however sophisticated a form, individual expressions of preference can never be taken to explain how those preferences came to be constituted. Such ontological auspices sit uneasily with conceptions of power.

It should also be evident by now that the question of what women's or men's 'real interests' are cannot reasonably be determined by reference to what a theory of patriarchy says they are or should be, any more than Marxist theory can determine what real interests are, without falling into the 'paradox of emancipation'.

What is to be done? One response on the part of both some Marxist and some feminist theorists has been to adopt a style of analysis known broadly and loosely as 'post-structuralism'. Post-structuralism is a very broad and loose label indeed but, following Giddens (1987: 74), one may note certain motifs or themes characteristic of the genre. These would include the centrality of conceptions of language, the relational nature of all totalities, the practices of linguistic signification, the de-centring of the human constitutive subject, and a concern with discourse. There is no one fixed meaning to post-structuralism, although it has generally applied to texts such as those of Derrida (1973; 1976), Lacan (1977), Kristeva (1984; 1986) and Foucault (1977; 1979a; 1979b; 1984; 1986).

POST-STRUCTURALISM AND FOUCAULT

Post-structuralism prematurely had its obituary written (Giddens 1987). Despite this, its central concerns still seem to be flourishing and nurturing debates on 'power'

(Weedon 1987). At the core of these debates is some conception of there being a significant relation between power and language. Language is the central focus of all post-structuralism. In the broadest terms, language defines the possibilities of meaningful existence at the same time as it limits them. Through language, our sense of ourselves as distinct subjectivities is constituted. Subjectivity is constituted through a myriad of what post-structuralists term 'discursive practices': practices of talk, text, writing, cognition, argumentation, and representation generally. The *meanings* of and *membership within* the categories of discursive practice will be constant sites of struggle over power, as identity is posited, resisted and fought over in its attachment to the subjectivity by which individuality is constructed. Identity is never regarded as being given by nature; individuality is never seen as being fixed in its expression. Post-structuralism admits of no rational, unified human being, nor class nor gendered subject which is the locus or source of the expression of identity. Membership in a category, as a particular type of subject, is regarded as the effect of devices of categorization; thus identity is seen as contingent, provisional, achieved not given. Identity is seen as always in process, as always subject to reproduction or transformation through discursive practices which secure or refuse particular posited identities. Identities are not absolute but are always relational: one can only ever be seen to be something in relation to some other thing. Identity is always defined in terms of difference, rather than as something intrinsic to a particular person or category of experience, such as worker, wife, woman, or whore. Each of these is a possible signifier of self, carrying complex, shifting and frequently ambiguous and contradictory meaning. All discursive practices (or language games) have historical specificity, particularly as the work of Foucault (1977) interpreted them. (The prevailing analytic, ordinary language philosophy of Wittgenstein's [1968] day tended to suppress an interpretation of the diachrony of language games in favour of their synchronic presence.)

The characterization in the preceding paragraphs is, of necessity, a broad-brush picture. To provide other than that, in a book whose focus is not post-structuralism *per se*, would be inappropriate. It is the implications of what has been termed post-structuralism for the analysis of power which are important. With post-structuralism there are evident dangers of a relapse into epistemological relativism, because of its tendency to dissolve all fixed points of reference. For instance, where structuralist theorists of language like Saussure (1974) regarded signification as fixed by the conventions of particular speech communities, post-structuralists like Derrida (1976) dissolved the focus on signs having an already fixed meaning to one in which there are no fixed signifieds or signifiers. Instead, meaning exists in the difference between relational terms to which current representations defer. However, there is no reason to expect that representations will remain contextually and historically stable but every reason to think that they will shift. Power will thus be implicated in attempts to fix or uncouple and change particular representational relations of meaning, a thrust which develops most explicitly from Foucault's (1977) historical ontology of some of the subjectivities which have been constituted through practices of power and knowledge. The knowledge that is used to structure and fix representations in historical forms is the accomplishment of power.

Feminist theory (e.g. Weedon 1987) has been one area of application where this post-structuralist analysis of power has been particularly well received. Clearly, if one's concern is with gendered subjectivity and its reproduction in relations which privilege male and subordinate female subjectivity, then a conception of power as existing in the very discourses by which subjectivities have been historically constituted and reconstituted will have evident potential. Knowledge which fixes the normal is evidently going to be knowledge which has a close relationship with power.

In constructing the knowledge/power relation as the object of analysis, one might seem to be celebrating a relativism in which any fixed point is dissolved, as some of Foucault's critics such as Perry Anderson (1983) insist. However, this is too extreme a reaction. What are dissolved are notions of any transcendent position which can be constituted outside of discursive practices. Within these, some representations will achieve a power far greater than others, which is an effect neither of a human subject and its volitions nor of a structure which works its will behind the backs of such subjects. It is the representations themselves, the fundamental discursively formed ways of constituting relations, which have a historically specific character and are the object of analysis. At base, the concern is with strategies of discursive power, where strategy appears as an effect of distinctive practices of power/knowledge gaining an ascendant position in the representation of normal subjectivity: forms of surveillance or psychiatry, for instance, which constitute the normal in respect to a penology or a medical knowledge from whose 'gaze' and rulings no one can subsequently escape, whether prison or medical officer, or one carcerally or medically confined.

To approach Foucault's work on power is no easy matter, and not just because, as Wickham (1983) has argued, the raw materials for the analysis are spread through a fragmented *oeuvre*. There is also a problem which soon becomes apparent as one reads the voluminous secondary literature on Foucault. It is the strange cult of obscurantism which has developed around his work. While that work is by no means always clear or lucid, it is rarely as impenetrable as some commentators would make it. The matter has been noted explicitly: 'Foucault is hailed as a revolutionary hero, and even his style is imitated, often resulting in incomprehensible English prose which is nothing less than a direct transliteration from French. Mystification is rampant: mysterious dogmas and *overthrows* are announced without explanation, and a dry genealogical erudition stretches as far as the eye can see' (O'Farrell 1982: 449). Such effects will not be sought here. Alternative interpretations are possible. Foucault may be treated as a very concrete and descriptive writer on power, in a line of scholarship in which Weber would not be unrecognizable. As such, one would regard his concern with power as seeking to establish the ontological foundations of modern institutions, the institutional sources of power. There are some writers who do grasp Foucault thus, in a way which is far more congenial to the temper of this volume. One thinks, above all, of Bauman's (1982) interpretation of Foucault's work as an historical account of modernity. It is principally, if not exclusively, in this manner that this ambiguous body of work will be interpreted here. (As a guide to bibliographic sources Smart [1985] is a concise introduction to Foucault; Dreyfus and Rabinow [1982] is the standard but 'heavier' introduction, while Kurzweil [1977] produces a very accessible overview of the *oeuvre* to that date, which can be complemented by the subsequent review by Gane [1986]. [Foucault died in 1984.] Cousins and Hussain [1984: 225–61], as well as Wickham [1983] provide an exposition of Foucault's often opaque and scattered views on power. Those who would prefer a critical comment from the left concerning the political implications of Foucault's work should consult Dews [1984].)

DISCIPLINARY POWER, BIO-POWER AND SOVEREIGN POWER

In Foucault's (1977) *Discipline and Punish* power is conceived of as a technique which achieves its strategic effects through its disciplinary character. Foucault (1977) sees the methods of surveillance and assessment of individuals, which were first developed in state institutions such as prisons, as effective tools developed for the orderly regimentation of others as docile bodies. This is so, he maintains, even when they provoke resistance. Resistance merely serves to demonstrate the necessity of that discipline which provokes it, according to Foucault. It becomes a target against which discipline may justify its necessity by virtue of its lack of omnipotence. These disciplinary practices become widely disseminated through schools, the army, the asylum, and eventually into the capitalist factory. They become strategic to the extent that they are effective constitutions of powers. As a form of knowledge they work through their own ontogenesis. Because they are knowledge constituted not just in texts but in definite institutional and organizational practices, they are 'discursive practices': knowledge reproduced through practices made possible by the framing assumptions of that knowledge. Moreover it is a very practical knowledge: it disciplines the body, regulates the mind and orders the emotions in such a way that the ranking, hierarchy and stratification which ensues is not just the blind reproduction of a transcendent traditional order, as in feudalism. It produces a new basis for order in the productive worth of individuals, as they are defined by these new disciplinary practices of power.

These new disciplinary practices of power are not, however, to be regarded as an intentional effect of any will, least of all of that traditional central condensation of power, the state.

> There is not, on the one side, a discourse of power, and opposite it another discourse that runs counter to it. Discourses are tactical elements or blocks operating in the field of force relations; there can run different and even contradictory discourses within the same strategy; they can, on the contrary, circulate without changing their form from one strategy to another, opposing strategy. (Foucault 1984: 101–2)

To assume that there are fixed interests on the one hand and definite discourses representing them on the other would be mistaken. The certainty of interests is not secured by mouthing what must in time, irrespective of content, become political platitudes. 'Discourses have no fixed referent in particular values or systems of morality', a point Weedon demonstrates with reference to eugenicist arguments, which

> have been used to support widely conflicting interests over the last eighty years, for women's individual rights to contraception in inter-war Britain, to Nazi sexual policy. Indeed, biological arguments are employed by widely contradictory interests, from radical feminism to the most conservative forms of sociobiology, with their strong investment in the reproduction of patriarchy. (Weedon 1987: 123)

If there is no given elective affinity between discourse, practice and interests, then power cannot be understood as a 'single, all-encompassing strategy' (Foucault 1984: 103). Power will be a more or less stable or shifting network of alliances extended over a shifting terrain of practice and discursively constituted interests. Points of resistance will open up at many points in the network. Their effect will be to fracture alliances, constitute regroupings and re-posit strategies (Foucault 1984: 95–6). In such formulations power is to be seen in

> the multiplicity of force relations immanent in the sphere in which they operate and which constitute their own organization; as the process which, through ceaseless struggles and confrontations, transforms, strengthens or reverses them; as the support which these force relations find in one another, thus forming a chain or a system, or on the contrary, the disjunctions and contradictions which isolate them one from another; and lastly, as the strategies in which they take effect, whose general design or institutional crystallization is embodied in the state apparatus, in the formulation of the law, in the various social hegemonies. (Foucault 1984: 92)

Central to Foucault's conception of power is its shifting, inherently unstable expression in networks and alliances. Rather than the monolithic view of power as a 'third dimension' incorporating subjectivities, the focus is much closer to Machiavelli's strategic concerns or Gramsci's notion of hegemony as a 'war of manoeuvre', in which points of resistance and fissure are at the forefront.

Particular concepts of power should not be viewed simply as an effect of a particular discourse. Such discourses are a means by which a certain theorizing power is itself constituted. For Foucault the discursive field in which formal academic theorizing about power has been constituted has been primarily derived from notions of sovereignty. In this context sovereignty refers to an originating subject whose will is power. The allusion is obviously to Nietzsche. (The connections between Foucault and Nietzsche are explored in Daudi [1986: 152–6].) Against this originary subject (which in western history becomes transmuted from the monarch into 'the state'), Foucault argues for a reversal of Hobbes' terms. Instead of concentrating on the sovereignty of power, he argues that, on the contrary, we should 'study the myriad of bodies which are constituted as peripheral subjects as a result of the effects of power'. The fact that theorists from Hobbes to Dahl might have conceptualized the subjects of power as 'individual(s), ... a sort of elementary nucleus, a primitive atom, a multiple and inert material on which power comes to fashion or against which it happens to strike, ... is already one of the prime effects of power'. In other words, the episodic and agency view of power cannot be taken as any kind of analytic fundamental or primitive conception. Foucault's conception of power attempts to break decisively with the 'mechanistic' and 'sovereign' view. He writes of the creation of new forms of social power which crystallize in the seventeenth and eighteenth centuries, beyond the terms which by now have become quite conventional for addressing and constituting 'power'. What emerges during this period is a 'capillary form' of power which 'reaches into the very grain of individuals', a 'synaptic regime of power, a regime of its exercise *within* the social body, rather than *from above it*' (Foucault 1980: 39).

'Disciplinary power' is one of two distinctive conceptions of power which Foucault (1979a) argues have characterized the 'modern' epoch, from the early nineteenth century onwards. The other is termed 'bio-power' (Foucault 1984: 140–4). Both are to be contrasted with the conception of 'sovereign power', a power tied irrevocably to the formal apparatus of the state in its complex organization. Whereas disciplinary power is targeted at particular individuals or collections of individuals, bio-power is oriented to the subjugation of bodies and control of populations in general. The area of bio-power on which Foucault concentrates is that of sexuality. Sexuality increasingly stands as the point of intersection of not only the expressivity of human beings but also the reproduction of the species as such. From the nineteenth century onwards, contrary to the hypothesis of 'Victorian repression', Foucault sees an outpouring of talk, concern and writing focusing on sex. The effect of this discourse, he argues, is the development of a whole new realm of discourse attending to the definition of what is and what is not 'normal' and what is and what is not available for individuals to do, think, say, and be. Indeed, Foucault may be said to be focusing on the range of professional discourses which increasingly limit, define and normalize the 'vocabularies of motive' (Mills 1940) which are available in specific sites ('situated contexts' in Mills' terms) for making sensible and accountable that which people should do, can do and thus do. Bio-power normalizes through discursive formations of psychiatry, medicine, social work, and so on. The terms of these ways of constituting the normal are institutionalized and incorporated into everyday life. Our own reflexive gaze takes over the disciplining role as we take on the accounts and vocabularies of meaning and motive which are available to us, while certain other forms of account are marginalized or simply eased out of currency.

The distinctiveness of Foucault's conception is that it presents, in its historical enquiry into disciplinary power, an alternative view of power practices. While the trajectory from Hobbes to Locke to Dahl remained fixated on the mechanics of apparent objects, Foucault is suggesting that, unviewed by this conception of power, a real world of new and distinct practices of power was in fact emergent, far from the sovereign concerns which had animated Hobbes. However, it was not this new, real world of capillary and disciplinary power which was intellectually victorious in those groves of academe devoted to the study of power, despite its transformation of the actual scene of power. Within the formal discourses available for the study of politics, it was the conception of sovereign power which continued to reign. From its genesis in Hobbes to its maturation in Lukes, the concept of power is primarily of something which denies, forestalls, represses, prevents. One may recall, for instance, that the central concepts of power around the non-decision-making debate were, not atypically, negative. Why should this continuity be so?

Foucault suggests that it may be because the discourse of power at its modern inception was so bound up with the institution of the monarchy, the sovereign power. Foucault argues that we are still very much in the thrall of a conception of sovereign power in which an 'episodic' notation has held sway for so long. Power has been conceptualized as being mostly absent except when exercised. It is exercised only intermittently in discrete episodes. Ultimately this conception of episodic power derives from the conditions under which sovereign power was initially exercised and sustained by feudal social relations. These conditions were such that it was

> a power which intervened in the life of the producer only on occasion; its sole function was to assure the periodical transfer of the product of labour – not the administration of labour itself. (Bauman 1982: 10)

The feudal monarch or lord was not implicated in the day-to-day subjugation of people:

> In such a society, surplus product was typically extracted from the producers, so to speak, in leaps and bounds; say, once or several times during the annual cycle of the essentially agricultural production, in the form of rent, or tax, or a levy, or a tribute or a tithe. The one function of power was to force the producer to part, of will or of fear, or of

both, with a fraction of his product. Once he had done that, he could be (and should be, if the production was to continue) left to his own resources. It was largely irrelevant for the circulation of surplus how he went about his daily business, how he administered and deployed his bodily and spiritual powers. The one thing which mattered for the 'sovereign' power – the availability of surplus – was quite adequately taken care of by the double pressure of natural cycle and the threat of what Ernest Gellner, this supreme master of the metaphor, once called 'the dentistry state' – a state specializing in extraction by torture. The sovereign power could remain distant from the body of the average producer, towering majestically at the far horizon of his life cycle. Its remoteness, not-of-this-world-ness was heavily underlined by the sacralisation of the royal reign, which ceremonially, in a timelessly repetitive fashion, symbolized the eternal order of social supremacy. In practice, this supremacy boiled down to the upward flow of agricultural surplus. In Georges Duby's words, the whole system of feudal power could well be portrayed as a method of keeping the stomachs of the barons and their retainers full. Otherwise, the customs and habits which ruled the daily life of the food suppliers were no concern of power. This era of merciless exploitation, of the organized universal theft of the surplus product, was also a time of rich and robust folk culture, which the church, so exacting and meticulous in its defence of the divine rights of secular powers, was quite happy to leave to its natural logic. (Bauman 1982: 40)

The absent, intermittent, episodic concept derived from sovereign power is all too evident in the incredulity and puzzlement of a contemporary power theorist, like Wolfinger (1971a; 1971b), when confronted with the seemingly bizarre idea that power is somehow present in its absence from the social terrain, in the normal routines of everyday organizational life generally. Sovereign conceptions of episodic power, constituted mechanically, mean that something has to be seen to have been done in order for it to be said that power has been exercised. The very verb-form of power's 'exercise' is redolent of the intermittent and episodic genesis of the applications of sovereign power.

Recall Hobbes' *Leviathan* and the solution proposed by Hobbes to what he saw as the 'state of nature': that architectonic power should be vested in the body of the sovereign. Hobbes was rationalizing and justifying the re-ascendancy of the English monarchy to the throne after the bloody Civil War and Cromwellian commonwealth. The context of Hobbes' theorizing may not be unimportant. It provided the background for a distinctive foregrounding of power focused on power's majesty. Foucault's (1980: 121) acknowledgment of this is both a question and a proposal. For one so sensitive to the corporeality of power, the proposal takes the form of a bloody and spectacular metaphor which invites us to wield the executioner's axe or to unleash the terrible power of the guillotine:

I wonder if this modern conception of power isn't bound up with the institution of monarchy. This developed during the Middle Ages against the backdrop of the previously endemic struggles between feudal power agencies. The monarchy presented itself as a referee, a power capable of putting an end to war, violence and pillage and saying no to these struggles and private feuds. It made itself acceptable by allocating itself a juridical and negative function, albeit one whose limits it naturally began at once to overstep. Sovereign, law and prohibition formed a system of representation of power which was extended during the subsequent era by the theories of right: political theory has never ceased to be obsessed with the person of the sovereign. Such theories still continue today to busy themselves with the problem of sovereignty. What we need, however, is a political philosophy that isn't erected around the problem of sovereignty, nor therefore around the problems of law and prohibition. We need to cut off the King's head: in political theory that has still to be done.

The radical nature of Foucault's enterprise thus becomes apparent with its demand for capital punishment to be performed on the theoretical corpus of power. It seeks to reverse the concentration of analysis on a mechanical and sovereign conception of power. Henceforth, power will not be seen simply in the familiar A-B terms and these terms will be neither conceptually over-extended nor yoked to a moral absolutism. Foucault refuses the option of moral absolutism: he does not presume to tell us what really is or should be. He does not embrace moral relativism. Instead, his project is extremely 'constitutive' but, unlike Lukes (1974) or Giddens (1984) the constitution is premised neither on 'agency' nor on the excluded 'structure'. Foucault seeks to show how relations of 'agency' and 'structure' have been constituted discursively, how agency is denied to some and given to others, how structures could be said to have determined some things and not others. The focus is upon how certain forms of representation are constituted rather than upon the 'truth' or 'falsity' of the representations themselves.

From the point of view of the argument being constructed in this book, it is the death-knell which Foucault sounds for the conception of power along 'sovereign' lines that is of most immediate interest in his work. At their furthest reach these sovereign terms embrace the fiction of that supreme power which can enable one to 'get another or others to have the desires you want them to have – that is, to secure their compliance by controlling their thoughts and desires' (Lukes 1974: 24). If only it were so simple! As has been argued in the preceding chapters, what Lukes implies with these terms is an acceptance of the Marxian problematic of 'hegemony' or 'dominant ideology', albeit without accepting the theoretical absolutism which would make this a coherent choice. As it is, Lukes' choice is not coherent because of the moral relativism that he simultaneously embraces. In a sense he may be said to attempt to eat his Marxist pie while trying to preserve his liberal decencies as he does so. However, as will be argued next, even if the niceties of liberalism had been abandoned for the unashamed pleasures of the 'Marxist pie' the analytical problems attaching to the over-extension of the sovereign power concept would still not have been resolved.

The over-extension of sovereign power can be seen when Lukes (1974) cites Gramsci's (1971) concept of hegemony to buttress the construction of the third dimension of power. At issue is the uneasy elision this entails with respect to what has come to be called a 'dominant ideology thesis' (Abercrombie et at. 1980): the notion that the most insidious, third dimensional aspect of power operates when a group 'for reasons of submission and intellectual subordination' cannot normally articulate its own interests (Lukes 1974: 47; citing Gramsci 1971: 327). The conceptual over-extension of the notion of sovereign power reaches its outermost limits in such conceptions through its denial of sovereignty to sovereign individuals. This is not to say that the moral and conceptual universe of sovereign individuals has some ontological primacy. On the contrary, it is simply to suggest that the denial of this sovereignty within a moral theory in which liberal, free and responsible individuals do hold conceptual sway is the ultimate act of negative, prohibitory power.

SOVEREIGN POWER AND ITS CONCEPTUAL OVEREXTENSION INTO DOMINANT IDEOLOGY

Minson (1986) has noted that the sovereign power concept has implications for modern power analyses. Sovereign power conceptions entailed that power was something possessed by unitary, 'sovereign' political forces. As we have seen, these were usually equated with human agents who possessed resources. Wolfinger (1971a) noted the propensity for this sovereignty to be diffused through conceptions of ideology in 'radical' accounts. Against these accounts one would argue that the contrast to this sovereign power is neither the 'non-decisions' concept, which Bachrach and Baratz (1970) extend the notion to include, nor the further extension by Lukes (1974), which leads ultimately to a problematic of hegemony or of ideology. It is important to grasp that Foucault's alternative to a concept of sovereign and intermittent episodic power would not reach into any putative third dimension. It is appropriate to put such conceptions of sovereign power finally to rest at their limit in Lukes' (1974) use of Gramsci's (1971) concept of 'hegemony'.

Gramsci has been interpreted, whether erroneously or not, as the theorist of hegemony *par excellence*. Bocock (1986: 106) recognizes Gramsci's importance as 'the fact that he emphasized that any "class" has to be constructed in order to be historically and politically a potentially active agent'. It is worth recalling the context in which Gramsci (1971) developed his ideas on hegemony, as both Davidson (1977) and Perry Anderson (1977) suggest. Gramsci did not accept, as had more mechanistic Marxists, that a proletarian revolution would of necessity occur in the most advanced capitalist countries. Instead, he argued that revolution might emerge in any country where certain structural weaknesses in the fabric of the system made it vulnerable to attack by the working class and its allies. By 'fabric of the system' Gramsci meant both the institutions of civil society and political institutions more generally. These would have to be attacked at their weakest point. The key to this approach lies in the emphasis on the organic relations between the political apparatus and civil society. Gramsci stresses the way in which the functions and effects of key institutions are influenced by their links to both the economic system and civil society. Class domination is maintained not only through coercion but also through consent, he argues. Surrounding the armed fortress of the coercive state is a complex web of hegemony woven into the very fibre of civil society. Hence Gramsci examines the hegemonic supports of state power in the economy (that is, hegemony in the factory), in civil society (that is, education/intellectuals) and in the state apparatus itself (the rule of law). Hegemony involves the successful mobilization and reproduction of the *active* consent of dominated groups. Thus, it involves the following four points:

1. Taking systematic account of popular interests and demands.
2. Making compromises on secondary issues to maintain support and alliances in an inherently unstable political system (whilst maintaining essential interests).
3. Organizing support for national goals which serve the fundamental long-term interests of the dominant group.
4. Providing moral, intellectual and political leadership in order to reproduce and form a collective will or national popular outlook.

Hegemonic practice is concentrated in certain organizations, for instance, the church, schools, trade unions, mass media, and is articulated by intellectuals who develop ideologies and set the parameters of the educational system.

According to Gramsci, hegemony has enabled the ruling class to deal with any threats to its authority. There is a need, therefore, to reconsider revolutionary strategy, to engage in a protracted attack on political and ideological structures rather than to attempt to capture state power *per se*. This implies a concern with the hegemonic apparatus of state power and the role of intellectuals in organizing the hegemony of the dominant class and in forming an historic bloc. The historic bloc becomes the normal mode for the exercise of power. It is only at times of crisis, when control through the hegemonic structures fails, that power is exercised directly in order to restore control. Gramsci's analysis seeks to explain why sovereign power does not normally have to be used.

Recently, Gramsci's concept of hegemony has come under renewed critical scrutiny as a mainstay of something which has been called the 'dominant ideology thesis'. That such a thesis may be said to exist has been the argument of a study by Abercrombie et al. (1980). They cite as the classical locus of the thesis the work of Marx and Engels (1970) on *The German Ideology* and the statement that the ruling ideas of every epoch are those of the ruling class. It is argued that the subsequent development of this idea compounds a mistaken emphasis on rule by ideas in the sociological literature into an almost canonical thesis of 'dominant ideology'. These authors recognize that Gramsci's theory of hegemony is far more sophisticated than a mere statement of the existence of a dominant ideology. None the less, they argue that Gramsci's concept of hegemony, as well as some other contributions, are based on this original Marxian notion. Subsequently, the dominant ideology thesis has been developed by Marxists to explain the deficiencies (that is, quiescence) of the western working class in terms of Marxist revolutionary theory.

In fact, having attributed the thesis to *The German Ideology* in the first place, they proceed to argue that Marx and Engels did not adopt a systematic theory of the incorporation of the working class in capitalist society. *The German Ideology* was rather more the exception than the rule in Marx and Engels' writings. After all, as Marx put it, it had been intended for the gnawing criticism of the mice rather than for posthumous publication. More typical of Marx and Engels' overall approach was Engels (1975) in *The Condition of the Working Class in England*. There he wrote that the bourgeoisie has more in common with that of other nations than with the working class in its own country, that the working class speak their own dialects, have their own specific ideals and thoughts etc. in short, they are like a foreign, unincorporated people. Elsewhere, in *Capital*, Marx (1976) argued that working class consent was founded primarily on the dull compulsion of economic relations. However, subsequent Marxists, at pains to explain why the working class has not taken up the revolutionary banner, have argued that the working class has become ideologically incorporated. Marcuse (1964), for instance, popularized the early research by the Frankfurt School into mass communication and argued that this incorporation took the form of 'one-dimensional thought', systematically promoted by the makers of politics and of mass information. Abercrombie et al. (1980) allocate the central role in the development of the dominant ideology thesis to Gramsci (1971). They do acknowledge that Gramsci's concept of hegemony was not seen purely as an ideological notion. Gramsci did, after all, argue that everyone is an intellectual in that everyone has some conception of the world. Gramsci also argued that the worker has a dual consciousness, as we have seen in Lukes' (1974: 47) citation of Gramsci (1971: 326). According to Gramsci, it is the consciousness forged in action rather than in thought which produces moral and political possibilities that can transcend normal conditions of subordination.

Gramsci (1971) is not the only target for Abercrombie et al. (1980) in their critique of dominant ideology theorists. Another theorist who, like Gramsci, rejects economism and emphasizes the importance of politics is Habermas (1976). Habermas' key concept is that of legitimation, defined as the acceptance by the population of a particular social system. Legitimation also comes under attack for its attachment to a dominant ideology thesis. Habermas' description of the legitimation process is not merely a matter of setting people to think in correct terms but also involves an increase in the level of material rewards. None the less, Habermas frequently makes reference to the impact of bourgeois ideology, to the effects of a technocratic consciousness, and to the question of manipulation and propaganda orchestrating the public for the purpose of legitimation.

According to Abercrombie et al. (1980), Habermas (1976) argues that any strain on the political system requires ideological solutions, the most effective being those mechanisms of formal democracy which can create the illusion of participation in decision-making. In order to ensure that this participation remains passive, it must occur only periodically (e.g., at elections) and be based on 'civil privatism' (i.e., people should mainly be preoccupied about their own private interests and not engage in broader social communication and resolution of problems). However, the fact that the state is constantly intervening into the private sphere (through, for instance, welfare, housing and planning schemes) can lead to a potential legitimation crisis. Abercrombie et al. (1980) are careful to acknowledge that Habermas' (1976) conception of legitimation is developed in opposition to a traditional model of the class struggle. On the other hand, Habermas (1976) does sometimes use terms which imply an acceptance of some form of what they term a dominant ideology thesis. In fact, he leaves unresolved the question of how ideology can come to serve the interests of one particular group or class over another. After all, Habermas claims that technocratic consciousness not only justifies a particular class's interest in domination and represses another class's partial need for emancipation but also affects the human race's emancipatory interests as such. This 'emancipatory interest' derives from his commitment to a conception of reason being intrinsic to the human project of communication.

Althusser (1971), whose view of how ideology can be produced independently of class interests but can still have consequences for those interests, is also regarded as a prime instance of the dominant ideology view. Like Gramsci (1971) and Habermas (1971), he rejects economism in the form of the simple-minded economic determination of ideas. Instead, he argues that there is a strong relationship between ideology and politics on the one hand and the economy on the other, such that ideology and politics are a 'condition of existence' of the economy. The modern abstract legal system, on this view, is a condition of existence of a capitalist economy. These arguments have been systematically undermined by Cutler et al. (1979a; 1979b) who convincingly demonstrate the great variation between the phenomenal forms which have sustained the mode of production that Althusser (1971) would call capitalist. In fact, they would argue that there is no such thing as capitalism *per se*, only distinct capitalisms.

In Althusser's (1971) analysis, ideology acts specifically as a condition of existence, which varies according to each mode of production. This is linked to the notion that the economy is the determinant in the last instance, in that it establishes which other structure is to be dominant. Thus, in the Middle Ages, ideology in the form of Catholicism, dominated; in ancient societies, it was politics that was dominant. In addition, ideology has the general function of relating people to their conditions of existence. Ideology achieves its effect by placing and adapting people to their structural roles as 'bearers' of structures of social relations. It does this by constituting individuals as particular types of subjects in a structure at the same time as it conceals from them their role as agents of that structure.

Althusser (1971) rejects the notion that ideology is generated by one class for the consumption or subordination of other classes. However, he also argues that the illusions of ideology do have consequences for class relations. As Abercrombie et al. (1980) point out, this leaves unanswered the issues of how ideology is formed and has consequences for specific class interests when it has been produced independently of them. The clearest expression of the dominant ideology thesis in Althusser's (1971) work is his essay on 'Ideology and Ideological State Apparatuses' in which he outlines the conditions which he sees as necessary for the reproduction of the economic system. Apart from the more obvious aspects, such as the reproduction of labour-power and labour skills, he stresses 'reproduction' of the submission by workers to the ruling ideology. This is reproduction of the ability to manipulate ruling ideology correctly on the part of agents of exploitation and repression. When achieved, this reproduction will provide for the domination of the ruling class 'in words'. The education system plays a key role in this scheme, according to Althusser. (Althusser has often been the subject of criticism: see Connell [1983a; 1983b] for instance, or for a more balanced appraisal, consult Elliot [1988].)

Proponents of the dominant ideology thesis, in its more blatant forms, give it a much more instrumental character. Ideology becomes an instrument in the hands of the ruling class. Miliband (1969), in his book on *The State in Capitalist Society*, argues that there exists an 'economically dominant class' which is also dominant in politics. The assumption of this and other versions of the thesis is that classes are origins of knowledge, belief or ideology.

Abercrombie et al. (1980) are dismissive of claims that a dominant ideology characterizes contemporary working class life, whether or not the claims come from Marxists such as Gramsci, Habermas, Althusser or Miliband. They also argue that very little has been said by its proponents about the impact of the dominant ideology on the dominant class. In fact, they go on to present a case which, on the one hand, argues that subordinate classes are not incorporated by the dominant ideology but, on the other hand, suggests that it is indeed the dominant classes who are deeply penetrated by and incorporated within dominant beliefs. The dominant ideology does exist, they conclude, but only for the dominant class. It is increasingly less relevant as capitalism develops (but see Perry Anderson 1964 and Wiener 1981). Against the influential arguments of much Marxism and sociology they conclude that as far as the working class is concerned there is no longer a requirement for a dominant ideology.

However, as Abercrombie et al. (1980) themselves admit, the dominant ideology thesis is subject to variable interpretation and the most influential non-Marxist expression of the dominant ideology thesis occurs in functionalist sociology, for instance, in Talcott Parsons' (1951) theory of socialization. It is through this process that dominant values are transmitted through the cultural mechanisms of family, church and school. These central, dominant values ('the central value system') are supposed to resolve the problem of social order. The weakness of such a theory is its inability to account for the emergence of other ('deviant') value systems. In a sense we have the paradox of emancipation in reverse. Deviant role behaviour, in Parsons' (1951) view, is simply a product of inadequate socialization.

Both Marxist and functionalist approaches face similar analytic problems. Functionalists are committed both to the notion of a common value system, which is necessary to sustain a social system, and to the theory of structural differentiation in modern societies, which creates pluralistic value systems; Marxists are committed to a theory of 'ruling ideas' and to a theory that each class, because of its own interests, has its own unique culture.

Abercrombie et al. (1980) draw on evidence from feudalism, early capitalism and late capitalism to support their critique of the dominant ideology thesis. Their analysis appears more persuasive about the first two when they show how the peasantry in Europe remained outside the ideological influence of Christian orthodoxy and how the debate over the nature of kinship served the purpose of defining a relationship between king and barons rather than king and peasants. One of their conclusions is both unsurprising and remarkably close to the model of hegemonic processes described by Gramsci (1971). In seventeenth-century England, in early capitalism, the dominant ideology was not the ideology of the dominant class but of an *ascendant class*. However, one could argue that the dominant class will always make use of, indeed, has always made use of, the ideology of an ascendant class in order not to be entirely overtaken by it. An often cited example is that of the land-owning aristocracy in Germany vis à vis the rising bourgeoisie and industrial capitalist revolution (Weber 1978).

Abercrombie et al. (1980) may, perhaps, be said to carry their critique too far in saying that late capitalism is a system which is in little need of ideology at all. While this is not quite the end of ideology, they are not too far from this view. Their argument is that in late capitalism there is no unambiguous pattern of beliefs providing comprehensive coherence; that there is, in fact, a considerable 'pluralization of life worlds'. They point to conflicts between different groups of capitalists (between small businesses, multinationals and state corporate enterprises). They argue that in late capitalism, unlike earlier stages of economic development, there is no need for the dominant class to have a dominant ideology since the nature of property relations has changed: private property in land and capital no longer requires a relatively stable marriage system, clear laws of inheritance, principles of legitimacy, adoption and re-marriage; thus, they suggest that the family structure is no longer of such importance.

They do not argue that ideology no longer exists; it is simply no longer as important. Perhaps the most obvious weakness of this lies in its failure to consider political processes.

Did Donald Trump, for instance, think that ideology is no longer significant in securing allegiance? He, and other political leaders, spent considerable effort in creating and responding to explicitly 'ideological' politics. Would they do this if ideology were so fluid and unimportant?

The critique of the dominant ideology thesis undoubtedly highlights the fact that many sociologists, particularly in the Marxist tradition, have side-stepped the problem of why the working class in western society have not revolted and have not taken that revolutionary action which so much, if not all, of Marxism had scripted for them. They have highlighted how hegemonic theory often leaves unanswered the question of *how* people's intentions are formed and how it often fails to do justice to the complex and contradictory nature of advanced capitalism. Recall, for instance, Lukes' (1974: 24) 'supreme and most insidious exercise of power', that which prevents grievances by shaping people's 'perceptions, cognitions and preferences in such a way that they accept their role in the existing order of things'. How on earth is the trick done? What is it that can culturally dupe people in this way? (At this juncture there is usually a retreat into notions of hegemony or a 'ruling culture', as in Connell [1976] for instance.) To the extent that the dominant ideology critics make us sceptical about such nostrums, they perform a useful service. However, the critics of the thesis tend to go to the other extreme of describing ideology as irrelevant.

The main contribution of Abercrombie et al. (1980) is to suggest that the situation in late capitalism is far more complex than any instrumental application of a dominant ideology view may suggest. They support this by citing research into British working class culture which tends to the view that working class consciousness has a dual character. Frank Parkin (1972) identifies three competing systems of meaning: a dominant value system, a subordinate value system (which promotes accommodative responses to inequality) and a radical value system (which promotes opposition). If Abercrombie et al. (1980) are aiming to modify the interpretation by many Marxists and sociologists of the Gramscian model, then their endeavour would appear worthwhile – but they themselves do not discard it entirely. Instead, in their own words, they turn it on its head, and apply it to the dominant class.

On the whole, they feel that the importance of ideological compliance in late capitalism has been exaggerated. In fact, they reach the same conclusions as Przeworski (1980), in his interpretation of hegemony, when they argue that consent or compliance has a material basis in everyday life. As they suggest, the fact that workers have to labour to live will itself constitute a permanent pressure towards their co-optation and participation. For Przeworski, hegemony is founded on material consent and constraint.

Although the majority of interpretations of Gramsci's (1971) theory of hegemony focus on ideology and consciousness, there are other interpretations which focus on material relations. Hegemonic theory does not, of necessity, have to be interpreted in the manner expressed by the so-called dominant ideology theorists. If we turn back to the four main elements of hegemony as outlined by Gramsci, we might wish to agree with him on at least two points. The perspective seems to be quite sound when we look at how dominant groups do mobilize consent. First, Gramsci suggests, they do this by taking systematic account of popular interests and demands while, second, they make compromises and alliances on secondary issues to maintain general support and existing alliances in an inherently unstable political system. His third element is open to some questioning, although it may be valid: that the dominant groups are able to organize support for national goals which serve their fundamental long-term interests. The fourth element is open to more doubt and forms the main platform for the critique by Abercrombie et al. (1980): the dominant groups provide moral, intellectual and political leadership in order to reproduce a form of collective will expressed as nationalist populism. Nationalist populism clearly plays a key ideological role in events such as Trump's political rallies, his opposing 'fake news', or in the mobilization of the UK Brexit vote. During the course of their consideration of the 'absence' of dominant ideology in the contemporary working class, they do recover a concern with the terms which so occluded Wolfinger (1971a) in the analysis of power. These terms focus on the dull compulsions of everyday organizational life.

Two implications flow from consideration of a 'dominant ideology thesis' with respect to the concept of sovereign power. First, the dominant ideology problematic of 'consent' should not wholly be located within the realms of consciousness in the terms implied by Lukes (1974). Second, the organization of consent is far more likely to be an effect of organizational necessity on the part of individuals, who have to make a living by hiring themselves on the labour market, than it is a conscious outcome of any sovereign power. As Przeworski (1980) argues, consent is not based on illusion. Although hegemony may be said to consist of exploitation with consent, this consent is not artificially manufactured and engineered by a sovereign power. It is founded on a material base, the wage earning and consumption capacities that workers enjoy, and the coercion on which this is based. It is in this way that Wolfinger's (1971a) inexplicable 'routines' become an apparent aspect of power.

DISCIPLINARY POWER AND THE DISSOLUTION OF THE SOVEREIGN POWER CONCEPTION

Foucault (1980), in the article 'Truth and power', indicates his opposition to the concept of 'ideology'. For him, it is a term of 'falsehood' whose relational opposition to a 'true' concept of 'science' can never be too far away. It is because his interest is less in issues of the truth and falsity of discourse and rather more in their functioning that he seeks to avoid the whole arena of concepts of 'ideology'. In fact, in a roundabout way, the concept of disciplinary power has this purpose because it seeks to demonstrate how the 'truths' and 'falsehoods' of particular discourses have been constituted historically. In *Discipline and Punish*, for instance, the focus is precisely on techniques whereby a whole new regime of truth concerning the nature of crime and punishment was constructed.

Foucault (1977) has shown how, during the eighteenth century, there occurred a shift away from an earlier regime of punishment based on the terror of sovereign power, one which could literally inscribe and inflict its penalty on the body of the juridical victim, to one concerned with what he terms disciplinary power. Disciplinary power saw a move to the identification and categorization of 'deviance', to the assignment of criminal responsibility, and to the design of appropriate rehabilitation and confinement for the criminal thus caught in the administrative web. This shift from physical torture to a highly regulatory apparatus of power, which seeks to structure the total institutional environment of the offender, is but one of a number of new forms of what Foucault termed disciplinary power. Disciplinary power works exactly through the construction of routine. Bauman (1982: 40–1) captures the processes of this new power perfectly, noting it as an aspect of a

general redeployment of social power; which entailed both the re-structuring of authority and a drastic shift in the scope of power and the method of its exercise. Power moved from the distant horizon into the very centre of daily life. Its object, previously the goods possessed or produced by the subject, was now the subject himself, his daily rhythm, his time, his bodily actions, his mode of life. The power reached now towards the body and the soul of its subjects. It wished to regulate, to legislate, to tell the right from the wrong, the norm from deviance, the ought from the is. It wanted to impose one ubiquitous pattern of normality and eliminate everything and everybody which the pattern could not fit. Unlike the sovereign power which required only a ceremonial reminder of the timeless limits to autonomy, the emergent power could be maintained only by a dense web of interlocking authorities in constant communication with the subject and in a physical proximity to the subject which permitted a perpetual surveillance of, possibly, the totality of his life process. Old forms were transformed into such authorities, while new authorities were brought to life to serve the fields old authorities were incapable of reaching. Thus families and sexual functions of the body are deployed in a new role; churches become teachers of business virtue, hard work and abstemiousness – and if old churches fail to hammer the lesson home, sects or dissident churches emerge to do the job; workhouses and poorhouses join forces in instilling the habit of continuous, repetitive, routine effort; idiosyncrasy and, indeed, any non-rhythmical, erratic behaviour is stigmatized, criminalized, medicalized or psychiatrized; individualized training by apprenticeship or personal service is replaced with a uniform system of education aimed at instilling universal skills and, above all, universal discipline – through, among other means, culling the individual *qua* individual from the guidance and authority of his group of origin and subjecting him to an external source of authority superior to this group and free from its control. No one of these many powers is now total, as that of the absolute monarch claimed to be. But together they reach a kind of totality which no power dreamed of reaching before. (Bauman 1982: 40–1)

Bauman (1982) is at pains to establish that it would be quite wrong to see this emergence of disciplinary power as an effect of any sovereign power. The notion of sovereign power used here, incidentally, must encapsulate not only the monarch but also all other putative loci of a ruling subjectivity. What one has in mind is the tendency of writers such as Marglin (1974) or Braverman (1974) to limit consideration of new forms of disciplinary power solely to factory settings. In this context they can be regarded as the outcome of the intentional acts of power of capitalists. While there is no doubt that some of the new forms of disciplinary power proved 'functional' for capitalists, as Weber (1978) argued, it is, as Bauman (1982: 42) suggests, far more difficult to establish that they were 'necessary'. The causality is all wrong. New forms of disciplinary power preceded the establishment of the factory system by at least two centuries, he suggests. In fact, as Kieser (1987) demonstrates, one should, as Weber (1978) suggested, chart the early religious roots of modern disciplinary power as they emerged in monastic discipline.

In the first century after Christ's death, some of his most ardent followers charted the route of ascetic religious virtuosi pioneered by John the Baptist. Many fell from the state of grace to which they aspired into beggary, although impoverishment and deprivation were in themselves insufficient for the religious vocation as sources of ascetic regard. Consequently, hermits began to design rules for an ascetic life such that it became enshrined in an organizational mode. The mode was explicitly and rationally oriented to other-worldly, spiritual concerns. Rational organizational design centred on the scalar principles of hierarchy, of discipline, of authority and of rules. Initially these had emerged to order the possibilities of other-worldly salvation from this-worldly existence which was encapsulated in the particular enclave of the monastery.

One of the first designers of a recognizably modern monastic form was the Egyptian Pachonius, who died in 346. Some of the rules he set up concerned the construction of a monastery. A big wall should isolate the monks from the outside world. The more mundane function of the wall was to guarantee the monks' purity. In addition, the gate, the only point of access, had to be controlled. It should be supervised by an especially reliable monk, who would also be responsible for the novices. The novices had to stay for some time in the boarding house for strangers. They had to receive preparation for the entrance examination. After passing it, they were to be dressed formally with a new gown. They received new names. All of these ceremonies symbolized that the monk was taking on a new identity. Other rules dealt with religious ceremonies and communal meals. Pachonius' principles solved the problem of how to lead an ascetic life. The structure of an ascetic life was no longer a personal problem. The solution was to be found in obeying the rules of the monastic order and obedience to these rules became the ascetic ideal.

The founding fathers of early mediaeval monasteries tried to minimize working time in order to optimize time for prayers. To do this, they organized work rationally. They planned the design of work and discussed alternative solutions to common problems; controversies over the best rules were quite common.

Controversy over work design was quite a new occurrence in western Europe. In the past, all religious thinking had been directed toward the preservation of old holy traditions. Now the preservers of those traditions, the monasteries themselves, became more oriented to new and more rational ways of thinking and doing. Between the years 500 and 800 after Christ, a kind of competitive environment existed in which those orders which developed rules that offered a more convincing ideal for a monastic life, thus attracting more followers, spread more quickly. Economic success was also important. Those monastic orders which were successful economically received more donations and more land held in fiefs and this enabled them to establish more new monasteries within their order.

Hand-writing became the crucial skill involved in the process of founding new monasteries and in incorporating new members. The monks advanced and developed the arts of literacy, with the aid of which they were able to provide blueprints for the duplication of monasteries from existing to new sites. By the seventh and eighth centuries, these skills had become well distributed and established within the monasteries. Monasteries grew quite large. As many as three or four hundred members and ancillaries were not uncommon. All of these people had to be provided for within the local economy of each monastery: this generated novel organizational problems. The solution which was most often pioneered was to bifurcate: to found new monasteries and new institutions. Given the development of literacy within the monasteries, those solutions which had proved profitable and useful in the past could be recorded and stored up for use in the future. The monasteries, in other words, were a repository of innovation, of learning, of development, of memory.

The success of a monastic order often led to its downfall. The economic success of a monastery meant that the ascetic goals were all too easily displaced. (Those who have read Umberto Eco's [1983] fine novel, *The Name of the Rose*, or seen the film, will have a good idea of this.) Consequently, schism and the growth of new, more ascetic, orders was rife. Amongst the most successful were the Cistercian monasteries. These were not only organized internally as rational bureaucracies but also found a collective expression, under the Cistercian order, as a bureaucratic *system* of inter-organizational units. Within the Cistercian system, the key reporting mechanisms were the annual accounts. The Cistercian order developed a rudimentary but, for the times, quite sophisticated accounting of the soul. Hence, when the royal households of the early western European kingdoms, such as England or France, began to differentiate the administration of the household from that of the kingdom, the first major department to be separated from the royal court was the treasury, and its first treasurers were frequently clergymen. 'Other-worldly' asceticism may not have escaped from the monastery into the factory but it did shape the state, its administration and politics. The reasons why this should have been so are quite apparent. In a system in which literacy was a vital skill in short supply then those institutions which could meet that demand were obviously going to be in a strategic position. The monasteries were such an institution. Clergymen were frequently recruited from the monasteries to become statesmen. The monasteries were, in fact, medieval loci of literacy, of numeracy, of knowledge. In short, they were the site of medieval disciplinary power.

The availability of disciplinary power mechanisms facilitated the development of capitalism, suggests Bauman (1982). Their availability was contingent upon transformations of the state form. As feudal rule disintegrated, both sovereign power and the fixity of rank and locale which went with it declined. The conditions which sustained a remote sovereign's occasional and intermittent displays of power were those of patrimonial rule. Sovereign power was patrimonial, a system in which power and rule were utterly fused with the royal household. This household was an organization controlled by personal servants of the ruler. Personal service was the rudimentary organizational mechanism for the extension of sovereign power which was premised on territorial rule, landed estates and patriarchal overlordship of a household. Rule was buttressed by religious precepts of 'divine rule'. Given the power of the Church of Rome as a complex transnational organization, divine ordainment was not a purely moral idea; the church sought to extend these moral ties to the relationship between rulers and ruled as being one of consent which drew upon Germanic tribal bonds of fealty.

The other effective limit on patrimonial power was what Giddens (1984) terms 'time-space distantiation', the problem of maintaining adequate surveillance and control over expansive territory. Mann (1986) argues that the limits of an army's route-march were very much the effective limits of the patrimonial ruler's core area of control; beyond these limits he might have authority but it would be of a far more contingent kind, less tightly enveloping and controlling, subject to greater resistance and requiring occasional pacification to continue to be effective.

Rulers had to delegate aspects of rule to authorities empowered with discretion, thus stretching and weakening patrimonial control and generating countervailing positions of power in the overall network of power. On this basis feudal relations, founded on increasingly reciprocal obligations, tended to develop where a territorial ruler could not ensure the subordination and control of those landed knights who acted as authorities of patrimonialism. Consequently, the relation between the patrimonial ruler and the vassals, who acted as authorities, was variably balanced. The vassal's contribution was to exercise authority (the collection of dues and taxes, pacification, and the maintenance of what was taken to be legal order) on behalf of the patrimonial ruler. The inducement for the vassal to do so was that, in exchange for an oath of fealty from the vassal, the ruler made a land grant of a fief or protectorate within which the vassal's rule might hold sway, through the exercise of certain judicial and administrative powers.

Where patrimonialism was at its strongest, the fiefdoms which the local notables enjoyed would be firmly embedded within the royal jurisdiction. Such holdings would be much less subject to subcontracting and to the devolving or parcelling out of parts of the fief. Where patrimonialism was at its weakest, at the other end of the continuum, relations between rulers and vassals would be based around some conception of mutual rights and obligations, usually sworn under sacred binding oath. The best example of this is Magna Carta. Characteristically, the system of medieval politics was divided between plural, unstable and sometimes countervailing powers.

Such networks of influence and power as there were were not necessarily stable. Stability would often depend upon the personalization of political relationships. The majority of people, of course, were just passive bystanders of these events. Power really involved only the patrimonial ruler and those vassals incorporated within the territory that was ruled. As Duby (1962) argues, in most of western Europe, with the exception of England, where feudalism existed, it was marked by an increasing fragmentation of the system of rule into smaller, ever more autonomous units. These would differ widely in methods of rule. There would be no necessary relationship between the top and the bottom. Relations between the king and vassals were expressed through particularized relationships. England differed. After the Norman invasion, the king of occupied England was the apex of vassal relations that conquest had brought into being under the monarch's banner. It was the disestablishment of existing land-rights which created a strong central power to which the post-1066 estates were beholden. Elsewhere it was much more difficult to distinguish powers of proprietorship from powers of landed possession.

Poggi (1978) suggests that, in general, the political, jurisdictional and proprietary prerogatives of fief holders were fused in such a way that the patrimonial elements became uppermost. In effect, what occurred was not a single system of patrimonialism but an overlapping, plural network of patrimonialisms in which the landed estate itself came to be seen as the bearer of semi-political, formal, public prerogatives. The monarch, lacking an effective monopoly of the legitimate means of violence over the given territory, had to rely for order in the land on the self-interested relations and conflicts of the nobles, and these relations would be cemented by plunder, by marriage and by other mechanisms for the consolidation of estates. Within feudal society, the majority of individuals had little in the way of rights other than to the domain of a particular landed noble or as members of a particular village. National concepts were largely abstractions in their experience. Such rights as existed were wholly contingent upon the status of the individual involved. Status would be defined either by heredity (for example, the nobles) or by membership in certain institutional orders which claimed and possessed certain rights and liberties (for example, municipal corporations). The vast majority of people, of course, were peasants.

Whatever rights the peasants held were constrained by the obligatory duties which they had to perform for the landlord to whose estates they were tied. In practice, rule and power were highly localized, highly particularized: dependent upon local practice and custom, in this particular town, in that particular guild, on this particular landed estate. As Perry Anderson (1974) puts it, feudal relations represented a situation in which economic and political exploitation and power were fused with political and legal coercion, and this all took place in the locale of a particular village or town or estate. The vast majority of people were born, lived and died within one very local area. Within medieval society some categories of persons were able to circulate freely but on the whole these were the exception. The major mass movements were forms of militarism. Beyond these extraordinary crusades, people were fixed in the surveillance of a local community which *knew* their place until death.

Sovereign power was organized around the 'institutional principle of perpetuity of bonds and obligations' (Bauman 1982: 43), bonds which tied people to a particular place, in a form of 'control-through-space'. If the peasants stayed put, then the peasants had some claims to communal support. However, there were pressures which offset the propensity of the peasantry to remain: the 'pull' of the free space of the towns and the 'push' of tightening servile dues imposed by a nobility confronting both periodic inflation and a decrease in its terms of trade. While people typically stayed put in their place, then in that context human behaviour in its totality was so clearly visible that keeping it on the customary course did not call for an organized, separately institutionalized surveillance (Bauman 1982: 45).

During the seventeenth and eighteenth centuries, as a result of increasing population pressure, the old immobility disintegrated. Bauman sees the consequent social production of 'strangers' to whatever communal conditions of membership prevailed, as the primary factor undercutting the 'normative' universe of sovereign power and rendering more problematic its infrequent incursions on settled people and places. The rapid swelling of urban life and populations becomes the impetus for the widespread adoption of forms of disciplinary power in Bauman's (1982) account (also see O'Neill 1987: 50–1). Subsequent capitalist industrialization thus simply modelled its forms of discipline on those which were already emergent. In particular, its time-discipline was forged in institutions for control of the surplus and uprooted population, drawing on those harsh regimes first constructed to keep erstwhile religious mendicants on the path of righteousness. The dark satanic mills of Yorkshire and Lancashire simply latched on to the disciplinary apparatus already let loose from the monastery into the poor house, the work house, the orphanage, the barracks, and so on.

Why was there this conjuncture of discipline and demography? North (1981) and North and Thomas (1973) provide some insight. (A critical discussion of this work may be found in Holton [1985].) They argue that during the years from 1500 to 1700, after the ravages of the Black Death had brought havoc to the feudal economies of Europe, it was not those states which sought to resolve their 'fiscal crises' through confiscation of assets or the sale of state monopolies but those which had recourse to a system of 'property rights', of 'open markets' in that property and its produce, which taxed transactions, which were to prosper and overcome the recurrent Malthusian tendencies of earlier centuries. A consequence of this shift to a property-based system of rights was the dissolution of the previous system of feudal rights. Serfs who were previously bondsmen were made free but for many their freedom consisted of little more than the necessity to roam the countryside seeking food, work and shelter from the owners of the emergent post-feudal property rights. In order to control the floating population of 'free' peasants, new institutions of containment and surveillance were innovated by the state, precisely because of the danger to the new order of property which was posed by vagabondage. Hence, when industrial capitalism developed upon the back of these new property relations, there already existed an institutional framework upon which relations in production might be modelled. These formed the new disciplinary power.

The ideal type of the new disciplinary power for Foucault is Bentham's proposal for a 'Panopticon'. The Panopticon was an architectural device consisting of a central, elevated watch-tower (the motif of The *Salvation* Army), a device which signals clearly the practical demise of the old sovereign concept. From this central point of inspection there was arranged a circular disposition of cells, radiating like spokes from the hub of a wheel to its rim. Each cell was illuminated with peripheral light which passed from the exterior rim of the building into the cell, making evident the person illuminated within. One observer, all-seeing but unseen in the tower, could in principle subject all in vision to surveillance. To the surveyed, surveillance would be less the actual superintendence, more the sheer impossibility of avoiding the observer's gaze and the realization of being always, in principle, subject to it. It would thus become, in principle, 'internalized'. Power would no longer be based on the constancy of place and normative ties, and the occasional act of power's expropriation. Power would now be regularized, routinized, cast not as an absent presence securing traditional norms but as a constant surveillance constituting a new discipline of norms and behaviour. Subject to the 'Panopticon', inmates of whatever institution would be acutely aware that their every action might be, and with no way of knowing if indeed it were, subject to the supervisory gaze of surveillance. This knowledge in itself might be sufficient to produce disciplined obedience, as subjects learned literally to survey themselves, to be reflexively self-regarding as if under the ever-present and watchful eye of surveillance. Moreover, coupled with the therapeutic incitement to speak and to provide an account of themselves in the terms made available by the new disciplinary practices, power was now able to work not simply by silencing people but by giving them voice. Power, rather than occasionally imposing itself on the subjectivity of its subjects, now 'in its actual exercise must be ever constitutive of the subjectivity of the agents of power relations' (Minson 1986: 113–14). Power subjects and, now, in its disciplinary mode, subjectifies.

The planned apparatus was quite cunning in terms of its design. However, although examples of the Panopticon were indeed built, it should be evident that a system of control which depends upon purpose-built and designed architecture is an expensive option and likely to be cast aside in favour of more cost-effective and flexible solutions. Very little flexibility attaches to a control system which can, by virtue of its design, hold only a specific number of inmates. For expanding commercial enterprises this was an especial barrier, although it could be argued that the principles of the Panopticon did find their expression in the design of some of the model industrial estates of nineteenth-century philanthropists such as the Cadburys of Bournville or the Salts of Saltaire. The inhabitants of these were under constant surveillance in their comings and goings from the neighbourhood. The purposeful design of the estates was to make the lives of those within them transparent and removed from temptations such as might be posed by the public houses of the traditional working class community. However, it is important not to attribute a greater effectiveness to the Panopticon than it actually had (which some of the over-enthusiastic and empirically untempered reception of Foucault has done). It is not as if, without the Panopticon, there was no discipline or control: it merely represents a particular condensation of these tendencies.

The subjectification which is identified with disciplinary power is regarded as operating primarily through enhancing the 'calculability' of individuals (Foucault 1977: 192–4). Minson (1986: 113) renders it clearly: 'The human individual constructed in such discourses is calculable to the extent of being subject to comparative, scalar measures and related forms of training and correction.' The objective of disciplinary techniques is normalization.

Wolfinger's puzzlement at the power of normalcy, of routine, fades. It represents the discursive 'fixing' of the conditions of subjectivity in particular places and times. Almost anything might become a resource in this process, from a religious vocation to the formation of discursive skills themselves (Clegg and Dunkerley 1980: 59–63). The social and economic history of early factory capitalism provides an instructive record of the normalization and resistance of a new disciplinary power, as Bauman (1982) bears warrant. The regulatory thrust was not so much towards rational organization *per se* as submission, domination, mastery over men, women and children, constituted as productive powers. From the school to the factory the game was to be learned and played 'for the state of its prizes' (Bauman 1982: 75). It was disciplined subordination.

Foucault's (1977) conception of disciplinary power developing to replace the older sovereign power, of which Machiavelli's (1958) precepts in *The Prince* were a veritable but sketchy handbook, is not inconsistent with Weber's (1978) account. Nor, as has been remarked elsewhere (for example O'Neill [1987]; Clegg et al. [1986: 57]), is Weber's account of the development of capitalist discipline and control inconsistent with recent 'labour process' descriptions of industrial discipline, provided that we relax certain assumptions which see this 'discipline' originating in the cunning of capitalists. (Clegg and Dunkerley [1980] make this error; also see Marglin [1974] and Stone [1974]: contrast with Rueschemeyer [1986] who arrives at similar conclusions via a different route.)

Disciplinary power, particularly in its 'time-discipline' (Thompson 1967), clearly emerged from the monasteries, as Kieser (1987) argues. However, it is equally clear that it was rapidly adapted in the competitive learning environment of early capitalist industrialization. A general transition may be said to have taken place from a domestic economy, premised on the 'putting out' system, to one which was factory based (Clegg and Dunkerley 1980: 49–56; 59–70), even though it is clear that (as O'Neill [1987: 47] observes, citing Laslett [1965] and Wall et al. [1983]) it would be a myth to regard the family as a 'natural' economy. However, it is evident that the chronology of the world was transformed, often in a generation, from one of Holy days, local feasts and the unremitting but seasonably variable rhythms of agricultural production into one based on the rhythms of the industrial machine, overseer, and the clock of factory discipline applied to factory 'hands'. (Workers were, literally, interchangeable 'hands', recruited as such.) In the competitive ecology of nineteenth-century production regimes, the possibilities for theft, casualness and ill-discipline in the putting-out system of domestic production compared unfavourably with factory control (Marglin 1974; Landes 1969). The keynote of this factory control was what Weber (1978) referred to as 'military discipline'. Equally, as we have seen, this discipline had not only military but also monastic roots, particularly in the subjugation of one's own time to an externally imposed discipline of the master's time.

O'Neill (1987: 47–8) notes, after Smelser (1959), that certain technological changes, such as steam power and mule spinning, cemented the loss of workers' control and the ascendancy of the masters' in the spinning trades. These changes were gradually emulated in the weaving trades, where women and children replaced the previously craft-based male labour whose resistance was stubborn, violent, political and drawn-out. Indeed, some writers who focus on class struggle at the point of production (Burawoy 1978; 1979; 1985; Littler 1982; Edwards 1979; Clawson 1980), see this as a battleground in which a dialectic of capitalist control and worker resistance to it is played out, one which is structurally irresolvable as long as capitalist relations of production are reproduced. Hence the dialectic of power and resistance is given a precise structural location in Marx's (1976) general theory of capitalism as relations of production. From this basis quite general theories of capitalist organization and control of the labour process have been developed (Clegg and Dunkerley 1980).

Foucault's (1977) conception of disciplinary power, although compatible with the Marxian focus on control and resistance in the capitalist workplace, differs from it in two important respects. First, control via discipline is not seen as developing initially in the factory but in various state institutions. It is adopted by the capitalist masters from the prison masters, the beadles, and the superintendents of asylums. Second, it is not a control which is functionally oriented to capitalist exploitation but to the creation of obedient bodies. Foucault spends considerable detail on the 'embodiment' of power. This focus was not entirely novel. Marx (1976) was only too well aware of the violence done to human bodies by the new capitalist discipline, as many of his more descriptive passages indicate. Gramsci (1971) was also aware of the impact of the 'Fordist' system on worker's bodies. Weber (1948: 261–2) too was aware of the 'tuning' of the 'psycho-physical' apparatus produced by the 'ever-widening grasp of discipline', although his focus was more on the role that Protestantism could play in producing a morally tuned and willing apparatus (Weber 1976; see the commentaries by Poggi [1983] and Marshall [1982]; also the studies by Thompson [1968], Hobsbawm [1969], Wearmouth [1939], Eldridge [1972], Anthony [1977] and Guttman [1977], all of whom stress the role that religion played in disciplining the workforce). Religion undoubtedly had a role to play, although as Eldridge (1972) notes, it is not always clear on the evidence of religious conviction that it was quite as dramatic as is sometimes assumed. Others see the Foucauldian stress on state institutions, rather than testament, as a more compelling locus of the new disciplinary power. Writing of the forced labour of the workhouses, which followed the breakdown of the Elizabethan Poor Laws under the increasing supply of surplus quantities of labour, driven off the land by enclosure, O'Neill notes that:

> When labour became increasingly plentiful, unemployed and driven to crime and rebellion, the houses of correction became even more punitive, while labour in the houses of correction was limited to intimidating and useless tasks so that no one would ever enter them voluntarily. The overall effect was to teach free labour the discipline of the factory outside and inside the factory.... Thus, the employed and the unemployed learn their respective disciplines. Thereafter, we might say that in the bourgeois social order the prison, the factory and the school, like the army, are places where the system can project its conception of the disciplinary society in the reformed criminal, the good worker, student, loyal soldier, and committed citizen. In every case, it is a question of reproducing among the propertyless a sense of commitment to the property system in which they have nothing to sell but their labour and loyalty. (O'Neill 1987: 51–2)

It is in this panoply of disciplinary organizations, in Foucault's account, that the new complex of bio-power emerges. It is this aspect of power, how it is tied up with new discourses of medicine, administration and so on, which is additional to either Marx or Weber's accounts, and which provides a framework for the carrying capacity of new forms of disciplinary power to spread like a contagion from their initial institutional sites. DiMaggio and Powell (1983) see the carriers of institutional isomorphism in this respect as primarily the state and the professions. Moreover, as certain 'radical' organization theorists have argued, it is these knowledges and the practices that they licence which produce what O'Neill (1987: 55) refers to as the *natural discipline* of the work place and the wage system (see, for example, Clegg 1977; 1979; Clegg and Dunkerley 1980). The Foucauldian twist is a useful corrective in making the process far less instrumental than these accounts presume.

These concrete histories of organizations, practices and institutions seem light-years from power, from As and Bs, from capacities and outcomes. What is the connection? Under the regime of disciplinary power, the 'capacity-outcomes' relationship of differential probabilities which agents might have is not so crucial to the analysis of power:

> It is not necessary to construe those differential advantages and disadvantages such as popular aspirations, morale, responsibilities, principles, rights or virtues as essential human or subjective factors belonging to a moral domain. Rather it is possible to treat these phenomena of the moral or personal life as always determined by the specific discourses and social relations in which they are formed and where they exercise definite, albeit limited effects. They are no less 'objective' nor more conditional than a policeman's powers of arrest or the power of a gun to penetrate a body or of a manager to sack an employee. (Minson 1986: 129–30)

Foucault's 'post-structuralist' historical approach to discursive practices is thus not the relativism it might appear to be. Whatever phenomena of fixity there are may be seen as an effect of those stabilized disciplinary powers and discursive practices which constitute them. In the terms of realist epistemology, the relatively intransitive causal powers of agents and the appropriate standing conditions for their expression must themselves be regarded as an effect of power. However, this should not be confused with any third dimensional conception of ideology masking 'real interests'. Post-structuralism dissolves this conception of ideology. The often esoteric concerns of post-structuralism, frequently unclear in their implications and outline (e.g. Derrida 1976), are thus of some consequence for notions at the centre of power analysis, such as the concept of ideology. Writers who have developed post-structuralist ideas in the direction of a critique of ideology are Ernesto Laclau (both individually and with Chantal Mouffe: e.g. Laclau and Mouffe 1985) and Goran Therborn (1980). However, Laclau and Mouffe (1985) distance themselves from Marxist structuralism by much greater reference to discursive post-structuralism than Therborn (1980).

FROM STRUCTURAL IDEOLOGY TO POST-STRUCTURALIST HEGEMONY IN LACLAU AND MOUFFE

The discourse of sovereign power unravels at its outer limits to a subjectivist problematic with its possible terminus in a conception of dominant ideology, one of two termini identified by Laclau (1983a; 1983b; 1980) with respect to the classical Marxist approaches to ideology. With Foucault, he opposes the coupling of ideology/truth; the attribution of being subject to ideology, and the economic determination of formulations of ideology. Consequently, for Laclau, neither the notion of ideology as a distinct level of the social totality nor as false consciousness is plausible in a post-structuralist universe. Both of these approaches are deemed unacceptable by Laclau in that they are ultimately grounded in an essentialist conception of society and social agency. The former approach requires a conception of society as an 'intelligible totality', in effect a classical Marxist base/super-structure model. Here the totality operates as an underlying principle of intelligibility through which social order can be recognized in the empirical variations on the surface of society. Against this version, Laclau insists on the

> *Infinitude of the social*, that is that... any structural system is limited, that it is always sur-rounded by an 'excess of meaning' which it is unable to master and that, consequently, 'society' as a unitary and intelligible object... is an impossibility. (Laclau 1983a: 22)

In place of society as a fixed system of positions and positionalities, Laclau argues that the social must be identified with the infinite play of differences, in effect through discourse:

> By 'discursive' I do not mean that which refers to 'text' narrowly defined, but to the ensem-ble of the phenomena in and through which social production of meaning takes place, an ensemble which constitutes a society as such. The discursive is not, therefore, being conceived as a level or even a dimension of the social, but rather as being co-extensive with the social as such. (Laclau 1980: 87)

Of course, the matter cannot rest here because the social, as an infinite play of differences, is subject to hegemonic principles in which the discursive elements are forever articulated in determinate, albeit unstable and transitory, ways. However, since these forms of determina-tion cannot be established in an essentialist a priori fashion, the base/superstructure division and the conception of ideology as a necessary level in the totality both fall.

The conception of ideology as false consciousness rests on a similar essentialism. The category of false consciousness is tenable only if the actor has a fixed and true identity which he/she is capable of recognizing, generally, as a consequence of his/her 'true inter-ests'. For Laclau, such a conception of social agency has had to be abandoned with the realization that

> any social subject is essentially decentered, that his/her identity is nothing but the unsta-ble articulation of constantly changing positionalities... But if any social agent is a decen-tered subject... in what sense can we say that subjects misrecognize themselves?

The theoretical ground that made sense of the concept of 'false consciousness' has evidently dissolved. (Laclau 1983a: 22)

The break with essentialism means that a concept of ideology can be retained only by 'inverting' its traditional content. Ideology would consist not of the misrecognition of a fixed positive essence but rather the opposite, the refusal to recognize the always unstable, articulated character of a social form: 'The ideological would consist of those discursive forms through which a society tries to institute itself as such on the basis of closure, of the fixation of meaning, of the non-recognition of the infinite play of differences' (Laclau 1983a: 24).

On this basis of identifying the ideological with the fixity of meaning, Laclau and Mouffe (1985) were subsequently to dismiss almost the entire Marxist tradition as ideologically essentialist: not without repercussions in terms of a fine and spirited display of polemic, vitriol and defence by Geras (1987). (See Laclau and Mouffe's [1987] more measured rejoinder, as well as Mouzelis' [1988] equally measured critique.) The conclusions reached by Laclau and Mouffe (1985: 112) are noteworthy: politics is about the articulation of meanings in forms which are only ever partially fixed. It is this which constitutes hegemony. Meaning can never be finally fixed, according to post-structuralist emphases on the relational quality of meaning, because meaning is relational and so it can never be wholly stabilized. In consequence, the impossibility of an ultimate fixity of meaning implies that there have to be partial fixations; otherwise, the very flow of differences would be impossible. Even in order to differ, to subvert meaning, there has to be a meaning.

One may acknowledge the advance made by this revisionist critique, but only to a point. In common with post-structuralism, it produces a contingent politics of articulation in opposition to the determinate certainties of classical Marxism. However, too many key concepts are left prematurely redundant by this dichotomous construction for it to be a viable alternative choice. A sociological framework is required in which neither the indetermination of the free-floating signifier nor the determination of the privileged economic subject holds sway. While recognizing the elements of contingency introduced by discursive analysis, this requires theorization in terms that analytically postulate strategic contingency, albeit not in the time-honoured fashion of materialist dialectics.

One may usefully commence by endorsing Stuart Hall's (1983) remarks on the discourse-theoretical construction of ideology and politics. Hall argues that the revisionist approach has, in effect, led to the abandonment of any concern with ideology as a process in political struggle. In place of the problematic notion of ideologies rigidly attached to specific classes, we now have, in his view, a construction which is just as limited because ideologies 'float' as disembodied discourses:

> The image of great, immovable class battalions heaving their ascribed ideological lug-
> gage about the field of struggle... is replaced here by an infinity of subtle variations
> through which the elements of a discourse appear spontaneously to combine and recom-
> bine with each other, without material constraints of any kind other than that provided by
> the discursive operations themselves. (Hall 1983: 79)

Hall develops this issue by skilfully exploiting the 'linguistic' dimension to the revisionist critique for materialist ends. The pitfalls inherent in an essentialist proposition, that
ideologies simply express an economic content, can be avoided by realizing that it is language which acts as the medium for ideological generation and transformation:

> In language the same social relation can be *differently* represented and construed. And
> this is so... because language by its nature is *not fixed* in a one to one relation to its refer-
> ent but is 'multi-referential': it can construct different meanings around what is apparently
> the same social relation or phenomenon. (Hall 1983: 71)

The circuits of capitalist production, for example, can be represented in a variety
of discourses. There are the vulgar 'apologetics' for capitalism with their 'spontaneous' or common-sense understandings; there is the discourse of political economy
in Smith and Ricardo and, of course, in Marx (1976). Much of *Capital*'s theoretical
content is taken up with exploring the limitations and inadequacies of the first two
discourses. 'Vulgar economy' dwells only on the 'phenomenal forms' or 'outward
appearances'; the task of science is to grasp the real relations. Such formulations occur
many times throughout the work.

Marx's achievement was to spell out the way in which the various discourses of capitalist production and exchange can be simultaneously real and illusory: real in the sense
that they do depict details of the actual lived experience of actors selling labour power
in commodity-producing societies; illusory in the sense that the same discourses also
systematically exclude alternative understandings of these circuits. If this is the case then
it is possible for a materialist account of ideology to remain compatible with the recent
theoretical 'deconstructions'. The issue, in short, is not the relation between 'true' and
'false' consciousness but is the mechanisms whereby a certain positioning of agents as
being this, that or the other 'consciousness' take place. As Hall (1983) elaborates:

> The same process – capitalist production and exchange – can be expressed within a dif-
> ferent ideological framework, by the use of different 'systems of representation'. There is
> the discourse of 'the market', the discourse of 'production', the discourse of 'the circuits':
> each produces a different definition of the system. Each also locates us differently – as
> worker, capitalist, wage worker, wage slave, producer, consumer, etc... All these inscrip-
> tions have effects which are real. They make a material difference, since how we act in
> certain situations depends on what our definitions of the situation are. (Hall 1983: 77)

The nature of identity is thus, to put it crisply, contingent upon discursive practices. Persons, as agents engaged in struggle, will strain over that which is constituted as arguable, according to the conditions of particular discursive processes, and will formulate their interests accordingly. It cannot be maintained that these interests are formulated outside the conditions of particular discursive practices and struggles, which a Marxian structuralist definition would seem to imply. In this view, class struggle is prioritized; other struggles might exist but they are merely contingent. This view not only over-determines class and underconceptualizes other sources of struggle over identity but also excludes other modes of interest representation.

As we have seen, Hindess (1982; also see 1986) has argued that unless interests figure as actors' reasons for acting, where that action has consequences, then the concept of interests is sociologically unsustainable. In other words, interests feature as elements of discursive availability. These stand in relations of articulation with those consequences held to flow from them discursively. As Laclau and Mouffe (1985: 113) put it, this 'practice of articulation… consists in the construction of nodal points which partially fix meaning'. Such fixity can never be immutable in the face of the indexicality of all expression, as Garfinkel (1967) has established. Interests arise from what is discursively available.

Interests, as reasons for action, are not necessarily fixed by the subject: there may be discursively available reasons for action other than those that a given subject articulates in a discourse. If reasons for action are situationally available as discursive vocabularies for accounting-for-action, a discussion of interests as reasons for action can focus on the structurally legitimate and socially available discursive frameworks in particular situations. These will be an effect of past struggles in which the 'interests' of certain forms of interest representation have been constituted in the constraints and pressures on discursive availability. Actors' reasons for action may themselves represent interests. Such reasons are thus effectively already the representation of some other interests besides those of the actors.

RADICAL CONCEPTIONS OF POWER COMPARED

One way of clearly seeing the theoretically radical implications of the positions advanced by Foucault and Laclau and Mouffe is to contrast them with Lukes' explicitly self-avowed 'radical view', which was expressed in the third dimension (Table 7.1).

The focus of analysis in both Laclau and Mouffe (1985) and Foucault (1977) differs markedly from Lukes' (1974) 'radical view'. Table 7.1 is designed to represent these differences as well as to demonstrate the difference in emphasis between the two types of post-structuralism which Foucault and Laclau and Mouffe appear to provide. Each view is developed out of a critique of some particular definition of the mainstream of analysis.

Table 7.1   Radical conceptions of power

Focus of analysis	Lukes	Foucault	Laclau and Mouffe
Critique of:	behaviouralism in political science	concepts of 'sovereign power' and their concern with ideology and the state	essentialism in Marxist analyses
Favoured objects of analysis:	thought control as the hegemonic third dimension of power	disciplinary practices for producing obedient bodies	discursive articulations of meaning and their representation in fixed practices
Key concepts:	hegemony and responsibility	surveillance and embodiment	necessary nodal points
Empirical agenda focuses on:	responsible individuals whose interests benefit from extant states of affairs	points of resistance in fields of force	the 'fixity' of the social field in discursive forms
Type of analysis:	an ethics of power	a micropolitics of power	a semiotics of power

Indeed, the nature of the objects of critique sets up the preconditions for the distinctive contribution each makes. For Lukes, the primary object of critique is the behaviouralism which Dahl foregrounded as the proper model for political science. The model was so seductive that even adversaries such as Bachrach and Baratz (1970) were implicated in it, according to Lukes' critique. Because of this, a third dimension of power has to be opened up at a deeper level of analysis than their second face of power. Behaviouralism must be thoroughly routed in order to uncover 'thought control' in operation and to identify those individuals who are responsible for it. For Foucault the conceptions of power which have to be opposed and contradicted are those which are equally at home in both classical political theory and Marxist analysis. These are identified as a view of 'sovereign power'. In classical theory this view is evident in a conception of power which allies its exercise far too closely to the will of the sovereign. In Marxism Foucault sees this emphasis as reproduced in the concern not with the ruling monarch but with the ruling class, the ruling state and the ruling ideology. It is to a diluted conception of the latter, with an endorsement of the concept of hegemony, that Lukes has recourse. Foucault, by renouncing this myopic obsession with an originary centre of power, seeks to free us to see power at work in a great many diverse sites and practices, as well as alerting us to the dialectic of power and resistance. This play of power and resistance can occur far removed from the materiality of the state and its ideology. Against any liberal or Marxist ethics of power, Foucault opposes a descriptive concern with the micropolitics of power. Whether explicitly or not, this entails a commitment to a pluralist view of power.

Laclau and Mouffe (1985) have clearly been influenced by the pluralist implications of Foucault's analyses. They do not regard power as having a necessary centre any more than does Foucault. However, the object of their antagonism is almost wholly the Marxist tradition, to which they themselves claim to belong. It is in this tradition, in both its theory and its political practice, that they see the major obstacle to the socialist pluralism which they espouse. For them socialism must be about power, not so much about winning it or seizing it but about deploying it in ways that extend the range of popular freedoms rather than restricting them in the name of an insuperable orthodoxy. In their view, the central traditions of Marxist analysis have become such an orthodoxy, acting as barriers to the recognition of sources of power and oppression which are not easily catechized in the context of the state, capital and ideology as the political, economic and ideological expression of a base/superstructure model. Consequently, they are opposed to the whole discourse of 'real interests' which Lukes embraces. They condemn almost the whole of Marxism for the 'essentialism' of its analyses: the way in which it smuggles in ungrounded prime movers to explain phenomena, entities such as the class structure, the state, and so on. In a move which is in some ways reminiscent of the Frankfurt school of critical theory, albeit expressed through elements of post-structuralism, they choose to see power as existing neither in specific individuals (as Lukes does) nor in concrete practices (as Foucault does) but in the way in which agents and practices are articulated in a particular fixed ensemble of representations. There is only representation; there is no fixed, real, hidden or excluded term or dimension. To the extent that meanings become fixed or reified in certain forms, which then articulate particular practices, agents and relations, this fixity is power. Power is the apparent order of taken-for-granted categories of existence, as they are fixed and represented in a myriad discursive forms and practices. Power is neither ethical nor micropolitical: above all it is textual, semiotic, and inherent in the very possibility of textuality, meaning and signification in the social world. It is from the latter position that the model of 'circuits of power', to be developed in the next chapter, will derive much of its inspiration, although its actual theorization will draw on an eclectic range of sources. At its core, however, is the insight that the central feature of power consists in this fixing of the terrain for its own expression.

CONCLUSION

Some problems of indeterminacy and pure contingency with the Laclau and Mouffe (1985) framework have been identified in this chapter. Others have also criticized Laclau and Mouffe (1985) for not observing that certain forms of 'strategic' contingency do in fact fix nodal points of articulatory practice. Bocock (1986: 108–9) observes the materiality not only of money in the economy but also of law in the state. Each of these stabilizes, constitutes and connects a disparate set of subjects, produced through the practices of civil society, into meaningfully fixed and stable totalities of, for instance, employers and employees, the lawful and the lawless, law enforcers and law breakers. Moreover, each of these practices is not merely discursive but has a high degree of materiality to it, which is constituted in offices, factories, shops, courts, prisons, and so on. On these points both Habermas and Parsons would agree: each would regard the law and money as 'circulatory media'. Habermas (1984) is of particular interest in his view of the law. He regards the law as the rationalized development of substantive culture and ethics, rather than as a functional necessity of the state. From the Middle Ages onwards, its rationalization is such that it develops an ever greater relative autonomy vis à vis sovereign will and power. It becomes, in Parsons' terms, ever more universalistic and decreasingly particularistic in its principles, as elements of tradition, religious belief and custom are diminished by the conscious reflections of juridical authorities. This constitutes what Foucault (1977) discusses as the new regulatory power of judgement. The push towards universalism and internal consistency is precisely what gives law its 'fixity' as an articulatory practice. Habermas' views tie in with the findings of recent historical scholarship (Macfarlane 1988) on why England became the first 'capitalist revolution'. (The term, incidentally, is shared by both Berger [1987] and Baechler [1975].) The argument suggests that it was the emergence of a single legal-national code (fixed in a stable space defined in national-geographic terms), together with the low level of taxes that this national stability allowed, which was decisive in constituting 'the cradle of capitalism' (Macfarlane 1988). This ties in with Mann's (1980) research on the record of national accounts which suggests that warfare was the major lever on the ratchet of tax collection. The fixing of the nodal points capable of creating these pathways to modernity would be a legitimate concern of a sociology of power.

The Laclau and Mouffe (1985) thesis of unstable articulatory practice evidently requires revision. The brief historical digression serves to make this clear. Some nodal points are capable of being fixed in remarkably stable ways when viewed historically. It ought to be possible to explain how such an essential nodality as the state's construction of rationalized law came to be fixed. Such a marriage between a conceptualization derived from some elements of post-structural critique and historical interpretation would be somewhat unusual, but the novelty of the exercise ought not to be sufficient reason for excluding it. That a liaison may be unusual is no reason for denying its consummation. Consequently, following Macfarlane's (1988) lead, the penultimate chapter of this book will explore the formation of the modern constitutional and legal state. It will do so by using a formal model of 'circuits of power' which will first be developed in chapter eight.

The key aspect of Laclau and Mouffe's (1985) work for the argument of the next chapter is the notion of 'nodal points' of discourse. This conception can be reached through a route other than the labyrinths of 'post-Marxist' and 'post-structuralist' debate which have been sketched here but there are certain advantages in having used this route. By doing so, the limitations of the route, leading from a one-dimensional concept of power via two faces to three dimensions, are apparent. The terminus of this particular maze is always the sovereign power of ideology and hegemony: the ultimate prohibition which forbids the subjects' recognition of the awesome power that subordinates them and which leads them to feel free as it entraps them.

Another route is via the sociology of science. In work done in that area by Michel Callon (1986) and various colleagues, the notion of 'obligatory passage points', a conception indistinguishable from that of necessary nodal points, becomes a powerful empirical tool. This tool will be wielded in the construction of an analysis which avoids the pitfalls of dialectics, dimensions and dualities of power, with their attendant traps of 'real interests', 'hegemony', and so on. In doing so, the revisions to the concept of power which were begun in this chapter will be continued. However, they will not lead in the direction of those earlier extensionary revisions made by Bachrach and Baratz, Lukes and others. The revisions which were previously encountered sought to extend episodic derivations from a sovereign concept of power. They functioned by extension of the basic concept in order to incorporate more 'radical' notions of interests and ideology and to show the dialectic or duality of power and structure. In this chapter the ontological limitations of these subjectivist treatments have been avoided through developing a 'post-structuralist' concern with power. At the focus of this concern has been an argument which established the practical decline of the conditions that could sustain sovereign power. However, the decline of sovereign power in the material world was not accompanied by a decline in the fortunes of sovereign conceptions of power within the formal academic community dedicated to the study of power. Here the discursive constituents of sovereign conceptions became the normal focus of analytical concern. At the same time, new forms of disciplinary power were emergent, inexplicable to the eye trained in the expression only of episodic derivations of sovereign power. Indeed, it is through the perspective of approaches deriving from organization theory and of historians of administrative rationalities that these newer forms of power become most evident.

What would the consequences be of the execution of the concept of sovereign power which Foucault calls for? We can speculate first on what would be dispatched. The important thing, of course, is not the literal execution of the sovereign but the negation of that concept of sovereign power which has held conceptualization in its sway for so long. Originally fixed in terms of mechanical metaphors, it is these metaphors which have held imaginations captive. For them, or at least their over-extension into places and concerns for which they are ill-designed, the axe or guillotine would be sharpened. What example would be set by such a metaphorical execution? One might anticipate a greater modesty in the ease with which a single concept of power could be extemporized for all purposes. Similarly, perhaps in consequence of the example of the sudden demise of sovereign power, there might in future be somewhat more rectitude and less absolutism in the determination of what others' real interests might be; no more interminable interrogation of the truth of those interests which others express; an abandonment of episodic, agency, causal, mechanical conceptions of power as if they were the whole of power. No more would one anticipate a metaphorical fixation on the ruler of a mechanical universe of obedient subjects. There would be no more metaphorical billiard balls biffing and banging into each other; no more cogs, flywheels, gears, levers and pulleys. There would be an end to the clumsy and obvious machinery of a bygone age in which the scientist was a mechanic, whose inspection of the moving and connected parts was sufficient to establish linkages. There would be no more mechanicalism, extended and stretched to illuminate those dark dialectical corners where three-dimensional objects might lurk or in which might be found those dualistic structures in which their agency might be trapped. The argument of this book thus far is that these frameworks may be beyond reasonable repair. The next chapter proposes an alternative framework, one which eschews the merely mechanical metaphors of the past in order also to embrace an imagery more redolent of the post-modern electronic age, an imagery suggested by its representation in a form which crystallized as a circuit diagram: circuits of power.

8
CIRCUITS OF POWER: A FRAMEWORK FOR ANALYSIS

INTRODUCTION

The episodic agency or, as Lukes (1974) calls it, one-dimensional view of power derives from those premises of sovereign power first clearly articulated by Hobbes. Against the current of recent scholarship, this book has not sought to extend the agency and episodic concept beyond its location in intermittent exercise of power. It has not, for example, sought to extend it to the shaping of consciousness, interests or ideology. In this respect one would see no fundamental problems with a revised version of an episodic, agency concept: revised, that is, to accommodate the realist critique of the regularity principle, and to incorporate some account of the necessary standing conditions for the realization of causal powers, in line with arguments raised and discussed in Harré and Madden (1975) and Benton (1981).

Restricted to its appropriate context of analysis and reformulated accordingly, there is much to recommend the careful analysis of causal power, in agency terms, of particular episodes. Where it has been over-extended into realms where alleged 'thought control' becomes a matter of serious concern, there is little to recommend it at all. It is not easily and unproblematically extended by hitching it to either moral relativism or absolutism, nor can it be so reduced to the constitutive agency of an ontologically instantiating human being.

Does this mean that there is no relation between power and structure? On the contrary, there are evident relations but they are neither of intentional agency nor of objective interests. Moreover, one also has to withstand any ontological impulse to restrict the category of agency only to human beings. In the terms of this book, agency is not a generic term for people: it may well often refer to collective forms of decision-making, such as organization. In fact, the terms organization and agency are necessarily coupled. Agency is entailed in most definitions of organization, which usually refer to purposeful goal-oriented action. From the perspective of this book, all forms of agency will be an achievement of control produced by discipline. Consistency, coherence and memory of self as such are not given but learned and accomplished. The agency of a person is no less an achievement of discipline than is that of an organization. It would be a naïve view of the transparency of language and the given nature of subjectivity, rooted in either a humanism of unique authenticity or a biologism of genus determination, which would insist otherwise.

Some areas of enquiry in the human and social sciences have been more aware of the achieved nature of agency than have others. In part this is because of the politics which surround the constitution of certain types of agency in certain ways. Wherever certain ascribed identities are premised on some aspect or other of the constitutive properties of an agent, such as ethnicity, sexuality or gender, then an important part of the politics of resistance by a group to the ascription of their identity will be the struggle to break free from the putative 'fixing' of a given identity ascription. Feminist post-structuralism, for evident reasons regarding the type of agency that has often been constituted as the normally feminine, is particularly aware of the 'achieved' nature of agency:

> If language is the site where meaningful experience is constituted, then language also determines how we perceive possibilities of change. Language in this sense consists of a range of discourses which offer different versions of the meaning of social relations and their effects on the individual. (Weedon 1987: 86)

While readers may accept the centrality of language with respect to a conception of agency which is still tied to that of individuals, what of the claim that agency may well be organizational? The claim has been implicit throughout this book and astute readers will recognize that the book has been marked by a certain reluctance to privilege people as the only forms of agency. Given the particular stress on organization which will characterize this chapter, this is an appropriate point at which to make this anti-subjectivist stress on agency wholly explicable. Not all agents are human actors. Agency may be vested in non-human entities as diverse as machines, germs, animals and natural disasters. These, and more especially organizations, may be agencies under the appropriate conditions. It will be argued that organization may constitute a form of collective agency and that there is no reason to make this a second-rate form of agency compared to that of the problematic human subject. Where organization achieves agency it is an accomplishment, just as it is for the individual but more so, because it involves the stabilization of power relations across an organizational field of action, and thus between many subjectivities, rather than simply within one embodied locus of subjectivities. Once more this is recognized in the ordinary language of organization theory. The common definition of organizations as formal and purposeful goal-oriented entities recognizes the contingent nature of this accomplishment. Such definitions are frequently problematic because they are constructed in such a way as to assume this purposefulness. Rationality is often conceived to be a constitutive feature of organizations. As should be clear, not only to radical critics, this purposeful organizational agency must in the first instance depend on the subordination of the constitutive individual parts of the organization (see Clegg 1975 and Clegg and Dunkerley 1980, especially chapter twelve). It is the ever variable achievement of this subordination (the variability of which will regularly be marked by a dialectic of power and resistance) which stands at the centre of any collective organizational agency. The implication of power with the dialectic of resistance resides in the realist view that power necessarily involves reciprocity because it is always constituted within a relational universe of meaning.

POWER IN ORGANIZATIONS

Power in organizations must concern the hierarchical structure of offices and their relation to each other, in the classical Weberian sense. Implicitly, this may be considered to be a concern with 'legitimate power'. However, in addition to this perspective, the literature of organizations has also highlighted what Thompson (1956: 290) termed 'illegitimate power'. In Weberian syntax one might think of this as a perturbation from and within the 'structure of dominancy' (Weber 1978): the formal, legitimated authority structure of hierarchical power, stabilized on distinct configurations of episodic power. Such perturbations need not necessarily represent a challenge to this structure but may instead be purely local struggles for autonomy and control, which pose no threat to the 'structure' *per se*. On empirically rare occasions, however, they might be such a challenge.

The dichotomy of the concepts of 'power' and 'authority' around the axis of legitimacy became constitutive of the 'contingencies' and 'resource dependence' problematic of power in organizations. Stages in the development of this have been traced elsewhere (Clegg 1977). Subsequently, in this tradition, a great deal of the discussion of the concept of power has been reserved for exercises of discretion by organization members which are not sanctioned by the members' position in the formal structure. Such exercises are premised on an illegitimate or informal use of resource control, access to which is given by the members' place in the organizational division of labour.

Nowhere is this tendency in the literature developed to a more refined pitch than in Mintzberg's (1983) 'System of Politics'. It can be encapsulated in the phrase 'insiders are not always... obedient' (Mintzberg 1983: 171). In Mintzberg's 'systemic' view of organizational life, politics is explicitly defined against the 'Systems' of 'Authority', 'Ideology' and 'Expertise'. Note, before proceeding further, that by creating a 'System of Politics' we can effectively evacuate its key concept, 'power', from the constitution of ideology, authority and expertise. In fact, the 'System of Politics' becomes the residual system which makes the other formal systems work in informal practice:

> Distilled to its essence, therefore, politics refers to individual or group behaviour that is informal, ostensibly parochial, typically divisive and, above all, in the technical sense, illegitimate – sanctioned neither by formal authority, accepted ideology, nor certified expertise (though it may exploit any one of those). (Mintzberg 1983: 172: emphasis removed)

The political nature of the 'structure of dominancy' (or 'Systems' of 'Authority', 'Ideology' and 'Expertise' as structurally sedimented phenomena which are themselves saturated and imbued with power) is not a perspective which is sharply observed in much of the literature of organizations (a point made at length elsewhere: Clegg 1975; 1977; 1979; Clegg and Dunkerley 1980), despite claims to the contrary (Donaldson 1985). In fact, a concern with the exercise of power from within a given structure of dominancy is not the same thing as a concern with mechanisms of dominance, strategies of power and regimes of control. The central concern of organization theories of power has been in a restricted conception of 'politics' which is premised on discretionary control of strategic contingencies or resource dependencies (Pfeffer 1981). Regarded in this way, power is a 'capacity' premised on resource control. It is also tautological. How is power to be recognized independently of resource dependency? Resource dependency of X upon Y is the function of Y's power. Equally, Y's independence is the function of X's dependence upon Y, given the previous X-Y relationship. The cause of power is resource dependency. At the same time, the consequence of resource dependency is equivalent to its cause. Hence notions of cause and consequence are meaningless in such formulae. Part of the problem is the pervasive tendency to think of power as a thing without considering that it must also be a property of relations.

MECHANISMS OF POWER: DISCIPLINARY PRACTICES OF SURVEILLANCE

Mintzberg's (1983) stress on 'obedience' is central to an analysis of the production of power in organizations, an insight which is shared by major precursors such as Weber (1978) and Etzioni (1961), which was subsequently deployed by Hamilton and Biggart (1985) in terms complementary to those under development here. Moreover, it is a focus which has received historical endorsement through not only the corpus of Weberian research (Matheson 1987) but also that recent and related work (encountered in the previous chapter) on the origins of disciplined obedience in monastic organizations. (Not only Kieser (1987) but also Assad (1987) is useful here.) A central theme of the latter's research stresses the connection between discipline and organizational virtue.

In contemporary and secular terms the latter may be conceptualized as the organizational achievement of that good order which displays the inward appreciation and enactment of one's duty as a member.

The mechanisms of this organizational achievement have come to be termed 'disciplinary practices'. The concept of 'disciplinary practice' derives, as we have seen, from Foucault (1977) but is implicit in Weber (1978). It is meant to render those micro-techniques of power which inscribe and normalize not only individuals but also collective, organized bodies. For instance, any comparative application of performance data or other forms of surveillance would capture the sense of this. Surveillance, whether personal, technical, bureaucratic or legal, is the central issue. Its types may range through forms of, for instance, supervision, routinization, formalization, mechanization and legislation Increasingly, these are rendered digitally. Multi-directional relations of 'veillance' emerge that constitute diverse relations between those watching and those being watched (Zorina et al., 2021). For instance, both digital and other forms of veillance can strive to manage the body, soul and commitment of those under veillance. As developed by Zorina et al. (2021), the *body* as an object of political economy is extended by IT tools enabling biometric identification, monitoring of biohealth markers such as blood pressure and heart rate, as well as closed-circuit television (CCTV) operation. Insight into the *soul* of the employee can be gained by company monitoring of employees' social media posts and the blogosphere. The *commitment* of those watched is gauged in non-standardized situations, such as creative tasks, independent and spontaneous actions, or activities with high complexity or communication requirements. Digitally performing HR tests devised to insure the organization against claims of sexual harassment, health and safety breaches, and other sources of litigation would be examples of attempts to control commitment, as organization members must consent to do these periodic tests.

These examples represent the extension of direct, personal supervisory control into notions of individual space which previously were private. However, surveillance is not simply about such direct control. It may range from cultural practices of moral endorsement, enablement and suasion to more formalized technical knowledge. At one particular level of application, these can include the use of digital technologies such as computer monitoring of keyboard output and efficiency or low cost drug-testing systems (Schachter 1987: 11). At another, more general level, one may be dealing with the development of disciplines of knowledge shaped almost wholly by the 'disciplinary gaze' of surveillance. Foucault (1977) suggests that this was the case in much nineteenth-century social science, particularly branches of social welfare, statistics and administration. Organizationally, the twentieth-century development of the personnel function, under the 'human relations' guidance of Mayo (1975) has had a similar tutelary role with respect to organizationally dependent members (see Clegg 1979; Clegg et al., 2006). By means of such mechanisms, individuals or bodies collectively, as well as abstract properties of goods and services, may be discriminated and categorized through diverse and localized tactics of ratiocination, which 'in their specificity of time, place, aims and objectives reinforce and borrow from each other to form an overall anonymous strategy of discipline' (Girdwood 1987: 22). At the more general level of discipline, this will form organizations into discursive locales of competing calculations. Each disciplinary practice, in its applications, will calculate organizational rationality from distinct auspices of power and knowledge. From such a potentially discursive babel, any formally efficient organization will normally attempt to construct the architectonic of some overall strategic practices of discipline. A storehouse of disciplinary techniques is available for organizations to achieve this aim. Not only are there the services of those many agencies who specialize in selling specific disciplinary techniques on a consultancy, advisory or sub-contracting basis but also the enduring sediments of previous practice which have been selectively structured into the rules of organization control (Clegg 1981). Such practices are capable of quite precise targeting within organizations. They are also buttressed by quite generalized but no less effective sanctions which are available as a result of the career structure and movement through it. In addition, there are 'the files', today digital, the repository of all that is formally recorded and known concerning an agent or agency, of whose potency as a device Weber (1978) was only too well aware; there are also the mechanisms of a 'span of control', of hierarchy, of divisional and departmental cleavage, and so on (see Barnes 1988: 117). Such practices are not simply constraining: they do punish and forbid but more especially they also endorse and enable obedient wills and constitute organizationally approved forms of creativity and productivity through a process both transitive (via authoritative externalities such as rules, superiors, etc.) and intransitive (via the acquisition of organizationally proper conduct by the member).

The transitive element in the production of disciplined obedience has long been the central focus of organization theory, as evidenced in the classical concern with the formal structure of organization, which is taken as a literal representation of what the organization's 'real' structure is. Doubtless, such representations do have a limited heuristic value when used by researchers. However, in practice, authoritative structures rarely if ever conform to their depiction in the organizational programme. The reasons for this are many: things change imperceptibly over time in ways which are not captured by a static idealization; organizational membership changes and so particularly competent 'power-players' may make more out of a position than a less competent predecessor, and so on. However, there is a more fundamental reason than these conjunctural events for the inadequacy of these depictions of the formal structure of the organization. Recalcitrance is implicit in the intransitive processes which constitute organizational disciplinary practices in an hierarchical field.

Any superordinate member of a complex organization will be just one relay in a complex flow of authority up, down and across organization hierarchies. Ideally, in any rationalistic view held by organization elites, planners and seemingly many theorists, such relays should be without resistance, offering no impedance whatsoever, no 'problem of obedience'. Rarely, if ever, will this be the case, as organization researchers have long known (Coch and French 1948). Resistance, to continue the metaphor, will tend to be pervasive. Authorities, to use the term as a plural noun, will rarely if ever be passive and resistance-free relays, as may be explained by appreciating the relationship between organization and agency.

ORGANIZATION AND AGENCY

Central to this relationship is the realization that the incorporation of agencies within organizations is normally secured on the basis of contract but that such contracts are rarely the reciprocal, conflict-free and equal exchanges that are axiomized in 'transaction cost theory' (Williamson 1981; also see 1985). Such axioms are profoundly unrealistic and, indeed, ill-conceived. One aspect of contracts, namely the resources that empower employees (e.g. the acquisition of specific skills and knowledge; collective organization; ownership of physical assets), is stressed as against the resources that empower employers (notably, ownership of the means and outcome of production, the support of the state and the legal system, and managerial prerogative within organizations). The overall lack of realism and the subsequent ill-conception of organizational reality in the 'transactions' framework is a result of concept construction which excludes and elides a central axiom of the more radical perspectives: organization means control.

Such control is never total, of course: indeed, in some formulations, the contradictions inherent in the evolution of regimes of control explain its development (Clegg and Dunkerley 1980). Control can never be totally secured, in part because of agency. It will be open to erosion and undercutting by the active, embodied agency of those people who are its object: the labour power of the organization. (Discipline is the major qualifying variable here.) To consider these people as 'labour power' as well as, or in opposition to, considering them as 'members' immediately portrays them not only as Durkheimian dwellers in an idealized moral community but also as labourers toiling to preserve their 'species-being' (resisting alienation), in Marx's metaphor. However, the locus of agency against organization is not only in Marx's view of the active, embodied person resisting the wasting of his/ her creative powers; it is also implicit in Durkheim's moral community. What is regarded as sacred and as profane depends utterly on relations of meaning. (Membership is the major qualifying variable here.) Such relations of meaning are as resistant to total control as are relations of production. This much has been clear ever since Saussure's (1974) project sowed the seeds for a de-coupling of any necessary relationship between the signified and the sign. Resistance to any attempt which seeks to freeze meaning in any specific regulation of it will always be intrinsic to the nature of language as a moral community. In the terms of Durkheim's heirs to the study of the moral order, ethnomethodology, indexicality may be shown to be present in even the most mundane utterance (Garfinkel 1967).

The implications for organizations of this double focus on the relations of meaning and the relations of production are evident. Organization encounters agency in at least two forms which have been prototypical for subsequent organization theory: the person as an agent of signification, in social action theory (Silverman 1970), and the person as an agent of production, in radical theory (Clegg and Dunkerley 1980). The separation of these concerns was an unfortunate aspect of earlier theoretical developments. It is important not to focus one-sidedly on conditions of organization participation. To do so is to resist the evident fact that the member of an organization is simultaneously and ineradicably a discursive subject, a contractual subject, and an embodied subject. Both meaning and body, fused in the person, are capacities for resisting the encroachment of organization control on individuals' discursive play and their ability to work. Consequently employers face at least three sources of resistance, by virtue of their employees having both discursive and bodily capacities, which require some disciplining if contractual control is to be achieved.

The central institution which rational employers will use to try to govern both relations of meaning and relations of production will be the contractual relation. In sociology, such contractual relations have been broadly conceived in terms of both the non-contractual elements of trust and power vested by employers and the discretion and autonomy gained by employees (Fox 1974). The impact of contractual relations is not only experienced by employees at the point of initial sale of their labour power: it is evident that contracting organizations frame the assumptions that structure both labour's purchase and its deployment, as Fox (1974) elaborates. This deployment is subject to contest as well as control, in terms of the variable conditions of autonomy and subordination which can be negotiated within the framework of the contract and its everyday constitution in the work routines of the organization. These will vary with the degrees of control that people have. Organizations are staffed by people who may be differentiated in terms of their variable control of methods of production, as well as through dichotomous categories of ownership and non-ownership of means of production. Inscribed in the former are the technical relations of production, embedded in diverse occupational identities. The latter constitutes the key social relations of capitalist modernity: those of production, of property, of ownership and control (Clegg and Dunkerley 1980; Clegg et al. 1986). Through this variable control are established variable abstract possibilities for interest representation, specified in terms of the 'rules of the game'.

Possible interests are seen at their most abstract in various models of capitalist production and reproduction, such as those presented by Harvey (1982). Whether or not such conceptions of interests are available as resources which people in organizations will use will depend upon how they represent what they take to be reality. Central to this will be struggles for the 'hearts and minds' of employees by competing representations which are constituted through agencies such as political parties, the various organs of the state, popular discourse in the media, employers' federations or trade unions. The comparative conditions of these struggles, even within the OECD countries, will vary enormously. For instance, only 10.1 percent of the United States labour force are presently trade union members, and the percentage is in decline. At the other extreme, about 68 percent of Swedish employees are trade union members and the numbers have been stable for some time. The explanation for these massive comparative differences in the political economy of organization membership has been addressed in considerable detail elsewhere (see Clegg et al. 1986) and need not be repeated here. It is sufficient to note that such structural differences of context will have a major effect on the availability or not of discursive formulations of membership conditions of organizations in terms of categories of 'interests'. 'Interests' are a variable discursive formulation. They are far more likely to be encountered in collective, rather than individual terms, where there are successful conditions for political class struggle. These will be achieved more readily by the labour movement in an ascendant social democracy than in its defeat or decline. The latter is typical of economic liberalism and its political expression. Indeed, the designation 'liberal' or 'market' democracy is meant precisely as the opposite form of political economy to that known as 'social democracy'.

In as much as conceptions of interest representation depict the arena of organizational life in terms of the leitmotif of 'class' and its social relations, they will be attuned to the general conditions of economic domination and subordination in organizations as theorists of the left from Marx onwards have defined them (see, for instance, Carchedi's [1987: 100] identification of these conditions). No necessity attaches to self-recognition in these general terms of class. In some circumstances, such as those which seem to prevail in much of the United States, self-recognition in class terms may well be much weaker than elsewhere. Wright (1985) makes this clear in his comparison of the United States and Sweden as archetypal liberal and social democracies respectively. General conditions will tend to be at their most pervasive as they impact upon the employment contract and its tacit conditions and informal 'effort bargains' (Baldamus 1961). These are not only located at the point of production, as Burawoy (1985) demonstrates, but they are also evident in their reproduction of the movements of the broader political economy which contextualizes them (Clegg et al. 1986). General conditions of economic domination are also overlain in particular cases by forms of domination endured by specific groups of people (Carchedi 1987). While this domination may be experienced in economic terms, as well as in terms of more general discrimination, it derives from criteria which are located outside the economy. Such discrimination is organized on the basis of salient aspects of social identity.

People are neither merely labour power nor signifiers of meaning. Necessarily they are subjects of both and subjected to both, signified as labour power and as the embodiment of differential and related social identities. Available identities are premised on the salience of issues such as ethnicity, gender, age, and phenomena which find expression in culture, which are distinct and hierarchized 'styles of life' (Weber 1978) that display elaborated 'positional goods' (Hirsch 1978) and 'cultural capital' (Bourdieu 1984). Together these form relational complexes which function as major limits on the discretion of organization action. Discretion may be thought of in terms of who may do what, how, where, when and in which ways to whatever objects or agencies. Customary and sometimes legally specific identities will be prescribed or proscribed for certain forms of practice. Embodied identities will be salient only inasmuch as they are socially recognized and organization-ally consequent. Other forms of embodiment, for instance, hair colour, size, or physiog-nomy, may be salient aspects of either individual corporeality or organizational cognition but are less generally and strategically so, except in particular circumstances. One thinks, for instance, of stipulations in the armed forces and the police and fire services regarding weight, height, or even the presence of facial hair (only beards or clean shaven faces are allowed in the British Navy; moustaches are proscribed). Other instances might be found in more informal organization definitions of 'front stage' actors (Goffman 1959), such as news readers or receptionists. However, few forms of embodiment achieve the generality of, for instance, age, gender, sexuality, ethnicity, religiosity and disability as recognizably embodied bases which serve to locate practices for stratifying organization members: this is evidenced by their being the precise target of various anti-discrimination laws.

From the person's point of view, the employer/employee relationship is central, as this constitutes the context in which other forms of organized social relations come into con-sideration (not least those incorporated in the form and actions of unions and the labour movement and in the state and its definitions of citizenship). Other forms of identity may achieve organizational expression through the ownership/non-ownership issue, as well as through the variable control of methods of production which is vested in people who are defined, in terms of both the formal and informal requirements of organization context, as differentially skilled actors.

Organizations may be not only hierarchically authoritative structures of class domina-tion but also structures of patriarchal domination, ethnic domination, and so on. Clearly such matters are contingent: most existing organizations may be structures of gender, ethnic and class dominancy but not all organizations necessarily are. Both 'meritocracy' and 'socialist organization' may be possible, in principle. A given structure of authority or class domination may be filled without regard to other forms of discrimination or one may seek to abolish it (Carchedi 1987). However, the empirical limits of such an alterna-tive have to be conceptualized (Clegg and Higgins 1987).

Although the vast majority of organizations are structured around an hierarchical cali-bration and relation of diverse social identities, it is all too easy to argue that this is in some way functional for the reproduction of the central principle of organization. Thus, for example, some neo-Marxists (e.g. Clegg and Dunkerley 1980) propose that gender and class structuration are necessarily reproductive of capitalist control of organizational means of production. The argument is one of 'divide and rule'. However, one could just as plausibly counter with an equally general and functional argument, which is as 'pro' capi-talist as the other is 'anti'; that equality is best advanced by the embrace of that efficiency and rationality which serves to reduce all identities to those of the market, thus purging particularisms through the universal calculus of unfettered market signals. Neither argu-ment is satisfactory, precisely because of their *general* character and their reliance on a con-cept of an expressive principle. For such reasons they are an unfalsifiable premise of faith.

Organizations should not be conceptualized as the phenomenal expression of some essential inner principle such as economic exploitation or rationality. Organization, just as any other locus for the accomplishment of agency, is better seen as a locus of deci-sion and action (Hindess 1987). Organizations do things as a consequence of decisions to act in certain ways by certain other agents. Organizations also do things that are not a consequence of a decision so to act, if only because decisions are shaped by struggles around competing substantive objectives – what may be called diverse modes of rational-ity. One cannot explain the politics of all organizations in terms of general theories of their rationality. Organizational action is an indeterminate outcome of substantive strug-gles between different agencies: people who deploy different resources; people whose organizational identities will be shaped by the way in which disciplinary practices work through and on them, even in their use of such techniques; people who seek to control and decide the nature of organizational action and those many things to which they will routinely have recourse in their membership, work and struggles. Consequently, the interests of actors in organizations and the decisions that they make are necessarily con-tingent on various forms of organization calculation. Thus, organizational action cannot be the expression of some essential inner principle: claims to such principles as prime movers necessarily neglect the actual complex and contingent conditions under which organizational action occurs.

One can no more explain the politics of all organizations in terms of general theories of labour exploitation than in terms of their rationality. For one thing, too much that hinges on aspects of identity other than those of membership or exploitation is left unconsid-ered in so many such theories. In specific organizational contexts the general conditions of economic domination may not necessarily be the most apparent focus of such resist-ance or struggle. More specific loci of domination may be organizationally salient; after all, divisions of labour are embodied, gendered, departmentalized, hierarchized, spatially separated, and so on. All of these actualities may give rise to struggle and resistance, power and consent. However, not only issues of identity limit the applicability of such general theories. Another important point must be the realization that, in many complex organizations, the politics of control and discipline are unlikely to be oriented solely towards people. Consequently, control is less oriented to the direct labour process than to the issues of product quality, equipment utilization, inventory supply chain managment and strategies for competitive advantage (Clegg et al, 2022). General strategy perspectives may well be of more explanatory use in such contexts.

Contingency reigns, albeit with a hegemonic personal cast; that is, one can say with a degree of empirical exactness (Heath 1981) that it is apparent, as far as people in organizations are concerned, that certain male identities which are constituted in socially and economically privileged contexts will be routinely more strategically contingent for organizational decision-making, access and success in hierarchically arranged careers. Equally, feminist scholarship (see Calás, & Smircich 1996) indicates that female identity should, in the aggregate if not in individual cases, be routinely regarded as a strategic handicap. This is not to say that either class or gender will necessarily function this way: simply that past sociological observation suggests that it probably will. What is of most interest here, of course, is, first, identifying which national state, legal and organizational characteristics and practices will produce systematic variation in stratifying outcomes that are constructed in terms of such key markers of identity and, second, studying the organization cultures in which they find particular types of expression.

STRATEGIC AGENCY

Implicit in the view being developed here is a conception of organizations as locales in which negotiation, contestation and struggle between organizationally divided and linked agencies is a routine occurrence, as Machiavelli saw so clearly. Divisions of labour are to be regarded as both an object and an outcome of struggle. All divisions of labour within any employing organization are necessarily constituted within the context of various contracts of employment. Hence the employment relationship, that of economic domination and subordination, is necessarily an organizational fundamental. It is the underlying sediment through which other organization practices are stratified. Often these will overlap with it in quite complex ways.

The sociological consequences of this view of organizations are evident. Divisions of labour plus their remuneration, as central aspects of the employment contract and effort bargain, will become foci of politics. In these politics, agencies interested in maximizing their strategicality must attempt to transform their point of connection with some other agency or agencies into a 'necessary nodal point': this would be a channel through which traffic between them occurs on terms which privilege the putative strategic agency.

Otherwise, strategic inclinations will be unconsummated. Strategic agency will not be successfully achieved. From these observations follow the central points of strategic contingency theory (Hickson et al. [1971]; Hinings et al. [1974]).

To achieve strategic agency requires a disciplining of the discretion of other agencies: at best, from the strategist's point of view, such other agencies will become merely authoritative relays, extensions of strategic agency (Law 1986a: 16). Whatever interests such relay-agencies might have would be entirely those that they are represented as having by the strategically subordinating agency. A totally disciplined army squad in the field of battle, obediently subject to higher authority and its commands, would be the extreme example of this evacuation from agency of interests other than those authoritatively attributed to them. The actual agents, in this case the army squad, remain literally non-actors in this process: the only action which is formally allowed is for them to obey unquestioningly, sometimes on penalty of death for mutiny, desertion or insubordination in the field of battle. Ideally, they become agents without interests other than obedience to others' commands. In this respect, the army, as Weber was well aware, represents only the most condensed and concentrated form of much 'normal' organizational power and discipline, at least along the transitive dimension as it applies to low-trust, low-discretion positions. It is expedient if one's military discipline is also buttressed by moral authority, such as a religious vocation: soldiers of God, as Anthony (1977) suggests, historically have been the highest expression of obedient organization membership. Commerce as a moral crusade would be, perhaps, the ultimate cultural evangelist's dream, as Weber (1976), of course, was aware.

High discretionary strategic agency is another matter, for which power will be less prohibitive and more productive, more facilitative of desired outcomes through the disciplined discretion of the agency of empowered authorities. Here the necessity is not so much to forbid or restrict or prohibit but to enable creativity which is imbued with positivity yet still constrained by discipline. The model, of course, is the classical conception of the professional discipline as a vocation, whose testament was so exquisitely conveyed by Weber (1948) in his declaration of faith in 'Science as a Vocation'.

The articulation of interests by strategic agencies is thus the medium and outcome of unique positioning over the discretion of others' positioning in the organization field. It must be reproduced in order for existing structures of power to be reproduced. Indeed, its reproduction is a significant component of the phenomenon of power; its transformation an effective resistance to it. It should be evident that such reproductions are always already structured: they are never flat, one-dimensional topographies. Topography in this instance will always be the result of previous and current contest. In organizational life, such field structure has to be reproduced by strategic agencies or it will be open to transformation.

Agency may be evident in any circuit in a network of practices. Typically, but not necessarily, these circuits will be human, but they may instead be departmental or inanimate. An example of the latter might be the undoubted agency exercised by the complex, highly coupled, computer decision-making systems monitored by the Securities Industry Automation Corporation for Wall Street trading. Some analysts regard these as a contributory factor in the stock market crash on Wall Street that heralded the global financial crisis whose full force was felt in 2008. Agency is expanded by digital affordances to actants such as ChatGBT and other AI devices.

One consequence of the position taken here is that organizational locales will more likely be loci of multivalent powers than monadic sites of total control: contested terrains rather than total institutions. Barnes (1986: 184) puts it thus: 'To retain discretion over a large number of routines requires delegation. But for the maximum retained discretion over any particular routine the requirement is that authority be delegated but not power.'

The theoretically most powerful delegation of authority depends upon the delegated agent acting as one who is 'obedient'. Other than this, there is no way that the delegated routines will be directed without discretion. 'Obedience' cannot be guaranteed, despite the search for a secular equivalent to divinely inspired obeisance, if only because of the complexity and contingency of agency, as a nexus of calculation. Discretion need not entail dissent: it may be organizationally creative, productive, reproductive. None the less, to increase the power of a delegating agency does mean authorizing delegated others and delegated authorities cannot be guaranteed to be loci of wholly predictable and controlled agency, other than if they are dutiful servants. Thus the problematic of 'power in organizations' centres not on the legitimacy or otherwise of subordinates' capacities, as in the conventional view, but on the myriad practices which *inhibit* authorities from becoming powers by restricting action to that which is 'obedient', not only prohibitively but also creatively, productively. Ineluctably, 'ideology', 'expertise' and 'authority', whether 'Systems' or not, are implicated in these practices.

It has been argued thus far that authority is an a posteriori concept to that of power. The enlargement of an agency's power, except in the unlikely event of omnipotence, must be organizationally achieved through delegation. Delegation implies that discretion attaches to delegates.

Important implications flow from the relationship between power and discretion. Power will always be inscribed within contextual 'rules of the game' which both enable and constrain action (Clegg 1975). These rules may be taken to be the underlying rationale of those calculations which agencies routinely make in organizational contexts. Action can only ever be designated as such-and-such an action by reference to rules which identify it as such. Such rules can never be free of surplus or ambiguous meaning: they are always indexical to the context of interpreters and interpretation. Where there are rules there must be indexicality, as has been demonstrated by texts as diverse as Wittgenstein (1968), Garfinkel (1967), Clegg (1975) and Barnes (1986). Rules can never provide for their own interpretation. Issues of interpretation are always implicated in the processes whereby agencies instantiate and signify rules.

'Ruling' is an activity. It is accomplished by some agency as a constitutive sense-making process whereby meaning is fixed. Both rules and games necessarily tend to be the subject of contested interpretation, with some players having not only play-moves but also the refereeing of these as power resources. Consequently, where rules are invoked there must be discretion. Thus, resistance is inherent in the regulation of meaning. The embodiment of labour power is also a source of resistance. It is so because of the gap between the capacity to labour and its realization. Power and the organization of control is implicated in closing this gap.

Here we confront the central paradox of power: the power of an agency is increased in principle by that agency delegating authority; the delegation of authority can only proceed by rules; rules necessarily entail discretion and discretion potentially empowers delegates. From this arises the tacit and taken-for-granted basis of organizationally negotiated order, and on occasion, its fragility and instability, as has been so well observed by Strauss (1978). Events and others must be rendered routine and predictable if negotiation is to remain an unusual and out of the ordinary state of affairs. Routines arise not so much by prohibition and intervention into states of affairs, but through the knowledgeable construction of these states of affairs so that subordinate agencies know what is to be done on their part if they are to minimize whatever sanctions might be directed at them by superordinates, or indeed by any others involved in their circuits of power. It is not only power that is premised on knowledge, or its exclusive control or privileged access. It is also subordination: as Barnes (1988: 103) puts it, such agencies 'must recognize that the output of appropriate action which they produce is what minimizes the input of coercion and sanctioning which they receive'. It is for this reason that, wherever questions of time-space extension become nec-essary for securing organization action, it becomes important that there be some form of rules of practice to which agents can be held. The freedom of discretion requires disciplin-ing if it is to be a reliable relay. Whether this be achieved through what Foucault referred to as 'disciplinary' or some other modes of practice is unimportant. It may be direct sur-veillance, the interiorized normalizing gaze of professional self-regulation, a standardized reporting scheme, common economic interest or client reports which serve as the rules of practice. In the absence of these, by their evasion or malfunction, organizations are ill-advised to put their trust in agencies, as Machiavelli knew only too well.

Power is implicated in authority and constituted by rules; the interpretation of rules must be disciplined, must be regulated, if new powers are not to be produced and existing powers transformed. In fact, given the inherent indexicality of rule use, things will never be wholly stable; they will usually exhibit tolerance to stress, strain and strife in rule con-stitution whose limits can only ever be known for sure in their ill-disciplined breach of regulation. By definition, wholly effective discipline admits no breach, no 'disobedience', total rule-boundedness. None of this is far from Weber (1978) or for that matter Foucault (1977), despite protestations to the contrary: see Foucault (1981). What is surprising is that aspects of Weber on 'discipline' which in themselves, while they do not connect with Durkheim's [1964] stress on 'moral regulation' articulate similarr themes not developed in the concern of the sociology of organizations with power.

Resistance to discipline will be irremediable not because of 'human nature', 'capitalism' or any other putatively essentialist category but because of the power/rule constitution as a nexus of meaning and interpretation which, because of indexicality, is always open to being re-fixed. This is what couples power/knowledge in Foucault's (1977) formulation, because, at its most pervasive, power positions the subject, through the organization of disciplinary practices which constitute the potentialities, incapacities and correlates of specific forms of agency.

Having now established the problematic basis for the expression of organization as agency and agency as organization, we can now move to a formal model for the expression of the dialectic of power and resistance, in terms of a reformed model of episodic power located within a general framework of circuits of power. With this framework, the issue of the relationship between power and structure, which has been at the centre of so much of this book, will be seen to be capable of dissolution in terms which require neither recourse to dualistic formulations of either concept nor reference to alleged attributes of these, such as conceptions of 'real interests'.

THE REFORMATION OF POWER: THE CONTRIBUTIONS OF CALLON, LATOUR AND COLLEAGUES

The relation between power and structure is best approached through an insight which was already present at the onset of modernity. It was developed in Machiavelli's approach to power. In chapter two this was distinguished from and compared with Hobbes' 'sovereign' concept. For Machiavelli, what was most striking about power was its strategic, contingent, extensional nature, a concept of power dependent greatly on alliances, on strategies, for its practical accomplishment. Against the fiction of *Leviathan*, which Hobbes was to engender, the analysis of power in Machiavelli conceptualized it in terms of networks, alliances, points of resistance and instability, using much the same military metaphors that Foucault was later to find congenial. However, not only Foucault has explicitly acknowledged the Machiavellian antecedents of his argument (Foucault 1981: 97); a group of sociologists of science, associated with Michel Callon and Bruno Latour at the *Centre de Sociologie de l'Innovation* in Paris, have systematically explored the Machiavellian dimension in the analysis of power.

Machiavelli is a conscious model for Callon et al. (1986) in their own ethnographic techniques. Machiavelli presents, they suggest, a method which offers a detailed and systematic description of the machinations of princes which flushes out their hidden designs... (in which)... he devotes himself, as a participant observer, to what would nowadays be called an ethnography of political action. Establishing his quarters in the palaces of Florence, and following the prince, Machiavelli succeeds in bringing Italian society to life and understanding its history and its conflicts. Paradoxically, in attaching himself to one person, the prince, he reconstitutes the cruel reality of a whole society. To be rigorous in such a project it is necessary to be audacious. In particular, it is vital not to let morality blind oneself in the study of how a society takes shape and is transformed from its strategic loci. (Callon et al. 1986: 5)

In Callon's (1986) work, the debilitation of moral relativism is opposed in practice by several explicit principles. Amongst these are the principles of 'agnosticism' and 'generalized symmetry'. The principle of agnosticism dictates that the power analyst be impartial between actors engaged in controversy while the principle of generalized symmetry demands that where one does encounter conflicting viewpoints one explains them in the same terms. There is a third principle, which is thoroughly consistent with the general realist auspices of this book. The principle of free association requires that one abandon all a priori distinctions between the natural and the social. (This would undermine the enterprise of Giddens at the root of his subjectivism.) These constitutive doctrines can steer a course of interpretation through the hitherto almost unnavigable channel bounded by moral relativism and moral absolutism. They undergird the remainder of this chapter and book.

The general approach which Callon (1986) develops goes by the name of a 'sociology of translation' or, as it is sometimes called, a 'sociology of enrolment' or Actor Network Theory (ANT). It receives its names through its method. The approach has been developed in empirical studies conducted in the sociology of science. At the focus of its concerns has been an empirical rather than moral approach to those interests which scientists display when doing science and which, at least in terms of some of the so-called 'philosophies' of science, have in the past been represented as if they were 'disinterested'. Such views are no longer sustainable in the face of empirical investigations of scientists at work. Some empirical sociologists of science have been concerned to demonstrates those 'interests' which are implicit in scientific work (see the debates between Woolgar 1981 and Barnes 1981a; also see MacKenzie 1978). This is not the position taken by Callon (1986; 1980) and his colleagues (see Callon et al. 1983 and 1986; Callon and Law 1982; Callon and Latour 1981; also see Law and Lodge 1984, part III, in particular).

Rather than imputing interests, on whatever theoretical basis, the approach favoured here is aligned to perspectives which seek to demonstrate how networks of interest are actually constituted and reproduced through conscious strategies and unwitting practices constructed by the actors themselves. Interests appear as 'temporarily stabilized outcomes of previous processes of enrolment' (Callon and Law 1982: 622). These may have been intentionally produced or they may not. Intention is not at all necessary to the model; the 'temporarily stabilized outcomes' may be practices historically encountered in their fixity and facticity which no one necessarily 'intended' in any relevant way. They may be no less real for that, and agents may come to have an interest in them for any number of reasons. Why they should do so is in itself not a necessary part of any explanation. Enrolling others to one's conceptions is a strategy in which formulation of one's own and others' interests may play a strategic role. It is one of the devices whereby we attempt to stamp our agency on others and other things (and especially others treated as reliable other things) through constituting networks of power. Interests thus have no ontological status; they are merely more or less stable devices for achieving relative social order.

The methodological approach which undergirds this position is prefigured in Machiavelli's descriptions which, it is maintained, are made through reference with 'neither fear nor favour of what it is that actors do' (Callon et al. 1986: 5). Without taking sides, without reducing all action to the manifestation of some agencies' putative intentions or interests, or making it the outcrop of some structure, the approach provides an empirical sociology of power, rather than a moral philosophy. By attending to politically engaged agents seeking to constitute agencies, to constitute interests, to constitute structures, the method seeks to map how agents actually do 'translate' phenomena into resources, and resources into organization networks of control, of alliance, of coalition, of antagonism, of interest and of structure. 'Translation' refers to the methods by which these outcomes are accomplished.

Four 'moments' of translation are identified in Callon's (1986: 196) approach. The first of these is *problematization*. Problematization involves the attempt by agents to enrol others to their agency by positing the indispensability of their 'solutions' for (their definition of) the others' 'problems': this is achieved when these others are channelled through the 'obligatory passage points' of practice which the enrolling agency seeks to 'fix'. The traces of post-structuralism are evident. (There is also a hint of the organizational 'garbage-can' approach of Cohen et al. [1972] in which 'solutions' seek 'problems' to which they might attach themselves.) Problematization seeks to construct 'hegemony' by fixing what Laclau and Mouffe (1985) call 'nodal points' of discourse. The term 'nodal points', introduced in the previous chapter, and the term 'obligatory passage points', introduced here from the work of Callon et al. (1986), will henceforth be used interchangeably in this book. They are meant to refer to the construction of a conduit through which traffic must necessarily pass. Power consists in part in the achievement of this positionality.

The second moment in the process of translation is termed *interessement*. This can be defined as the process of 'interesting' or 'recruiting' another agent to one's own agency: one agency 'attracts a second by coming between that entity and a third. Interessement is thus a transaction between three entities' (Callon et al. 1986: xvii). It seeks to achieve the 'fixing' or 'locking in' of membership and meaning in certain 'categorization devices'. The 'membership categorization devices' or MCD approach, developed by ethnomethodologists such as Sacks (1972), would be a useful research tool here. How does a universe of categorical possibilities for membership become aligned with a universe of possible members?

The third moment in the process of translation is termed *enrolment*. This is the process whereby agencies seek to construct alliances and coalitions between the memberships and meaning which they have sought to fix. Finally, there is *mobilization* which refers to the set of methods that agencies use to ensure that the representations of interest which other enrolled agencies make are in fact themselves fixed, that the agencies in question do not, as it were, betray or undercut their representatives and representations.

The above is a slight reworking of the terms of the translation approach but it does not undermine its representations. Of the work done under the translation approach, the most easily accessible and interesting study is that conducted by Callon (1986) of the 'domestication of the scallops and the fishermen of St Brieuc Bay'. In this study, a complex interpretation is built up of the relations constituted between three marine biologists, a fishing community at St Brieuc Bay in Brest, and, the major actors in the story, the scallops which are harvested and researched in the bay. The scallop harvest was diminishing; the fishermen's livelihood was threatened. Little local knowledge of the scallop's life-cycle existed. A conference was held in Brest at which the three marine biologists reported on the latest scientific knowledge of the scallop's life-cycle to representatives of the fishing community.

Over the subsequent ten-year period, the marine researchers sought to construct 'obligatory passage points' enrolling the 'interests' of the fishermen, the scallops and their scientific colleagues, in stable representations to form an 'organizational field' in which 'agencies were defined, associated and simultaneously obliged to remain faithful to their alliances' (Callon 1986: 224). It is a fascinating study which repays careful consideration and whose general methodological precepts will be drawn on in the construction of a formal model of 'circuits of power' in this chapter. In the following chapter, the model will be illustrated with reference to the emergence of the circuit of power which is the modern capitalist state.

One insight vital for the reformation of the sociology of power is that strategic emphasis which, it has been argued, was first encountered in Machiavelli and most fully developed as a 'sociology of translation' by Callon and his colleagues. A second important insight, which may be attributed to Foucault (1980), is the distinction between the sovereign conception of power and the notion of disciplinary power. In this chapter the notion of disciplinary power will be conceptualized as a distinct 'circuit of power' in which disciplinary technique, in the broad sense that Foucault suggests, structures the relations of power through its diffusion according to principles of competitive ecological pressure and institutional isomorphism. Although the concept of 'institutional isomorphism' (Meyer and Rowan 1977) appears to be of more recent provenance than the more familiar evolutionist idea of ecological pressure, something very like the process which the concept describes was in fact present in Machiavelli (1958: 49) when he observed that 'Men nearly always follow the tracks made by others and proceed in their affairs by imitation, even though they cannot entirely keep to the tracks of others or emulate the prowess of their models. So a prudent man must always follow in the footsteps of great men and imitate those who have been outstanding. If his own prowess fails to compare with theirs, at least it has an air of greatness about it.' If 'organizations' were to be substituted for 'great men' in this formulation, it would not be unrecognizable to one familiar with modern institutional theory.

The effectiveness of forms of disciplinary power in the nineteenth century, which both Bauman (1982) and Foucault (1977) discuss, had to do with the pressure to innovate techniques of discipline appropriate for more impersonal, large-scale settings in which the *gemeinschaft* conditions whereby each person knew his/her place no longer prevailed. Such localized moral regulation, premised on the transparency of the person to the gaze of the community, was no longer viable. Many new forms of state institution were developed which sought to process categories of surplus population. No grand plan caused these institutions to adopt similar forms of disciplinary technique, which the factory masters belatedly took up. The process is perhaps best seen in terms of the pressures of institutional innovation (Meyer and Rowan 1977). The disciplinary techniques which had been readily available in the monastic milieu of religious vocation had already constituted institutional forms of schooling, poor houses, etc. Their effectiveness in producing soldiers and marines out of peasants had been established during the previous two centuries. Practices of institutional isomorphism would tend to reproduce similar relations of meaning and membership as the basis for social integration in the new institutions of the state (Meyer and Rowan 1977). Because certain forms of technique were already available and known, they had a certain legitimacy which enabled them to be more widely dispersed than they might otherwise have been. One could also, following Aldrich (1979), point to the similarity of 'niche space' of these institutions. In Goffman's (1961) terms they were all 'total institutions'. (Incidentally, although Goffman never made it explicit, it has been suggested that there is an implicit view of power in his writing. Interested readers might refer to Rogers [1977] and Clegg et al (2006).) Environmental pressures served to structure system integration into a limited range of organizational forms.

POWER AND RESISTANCE

It has been argued at the outset of this chapter that an appropriate point of departure for an analysis of power would be not agency but the social relations which constitute effective agency, particularly where it is organizational in form. In fact, as we shall see, the relational focus needs to be broader even than this: what is required is a consideration of the relational field of force in which power is configured and in which one aspect of this configuration is the social relations in which agency is constituted. The key to understanding resides in thinking of power as a phenomenon which can be grasped only relationally. It is not a thing nor is it something that people have in a proprietorial sense. They 'possess' power only in so far as they are relationally constituted as doing so. To the extent that the relational conditions which constitute power are reproduced through fixing their obligatory passage points, then possession may be fixed and 'reified' in form.

The greatest achievement of power is its reification. When power is regarded as thinglike, as something solid, real and material, as something an agent has, then this represents power in its most pervasive and concrete mode. It is securely fixed in its representations. However, reified power will rarely if ever occur entirely without resistance. To this extent power is infrequently the complete reification that it is sometimes assumed to be. Reification is rarely achieved in terms of that 'forgetting' of it as even existing as such which, for the classical critical theorists, was the apotheosis of power achieved through the negation of freedom. Resistance to power may be of two kinds. Sometimes, under rare conditions of what will be termed 'organizational outflanking', resistance to power may consolidate itself as a new power and thus constitute a new fixity in the representation of power, with a new relational field of force altogether. On the other hand, it may be resistance to the exercise of power which leaves unquestioned the fixity of the terms in which that power is exercised. It merely resists the exercise not the premises that make that exercise possible. In this respect resistance is compatible with reification and the exercise of power. What is reified is the fixity of powers terms, the representations which constitute it as such, centred on particular obligatory passage points.

Implicit to the conception of episodic agency power is the assumption of resistance. As Wrong (1979: 13) has put it, 'Politics includes both a struggle for power and a struggle to limit, resist and escape *from* power'. Consequently, as power always involves power over another and thus at least two agencies, episodic power will usually call forth resistance because of the power/knowledge nature of agency. Power and resistance stand in a relationship to each other. One rarely has one without the other. It might be thought that, in the absence of an overt conflict, there will be no resistance to power. This would be to confuse the notion of resistance *per se* with a particularly dramatic expression of it. Excessive politeness in dealing with one to whom one is subject may well ironicize resistance; working to rule may not produce overt conflict with a superior, if one can legitimate one's actions with reference to a rule book governing what one should be doing, but it may well be an effective form of resistance, as many unionists will attest (also see the discussion in Clegg 1987). Barbalet (1985: 531) has characterized that resistance which imposes limits on power as 'frictional' – an absence of interest in the realization of the goals of power in contrast to intended or direct resistance.

Barbalet's (1985) treatment of 'power and resistance' is of particular interest for the clarification it provides of the relation of power and resistance in Weber's (1978: 53) definition of power. It is convincingly argued that these terms stand for distinct but interdependent aspects of phenomena within the power relation, in which resistance should be regarded as a phenomenon in its own right which will be directly implicated in power relations. From this perspective, resistance would be the 'efficacious influence of those subordinate to power' (Barbalet 1985: 542). Some conceptions of resistance are over-extensions of a sweeping concept of power itself, a criticism justifiably made by Dews (1979: 165) when he notes Foucault's (1977) 'tendency to slide from the use of the term "power" to designate one pole of the relation power-resistance, to its use to designate the relations as a whole'. More calibrated conceptions are important because they acknowledge that capacities can never be sure to determine outcomes. Power, as the realization of outcomes, cannot simply be assumed from the capacities of those exercising power, as we have seen in Hindess' (1982) argument. There is always a dialectic to power, always another agency, another set of standing conditions pertinent to the realization of that agency's causal powers against the resistance of another. Consequently, as Barbalet (1985: 539) has suggested, the power of an agent will always be less than the capacities that agent mobilized when attempting to achieve a specific outcome. Rarely will intentions be realized, if we mean by intention the outcome projected by the agency at the outset. Without resistance, we would note either that there is a genuine consensus of wills and thus no antagonistic agency or that there is a capitulation on the part of Bs and their strategic subordination to A. Such a situation would correspond to that relational subordination of B to A routinely secured through dispositional power.

While episodic, one-dimensional conceptions of agency and power may tell us something about the nature of power relations between an already constituted A and B, it can tell us nothing about the constitutive nature of the relational field in which A and B presently are nor how this privileges and handicaps them respectively, in relation to those resources that are constituted as powerful. Contrary to some conventions of power analysis, there is little point in constructing a priori abstract lists of specific resources as power resources. Whether they, whatever they are, are power resources depends entirely on how they are positioned and fixed by the players, the rules, and the game. This point is at the centre of the translation approach.

RULES AND POWER

Realism would have been greatly facilitated in the past if some conception of structural power had metaphorically skewed and made uneven and fissured that level table on which conceptual billiard balls from Locke to Dahl have moved so easily. To skew the table is simultaneously to advantage and disadvantage players dependent upon their relation to the table and the moves they wish to make. It disturbs the equilibrium upon which the rules of the game may fairly be applied, by skewing the rules to the advantage of whomsoever has management of the skewed table. Of course, only in pure games of skill or chance is it ever the case that games are played on a 'level table' or a 'level playing field'. Social games rarely if ever correspond to the ideal conditions of pure games *per se*. The rules will not be as static and idealized as in chess or some other game but will instead be far more fragile, ambiguous, unclear, dependent upon interpretation, and subject either to reproduction or transformation depending on the outcome of struggles to keep them the same or to change them this way or that (see Doyal and Harris 1986: 80–6 for a general discussion of 'rules').

The application of metaphors drawn from an analogy with games to the analysis of power is not uncommon amongst theorists. Hoy (1986: 135), for example, interprets Foucault's (1982) explanation of strategy in terms of a game of chess, an analogy which the present author also introduced in an earlier book on *Power, Rule and Domination* (Clegg 1975). In that text a concern with rules was closely linked to the analysis of power and domination (derived from Wittgenstein's [1968] analysis of 'rules', 'language games' and 'forms of life'), as the title denotes. For instance, following Wittgenstein (1968), the argument was made that behaviour is largely rule-guided: that the fact that policemen or traffic lights can cause traffic to stop makes sense only within reference to a set of explicit and implicit rules with which there is a widespread familiarity within a jurisdictional universe. Jurisdiction implies the probability of sanction of its breach in this formulation. Rules are not absolute; they are open to diverse interpretation. Moreover, not all interpretations are equal. One can draw on the analogy with the game of chess. 'Obviously, in an ongoing game, a piece like the queen would start in a more privileged position than a pawn, simply because the extant rules, which are now open to interpretation, enable her to begin the sequence with more potential moves to make' (Clegg 1975: 49). In metaphorical terms, if the power of a queen derives from the 'rules of the game', then the basis of these rules has to be established. In other terms, if the queen's episodic power is greater in scope than that of a pawn, then on what basis are their respective dispositional powers fixed so that their capacity to make their respective moves is rooted and routinized? To raise this question is to move into the circuit of dispositional power.

In fact, the chess analogy employed by Clegg (1975) could and should be extended further, as Saunders (1979: 61) has pointed out: 'it is not simply that powerful actors have greater scope in their permissible actions, but also that they can authoritatively reinterpret (within limits) what the rules mean. In everyday life, queens may begin to move as knights.' Moreover, because of their power, as given by the rules, they are at much greater liberty to make their interpretations of rules stick than those for whom the rules of the game allow only a much more limited set of moves. Indeed, a huge industry of lobbying governments, pressuring them to change the rules of various activities or leave them the same, exists, paid for by wealthy organizations and their institutional expressions.

The concept of rules also relates to that of intention. Talk of outcomes in the episodic power model implies that intentions are implicated in power. However, it should be clear that intention is not to be regarded as something interior to private mental states of persons or even as equivalent to what persons tell us comprise their private mental states. For the former we cannot indubitably 'know' another's mind and mental constructs because they remain unarticulated. Nor is our conception of agency at all equivalent with that of another person. When intentions are articulated, they can only be so through whatever forms of discourse are socially available regarding what intentions can sensibly be taken to be, in the forms of language, reasoning and accounting for action. In this respect, talk about intentions that others might have is a reference less to their interior mental states as causal springs of putative action than to currently 'fixed' representations for making sense of what people do. It is to report on the availability and applicability of discursive formulations that are available for identifying behaviours as specific types of social action, to which agents may lay claim with respect to their own actions and which others may judge as 'vocabularies of motive' (Mills 1940; also see Taylor 1972).

In regarding a behaviour as a specific type of social action which can be said to have been intended to be such and such an action, we necessarily make reference to our interpretations of social actions by reference to social rules. That certain types of behaviour can be interpreted as moves in a game of sexual arousal depends upon their being interpreted in terms of the conventions of a game defined as sexual etiquette. Of course, as in many if not most social games, the rules may not be clear and the players may be playing different games unknowingly or unthinkingly. One way of resisting power play is not even to acknowledge the game that one thinks that the other thinks is being played. The point is that an intention to arouse sexually is not necessarily intrinsic to whatever is constituted as sexually arousing action: it resides in the way in which demeanour, appearance, clothes, embodiment, gestures, talk can all be interpreted in terms of available representations and arenas of behaviour. It will be rare indeed that the meaning of these is universally fixed, although, of course, it may be. A major strategy for resistance will always be to try to resist the meaning in which one is being implicated by the other's moves.

If intentionality requires reference to rules on this account, one should have equal recourse to discussion of rules in order to provide an appropriate concept of 'social causality'. Social causality is introduced to distinguish a conception of causality that is different from the implicit model of Humean causality which was found in Dahl's stress on event causation. The stories of the semiotics of traffic lights or of police uniforms and hand signals serve to differentiate this notion of social causality. Neither traffic lights nor policemen are inexorably and infallibly bound by universal causal law in the effects they might produce. These effects are contingent upon a rule being reproduced by being widely obeyed by those who should be subject to it. It is, in this sense, a normative rather than a causal imperative. It will be reproduced for just as long as people choose to obey it. One can easily imagine extraordinary situations of panic or lawlessness in which such rules might not be reproduced: war, a natural disaster such as an earthquake, or widespread social upheaval. Choice is essential to rules, irrelevant to law of a Humean kind (Ball 1976: 207; Harré 1970: 85; Clegg 1979: 39–40).

EPISODIC AGENCY POWER: THE 'NORMAL POWER' OF SOCIAL SCIENCE

One should conceive of episodic instances of agency power as the most apparent, the most easily accessible and most visible circuit of power. It is the 'normal power' of most social science, that conception which has been identified as stretching from Hobbes right through to the 'dimensional' approach of Lukes (1974). However, it is neither the foundation of the totality of power in the terms that Lukes' dimensional approach suggests nor a free-standing circuit as in the formal model that Dahl (1957) advances. Power, viewed episodically, may move through circuits in which rules, relations and resources that are constitutive of power are translated, fixed and reproduced/transformed. These other circuits of power, which will be termed the circuits of social and system integration in which are implicated dispositional and facilitative power respectively, constitute the field of force in which episodic agency conceptions of power are articulated. Fixing these fields of force is achieved through enrolling other agencies such that they have to traffic through the enrolling agencies' obligatory passage points. Power involves not only securing outcomes, which is achieved in the episodic circuit of power, but also securing or reproducing the 'substantively rational' conditions within which the strategies espoused in the circuit of episodic power make contextual good sense (see Biggart and Hamilton [1987; 1984]; Hamilton and Biggart [1985; 1984] and Hamilton [1986] for complementary discussions of 'substantive rationality').

Different theoretical perspectives diverge on the temporality within which the contextualization of action is conceived. At one level there is the ethnomethodological school which tends to see the reproduction of substantive rationality as occurring within immediate temporal contexts of action; in the least immediate conceptualization of substantive rationality is the concern with long, slow, cyclical and enduring change which characterizes the *Annales* school of historians. It is not a question of which one of these extremes is correct or of the interim point at which one should arrest the temporal flow. In the appropriate empirical context of analysis, any point might be correct. It will depend in part on how efficaciously secured is the substantive rationality which both contextualizes particular strategies of episodic power and undercuts strategic opposition. Some highly structured procedural contexts of action within which questions must elicit accountable answers, such as courtrooms or judicial hearings, have an immediate co-presence of strategy and temporality. Ethnomethodological conversation analysis will thus be a useful research technique for such occasions. Others, such as a particular context of political economy, may show no such strategic returns in the normal course of affairs. Under these conditions, the *longue durée* may well be a more appropriate frame of reference, and the rich narrative, description and data of the *Annales* historian a more apposite technique.

Irrespective of mode of analysis, an adequate framework of power should enable us to sketch a plausible narrative, where plausibility is not brought into question by recourse to devices such as analytical prime movers, or hidden and inexplicable mechanisms of thought control. Episodically, power may be conceived as occurring within a reasonably well delimited framework in which there are systematic relationships between agencies and events. From what has been said beforehand, it should be clear that while this framework may be existentially real, it should also be regarded as the effect of a successful translation in its own right. Thus, it is no eternal set of relations. Systematicity derives from agents' differential control over and interest in events and each other. Interest carries no epistemological baggage in this formulation. It does not refer to an evaluative conception. The reference is only to the representations of interest which agencies make. These are not to be considered as identical to an individual actor's reasons for acting. Such a position brings one too close to a constitutive phenomenology of the subject, premised only on the subject's own discursively available categories. A representational concept of interest, constituted by agency, is clearly not the same thing. It refers to agencies not an actor. Agencies may represent interests precisely as the result of a process of 'translation'. Consequently, reference to interests in this schema is not to be taken as referring either to individual agent's 'reasons' or to their unknown but 'real' interests.

The two defining elements of any power system are agencies and events of interest to these agencies. As a provisional and conventional point of departure for discussion of episodic power in this section we shall begin with some artificial and unrealistic limiting assumptions. The precedents for doing this are obvious. They derive from neo-classical economics, in this instance via the work of Coleman (1977). However, unlike the neo-classical economists we shall progressively drop the unrealistic limiting assumptions as we proceed. At the outset, a 'principle of action' may be specified whereby agencies 'act so as to gain control of those events in which they have an interest.... The way in which actors gain control of those events that interest them is to give up control of those events over which they have little or no interest' (Coleman 1977: 184). They engage in exchange such that each agency has control over events that interest that agency, subject to the resources with which that agent began: that is, the control over events held as a resource capacity at the outset. This is represented in Figure 8.1, together with the other circuits of power. It may be useful to refer to this representation subsequently, when the other circuits of power are being discussed.

Power is represented in the circuits framework in a number of ways. (Incidentally, the configuration of this model has a distant lineage in earlier models of 'power, rule and domination' [in Clegg 1975; 1979] although the present articulation is not structural but prcessual) Power is evidently present as each specified modality of episodic, dispositional and facilitative power. It is also present in the overall flow of action through the circuits of power, the relational articulation which will constitute the calibration of this flow. Empirically, power may be contained within the episodic circuit only or it may flow through the dispositional and facilitative routes. These are properly thought of as aspects of the overall framework of power phenomena and are signified as 'rules' and 'domination' in order to differentiate them from the most frequently conceptualized circuit of power which is so often taken to be power *per se*.

A very brief word on the derivation of the terminology of power, rule and domination may be in order. It is derived from Weber's (1978) discussions of *macht* and *herrschaft*, via Clegg (1975). Where domination is institutionalized through the circuit of dispositional power as a substantive modality of rule, such as patrimonialism or legal rationality, it is conventional to speak of it as authority. It should be clear from the earlier discussion of authority in this chapter that the conventional conception of authority as a legitimating source of power is being dispensed with in favour of a concern with the processes whereby authority may be empowered. Hence the translation of *herrschaft* as 'authority' is displaced in favour of a more accurate rendering as 'domination', leaving open as a matter for investigation whether or not this is accompanied by authority.

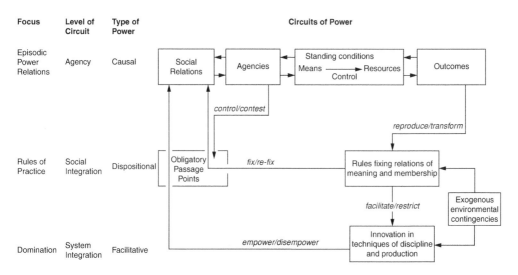

Figure 8.1 Representing the circuits of power

In the circuits framework, power is multifarious: it is episodic power; it is also the circuit of power through rules and domination, as well as the overall empirical articulation which configures the theoretical circuits in any application of the model. If this seems complex, one can only submit that the law of 'requisite variety' may well be appropriate here: the complexity of the phenomenon is mirrored in its representation. Certainly, simpler formulations are entirely possible: the earlier chapters of this book bear warrant to that eventuality. They should also have alerted us to some of the drawbacks that such formulations contain.

Existing social relations constitute the identities of agencies, whether individuals or some collective loci of decision-making and action. Agencies' causal powers will be realized through the organization of standing conditions. These require that agencies involved in what Hindess (1982: 501) terms 'arenas of struggle' are capable of utilizing means in order to control resources which have consequential outcomes for the scope of action of these agents. Each agency is operative in a highly complex environment of standing conditions. Each is among many others with strategic interests in each other and in the relations that constitute them as actors in the same system. Agencies possess varying control of resources which they have varying means of effectively utilizing in order to produce consequential outcomes for their own and others' agency. Power at this level will invariably be accompanied by resistance, which is indicated in Figure 8.1 by pairs of arrows connecting the boxes in the model of episodic power relations. Those pointing to the right-hand side indicate social relations constituting agencies, agencies utilizing standing conditions, and standing conditions utilized by agencies causing outcomes. The arrows which point to the left-hand side indicate resistance. (If it were not that it would have unnecessarily complicated an already complex figure, lines of resistance could have been drawn from outcomes to agencies and social relations, as well as from standing conditions to social relations.) Power which proceeds at the level of these episodic power relations is the most apparent, evident and economical circuit of power. It is 'power over' which, however, necessarily trades off some extant 'fixing' of facilitative and dispositional power. Rules of practice are at the centre of any stabilization or change of the circuitry. Through them, all traffic must pass. However, it is not only as a result of struggles which occur explicitly over relations of meaning and membership that social change occurs. It can also be a function of those changes in the process of innovation which always pose potential transformations for the extant structuring of empowerment and disempowerment, dependent upon extant techniques of production and discipline. The techniques are not only carriers of innovation but almost invariably bearers of domination. Thus, domination is never eternal, never utterly set in time and space: it will invariably be subject to processes of innovation which may as readily subvert as reproduce its functioning. Even in the most closed of systems, where sources of external contingency rarely penetrate (for example, the Japanese empire prior to its forcible opening to the West under the direction of Perry's guns), the domination of particular relations of meaning is neither timeless, static nor unchanging.

Let us return to the formal model and some familiar tactics of analysis. Consistent with the artifice of assumptions, imagine an absence of resistance, the economists' rational norm. A situation of non-antagonistic agency would be equivalent to a deal freely entered into by each party to the relationship, where the relationship is a balance of 'inducements' and 'contributions', a fair exchange. In such a situation of fair exchange, the final control of events would leave the two agencies in a similar position of balance vis à vis the 'scope' of their agency. For instance, A may have contracted to provide 100 units of X at $10 per unit cost to B. For A, the loss of 100 Xs would be equivalent for A to the receipt of $1000 while, for B $1000 outlay would secure the balanced satisfaction of 100 units of X. The fiction that economists call a perfect market would prevail.

In this fiction, as Coleman (1977: 184) argues, controlling events would be analogous to 'control over the disposition of a good in a private market'. A price or value of control for each event is negotiated through exchange. Each agency 'can be described as having a certain amount of power, depending on the value of the events', over which control is exerted. There is, as he argues further, 'a simultaneous definition of value and power'. Value is defined by the interest that agents have in an event, weighted by the agents' power. The power of an agent would be equivalent to that agent's control over events, weighted by the value of these events (Coleman 1977: 184). As is clear from the definitions, Coleman's conception of power is developed on an explicit analogy with the conception of wealth in an economic system. It is a neo-classical conception of 'fair exchange'. Adherence to a reality principle requires the abandonment of these limiting assumptions. We shall proceed to do this by first noting the obduracy of resistance as a social phenomenon. Such a 'fair exchange', viewed episodically, would not be consistent with a notion of power ineluctably linked to resistance. If A and B are agencies who freely entered into a relationship with each other (the ideal of this being a spot-market transaction between a buyer and a seller of a good), it is difficult to talk of a relationship of power. The 'perfect market assumptions' ensure that. Beyond a number of highly specific and mostly atypical markets, these conditions do not prevail. They certainly do not prevail on that most important of markets, the labour market. (See the discussion in Clegg et al. [1986: 52–66; 214–49; 259–96]. While this discussion will not be repeated, it is a necessary backdrop to the conception of labour markets which is implicit in this book.) Such exchanges will be more or less unequal. Consideration of power requires consideration of imperfect exchanges under imperfect market conditions. Whether or not an agent's causal powers are realized will depend upon the standing conditions for their utilization of and access to means and resources. These will invariably be distributed unequally.

In an imperfect market, means and resources will be inequitably distributed. Realization of an agency's causal powers will entail gaining an outcome in opposition to the preference of another agency in the exchange. What an agent is able to achieve as an outcome thus depends in part on the causal powers that are constitutive of that actor and, in part, on the standing conditions of access to means and resources which may restrict or enable the achievement of outcomes. Just as in the natural sciences, the arrangement of standing conditions has to be organized experimentally in order to achieve that threshold of action beyond which causal powers can manifest themselves. The difference, of course, is that for social phenomena the agencies who comprise the field of study are also the 'experimentalists', seeking to organize the standing conditions in order to realize their constitutive causal powers.

Where the exchange relationship is unequal, as a result of neither chance nor error but of the constitutive nature of the agencies and the relationships between them, we can say that an A can get a B to do something that B would not otherwise have done. Alternatively we might say that A can get B not to do something that B might reasonably have been expected to do. The important thing is that the episodic conception is now grounded in a less fictional conception of power. Episodic power is seen to derive from the capacities of agents grounded in resource control. The constitutive relations which prevail between agents can be seen to determine the nature of resources. Resources, under the appropriate standing conditions, can empower A vis à vis a specific scope of B's agency, when utilized through means which implement them. The episodic power circuit may thus be conceptualized as both a relatively coherent and an important circuit of power in its own right. Conceptual closure can thus be admitted at this level of power relations. However, closure at this level is not to be taken for closure of consideration of power phenomena *per se*.

A's power attempt and B's resistance to power must have some basis, some resources, which can be activated in the struggle. Moreover, the protagonists must have some means available to them to activate these resources. Such resources are generally deployed not promiscuously but with a target in view. For the protagonist, such a target would be that scope of the other's actions over which the exercise of power is sought. Protagonists may be more or less effective in achieving their target and restricting the scope of the other's actions just as they may be in resisting attempts by others to achieve the same compliance with respect to their own actions. The more successful a protagonist is in achieving means of effective activation of resources, accurately targeted at restricting the extent of options within the scope of another, the more 'integral' the protagonist's power will be. The more successful is resistance to power, the more 'intercursive' or countervailing power will be. (The distinctions between 'integral' and 'intercursive' are made by Wrong [1979: 11; also see 260, ch. 1, n. 28].) The former situation would correspond to the cohesive oligarchic structure of rule which elite theory routinely represents, while the latter would be pluralist. In the pluralist, intercursive situation, both power and resistance may be evident in the same agencies with respect to differing scopes of behaviour of the other agencies.

Resistance to oligarchic or integrative power, when viewed episodically, can take a number of forms. It may seek to exercise countervailing power on the basis of more effective means of utilization of its existing resources; more precise targeting of the other agencies' more powerful scopes for action and their preferred options within these; enrolling other agencies to its cause and thus making more extensive any episodic attempts at power by the antagonistic agency, and so on.

Terms such as these can be clearly specified. To this extent they do aid us in constructing research into power. However, while some terms, at least, can be quantified, it is doubtful whether quantification is of much use as an end in itself, although it may be a valuable strategy of research which contributes to the overall qualitative picture that investigation into episodic power tries to build up and develop. The quantitative problem is simply that, as we have seen, such terms as 'scope' are difficult to quantify in ways that do not leave the comparative rankings vulnerable to weighty matters of qualitative consideration which cannot be so easily quantified and compared in terms of any single unit of value. None the less, some researchers will always be disposed to counting, since, for many, numbers have their own power. As long as the overall context is considered, so that facile aggregation of inherently and qualitatively non-equivalent phenomena (such as the number of Bs or the number of scopes) is avoided, then no great harm to understanding will be done by this comparative ranking. Indeed, it may well be aided.

ORGANIZATIONAL OUTFLANKING OF RESISTANCE: MANN'S CONTRIBUTION

Mann (1986) has conceived of 'societies as organized power networks'. One premise of his approach has already been implicit here in the refusal to regard ordered totalities as the prior framework in which power operates. These are an achievement of power, not its generative principle. Communities, or societies, cannot be reduced to a single systemic ordering principle, to a single, bounded, space-time continuum as the a priori from which power is generated. This is the mythical premise of Hobbes' political community, which this book has been slowly unpicking in favour of a more strategic, more 'Machiavellian' concern in which totality may be an ultimate but rarely achieved objective.

Mann (1986: 2) argues that there are likely to be some relational practices which are of greater significance than others as pathways or conduits of power. For Mann there are four sources, bases or resources of social power. These are defined as ideological, economic, military, and political relationships. Although very nearly in agreement with Mann's neo-Parsonian schema on this, I would argue for circuits of power, not sources, and would see the circuits mobilizing relations of meaning and membership (equivalent to the ideological and political in Mann) and techniques of production and discipline (equivalent to the economic and military in Mann). There is most discrepancy in the latter pairings.

The purpose of this book is to develop a formal model for analysis of power, irrespective of substantive content. Consequently, while relations of meaning and membership, as well as production, are universals which can be applied to all substantive organized settings, military relationships are far more specific to the large-scale comparative and historic study of state formation in which Mann (1986) is involved. While not eschewing the importance of military relationships, force, violence and war in general (which a number of writers such as Giddens [1985] and Turner [1986b] have reiterate), the conception of military relationships remains too restricted for formal purposes. It is for this reason that 'force' is conceptualized in terms of techniques of discipline, as the organizational conduit for what Przeworski (1980) terms the 'material bases' of consent (the affinities with Lockwood should be evident). The point of force or military violence is to secure outcomes which cannot be achieved through circuits of social integration, particularly against those constituted as 'others' or as 'outsiders' in terms of their membership. For such 'strangers', the circuit of integrative, dispositional power is so much more difficult to achieve, precisely because of this 'difference'. It has long been evident that consent is usually underlain by force, at least since Gramsci's (1971) reflections on Machiavelli and the 'Modern Prince' became available, as Przeworski (1980) has argued.

In this text, 'force' is conceptualized in terms of that configuration of both power and knowledge that Foucault (1977) terms 'disciplinary power'. The reasons for this are evident. Productive power requires what an early writer, Andrew Ure (1835), called for in *The Philosophy of Manufactures*, namely the 'distribution of the different members of the apparatus into one co-operative body', by 'training human beings to renounce their desultory habits of work, and to identify themselves with the unvarying regularity of the complex automation' (cited in Thompson 1968: 395). The extension of any agency's governing power over time, over space and over other agencies will require the diffusion of disciplinary techniques throughout the apparatus or organization, whether it be a military apparatus or any other kind of formal organization. In Foucault (1977), we see how the disciplines involved eventually constitute a general formula of domination, built up from many local, unconnected micropolitics of episodic power, into an overall configuration tracing its network of power and resistance across a multiplicity of fields of force. The present author's conception of the circuits of power derives from this. It consists of processes for stitching-up particular configurations of state, economy and civil society (see Clegg et al. 1986: 63–6 and chapters 9 and 10 below).

To the extent that power stays purely within the episodic circuit, it automatically reproduces the existing configurations of rules and domination because it challenges neither social nor system integration and thus cannot innovate. This will be the case irrespective of whether it is the putative A or the putative B which 'wins'. This involves a proposition. Conceive of an agent which may be either the putative A exercising power or the putative B resisting it. Questions of transformation arise only when practices of rule and/or existing techniques of domination are challenged. Under such conditions it may well be that the relational field which constitutes agencies, means of control, and resources is reconfigured. Independent support for this proposition can be found in a number of studies. First, one can return to Lukes' (1974: 47) citation of Gramsci (1971: 327) on the contrast between a conception of the world affirmed in words and another held in effective action taken at periods of crisis. At such times it is precisely the inability of the extant episodic power's relational field to contain power within its customary circuit which is the locus of the disjuncture. Therborn's (1977) study of the link between capitalism and democracy would also be a case in point. The democratic state, he argues, usually develops either where there has occurred a destruction of a pre-existing, non-democratic state form in warfare or where a wartime mobilization with a national popular impetus has been sustained into a struggle for representation across a broad front in the post-war period. In either case, conditions of material crisis severely weaken the pre-existing state form and its representations. In such a conjuncture, where the organization field has been either severely weakened in defeat or organizationally outflanked by the unanticipated consequences of the organizations raised to win the victory, transformations have occurred, leading to a new 'constitution' of the power configuration.

In the 'normal' course of affairs, we see once more the economy of a power which raises questions neither of rules nor of domination. Additionally, we may note the susceptibility of such power to resistance which is able to raise such questions. If 'susceptibility' is merely a matter of raising questions concerning social and system integration, why do agencies not routinely do so? Rather than answer this question by recourse to notions of a captive consciousness, one should look elsewhere. The notion of 'organizational outflanking', to use the term coined by Mann (1986: 7), provides a serviceable answer to why the dominated so frequently consent to their subordination and subordinators. It is 'because they lack collective organization to do otherwise, because they are embedded within collective and distributive power organizations controlled by others'. It is because they are so frequently 'organizationally outflanked'. Effective agency invariably implies organization of other agencies in a process implicit to 'translation'. Organizational outflanking will be used as a key concept in what follows, not just as a strategy of hierarchical containment but also as a strategy which is equally efficacious on a more horizontal plane.

Organizational outflanking can be thought of in at least two related ways: one concerns the absence of knowledgeable resources on the part of the outflanked, the other concerns precisely what the organizationally outflanked may know only too well. First, let us consider the most evident absence of knowledge: ignorance. Frequently those who are relatively powerless remain so because they are ignorant of the ways of power: ignorant, that is, of matters of strategy, such as assessing the resources of the antagonist, of routine procedures, rules, agenda setting, access, of informal conduits as well as formal protocols, of the style and substance of power. It is not that they do not know the rules of the game; they might not recognize the game, let alone know the rules. Of course, this is a particular problem where an overwhelmingly technologically superior form of life meets one which is by contrast less developed in technical terms. Historically the vast majority of cross-cultural contact has occurred on this basis: consequently it has been the force of arms and the soundness of strategy which has settled the outcomes. However, as will subsequently be argued, it should not be assumed that overwhelming resources will necessarily ensure success. To do this means that they must be deployed on a battlefield suited to their deployment: strategically minded opponents will flee rather than fight until they have enticed the match into a timing, duration and a terrain more of their own choosing.

Ignorance often extends to a simple lack of knowledge of other similar, powerless agencies with whom one might construct an alliance. Here resistance cannot be part of a concerted action but remains an isolated occurrence, easily surmounted and overcome, even when its irruption is not infrequent across the whole canvas of power's scope. As long as the outbreaks remain uncoordinated, they can easily be dealt with by defeat, exile or incorporation. An absence of knowledge may be premised on isolation. One would resist or could do so more effectively if one were not so isolated. An agency may simply be unaware of the other agencies that might enter its calculations as potential allies, yet be only too aware of who its opponents might be. Even though the allies might easily outweigh the opponents if they could only connect, they cannot because they do not know of each other's location, although they might surmise their existence.

One step further from isolation is division. Time and space may be ordered and arranged to minimize the interaction and mutual awareness of subordinates, or even to render one group of subordinates invisible to another (Barnes 1988: 101). Complex divisions of labour may achieve this, in global supply chains, as may the extreme experience of competition. An example of the latter might be the arrangement of concerted action within an organization in such a way that it is experienced in individuated rather than collective terms through competitive individual bonus systems of payment or through other mechanisms for constructing an egocentric environment.

Organizational outflanking on the basis of knowledge operates in a quite distinct manner from those instances premised on ignorance. At issue is knowing not only what is to be done but also that the costs of doing it may be far in excess of the probability of either achieving the outcome or, if achieved, the benefits so obtained. Barnes (1988: 43–4) offers the unpleasant if apposite example of an extermination camp, one of the last century's more successful techniques of power. The Heart of Darkness' deals with these matters (Clegg et al, 2006). Within such a camp, the thousands of inmates might succeed in concerted action against the relatively few armed guards, depending, of course, upon the vulnerability of the watch-towers, the security of the perimeter, and the strength of arms on the part of the guards. With sufficient sacrifice, the inmates might overcome these obstacles but knowledge of two sorts may be said to operate in order to minimize this probability. First, there is the technical difficulty of achieving concertation among the inmates when they are unable to be seen to organize explicitly. Implicit organization is perhaps possible on the basis of contained sub-units, such as dormitories, but exceedingly difficult in the absence of either mechanisms or an arena of organization. In prisoner-of-war camps by contrast to death camps, the existence of a recognized command structure, its disciplines and rules, make this organization that much easier to achieve.

Second, there is a problem of some magnitude. Existing in severe deprivation, under a regime of brutality, terror and horror, is not conducive to closely organized ranks of relatively undisciplined individuals. Knowing that it is easy for the will to power to be broken by disparate acts of recalcitrance makes its achievement more fragile and precarious a probability. While there may be little or no chance of organizing for success, there is every chance that the attempt at organization will lead to certain failure and death. Even if it were successful, the confines of the camp may be breached only for an individual to be picked out, as part of the fleeing mob of inmates, at the leisure of the authorities who command the environs of the camp. For these reasons, opportunism will always be a problem. Few may be willing to sacrifice themselves for the altruistic good of others by initiating a charge on the armed guards. Some may hope to save their own skins by ensuring that others are exposed by them to the authorities. While routinized circuits of episodic power, fixed on particular points of passage, are always open to challenge and transformation through concerted action, this is an eventuality that remains in the abstract. If the organization of concerted action cannot be attempted or envisaged as a feasible form of resistance, routine relations, agencies, means, standing conditions, resources – in a word, powers – will be likely to endure. The resources will be judged all too frequently and accurately to be unavailable or insufficient to overwhelm extant circuits of power.

Finally, organizational outflanking may operate not so much on the knowledge of what can reasonably be anticipated to be achieved as on the fact that conditions exist which render any such knowledge useless. The necessity of labour's dull compulsion in order to 'earn' one's living, and the nature of that dull compulsion as busy work, as arduous exertion, as ceaseless activity, as routinely deadening, as compulsory and invariable, are such techniques of power that may easily discipline the blithest of theoretically free spirits when the conditions of that freedom become evident. The most resistant of wills may bend in time when it is without the remotest chance of increasing the freedom to manoeuvre through recourse to some alternative. Time is double-edged here: both using up the time of an agent on the routine performance of routine tasks as well as producing habituation over time, as the routines take on their own ritual nature as one of the bulwarks against the encroaching meaninglessness of the routine imposed from without. Such rituals may be both informal and formal, the former a kind of resistance to the meaning of the latter, as Burawoy (1979) charts. Formal rituals, myth and ceremony serve to reinforce and make meaningful the routines of everyday subordination, just as those of resistance may seek to ironicize, distance or undercut the more formal instances. In this way the formal rituals of power may be endured.

Mann's (1986) account stresses that historically, organizational outflanking of resistance has consisted of being capable of constituting a stable organization field of extensive, coherent and solidaristic alliances and nodal points. Historically this is something only rarely achieved by subordinate strata. Usually it has been achieved only in the face of division and access through marginalized but pervasive nodal points into some relations of meaning that are capable of fixing many disparate, subordinated entities into some coherent organization field (for example, various religious movements based on the transcendent ethic and organization capacities of Christian ideology, much as in Poland's 1980s struggle against Soviet rule). For the moment, let us leave the historical detail to one side. The next chapters of this book will attempt a descriptive sketch of the role of the circuits of power in constituting the central features of our modern world. For now the purpose is to develop the formal model which will guide that narrative.

SOCIAL INTEGRATION AND SYSTEM INTEGRATION: DISPOSITIONAL AND FACILITATIVE POWER RESPECTIVELY

One of those conceptual distinctions which seems to lend itself to constant re-working is that made by Lockwood (1964) in his famous paper on 'Social Integration and System Integration' (for example, see Parkin 1972b and 1976; Habermas 1976; Giddens 1979; Clegg and Dunkerley 1980; Barbalet 1987). As Barbalet (1987: 13) says 'Lockwood's treatment of social and system integration… offers a distinctive approach for understanding the relationship between social structural resources and power relations.' However, no single one of these 're-workings' will be adopted here, as it is necessary to conceive of Lockwood's (1964) 'institutional order' in quite specific terms. These conditions will develop a conception of social integration in terms of relations of meaning and membership, as these have been derived from debates about post-structuralism. System integration will be conceptualized in terms of 'material conditions' of techniques of production and discipline, in a conception quite consistent with Lockwood's Weberian formulation:

Material conditions most obviously include the technological means of control over the physical and social environment and the skills associated with these means. They include not only the material means of production, but also what Weber frequently refers to as the material means of organization and violence. (Lockwood 1964: 251)

Social and system integration can thus be conceptualized as the pathways through which fields of force are fixed and stabilized on 'obligatory passage points' in the circuits of power. What the actual conduits will be cannot be specified in advance but they will be contingent upon what flows through the circuits.

The circuit of social integration is concerned with fixing or refixing relations of meaning and of membership, while the circuit of system integration will be concerned with the empowerment and disempowerment of agencies' capacities, as these become more or less strategic as transformations occur which are incumbent upon changes in techniques of production and discipline. However, the latter circuit cannot, of course, escape relations of meaning and membership. It has to be fixed on obligatory points of passage through these if it is to have any effectiveness. It functions as a potent source of resistance to the stabilization of existing memberships and meanings by generating new techniques of production and new modes of discipline, which, if they are not already present within existing rules of practice, have the capacity to transform these. Existing structures of dominancy are thus in principle always open to subsidence, disruption and innovation, since new techniques may open up new conduits and passages which undermine the presently entrenched structures.

Changes in both social and system integration may be either endogenous or exogenous. If endogenous the changes occur as a result of episodic power outcomes achieving either transformations in the rules that fix relations of meaning and membership or enhancement in the process of innovation of techniques of production and discipline. Exogenous change occurs as a result of environmental contingencies which interrupt and disturb the fixed fields of force of the circuit of either social or system integration. It should be apparent that these circuits may be termed 'integrative' but they should always be viewed as double-edged: they may be disintegrative as well as integrative, particularly where exogenous sources of change are involved. No necessity attaches to exogenous disruption. Whether or not exogenous factors achieve impact will depend upon what Holton (1985: 212) has termed 'a highly complex interrelationship between the exogenous influence of innovations and the receptivity or otherwise of the endogenous unit in question'. Receptivity will always be dependent upon securing conduits through which traffic in the circuit of social integration must pass; hence the centrality to the model of the obligatory passage points and the rules of membership and meaning. Obligatory passage points represent the securing of particular 'indexical' interpretations of what these rules are.

The pathways of these circuits, as fields of force, will be carried by organization. It is for this reason that 'organizational outflanking' is basic to both social control and social change. Hence, each of the circuits of social and system integration will have to reproduce stable relations of episodic power, through fixing obligatory passage points, if they are to reproduce the extant organizational carrying capacity. (This is not represented in Figure 8.1, in order to avoid unnecessarily confusing detail.) The centrality of organization to the schema suggests that the sources of change therein will be organizational. Indeed, each circuit of social and system integration has a characteristic mode of organization change. For the circuit of social integration in which rules fix relations of meaning and membership, the characteristic device is what Meyer and Rowan (1977) term institutional isomorphism. Certain fixtures of meaning are privileged, certain membership categories are aligned with these meanings (Sacks 1972 on 'membership categorization devices' is relevant here) and, consequently, a specific organizational field (DiMaggio and Powell 1983) or what Callon et al. (1986: xvi) term an 'actor network' is constructed. Indeed, these two labels seem co-terminous. An 'actor network' concerns the interrelated set of entities successfully translated by an actor. This book has sought to avoid adopting the actor's perspective, in recognition that agency may well be organizational rather than a human, and so it will deploy the notion of an organization field, somewhat akin to a Foucauldian 'field of force', as a 'recognized area of institutional life' in DiMaggio and Powell's (1983) terms. Such fields exist only to the extent that they are an achievement of episodic power in the institutional field, stabilizing relations of power between organization agencies A, B,... N. Episodic power's achievement will consist, first, in constituting a relational field by 'enrolling' other organizations and agencies; second, in the 'stabilizing' of a network of power centrality, alliance and coalition among agencies within the field; third, in the 'fixing' of common relations of meaning and membership among the agencies within that field, such that they are reflexively aware of their constitution as a field.

As Stinchcombe (1965) has argued, the time at which organizations, and one may add organization fields, are constructed constrains the reproduction of their structural characteristics. Time functions here as a form of shorthand for the disciplinary techniques available at a specific conjuncture. However, this is constraint, not static reproduction of the same field of force. The general idea is well understood by organization ecology theorists who have argued that, as organizations age, their reproducibility and structural inertia will increase as meanings become more fixed on local membership conditions. Consequently, older organizations are favoured by selection processes because they have lower death rates than do newer organizations. New organizations are more liable to an imminent end to their mortality. Hannan and Freeman (1984: 152–7) term this the liability of newness thesis. This is not to say that older organizations should be regarded as immutable. There will invariably be competitive pressures from other organizations to improve performance by adopting innovations, but, as has been argued by Meyer and Rowan (1977), the spread of an innovation rapidly pushes to a threshold 'beyond which adoption provides legitimacy rather than improves performance' (DiMaggio and Powell 1983). Of course, this will particularly be the case for those public sector organizations which are not as subject to 'market discipline'. It is precisely these types of organizations that have most frequently been studied by writers associated with Meyer and Rowan's (1977) 'institutional' perspective. The general point would be that issues of social integration, achieved through fixing rules governing relations of meaning and membership, become more predominant both within organizations and in organization fields as they age. The fix is achieved by agencies exhibiting isomorphism in their adoption of innovation. The field becomes stabilized on certain rules of practice guiding innovation, such that membership and meaning characteristics tend towards a norm. Note, however, that all norms are temporal not eternal. Even though agencies may try to innovate constantly, the aggregate effect of these many individual agency changes may well be to lessen the diversity of the field of organizations: their membership and meaning characteristics in terms of personnel, formal structure, culture, goals, etc. tend towards homology, at least temporally. Structural inertia or reproduction may well be seen as a consequence of selection processes, as Hannan and Freeman (1984) have argued.

The above offers a formal framework for understanding the pressures in the circuit of social integration towards the stabilization of episodic power configurations in an organization field. It thus addresses pressures towards temporal stabilization of episodic power configurations of organization fields. Moreover, it is thoroughly consistent with Mann's (1986) argument that the reason that radical social change is rare is because of organizational outflanking. Compliance is premised on an absence of collective organization to do otherwise. Once a given configuration of an organization field has been stabilized, the pressures are such as to reproduce it that way (an implicit 'all things being equal' clause must be instanced here, before going on to discuss counter-tendencies). Not only can the evidence which Mann (1986) adduces be cited as relevant here; one might also, as Barbalet (1987) suggests, consider Stinchcombe's (1965) insight, as well as empirical support in Carroll and Delacroiz (1982) and Singh et al. (1986).

The theoretical approach in the literature of organization theory, which has focused on the circuit of social integration, has developed from the institutional perspective outlined by Meyer and Rowan (1977). A central mechanism of transformation and reproduction within this literature has been identified as 'institutional isomorphism' by DiMaggio and Powell (1983). Institutional isomorphism is concerned to understand how an innovation, once made, becomes widely adopted throughout organizations in a specific field. The issue of what is institutionalized, while not being addressed in institutionalism's neo-functionalist theory, is the central issue for the 'circuits' framework. What becomes institutionalized depends precisely on the power of agents' 'translation'. The circuits framework seeks to depict how this is accomplished. Institutional theory is not concerned with the nature or source of innovation itself. (In the 'circuits' framework, the circuit of facilitative power through system integration is the locus of this concern with 'social change'.) The institutional perspective is particularly concerned with 'politics' and 'ceremony', the focus which has been referred to here as rules of practice. Flow through these is a necessary route for both social and system integration in the circuits of power, once these are activated outside the episodic circuit. The circuit of social integration focuses on the mechanisms of institutional isomorphic change which DiMaggio and Powell (1983) identify in terms of three processes of coercive, mimetic, and normative pressure. (A useful review article on the 'institutional' perspective has been produced by Scott [1987]. The field of institutional theory has grown and developed considerably, becoming the dominant organization theory (see Greenwood et al., 2017.)

Coercive pressure tends to come from centrally configured agencies in the organization field and will be applied to dependent relations in the network. Changes of whatever kind are required by agencies that are able, as a result of existing configurations of episodic power relations, to demand their implementation. Obvious examples of these would be state legislation or routines requiring an organization response, such that organization structures stabilize and are fixed on rules institutionalized by state agencies:

> As a result, organizations are increasingly homogeneous within given domains and increasingly organized around rituals of conformity to wider institutions. At the same time, organizations are decreasingly structurally determined by the constraints posed by technical activities, and decreasingly held together by output controls. Under such circumstances organizations employ ritualized controls of credentials and group solidarity. (DiMaggio and Powell 1983: 150–1)

All forms of standardized reporting, co-ordinating or control mechanisms, within a circuit of social integration, will tend to reproduce existing configurations of power within a given organization field. It will not only be the case where external mechanisms are 'imposed'. In order to secure resources from the environment, agencies may well have to conform to those rule practices which the nodally positioned agencies in that environment require before they will ensure that the resources are forthcoming. If agencies want certain resources then they will have to do certain things, adopt certain practices. An interesting instance of this occurred historically in Australia.

The Australian Federal Government, as the sole supplier of funding for all tertiary education in Australia (bar a few donations, research company earnings, and what are at present other marginal inputs) in the late 1980s devised rules of practice in that organization field to transform radically the characteristics of the organizations within it. However, the government did not 'impose' these changes on the field. The situation was as follows. If agencies already within the field chose to remain within that field in the future, as the government transformed and reconstituted it, then they were obliged to comply with the rules that the government propounded. These involve detailed individual organization re-structuring and the preparation of 'profiles' by each tertiary organization. On the basis of these profiles, the organizations would 'bid' competitively for resources from a central government fund, over and above a diminishing pool of recurrent funds. Bids would be assessed on the basis of these profiles and their congruence with governmental priorities. An increasing fund of discretionary money would then be distributed accordingly.

The government was at pains to stress that these agencies were by no means being compelled to join the new 'national unified system'. They were free to choose to exist outside it. However, if they so chose, they would not be resourced by the government, given that they made the choice to step outside the rules of practice. Not surprisingly, not one of the sixty-four existing government-funded tertiary organizations chose to 'step out' of the system. The outcome was an organization field which display strongly enhanced features of institutional isomorphism.

Agencies may experience mimetic pressure by responding to environmental uncertainty or ambiguity, as is well understood in the contributions of March and his colleagues (e.g. March and Olsen [1976]; Cyert and March [1963]; Cohen et al. [1972]). Mimetic pressure can be seen in Japan's Meiji Restoration, when European examples, particularly that of Bismarck's Germany, were consciously mimicked (Westney 1987; Ketcham 1987). More recently, the proliferation of attempts to produce clones of Silicon Valley by various national and regional authorities around the world is a further example.

Mimetic pressure is a constant reminder that in order to outflank organizationally existing configurations of power, one of the few examples of innovation from which to learn is existing configurations. Another historical instance drawn from the political arena may serve to make the case clear. In post-war Australia, both the Menzies Liberal government and the Hawke Labor government were particularly good examples of mimetically innovating the opposing party's best policies. This form of fixing and stabilizing rules of practice does make innovative and successful opposition extremely difficult on anything other than a 'principled' basis. Such a 'principled' basis tends towards an 'articulatory' rather than an 'aggregative' politics. As has been argued elsewhere, it is the latter which tends to be more electorally successful because of its 'catch-all' character (Clegg et al. 1986). Another instance drawn from the formal arena of politics may be noted. In new nations, the pervasiveness of certain forms of rules of practice, membership and meaning can be understood because of their being not so much the most efficient mode of organization but the symbols of the 'imagined community' of 'proper' nations to which elite agencies in emergent states aspire. (B. Anderson's [1983] study of nationalism under the title of *Imagined Communities* is a sustained series of examples of this process and their often incongruous results. This study is considered in the next chapter.)

In the contemporary world, suggest DiMaggio and Powell (1983), the pressure of normative isomorphism is sustained mainly through the processes of professionalization. These ensure that common networks of discursive practice spread from universities and tertiary institutions generally throughout the organizations that employ professionals, as professionally sanctioned rules of practice. Such professional projects frequently enrol the state in their aid. As Boreham (1983) has argued, the claims of 'indetermination' (and thus non-substitutability) in the professional project have frequently enjoyed active state support, particularly amongst the 'new' rather than the 'traditional' professions (also see Johnson 1972).

Other sources of pressure for isomorphic rules of practices will be the structure of labour markets generally and especially the competitive filtering pressures that operate through phenomena such as 'credentialling' and 'internal labour markets' to produce low levels of variation in the salient membership characteristics of employees. Moreover, labour markets provide another example of the way in which episodic power configurations may be reproduced as a structurally unequal field of agencies. Good discussions of this exist in work by both Kreckel (1980) and Offe and Wiesenthal (1981): they are discussed in detail in Clegg et al. (1986: 259–69). The constitutive organizational properties of the 'countervailing power' of labour and capital on capitalist labour markets are such that they are pervaded by a distinctive configuration of episodic power as a 'primary asymmetry', as Kreckel (1980) terms it. Both in individual employment and in the possibilities for collective action, the rules of practice are heavily weighted against labour. The formal relationship may appear to be one of apparent reciprocity in terms of the exchange relation between employer and employees, yet, as Kreckel (1980) puts it

> their relationship is an asymmetrical one. First they do not need each other for the same purpose. Second, and more important, the conditions of their encounter are unequal for a very simple reason: unemployed labour in a capitalist system loses its exchange value more quickly than unemployed capital. Whenever the selling of labour power comes to a halt, be it voluntarily (e.g. a strike) or by force (e.g. lock-out; unemployment) this typically leads to immediate crises of personal income, if not personal identity, labour power being a relatively inflexible and 'perishable' commodity. Capital, on the other hand, is more flexible and more durable. In each case labour is temporarily unavailable, capital can 'wait', and it may also be transferred to alternative productive or even consumptive uses. Furthermore, a reduction of the labour force may very often be to the employer's advantage; it very rarely is to the workers. (Kreckel 1980: 529)

Here we have the source of those empirical tendencies towards mimetic interest isomorphism within each 'interest association', within peak organizations of labour against capital. One might refer to this as a constitutive feature of the rules of practice of the organizational field in which capital meets labour. However, these relations of membership are also always relations of meaning. Whether relations of meaning can be fixed across the many diverse sites of potential struggle, in organizationally stable forms, will be highly contingent. A great deal depends on the arena through which power in the circuit of integration is routed. In the industrial arena organizational outflanking by employer's associations of labour that is employed in many sites and belongs to multiple unions whose members have multiple preferences, will not be difficult for a few well-organized employers. The latter have not only the power of small numbers but also the ability to reduce all issues to a single interest in profitability to assist them. However, as Korpi (1979; 1983) and Clegg et al. (1986) have argued, if the power episodes of labour versus capital can be switched from the industrial to the political arena, then the structural asymmetry can be greatly reduced because it occurs in a more balanced organization field and configuration. Indeed, as Clegg et al. (1986) argue in their concluding chapter, it may even open up the possibility of transformation to a new game, because new dispositional capacities can be achieved. (Also, see Dow et al. 1984.) This is not an argument for an unproblematic conception of class interests (with all the attendant problems of absolutism), as some have argued (Hindess 1989; also see 1987). On the contrary, the argument proposes that agencies can form a collective representation of 'interests'. These may then be the basis for policies which contain calculations of the effects necessary to secure these putative interests. Where these effects can be demonstrated to be secured in whole or in part, it is not unreasonable to speak of interests being realized, more or less, in comparative cases.

Politics consists of coupling calculations, beneficial claims, and discursive categories in such a way that traffic in these has to pass through the network constructed by the representation of the interests thus secured. For instance, social democratic parties which claim to represent the interests of certain categories of people constituted in their discourse, such as 'families', 'workers', etc., will have to ensure that they show that these very categories are mobilized and benefited through their policies. Achievement of this produces a positioning of political actors and subjects, calculations and benefits, which then constitutes an aspect of the arena of politics through which the party in question can claim a 'privileged' position. Counter-claims thus have to traffic through the network so established, hence securing the legitimacy of certain categories, actors, calculations, etc.; in short, securing certain discursive forms on the basis of certain material benefits. (Concrete instantiation of this position is argued at length in Clegg et al. [1986] and Emmison et al. [1988].) System disintegration consists precisely in losing this positionality to competing discursive couplings which succeed in organizational outflanking through the new pathways. The mechanisms of integration and disintegration are the same.

Clear examples of an attempt at disintegration through resistance, which is premised on problematizing existing circuits of power with their implicit rules and domination, would be the seizure of 'innocent bystanders' as 'hostages' or an attack by the random violence of the car-bomb on the part of a 'terrorist' group. Such seizure or attack immediately implicates those ordinary people involved as resources in a deadly game with frequently unstable and unclear rules. The logic of the game is to undercut the normal circuits of politics by gaining access to the circuit of episodic power in order to achieve whatever are the group's desired objectives, despite the formal absence of the group from the conference chambers. To do this, the group seizes, as leverage, agents who invariably have not been directly implicated in whatever issues it is that the group seeks to advance. Terrorist action seeks to transform the extant circuits of power, to short-circuit existing rules and membership, and to handicap existing practices of domination within the web of the legitimacy which these practices claim. Its innovation is to claim legitimacy on the grounds that the sheer terror and illegitimacy of the action pursued are justified strategically in order to address the historical wrongs committed and the ultimate values denied. If the demands are not heard, legitimate voice not given to the excluded grievances, then the strategy is that of 'assault'. (Perhaps 'exit', 'voice' and 'loyalty' ought to be stretched to include 'assault' as another category of rational action.) Terror is the most fundamental assault on power imaginable, precisely because it neither conforms to isomorphic pressure nor heeds the evident superiority of disciplinary technique which it faces in the environment. Hence it is not easily defeated in the normal way through overwhelming superiority of force or resources by its opponents because it refuses the circuits in which these capacities can determine outcomes. Typically, it is the resignation of the opposition from a battle and field not of their design, rather than by defeat *per se*, through which the terrorist group enters into the episodic circuit in an institutionalized way and becomes a heroic force of whatever ultimate value was claimed to have guided them. Prior to this, particularly where the struggle is over ground which both sides hold to be sacred and to be theirs, a long war of attrition and position will usually prevail *if* the organizational resources to sustain it are available to both the occupants and the would-be outflankers.

System integration concerns the circuit of power through techniques of domination: that facilitative conception of power which sees episodic exercise of power beginning always from conditions other than rest, conditions of relative empowerment and disempowerment in terms of power's productive capacities. The organization of techniques of production and discipline, what Foucault (1977) calls disciplinary power, is subject to both competitive ecological and institutionally isomorphic pressures. It should be clear that discipline is not being used in a way which is designed to be synonymous with Foucault (1977). The conception of discipline is much less schematic than simply hierarchical observations, normalizing judgements and examinations. In this respect perhaps, if not in others, the conception used here is closer to the Weberian notion of discipline with its overtones of rationalized obedience. In tying discipline and production together in one circuit of facilitative power, one is mindful of the stress both in Foucault (1977) and in Parsons (1963) on power as productive. Because in this view power produces power, its effects can always be seen in terms of the relative empowerment and disempowerment of agencies in a relational field. Frequently this will occur through a 'zero-sum conflict', but it need not do so. It is conceivable that empowerment may occur of both the relatively more powerful and the relatively less powerful in the relational field of force, an outcome much sought after by management consultants, who refer to it as a 'win/win' situation. Certainly, it may well be so, but it is sociologically important to be unapologetic about the need to see this limited conceptualization within the broader relational picture. The practice of sociology without apologies is vital if we are to grasp the representation of power, rather than remain trapped within representations, tracing only the frame of that which fixes without ever grasping that which is fixed and the mechanisms whereby that fixity is achieved.

The two concepts of discipline and production are inseparable: this is one of the main lessons both of Foucault's concern with 'disciplinary power' and the whole 'labour process' perspective derived from Marx (1976) and Braverman (1974). Methods of production entail methods of discipline (Clegg and Dunkerley 1980). A number of schemata are available in the contemporary 'labour process' literature under the rubric of either types of 'control' (Edwards 1979; Friedman 1977; Clegg 1981) or 'factory regimes' (Burawoy 1985). In this useful literature, the dialectics of power and resistance are now well understood, although at the time of the first edition, little cross-fertilization of the post-Braverman and Foucauldian concerns (had occurred, although subsequently Knights and Vurdubakis, [1994], fostered an early rapprochmen that was to gather considerable support in the pages of *Organization Studies*). One point of continuity between Foucault's (1977) concern with 'disciplinary power' and theorists of the labour process and institutionalism has been agreement that, as Marglin (1974) argued with respect to early forms of the factory, efficiency arguments alone are insufficient to explain why certain types of technique of production and discipline were adopted. These approaches note not only competitive pressure but also institutional sources of isomorphism.

The circuit of facilitative power is the major conduit of variation in the circuits of power. Transformation of an existing configuration of episodic power networks both within any given agency and in terms of agency networks in a field of force, will, as Lockwood (1964: 252) originally suggested, arise 'from a "lack of fit" between its core institutional order and its material substructure', and 'will be characterized by a typical form of "strain" arising from the functional incompatibility between its institutional order and material base'. Social integration tends, within specific temporal parameters, to the stabilization of rules of practice. Lockwood termed the outcome of this the institutional order, while DiMaggio and Powell (1983) prefer institutional isomorphism. System integration, premised on disciplinary techniques of production, will be a potent source of transformation and strain, posing new conduits, new obligatory passage points which extant stabilizations of social integration may find difficult to escape or resolve. It will do this primarily through the production of new organizational forms, as Singh et al. (1986) argue. System integration will thus be a locus of potential instability and transformation, developing through the specific forms constructed around the core techniques of production and discipline. However, there will be a 'liability of newness' attached to these transformational forms.

The transformation of a given configuration of episodic power capacities has three distinct processes involved in it: variation, selection and retention. Variation consists of sources of difference in techniques of production and discipline. The sources of difference may be multifarious. They may be strategically innovated in the case of those agencies able to exert some control over their relevant environments (Child 1972) or they may have a more relatively independent, exogenous dynamic. Innovations in the techniques of production and discipline may well serve to empower or disempower significantly the existing power capacities which agencies might have. The whole labour process debate on 'de-skilling' is an instance of this (see the papers collected in Wood 1982). As Child's (1985) research into 'managerial strategies' suggests, the probability of disempowerment of an agency depends greatly on the position that that agency has constructed in the existing network configuration of episodic power as well as in the circuit of social integration. One would anticipate that this hypothesis would hold both intra-and inter-organizationally. Control of extant obligatory passage points, as by doctors in hospitals, will serve to reproduce institutionally system-transforming change in empowering rather than disempowering ways. For shop assistants, however, who are merely traffic through conduits controlled elsewhere, the impact of 'new technology' is by no means so empowering.

The source of innovation may be due to competitive cost-cutting pressures by capitalist entrepreneurs, for instance, or it may result from an ecologically transformed demography, such as the 'Black Death' of the fourteenth century which radically altered the balance of power between peasant and feudal lord. Through depopulation of the former and relative economic decline of the latter, it transformed the relational ties that bound them, opening up possibilities for fight and flight which had not hitherto been present to anything like the same degree (P. Anderson 1974). This example will be elaborated in the following chapter. In contemporary times, the effects of COVID-19 have been testament to a virus that has been not only a deadly actant but has produced remarkably innovative effects on many of those that did not succumb to it in terms of state responses to the virus. Governments locked down communities, requiring those organizations and employees that could, to organize working from home, creating an innovation with multiple effects. As Spicer (2023) notes, a revolution in working life has occurred. Home working became common during the pandemic, seemingly not as a temporary change. The UK Office for National Statistics reported that "between September 2022 and January 2023, 16% of the workforce still worked solely from home, while 28% were hybrid workers who split their time between home and the office. Even more than this – 40% – had worked from home at some point in the past seven days, compared with just 12% in 2019." (Spicer, 2023). A survey conducted in 27 countries and reported in Aksoy et al. (2022) reports it as a new norm. The effects of COVID-19, especially in terms of the circuits of power available to the state, are discussed in chapter 10. The pandemic reinforced both the powerfulness and the powerlessness of the state. The analytical point of these examples is that innovation may be a result of either strategic action or environmental chance. Where it is a result of purely contingent features, no strategy could have foreseen it beforehand. Contingent sources of innovation always have the potential to transform existing strategic relations.

The circuit of power through system integration is conceptualized after the model of the population ecology perspective in organization analysis (Aldrich 1979; Hannan and Freeman 1977). Competitive pressure for resources is hypothesized to be the major mechanism generating change and stability, through practices of innovation and isomorphism. However, it should be clear that what is being constructed is not a 'pure' population ecology argument *per se*. It is not only that there seem to be severe limitations to the applicability of these ideas in organization theory, as Young (1988) has cogently argued, but also that the strategic aim of this text is more an exercise in the imaginative application of some general ideas to the circuits of power framework, in an attempt to explain processes underlying change, than an application of population ecology or any other specific 'school' of organization analysis.

Innovation may depend on factors which at the time were wholly contingent. Not all sources of change will be selected. 'Organizations fitting environmental criteria are positively selected and survive, while others either fail or change to match environmental requirements' (Aldrich 1979: 29). Environments consist of resources for which agencies compete. Selection will occur through relative superiority in controlling and deploying resources, where control will usually be achieved through some extension of both inter- and intra-agency power. Retention is favoured by reproduction of the selective variation, such as Foucault (1977) and Bauman (1982) saw happening with the Panoptican form of disciplinary power in the nineteenth century. Prisons present interesting problems for organization theorists. That we still use the prison as a mode of disciplinary organization and as a major penal mechanism in the twenty-first century cannot be because it is so efficient at rehabilitating criminals, which invariably is an element in the 'mission statement' or 'formal goals' of most prison systems. On the contrary, recidivism rates everywhere suggest that prison functions only too well as a training ground for further criminality. As Foucault (1977) argues, the survival of the prison is premised on something other than efficiency in this respect. Incarceration along traditional lines serves only to tighten the webs of criminal membership and meaning for most inmates of the institutional form and to reproduce careers for those who work in and around it.

The prison functions as a substantive instance of the important point made by Astley (1985) that there is not just one type of ecological argument but two. From a perspective of 'community ecology' rather than 'population ecology', the prison's longevity becomes much more apparent. According to Astley (1985: 224), a community ecology perspective 'encompasses and complements the population ecology perspective'. Unlike the population approach, change from the community ecology perspective is perceived as being discontinuous. It operates through the colonization of new niches rather than through adaptation to existing ones. The colonization processes are described as being essentially random, dependent upon chance, opportunism and choice. Hence the focus is once more thrust back upon the rules of practice because it is these which both constrain and enable the occurrence of randomness. Thus, the prison was fixed on the basis of available disciplinary techniques that were loosed from the religious world and located within the regulatory web of the state as a monopoly supplier of the organizational form. Within the niche thus created it flourishes without rivals, having incorporated other forms of practice like probation as subsidiary to its penal task. Just as the onset of de-regulation typically produces a rapid proliferation of new population forms, one might assume that regulational fixity will produce a lack of innovation, especially where no 'incentive' exists to open up the rules of practice to incorporate competitive disciplinary techniques. Community ecology would focus, precisely, on 'the birth of the prison' and the birth of population forms generally as niches are constructed. Rules of practice are thus at the core of games of power.

The circuit of social integration generates tendencies towards the reproduction of extant configurations of episodic power. The circuit of system integration is altogether more dynamic and unstable: selection through market competition, niche changes and goodness of fit of agency and environment characteristics introduces a potent source of innovation from optimizing environments which will favour certain forms of technique of production and discipline. The economic theory of the firm of writers like Friedman (1953) would be an idealized model of these processes. Certain forms of technique of production and discipline will fail to flourish in certain environmental conditions because they are 'crowded out' by more successful forms which better compete for essential resources. Selection is not about pure competition and efficiency, however. It is through the facilitative circuit of power that domination is produced as certain forms of agency are empowered and disempowered. The process of empowerment/disempowerment is double edged. It is oriented to what are constituted as environmental resources, which are selected: however, to be retained they have to become stabilized in rules of practice as an 'obligatory passage point' through which an agency's reproduction must pass in the circuit of social integration.

System integration is thus a circuit of power which introduces a potent uncertainty and dynamism into power relations, by offering opportunities for empowerment and disempowerment, through the development of techniques of production and discipline. Crozier's (1964) classic study of the French government Tobacco Monopoly is a case in point. In an almost wholly bureaucratic system, in which the techniques of production were fully rationalized around the moving conveyor belt, and the techniques of discipline centred on a wage payment system of production-related bonuses, a potent form of resistance was presented to the only workers, maintenance men, who had not been subject to these increasingly rationalized techniques. Outside its normalizing power, they proved to be a powerful source of resistance to the whole rationalized system. Their resistance was premised upon the obligatory nature of their knowledge to the realization of everyone else's disciplined power within the system.

The circuit of power through system integration is a source of new opportunities for undermining established configurations of episodic circuits of power, as it generates competitive pressure through new forms of technique, new forms of disciplinary power, new forms of empowerment and disempowerment. However, no automaticity attaches to these processes (the functionalist and the Marxist error), no matter how long the long run to the lonely hour of the last instance may be. Agencies have to be able to position themselves in order to control the 'nodal' or 'obligatory passage points' that system (and social integration) circuits potentiate. Techniques of production and discipline generate pathways through emergent issues which can, through the construction of networks of alliance and control by agencies, become a new set of standing conditions redefining both social relations and agencies' causal powers. Whether or not these are realized becomes contingent upon the construction of those alliances and networks which can sustain the standing conditions: a process of some indeterminacy.

System integration and contradiction are obviously two aspects of the same process. Parkin (1976) has suggested that the tendencies towards contradiction will be contingent upon what are termed here relations of meaning and membership. Where these tend to be characterized by higher degrees of isomorphism, this congruence within a system of relations of meaning and membership will typically produce more of an equilibrium in the circuit of episodic power. In such circumstances, capacities will be more likely to determine outcomes. Isomorphism in this respect produces circuit stability; it is this tendency which the stress on 'thought-control' and 'hegemony' articulates in the literature. Where there is a plurality of relations of meaning and membership, there will be competitive bases of legitimation centred on the fixing of alternative nodal points, giving rise to differential resource-based capacities that enter into the episodic circuit of power. These will carry a highly uncertain potential for securing desired outcomes. Only in highly isomorphised circuits can outcomes be probabilistically determined by resources; more pluralistic circuits will be characterized by far more contingent and far less strategic calibrations of capacities and resources. Once more the nub of power resides in the relations of meaning and membership: if these are tightly keyed then loose coupling of elements in the circuit of system integration will not generally entail a threat to the social order, as Parkin (1976: 129) suggests. System contradictions, he says, are most likely to generate pressures for change when the relations of meaning and membership are strongly differentiated and classified with strong framing of the disparate meaning-elements, such that little boundary-spanning traffic occurs (Parkin 1976: 141; also see Bernstein [1971] on 'classification' and 'frame'). In these circumstances, competitive elites are likely to define their membership and meaning in terms of the competitive advantage and disadvantage that innovation in the techniques of discipline and production will entail for them. Thus, systems whose circuits of social integration are highly isomorphic will hypothetically be better able to respond to system innovation in a productive fashion. Other things being equal, the more open and competitive is the access to membership criteria, and the more stable the terms of that membership are, then the more secure the existing circuits of episodic power will be. Parkin (1976) elaborated his argument with a comparison of the relative stability of 'modern capitalism' compared to the relative instability of Eastern 'state socialism'.

While a stress on the circuit of system integration and the emergence of forms of innovation and domination would tend to orient one towards a model of 'efficiency' pressures, a stress on the circuit of social integration and the stabilization and fixing of rules of practice would tend to orient one towards a model of 'rationality' pressures (M. Meyer 1987). As Meyer argues, the efficiency argument tends to incoherence compared to the rationality argument. In the organizations literature, there is now no widespread agreement with classic writers like Weber (1978) that a particular organization form, such as bureaucracy, is predominant because of its competitive efficiency. Some contrary arguments have focused almost exclusively on the 'dysfunctions' of bureaucracy, identified on efficiency grounds. The well-known revisions to Weberian theory by writers such as Crozier (1964) would be instances of this negative view of the efficiency of bureaucracy. Another source of objection to the classic Weberian theme of bureaucratic efficiency would be the influential de-regulatory thrust of the 'public choice' literature widely disseminated through the pages of the journal, *Public Choice* (for example, Nellor 1984). By contrast, rationality models of organizations have considered efficiency to be less consequential than those pressures exerted on organizations as they attempt to manage and control contingencies. These may be of both an intra-organizational nature, such as the achievement of disciplined control over a labour process or a technology, as well as environmental. The latter would consist of attempts to master and exert control over equivocal, uncertain and dynamic environments. Such environments are seen as posing problems for which rarely if ever are there any immutable or definitive solutions. Rationality is thus the outcome of organizations exerting agency under conditions of some uncertainty as to how they should handle whatever it is that they might be handling. Rationality will always be expressed plurally in terms of shifting 'modes of rationality', as argued elsewhere (Clegg 1975; Clegg and Dunkerley 1980). There can be no single, rationally best way of organizing in a world characterized by flux and change. The emergence of rules of practice as identifiable 'modes of rationality' is thus important. These modes of rationality are not absolute but are recognizable and replicable solutions to problems which organizations are persuaded that they face. They may be mistaken in their prognoses, of course. To the extent that modes of rationality are seen to be successful solutions elsewhere, they acquire a cultural capital: they become a positional good to be aspired to as an end in itself.

The argument in terms of modes of rationality is able to be far more consistent than is that from efficiency because instances of a prevalent form being regarded as inefficient are not sufficient to disconfirm its explanatory thrust. Inefficient forms may be culturally valued. Rules of practice fix on them as obligatory passage points irrespective of the efficiency characteristics. In effect, the argument from modes of rationality is superior in explaining the persistence of organization forms. Modes of rationality have to be stressed in order to ensure that no mistaken conception exists that there is such a thing as rationality per se. However, an argument from modes of rationality can never explain organization innovation and how a certain practice of domination first emerged. Some form of efficiency argument in terms of the circuits of system integration is necessary in explaining where dominant modes of rationality come from: otherwise there would be no conceptual space for innovation in organization forms, modes of rationality and changes in domination. It is for this reason that innovation is always associated with the relative empowerment of some agents vis à vis the relative disempowerment of some other agents. It is also why the circuit of social integration is central to the model of circuits of power, because it cannot be avoided by any potential innovation, even where it has been exogenously produced with respect to any specific system of circuits.

CONCLUSION

We are a long way from fixing 'real interests' or delving into 'third dimensions' or exposing 'dominant ideologies'. These conceptions have not sustained this chapter. What has generated it has been the realization that the concept of power, in a singular sense, only appears to be an essentially contested concept. Parsons (1967) and Foucault (1977) have distinctly different (albeit with some family resemblances to each other) conceptions of power to the agency conception which has been mainstream. Additionally, writers like Wrong (1979) and Harré and Madden (1975) have pointed towards a dispositional conception of power, different again from the facilitative conception of 'power as productive' which both Parsons and Foucault develop. The strategy of this book has been to admit an insight to each distinct conception which the others do not share. On this basis, power can be understood analytically as moving through three distinct circuits, carried always by the organization of agencies. However, contrary to a view of organization as effortlessly rational or powerful, the carrying capacity is itself opened up for scrutiny in power terms.

The representation here of power, rather than monolithic, is altogether more contingent, more realist and more subject to those tendencies that Machiavelli saw only too well. It is not an over-extension of any single sovereign power conception. Instead it argues for the distinct circuits of episodic, facilitative and dispositional power, distinctions clearly grounded in the grammar of power as a concept. Central to each of these circuits, it has been argued, is effective organization, whose form is both simultaneously subject to pressures of reproduction and transformation in each of the circuits of social and system integration. The relation between the two is contingent upon organization. Whether sources of system disintegration or contradiction actually lead to transformation and a new practice of rules will depend upon the network of power and passage points that are achieved through episodic power's configuration of the organizational field at the level of social organization.

System integration is the source of resources for power, subject to competitive pressure (Hall [1986] argues this extensively in a major comparative and historical exercise). However, competition will not necessarily prevail as readily as in Friedman's (1953) highly idealized account of it. It will depend on the passageways made obligatory by the fixing of rules of practice at the facilitative core of power. At its centre lies the insight that post-structuralism makes available: our irremediable entrapment within webs of meaning together with our organizational capacity to transform these. This is the dialectic of power and structure.

In the next chapter of this book the general framework provided for the analysis of power is used to weave a narrative concerning the construction of the key nodal points of power in modernity: the state, organization and the market.

9
CONSTITUTING CIRCUITS OF POWER IN MODERNITY

INTRODUCTION

It is often argued that power is the central concept of the political sciences. If this is so, to the extent that analysis is restricted to any one of the one-dimensional, two-dimensional or three-dimensional models reviewed here, it is difficult to see how we could sensibly address some of the most important political phenomena which constitute modernity, such as the modern state, the very crucible of power according to almost all accounts. How can we turn the 'circuits of power' argument of the preceding chapter to the task of addressing what Foucault (1979a: 20) terms the emergence of 'governmentality'? How can one eschew 'the model of the *Leviathan* in the study of power' (Foucault 1980: 102) and still address the state?

The predominant contemporary forms of analysis of the state have been Marxist. The state has been regarded as an expressive totality redolent with imagery of exploitation and repression, both ideological and forceful, whose project would be terminated by that heir to the enlightenment quest for an emancipatory subject: the transcendent prole-tariat. Frankel (1983) has identified seven 'misconceptions' in this tradition of analysis, which any alternative approach should try to avoid. The assumptions under challenge are those that hold the state as an ideal-type; the state as a subject; the state as an instrument; the state as a derivative part of capital; the state as an object of morality and the state as a locus of ideological or hegemonic reproduction (see Frankel 1983: chapter one; also Jessop 1987). Avoidance will be attempted.

The key to the model of circuits of power is clearly that juncture at which social and system integration 'meet', as it were, in the construction of obligatory passage points in an organization field. The stabilization and fixing of rules of meaning and membership, and techniques of production and discipline, in an organization field which is capable of extensive reproduction over space and time are the central issue. The analysis should be able to fit together into one coherent framework both the competitive ecological and the institutionally isomorphic sources of change, and the organizational treatment of these, without reducing the organizational phenomenon to the status of a means or instrument manipulated by some other interests. Organization has irreducible power properties of its own and it is to the achievement of these that the account must be geared, so that the various factors of explanation such as the economic, the political, the ideological, and so on, can be seen as an integral part of the argument. It is in the constituting, fixing and re-fixing of certain obligatory passage points that an organization field, which is a stable configuration of episodic power, is evidenced as a stable and authoritative structure of dominancy. How was this achievement secured? By what means was organizational out-flanking, the central mechanism of social transformation, secured?

Contributions by Poggi (1978), Hall (1986), P. Anderson (1974), Giddens (1985) and others enable one to construct an account of the circuits of power which constituted the modern state. The point of considering this in detail is that it provides a sustained histori-cal case study of the way in which the stable configuration of episodic powers, which we know as the authoritative state, was developed. Organizational outflanking and the fixing of organization fields play a major role in the story. For the purposes of this account, the story begins with the role of the towns in the feudal sphere.

In this chapter, extensive use is made of existing historical sociological materials in order to illustrate a contribution to an analysis of the power of the state which is neither reductive in terms of interests nor purely descriptive. Of necessity the argument must be sketchy and it must be illustrative. In this context there is neither the space nor the resources to do other than this. To be explained is how what is now ordinarily referred to as 'the state' came into being. If, in the course of this discussion, it is clear that the matter was a result not of intentional action, a realization of some other, 'real', interests, but of complex, contingent, strategic action in constituting networks of power for many diverse but sometimes explicable reasons, then the purpose will be served.

URBANISM AS A FEUDAL NODAL POINT

Recent sociological history has pointed to decisive conditions of occidental dynamism being sustained in European history by virtue of a competitive ecology of autonomous states which developed in the niche space that Christianity, as an overarching relation of meaning, constituted (Hall 1986: 133–5). The states in question, those that became pathways of capitalist development, had as their only common feature what Holton (1985: 186) has referred to as 'an effective degree of centralization and national political coherence' which the less dynamic states did not achieve. However, it would be entirely mistaken to assume that there was any one privileged pathway to this effective organization. The distinctiveness of the space in which European state formation developed after the break-up of the Roman empire was twofold. First, the Church of Rome never succeeded in becoming an imperial power but its existence was sufficient to sustain relations of membership within a single community of overarching meaning, even when relations of force were reproducing a pluralized system of states. The development of these states had been contingent on the break-up of the Roman empire at the hands of those various northern tribes who were to found numerous realms on what had been its territory. Second, the existence of a competitive ecology of states, engaged in military technology and warfare, overlapped the dynamic of a competitive market system which had emerged out of the changing balance of power between landlords and peasants that was transformed by changes in the natural ecology of pestilence and productivity (P. Anderson 1974; Hall 1986).

Two competitive loci thus overlapped. In turn, they were faced by two comparatively structurally weak points of resistance. One point of resistance to both state and market power was the system of kinship relations. Extensive kin with extensive obligations of fealty and economic support are an excellent insurance against both an aggressive state and an unkind market. By comparison with other world civilizations, in Europe these tended to be less extended and more nuclearized than elsewhere. The reason for this concerned some European particularities of the relation of procreative activity to resources as they became established under the guidance of the Church. Laslett (1988: 235) identifies a 'specifically European system; one which ensures that normatively procreative activity will only take place between spouses who are required to create their own households'. An outcome of this was to ensure that 'European populations were sensitively and stably related to their economic and physical environment'. Some important consequences flowed from this.

Unlike among populations elsewhere, the pestilence of the Black Death in the fourteenth century was not a recurrent, routine event but extraordinary. Hence the human resource base grew steadily rather than shrinking and expanding in cycles. The requirements of household formation imposed a discipline of work and saving on most people. To marry one had to form one's own household: it was a correlate of marriage. In turn, marriage was a correlate of adulthood. Two consequences of this were evident: one was the spirit of parsimonious rectitude upon which a religious ethic would later bite (Weber 1976), the other was what Laslett (1988: 237) describes as a high degree of geographical mobility occurring amongst young people who worked in service prior to marriage. The capacity for generational learning which this produced in an otherwise highly geographically circumspect social world (apart from military adventures or Crusades) would have been a significant source of variation in new techniques of production and discipline.

While Laslett (1988) describes the nature of kinship in Europe, Hall (1986) argues that it became structured as it did in part because of church teaching which stressed the spiritual value of land bequests. To the extent that holdings sustained less densely tied kin, they might more reasonably be bequeathed. In addition, the Church itself, through the monastic discipline, became a network of interconnecting points of trade and distribution criss-crossing Europe, particularly those of the order of Cluny (Werner 1988: 174). Hall (1986: 136) has argued that it was the depth of penetration of markets throughout Europe which gave the European city its autonomous dynamic, agreeing with Weber (1978) in this respect. In Foucault's (1977) terms, these urban nodes became points of resistance (in comparison to elsewhere) to the reproduction of feudally bonded relations. They were dense, local points of pressure through which innovation in social relations took effect, according to Poggi's (1978) account. Perry Anderson (1974) also gives a particular effectiveness to the place of the towns. By his account, the humble rat was one of the principal agents of these transformations, as it was the 'Black Death', the bubonic plague virus carried by infected rats, which altered the balance of feudal power on the land between lord and peasant by weakening the taxable capacities of lords and strengthening those of the towns.

What agency did the rat play? To understand the answer to this question, we should appreciate the nature of agrarian production under feudalism. The limits of feudal production were ecological. Ecologically the limits to productive utilization of any land will always be expressed through a consideration of the amount of land surface in production relative to the available levels of technique. Under feudal property relations of agricultural production, the available technique depended upon the effective disciplining of peasant labour to bonds of feudal fealty and reciprocal obligation. The landed lord had a relative superiority of resources available for subordinating and pacifying the peasantry in order to extract a surplus from them. However, this was not power exerted upon an inert mass. The probability of peasant resistance was a function of the mass of disposable labour power that any given lord could bring into production. The procreative patterns already limited the amount of labour power, as did extant patterns of mortality. In the fourteenth century, the balance between mortality and reproduction was transformed as the bubonic plague virus latched on to a population which had become misaligned with the resources capable of supporting it. The limits of rural reclamation had been reached under the existing techniques of drainage and cultivation; the productivity of the available land had reached its outer limits and the size of population which could be sustained during famine was exceeded by that which had been reproduced. It could be said that biological reproduction of the species exceeded the agrarian production capacity of the land during the fourteenth century. The 'Malthusian' scenario was enacted. At the same time, exhaustion of the mines which yielded precious metals for currency led to widespread currency debasement and consequent inflation. On the one hand, there was a slowly increasing demographic base and a slowly decreasing agrarian base which could support it, as land became exhausted and over-exploited. On the other hand, there was spiralling inflation as less and less money was available for circulation and was chasing a decreasing supply of foodstuffs at ever more expensive prices.

It was during the first quarter of the fourteenth century that a number of factors began to transform the balance of feudal power. First, the rats: as carriers of bubonic plague, they were a normal health hazard. However, in times of famine, the population was increasingly at risk. Periods of famine, as P. Anderson (1974) notes, were increasingly prevalent because of the technical and ecological barrier of a fixed amount of cultivable land sustaining an increasing population. As a result of relative starvation, calorific shortfalls made the population more than usually susceptible to the plague. The loss of population in Western Europe was considerable: some estimates are about 25 percent overall. This solved the starvation problem readily because there were less mouths to feed as the century drew to a close than had been the case at the beginning. However, for those manorial lords who were dependent on grains for their income, less demand for agricultural staples led to a decline in revenue and income available for consumption of those luxury goods that were produced and marketed in the towns. Simultaneously, inflation was increasing the price of urban commodities and thus sustaining urban incomes, as the terms of trade turned against agricultural producers.

Those nobles who attempted to be rational actors were left with an obvious course of action. They could obtain more agricultural produce in order to maximize income. To do this meant either appropriating a greater surplus produce from the peasantry on their land or increasing the surplus being produced. However, the problems with the latter were ecological, not only with respect to the carrying capacity of existing technique and lands but also regarding population and social relations. In terms of the population ecology, fewer peasants were available than previously because of the ravages of plague. As it was, the rational choices made by the nobles slowly transformed the social relations constituting the universe of meaning and feudal membership. The peasants were the source of surplus; if surplus was to be increased from a diminished supply of peasants then the peasantry had to retain less and/or produce more. The extant bonds of extractive norms, fealty and reciprocal obligation were under attack from the asymmetrically stronger party.

Rational peasants would resist in such circumstances by seeking to retain what had traditionally been theirs and this is precisely what some of them did. They fought through peasant rebellions and, more especially, they took flight from a set of feudal relations in which one partner was reneging on what had traditionally been the rules of the game. Flight out of feudal relations could only be flight into urban centres or into vagrancy. There was nowhere else to go. Consequently, the urban centres received the advantage throughout the century of inputs of cheap, landless labour for whom exit from the urban sphere was not a realistic option, at least until they had become 'free' to move safely outside the town and through the feudal sphere. The response of the nobility was equally predictable: from the mid-century on, as P. Anderson (1974) notes, a wave of repressive legislation sought both to batten down peasant demands and to restrict the peasants more tightly to the land. This had major and variable consequences throughout Europe. Where urban forms had developed in the interstices of feudalism, the possibility of flight increased for the local peasantry, as did the probability of their rebellion (Anderson [1974: 205]; on the general conceptual point see Banaji [1977: 18]; on the general theory see Kula [1977]). The influence of urban centres was twofold:

> For, on the one hand, it was the prevalence of these market centres that rendered a flight from serfdom a permanent possibility for discontented peasants... On the other hand, the presence of these towns put constant pressure on the embattled nobles to realize their incomes in monetary form. The lords both needed cash, and, beyond a certain point, could not risk driving their peasants wholesale into vagrancy or urban employment. They therefore were compelled to accept a general relaxation of servile ties on the land. The result was a slow but steady commutation of dues into money rents in the West, and an increasing leasing-out of the demesne to peasant tenants. This process developed earliest and farthest, in England. (P. Anderson 1974: 206)

There were several consequences. First, feudal bonds and feudal revenues were greatly weakened. Second, an independent peasantry became self-interested and disciplinarily disposed towards productive and facilitative power rather than towards resistance as subservient producers. Hence, for the peasant units of production, there became compelling pressures for increasing productivity and returns, since the surplus produced would be enjoyed by the producers rather than by their feudal masters. Third, the subsistence economy declined and the market economy flourished under the impact of both the increasing market of urban growth and an emergent attitude more conducive towards increasing the efficiency of agricultural production and marketing. Fourth, the nobility increasingly switched out of a subsistence and into the market economy through, for example, enclosure for wool farming, oriented to servicing the clothing industry that was developing in the market economy. Fifth, to the extent that all of this occurred, the bonds of servility which sustained feudalism were weakened further.

Consequences of the decline of landed feudal relations can be identified for the state system. From the point of view of the sovereign power of the monarchy, the main feature of entitlement to territory was the ability to tax it in order to sustain the dedicated pursuit of warfare, the major monarchical recreation of Europe in the fourteenth and fifteenth centuries. War was costly and taxation was the key issue in its contrivance (Wallerstein 1974). Above all, feudal rule required military force to confront other hostile states and would-be rulers. Military force required taxes to pay soldiers, purchase equipment, and so on. At the same time as the social changes already discussed were occurring, changes in military technique and discipline were also weakening the basis of feudal armies of loyal medieval knights and ill-disciplined peasants. Large standing armies, trained in disciplinary formations of pikemen, were costly. They required centralized funding, training and provision. Centralizing tendencies favoured those states whose extractive capacities were best regularized.

Giddens (1985) argues that there are a number of extremely important and inter-linked military developments in techniques of production and discipline which facilitated the strengthening of circuits of power through the tax-raising capacities of the ruler. First, changes in armaments rendered obsolete certain traditional siege-based techniques of war. Second, armed bodies of men became themselves the object of disciplinary techniques, through drill and formation. Third, there was the development of European naval strength, which in itself was dependent upon specific navigational and shipbuilding techniques that were developed during the sixteenth century (Law 1986b). The gun was the most important new innovation. It transformed both war and urban life, outflanking both the castle and the city walls as defensive fortifications. Giddens (1985) also emphasized the importance of cannon at sea on warships. These contingent innovations, as well as the competitive ecology of states which fostered them through the fortunes of war, were to shape decisively the pattern of European state formation (Giddens 1985: 111–12). Hence one can agree with the centrality which Mann (1986) attaches to the military: its innovations were frequently a major source of outflanking organization of one state by another and its financing was the major pressure on state capacities (Mann 1980).

War is absolutely decisive for Giddens' account. War and preparation for war was the initial competitive pressure that shaped the ecology of states in Europe. This led to the reorganization of administrative and organizational capacities which could generate the surplus sufficient to continue waging war. At the same time, changes in productive forces and disciplinary techniques were carried primarily through states competing at war, rather than, as many Marxist accounts would have it, through purely economic changes. Thus, for Giddens, the source of system disintegration is, in terms of what have been referred to in the 'circuits' model as techniques of discipline and production, the circuit of competitive innovation. Another source of competitive pressure for innovation resulted from certain other forms of violence: persecution and bigotry. Persons whose agency was limited by war or persecution were not captives of the state as an all-embracing totality, as would have been the case had there not been a competitive plurality of states. Those whose resources of cultural or financial capital were threatened by the state which presently enveloped them could escape elsewhere. If a given niche space proved hostile, one could readily migrate to an alternative space. Hence, techniques of production and discipline could be transmitted and reproduced even when existing niche spaces were not environmentally supportive.

In raising money for warfare, the prosperity of the towns made them an obvious target for taxation. However, unlike the chain of particularistic pressure that could run directly from monarch to vassal and from vassal to peasants on the landed estates, in order to produce fruitful, if painfully and intermittently extracted, surplus produce, no such chain of 'fealty', or circuit of power, laced together the urban burghers and the monarch. The towns were interstices of feudalism within which strongly organized fields of force could be contained inside the city walls. Poggi (1978) regards them as organized corporate agencies, which were a potent site of resistance to feudal restrictions on commerce, production and trade. Resistance was organized through the corporate bodies known as the estates, representing the free burghers of the town. As a corporate body, representation in and of it was relatively formal and public. The publicity of corporate rule in the burgher estates was in marked contrast to the central locus of power around the court. The nobles gained representation only on a basis of particularistic and often private exchange with the king. Vassal and monarch consorted relatively privately at court. Monarch and estates necessarily related in public not only because of the representational and organizational qualities of the estates but also because of their absence from court. The public nature of the estates' relation with the territorial ruler tended to outflank organizationally the particularism of vassal-monarch relatios. The public quality made the relation more accountable and less likely to sabotage, undercutting and deceit, precisely because the relation was less particularistic.

Public, corporate, representative functions were organized through elected representatives who governed by enacting statute and who administered by developing differentiated offices. Offices were functionally distinct from incumbents. Typically these incumbents were drawn from the free burghers; the prosperous lawyers, merchants and other literate people for whom public life was an emergent civil sphere outside of state control and distinct from domiciliary affairs. A plurality of public domains in the towns began to emerge as an organizational field with distinct rules of membership and meaning. Representation of a public, ordered, procedural nature was developing in urban nodal points, which was distinct from that circuit of power that tied the nobility to monarchical grace and favour and that was located in and centred on the scheming, the sycophancy and the particularism of court. As modes of organizing estate rule and of resisting incursion from either nearby nobles or a distant monarch, the towns necessarily constituted new fields of force through which power was deployed. As such, they could not for long be ignored by monarchs who increasingly had to extend their rule through these public nodal points, producing a rule which required that a royal household be oriented less to the court and more to the administration and defence of the realm.

The defence of the realm was the central business of rule (Mann 1980). From the fourteenth century onwards, in what were to become the major centres of western Europe, this rule increasingly bypassed the feudal lords and came to centre on the courts of patrimonial rulers. Hence the monarch frequently sought to constitute 'estates (representative urban assemblies) in order to construct a network of power through which taxes might be procured', as Poggi (1978) argues. However, to constitute such assemblies was to implicate one's self as ruler in an organization field quite distinct from that of the court. It was a public rather than a private field of force; in such an assembly, a ruler met not one subject whose loyalty could be bought by particularistic favour but a representative agency that was relatively immune to particularistic deals and settlements, precisely because of the corporate constitution of that agency. Yet, rulers seeking to sustain military power had no option other than to enter this organization field and navigate its circuits and seek to constitute control over points of passage through it. Consent for sequestration on an orderly basis of taxation had to be sought if monarchical militance was to sustain the basis of orderly rule within a given territory, against other claimants. Monarchs could not simply plunder from the towns the resources they required, in part because of the way in which the towns were constituted. Towns were a definite urban space, sharply delimited by fortification and easily defended. The spatial configuration that favoured the constitution of an urban organization field also favoured a defensive strategy for maintaining control of it. In addition to the city walls there was an urban militia, a distinct and effective technique of military production and discipline. It was useful not only for defence but also for occasional offence, which was pursued through urban alliances between towns against a common threat of feudal depredation.

The centrality of the estate system as an organizational field, defining and constituting resources, was not immutable, as is evident in Poggi's (1978) account of how they were outflanked in Prussia. Here, he suggests, the key move was the creation of a new tax. The tax in question was an urban excise on consumption goods, the collection of which was placed in the hands of the ruler's personal agents. Consequently, neither vassals nor estates remained the primary conduits for the upward flow of resources. These resources were of revenue directed chiefly to the ruler, with which the ruler was able to sustain the costs of maintaining a standing army capable of resisting Swedish expansionism against Prussian dominion. Now the key point of the organizational changes was to bypass the estates in commandeering a fiscal flow and putting it to military use. Consequently, the ruler was increasingly able not only to dispense with the necessity to assemble the estates but also to ignore their resistance to this marginalization. What the ruler wanted could now be obtained in other ways more facilitative of circuits centred on obligatory passage points under monarchical control. Both the vassals and the estates were organizationally outflanked. The vassals were also effectively settled with a compact whereby the Junkers 'maintained jurisdictional authority over local government, while also becoming incorporated into the army and bureaucracy' (Holton 1985: 183). In the longer term, the personal agents of the prince were themselves to be outflanked by the developing bureaucracy.

As Poggi (1978) notes, the ruler was not only a single symbol personified in the monarch but also incorporated the total administration of the royal household. To the extent that rulership could sequester economic resources without consent and use these to generate a superior military might, the resistance of the estates could be marginalized. To quote him: 'Progressively this household became the centre of a new, even larger body of political administrative personnel, all of whose members, however exalted and handsomely rewarded, stood in a relation of greater dependence on and submission to the ruler than was ever the case with feudal vassalage' (Poggi 1978: 53). Within this body of personnel, three distinctive but sometimes overlapping strata may be distinguished. They were those who shared the near monopoly of literacy in feudal society as their key resource: clerics, university-trained lawyers, and those nobles who were seeking advancement at court. Through such 'delegates', the ruler was able to consolidate territory and rule. Sovereignty was staked against external claimants with an avaricious eye upon a territory; internally it was posited against feudal magnates, other pretenders to the throne, and eventually the estates themselves.

The outcomes of these political processes were various, as Poggi (1978) suggests. In France it led to the development of the strongest absolutist state in Europe. Here a territorial ruling dynasty progressively centralized power, politically weakened the estates and built an increasingly effective apparatus of rule around the monarch. This reached its peak, of course, with the Sun King, Louis XIV. In England, after the consolidation of the Norman conquest, the monarchy met progressively stronger opposition. Despite this opposition, it had achieved by the twelfth century a strong unified position. Eventually, of course, opposition was to produce the Cromwellian rebellion and state seizure. After the fall of the Stuarts, it was Parliament which continued the centralization of the English state and which became the obligatory passage point through which key relations and resources had to flow. Unlike in Prussia, where the growth of the estates was outflanked, Parliament could no longer be detoured. In Prussia, the extension of rule though formal administration and tax collecting extended the episodic power of the ruler in routinized ways. Rationalization occurred extensively in the service of external state-to-state relations, primarily through the diplomacy of arms, as Giddens (1985) observes. Other techniques became modelled on military discipline, establishing an ethic of rigour and discipline which was not contained among the ranks of the army but spread into the general business of rule, into administration, into economic action and into moral and spiritual regulation, as Holton (1985: 187) and Oesterich (1982: 270) observe. Holton (1985: 182) notes: 'The comparatively spare and frugal character of the Prussian bureaucracy reflected, at least in part, the limited financial resources available to the state – especially once military needs were met.' Holton follows Oesterich (1982) in seeing not only the protestant origins of this discipline but also the impact of ascetic Dutch humanism and political philosophy. The remarkably disciplined effects impressed almost all contemporary observers, not least Hegel. The contrast with French absolutism in its ill-discipline could not have been more marked.

A significant factor in the growth of Prussian absolutism was the Reformation, which fragmented the religious unity of the Christian community and undermined the theocratic status of the Holy Roman Empire. Important consequences followed. The maintenance of order and the protection of life became the internal functions of the state, rather than the imposition of one religious truth. With the Reformation came the general realization that scripture was not a sacred holy writ of tradition but could be subject to systematic interpretation. In addition, that interpretation was no longer to be seen as simply the monopoly of the Pope and his bishops. With the democratization of religious conscience that the Reformation unleashed, there also developed the parallel critique of the traditional conception of the ruler as a judge of established rights. In the new absolutism, the ruler increasingly became a source of new law, legislating with respect to civil law. Law became increasingly an instrument of rule rather than simply a traditional framework for rule. It was a law that applied to all within a territorially delimited area. It became increasingly more universalistic, helping to de-personalize state authority from the ruler, thus providing a basis for abstract rights and duties to be conceived separately from the cumulated prerogatives and rights of the historically distinct status groups of feudal society.

CENTRALIZED STATES AND THE EMERGENCE OF 'PUBLIC' ADMINISTRATION

The system of feudal states that were dotted across Europe were linked mainly through markets (Wallerstein 1974) and through the circulation of elites between courts (Elias 1983). For the majority of the population, hardly any connections existed. Under absolutism on the continent and the centralizing parliamentary state-form emergent in England (Macfarlane 1988), the routinization of rule took on what Foucault (1977) and Bauman (1982) term a more capillary form. It began to reach down slowly into the everyday lives of its subjects, taking the shape more of a series of conduits than of a 'capstone' in John Hall's (1986) phrase. To maintain the flow of traffic in these conduits, mainly of taxation revenues and military expenditures, a new organization field began to be stabilized. Rulers who followed the Prussian route might outflank estates and vassals but their constitution of power required delegation to a body of permanent and dependent officials. The existence of these increased enormously the efficiency of rule through fixing standing conditions under which resources could be effectively garnered, delegates empowered, offices authorized and state capacities increased (Poggi 1978; Giddens 1985; Dyson 1980).

The major innovations that created the new centralized absolutist state of the six-teenth century included disciplinary techniques, such as the introduction of standing armies; the development of a permanent bureaucracy, initially based on the venality of office; the strengthening of public taxation; the emergence of stable rules of meaning and membership through codified law; the emergence of a common set of relations of trading membership within the beginnings of a unified common market based on European-wide trade in cereals and grains. The emphasis of different writers varies. While Wallerstein (1974), for instance, stresses the common market aspects, Giddens (1984) the military, and Poggi (1978) the administrative, P. Anderson (1974) places particular emphasis upon the importance of the reception of Roman law in continental Europe. His focus is on its rediscovery in those territories which had been subject to the Roman Empire. It was in Roman law that the justification for overriding traditional feudal rights and creating new relations of meaning and membership was to be found. Within Roman law could be found traditions of equity, the idea of rational canons of evidence, and the notion of a professional judiciary. It enabled the emergence of a codified body of practice. On this basis, 'public' law, pertaining to the impersonal, abstract character of the state, could emerge equipped with distinctive procedural and administrative rules. This occurred throughout continental Europe but not in England, where law was made initially by stat-ute and latterly, after the revolution of Cromwell, through Parliament.

The circuits of law and taxation may be taken as efficient indices of the circuit of power. In terms of state formation, law is the formalized circulatory medium of rules of meaning and membership, while the conduits of tax revenues frequently serve as points of resistance to rule. In absolutist France, the circuits all passed through the monarch. One consequence of this was the enormous public projection of power that was disposed through this one body. Poggi (1978), in a marvellous passage, perfectly captures the fla-vour of this centralized and patrimonial state:

> Rule now rested solely with the monarch, who had gathered all effective (as against formal) public prerogatives unto himself. To exercise it, he first had to increase his own prominence, had to magnify and project the majesty of his powers by greatly enlarging his court and intensifying its glamour. The absolute ruler's court was no longer the upper section of his household, a circle of relatives, close associates, and favoured dependents. It was an extensive, artificially constructed and regulated, highly distinc-tive world that appeared to outsiders (and to foreigners) to be a lofty plateau, an exalted stage at the centre of which the ruler stood in a position of unchallengeable superiority. The ruler's person, to begin with, was continuously displayed in the glare of the condensed and heightened 'public' world embodied in the court. Let us consider this phenomenon in the seventeenth-century French court, which best exemplified it. The king of France was thoroughly, without residue, a 'public' personage. His mother gave birth to him in public, and from that moment his existence, down to its most trivial moments, was acted out before the eyes of attendants who were holders of dignified

offices. He ate in public, went to bed in public, woke up and was clothed and groomed in public, urinated and defecated in public. He did not much bathe in public; but then neither did he do so in private. I know of no evidence that he copulated in public, but he came near enough, considering the circumstances under which he was expected to deflower his august bride. When he died (in public), his body was promptly and messily chopped up in public, and its severed parts ceremoniously handed out to the more exalted among the personages who had been attending him throughout his mortal existence. (Poggi 1978: 68–9)

If the monarch was the personal emblem of this rule, the centre of absolutist administration was the court, the most influential of which was in Paris. From there, codes of conduct, of manners, of taste, of deportment, of language, of clothing, of all manner of relations of meaning and membership of an elite, were to spread in varying periods to all the other European courts. These relations of meaning and membership spread through 'emulation' (or mimetic isomorphism, as it has been termed in the 'circuits' model) between elites within the competitive state system. Hall (1986) sees this process of emulation most clearly in the history of art, from the late-fifteenth century spread of the Italian Renaissance styles throughout Europe as a result of French conquest. As he observes,

> emulation was not confined to artistic matters, but extended to the establishment of various scientific clubs in eighteenth century France in conscious imitation of their English rivals. Such emulation is ultimately only possible between states which recognized each other as of more or less similar standing. (Hall 1986: 139)

Europe became a diplomatic network of power, with power centred on and through the courts of the various states. Internally, the conduits were fiscal and administrative. They involved the flow of revenues and laws. Externally, they centred on the rarefied heights of the court and a courtly society constituted around the most elaborate and subtle distinctions of status. In the terms of Elias (1983), the many individual courts of the west, with their relatively uniform manners, can be seen as communicating agencies in European society at large. 'Society' was composed of a courtly aristocracy embracing western Europe, with its centre in Paris, with dependencies in all other courts, and with offshoots into all other circles that could lay claim to belong to that 'society'. This new and emergent concept of 'society' incorporated the upper stratum of the bourgeoisie as well as some broader layers of the wealthy middle classes. Elias (1983) suggests that the members of this courtly society, spread throughout Europe, had far more in common with each other than with the subjects of rule of the individual and different courts. For one thing, they all spoke the same language, French. They read the same books, displayed the same taste, had the same manners, and, with differences of degree, the same style of living. They intermarried and thus consolidated interlocking property and kinship ties: sometimes they fought each other.

At the height of French absolutism, the ruler ruled from his court rather than through it, to use Poggi's (1978) phrase. The court, with its exquisite etiquette of status, became a privileged arena to which all who aspired to the political game must want to belong. It was *the* conduit of power, *the* obligatory passage point, which also served to shield the absolute ruler against attempts to regain corporate rights of rule. In ruling from the court, rather than through it, the monarch also exercised power through councils of government, which were so important in managing and maintaining the diplomatic arrangements between the constellation of nation states that characterized the European landscape by the sixteenth century.

Particularly under French absolutism, officialdom was premised in part on administration based on nomination and merit, as for example *les intendants*, and in part on the 'venality of office'. With respect to the latter, some rights to collect revenue in the form of taxes were sold. The assumption behind the 'auction' was that someone working to collect taxes on the ruler's behalf would make sufficient surplus income out of the exercise that it would be worth their spending a considerable amount of money to buy the rights which enabled them to exercise that office. Some elements of taxation sustained the office-holder, some sustained the monarch, while others reproduced and extended state capacities. Offices of the royal administration which had been bought could become hereditary through payment of an annual fee. At times of financial crisis, the ruler would create offices *en masse* whose sole purpose was to raise additional funds. This system not only proliferated administrative posts but also increased the rapaciousness of officials, who tried to get their money back as quickly as possible before the creation of more offices lowered the value of the existing ones.

In a situation where the monarch was constrained fiscally and did not want to put his private fortune and income at great risk, the sale of offices was an effective way of both securing funds and strengthening the state. While the practice of selling offices met the costs of state-building, it also created a fourth estate of office-holders whose interests were allied to the ruler in an organization field fixed on the flow of revenues. However, the creation of a hierarchy of such offices posed a threat to the traditionally powerful noble families who staffed the ranks of the nominated *commissaires*. The sale of office opened a route of social mobility for the burgher strata of society, who might seek ennoblement on the basis of tax-farming services rendered. Although the sale of office was hardly procedurally meritocratic, it was somewhat less particularistic in its recruitment of office-holders than the practice of filling office only through members of the aristocratic lineage. To substitute the power of money for the power of blood would have been a marginal democratization: as it was, however, both money and blood were necessary for those who aspired to the most important offices, which gave access to the nobility, such as the judges of the *Parlements*. In the terms of modern sociology, the sale of office created a form of 'clientelism' (Dyson 1980; Ferraresi 1983) alongside and interpenetrated with the older feudal system of nomination and merit.

Courtly society was the major instrument of rule under the absolutist regime of the French king. In Prussia, by the eighteenth century, the mechanisms were far more pervasive and less centralized. Modern forms of rule were being constructed, prefiguring the rule of bureaucracy in its more modern and rational-legal form. At the centre of this bureaucracy, which began to emerge with Frederick William I of Prussia, was a new type of public law. It was specifically concerned with the construction and operation of a system of administration. Unlike the earlier French patrimonial bureaucracy, offices were not sold. Members operated neither directly under a commission from a ruler nor under the arbitrary rule of personal command. Instead they worked under the guidance and control of a body of administrative law. In what was to become the classic model of bureaucracy, the individuals who staffed such administrative organs were functionaries. They did not own the posts that they occupied, nor were they supposed to sequester them or any revenues that accumulated from them. The salaries were fixed according to a strictly determined scale. How they were to relate to superiors, subordinates, colleagues, and the public at large, was laid down and specified quite precisely in the administrative law. Decision-making of all sorts was to be reached through juristic reasoning, applying general legal provisions to particular circumstances. All decisions were to be recorded and transacted in writing and placed in the files. It served as part of the basis for Weber's (1978) characterization of an ideal type of bureaucracy as *the* disciplined instrument and technique of rule. Increasingly, under such a system, administration operates as the instrument not so much of the rule of the court and of the courtly society but of its own laws. It begins to outflank the court's privileged *rites de passage* and obligatory positioning, in large part through its sheer technical efficiency. No other existing system of rule could compete with it.

The state as an abstract entity became increasingly 'public'. It could be seen as a set of statutes and codes that were available for all to inspect. It was manifested and embodied in officials who were bound by these statutes and codes and who often displayed their status and position in the hierarchy of officialdom through the uniform or insignia of rank which they wore. (Contrast this outer embodiment with that of the King of France in the seventeenth century.) Visible signs of office constituted them as officials. The state was increasingly separate from what became known as civil society. From the vantage point of the state, those admitted to be under rule were civil individuals who were constituted as subjects and subject to tax, subject to military service, subject to juridical regulation, etc. What constituted them was precisely their status as subjects of rule, subject to rules. Major objects of intervention and regulation were to be the varying economic restrictions and practices which the guilds and corporate bodies of the towns had developed over the preceding centuries.

Running a state became increasingly costly, both in its courtly excrescence in France and in its more routinized form in Prussia. Consequently, it became a prime necessity of the state to ensure the production of the taxable surplus with which the state could continue to reproduce itself. Civil society, thus constituted, was not maintained at arm's length for long. Eventually, demands for an active participative role in the public/political process from an emergent class, a new public, the bourgeoisie, were to transform the system of rule. New conduits of economic power arose which were not initially subject to complex transnational ties. However, they were to produce a new basis for such ties, which moved through neither the court nor blood-lines, nor even the administratively public bureaucracy but through industry, trade and commerce. From about the middle of the eighteenth century onwards (earlier in one country, somewhat later in another) there was a gradual displacement of the centre of gravity from courtly society on a European scale to various national bourgeois societies. Symptomatic of these changes, above all else, was the way in which the French language gave way as a language of courtly society to a bourgeois vernacular which increasingly became a national language, even among the upper classes.

MARKETS AND STATES AND POWER

While there may be disputes between different theorists as to the role of warfare, military technology and the development of capitalism in the rise of the modern nation state, it is clear that the western absolutist and centralist state was of fundamental importance in providing the legal, political and military framework for the development of capitalist economies. Some writers, such as Holton (1986), join Wallerstein (1974) in arguing for the centrality to the process of state formation of those new forms of surplus appropriation which Wallerstein describes as a capitalist world economy. This surplus appropriation was based not on the direct appropriation of agricultural surplus, in the form of tribute or in terms of feudal rent, but on more efficient and expanded productivity, initially in agriculture, later in industry. For Wallerstein, a crucial component of this was the existence of a growing trans-European world economy in exchange and trade between that plurality of competitive states which occupied the world market as it began to be formed. From the very beginning, he argues, this world market was a capitalist world economy. (Evident empirical problems in this framework have been signalled by O'Brien's [1983] research which indicates that there were in fact quite insignificant amounts of international trade recorded at precisely the time that this 'world-economy' was supposedly being constructed.) Several factors are identified as essential in this establishment of a capitalist world economy. These include the territorial expansion of Europe; the development of different forms of labour control for different products in different zones of the world economy, in particular the maintenance of feudal relations of production in eastern Europe and the development of plantation economies based on African slavery in the newly discovered territories of the Americas. The longevity of these feudal organization forms in the lands east of the Elbe contrasts with the creation of relatively strong state machineries in what would become the core states of the capitalist world economy. The strategy which these states followed sought to try to maintain nationally favourable terms of trade. According to Wallerstein, the distinctiveness of the new world system was that, as an economic entity, it was much larger than any political unit within it. Hitherto, political entities in the forms of imperial systems had transcended economic entities; henceforth, this polarity was to be reversed. A competitive ecology of states and a facilitative circuit of power, as the basis of system integration, had emerged.

Wallerstein's (1974) book, *The Modern World System*, charts the transition from a world in which the core was the economic activity clustered around the northern shores of the Mediterranean to one in which the central axis shifted to the maritime provinces of north-western Europe. At the centre of his account is the importance of the nation-state within an increasingly competitive international context, in which endogenous intrastate factors were contingencies that could relatively empower that state in the competitive struggle. However, none of the states emergent from the fifteenth century onwards was sufficiently strong in absolute terms to overwhelm the other states – hence the ecology was set for a competitive struggle. Frequently this was manifested in terms of warfare over control of those regions within the expanding world economy that were not yet consolidated in state form, initially in Europe and then increasingly in the rest of the world. Additionally, and as a necessary basis for successful armed struggle, economic innovations were also competitively engendered, both through isomorphic pressures, once innovated, as well as pioneering innovation. The conditions of innovation for 'pioneers' were of course very different from those that facilitated isomorphic diffusion and adoption. The latter can selectively learn and adapt from pioneering efforts. On the other hand, as Holton (1985: 210) has observed, the mimetic followers 'also face competition and pressure from already established capitalist nations, pressure which may be sufficient to inhibit or distort subsequent processes of transition to capitalism'.

The pace-setter in this transition was England, where the leading edge of export trade was textiles. Certain features of the English state helped to assure its advantage, as did the importation of many diverse disciplinary techniques from elsewhere. The confiscation and sale of church lands by Henry VIII had expanded the amount of land available on the market, particularly for agricultural production, and had accelerated the extension of capitalist modes of production, in part by throwing new sources of capital into circulation. With the exception of the Irish problem, which was subject to periodic renewal, England was exceptionally unified. It was administratively and fiscally efficient, politically stable and, prior to the seventeenth century, had no overseas possessions which required defence or administration. Moreover, it was unified under the rule of a strong capital city. Unlike some of its continental neighbours, until the latter part of the eighteenth century it had no massive standing army which required high taxation and a bureaucracy to maintain it, although it did have a navy which was able to ensure the safety of trade. Its causal powers were assured, its standing conditions fixed, its sources of internal outflanking minimized. It proved fertile soil for the growth of the new institutions of market society.

The critical element in most accounts of the marketization of English life is the elimination of the peasantry. For instance, for Barrington Moore (1968) the crucial fact was the destruction of the peasantry and the traditions of village life which occurred in England as a result of the movement of enclosures. This removed the peasantry as a reservoir of resistance to market capitalism of the kind which continued to be experienced in France well into the nineteenth century. The absence of a peasantry opened up the possibility of a more successful agrarian capitalism. The landed classes thus had no need to rely on repressive political action to sustain a competitively and organizationally outflanked agricultural economy premised on feudal relations. This was the lot of the Prussian Junkers, for example.

From the seventeenth century onwards, England differed quite markedly from the rest of Europe in its political development. Monarchical authority was limited. It never achieved absolutism as in the European examples. Political accommodation between traditional and rising economic elements, in the context of a state machinery which was both sufficiently strong to provide external security and sufficiently weak not to favour the landed nobility or the new state administrators over and above the emergent capitalist class, enabled England to become the first industrial nation. The outcome of the English civil war in the midseventeenth century had enabled the gentry to establish the power of Parliament as a set of limits on monarchical expenditures. Because of the monarch's inability to tax without Parliamentary approval, it became the obligatory passage point in the circuits of power. It was a national, organizationally unified parliament premised on territorial representation rather than on the continental model of an organizationally divided parliament of estates. It constituted both an arena into which newly emergent classes of social actors could be drawn and a mechanism for settling conflicts of interest between these and other groups. Neither gentry nor military consumed the 'capitalist' economic surplus which resulted from this specific conjuncture of political and commercial opportunities. Being a gentleman was not considered to be incompatible with being an improving farmer (King 1986: 43–7).

Barrington Moore (1968) and Wallerstein (1974) stress economic factors in explaining developments in the political structure. However, this minimizes both agency and the constitution of an organization field by the state as an administrative complex. The organization of the state itself may be an important determinant of political structures. This point has been raised in the work of Skocpol (1979), who stresses the relative autonomy of the state, a concept derived from contemporary Marxian theorists of the state (see Evans et al. 1986). Historically states have not 'reflected' dominant economic interests but have served to organize internal control of a particular configuration of space and people, and external control of an environment of other states. These international relations have frequently involved the use of warfare as a form of diplomacy by other means. From this perspective, the comparative strength and weakness of a state may be explained by reference to factors such as administrative efficiency, political capacities for mass mobilization, or international geographic position, as much as by reference to the strength of the economy. Skocpol suggests that modern social revolutions have provided particularly good examples of this: where existing state authority has been undermined by events, such as defeat in war or threat of invasion or struggle over colonial controls, successful revolutions have occurred, she argues (in agreement with Therborn [1978]). Once more we see the conditions of organizational outflanking. Revolutionary crises occur when organization fails. The failure may be economic or military. It occurs when states are weakened by losing competitive struggles and when they lack the capacity to carry through political reform in the face of entrenched opposition, such as would emanate from a feudal stratum dependent upon continuing peasant subordination. Such opponents, she suggests, are more concerned with preventing the increase of their own taxation or with using possession of state offices to procure personal revenue than with facilitating organizational reforms with foreseeable commercial and industrial benefits. We can see, on this reckoning, why the civil war and defeat of the landed gentry in England should have been such a decisive factor in the development of England as the first capitalist nation. It removed the major source of resistance to the exercise of a unified causal power in a fixed organization field.

Once the first industrial nation had succeeded, in an international system of states it presented rulers of other states with considerable dilemmas and obvious answers. Henceforth, they were faced with intensifying military competition from a nation state with greater power based on capitalist breakthrough. Mimetic or coercively attained isomorphism was the evident answer, if they were not to wait for the competitive forces of 'natural development' to produce capitalism in their own sphere. The success of the first capitalist state became an important pressure towards mimetic institutional isomorphism of other state forms premised on the capitalist model. Such isomorphism was encouraged by the economic doctrine of free trade, which argued that the best route to capitalist development was that which dismantled whatever regulations currently existed. English commitment to a 'no-rules' set of rules was clearly not unconnected with the self-interest in prosperity of the emergent bourgeois class in the first industrial capitalist heartland. It is worth observing however, that the mimetic followers rarely had the bad sense to adopt free trade, preferring instead to employ protectionist tariffs.

Coercive isomorphism was pioneered by two nations in particular, Prussia and Japan, who produced capitalism by regulation rather than de-regulation. Prussia served as the explicit mimetic model for Japan in doing this. As Gerschenkron (1962) has argued, this isomorphism in results was achieved through highly innovative 'institutional instruments' and 'ideologies' which were developed by the state rather than by autonomous economic agencies within these states. The revolutions from above which occurred in Prussia and Japan showed that authoritarian political rule could organize a declining economic base into a competitive machine. With the support of a weak commercial bourgeoisie allied with the landed upper classes, such capitalist revolutions could literally be organized by the state rather than by civil individuals developing the conditions for capitalist breakthrough. Not least in this process was the introduction of the manufacture of armaments and heavy industry as a locus of capital accumulation. The upshot was regimes with an authoritarian military ethic and with bureaucratic organization capacities vested in the state, before which civil society was relatively much weaker.

Contrast this with France. Here the *ancien régime* which existed prior to 1789 was defeated by the opposition of those politically powerful landed gentry who had resisted the king's attempts at reform. One consequence of this was the maintenance of a large peasant sector, providing the surplus to support this privileged stratum. At the back of the opposition of the landed gentry stood absolutist power. Thus the highest echelons of the society depended on proprietorial privilege. Courtly society had a vested interest in opposing reform, although the fact that economic surplus increasingly was incapable of being extracted from the peasantry in sufficient quantities might equally have disposed them to a better sense of their own self-interest in this matter. In large part, the exhaustion of the agrarian surplus-yielding capacity was because of the enormous costs associated with participation in not only courtly life and society but also that most courtly of pursuits, war. The peasantry had already been impoverished by a rapacious and primarily parasitic stratum with little or no improving interest in the land other than as an arcadian retreat and fantasy world of nymphs and shepherds in the ever more bizarre games enacted out of Versailles. The lack of interest was explicable given the fact that often their ownership of the land was more by way of legal title than effective control. The latter was vested in the peasantry who had traditionally held but not owned the lands. The peasantry had no effective motivation for agrarian reform while the gentry had little opportunity not only because of the distractions of court but also their lack of effective control other than as occasional expropriators of peasant production. Brenner (1982) has argued that this effective hereditary peasant tenure was the obstacle to reform, because it blocked the possibilities of the agrarian capitalism which developed elsewhere. For this reason, the venality of office was an attractive income option for the lesser elements of the French aristocracy who could not prosper on the backs of a recalcitrant and effectively independent peasantry. Moreover, they were unable to displace the peasantry from the land, owing to the latter's protection by the French court as the base of the tax-collecting pyramid which raised revenues for military adventurism. When, in the late eighteenth century, the system's economic foundations collapsed, Louis XVI presciently remarked,

'Apres moi, le deluge'. Indeed, inability to secure reform against the landed resistance of the peasantry and the tax-collecting proclivities of the court led to the collapse of the royal administration and paved the way for social revolution in 1789 (Skocpol 1979). It was precipitated by the recalling of the estates general to give consent to the king for new taxes. These were the nodal point through which resistance erupted. Its central social thrust, however, was provided by the peasant revolt against the heavy rents and dues which they, as the base of the economic pyramid, had to support. This finally forced the deputies in the Constituent Assembly to sweep away feudal rights and the privileges of medievalism. The remainder, as the saying goes, is history.

From the point of view of a sociology of circuits of power, the most important absolutist innovation was the development of rules based on organization by state officials. Its field of force became a more densely populated organization field, with a multiplicity of networks and nodal points. Political stability came to depend upon state officials ensuring that the regime continued to function without major disturbance. However, as the calling of the Estates in France shows, with the development of bourgeois political claims in civil society, these old nodal points could not contain and control the traffic that the new claims to membership raised for admission into the circuit of power that fixed and deployed the obligatory points of passage of tax and law.

Poggi (1978: 79–85) notes how, within absolutism generally, there began to emerge a sphere of civil society contingent upon the development of a European bourgeoisie. These people, he suggests, had been redefining their social identity as that of a class, no longer as that of an estate. Poggi describes class in the following terms.

> A class is a collective unit more abstract, more impersonal, more distinctly translocal than an estate. Its visible boundaries are set not by a style of life nor a specific mode of activity, but by the possession of or exclusion from market resources that give their possessors a claim to the appropriation of a disproportionate share of the social product, and that as a consequence can be accumulated and continuously redeployed on the market. In the case of the groups we are considering, the resource in question is capital, privately owned. The unity of a class, unlike that of an Estate, is not maintained by internal organs of authority that guard the traditional rights, particular and common, of the collectivity and enforce discipline on its individual components. A class presupposes and admits competition for advantage among its components, who are all private, self-interested individuals. However, such competition is supposed to be self-equilibrating: it thus limits and legitimizes a given component's advantage over others. Moreover, competition within a class is limited by the recognition of certain shared interests among all components in the face of antagonistic classes on the market. (Poggi 1978: 79)

Poggi goes on to differentiate the ways in which a bourgeois class differs politically from an estate. The most crucial difference seems to be that while this class does not claim a facility to rule, to be part of the network of power, as does an estate, it cannot dispense with rule altogether. It requires the state to function as an agent of rule within the territory. As he goes on to add, however, this is not rule as it had been constructed through the terms of absolutism: rule characterized by a resolute emphasis on purposeful intervention in business matters, on monopolies, on restraints on competition, and on the direction of trade. All of these interfered with the fluidity and autonomy of the newly emergent market mechanism. The market is where the new class maintains collective advantage by accumulating and utilizing resources and moderating internal competition through internal contracts. For this new class the market and its extension represents the points of passage around which the whole organization field is to become fixed. Henceforth it will be the 'health' of the market on which will depend the fiscal capacities of the state.

Poggi (1978) is at pains to note that something more than just bourgeois class interests centred on the autonomy of the market and led it to pose a radical political challenge to absolutism. In the explanation that he provides, he comes quite close to that which Benedict Anderson (1983) was later to argue in *Imagined Communities: Reflections on the Origin and Spread of Nationalism*. Poggi says that we need to assess additional factors to explain why various national bourgeoisies did pose a challenge to their respective *ancien régimes*. Those factors point, once more, to the centrality of an organized field of relations of meaning and membership. Hitherto, these had typically been local. The loci of identity in preindustrial agricultural societies had been overwhelmingly civil in terms of family, class or village. With the development of industrial capitalism, these secure markers of identity, rooted in the close surveillance of the *gemeinschaft* (Bauman [1982; 1983]; Gellner [1983]), were massively eroded. In these absolutist agrarian societies, as Gellner (1983) argues, a small ruling class, often ethnically and linguistically alien to the subordinated population of the territory in question, occupied an hermetically sealed culture at the apex of the society, otherwise peopled mostly by a vast culturally distinct stratum of peasants and agrarians. Only amongst the elite did the solidarity of an organization field occur through relations of meaning and membership which were secured by a unifying high culture, premised on a distinct linguistic community that was cemented through print. At the level of the agrarian stratum, people's identities were contained within their vertically insulated communities, differentiated on regional, communal, ethnic, linguistic and other bases. Not only were the rulers alien to the populace but the people were also alien to one another from community to community. Unlike the ruling elite, no intellectuals composed homogenizing forms of cultural reproduction.

In the space of a few decades, capitalist industrialization transformed the formal basis for the cultural and social differentiation between the rulers and the ruled. The major mechanism of this transformation was the vernacular market produced by 'the convergence of capitalism and print technology on the fateful diversity of human language (which) created the possibility of a new form of imagined community' (B. Anderson 1983: 49). The book was thus the first modern industrial commodity and it enabled the formal homogenization of culture along a national axis of a common language and common relations of meaning and membership. There were some interesting developments on these lines in Australia in the 1890s, particularly around the journal, *The Bulletin* (see Lawson, 1983; Cantrell, 1977). In Australia, democracy incorporated everyone other than those who were not 'White Australians', notably Chinese migrants, indentured Kanaky labourers from the Pacific Islands and, of course, the original inhabitants. (In this respect it is interesting to compare the effects of the absence of any treaty with the original inhabitants of Australia, at the time it was first settled, with the effects of the Treaty of Waitangi, which was signed in neighbouring New Zealand by a coalition of Maori people and the occupying British forces. The latter provides an indubitable contemporary basis for a legal claim and access to the circuits of power, which is absent from the overall organization field in Australia. There, issues of aboriginal land rights have to be laboriously constituted in each case and no central document stands as an indexical resource over which, around which and through which struggle and resistance of the many interested parties may occur.)

In Benedict Anderson's (1983) terms, what made possible a relatively coherent and homogeneous nationalist project was the development of what he terms 'vernacular print capitalism'. This provided the mechanism for the production of the mobile, literate workforce that was required by industrialism. Industrial society produces a universal culture but it is 'boundedly universal'. Its universality is bounded by the variety of human languages and the necessity of presenting the standardized education in a tongue that all will understand. In Poggi's view

> such bourgeoisies were politically radicalized and 'energized' by components of them distinct from the entrepreneurial groups... (though sometimes overlapping with them). These components were involved particularly in intellectual, literary, and artistic pursuits, and had been developing a distinct social identity that of a *public*, or rather, at first, of a variety of 'publics'. They had been increasingly carrying out their pursuits in distinctive settings and media (from scientific societies, literary salons, Masonic lodges, and coffee houses, to publishing houses, and the Daily and Periodical Press) that were public in being accessible to all interested comers or at least all those possessing appropriate objectively ascertainable qualifications, such as learning, technical competence, relevant information, persuasive eloquence, creative imagination, and capacity for critical judgement. Furthermore, all participants were allowed to contribute to the open-ended, relatively unconstrained process of argument intended to produce a widely held, critically established 'public opinion' about any given theme. (Poggi 1978: 81)

Culture that is considered universal within its own confines will be particular in extent. That is, it will extend only to the linguistic community able to be educated within it. With the extension of literacy to the proletariat, the market begins to organize new classes which not only seek to incorporate themselves politically, as the bourgeoisie and as the proletariat, but also can eventually imagine a community of interest amongst themselves as a people and a nation, particularly where the soil can be made sacred or the bond blessed by national and competitive blood-letting through war. While the tensions of class can be imaginatively resolved through the notion of the people, there are other loci of tension which are somewhat less open to the communitarian imagination. State formation in a culturally heterogeneous society will produce tensions which will engender 'sub-nationalism' where the state formation does not map a universalistic relation of citizenship on to civil cleavages. This will usually be the case where there is an attempt at hegemony, which is premised on a ruling ethnicity and tongue, and where there also exist subordinated ethnicities and languages with a claim, which may be construed as 'legitimate', to the rule of a territory. As can be seen in the example given of the Treaty of Waitangi, the legitimacy of these subordinated claims is greatly aided if the subordinated people's prior occupancy of the land in question was legally recognized by the occupying power, thus facilitating access to extant circuits of power.

Initially, through the mechanisms of print capitalism, it is not so much a national ethos which is forged but a male bourgeois ethos to which women and the respective proletariats will eventually be admitted. Print capitalism begins to fix relations of meaning and membership in a distinct organization field. Through this enterprise is created a public sphere to complement that created from above by the state. It is formed by individual members of the civil society who develop a public opinion expressed through the mechanisms of print. Not only the availability but also the subject of print capitalism was important. The new media contained a bourgeois attack on the notions of privilege, of ascribed rights, particular to certain ranks. The writings of *les philosophes* are replete with such critical activity (Bauman 1987). This was a direct attack on absolutism and upon its policy of maintaining traditional estates. The creation and advocacy of national interest by this newly emergent bourgeoisie, this public opinion-making sphere, and the suggestion that this national interest should guide state policy were an embarrassment to monarchs vestigially attached to dynastic interests and still surrounded by the absurdly wasteful pomp of their courts (Poggi 1978: 83). Moreover, as Benedict Anderson (1983) points out, the courts themselves would frequently be quite alien from the notion of the people being constructed in this bourgeois sphere of print capitalism. Through these mechanisms, visions of new constitutional designs for fixing the organization field abounded toward the end of the eighteenth century, particularly in France. They projected the distinctive claims and aspirations of the bourgeoisie as the new public. These were the 'legislators' that Bauman (1987) so ably characterizes.

THE MODERN CONSTITUTIONAL NATION STATE

There were several pathways to constitutional statehood. Some of them we have indicated already. We shall not go into detail here. Suffice to say of the state that did emerge in the nineteenth century, first, that it was a centralized power which attempted to overawe all other powers in a given territory through the use of various forces, agencies, etc. Second, it was ideally to be founded on consent. State power must be legitimated and turned into authority. Consent by those whose state it was meant that it could still use force against those within its borders whose state it was not. Workers, socialists, unionists, suffragettes and national liberationists were all fair targets. For the bourgeois citizens of the bourgeois state, episodic power relations had to take on a distinct configuration rather than be merely contingently intermittent. The 'dentistry state' had become the rational legal state. Moreover, this transformation took place within the context of an international system of states which was consolidated throughout the world economy during the nineteenth century. On the one hand, the world had become politically one economy while, on the other hand, it was fragmented into many competing state forms, both at the European core and in the African, Asian, American and Australasian and Pacific peripheries. At the periphery, competition between core European states was easy enough to understand. It was competition for spoils, for resources, for territory which might be aggrandized on a monopoly basis for the colonizing power. At the core, competitiveness was organized much more around the principles of 'nationality' and of 'natural borders'. Often, the two claims could articulate in a contradictory way. States would claim that populations currently subject to a neighbouring state were nationally the same as its own population. This could lead to someone being born French, perhaps, in Alsace Lorraine, growing up German, and dying French while fighting for France against Germans as state boundaries shifted with the fortunes of war.

Closely allied to the plea for national integrity, in terms of the imagined community of the nation, was a cry for natural borders, for physical boundaries. Such boundaries were sought as would make the nation, identified as the state, defensible and would provide a sense of completeness and integrity. The ramifications of this claim are still being felt in some parts of the European system of states, particularly in Ireland and the Basque provinces of France and Spain. The state form constituted an organization field whose fixity was capable of being undercut and organizationally outflanked by rival states with more productive and disciplinary resources. However, a material basis in itself would be insufficient if the relations of meaning and membership could not be fixed in a stable organization field of force, in which linguistic community was the main obligatory passage point. The limits of the sovereignty of one state were the claims of another state to sovereignty over that same territory and those same people.

What are some of the attributes of this new form of state that emerged in the nineteenth century? First, it is characterized by a public causal power, which is quite distinct from other powers and other office-holders, including the monarch. States are characterized by authority backed up by the rule of law, the law itself being contingent upon effective monopoly of the means of violence in a given territory. Clear territorial boundaries mark out the state. Within this unified state, we might expect to find a unified national police force, a uniform currency, a unified legal system, a national flag and a national anthem. One would anticipate a large public-sector educational system employing a single unified language. (Of course, some exceptions were to prevail, for example in Belgium and in Canada in the twentieth century.) National language is the means whereby a literary tradition is constructed, which erodes cultural particularisms. It is instrumental in the formation of the imagined community that becomes the nation of the state. National armed forces are another powerful mechanism not only for national defence but also national formation. Each of these forms a capillary power reaching down into 'the people'. A further distinction, in contrast to absolutism, would be a far more profound separation of the economic and the political, premised on the contract between formally free labour and private capital and on the increasingly juridical equivalence of these individuals as identical citizens, being constituted as such as rights are fought for and won, initially by white, property-owning males. Later struggles, of course, were to extend this constitution of society. Extension, however, stayed within the political sphere that was differentiated from the economy. In economic relations, citizenship remained remote (see Abrahamsson and Broström 1981). These were the terms on which the organization field of force became fixed.

States are formal complex organizations. They have hierarchically arranged offices. They have a formalized division of labour. Within this division of labour, within this hierarchy, administrative tasks are themselves depersonalized. Administrative decision-making is by reference to procedure, to rule, rather than to person. Poggi (1978: 108–12) distinguishes some of the processes at work in this 'rationalization'. First we can note the development of civility. By this is meant the outcome of that long process which Elias (1982) has referred to as the civilizing process. Although the state is founded upon a legitimate monopoly of the means of violence, it is less and less likely to use these on a routine basis against its subjects, except when the rule of law can itself be said to be under threat from strikers, demonstrators, nationalists, etc. The military and the police, as repositories of the means of violence, become rationalized means of control in which the means of violence are themselves the ever present but seldom used backdrop. In other words, there is a growing trend towards civility in the spheres of public life, as they become organizationally fixed, as long as the rules of the game are adhered to and existing privileges are preserved in the episodic circuits of power.

Second, we can point to the ways in which the political process becomes differentiated. The state becomes a machinery of many complexes of organization, with many distinct foci, offices, agencies. There is a plurality of foci in the state's administrative machinery. Rather than being a repository for the reproduction and maintenance of tradition and of time-honoured beliefs and practices, the state becomes much more discursively rational. It becomes a locus in which decision-making, based upon relatively unconstrained discussion and legal elaboration, is the basis for the decisions made. This can be characterized as an increasing open-endedness. The state becomes a set of formal machinery and mechanisms for articulating order within the wider civil society but at the same time it constitutes an arena in which controversies may be legitimately cooled off, differences may be aired, and constraints may be exercised on the business of rule. Unlike the absolutist state, where representation was a matter of corporateness, of being incorporated within one of the traditional estates, the modern liberal, constitutional state achieves representation through parliamentary assemblies in which the individual as a pristine, juridical, citizen-subject is claimed to be represented. Claims to constitute a social relation between state and citizen, which is based upon consent, are central to the legitimacy of the modern constitutional state. Compared to absolutism, this is clearly a quite novel claim. It raises quite novel problems of membership and meaning as well. Who belongs to the political community? Who is able to give their consent? And on what rational basis are those members of a given territory to be excluded from the political community, to be excluded from citizenship, to be excluded, as it were, from the state? These have been important historical questions with interesting implications for certain categories of people, such as women, non-property holders, blacks, aborigines, guest workers, all of whom have been, or indeed still are in some places, constituted as lacking in some respects the full pantheon of subjectivity which would qualify them as citizens of a given state. This then raises the question, how do certain categories of individual subjects come to be included and or excluded? How it is that the excluded may later come to be incorporated within the definition of citizen and thus fall within the sphere of the state? This question has been addressed by Turner (1986b).

The argument of Turner's (1986b) book is straightforward. It can be summarized in the following words. The critical factor in the emergence of citizenship is violence, which he sees as being of two kinds. First, it can be struggle by social groups to achieve social participation. An instance of this would be the struggle of the working class to gain admission to the franchise or, somewhat later, the struggle by women to become enfranchised. The major instance of this kind of struggle is that of class conflict. However, class and class structure, while important determinants of citizenship, are clearly not the only social movement with implications for citizenship. The feminist struggle of the suffragettes for the representation of women has already been mentioned. Social movements like these, suggests Turner (1986b), historically have had their most significant impact under conditions of war. Therefore, he regards warfare as a second illustration of the importance of violence as the basis for citizenship. Turner (1986b) proposes a third factor which he sees as contributing to the emergence of citizenship under conditions of conflict. Migration, he believes, undermines the hierarchical and stable social relationships that are formed in the tyranny of the *gemeinschaft*. This view is of particular importance in looking at a society such as Australia. Australia is one of a number of important modern societies which has no feudal background, no prior history of the state, and which has been largely the outcome of settler-capitalist development and migration. Another aspect of Australian state formation which is particularly interesting is the way in which the territory that was settled was initially a series of independent colonies which found unity and nationhood under a federal form. This federal form could be seen as a kind of resistance, on the part of the landed pastoral interests in the Australian social formation at the end of the nineteenth century, to the push for expanded rights for citizenship, contingent upon the working class struggles of the 1890s. At the core of this were the shearers' strikes and the birth of the Australian Labor Party (ALP) (Connell and Irving 1980).

Against Turner's (1986b) thesis it should be argued that, if warfare is seen by him as being the single most important factor in influencing the development of citizenship rights, one obvious counter-factual example is that of Sweden. That society is arguably the most advanced in terms of citizenship rights of all the western social democracies (see Abrahamsson and Broström, 1980) but it has been quite immune from warfare for a period of two hundred years or so. Hence, to assign causal primacy to military force or to violence alone in the circuits of power is inadequate. What is important is the fixing of an organization field, a process in which rules of meaning and membership as well as techniques of production and discipline have a contingent role to play. Sweden represented a particular configuration of these, as explored elsewhere (see Clegg et al., 1986: ch. 9).

Returning to Poggi's (1978) consideration of the nineteenth-century constitutional state, he observes several significant political issues which were tied up with its development. First amongst these he notes a number of constitutional issues. Should the head of state be a president, be elected, or be an hereditary monarch? What passageways to power are to be privileged? What should the powers of the person be? These issues also involve questions about the distribution of powers between legislature, executive and judicial agencies as well as the allocation of tasks and resources to central and local administrative agencies. A final set of constitutional issues concerns relations of membership and meaning in the state and church, and in the extension of the franchise, and how these are to be fixed in the organization field of the state vis à vis the facilitative powers of the military. Second, there was a set of foreign policy issues. These concerned questions of alliances, tariffs, armaments, and directions of colonial expansion: questions about the international management of a system of states, of state-to-state relations, as an organization field. As Poggi (1978) notes and as Giddens (1985) outlines in detail, these indeed were the central issues of the nineteenth-century state system which brought about its disastrous collapse in 1914.

A further set of issues, which began to take prominence in the nineteenth century, are what may be referred to as social issues arising from the economic development of capitalism as a mode of production within the confines of this constitutional state. Phenomena such as demographic pressure, proletarianization of the populace, urban epidemics, growth in criminality, destitution, industrial accidents, secularization, growth of union-ism and socialism, illiteracy, vice in the form of prostitution, industrial disease and illness, became emergent matters for state management in the nineteenth century. Marx's (1976) discussion of the 'Factory Acts' in *Capital* is an example of this sphere of management. Indeed, as good an index as any of the growth of these concerns is the initiation of the systematic collection of official statistics, as both Foucault (1977) and Giddens (1985) sug-gest. As the state begins to fulfil more functions in this respect, this is an indication of the accomplishment and deepening of liberal constitutional statehood. In the period of abso-lutism, such data-gathering was largely concerned with finance and taxation, and popu-lation statistics. Finance and taxation clearly stretch back to the importance of financial management for the absolutist state. The development of population statistics is tied up with state control of the dislocated, displaced population that industrial capitalism was producing (Bauman 1983). The problems of rebellion, vagabondage, the mob, were tied up with increasing state surveillance of the populace through the formation of population statistics. By the middle/late-eighteenth century, all states began to keep these sorts of sta-tistics but, as the nineteenth century wore on, the statistics ranged over many sectors of social life. They became more detailed, systematic and complete. Developments included the centralized collection of materials that registered births, marriages and deaths; statis-tics pertaining to residence, to ethnic background and to occupation. Also, what some authorities came to call 'moral statistics', relating to suicide, delinquency, divorce, and so on, were part of this development.

Certain influential conceptions of sociology were to see the discipline as ineradicably tied in to the development of moral statistics and social questions. Some commentators suggest that these concerns with questions of moral and ideological community were to be regarded as a response and a bulwark to their politicization by socialists (Therborn 1976). The extent to which the social question was regarded as political was itself a highly political and contested question and concerned the relationship between the liberalism which underlay the notion of the nineteenth-century constitutional state and the frontal attack that socialism made upon it during the nineteenth century. Socialism, as a sys-tematic conception of new networks of relations of meaning and membership, became the major vehicle for attending to new and presently suppressed aspects of citizenship. These centred upon the social rights of citizens and upon the assumption that the state had some responsibility for ameliorating social problems, rather than leaving them to the invisible hand of the market to adjust. Controversy, channelled appropriately and contained within arenas such as Parliament, becomes a measure of the issues of the day as they are represented in and through parliamentary forms. Of course, throughout the century, exclusion (of the working class, of women, of non-property holders) was of more moment in the circuits of power than was representation. As the extension of the fran-chise fixed the parliamentary arena as the nodal point, it developed the possibility of slow, incremental organization outflanking of extant configurations of power and organization field by a market premised on explicitly political considerations, ones oriented not to the 'naturalization' of the market's rules of membership and meaning but to their transformation into a new field, through new techniques of production and discipline. For many this was a hope, a beacon on the hill, an active utopia, while for others it was a fear whose consummation was to be strenuously resisted. For both dreamers and visionaries, as well as those who feared the new issues and agenda, the state and its circuits were the field in which power was to be fought for or against.

The legacy of different phases in the development of the state may be seen as Poggi (1978) suggests. The state is a temporally sedimented, complex organization much as Stinchcombe (1965) argued that organization fields would be. The constitutional issues relate back to the question of the allocation of powers that preoccupied the feudal and the Estates systems of rule. Foreign policy issues concentrate upon the international system of states, while the issues of economic management and the social question are undoubtedly tied up with the development of the capitalist mode of production within the envelope of the nation state itself. Each represents a different nodal point for interest representation. Economic management concerns the management of the infrastructure for the new capitalist class. The issues making up the social question are placed firmly upon the state's agenda by the new organized resistance from the working class party and union movements of the nineteenth century. Indeed, Poggi (1978) suggests that all of these issues had to be confronted within the framework set by the institutions of capitalism and by the logic of capital accumulation. The sleight of hand of making non-organization appear to be the principle of organization in the fixed field of force of the market had been achieved. Of late it is increasingly *the* nodal point through which the circuits of power must flow in the advanced industrial capitalist states, as well as increasingly in state socialism.

CONCLUSION

The familiar phenomenon of not only 'substantive' but also 'limited rationality' has been all too evident in this chapter. In the terms of this text, it is to be expected as an attribute of power, which rarely is as omnipotent and all-knowing as its mythology suggests.

Consider the following examples of power. Church tutelage did not intend the modern state, although its effects on procreative activity and household formation were organizational and this form of organization sustained both European trade and peoples in ecological disasters which were economically crippling elsewhere. *Rattus rattus* did not mean to aid the transformation of the balance of power of the European landscape in order to weaken lords against peasants and to strengthen towns against country. These towns, in developing as centres of commerce and corporate relations, did not intend to undermine feudal power through setting up an alternative, public conduit of representation. These centres of representation did not intend to become prosperous sites of taxation in order to sustain princely military adventurism. Technological and disciplinary advances in the pursuit of these military adventures were not intended to facilitate more centralized, higher-taxing states. Rulers did not wage war in order to ensure that the ecology of organization forms was made more environmentally fit, both in states and in markets. The Reformation and Counter-Reformation had no interest in producing bodies of abstract law which would henceforth constitute all organization fields, thus strengthening secular against church authority. The Sun King, Louis XIV, did not intend to create a centralized system of administration which was incapable of ruling efficiently or effectively on the extant tax base of his successors, who were thus obliged to call the Estates. Nor, in so doing, did Louis XVI seek to have his head guillotined and a revolution set in train. In addition, his august forebear did not mean to create a network of civility through which institutionally mimetic isomorphism would be facilitated across the whole ecology of European states. Frederick William I of Prussia did not intend to create some elements for an ideal type of bureaucracy to administer modern states and thus outflank the court as an organization form surviving in the competitive ecology of states. It was not intended that the English peasantry be weakened so that capitalism might first develop there and outflank more agriculturally based social relations of the state and production elsewhere. Nor did Cromwell's 'Model Army' intend its discipline to create a state enveloping and enabling this spectacular secular force. The development of printing from Gutenberg onwards was not intended to produce a capillary rather than a capstone power, capable of reaching down into and constituting the framework of national subjects and national states. And so on.

The modern state emerges from a series of circuits of power in which both ecological and isomorphic pressures contributed to the stabilization of various organization fields of force and to their outflanking. The actors or agents were many and varied, and frequently highly contingent, ranging from the humble rat and bubonic virus to the majesty of the Sun King. Organization, of many kinds, was the raw material for agents who sought state power for whatever purposes. Organization, as has been remarked elsewhere, is basically about control (Clegg and Dunkerley 1980). This means that in extending power through delegation one must be able to bind delegates to the power that authorizes. Various modes of organization are attempts to achieve this. As the argument has been constructed, no one method of organization is sacrosanct. Some simply proved more effective in certain conditions. The hypothesis that one may derive from this is that the rise and fall and management of states in the past appears to have been contingent on more or less blind organization ecology and adaptation. In the past the state may have developed less as conscious design and more as expedient, adaptive organization. Today, with a much more sophisticated knowledge of causal powers, we can afford to be less ignorant in managing the state, as has been argued elsewhere (Clegg et al. 1986). Without repeating these earlier arguments, it seems evident that despite the capacities which now exist these powers are today still less than fully realized in the management of some states. The circuits of power framework enables us to analyse how this is so. Why it should be so is another question, suited to more polemical occasions than this text allows.

In conclusion, suffice only to say that the framework of circuits of power can be used effectively to discuss the emergence of the modern state in a way that does not leave us hostage to the forms of either interest-reduction or the various extensional formulae of dimensions, faces, levels, dialectics and those sundry other concepts which have so often characterized power analysis in the past. The model of circuits of power is capable not only of carrying analysis in ways in which these earlier formulations are not but also of incorporating diverse secondary materials within a coherent framework in which may be addressed central issues of sociology.

10
A HISTORY OF THE PRESENT

INTRODUCTION

During 2022, at the time of writing, the world faced three global threats, one possibly receding, another certainly advancing and one whose trajectory was unclear. Receding was the COVID-19 pandemic, in those countries in which efficient vaccines had been widely administered, although the virus will continue to mutate and new variants will emerge. Viral pandemics never die; at best, they just fade away. Advancing is the threat of climate change. What is unclear is the outcome of present events in Russia and Ukraine. These events, labelled on one hand as a 'special military operation', on the other hand as an unwarranted invasion of a national sovereign space by an imperial power, are unfolding with deadly and destructive consequences. I will connect these three aspects of the present in an analysis, premised on the circuits of power model. My analysis will focus on questions of social and system integration (Lockwood 1964). Social integration refers to the principles by which individuals or actors are related to one another in a society; system integration refers to the relationships between parts of a social system; these relations will be analyzed in terms of concepts of circuits of power and the paradoxes they constitute.

Lockwood's (1964) concepts have been subsequently addressed by many authors, including Margaret Archer. Archer (1996: 698), proposed an analytical dualism in which 'social transformation/social reproduction can only be explained by examining the interplay between two sets of emergent, irreducible and autonomous causal powers pertaining respectively to structure and agency'. As Archer (1996: 692) writes, 'the fate of "systemic" tendencies is at the mercy of their confluence with "social" integration', the fundamental relationship to be explored in this chapter. I will provide a history of the present, loosely composed in these terms. Any conception of the present will be a condensation of an infinite number of questions and challenges. Specialization on different levels of analysis, marking so much of our professional lives, needs to take heed of the fact that these questions and challenges do not always present themselves neatly wrapped up for analysis by specific disciplines or at different levels of inquiry. Instead, the world presents as a flat ontology, albeit one that is frequently paradoxical. Three paradoxes are singled out for investigation: the Russian invasion and war in Ukraine, the COVID-19 pandemic and the encroaching climate crisis.

First the war in Ukraine. Kurnyshova et al. (2022) note that the war is 'full of paradoxes'. They note as a first paradox, that although Vladimir Putin was preparing for the war for months before the invasion, few observers expected these preparations to be more than a performative 'storytelling, disinformation and fake news' simulacrum. It turned out to be a simulacrum with deadly consequences. In this respect, these commentators were following a long line of tolerance of Putin's politics by other means. For instance, that Putin was appeased on so many prior instances, including the invasion of Crimea and its annexation in 2014, the poisoning and murder of dissidents at home and abroad, the downing of MH17, the devastation of Aleppo and the cyber interference in Western election, did not make his subsequent actions more but less reasonable. A further paradox is how the consequences of Russia's invasion of Ukraine have struck many Western observers. As Helimi (2022) states in *Le Monde*, 'the paradoxical result of the invasion of Ukraine is that it will lead to a strengthening of the Western military alliance on Russia's own doorstep'. A third paradox is noted by historian of Ukraine, Timothy Snyder (2022), who is quoted as saying, 'Russia wins by losing. Russia really needs to lose this war, and to lose it decisively … The whole colonial move towards Ukraine is a distraction, a substitute for the internal changes which Russia really has to make' (Rankin 2022).

While the issues that the war raises might seem paradoxical, not all the 'paradoxes' mentioned by the commentators are true paradoxes either in a logical sense, where apparently correct premises lead to a patently false conclusion or as contrasting but interdependent requirements. The issues are paradoxical in the sense that they denote a counterintuitive or surprising event. In terms of paradox theory (Cunha et al. 2022; Cunha et al. 2021a; Berti et al. 2021) there are other evident paradoxes, ones consisting of contrastingly interdependent poles. The need to defeat Russian imperialism decisively and at the same time to negotiate a peaceful conclusion is a real paradox, as is the fact that fighting Russian nationalism fuels Ukrainian nationalism and *vice versa* or supplying armaments to pursue peace because appeasing Putin's Russia would in all probability extend his imperial ambitions, causing additional conflicts.

To be successful, wars require a clear and vital strategic purpose, with some probability of achieving that purpose. Two ways of exploring purpose suggest themselves in relation to Russia's imperial ambitions. First, there is what it is stated as being, in analogy with the Great Patriotic War, a key Putin antenarrative (Boje 2001), linking a retrospective story to an imagined future, albeit embedded in a less than wholly coherent account.

Second, there is the argument that it is key beliefs that define and drive actions. The key beliefs that Putin has advanced as the purpose of the war are to defeat external enemies that wish Russia ill. His operational code (Leites 1951; 1953; see Walker 1990), confirms the sociological adage that, if situations are defined as real, they are real in their consequences (Thomas and Thomas 1928). The default position of paradox scholarship is to embrace both poles of a paradox (Bert et al. 2021). In the situation of Western responses to the war in Ukraine, this amounted to a morally ambiguous policy of Western appeasement with respect to kleptocratic investments in London property and politics, while opposing the war that the oligarchs support. There was a history to this appeasement. Putin has routinely blamed 'Russia's woes on American imperialism and the moral decay it hastens, on liberals, fascists, Islamic terrorists, the Baltic states and most recently on Ukrainians, especially their relatively recent reorientation to Western institutions such as NATO and the EU. Ukrainian political elites' sensemaking of the Western position, encouraged by some of its institutional political and military leaders, legitimated the mobilization of force in Russia against the constitutional goal of seeking either EU or NATO affiliation. The Ukrainian parliament approved amendments to the constitution in September 2018 that made the accession of the country to NATO and the EU a central goal and foreign policy objective. Such action contradicted the belief in the paramount right of Russia to rule its domestic sphere of influence. 'For years Ukraine was feminized in the Russian mainstream discourse of a big Slavic "family" that implicitly implies the "right" for domestic violence (which, by the way, has been de-criminalized in Russia)', as Kurnyshova et al. (2022) suggest, drawing on the works of Lacan, as these have been explored by Stavrakakis (2002).

While it may prove impossible to dislodge Russian invading forces from some of the areas unlawfully annexed, such as the Eastern Donbass or Crimea, Balkanization of the Ukrainian state and enhanced social integration of NATO under US hegemony seems most likely to be the result of the crisis caused by the Russian invasion. The nostalgic attempt to reinstate the reimagined system integration of past Soviet and Tsarist borders appears to be destined to fail in the terms promoted by Putin. The military failing may be drawn out; any social integration will certainly be a long time coming, achievable only on the Baltic model of colonizing captive states. Moreover, as *The Washington Post*'s Democracy Editor, Gritte Witte (2022) writes, by 'overestimating his military's capabilities and misjudging his adversaries', Putin appears to be repeating the errors of the Soviet campaign in Afghanistan, a point reinforced by Milton Bearden (2022 March), ex-CIA chief in Pakistan at that time.

The issue of power relations has been 'a major vacuum in paradox studies' (Cunha & Putnam 2019: 100). Considering that matters of choice, responsibility and decision-making are essential to the ways in which paradoxes are approached, this is surprising. The relation between power and paradox is now attracting considerably more attention

(Berti & Simpson, 2021; Cunha et al. 2021a; Julmi 2022; Pamphile 2022). There are at least four ways in which power shapes paradox. First, by moderating the degree of opposition and interdependence of underlying tensions; second, by determining their 'undecidability', that is, the possibility of providing rational accounts for action; third, by affecting actors' possibility to respond to the paradox generatively or pathologically; fourth, by framing the possibility that the tension can result in a dynamic equilibrium or in a radical, dialectical transformation (Berti & Cunha 2022).[1]

The other two crises which I will discuss are also graphic in their representations on the screens of our televisions, through images of floods and fires and overburdened health services as well as being no less real in their paradoxicality. COVID-19 has shaped lives globally in different ways for a period of two years or more. The crisis of the present pandemic will recede, slowly. In the face of the challenge of the climate crisis, the major paradox in democracy occurs when elected populist leaders simply deny reality. The elections of Trump, Modi and Bolsonaro are symptomatic of the weakness of democracy in making hard decisions that are often seen as involving immediate costs for uncertain future benefits. Despite the ample opportunities for organizational learning that the pandemic has provided, such opportunities to learn have been difficult both for political party organizations in democracies with a short incumbency and an even shorter focus on history and autocracies. While democracy has its costs, a stable public service can minimize these for the longer run – if expert advice is heeded in political decision-making, whether such advice comes from within either a public service or from a consultancy hired to replace the capabilities and capacities that such states might once have had, but which new public management has eroded. Autocracies can exercise more sweeping powers than democracies, more readily, but these can easily lead to unlearning. In China, during the first weeks of the pandemic, tens of millions of people were locked down to stop the spread of the virus out of Wuhan. Almost three years later, these lockdowns have spread to many other cities, despite the number of cases still rising, as are protests challenging the lockdowns, while the number of people vaccinated remains comparatively low. Neither the lockdowns nor the use of the Chinese Sinopharm vaccine are proving efficient in halting the spread of the virus and state ideology, that the Party is always correct, limits organizational learning.

For the crisis of climate change, the bleak prospect is that too little, too late is being done in the way of restricting carbon contamination and translating to a zero emissions future. If this continues to be the case, the leaders of the world's nation states will condemn the planet to a future of increasingly more hyper-critical uncertainties of fire and rain, aridity and floods. Here, the paradox is that for the short-term advantage of declining branches of capital, our descendants will endure increasing misery that we have bequeathed them. While there are many expert voices warning of the perils of climate change, many political and business organizations have still not taken heed of the fact that the temperature is inexorably rising. Akin to frogs in slowly boiling water, these organizations and their leaders seem blissfully unaware of the medium in which they are situated. That this paradox is occurring for a species with more reflexive capabilities than amphibians should concern us most in the present.

In this gallery of paradoxes, the invasion of Ukraine by Russia and the Western response has a long-term potential to be a local circuit breaker of the lack of reflexivity associated with the death wish of a slowly warming planet. Wealthy European nations are presently greatly dependent on oil and gas, while the reliance on coal, another fossil fuel, is rapidly receding (even as it grows in countries in Asia, which are importing it from Australia). In much of Western Europe, having energy frequently means a choice of supporting either Russian or Middle Eastern autocracy. As energy prices escalate in response to the events associated with the war in Ukraine and the sanctions being applied to Russian sources of energy, in the short run those applying the sanctions have been funding the war as prices and profits climbed. That is a paradox that is all too obvious. In the long term, however, it prepares a compelling political and economic rationale as to why states should go green, to add to those reasons that are obviously ecological. Crucial policy aspects of social and system integration are in play.

The crisis of capitalism that occurred in the Global Financial Crisis of 2007 onwards was one of both social and system integration. Despite its intellectual register in the works of left critics such as Piketty (2018) and Stiglitz (2015) as system disintegration, this was not a crisis producing major progressive social change in the sense that Habermas (1976) or O'Connor (1972) anticipated (Clegg 2015). A groundswell of withdrawal from democratic consent and resentment towards elites that culminated in Trumpian and Brexit populism was created, leading to diminished social integration in these countries but no system disintegration, at least at the time of writing. Instead of political economy veering left, a tilt to the right in populist responses has been more successful. In the autocracies of the East, in Russia and its subordinate states, as well as in China, the global financial crisis emboldened autocracy in the conviction that the West was weakening (Rachman 2022). It is to Russia that this chapter turns first.

DIS/INTEGRATION AND DOMINANT MYTHS

Before the federation of Russian states existed, there was the USSR. While the USSR centred on one dominant institution of the Party, Western capitalism had one dominant institution of the market. Dominant institutions easily become mythical (Zeraffa 1976). The 'rational myth' (Meyer and Rowan 1977) of a cybernetically planned economy in the east (Spufford 2010) or the divine invisible hand (Hill 2001) in the West play, as obligatory passage points, much the same legitimating purpose. Circuits of system integration built around ever-expanding imaginaries and institutions of either cybernetics or markets offer a seemingly secure basis for social ordering. While market myths are no more immune to crises than circuits that are largely socially integrated by long-range planning, they are more resilient. In Russia, the Party as the medium of system integration closed off formal possibilities for plurality and prosperity, while in the West, the market creatively spun these possibilities out and celebrated them, producing a bounty of plenty (including an excess of often limited use value).

The USSR Communist Party's rational myths concerned the superiority of state planning and central control of the economy under the direction of a Party with a monopoly of state power. These claims to legitimacy became widely adopted and diffused in the institutional field of East European and Soviet state politics. The Soviet Union had been built as a complex system of networks dominated by a single elite organization, the Communist Party. The Party was centrally planned, ideologically controlled and coercively regulated through state apparatuses for which the Party 'presided over every section, department and division' (Soldatov and Borogan 2010: 4). As Kostera and Wicha (1996: 81) noted, 'economic organizations relied primarily on a symbolic doctrine', a rational myth framed in terms of social or state interest as overlapping. The central element of social integration was the communication of an ideology that sought to connect different levels of practice, from the micro to the macro, through a vast system of surveillance of people's capacity to act as if they believed what they were told. It was an interlocking network of communication events and episodes that formed the organization of the system (See the discussion of the German Democratic Republic's Stasi in Clegg et al., 2006, pp. 172–5 for a detailed analysis of a similar system in a satellite state of the USSR).

Communication flowed from the elite of the Party centre (Chirot 1990/1991; 1991) to impose the Party's managerial control of communicative practices. These flows were shaped by the putative state monopoly command of the means of communication. The coercive elite of the KGB and other repressive state apparatuses were on hand to attend to communication breakdowns. As Scott (1996: 40–7) argues, clusters of overlapping 'command situations' generate and sustain elite 'power centres' linked to one another through processes of interaction and circulation (Clegg and Hardy 2006). These power centres strove to maintain the appearance of their legitimacy in the judgements of their citizens. However, events can disrupt legitimacy. Social integration, built around a mythical ideology, as the USSR discovered, is a fragile construct. Recurrent episodes of power to normalize and restore order are required, as demonstrated in interventions in Hungary in 1956 and in Czechoslovakia in 1968. The April 1968 Action Programme of liberalizing the press in Czechoslovakia, allowing increased freedom of speech and the possibility of multiparty government (see Dubček 1968; Williams 1997) opened fissures that threatened the rational myth of Party sovereignty.

For the Soviet elite, intervening in Czechoslovakia was 'normalization'. Intervention by Soviet tanks forcibly normalized the changing basis of social integration that was occurring in Czechoslovakia. Repression of the Prague Spring of 1968 by the Red Army was understood by students and workers as the brutal repression of demands for liberties and for socialism with a human face. The imposition of violence by the Party violated local institutional reform by Czechoslovakian intellectuals and students. Liberalizing Czechoslovakia in 1968 threatened the fragmentation of Soviet hegemony. By 'normalizing' the situation through the barrels of Soviet tanks and guns, as well as the communications of Soviet apparatchiks and their local puppets, dissent was contained. For Czechoslovakia, the Brezhnev-led Soviet Communist Party was an event crushing endogenous reform. It was nationally exogenous, a contingency waiting to happen, that led to the ascent in 1969 of Husák to leadership of the Czechoslovakian Communist Party, which imposed 'normalization', following Soviet 'liberation', squashing Czech 'freedoms' for a further twenty years.

FROM INTEGRATION BY REPRESSION TO DISINTEGRATION BY REFORM

By the late 1970s, the Soviet elite was increasingly a gerontocracy. Mann (2011: 88) suggests that at the end of the gerontocracy, the Party had become 'a set of bureaucratic apparatuses incapable of reform or of generating a political debate about reform'. When Gorbachev assumed the presidency in 1990, he represented a generational change, signalled by the introduction of *glasnost*, an attempt to promote reform. Potentially, *glasnost* opened new circuits of power reaching from the micro-level of everyday talk to the commanding heights of the state. As such, it was a significant change within the communication system of the Party. Gorbachev's talk of a socialist market economy in the late 1980s saw the Party scramble to be in the vanguard of events it could not control (Judt 2005: 602–3). Gorbachev's reforms sought to allow elements of a small-scale market economy while maintaining a one-party state organization and a command economy (Kenez 2006: 47–8). These responses did not make sense in terms of the Party's past practices; they were, indeed, paradoxical, a communication breakdown in terms of past coding.

The communication effects of the 'market reforms' were more significant than their real import. It has been suggested that Gorbachev launched 'a relentless process of public desacrilization' which led to a 'partial destruction of the Brezhnevite political–economic and socio-political orders' (Breslauer 2002: 60; see Grint 2010: 95). Doing so enabled what had hitherto been underground and samizdat communication to become publicly acceptable; nonetheless, albeit necessary for structural change, the change was insufficient. 'Serious economic reforms implied the relaxation or abandonment of controls'

(Judt 2005: 596). Loosening control initially exacerbated the problems it was designed to solve, as well as threatening the basis of the Communist state system. The expertise of the technocratic, military and security elites that held the state's communication networks together 'became increasingly difficult, if not impossible, to sustain' (Reed 2012: 217). The 'imminent collapse' of the Soviet system 'revealed an organizational reality characterized by internecine rivalries and structural decomposition' (Reed 2012: 217).

Gorbachev sought to control and manage widespread change of the Soviet system through leadership of the Communist Party organization, instituting *glasnost* and *perestroika*. *Glasnost* weakened the tight social integration that had characterized the USSR and its satellite system during the height of the Cold War, while *perestroika* weakened system integration. At the same time as *glasnost* and *perestroika* were being introduced, the practice of building the Communist Party organization on nationalist lines in the subordinated republics, especially those in the Caucasus and in the central Asian republics, produced new forms of secession organized in terms of alternatives to those of the Party: ethnic and language nationalism. Gorbachev's reforms unwittingly initiated fragmentation of the USSR (Judt 2005: 603) and once the Party began to fragment, the centrifugal pull of anxious local administrators, protecting their own interests, fractured it further. *Perestroika* and *glasnost,* redefining social and system integration, could not be easily controlled once introduced: they hastened fragmentation and change.

As Spufford (2010) evocatively characterizes it, the organization of the Soviet Communist Party could be thought of as a gigantic coding machine, spewing out official codes, a vast system in which autopoiesis, in Luhmann's (1995) sense, was dysfunctional. Feedback did not lead to reform so much as further action to maintain the myth of the plan. Social integration was undercut by deep cynicism, popular distrust and systematic blockages in supplies as well as systems' breakdowns, signified most dramatically by the mishandling of communications about the Chernobyl disaster in 1986. The Party became increasingly incapable of maintaining mechanisms of stability and planned change.

Whatever quiescence local elites exhibited was a form of 'pragmatic submission' (Scott 1985). When the threat of compulsion seemed real, apparent order prevailed on the surface. When forcible intervention seemed increasingly distant and unlikely, which was the case by the end of the 1980s, resistance began to break out in many places, articulated by ethnic and language nationalism as well as resistance to the dominant myth. Paradoxically, Gorbachev's *glasnost* and *perestroika* might have been successful if it had been applied in a less fragmented field, in which countervailing national narratives flourished; if the field had been less fragmented, however, it would have been less necessary. The result of their introduction was a spark that led to the collapse of the system. Out of the chaos emerged a kleptocracy of ex-apparatchik become oligarchs and eventually a Putin presidency of a Russian-led confederation that, over time, sought to reaccumulate the powers that the Party had once assumed. In this third act of Russian autocracy, after the tsars and the Soviets, power was now concentrated on Putin and an oligarchical centralization and conservation of control of judicial, media, police and surveillance powers (Service 2019; Wood 2020).

Snyder (2018) defines the interregnum after the collapse of communism in the Soviet Union as one in which the old inevitabilities of capitalism's superiority to communism became fused in the West into a neoliberal end of history thesis, most popularly by Fukuyama (2006). There were several versions of this story of progress. In the American dominated neoliberal version, the market behaved in ways akin to a law of nature. A corollary of the democracy of market competition was the associated political democracy, which brought happiness, a constitutional right. In the Western European version, after two World Wars Europe learned that peace was good, choosing cooperation and prosperity in a common market as an extension of the Westphalian settlement that had so obviously failed to limit interstate conflicts. As the implications of the global financial crisis played out in everyday lives of despair about the future, there were those who sought to exploit popular discontent by making America great again or that sought to regain their freedoms by taking back control through Brexit. In such translations, teleology was reversed and the utopia of the desired future state became a Retrotopia, as Bauman (2017) explained (see Clegg 2018). Such myths of nostalgia limit the possibility of acknowledging persistent paradoxes, thus blocking the capacity to navigate and learn from them.

In the ashes of the socialist utopia that had been built and imposed by the Soviet Union, an alternative worldview emerged. It echoed tropes thought long eliminated with the end of fascism. Putin's imperialism sought to present an ordered, one-dimensional vision of the world, in which past and present collapsed and an eternity beckoned, in which clarity was provided through submission to absolute leadership and an unambiguous view of the enemy: 'Whereas inevitability promises a better future for everyone, eternity places one nation at the center of a cyclical story of victimhood' (Snyder 2018:8).

INTEGRATIONS' CONSEQUENCES, WEST AND EAST

The myth of the market contains the powers of creative destruction which have crisis and failure already normalized, as a regular occurrence. No armed state interventions are necessary. In the West, system integration is founded on market fictions that have become ever more abstracted, particularly in financial markets, while social integration, premised on identities sharing and differentiated by symbolic meanings and a plurality of language games, categorization devices and discourses, is increasingly organically dynamic. On the one hand, individual identities, particularly of young people, became founded on virtual celebrations of individually distinct identity expressed through social media posting and following defining different styles of life. On the other hand, identities were collectively orchestrated through whatever major forms of collective sentiment, combining spectacle and ethics, command attention, with sport being the major conduit. Supporting national teams in international level competitive sports tournaments, as well as specific national competitors, is the classic case of contemporary spectacles. In both cases, media effectively 'colonize the lifeworld'. One consequence, is that the democratic power of the multitude to grasp the critical moments in which we live is increasingly focused on immediacy, presence and individualism.

In twentieth-century capitalism, social integration within a fundamentally unequal society was justified in relation to the principle of meritocracy. The obligatory passage point justifying the inequalities of capitalist societies was the idea that privilege was a fair reward for hard work and ability. However, in the twenty-first century, with the undermining by economic neoliberalism of the welfare state, the effects of policies enabling working-class social advancement through educational reform declined. The lack of legitimacy of meritocratic inequality was further undermined by the realization that a small elite (the 1 per cent) are becoming comparatively wealthier relative to the middle-classes, as Stiglitz (2015) and Piketty (2018) elaborate. It was the middle classes who were the main consumers and purveyors of the idea that inequality could be justified by meritocracy (Markovits 2019; Bloodworth 2016). The argument that the wealth of the wealthy is not an issue because of trickle-down economics appears increasingly implausible; however, perceptions of illegitimacy have yet to be translated into much concrete social action by the political elites voted into office by democratic populaces; these elites have yet to promote a sustained new basis for social integration.

The comparative lessons are evident. In the West, circuits of power that govern through freedoms, however illusory, are more efficient than repressions and this applies across all levels of analysis from the organizational to the societal. In Western capitalism, circuits that stress system integration and allow for diversities, pluralities and freedoms of identity in social integration are more resilient and robust than those that are tightly policed. In the East, in post-communist state capitalist Russia and China, where the levers of ideological hegemony producing dominant ideology are state centred, censored and sanctioned, paradoxically, the Marxist critique of ideology rings most true. The absence of pluralism in media inculcates social integration around a dominant ideology that in both cases is increasingly nationalistic. To the extent that extensively networked system integration relies on tightly coupled flows through limited nodal points, system shock absorbers do not function well.

It is not ideological myth and social integration that is central in the liquid modernity of the West, so much as system integration. The reliance of financial institutions on algorithmic devices caused a near-global crisis in 2008, with subsequent limited attempt at delegitimation signalled by some elements of carnival associated with Occupy and related social movements. In the West, meanwhile, not a thousand but millions of flowerings of identity bloomed, aided by digital devices and their software. Paradoxically, a dense plurality of circuits of social integration can both cushion, compartmentalize and rationalize those crises that ensue as well as amplify them. While online chat groups can function as circuits of local integration among commonly interested participants, they can also be sources of overall social disintegration. Think of the QAnon conspiracies and their role in fermenting the January 6, 2021 insurrection in the USA. The internet reaffirms cognitive bias through the various algorithms that drive its traffic. Enquiry about any aspect of the QAnon stories on Google will simply take one deeper into the looking-glass of whatever conspiracy is being promulgated. In terms of system integration, the pluralities of social integration online afford opportunities for any specific community of practice to swarm physically, as well as virtually. Whether the swarming is a positive or negative for overall social integration is a matter contingent on the beliefs that motivate the swarming and the conditions under which the swarm forms.

In the East, in Russia, before the internet, state steering of identity politics was critical for social ordering because the central conduit of politics was reliant on social integration, which it was the role of the Party to regulate (see Spufford 2010). Putin's regime, which replaced Soviet Marxist–Leninist ideological control with oligarchic kleptocracy and legitimations of nationalism and Orthodox religiosity as ideology, is learning this anew (Wood 2020). Putin's Russia is marked by its extreme nationalism. Religion plays its role also: the Orthodox Church supports and reproduces the discourse of nationalism, something Solzhenitsyn knew well (Smith 2022). For Solzhenitsyn, Russia's future was unlikely to be one of liberal democracy; too much Tsarist and Soviet history made that unlikely. In Russia, the shift of social integration from the rhetoric of the Party to that of national, patriarchal and religious identity seeks to channel social identity through restricted obligatory passage points disseminated through centrally controlled media, a control that touches social media. The conduits may have changed, but the dynamics remain very similar.

The contrast in the role that Christianity plays in the US and Russia is striking. In the US, Christianity is plural, fragmented and individualistic, with strong popular undercurrents of a fundamental evangelism, while in Russia it is centralized, homogenous and traditionalist for elites and masses alike. Expressions of religious faith convey remarkable truths deemed sacrosanct. Such reification socially constructs believers' claims to a truth divine, beyond doubt and incontestable. In liberal democracy, fallibility – the idea that all our beliefs can be contested – can keep the authoritarianism of such reifications in check, as we agree to disagree. Extreme claims to spiritual possession of infallible truth, of whatever religious persuasion, can threaten this democracy when it is enacted to resist plural and diverse opinion. Such enactments can be increasingly digitally mediated and publicly shared among the communities of faith. Where faith is seen as essentially arbitrary and therefore a deeply individual and personal act, more tolerance of pluralism can be expected. Faith is a highly singular basis for social integration by contrast, the essence of modern power/knowledge relations resides in their condensation and differentiation through many organs and capillaries of transmission, rather than being faith-based.

Modern democratic power is abstract not personalized – it mostly flows through things and devices rather than targeting specific dissident individuals (although there are always exceptions as the case of Julian Assange demonstrates: see Logue and Clegg 2015). The devices may be symbolic, as is money, something that kleptocratic regimes recognize well as they invest the billions of surplus incomes available to them in real estate in London, Monaco and elsewhere, in places where they moor their yachts and park their planes, ably assisted by Western, especially London, institutions (Belton 2020). Devices may also be material, as tanks, missiles and bombs, as Putin commands. Or they may be nightmares that are potentially real, such as the threat of mutually assured destruction, which Putin provokes.

On one hand, disrupting the status quo creates uncertainty that can be exploited as a source of agentic power (this is what Putin did in invading Ukraine: using military power to disrupt 'Western order', to create new space for himself to exploit tyrannically). At the same time, such disruption can undermine the very flows of systemic power (namely, global trade and resource-based needs) that constitute the energy of Putin's power. Indeed, this is a very dangerous and (hopefully) self-defeating strategy, in which attempts to create new power opportunities (creating in the meantime unspeakable suffering) end up destroying power advantages.

Two cautionary notes can be sounded. First, circuits of social integration – the more centred they become on obligatory passage points that stress conformism and convergence, the more they stifle social innovation and have a low capacity to absorb shocks that do not conform to their constructions of reality. The recent history of Ukraine can be seen in these terms. Ukraine's misfortune is to be adjacent to a specific geography and history, both haunted by Russian nightmares and European dreams. After the collapse of the USSR, Ukraine became a failed state that the hyper-inflation of the decade after the break-up of the USSR created. The Church then broke into Ukrainian and Russian Orthodoxy with the allegiances of the breakaway provinces of the Donbas being more Russian-oriented and supportive of the Eurasian Economic Union that Russia helmed, while under Zelensky and his predecessor, the 'irrational dream' of joining the European Union and NATO was floated. The latter was the Russian nightmare; its counterpoint, grounded in realism, was that Ukraine should be a buffer state between East and West, something that 'a narrowly Ukrainian, anti-Russian form of nationalism, reflected in language policy, "de-communisation", and the secession of the Ukrainian Orthodox church from its Russian "mother" church made "impossible" (Jones 2022). Two rival forms of social integration were competing in the same national civic space and neither recognized the legitimacy of the other. To bolster their respective legitimacies, the parties and the oligarchical elites of each oriented increasingly, respectively, West and East, furthering the Ukrainian system disintegration that hyper-inflation, local kleptocracy and external influences had fostered. Cyber-factories, dispensing digitally malevolent mischief and disorder, were also rife within Russia, targeting the West and its allies, including Ukraine (Greenberg 2022), adding further disinformation.

Second, circuits of system integration that display network complexity and extensive interlocking can rapidly relay circuit-breaking events. Using tightly coupled and heavily programmed subsystems, such as the way in which Europe and the US have used the Swift system and financial and insurance sanctions to cripple the Russian economy, make foreign exchange holdings 'a kind of financial suicide bomb' (Foroohar 2022). As major source of system integration, fixed networks of pipelines, rather than digital networks, become a potential liability. The decision to block the Russian central bank from international financial markets, which effectively freezes its foreign exchange reserves, with even Switzerland doing so, has major implications for the Russian economy and ultimately for global social integration.

Russia is a failing post-communist state; the other post-communist capitalist state is China, which embodies authoritarian policies with significantly greater success than Russia. As O'Neill (2022) argues, 'China must be alarmed and displeased by the audacity of both Russia's war and the Western reaction to it'. Doubtless, this is the case but it might also be that China is gathering intelligence from the approaches applied, as well as global responses to them, not all of which are condemnatory. Should China invade Taiwan, the same lock-out from the global financial system by the West is probable, coexistent with accommodation elsewhere, a fate potentially presaged by sanctions on Russia. While Europe abandoning oil and gas that is convenient for other sources of supply that are not, is a costly move in the short-term, it is, perhaps, less so in terms of long-term strategy.

What might eventually work for the West against Russia is less likely to do so in China. While China may be alarmed by EU reactions to the invasion of Ukraine, should China invade Taiwan it is doubtful that Europe and the United States could maintain sanctions of this magnitude against China. Furthermore, China might well learn from Russia's mistakes. It certainly has in terms of fragmentation. China's Han nationalism combines with expressions of belief in the will of the Party in steering integration. In China, both the media and the content of ideology are more effectively controlled than in Russia. Social integration is achieved through enforced ideological incorporation and where that fails – for instance, in Hong Kong – draconian policing, judicial action and coercion reinforce pragmatic consent, while among the Uighur minority in the far West, exclusion through concentration camps for re-education is favoured. The empire is far more integrated, less fissiparous and better repressed than Russia, although the increasing antipathy of locked down populations to the conditions of the lockdown is making dissent more public (Carey 2022). China is also better buttressed by reefs and islands claimed in its name to bolster maritime command of sea lanes in the Pacific and is not reliant on access to seas controlled by adversaries.

Globally, China's policy is one of essentially buying foreign local elites with its Belt and Road strategy (for more on which, see Clegg et al., 2022). The largesse of this project appears to be a highly effective form of imperialism, which may enable China to take over many of the Asia-Pacific countries as well as Africa by offering the lure of megaprojects built with Chinese labour and paid for by loans from China, that end up imposing constraints through long-term indebtedness. Sri Lanka is testament to the socially disintegrative effects of this form of system integration. For those societies subject to these overtures, where liberal democracy exists, it will be undermined, with the Chinese command economy being positioned as a new norm.

SOLIDARITIES

Updating Durkheim (1893), contemporary Russia is based, ideologically, on modern mechanical solidarity, as depicted in Table 10.1.

Russia is not a liquidly modern society; indeed, in some respects it is a premodern state, riddled with 'fluid fiefdoms' (Sussex 2022). The contrast with the West is striking. Societies of Western Europe and the United States are based on a postmodern organically liquid solidarity. System integration also differs markedly. In contemporary Russia, it flows through pipelines as oil and gas that are the major resource forming the basis for a network of system integration that is state controlled. While before the conflict, the EU imported about 45 per cent of its gas and 25 per cent of its oil from Russia, the combination of sanctions and voluntary withdrawals from the market is having destabilizing effects not only on them but more so on Russia. If Russian integration of its pipeline

Table 10.1 Contemporary mechanical and organic solidarity

Modern mechanical solidarity	(Post)-modern organically liquid solidarity
Solidarity through claims of essential likeness	Solidarity through claims of essential difference and pluralism
Strong collective consciousness; a national(ist) identity; ritual value of a single religion	Weak collective consciousness; diverse freedoms of identity; abstract value of individualism as religious pluralism (USA) or secularism (Europe).
Repressive and tightly controlled ideological state apparatus	Pluralistic ideological market apparatuses
State-centred vertical integration	Market-centred networks integration
Dominance of industrial manufacturing and mining sectors	Dominance of digital service sectors

network to Europe is permanently ruptured, the consequences would be extreme, especially so for Russia, starved of foreign capital from export sales in the long term. As the politics of democratic sentiment wash over the parliaments and peoples of Europe and America, leading to a minimizing of gas and oil supplies from the East, the consequences will be a major long-term shock to Russian system integration, especially on the part of Germany.

In the short term, sanctions have had the perverse effect of driving up the receipts from Russia's oil and gas exports as their cost rises, boosting its trade balance and thus financing its war effort (Elliott 2022). For as long as gas flows and oil are shipped and insured, Russia will have monetary resources to sustain a long campaign of deadly attrition and destruction, even if only cashed out in roubles, in which China may well sustain them by buying globally cheap Russian energy. Russian energy exports are also flowing East, as well as to impoverished states such as Sri Lanka, and its more prosperous neighbour, India, eager for the cheapest energy they can buy, irrespective of its source (Mushtaq 2022).

In the West, the USA and Europe's primary means of system integration is through complex global market networks that are far less material, are digital and much more pervasive, with the sanctions regime these afford having the potential to shut Russia's oligarchy out of global capital markets. These Western countries have every motive to divest from the carbon economy; Russia has not. In the short-term, the sanctions regime on Russian energy will unleash the spectre of stagflation in European treasuries, while in the longer term, moves to non-carbon energy sources will control these tendencies. Some countries in Europe, especially Norway, with its hydro-power resources, as well as its oil and gas, are prefiguring an increasingly decarbonized economy and society. Others, such as Germany, will follow if their politicians and business elites are smart. The future belongs to the investors in and the exporters of green energy rather than those that retain fossil fuel as an energy source.

New forms of social integration are promised by green energy sources. Green hydrogen can almost eliminate emissions by using renewable energy – increasingly abundant and often generated at less-than-ideal times – to power the electrolysis of water. When the electricity comes from renewable sources, the hydrogen is effectively green; the only carbon emissions are from those embodied in the generation infrastructure. The cost per kilogram of producing green hydrogen is forecast to be cost competitive by the end of the decade at almost 70 per cent of the present cost (Longden et al., 2020). Where electrolysis is powered by green energy, its cost, once the electrolyzer is purchased, will be minimal. For instance, in Australia the AUD$51 billion Asian Renewable Energy Hub, will produce 26 gigawatts of cheap solar and wind power in the Pilbara region of Western Australia, producing more power than all the nation's coal-fired power stations. The Pilbara is a major site of iron ore mining, so that with a plentiful supply of hydrogen, 'green steel' can be produced in towns like Port Hedland or Karratha and exported globally. For those countries that do not have considerable solar capacity, where wind and wave sources of energy are insufficient or unreliable, hydrogen can be converted into ammonia for transport and then reconverted at destination to overcome safety issues in hydrogen's transportation (Purtill 2021). Thus, green energy can produce ammonia to be imported from solar-rich countries closer to the equator which can be exported globally in hydrogen powered ships.

The disruption of European system integration by the diminution in use of Russian oil and gas will not only enfeeble Russian autocracy further, but also hasten technological innovations that will reconfigure system integration that is based on non-fossil energy. From the Western point of view of liberal democracy this is the optimistic outlook. More pessimistically, it is possible that the result of EU sanctions will be that Russia becomes a vassal state to China, as it reorients its economy East. If so, if China remains stable, Russia will be able to continue with its own authoritarian kleptocracy.

Returning to social integration, with reference to Table 10.1, it should be noted that it works through different solidarities, ideal typically represented here as modern and postmodern, or, one could say, in this instance, as Russian and Western. Of course, social integration can always construct an Other on whom the unleashing of episodic power can be justified: for Russia, at the present, the Ukrainian state is the Other. The irruption of episodic power disrupting and destroying this Other strengthens social integration at home through rallying nationalistic opposition, antagonism and violence to Western European-oriented political projects, such as those of the majority fraction of the Ukrainian political elites. The Ukrainian minority elite fraction that mapped its support closely onto social identity claims premised on language, religion and ethnicity sprung from Mother Russia have little legitimacy in either Ukraine or the West in the face of Russian coercive power.

The claims of Russian and Ukrainian social integration create the paradox that if the claim is that Russian social integration is pan-national, then the invasion of Ukraine is a declaration of war on a shared social identity, a civil war. It is important to note, as did Parsons (1963), that creation of power within a system normally presupposes consensus on goals, providing a framework within which facilitative power operates. The Ukrainian state has not shared goals with Russia since at least 2014 and the Maidan Revolution. Social and system integration clash on Ukrainian soil.

To summarize: in the East, where there is centrality of circuits of social integration, social ordering is marked by too much state and too little market, while in the West, or at least in its most neo-liberally economic expressions, there is centrality of circuits of system integration and social ordering is marked by too little state and too much market. Of course, states are dense collections of fields, characterized by complex relations. As circuits of social and system integration traverse these relations, each is liable to circuit breaking from events. Where social integration is central, power over deviant subjects defined in terms of dominant conceptions of normal power/knowledge will be forcibly exercised, even against resistance. Doing this may undermine system integration, as in the case of Russia, while its effectiveness in silencing dissent in China remains an open question at the time of writing. Where system integration is achieved not just through material but also digital infrastructure with its abstract and pluralistic coding, while the system may be confounded when confronted with events, it may not face rupture.

Crisis in either market-led system integration or in state-led social integration can destabilize existing knowledge, resource dependencies and pattern of interaction. In such conjunctures, while system disintegration can be fixed by states learning new routines, such as quantitative easing, social disintegration is far more problematic where no higher order organization (other than potentially religious institutions such as the Orthodox Church in Russia) exists to fix internal problems of integration. However, these can be displaced externally through projections of power, seeking to rupture system integration in the process, as in Ukraine.

Neo-economically liberal states weather crises much more resiliently than do states in which system integration is subordinate to social integration. The former situations are far less ideological, while the latter are far more ideological, contrary to the lessons of Western Marxism. Thus, contradictions in system integration have not destroyed capitalism because of capitalisms' relative autonomy as a circuit of power/knowledge, especially in the most central global states; in addition, the plurality and diversity of social integration within such nations make them far more resilient, even when all the preconditions of fiscal and legitimation crisis are present, as they have been in recent times, with the impact of the COVID-19 virus.

THE COVID-19 CRISIS

In terms of public policy, it should be evident in ways that perhaps was not the case previously, that we really do live in a global risk society, as Beck (1992) argued. Nuclear accidents, viruses and climate change are no respecters of national borders that cannot protect their citizens (Beck 1992). Nonetheless, COVID-19 highlighted the interdependent oppositions facing decision-makers: should we protect people or protect the economy? Display strength or vulnerability? Keep calm by expressing confidence or transmit confidence by embracing doubt? These irresolvable choices are typical of paradoxes that present themselves as interdependent persistent oppositions (Schad et al. 2016).

The pandemic promoted a paradox premised on circuits of power: those powers steering the state were able to exemplify their powerfulness against citizens by being able to impose lockdowns, which were made legitimate by appeals to a state of exception.

The social construction of a state of exception afforded an opportunity for authorities to indulge in power. Autocracies such as Xi Jingpin's China took this furthest, although autocracy appeared in several forms and shapes. In India, Modi used the opportunity to advance his Hindu first agenda (Prasad 2020). In the UK, Boris Johnson became a victim of the contagion in whose power he had initially doubted and recovered to lead a largely successful vaccine programme. In the US, Donald Trump presided over belief in miracles and miracle cures as the contagion raged in the incompetence he nurtured; after he was infected, he claimed that God rather than science had spared him. The King of Thailand, Rama X, found refuge in the German Alps, in the company of his harem, while demonstrators in Bangkok faced the threat of arrest in a country still characterized by *lèse majesté* legislation. China, facing an outbreak in 2022 of the Omicron variants, has seen officials adopting ever more extreme measures to stamp out the highly infectious variant as part of President Xi Jinping's strict zero-COVID policy. Shanghai, China's most important economic hub and the world's busiest port, came to a standstill. Multinationals such as Apple, Tesla and General Electric, Amazon, Adidas and Estée Lauder have seen their supply chains disrupted due to the lockdown of China's major export hub, as the country applies a zero-COVID policy that confines workers to their homes and dormitories, against which increasingly fractious protest is occurring.

The pandemic confronted leaders with hard choices, twixt the fire and the sword (Tourish 2020): act too rapidly and be accused of exaggeration; be too lax and be accused of carelessness. Elites often oscillate towards concentrating power further, not only authoritarians such as Xi Jinping. For instance, the elimination strategy that New Zealand initially embraced went against that scientific advice that stresses that one cannot fight a pandemic by eliminating it in a single region and that, in the long term, doing so can be extremely counter-productive by fostering an 'every nation for itself' attitude, chasing the illusion of 'cleansing through isolation', the China syndrome. The WHO, among others, specifically advised against border closures or excessive use of lockdowns, as these measures can only be justified in extreme cases and for short periods of time.

Pandemic organizing oscillated purposefully between strong measures and relatively more 'relaxed' periods in which activities could be carried out in a semi-normal way. Strong measures included initiatives of temporary but total and well-enforced lockdowns aimed at slowing the epidemic; working on retrofitting social structures to cope with the pandemic's effects in the long term, such as adding ICUs, reinforcing remote working and teaching capabilities, improving sanitation protocols, especially on public transport, while developing new practices that minimize social distance without keeping everyone at home, stressing the necessity to be vaccinated in order to safeguard life and health, while also sending a strong message to the population that these measures are serious, not to be lightly dismissed. In time, reopening of theatres and restaurants with new stringent distance protocols became part of relaxing regulation, albeit with a readiness on the part of states to lock down again if there were further increases in transmission. Doing this allows both educating the population and maintaining a semblance of normalcy: if people see no end to lockdown, panic and fear will escalate; if they are not given the opportunity to experience a lockdown, they do not take things seriously enough.

What all governments and their leaders had in common was that their being in power did not correspond to being in control. In a pandemic, no one is in control. To use a famous leadership conceptualization, the context leads (Yukl 2006). The fact that this condition is explicit creates a problem: 'those in charge of the state are in a panic because they know that not only that they are not in control of the situation, but also that we, their subjects, know this. The impotence of power is now laid bare' (Žižek 2020: 123). Here is the irony: leaders need to project power yet know that everybody is aware of their condition of powerlessness in the face of the pandemic. Some authoritarian leaders such as Xi Jingpin chose to display performances of strength, others such as Jacinda Arden performed empathy, while many democracies adopted the mantra of believing in the science until its recommendations did not fit the politics of the government in office or what their focus groups told them. An excess of strength in the face of highly volatile conditions proved to be a recipe for disaster, given that conditions changed so fast that today's orders were rapidly contradicted by tomorrow's needs.

Pandemics perturb power, the uncertainty nurtured by pandemic threatens dictatorial regimes by showing the limits of their certainties and their control, as a threat to the very legitimacy of the established order. People who contracted the virus were sometimes categorized as careless and antisocial (ironically, because of their failure to maintain social distances); foreigners became characterized as potential threats as carriers of virus; in some extreme cases, such as in Australia, even citizens who desired to venture interstate or overseas were treated with disdain and suspicion. If overseas, they were unable to return; if at home many were banned from venturing outside exclusion zones established by their state government. Failure to observe these rules led to substantial fines (subsequently rescinded, as Taouk, 2022, reports). Episodic power, centred on containment and surveillance, was the order of the day. The need to protect public health became construed as legitimation for unprecedented surveillance and disciplining of the population using digital proofs of vaccination functioning as a kind of internal passport to venues. This became the other arm of policy, to containment, heightening digital veillance of movements among sites of infection. Interestingly, some of the most extensive powers have been advocated in countries that, because of their peripheral location, were relatively less affected by the pandemic.

The virus was an 'exogenous environmental contingency' that perturbed system integration. The system was shown to be inadequate relative to the 'facilitative' capacity of the system to deal with a new external threat of COVID-19. Social actors in positions of dispositional power reacted by deeming this a state of exception, which called for a redefinition of the 'rules of practice', fixing relations of meaning and membership. The 'dispositional' powers of the system had to be changed and, with it, the rules of 'membership and integration' were shifted. Suddenly, those who were too mobile became suspect, relative to social integration. From a situation where flying to other countries or flying in from other countries was a source of status, flying from anywhere could make the social subject excluded rather than exclusive. The abnormal rules of lockdown and the virtual ban on international travel became the new 'rules of practice' of the dispositional power circuit.

Medical experts, following 'the science', stipulated the 'obligatory passage points' for policy. Policy makers justified their actions relative to claims to truths held to be scientifically sound, derived from epidemiological and medical science, rather than, as was previously typical in the neoliberal order, relative to the claims of economic orthodoxy. The citizens watching the news became familiar with whoever featured at the national level as experts drafted into COVID advisory panels of expertise – for example, Sweden's Anders Tegnell. At the episodic level, social actors in discriminated locales suddenly felt the power of the state the moment they walked outside their house. The local police officer could tell them it was illegal to walk in the park. Indeed, even inside their homes the local police could exercise episodic power by breaking up a birthday party or other personal celebrations. In Italy, dogs became valuable assets, resources of episodic power, enabling owners to walk in the park. Indeed, these dogs became passed around the neighbourhood, to facilitate strategies of episodic resistance to the newly assumed dispositional powers of the state. As observed by Foucault, wherever there are new circuits of power created, at an agency level, social actors will find modes of resistance.[2]

The surveillance society analyzed by Zuboff (2019) benefitted significantly from the 'windows of opportunity' created by the COVID-19 pandemic, by creating a 'normality of exception' in Santos' (2020) phrase. The social construction of COVID as an exception created the conditions of possibility for the state to assume new dispositional powers, which under 'normal' circumstance would have been characterized as authoritarian, thus outside the conditions of possibility for any liberal democratic state. Not only states: new modes of surveillance were adopted by companies to control their employees (Bhave et al. 2020).

Responding to COVID-19 has tapped into the many affordances of IT-based monitoring. For example, during the COVID pandemic, contact-tracing programs that require significant monitoring (so that individuals can be notified if they have been in contact with an infected individual) were assumed to be critical for controlling the spread of the virus and allowing economies to open (Servick 2020). Interestingly, these contact-tracing programs have been implemented in very different ways across the world, sparking debates about the role of surveillance in societies. Amnesty International, concerned about the surveillance implications of these apps, devised an eight-point framework that governments should follow if privacy concerns were to be allayed (Amnesty International 2020). Data protection regulators in Norway vetoed the use of a health authorities contact-tracing app that used location data as well as Bluetooth, processing proximity data centrally rather than on individual smartphones, for instance (Browne 2020).

Monitoring increasingly does not position specific actors as central; what matters are data flows associated with them. Thus, dataveillance implies building on the digital data traces left with IT-based automated decision systems that can access, interpret and monitor people's behaviour (Mayer-Schönberger and Cukier 2013; Van Dijck 2014). Likewise, for surveillance assemblages (Gilliom and Monahan 2012: 22), the 'central idea is that there is no central force. There is no Big Brother, no panopticon, but a shifting, moving observation, presentation and regulation of the self by countless measures in countless locations.' In these circumstances, power becomes increasingly abstract.

Being locked down, working from home, with its attractions, came into vogue. It also had its downside. As observed by Foucault (1982), to be effective, power must not simply say no or assume the form of interdiction. It must facilitate new freedoms, which creates attraction to the new dispositional power. Working from home became a force of 'enrolment', drawing social actors into the new structures of power. As the COVID crisis unfolded, employers postponed or cancelled plans for a return to the office, with some managers deploying increasing levels of surveillance to re-create the oversight of the office at home, reported Alex Hern (2020) in *The Guardian*. For people who were home-working, many organizations began to track what their employees were doing. Freedom became tied to restraint and accountability. The power of enrolment had its disciplinary side. Some surveillance is as simple as 'checking in' or stamping your timecard in a digital sense. Tools such as Slack and Microsoft Teams report when an employee is 'active' and failure to open apps first thing in the morning is often taken by managers as the same as being late for work. Some employers require all staff to join a video conference every morning, with their webcams switched on. Organizations that practise low trust/high control management at work strove to emulate it for homeworking. PwC came under fire for developing a facial recognition tool that logs when employees are away from their computer screens while working from home. According to PwC, it is designed to help financial institutions meet their compliance obligations, as workers would normally be monitored for security purposes on trading floors but mightn't one expect them to say that?

The coronavirus presents an existential challenge to cultural boundaries. Strategies to prevent its further spread (e.g., handwashing, 'social distancing' and closing national borders) are culturally significant. As observed by sociologists of food and etiquette (e.g., Mennell 1996), major social changes at the macro system integration level are accompanied by significant changes in everyday norms of etiquette and behaviour. The virus creates boundaries around people and exclusionary social hierarchies, changing the rules of social integration. Collateral consequences of protective measures vary across regions and social groups, creating and exacerbating social inequalities. People engaged in body work seem most vulnerable: hairdressers, beauticians, nail-bar technicians, carers, uber and taxi drivers, mortuary workers, nursing and medical staff, trainers. Not exclusively, but often the bodies at risk are marked by gender, caste and status ascription. The virus creates a hybrid of threatening pathogen and human bodies; these bodies, once infected, suffer additional exclusions, discrimination and disrespect.

The differential consequences of the management of COVID-19 have been pointed out: the poor and essential workers, often the same, suffered far more than the knowledge workers, those able to continue working from their keyboards, despite being locked down at home. Those who cleaned, nurtured and tended to the impurity of society; those who assisted and cared for aged and frail people; those who toiled physically in manual labour or confined spaces; those who did the body work that defines the various skin trades as lower caste (O'Neill 1972) had no such options. For such people, their everyday life was already defined as being lived in dangerously marginal relationships to hygieneism (Zulfiqar 2019); the pandemic made their marginality more salient and revealed the scale of contagion spread through body work.

As is often the case with shifts in etiquette that define status, those at the bottom of the social hierarchy were most subject to the new norms and were least able to conform to them, given that the precariousness of their economic status exposed them to more travel and to a more precarious patchwork of employment. Their inability and reluctance to conform set them apart as marginal. From a sociological perspective, it is important to understand that such norms are not only about medical hygiene; they are also rules of distinction that confer status (Bourdieu 1984). The rules concerning hand washing and so on have strong resonance with the types of rules found in religious practices and those of caste systems, excluding them from physical contact with those of higher status for whom socially constructed uncleanliness is a sign of profane and low status. Even though most scientists are agreed that the virus is spread by small airborne liquid particles, not by touch, the first reaction assumed it was touch that spread contamination, which has strong resonance with rules of distinction. In other words, the rules of touch make more sense sociologically than they do medically.

More than this, the nature of everyday security in working life was transformed. Practices of hot-desking, open-plan offices, air-conditioned offices with windows that do not open, lifts that have keypads that everyone touches, all become extremely uninviting in a pandemic. Until such time as almost everyone is vaccinated and mutations cease to be as dangerous, homeworking is likely to be preferred. For some, this worked well; for others, there were the drawbacks of loneliness, threats to mental health and the lack of social solidarity that ensued, not to mention the unequal costs in terms of the gendered nature of domestic and childcare, as well as childminding duties of children no longer able to participate in childcare, kindergarten or school. These are some of the shocks to social integration; there were also major system integration consequences.

Modern normalcy became premised on going to work elsewhere from where one lived. Work and home, inseparable under the pre-capitalist putting-out system, became separate zones of exclusion, each of the other, in the nineteenth century (Marglin 1974), as merchant capitalists incorporated domestically based weaving and spinning into manufactories under the super(ordinate)vision of the business owner. Prior to the First World War, those women in middle- and upper-class homes were largely confined in status to domestic management. That war liberated working-class women from domestic service, giving rise to the 'servant problem' of the inter war years (Clegg and Dunkerley 1980/2013), changing social mores considerably. In the post-Second World War period, dormitory suburbs, shopping malls and industrial or tech districts shaped development, based on rail and automobile mobilities. Post-COVID, in the twenty-first century one can speculate whether this separation of work and home is to become a thing of the past. The freedom of being able to work from home becomes coupled with surveillance of the home. It is possible that COVID-19 has created conditions for the possibility of a new type of society, with new dispositional powers, concerning the management of space.

COVID-19 has had a global impact. At one level, the lockdowns, the social isolation and exclusions disrupted norms of local and global networks, massively threatening global system integration. More than this, however, Santos (2020) saw the virus as sundering 'hypercapitalism', as for instance, in the closure of the port of Shanghai, a central node of global trade. In COVID-19 society, a 'new barbarian capitalism' (Žižek 2020: 127) flourished, in which the old and weak were left to die in 'aged care' facilities in which the virus spread like wildfire, in part because of the casualization of a workforce that could unwittingly spread it between different locations of work. As Žižek recounts, in socialist utopias, this was nothing new: at some point in Ceausescu's Romania, retired people were not admitted to hospitals because they were no longer productive (2020: 101).

Old age in hypercapitalism affected by a contagion differs from Ceausescu's Romania; it is less that people are abandoned by the state as the fact that the market kills them. The issue has been sometimes presented as a dilemma between the need to shelter frail, elderly people through isolation, versus the unbearable psychological cost of such isolation, as if the choice was between risk of dying because of COVID-19 and the risk of being deprived of social contact. While this trade-off is unmistakably present, the real cause of the diffusion of the virus in aged care facilities has been the reliance on a privatized model of aged care, employing a visibly precarious workforce (e.g., Peticca-Harris 2020), whose movement between different facilities contributed to the contagion. Private-sector aged care maximizes surplus value by minimizing the value attached to old folk. Low-waged, relatively unskilled care-providers, often casual and precarious employees, often uninsured medically because of the nature of their casual employment, spread the virus through the workings of the aged care labour market. For these less privileged workers, lower standards of living were the norm.

Society is composed of different demographics. We have become much more aware of the terrible total institutions to which older citizens are confined as they age; these became death traps under the virus. One should stress the word 'citizens'; we ought ethically to owe obligations to citizens at every stage of the life course, from kindergarten to aged care facility; for either of these to be conceived purely as profit centres is inhumane. In aged care, as Flybvjerg (2020) argues, the safety of both employees and patients has been compromised in inhumanely unimaginable ways, at least in terms of pre-pandemic imaginings. During the pandemic class and ethnic distinctions became even more acutely matters of life and death. Poor neighbourhoods were more exposed to the virus than the wealthier. Death stalked the disproportionately black, brown and poor. The pandemic revealed that the notion of the periphery (Day and Schoemaker 2004) includes not only organizations and markets, but also a huge group of people. Santos (2020) dedicated significant attention to the groups formed as disempowered, disenfranchised people: women, the precariat, street workers, the homeless, people from poorer neighbourhoods, refugees, older people, people with disabilities. Some of these people do jobs latterly described as 'essential', as distinct from the knowledge workers, the core of organizational 'wars for talent', working from home. These people do not do what 'essential workers' sustain. They do not clean, tend, teach, toil and transport.

Services and careers need rebuilding and rethinking in the wake of the virus. Any national society is composed of complex divisions of labour that are, in Durkheim's (1893) words, 'organic', in which we all depend on others. In the past, the social categorization of some jobs as more important than others resulted from categorization devices premised on earnings; the pandemic has privileged different categories of 'essentialness'. A revalorization of divisions of labour is overdue and one upshot of the pandemic may be to achieve that. People who were formerly invisible, suddenly have become visible. Categories of people, including working mothers (especially affected by working from home), the old and retired, people with disabilities and the homeless must also be added to the ranks of the invisible. If organizations are to be transformed by the pandemic, then policies dedicated to the inclusion of marginalized groups will need to be embraced, if only because, as Ibarra (2020) notes, COVID-19 poses specific problems for vulnerable minorities. When knowledge work is now known to be doable from anywhere, independently of an urban infrastructure of transport, cafés, bars, offices, etc., the masses that lived off these knowledge workers, the service sector employees, the homeless and charitably supported persons, will be a new, resentful sub-proletariat freshly joining the reserve army of the unemployed.

Critically, the privatization of public sector work left many states devoid of adequate tools, capabilities and dispositions with which to fulfil their mission in the pandemic.

Hollowed out neoliberal states presided over systems of disintegration rather than integration in areas of residual welfare. The weakness of the neoliberal state exposed the need to find a new logic of social organization. While neoliberal capitalism incapacitated the state in responding to emergencies is advanced by Santos (2020), it is easy to defend the opposite, that the crisis over-empowered the state, throwing ideology into question, making things more fluid, more liquid. In the Western world, we live an ideology that Bauman (2000) called 'liquid modernity'. For Bauman, to 'be modern' means to modernize – compulsively and obsessively, forever 'becoming', avoiding completion, staying undefined. In liquid modernity, change is the only permanence and uncertainty the only certainty. Progress denotes a condition of perpetual motion, new desires, novel technologies. Neoliberal capitalism is a solvent that liquefies the norms of social integration until they seem to be melting away.

One consequence is the defence of cultural traditions in the face of liquidity, through religious conservatism in diverse expressions, such as reactionary Catholicism in Europe, Pentecostal evangelism in parts of Latin America, radical Buddhism in Myanmar, radical Islamism in the Middle East and fervent Hindu nationalism in India. With the stated goal of rescuing the economy, these groups sought to eliminate parts of the population not subscribing to their beliefs, dispossessing them productively and economically, in a demonstration of the limits of social integration. In moments of crises, regression to basic forms of defence against a real or imaginary enemy (Kets de Vries 2020) creates Others as threats to bolster social integration.

The pandemic exposed the importance of thinking paradoxically to face important organizational and societal grand challenges. For example, the issue of border controls can be represented as a contraposition between a collective need (protecting the public from the risk of importing the disease) and an individual one (the right of free movement). Statistics showing the frequency of transmission caused by overseas travellers have been used in Australia to justify strict limitations in the number of residents allowed back in the country: the distress caused by these policies is justified as the need to safeguard public health. Yet, it is equally possible to pinpoint the 'true' cause of these imported infections as residing in the inadequacy of quarantine and screening protocols, determined by poor management and by the choice of relying on cheap labour and private subcontracting of quarantining in hotels.

There were public implications of the pandemic for economic policy. The politicians promoting austerity budgets on the basis that a state is akin to a household and cannot afford to go into debt, are no longer able to maintain that fiction. The argument that governments cannot afford to support both the economy and society no longer cuts much ice in view of the massive borrowings that have been made. In extraordinary times, many states were able to create extraordinary amounts of money to do extraordinary things with extraordinary effects, such as mass vaccine rollouts. The COVID-19 related debt that accrued is not a metaphorical 'black hole' to be filled as quickly as possible by ceasing expenditure to create austerity; the debt will in due course be diminished by inflation as well as by productive Keynesian investment (Clegg et al. 1985/2013; Sohda 2022).

The coronavirus has laid open the failure of the state in so many places; yet, paradoxically, this relative powerlessness demonstrates the importance of the state. While markets can deliver some things, they cannot deliver public security. One of the morbid symptoms to appear in many societies globally in the recent past, with the advent of a populism harnessed by political leaders, was the mantra that there was no more need for 'experts', something that has for a while been a dominant part of political rhetoric in some liberal democracies in which politicians have railed against scientists, whether social scientists in Brexit Britain or climate scientists in Australia and the United States. No more is this the case; for those on the liberal democratic side of the spectrum, there is a realization that scientific expertise is essential to the management of a complex society at the best of times; even more so at the worst of times and in the worst of places, for those countries that are governed by political 'dilettantes' (Weber 1946). Yet, for the followers of the types of conspiracy theories that populist leaders promote, such as Trump and Bolsonaro, experts are the problem. Ordinary citizens that resist the state's appropriation of new powers during COVID that are interpolated by and accept these conspiracy theories, 'experts' become agents of their oppression. Curiously, while modern capitalism was built on the triumph of scientific reason, COVID reinforced popular and populist scepticism towards science, which is currently harnessed by right-wing populists.

Precautionary principles will entail maintaining stockpiles of adequate supplies of essential equipment, drugs and sanitizers. Contingency planning will need to be rethought; pandemics are not the only instance of crises that can be acute, unpredictable and generalized, and we need to plan for their eventuality and be able to act fast and act at scale when these crises occur (Flyvbjerg 2020). The pandemic revealed global institutional voids in the supply of essentials such as PPE and vaccines (Sarkar and Clegg 2021) when long outsourced supply chains that worked on normal expectations of what was needed just-in-time could not meet the demand. The institutional void was filled by curated and distributed designs through the internet, which FabLabs and other makers could produce locally.

Vaccine uptake is particularly revealing and important. In a global viral pandemic, none of us is safe until all of us have the modicum of protection that a vaccine can offer. For as long as countries in continents such as Africa remain at dismally low vaccine levels, not only does this pose a future scenario for these nations, such as Nigeria, that is bleak and dismal, but it also threatens the global world. In many parts of Africa, the low vaccine take-up is not simply a question of supply, but also of populist resistance to the dictates of scientific expertise, which in that continent also has an association with the European colonial project. The pandemic has threatened both social and system integration, killing over six and a half million people globally through failures on both fronts. It is clear evidence of Beck's 'risk society'. Without the system integration delivered by high rates of effective vaccination, social integration will be punctuated by state actions of dispositional power striving to reconfigure standing conditions to maintain or isolate the spread of the virus, creating lockdowns and the inevitable resistance to them that is to be expected as individual freedoms are constrained.

While viruses respect no borders, people can be vaccinated against their effects and communities of contagion can be isolated. The third crisis that I will address admits of no single guarantor of immunity such as a vaccine, nor can it be isolated or contained. Climate crisis is experienced by all, everywhere – truly a global risk (Beck 2009).

THE CLIMATE CRISIS

In Australia, the pandemic was preceded by frighteningly exceptional bushfires in 2000 and accompanied by equally frightening and exceptional floods in 2022. Like the major flooding that occurred at the same time in Pakistan, these are acknowledged to be the effects of anthropocentric climate change that has been both socially integrating and disintegrating. The social integration has come from communities fighting the fires and floods themselves, rather than government assistance coming rapidly and doing it for them. While community resilience and solidarity can be built this way, it creates a degree of social disintegration from the body politic, especially as the costs of climate change are escalating, not only in every social sense, but also in an economic sense as well. The communities ravaged by floods in the northeast of New South Wales have been subject to substantial inundations in the city of Lismore, with two floods in the space of the two months of February and March 2022 of 14.4 metres and 9.7 metres height respectively. Extensive flooding in the continent on an unprecedented scale has persisted throughout 2022.

At a time when state responses to the pandemic have created a debt-laden future, one possible way of reducing the debts is to become economically serious about climate change. Anthropocentric climate change, the result of human interaction with the biosphere, is in large part due to the burning of fossil fuels. These are a major causal factor in global warming in a spectacular instance of the system integration circuit of power having unintended effects, ultimately undermining the stability of that circuit. Rich nations are presently greatly dependent on oil, gas and coal for energy. There are political and economic reasons why states should invest substantially in going green, in ecological Keynesianism, despite, at present, some harbouring liberal technological imaginaries of carbon capture. Let us leave these imaginaries to one side and consider the ecological reasons and possible responses to them.

Life on earth flows through systems of systems contained within the biosphere in which all forms of agency inhabit a flat ontology (Collinge 2006; Latour 1999a, b; Latour 2009; Pickering 1995). The networks these systems link are ones in which organizations provide key nodal points, as sources and distributors of global warming and change to the planetary boundaries of life on earth. While all forms of life are enfolded within this biosphere, there are evident power asymmetries not only among different forms of being, but also between different regions, groups and social classes of humans, the dominant form of life (Malm and Hornborg 2014; Moore 2017). The global command of wealth and other organizational resources in organizational and actor networks straddling the globe inscribe some powerful actors with enhanced strategic choices over the vast range of organisms, materialities and possibilities within which all life thrives and dies (Anderson and Cavanagh 1996; Malm and Hornborg 2014; Ulvila and Wilén 2017; Vital et al. 2011).

Sociologically, humans and non-humans are inextricably implicated in acts of agency in which humanity's reflexive capabilities, by developing new scientific, social and ethical approaches to living in the world, can work towards the collective good. Being is 'inevitably endowed with a moral and political history' (Latour 2014b: 4), one that is earthbound, inescapably tied to this earth. The earth sustains those standing conditions that enable life; human interaction with the earth can deplete or complement those standing conditions. Sciences' reflexive capacity in grasping how climate interacts with humans in sustaining or threatening forms of life increasingly understands the importance of these standing conditions. Understanding is channelled through technical discourses of climate science and intellectual discoveries based on detailed research investigations made within multiple disciplines (Latour 2014c). Assembled into new sets of actions, these insights and creative ideas have the potential to lead to the development of novel competences and more responsible agency.

Contemporary reflexive capacities in the biological, ecological and climate sciences are increasingly oriented to the planetary boundary (PB) framework (Rockström et al. 2009; Steffen et al. 2015). The PB framework details what are the standing conditions for life on earth, the consequences of crossing which are potentially catastrophic. While the PB framework directs academic and practitioner attention not merely to climate change (the topic currently attracting the most attention), it is also relevant for other earth systems related to sustainable change: the rate of biodiversity loss (terrestrial and marine); interference with the nitrogen and phosphorus cycles (e.g., from the nitrogen used in fertilizers); stratospheric ozone depletion; ocean acidification; global freshwater use; change in land use; chemical pollution, and atmospheric aerosol loading (see, e.g., Hoffman and Jennings 2018). Embracing radical ecological relationality, identifying global hotspots, acknowledging interactions far beyond the knowledge of any singular discipline, the PB model sees the role of scientific knowledge in the preservation of the planet as a pragmatic and legitimate process requiring urgent action (Van den Bergh and Kallis 2012; Whiteman et al. 2013).

The PB framework is shedding new light on 'the problem of scale' (Perey 2014: 215), providing insights into how to address connections between the different systems or hierarchical scales that constitute the planetary system (Boulding 1966). The boundaries of these are framed by strategic devices that bind and divide through acts of defining, separating and assimilating; that stabilize through acts of fixing, delimiting, controlling, and that make visible through acts of empirical recognition by technologies of representation and control (after Campbell et al. 2019). In this way, boundaries are constituted that stretch from 'ocean basins/biomes or sources/sinks to the level of the Earth system as a whole' (Steffen et al. 2015: 2). Steffen et al. (2015) observe that at least four system boundaries (rate of biodiversity loss, climate change, human interference with the nitrogen cycle and land-system change) appear to have already been transgressed in ways that cannot be repaired or will be extremely challenging to reverse (see also Rockström et al. 2018). These, in common with the other PBs, entail practices connecting individuals, organizations, societies and global networks. Seen this way, life on earth depends on the integration of systems of systems.

The impact of organizations on earth systems (e.g., ocean acidification, ozone layer depletion and climate change) and on sub-global processes, such as land and water use, is well known, as are the consequences of environmental degradation for human society (Steffen and Smith 2013; Steffen et al. 2015). The boundary framework embeds reflexive actors in an ecological network of planetary processes (e.g., Waddock 2011). These processes have political implications (Hoffman and Jennings 2018; Orssatto and Clegg 1999) – for example, processes of ecological destruction cause severe problems for earthbound actors, for whom the associated risks are not equally distributed. These risks are not just here and now because they present temporal implications for futures unfolding. Various actors and actants are capable of different projective reach in shaping these futures.

At the outer temporal limits, some technologies can be powerful autonomous actants with temporal effects that project into futures not envisaged at the moments of their design and use. Energy sources are a case in point; the shift from wind and water as power sources for industry to fossil fuels made a great transformation in industry and life possible (Ellul [1954] 1973; Vadén 2014). The polluting effects of the industrial revolution were evident in the soot-blackened Yorkshire stone buildings of my youth as well as in the multitude of furnaces belching smoke out of mill chimneys not yet shut down by shifts in global manufacturing. Being schooled in the 1950s and 1960s, however, one learnt of an optimistic future of peaceful uses of nuclear energy, the new source of industrial progress. It was a popular refrain at that time (Moriarty 2021).

The 1986 meltdown of the No. 4 reactor at the nuclear plant at Chernobyl, in Soviet Ukraine, punctured optimism profoundly. The Soviet authorities failed to publicize what had happened and it was only alert Scandinavian climate scientists that informed the world of a large and inexplicable radioactive cloud heading their way. The 1986 Chernobyl nuclear reactor meltdown had a continental projective reach, rendering adjacent zones of life critical for all foreseeable futures for those who occupy them. By contrast, fossil fuels are less dramatic in their single use (what difference does a single coal or wood fire make is a common refrain) despite the blackened buildings, scarred landscapes, communities and people. In terms of the temporal horizon of effects, the cumulative consequences of fossil fuel extraction and use have, in the *longue durée*, been far more global than a single nuclear accident.

Nuclear meltdown, nonetheless, poses infinite dangers in terms of generational lifespans that energy policy must countenance. After Chernobyl, and especially the 2011 Fukushima Daiichi nuclear accident, caused by a tsunami whose effects were a series of equipment failures, nuclear meltdowns, and releases of radioactive materials, energy policies shifted in many countries, precipitating the German reliance on Russian energy. In the wake of Fukushima, Germany decided to abandon nuclear power and turned to the plentiful supplies of oil and gas produced to its north by Russia, setting up the conditions for a future conjuncture few had contemplated until Russia invaded Ukraine. The causal powers of past decisions as to what actants frame life are always unknown at the time of choice.

BECOMING REFLEXIVE ABOUT ACTANTS' EFFECTS

While all actants exist together in a horizontal and vertical 'web of life' (Capra 1995; Waddock 2011), they do not exist equally in temporal terms: the projective reach of a nuclear plant far exceeds that of a mosquito, for instance. The mosquito might give one a bite; the bite might produce inflammation at best; at worst, it might produce a debilitating virus in a human subject. Should that subject, in a fever, have recourse to fly a plane or drive a vehicle, the impact of that small insect might be far greater than one initially might envisage. The mosquito, for all intents and purposes, however, does not intend to cause harm. It has no language game that translates to humans and in which the idea of harm would make sense; instinctually, it merely seeks preferential food. While mosquitos and their habits and habitat are of scientific as well as everyday interest, it is the intentional effects of humans' causal powers and their interactions with the causal powers of other actors that are of concern to social scientists. Such causal powers contain potentialities with possible multi-scalar impacts for a diverse range of interests.

In multi-scalar Anthropocene society (Hoffman and Jennings 2018), processes of organizing and the designs that we make material link those near to those distant, us to them, we to others, while maintaining pragmatic network boundaries necessary for respecting the uniqueness of all actors and their powers. Informed by Perrow (2011), Hoffman and Jennings (2018) propose that there is a need for more sophisticated ideas of resilience, modularity and decoupled institutions in which the welfare and rights of wider subsystems should be counted as stakeholders in terms of the temporal effects of these materialities (Jones et al. 2007: 138). Such ethical ideas inform actions concerned with the well-being of non-human as well as human stakeholders, enlarging managerial responsibility beyond sophisticated ideas of procedural and distributive justice under-lying notions of corporate perceptions of fairness and increased contribution to social welfare (Bosse and Phillips 2016). These management approaches to the treatment of employees (Bergström and Diedrich 2011; Pinnington et al. 2007) can be linked to the treatment of wider networks of community, ecology and sustainability.

In the framework of 'circuits of power', responsibilities for the pursuit of future perfect conditions that explicitly demonstrate care directed towards multiple stakeholders, includ-ing ecosystems, are variously assigned. First, the episodic circuit captures visible exercises of power by actors seeking to obtain outcomes favouring their definition of interests in terms of phenomena such as carbon emissions. Episodically, in terms of organizational impact on planetary boundaries, for responsible management the precautionary princi-ple needs to be paramount in relation to all stakeholders in various ecological systems, whatever their agential status as living beings and media sustaining life. Dispositionally, in terms of social integration, new rules and meanings for audit accountabilities need to be routinized. Facilitatively, in terms of system integration, the conception of relevant network systems needs expanding from a focus simply on socio-technic, human and organizational systems to embrace wider systems. Social systems set normative limits to agency: for instance, what can and should be done with respect to other systems in the biosphere (see Waddock 2011).

Exercises of power depend on the configuration of the network of relations stabilized through the two circuits of social and system integration. The acuity that knowledge of emissions has for organizational strategies is embedded in the circuit of social integra-tion. Prevailing rules of practice shape actors' dispositions to behave in certain ways. Both explicit and implicit rules of meaning and membership defining taken-for-granted responsibilities, encapsulated in specific language games whose rules guide actors in making sense of the world, events, others and themselves, will shape actors' knowledge, which, in turn, underlies their (re)actions. In a nutshell, people's discursive consciousness needs to be fixed and accordingly audited and accounted in terms of the planet as well as profits. Actors' appropriate action, in the context of identity assumptions and claims, given their (actual or desired) status as members of certain groups follow. Strategic choices are there to be made – either subscribe to the principle of a circular economy or be respon-sible for the consequences of not doing so.

Those language games registering different forms of social integration and their obligatory passage points will frame the institutional field in which actors episodically exercise power in specific interactions, as Hoffman and Jennings (2015) acknowledge.

Organizations need strategically to reposition the language games they are involved in because these offer the primary point of inflection. For instance, are they involved in the exploitation of nature or in the search for sustainability? Are they building a circular economy or simply churning out more produce to be marketed and end up as landfill? For organizations to contribute to sustainable change, they must play their part in these new language games, implementing collaborations across assemblages of multilevel social and physical networks, supporting human development consonant with flourishing ecosystems. At the level of system integration, techniques of production and discipline applied to production machinery, information systems, organizational structures and business processes will need to convey power as facilitative, productive and positive. Material, social and knowledge responsibilities will need to be assigned appropriately in the circuit of system integration as organization designs reflect system requirements, shifting from power over by hierarchs and shareholders to more coactive and collaborative power shared with employees and broad-based stakeholders, especially those advocating and defending planetary interests.

Failure to reform organizational circuits of power implies that transgressing planetary level boundaries will have the consequence of triggering causal powers best undisturbed, standing conditions that should not be breached, the consequences of which are enhanced global warming, climate change, with ferocious fires and floods. Any specific organization or nation may argue that their individual actions are unlikely to make much difference in the overall scheme of things. This may be so, but of course, if every agency acted this way, solipsism would rule the fate of the planet. Managers, as actors amid other earthbound beings and forms of life, either act in ways that are planetarily responsible, or they do not. In consequence, organizational decision-making must understand human agency as being networked with systems of fellow humans and their organizations as well as being enmeshed with non-human actors and their systems.

To understand human agency as something enmeshed with non-human actors, in addition to other fellow humans and organizations, then dominant discourses and language games must change; being in the language games of politics and being in the ontology of the Anthropocene require reconciliation. The reconciliation cannot be one wholly of social construction; if that were the case, climate sceptics would have as much validity as climate scientists. The latter's grounded, modelled and empirical understanding of the causal powers of Earth's materialities, such as climate-dependent ecologies and the impact of climate-induced 'natural' disasters on them are based on realism in science. Both materiality and language matter in their relation to realist science.

The boundaries of actor networks require collective attention and consequently new deploying of standards, ideas, tools and approaches that constitute less destructive collaborations across multilevel networks and assemblages. Without a changed understanding of powerful organizations' agency and impact on other forms of life, they are likely to continue resisting the accountabilities and controls of environmental laws and regulatory conditions that seek to keep earth safe. The complexity of the Anthropocene requires holistic modes of thinking (Waddock 2011; Hoffman and Ehrenfeld 2014; Hoffman and Jennings 2018). To meet the challenges of the new geological epoch requires consideration of the aspects of both nature and culture. In addition, 'partnerships, materials use and supply chains, domains of corporate activity, organizations' as well as the 'economic models and the metrics that are used to measure them' (Hoffman and Ehrenfeld 2014: 2) need rethinking.

RESPONSIBILITIES AND POWER

Elite business leaders should be astutely aware of their responsibilities, as well as the power of their cooperation since 'nearly 4/10 of the control over the economic value of TNCs in the world is held, via a complicated web of ownership relations, by a group of 147 TNCs in the core, which has almost full control over itself' (Vital et al. 2011: 36). Network 'strength arises [exactly] when an entity manages to assemble as many allies as possible, while weakness emerges when it is isolated or cut off from alliances' (Harman 2007: 33). In close connection with state actors, the elite group of global business organizations can successfully strengthen their agency and power across the scales. Some individual members of this central group are taking sustainability action with the support of, for example, multiregional input–output models (Lenzen et al. 2012). Their language games are changing to make a collective effort, through which business actors gain momentum by assembling alliances whose agency demands changes in industry and supports democratic mechanisms to ignite change at large (Heikkurinen and Mäkinen 2018).

An example of repositioning can be seen in Wiesner et al.'s (2017: 21) study of leaders of small and medium-sized companies who have a reputation in their industries for environmental sustainability, and commit to continuous learning and improvement, influencing others and becoming 'innovators' in environmental sustainability. Bennett notes that 'corporate regulation is one place where intentions might initiate a cascade of effects' where, perhaps, 'the ethical responsibility of an individual human now resides in one's response to the assemblages in which one finds oneself participating' (Bennett 2010: 37–8). If we are to survive as a species, the technical and the moral need to be inseparable in the new circuits of power because together they constitute the obligatory passage points. Unlike in industrial capitalism, where the obligatory passage points were premised on the exploitation of profit, we must accept sustainability becoming an obligatory passage point for the justification of policy choices, a new truth, a new language game.

While acknowledging the limits of state-oriented solutionism (e.g., Scott 1998), there must be limits to capital and it seems that only the state could ensure them. For sustainable development to be more than an oxymoron, as Banerjee (2003) argues, organizations of different sizes, forms and ownership types must share responsibility for restraining action within the boundaries of safe operating spaces. Of course, as Campbell et al. (2018) assert, these boundaries may already be irretrievably breached, in which case pessimism of the intellect must retain hope in the optimism of the will (Gramsci 1971) contributing to sustainable change. For optimists, institutional legislative and regulatory measures need rethinking (see e.g., Hoffman and Jennings 2018). The state must play the central role.

Giddens (2008) argues that the state has a prime function in tackling climate change, especially in terms of negotiating international treaties and enforcing them, advocating the creation of an enabling state that is 'expected or obligated to make sure ... processes achieve certain defined outcomes – in the case of climate change the bottom line is meeting set targets for emissions reductions (Giddens 2008: 8–9). It is important, however, not to fall prey to naivety. Capitalism is still capitalism and without social democratic limits to its principle of freedom to consume, we may well witness the sixth mass extinction (see Cebellos et al. 2015). Human agency must impact upon system integration to avert disaster. Aversion cannot simply be ritual, in terms of individual, one-off episodic exercises of power that are only symbolically meaningful (such as treaties that set emission targets well into the future, thus postponing climate action). These ritual actions enable postponement of climate action here and now by projecting it onto the next generation who must live in the history of the past generations' betrayal of their futures. A profound change in the configuration of system and social integration is required. As the obligatory passage points of the system shift from profit to sustainability, social integration shifts from individuals' economic utility to their value as living beings within fragile ecosystems.

Currently, abundant information and management tools are available for reducing the use of natural resources and climate emissions (e.g., Lenzen et al. 2012). Effective action in response to the challenges to life on earth requires not only highly collaborative and insightful ways of enacting responsible organizational agency (rather than merely publishing attractive reports on corporate sustainability), but also political will and direction, a strong public sector and an enabling state (nationally and internationally through climate-centred conferences of the parties' meetings), although there are no guarantees that such knowledge *will* lead to responsible action.

Humans can project different versions of a future perfect and typically, in democracies, they strive to do so through pluralist political contests. The results of these, in terms of electoral politics, must see capacities become practicalities. For instance, proposals for states to implement ecotaxation become relevant, as a nudge that may be required. The powers of the state include the monopoly of the right to taxation. The rate and principles of taxation are a piece of social construction in which various imaginaries can be encoded. As such, taxation changes become exogenous environmental contingencies with which all organizations are obliged to deal. At present, some jurisdictions, including the United States and Australia, extend the right to tax profits globally. Taxing the foreign profits of TNCs (Trans-National Corporations) on a global basis could be extended in several ways.

First, it could be recognized, as the French government has proposed, that companies lacking physical presence in a country in which they are accruing profits through large numbers of online users or customers, should be taxed at the same rate as bricks and mortar businesses. If this proposal were adopted by various national governments, then the beginnings of a global tax scheme would be in place. Such a scheme could be extended to include ecological taxation – ecotax – that could be levied as an excess and additional tax on those business actions whose activities anywhere in the world were endangering planetary boundaries. The state is also the only actor that could establish caps on production either directly or through Pigouvian taxes, which Alcott (2010) sees as necessary to guarantee policy success for sustainable change.

The Global Resources Dividend (GRD) proposed by Pogge (2001) might be a base model for policy innovation. Businesses would pay a tax on any services or resources that they use or sell rated proportionately to the harm that they create in extraction or production. Those business organizations that could establish that they had enacted policies that minimized the harm to the lowest rated harm decile of the tax register would pay a disproportionately lower tax than those businesses that could not so demonstrate that they qualified. Proportionality would vary with the demonstration of performance. Those organizational actors that could demonstrate commitment to circular economy principles would clearly be advantaged.

Landrum's (2017) stages model of sustainable development has the aim of moving from weak sustainability, typical of compliance and business-centred corporate approaches, towards regenerative and co-evolutionary sustainability. The emphasis is on absolute reductions of production and consumption activities (Bonnedahl and Heikkurinen 2019) through ecotaxes that will have to be multidimensional in their criteria. So, for instance, while an electric car will score well on driving emissions, account must be taken of the environmental costs of production and end-of-life recycling (Orsato et al. 2002).

The onus is on business organizations to demonstrate why they should not be taxed at the highest band. Tax will act as a nudge to the adoption of policies with transformative potential. Implementing some version of such an ecotax would entail not only discussions about practicality, but also a normative affirmation of the power of projective reach. Again, the onus is on companies to demonstrate the precautionary principle in practice; those that fail to do so would be subject to highly discriminate taxes. If most organizations were paying their GRD, the tax benefits of doing so would help deter deviance as self-interest drove responsible action. There would be added pressure on each country to enforce the gathering of GRD funds within its borders because of the tax advantages of so doing; the hosting of rogue businesses by non-compliant states could lead to these businesses being singled out for preferential and discriminatory tax treatment in the more developed states that implemented.

The climate crisis and COVID-19 are no respecters of national boundaries, any more than is Russia, with its leadership memories of tsarist and Soviet past imaginaries. Borders are lines on maps that serve as markers of the power contained therein, overlain by international relations' networks of power. If the fragile system integration afforded by oil and gas from a nearby autocracy for European countries such as Germany is no longer sought, then it provides a massive stimulus to its replacement by green alternatives, such as wind, wave and solar power, battery storage and the production and import of green hydrogen to power heavy industry, affording an alternative basis for system integration that is positive for the climate crisis. Climate crisis is *the* persistent processual crisis of our present and future, which will be threatening long after COVID-19 has been superseded by other viruses and Putin by other leaders. Furthermore, by learning from pandemic lessons in the West, we understand how the imperative of investment in a stable public sector, building system redundancy and social solidarity around health and learning from pandemic lessons can translate to ecological futures.

Social integration, through the various COP meetings, has been essential in communicating the science of climate change to a broader public audience. The audiences that have been least amenable to these communications have, not surprisingly, been those most dependent on fossil fuels and carbon emissions for their employment in mining and manufacturing communities in which fossil fuels are a major input and carbon emissions a major output. Such communities tend to want to defend their livelihoods against any risks to continuing employment. Given this sticking point, an often-unscrupulous lever for manipulation to electoral advantage by non-Green parties of any persuasion, how can a just transition occur?

To the extent that fossil fuels define modern industry and sustained modern society they need to be made unacceptable for social integration in a postmodern society. Past precedents for the extinction of activities such as coal mining in the United Kingdom, during the Thatcher government were neither wise nor acceptable. There, coal mining was terminated with no regard for a transition to alternative sources of employment or the civil sustainability of the communities abandoned (Parker 2000; Turnheim and Geels 2012). While this example followed the favoured neo-liberal mode of operation, leaving transition to the 'market', it is not an appropriate mode in which to manage transition equitably.

A strong state can manage the transition by making evident to society, especially its investors, that carbon intensive fossil fuel-based industry will comprise future stranded assets. Stranded assets are inhospitable sites for investment, leading to their evolutionary extinction. Making an industry extinct must not mean making people's employment opportunities extinct, as happened in Thatcher's United Kingdom. There are sound policy approaches that can strive to minimize this possibility.

States that have developed compulsory national superannuation policies, of which Australia is the exemplar, create substantial membership wage funds to provide retirement income contributed by both employees as deferred income as well as by employer contributions. The state develops a wage-earners funded model of superannuation supplementing traditional pension benefits, ultimately replacing these for most citizens. These funds, which are major institutional investors, direct their investments to create collective capital formation for retirement benefits for their members. Many of these funds are industry-based, often containing union representatives on the board. An industry super fund is run only to benefit its members rather than the interests of external shareholders. Profits are returned to the fund and its accountholders, instead of being paid out in dividends as is the case with retail (e.g., bank-owned) funds.

Collective capital formation through mandated superannuation can be invested as an active labour market fund to speed the transition to a net-zero economy. Many such funds are directing future economic activity into green industry located in the regions where fossil fuels and carbon emissions are a major issue. Employees increasingly blighted by employment in assets fast becoming stranded can be retrained for employment in new economic opportunities, based on green industrial development. Especially where funds are industry-based, that members that can see the end of the road for their carbon intensive activities and the need for new models of system integration, should ensure support for transitional investments. Where the normative environment of social integration has been well prepared, communities realize that the past does not point to the futures unfolding that risk extinguishing their employment. Rather than treating employees and citizens as akin to frogs sitting in slowly boiling water, blissfully unaware of the medium in which they are situated, a just transition out of a fossil fuel-based economy, is entirely feasible. It can be led by institutional investment and an active labour market policy that seeks to ensure that citizens are not stranded along with assets.

Successful contestation around the necessity of net zero emissions establishes the obligatory passage points of social integration through which the processes of systems integration must proceed. System integration of a green economy is analytically separable from the social integration making it possible. As a result of the war in Ukraine driving up global gas prices, those companies shipping gas have seen windfall profits because it is the market shortages rather than the costs of production that are determining the commodity price. In most cases, the global price sets the price charged to domestic consumers. Again, these market practices make strong state actions sensible in both taxing windfall profits and using the revenue to develop national sustainable wind, wave, thermal and solar power, depending on availability. As Denniss (2022) argues, 'Renewable energy with storage is not just cleaner and more reliable than gas and coal, it's cheaper as well.'

Windfall gains taxes can be the state-sponsored arc of sustainability, supporting the development of renewable energies in which the systematic accumulation of wage earners' funds in superannuation schemes can be invested. Investment decisions, premised on a 'green' obligatory passage point for social integration can be increasingly premised on an alternative basis for system integration that will create a just transition of employment opportunities. That is how climate change might be arrested and a more beneficial environment be structurally elaborated.

IN CONCLUSION

A greening economy on the way to net zero does not require the stimulus of invasion, destruction and consequential sanctions on fossil fuel exports, as is presently occurring in Europe. It does not require a war that raises the cost of carbon-based energy precipitously. There is a more peaceful way. All it takes is a developmental state using ecotaxation to nudge organizational investments and behaviours and the creation of wage earners' funds to build a state-mandated superannuation scheme, as the systemic elements making possible social integration around the agenda of net zero. A green social democracy is eminently possible (Clegg et al., 1985/2013), one that does not have to wait till the last ton of fossil fuel has been burnt (Weber 1976).

The obligatory passage points of social integration are fixed and refixed politically and economically by democratic deliberations by electorates and institutional investors, among whom wage earners' funds boards set standards. In the present, the necessary conditions that allow sustainable system integration in response to the exogenous environmental contingencies of climate change and the system disintegration effects of sanctions on Russian energy supplies are in place. The *circuits of power*, in every sense of those words, are transforming. The history of the present is 'being made as changing obligatory passage points refix and empower different circuits of power. While this history of the present has a green telos, no historically constructed end unfolds naturally. Achieving substantial changes requires boldness of politics, pessimism of the intellect, as well as optimism of the will (Gramsci, 2011, p. 300). While the future will always be uncertain, what we do and strive for in the present frames its possibilities.

NOTES

1   Thanks Marco Berti, for this clarification.
2   Thanks to Mark Haugaard for these observations.

POST-MODERN POSTSCRIPT

A final few words are in order in view of the material chosen to make the argument in this book. Strategic reasons were involved. These concerned the past centrality of the theory of the state to the theory of power, as well as the recent centrality of approaches to power which were not closely related to the state at all. Drawing on these may have made the applicability of some newer approaches to some traditionally central questions clearer than they might otherwise have been. In the past, power centred on stabilizing and fixing obligatory passage points for the stable organization of production and state management. In a word it centred on 'domination', the fixing of which was 'legitimation'. One consequence of choosing to concentrate the discussion on the historical case of the modern state is perhaps to make it seem as if power is treated as a massively reified thing, despite the frequent disclaimers and protestations to the contrary. To re-iterate what has been implicit throughout the latter part of the book: this has been posited as a post-modern analysis of the modern condition, post-modern because of its relentless stress on the relational quality of power, the representation of power and the fixing of power as its encompassing frame. However, it has equally been applied to an extremely modernist set of issues: the emergence of those privileged pathways which have become the modern state, organization and market.

Today, for much of the post-modern world, there are indications that of these central institutions it is the market which has emerged the dominant term of the trinity, the architectonic around which both the state and organization have increasingly come to be articulated. That it need not rationally be so to such an extent as has become fashionable is not an issue which we can address here: for one thing, it has been considered at length elsewhere (Clegg et al. 1986); moreover, in much of this world it is no longer clear that rationality, as it might once have been considered, is an appropriate category with which to study political action. If it were, then certain nostrums about the relations of politics and markets, those which stress the rationality and morality of small public sectors as pathways to full employment, low inflation and sustained economic growth, would be far less readily peddled and consumed.

Bauman (1988a: 807) argues very clearly that the shift to post-modern society is premised on the replacement of older modernist and intellectual notions of rationality with the reality of the marketplace as the privileged pathway through which all traffic increasingly must pass. This obligation is such that 'consumer freedom', premised on and geared to the market, has become 'the cognitive and moral focus of life, integrative bond of the society, and the focus of systemic management'. If this was correct as a reading of tendencies present at the time and place that these words were coined (in the United Kingdom during the consumer boom of 1988), then it would have major implications for the project of power. While, in the era of modernist power, the central focus and problems concerned stabilizing the obligatory passage points of state and organization generally on issues of disciplined work, production and surplus, in both the state and economy, in post-modernity the pathways would seemingly have become far more plural and diverse. In part, surely, this is because of the successful reification of power which modernism has accomplished in the state and in organization control. Within this encompassing frame of stable national and organizational entities, new post-modern freedoms from power can seemingly develop.

'Seemingly' should be taken advisedly in the previous paragraph. If consumer freedom has taken over 'the crucial role of the link which fastens together the lifeworlds of the individual agents and purposeful rationality of the system' (Bauman 1988a: 808) with an attendant shift from production to distribution, from control to consumption, this newly found freedom has been premised, as Bauman (1988a; 1988b) rightly argues, on the power of seduction rather than repression. Where domination no longer requires legitimation, power can shift increasingly out of circuits of repression and prohibition into more productive and positive forms. Consequently, the focus of post-modern power shifts from the episodic agency circuit, the repressive power par excellence, to the dispositional and facilitative circuits. Increasingly, in the post-modern era, power comes to be oriented not to fixing the passage points of a small number of stable and tightly coupled pathways but, on the contrary, to focusing on proliferating and endlessly reproducing privileged pathways, only to devalue them deliberately with the next conceit. 'Shelf-life' is remorselessly shortened not by shoddy work but by the pleasures of consumption. In consumer society, far from the consumer being a sovereign subject, subjectivity can never be achieved through the subjection and appropriation of objects because the possibilities of the object world are endlessly proliferating, spinning off, opening new paths to sovereign power on a terrain which unceasingly shifts. In such a world, 'seduction' becomes 'the paramount tool of integration (of the reproduction of domination) in a consumer society'. As Bauman (1988b: 221–2) goes on to say, seduction 'is made possible once the market succeeds in making the consumers dependent on itself', a dependency 'achieved through the destruction of such skills (technical, social, psychological, existential) which do not entail the use of marketable commodities; the more complete the destruction, the more necessary become new skills which point organically to market-supplied implements'. At its most sublime (and surreal), men and women become slaves to the rhythm of the market, held in its bondage.

In the post-modern world, power consists less in the control of the relational field of force in each circuit and more in the way in which the obligatory passage point of the market has become a 'black hole', sucking in ever more agency and spewing out an ever more diffuse power as the pursuit of things becomes an all encompassing passion. When things are needed so much for their own sake, for what they can only ever fleetingly signify, power can be relaxed in terms of its repressions, except at the margins of post-modern life, for those for whom membership in the new order has either not been proffered or rejected where it was offered. The disposition to consume and the enjoinment to produce pleasure through the domination and innovation of things are facilitative not of any generalized systemic resistance so much as a satiation which knows only how to feed on itself, which knows only too well, one might say. Such a system is marked by the absence of widespread interventions on behalf of episodic power, other than on the peripheries of civil (i.e. market) society. There it serves to repress 'the considerable margin of society which cannot be absorbed by market dependency... people whose business of life does not transcend the horizon of survival' (Bauman 1988b: 222). Consequently, the decline in the exercise of power, in the familiar mode of A getting B to do something that B would not otherwise have done, does not signal the end of power or its consignment merely to a memory chest. On the contrary, it signals a newer and even greater economy of power than its one-dimensional form. In the multi-dimensional pleasure dome of post-modern society, as the traditional spectacle of power retreats to the margins, the centre stage is increasingly occupied by the dispositional and the productive in a plethora of new capacities, empowerments and pathways which are immune to any pretensions to 'painterly architectonics' that sovereign power might once have had. The canvas is not fixed; the palette not given; the style not dictated. Representations can be fixed anywhere, anyhow, anyway. This is the post-modern democratic freedom of the market. The conceptual execution of sovereign power heralded only superficially a new realm of freedom; the easing of surveillance seems sure to offer even less freedom if these old concepts are reborn in the unity of the self-regarding and ceaselessly restless consumer sovereign reflexively monitoring the appearance of things through one's self and one's self through things. In such a world, as Bauman (1988b) suggests, legitimations based on the fixity of hegemonic pathways cease to matter. As a corollary, one may note that debates over the concept of power would acquire more of a historical than present-day interest.

Perhaps this 'forgetting' of power may yet be the 'fate of our times'?

I posed this question at the end of the first edition; these days it seems less relevant as the crises that the last chapter discussed mount. Few but the most ideologically blinkered would still have faith in markets to resolve these crises; few others would doubt the powers that the state can exercise, despite the heavy weight of freedom defined by markets and their rhetoric.

REFERENCES

Abercrombie, N., S. Hill and B.S. Turner (1980) *The Dominant Ideology Thesis*. London: Allen & Unwin.

Abrahamsson, B. and A. Broström (1981) *The Rights of Labour*. London: Sage Publications.

Adrian, C.R. (1973) 'Narrow Class Concerns and Urban Unrest', *American Politics Quarterly*, 397–404.

Agger, R.E., D. Goldrich and B.E. Swanson (1964) *The Rulers and the Ruled: Political Power and Impotence in American Communities*. New York: John Wiley.

Aksoy, C.G., Barrero, J.M., Bloom, N., Davis, S.J., Dolls, M. and Zarate, P. (2022) Working from Home around the World, *National Bureau of Economic Research*, https://www.nber.org/system/files/working_papers/w30446/w30446.pdf, accessed 15.02.23.

Alcott, B. (2010) 'Impact Caps: Why Population, Affluence and Technology Strategies Should Be Abandoned', *Journal of Cleaner Production*, 18(6): 552–560.

Aldrich, H. (1979) *Organizations and Environments*. Englewood Cliffs. NJ: Prentice Hall.

Alford, R.R. and R. Friedland (1985) *Powers of Theory: Capitalism, the State and Democracy*. Cambridge: Cambridge University Press.

Althusser, L. (1971) *Lenin and Philosophy and Other Essays*. London: New Left Books.

Althusser, L. and E. Balibar (1970) *Reading Capital*. London: New Left Books.

Anderson, B. (1983) *Imagined Communities: Reflections on the Origins and Spread of Nationalism*. London: Verso.

Anderson, P. (1964) 'Origins of the Present Crisis', *New Left Review*, 23: 26–53.

Anderson, P. (1974) *Passages from Antiquity to Feudalism*. London: New Left Books.

Anderson, P. (1977) 'The Antinomies of Antonio Gramsci', *New Left Review*, 100: 5–80.

Anderson, P. (1983) *In the Tracks of Historical Materialism*. London: Verso.

Anderson, S.D. and Cavanagh, J. (1996) *The Top 200: The Rise of Global Corporate Power*. Washington, DC: Institute for Policy Studies.

Anthony, P.D. (1977) *The Ideology of Work*. London: Tavistock.

Archer, M.S. (1982) 'Morphogenesis Versus Structuration: On Combining Structure and Action', *The British Journal of Sociology*, 33(4): 455–83.

Archer, M. (1996) Social integration and system integration: developing the distinction. *Sociology*, 30(4), 679–699.

Ashley, D. (1982) 'Historical Materialism and Social Evolution', *Theory, Culture and Society*, 1(2): 89–92.

Assad, T. (1987) 'On Ritual and Discipline in Medieval Christian Monasteries', *Economy and Society*, 16(2): 159–203.

Astley, W.G. (1985) 'The Two Ecologies: Population and Community Perspectives on Organization Evolution', *Administrative Science Quarterly*, 30: 224–41.

Bachrach, P. and M.S. Baratz (1962) 'Two Faces of Power', *American Political Science Review*, 56: 947–52.

Bachrach, P. and M.S. Baratz (1963) 'Decisions and Nondecisions: An Analytical Framework', *American Political Science Review*, 57: 641–51.

Bachrach, P. and M.S. Baratz (1970) *Power and Poverty: Theory and Practice*. Oxford: Oxford University Press.

Baechler, J. (1975) *The Origins of Capitalism*. Oxford: Blackwell.

Bailey, F.G. (1977) *Morality and Expediency*. Oxford: Blackwell.

Baldamus, W. (1961) *Efficiency and Effort*. London: Tavistock.

Ball, T. (1975) 'Models of Power: Past and Present', *Journal of the History of the Behavioural Sciences*, July: 211–22.

Ball, T. (1976) 'Power, Causation and Explanation', *Polity*, Winter: 189–214.

Ball, T. (1978) 'Two Concepts of Coercion', *Theory and Society*, 5(1): 97–112.

Ball, T. (1988) 'The Changing Face of Power', in T. Ball, *Transforming Political Discourse: Political Theory and Critical Conceptual History*. Oxford: Blackwell. pp. 80–105.

Banaji, J. (1977) 'Modes of Production in a Materialist Conception of History', *Capital and Class*, 3: 1–44.

Banerjee, S.B. (2003) 'Who Sustains Whose Development? Sustainable Development and the Reinvention of Nature', *Organization Studies*, 24(1): 143–80.

Banfield, E.C. (1966) *Political Influence*. New York: Free Press.

Bansal, P., Kim, A. and Wood, M.O. (2018) 'Hidden in Plain Sight: The Importance of Scale in Organizations' Attention to Issues', *Academy of Management Review*, 43(2): 217–41.

Baratz, M.S. (1977) 'Review of J.H. Nagel (1976), *The Descriptive Analysis of Power* and S. Lukes (1974) *Power: A Radical View*', *American Journal of Sociology*, 82(5): 1165–68.

Barbalet, J.M. (1985) 'Power and Resistance', *British Journal of Sociology*, 36(1): 521–48.

Barbalet, J.M. (1987) 'Power, Structural Resources and Agency', *Perspectives in Social Theory*, 8: 1–24.

Barnes, B. (1981a) 'On the "Hows" and "Whys" of Cultural Change', *Social Studies of Science*, 11: 491–8.

Barnes, B. (1981b) *T.S. Kuhn and Social Science*. London: Macmillan.

Barnes, B. (1986) 'On Authority and its Relationship to Power', in J. Law (ed.), *Power, Action and Belief: A New Sociology of Knowledge?* Sociological Review Monograph 32, London: Routledge & Kegan Paul. pp. 180–95.

Barnes, B. (1988) *The Nature of Power.* Cambridge: Polity Press.

Barnes, J. (ed.) (1984) *The Complete Works of Aristotle: The Revised Oxford Translation.* Princeton, NJ: Princeton University Press.

Bauman, Z. (1976) *Towards a Critical Sociology.* London: Routledge & Kegan Paul.

Bauman, Z. (1978) *Hermeneutics and Social Science.* London: Hutchinson.

Bauman, Z. (1982) *Memories of Class: The Pre-History and After-Life of Class.* London: Routledge & Kegan Paul.

Bauman, Z. (1983) 'Industrialism, Consumerism and Power', *Theory, Culture and Society,* 1(3): 32–43.

Bauman, Z. (1987) *Legislators and Interpreters.* Cambridge: Polity Press.

Bauman, Z. (1988a) 'Viewpoint: Sociology and Postmodernity', *Sociological Review,* 36(4): 790–813.

Bauman, Z. (1988b) 'Is There a Postmodern Sociology?', *Theory, Culture and Society,* 5: 217–37.

Bauman, Z. (2000) *Liquid Modernity.* Cambridge: Polity Press.

Bauman, Z. (2017) *Retrotopia.* Cambridge: Polity Press.

Bearden, M. (2022) Putin's Afghanistan: Ukraine and the Lessons of the Soviets' Afghan War, *Foreign Affairs,* March 24, www.foreignaffairs.com/articles/afghanistan/2022-03-24/putins-afghanistan, accessed 02.12.22.

Beck, U. (1992) *Risk Society: Towards a New Modernity.* London: Sage.

Beck, U. (2009) *World at Risk.* Cambridge: Polity Press.

Belton, C. (2020) *Putin's People: How the KGB Took Back Russia and Then Turned on the West.* London: William Collins.

Bennett, J. (2010) *Vibrant Matter: A Political Ecology of Things.* Durham, NC and London: Duke University Press.

Benton, T. (1977) *The Philosophical Foundations of the Three Sociologies.* London: Routledge & Kegan Paul.

Benton, T. (1981) '"Objective" Interests and the Sociology of Power', *Sociology,* 15(2): 161–84.

Berger, P. (1987) *The Capitalist Revolution.* London: Wildwood.

Berger, P. and T. Luckmann (1966) *The Social Construction of Reality.* New York: Doubleday.

Bergström, O. and Diedrich, A. (2011) 'Exercising Social Responsibility in Downsizing: Enrolling and Mobilizing Actors at a Swedish High-Tech Company', *Organization Studies,* 32(7): 897–919.

Berlin, I. (1969) *Four Essays on Liberty.* Oxford: Oxford University Press.

Bernstein, B. (1971) 'On the Classification and Framing of Educational Knowledge', in M.F.D. Young (ed.) *Knowledge and Control: New Directions for the Sociology of Education.* London: Collier-Macmillan. pp. 47–69.

Berti, M., and Cunha, M. P. e. (2022) Paradox, Dialectics or Trade-Offs? A Double Loop Model of Paradox. *Journal of Management Studies*, https://doi.org/10.1111/joms.12899.

Berti, M., and Simpson, A. V. (2021) The Dark Side of Organizational Paradoxes: The Dynamics of Disempowerment. *Academy of Management Review*, 46(2): 252–274.

Berti, M., Simpson, A., Pina e Cunha, M. and Clegg, S.R. (2021) *Elgar Introduction to Organizational Paradox Theory*. Cheltenham: Edward Elgar.

Betts, K. (1986) 'The Conditions of Action, Power and Interests', *Sociological Review,* 34(1): 39–64.

Bhaskar, R. (1975) *A Realist Theory of Science*. Leeds: Basic Books.

Bhaskar, R. (1979a) 'On the Possibility of Social Scientific Knowledge and the Limits of Naturalism', pp. 107–37 in J. Mepham and D.H. Ruben (eds), *Issues in Marxist Philosophy*. Brighton: Harvester Press.

Bhaskar, R. (1979b) *The Possibility of Naturalism*. Brighton: Harvester Press.

Bhave, D.P., Teo, L.H. and Dalal, R.S. (2020) 'Privacy at Work: A Review and a Research Agenda for a Contested Terrain', *Journal of Management*, 46(1): 127–164.

Biggart, N.W. and G.G. Hamilton (1984) 'The Power of Obedience', *Administrative Science Quarterly,* 29(4): 540–9.

Biggart, N.W. and G.G. Hamilton (1987) 'An Institutional Theory of Leadership', *Journal of Applied Behavioral Science,* 23(4): 429–41.

Black, M. (1965) *Models and Metaphors*. Ithaca, New York: Cornell University Press.

Blalock, H.M. Jr. (1964) *Causal Inferences in Nonexperimental Research*. Chapel Hill: University of North Carolina Press.

Bleicher, J. and M. Featherstone (1982) 'Historical Materialism Today: An Interview with Anthony Giddens', *Theory, Culture and Society,* 1(2): 63–77.

Bloodworth, J. (2016) *The myth of meritocracy: Why working-class kids still get working-class jobs*. Hull: Biteback Publishing.

Bocock, B.J. (1986) *Hegemony*. London: Tavistock.

Boje, D.M. (2001) *Narrative Methods for Organizational & Communication Research*. London: Sage Publications.

Bonnedahl, K. and Heikkurinen, P. (eds) (2019) *Strongly Sustainable Societies: Organizing Activities of a Hot and Full Earth*. London: Routledge.

Boreham, P. (1983) 'Indetermination: Professional Knowledge, Organization and Control', *Sociological Review,* 31(4): 693–718.

Bosse, D.A. and Phillips, R.A. (2016) 'Agency Theory and Bounded Self-interest', *Academy of Management Review*, 41(2): 276–97.

Boulding, K.E. (1966) 'The Economics of the Coming Spaceship Earth', in H. Jarrett (ed.), *Environmental Quality in a Growing Economy*. London: Johns Hopkins University Press.

Bourdieu, P. (1977) *Outline of a Theory of Practice*. Cambridge: Cambridge University Press.

Bourdieu, P. (1984) *Distinction: A Social Critique of the Judgement of Taste*. London: Routledge & Kegan Paul.

Bradshaw, A. (1976) 'A Critique of Steven Lukes' "Power: A Radical View"', *Sociology,* 10: 121–7.

Braverman, H. (1974) *Labour and Monopoly Capital: The Degradation of Work in the Twentieth Century.* New York: Monthly Review Press.

Brenner, R. (1982) 'The Agrarian Roots of European Capitalism', *Past and Present,* 97: 16–113.

Breslauer, G.W. (2002) *Gorbachev and Yeltsin as Leaders.* Cambridge: Cambridge University Press.

Bridgman, P.W. (1927) *The Logic of Modern Physics.* London: Macmillan.

Browne, R. (2020) 'Why Coronavirus Contact-tracing Apps Aren't Yet the "Game Changer" authorities hoped they'd be'. Available at: www.cnbc.com/2020/07/03/why-coronavirus-contact-tracing-apps-havent-been-a-game-changer.html, accessed 04.07.20.

Burawoy, M. (1978) 'Towards a Marxist Theory of the Labour Process: Braverman and Beyond', *Politics and Society,* 8: 247–312.

Burawoy, M. (1979) *Manufacturing Consent: Changes in the Labor Process under Capitalism.* Chicago: University of Chicago Press.

Burawoy, M. (1985) *The Politics of Production: Factory Regimes under Capitalism and Socialism.* London: Verso.

Burawoy, M. (2005) 'For Public Sociology', *American Sociological Review,* 70(1), 4–28.

Burawoy, M. (2008) 'Open Letter to C. Wright Mills', *Antipode,* 40(3): 365–75.

Burrell, G. and G. Morgan (1979) *Sociological Paradigms and Organizational Analysis.* London: Heinemann Educational Books.

Butler, J. (1990) *Gender Trouble: Feminism and the Subversion of Identity.* London: Routledge.

Butters, H. (2010) Machiavelli and the Medici. In Najemy, J. N. (Ed.) *The Cambridge Companion to Machiavelli,* Cambridge: Cambridge University Press, pp. 64–79.

Calás, M. B. and Smircich, L. (1996). From the woman's' point of view: Feminist approaches to organization studies, in S.R. Clegg, C. Hardy and W.E. Nord (eds) *Handbook of organization studies,* 218–257.

Callinicos, A. (1985) 'Anthony Giddens: A Contemporary Critique', *Theory and Society,* 14(2): 133–66.

Callon, M. (1980) 'Struggles and Negotiations to Define What is Problematic and What is Not: The Socio-logic of Translation', in K.D. Knorr-Cetina, R. Krohn and R.D. Whitley (eds) *The Social Processes of Scientific Investigation.* Sociology of the Sciences Yearbook, Vol. 4. Dordrecht: Reidel. pp. 197–219.

Callon, M. (1986) 'Some Elements of a Sociology of Translation: Domestication of the Scallops and the Fishermen of St Brieuc Bay', in J. Law (ed.), *Power, Action and Belief: A New Sociology of Knowledge?* Sociological Review Monograph 32. London: Routledge & Kegan Paul.

Callon, M. and B. Latour (1981) 'Unscrewing the Big Leviathan: How Actors Macrostructure Reality and Sociologists Help Them to Do So', in K.D. Knorr Cetina and A. Cicourel (eds) *Advances in Social Theory and Methodology: Towards an Integration of Micro- and Macro-Sociologies.* London: Routledge & Kegan Paul. pp. 227–303.

Callon, M. and J. Law (1982) 'On Interests and their Transformation', *Social Studies of Science,* 1: 615–25.

Callon, M., J.P. Courtial, W.A. Turner and S. Bauin (1983) 'From Translations to Problematic Networks: An Introduction to Co-Word Analysis', *Social Science Information,* 22:199–235.

Callon, M., J. Law and A. Rip (eds) (1986) *Mapping out the Dynamics of Science and Technology: Sociology of Science in the Real World.* London: Macmillan.

Callon, M. (2007) 'What does it mean to say that economics is performative?', in D. MacKenzie, F. Muniesa and L. Siu (eds) *Do Economists Make Markets? On the Performativity of Economics.* Princeton, NJ: Princeton University Press. pp. 311–57.

Campbell, N., McHugh, G. and Ennis, P.J. (2019) 'Climate Change is not a Problem: Speculative Realism at the end of Organization', *Organization Studies,* 40(5): 725–44.

Cantrell, L. (1977) *The 1890s: Stories, Verse, Essays.* St Lucia: University of Queensland Press.

Capra, F. (1995) *The Web of Life.* New York: Anchor Doubleday.

Carchedi, G. (1987) *Class Analysis and Social Research.* Oxford: Blackwell.

Carey, A. (2022) China protests: What on earth is that alpaca meme all about?, *Sydney Morning Herald,* December 2, www.smh.com.au/world/asia/china-protests-what-on-earth-is-that-alpaca-meme-all-about-20221130-p5c2jo.html, accessed 02.12.22.

Carmichael, S., and Hamilton, C. V. (1967) *Black Power: Politics of Liberation.* New York: Vintage Books.

Carroll, G.R. and J. Delacroiz (1982) 'Organizational Mortality in the Printing Industries of Argentina and Ireland: An Ecological Approach', *Administrative Science Quarterly,* 27: 169–98.

Caton, H.P. (1976) 'Politics and Political Science', *Politics,* 11(2): 149–55.

Ceballos, G., Ehrlich, P. R., Barnosky, A. D., García, A., Pringle, R. M., and Palmer, T. M. (2015) Accelerated modern human–induced species losses: Entering the sixth mass extinction. *Science advances,* 1(5), e1400253.

Chamberlain, C.W. (1982) *Class Consciousness in Australia.* Melbourne: Allen & Unwin.

Cheibub, J.A., Hong, J.Y.J. and Przeworski, A. (2020) 'Rights and Deaths: Government Reactions to the Pandemic'. Available at SSRN 3645410.

Child, J. (1972) 'Organization Structure, Environment and Performance: The Role of Strategic Choice', *Sociology,* 6: 1–22.

Child, J. (1985) 'Managerial Strategies, New Technology, and the Labour Process', in D. Knights, H. Willmott and D. Collinson (eds.) *Job Redesign: Critical Perspectives on The Labour Process.* Aldershot: Gower. pp. 107–41.

Chirot, D. (1990/1991) 'What Happened in Eastern Europe in 1989?' *Praxis International,* 10: 278–305.

Chirot, D. (1991) *The Crisis of Leninism and the Decline of the Left: The Revolutions of 1989.* Seattle, WA: University of Washington Press.

Chotiner, I. (2019) 'Bernard-Henri Lévy on the Rights of Women and of the Accused', *The New Yorker*, 18 March. Available at: www.newyorker.com/news/q-and-a/bernard-henri-levy-on-the-rights-of-women-and-of-the-accused

Clark, T.N. (1972) 'Community Power and Decision-Making', *Current Sociology*, 20(2): 6–53.

Clawson, D. (1980) *Bureaucracy and the Labor Process: The Transformation of U.S. Industry 1860–1920.* New York: Monthly Review Press.

Clegg, S.R. (1975) *Power, Rule and Domination: A Critical and Empirical Understanding of Power in Sociological Theory and Organizational Life.* London: Routledge & Kegan Paul. Reprinted 2013 as *Power, Rule and Domination: A Critical and Empirical Understanding of Power in Sociological Theory and Organizational Life.* London: Routledge Library Editions: Organization: Theory and Behaviour (Volume 6).

Clegg, S.R. (1976) 'Power, Theorizing and Nihilism', *Theory and Society*, 3: 65–87.

Clegg, S.R. (1977) 'Power, Organization Theory, Marx and Critique', in S.R. Clegg and D. Dunkerley (eds) *Critical Issues in Organizations.* London: Routledge & Kegan Paul. pp. 21–40.

Clegg, S.R. (1979) *The Theory of Power and Organization.* London: Routledge & Kegan Paul.

Clegg, S.R. (1981) 'Organization and Control', *Administrative Science Quarterly*, 26(4): 545–62.

Clegg, S.R. (1983) 'Organizational Democracy, Power and Participation', in C. Crouch and F. Heller (eds) *The International Yearbook of Organizational Democracy.* London: John Wiley. pp. 134.

Clegg, S.R. (1986) 'Review of A. Giddens, "The Constitution of Society"', *Australian and New Zealand Journal of Sociology*, 22(1): 167–9.

Clegg, S.R. (1987) 'The Power of Language, the Language of Power', *Organization Studies*, 8(1): 60–70.

Clegg, S.R. (1989) *Organization Theory and Class Analysis.* Berlin: De Gruyter.

Clegg, S.R. (1989) 'Radical Revisions: Power, Discipline and Organizations', *Organization Studies*, 10(1): 97–115.

Clegg, S. (1992). 'How to Become an Internationally Famous British Social Theorist,' *The Sociological Review*, 40(3), 576–598.

Clegg, S.R. (2014) 'Circuits of Power/Knowledge', *Journal of Political Power*, 7(3): 383–92.

Clegg, S. R. (2018) Reading Bauman and Retrotopia. *Scandinavian Journal of Management*, 34(4), 354–363.

Clegg, S. R., Cunha, M. P.e., and Berti, M. (2022) Research movements and theorizing dynamics in management and organization studies, *Academy of Management Review*, 47(3): 382–401.

Clegg, S.R. and D. Dunkerley (1980) *Organization, Class and Control*. London: Routledge & Kegan Paul.

Clegg, S. R., and Hardy, C. (2006) Representation and reflexivity. In S. R. Clegg, C. Hardy, W. Nord, and T. Lawrence (Eds.), *Handbook of organization studies* (2nd edition) (pp. 423–444) London: Sage.

Clegg, S.R. and W. Higgins (1987) 'Against the Current: Sociology, Socialism and Organizations', *Organization Studies,* 8(3): 201–21.

Clegg, S.R. and Haugaard, M. (eds) (2009) *The SAGE Handbook of Power*. London: Sage.

Clegg, S.R., Courpasson, D. and Phillips, N. (2006) *Power and Organizations*. London: Sage.

Clegg, S.R., P. Boreham and G. Dow (1983) 'Politics and Crisis: The State of the Recession', in S.R. Clegg, G. Dow and P. Boreham (eds) *The State, Class and the Recession*. London: Croom Helm. pp. 1–50.

Clegg, S.R., P. Boreham and G. Dow (1986) *Class, Politics and the Economy*. London: Routledge & Kegan Paul.

Clegg, S.R., Pitelis, C., Schweitzer, J. and Whittle, A. (2022) *Strategy: Theory and Practice* (4th edn). London: Sage.

Cloward, R.A. and F. Fox-Piven (1988) *Why Americans don't Vote*. New York: Pantheon.

Coch, L. and J.R.P. French Jr. (1948) 'Overcoming Resistance to Change', *Human Relations,* 1: 512–32.

Cohen, J. (2009) 'Reflections on Deliberative Democracy', in T. Christiano and J.P.

Collins, P. H., and Bilge, S. (2020) *Intersectionality*. London: John Wiley and Sons.

Christman (eds) *Contemporary Debates in Political Philosophy*. London: Wiley-Blackwell. pp. 17–247.

Cohen, M.D., J.G. March and J. Olsen (1972) 'A Garbage-Can Model of Organizational Choice', *Administrative Science Quarterly,* 17(1): 1–25.

Cohen, P. (1968) *Modern Social Theory*. London: Heinemann Educational Books.

Coleman, J. (1977) 'Notes on the Study of Power', in R.J. Liebert and A.W. Imerskein (eds) *Power, Paradigms and Community Research*. London: Sage Publications. pp. 183–98.

Collinge, C. (2006) 'Flat Ontology and the Deconstruction of Scale: A Response to Marston, Jones and Woodward', *Transactions of the Institute of British Geographers,* 31(2): 244–51.

Connell, R.W. (1976) *Ruling Class, Ruling Culture: Studies of Conflict, Power and Hegemony in Australian Life*. Cambridge: Cambridge University Press.

Connell, R.W. (1983a) 'Complexities of Fury Leave … A Critique of the Althusserian Approach to Class', in R.W. Connell (ed.) *Which Way is Up?* Sydney: Allen & Unwin. pp. 98–139.

Connell, R.W. (1983b) 'The Black Box of Habit on the Wings of History.Reflections on the Theory of Social Reproduction', in R.W. Connell (ed.) *Which Way is Up?*. Sydney: Allen & Unwin. pp. 140–61.

Connell, R.W. and T. Irving (1980) *Class Structure in Australian History*. Melbourne: Longman Cheshire.

Connolly, W.E. (1972) 'On "Interests" in Polities', *Politics and Society*, 2: 459–77.

Connolly, W.E. (1988) *Political Theory and Modernity*. Oxford: Blackwell.

Cousins, M. and A. Hussain (1984) *Michel Foucault*. London: Macmillan.

Cox, A., P. Furlong and E. Page (1985) *Power in Capitalist Societies: Theory, Explanations, Cases*. Brighton: Wheatsheaf.

Crenson, M.A. (1971) *The Un-politics of Air Pollution: A Study of Non-Decisionmaking in the Cities*. Baltimore, MD: Johns Hopkins University Press.

Crick, B. (1958) 'Introduction', in N. Machiavelli, *The Prince*. Harmondsworth: Penguin. pp. 13–73.

Crozier, M. (1964) *The Bureaucratic Phenomenon*. London: Tavistock.

Cunha, M.P. e, Clegg, S.R., Rego, A. and Berti, M. (2021a) *Paradoxes of Power and Leadership*. London: Routledge.

Cunha, M.P. e, Berti, M. and Clegg, S.R. (2021b) 'European Social Theory Reflecting on a Time of Contagion: A Book Review Essay', *Journal of Political Power*, 14(2): 372–82.

Cunha, M. P. e, Clegg, S. R., Gaim, M. and Guistiniano (2022) *Elgar introduction to Designing Organizations*. Cheltenham: Elgar.

Cunha, M. P. e, and Putnam, L. L. (2019). Paradox theory and the paradox of success. *Strategic Organization*, 17(1): 95–106.

Cunha, M. P., Rego, A., Simpson, A.V., and Clegg, S. (2020) *Positive Organizational Behavior*. London: Routledge.

Cunha, M. P. e., Simpson, A. V., Clegg, S. R., and Rego, A. (2019) Speak! Paradoxical effects of a managerial culture of 'speaking up'. *British Journal of Management*, 30(4), 829–846.

Cutler, A., B. Hindess, P.Q. Hirst, and A. Hussain (1979a) *Marx's Capital and Capitalism Today*, Vol. 1. London: Routledge & Kegan Paul.

Cutler, A., B. Hindess, P.Q. Hirst, and A. Hussain (1979b) *Marx's Capital and Capitalism Today*, Vol. 2. London: Routledge & Kegan Paul.

Cyert, R. and J.G. March (1963) *A Behavioural Theory of the Firm*. Englewood Cliffs, NJ: Prentice Hall.

Dahl, R.A. (1957) 'The Concept of Power', *Behavioural Science*, 2: 201–5.

Dahl, R.A. (1958) 'Critique of the Ruling Elite Model', *American Political Science Review*, 52: 463–69.

Dahl, R.A. (1961) *Who Governs? Democracy and Power in an American City*. New Haven, NJ: Yale University Press.

Dahl, R.A. (1963) *Modern Political Analysis*. Englewood Cliffs, NJ: Prentice-Hall.

Dahl, R.A. (1966) 'Further Reflections on "The Elitist Theory of Democracy"', *American Political Science Review*, 60(2): 296–303.

Dahl, R.A. (1968) 'Power', in *International Encyclopaedia of the Social Sciences*. New York: Macmillan. pp. 405–15.

Dahl, R.A. (1971) 'A Critique of the Ruling Elite Model', in F.G. Castles, D.J. Murray and D.C. Potter (eds) *Decisions, Organizations and Society*. Harmondsworth: Penguin. pp. 354–63.

Dahl, R.A. (1986) 'Power as the Control of Behaviour', in S. Lukes (ed.) *Power*. Oxford: Blackwell. pp. 37–58.

Dallmayr, F. (1982) 'The Theory of Structuration: A Critique' and 'Rejoinder to Giddens', in A. Giddens (ed.), *Profiles and Critiques in Social Theory*. London: Macmillan. pp. 8–25, 27.

Daudi, P. (1986) *Power in the Organization*. Oxford: Blackwell.

Davenport, S. and Leitch, S. (2005) 'Circuits of Power in Practice: Strategic Ambiguity as Delegation of Authority', *Organization Studies*, 26(11): 1603–23.

Davidson, A. (1977) *Gramsci: Towards an Intellectual Biography*. London: Merlin.

Dawe, A. (1973) 'The Role of Experience in the Construction of Social Theory: An Essay in Reflexive Sociology', *Sociological Review*, 21(1): 25–56.

Day, G.S. and Schoemaker, P. (2004) 'Peripheral Vision: Sensing and Acting on Weak Signals', *Long Range Planning*, 2(37), 117–21.

Denniss, R. (2022) 'If Australia taxed windfall gas profits we could invest billions in renewables and get off fossil fuels for good', *The Guardian*, 8 June. Available at: www.theguardian.com/commentisfree/2022/jun/08/if-australia-taxed-windfall-gas-profits-we-could-invest-billions-in-renewables-and-get-off-fossil-fuels-for-good, accessed 10.06.22.

Deroy, X. and Clegg, S.R. (2015) 'Back in the USSR: Introducing Recursive Contingency to Institutional Theory', *Organization Studies*. 36(1): 73–90.

Derrida, J. (1973) *Speech and Phenomenon*. Evanston: North Western University Press.

Derrida, J. (1976) *Of Grammatology*. Baltimore, MD: Johns Hopkins University Press.

Dews, P. (1979) 'The Nouvelle Philosophie and Foucault', *Economy and Society*, 8(2): 127–71.

Dews, P. (1984) 'Power and Subjectivity in Foucault', *New Left Review*, 144: 72–95.

DiMaggio, P. and W. Powell (1983) 'The Iron Cage Revisited: Institutional Isomorphism and Collective Rationality in Organizational fields', *American Sociological Review*, 48(2): 147–60.

Domhoff, W.G. (1978) *Who Really Rules? New Haven and Community Power Re-examined*. Santa Monica, LA: Goodyear.

Dow, G., P. Boreham and S.R. Clegg (1984) 'From the Politics of Production to the Production of Polities', *Thesis Eleven*, 9: 16–32.

Doyal, L. and R. Harris (1986) *Empiricism, Explanation and Rationality: An Introduction to the Philosophy of the Social Sciences*. London: Routledge & Kegan Paul.

Dreyfus, H.L. and P. Rabinow (1982) *Michel Foucault: Beyond Structuralism and Hermeneutics.* Brighton: Harvester.

Dubček, A. (1968) 'Action Plan of the Communist Party of Czechoslovakia', *Marxism Today*, 12(7), 205–17.

Duby, G. (1962) *L'Économie Rurale et la Vie des Campagnards dans l'Occident Médiéval.* Paris: Presses Universitaires Françhises.

Durkheim, E. (1893) *The Division of Labour in Society.* London: Macmillan.

Dyson, D. (1980) *The State Tradition in Western Europe.* Oxford: Martin Robertson.

Eco, U. (1983) *The Name of the Rose.* New York: Martin Secker & Warburg.

Edwards, R. (1979) *Contested Terrain: The Transformation of the Workplace in the Twentieth Century.* New York: Basic Books.

Ehnmark, A. (1986) *Maklens Hemligheter: En essä om Machiavelli.* Stockholm: Norstedts.

Eldridge, J.E.T. (1972) *Max Weber: The Interpretation of Social Reality.* London: Nelson.

Elias, N. (1978) (trans. Edmund Jephcott) *The Civilising Process: The History of Manners and State Formation and Civilisation.* Oxford: Blackwell.

Elias, N. (1982) *State Formation and Civilization.* Oxford: Blackwell.

Elias, N. (1983) *The Court Society.* Oxford: Blackwell.

Elliot, G. (1988) *Althusser: The Detour of Theory.* London: Verso.

Elliott, L. (2022) 'Russia is winning the economic war – and Putin is no closer to withdrawing troops', *The Guardian*, 2 June. Available at: www.theguardian.com/commentisfree/2022/jun/02/russia-economic-war-ukraine-food-fuel-price-vladimir-putin, accessed 03.06.22.

Ellul, J. ([1954] 1973) (trans. J. Wilkinson) *The Technological Society.* New York: Vintage Books.

Emmet, D. (1953) 'The Concept of Power', *Proceedings of the Aristotelian Society,* 54: 1–26.

Emmison, M., P. Boreham and S.R. Clegg (1988) 'Against Antinomies: For a Post-Marxist Polities', *Thesis Eleven,* 18: 124–42.

Engels, F. (1975) 'The Condition of the Working-Class in England', in *Karl Marx/Frederick Engels: Collected Works.* London: Lawrence & Wishart. pp. 295–598.

Etzioni, A. (1961) *A Comparative Analysis of Organizations.* New York: Free Press.

Evans, P.B., D. Rueschemeyer and T. Skocpol (eds) (1986) *Bringing the State Back In.* Cambridge: Cambridge University Press.

Faulconbridge, G. (2022) Video shows sledgehammer execution of Russian mercenary, Reuters, November 14, www.reuters.com/world/europe/sledgehammer-execution-russian-mercenary-who-defected-ukraine-shown-video-2022-11-13/, accessed 30.11.22.

Ferraresi, F. (1983) 'The Institutional Transformations of the Post Laissez-Faire State: Some Reflections on the Italian Case', in S.R. Clegg, G. Dow and P. Boreham (eds), *The State, Class and the Recession.* Beckenham: Croom Helm. pp. 129–51.

Fleming, P. and Spicer, A. (2014) 'Power in Management and Organization Science', *Academy of Management Annals*, 8(1): 237–98.

Flyvbjerg, B. (2020) 'The Law of Regression to the Tail: How to Survive COVID-19, the Climate Crisis, and Other Disasters', *Environment Science and Policy*. Available at: https://doi.org/10.1016/j.envsci.2020.08.013

Follett, M.P. (1987) *Freedom and Co-ordination*. New York: Garland.

Follett, M.P. and Metcalf, H.C. (1941/2003) *Dynamic Administration: The Collected Papers of Mary Parker Follett: Early Sociology of Management and Organizations*. Abingdon: Routledge.

Foroohar, R. (2022) Ukraine reveals nature of war in the age of weaponised networks, *Financial Times*, March 7, www.ft.com/content/14511f47-103a-4fce-b87e-4c26877a33c5, accessed 02.12.22.

Foster, C. (2020) 'Coronavirus Pandemic is a Disaster for the World, but a Few Good Things Might Emerge From It', *The Conversation*, 19 March. Available at: https://theconversation.com/coronavirus-pandemic-is-a-disaster-for-the-world-but-a-few-good-things-might-emerge-from-it-133723, accessed 10.10.20.

Foucault, M. (1969) *The Archaeology of Knowledge and the Discourse on Language*. London and New York: Vintage Books.

Foucault, M. (1982) 'The subject and power', *Critical Inquiry*, 8(4): 777–95.

Foucault, M. (1994) *Dits et Écrits*, 4 vols. Paris: Gallimard.

Foucault, M. (1972) *The Archaeology of Knowledge*. London: Tavistock.

Foucault, M. (1977) *Discipline and Punish: The Birth of the Prison*. Harmondsworth: Penguin.

Foucault, M. (1979a) 'Governmentality', *Ideology and Consciousness*, 6: 5–21.

Foucault, M. (1979b) 'What is an Author?', *Screen*, 20(1): 13–33.

Foucault, M. (1980) *Power/Knowledge: Selected Interviews and Other Writings 1972–1977*. Brighton: Harvester Press.

Foucault, M. (1981) 'Questions of Method: An Interview with Michel Foucault', *Ideology and Consciousness*, 8: 1–14.

Foucault, M. (1984) *The History of Sexuality: An Introduction*. Harmondsworth: Peregrine.

Foucault, M. (1986) 'Disciplinary Power and Subjection', in S. Lukes (ed.) *Power*. Oxford: Blackwell. pp. 229–41.

Fox, A. (1974) *Beyond Contract: Work, Power and Trust Relations*. London: Faber & Faber.

Frankel, B. (1983) *Beyond the State: Dominant Theories and Socialist Strategies*. London: Macmillan.

Freire, P. (1972) *The Pedagogy of the Oppressed*. Harmondsworth: Penguin.

Frey, F.W. (1971) 'Comment: '"On Issues and Non-Issues in the Study of Power"', *American Political Science Review*, 65: 1081–101.

Friedman, A.L. (1977) *Industry and Labour: Class Struggle at Work and Monopoly Capitalism.* London: Macmillan.

Friedrich, C.J. (1937) *Constitutional Government and Democracy.* New York: Gipp.

Friedman, M. (1953) *Essays on Positive Economics.* Chicago: University of Chicago Press.

Fukuyama, F. (2006) *The end of history and the last man.* New York: Simon and Schuster.

Gallie, W.B. (1955) 'Essentially Contested Concepts', *Proceedings of the Aristotelian Society,* 56: 167–98.

Gane, M. (1983) 'Anthony Giddens and the Crisis of Social Theory', *Economy and Society,* 12(3): 368–98.

Gane, M. (1986) 'Review: The Form of Foucault', *Economy and Society,* 15(1): 110–22.

Garfinkel, H. (1967) *Studies in Ethnomethodology.* Englewood Cliffs, NJ: Prentice Hall.

Garson, D. (1973) 'Automobile Workers and the American Dream', *Politics and Society,* 3: 163–79.

Gaventa, J.P. (1980) *Power and Powerlessness: Quiescence and Rebellion in an Appalachian Valley.* Urbana, IL: University of Illinois Press.

Gellner, E. (1983) *Nations and Nationalism.* Ithaca, NY: Cornell University Press.

Geras, N. (1987) 'Post-Marxism?', *New Left Review,* 163: 40–82.

Gergen, K. J. (2015) From mirroring to world-making: Research as future forming. *Journal for the Theory of Social Behaviour,* 45(3), 287–310.

Gerschenkron, N. (1962) *Economic Backwardness in Historical Perspective and Other Essays.* Cambridge, MA: Harvard University Press.

Gibson, Q. (1971) 'Power', *Philosophy of the Social Sciences,* 101–12.

Giddens, A. (1968) ' "Power" in the Recent Writings of Talcott Parsons', *Sociology,* 2(3): 257–72.

Giddens, A. (1976) *New Rules of Sociological Method.* London: Hutchinson.

Giddens, A. (1977) *Studies in Social and Political Theory.* London: Hutchinson.

Giddens, A. (1979) *Central Problems in Social Theory.* London: Macmillan.

Giddens, A. (1981) *A Contemporary Critique of Historical Materialism.* London: Macmillan.

Giddens, A. (1982) 'A Reply to my Critics', *Theory, Culture and Society,* 1(2): 107–13.

Giddens, A. (1984) *The Constitution of Society.* Cambridge: Polity Press.

Giddens, A. (1985) *The Nation State and Violence.* Cambridge: Polity Press.

Giddens, A. (1987) *Social Theory and Modern Sociology.* Cambridge: Polity Press.

Giddens, A. (2008) 'The Politics of Climate Change: National Responses to the Challenge of Global Warming', *Policy Network Paper.* London: www.policynetwork

Gilliom, J.T. and Monahan (2012) *SuperVision: An Introduction to the Surveillance Society.* Chicago: University of Chicago Press.

Girdwood, J. (1987) 'On Reading Foucault, Genealogy and Power-Knowledge'. Honours paper, Department of Sociology, Armidale, University of New England.

Goffman, E. (1959) *The Presentation of Self in Everyday Life*. New York: Doubleday Anchor.

Goffman, E. (1961) *Asylums: Essays on the Social Situation of Mental Patients and Other Inmates*. Harmondsworth: Penguin.

Goffman, E. (1974) *Frame Analysis: An Essay on the Organization of Experience*. Cambridge, MA: Harvard University Press.

Gramsci, A. (1971) (ed. and trans. Q. Hoare and G. Nowell) *Selections from the Prison Notebooks of Antonio Gramsci*. London: Lawrence & Wishart.

Greenwood, R., Meyer, R. E., Lawrence, T. B., and Oliver, C. (eds) (2017). *The SAGE handbook of organizational institutionalism*. London: Sage.

Grint, K. (2010) 'The Sacred in Leadership: Separation, Sacrifice and Silence', *Organization Studies*, 31: 89–107.

Gross, D. (1982) 'Time–Space Relations in Giddens' Social Theory', *Theory, Culture and Society*, 1(2): 83–8.

Guttman, H.G. (1977) *Work, Culture and Society in Industrializing America*. Oxford: Blackwell.

Habermas, J. (1970) 'Toward a Theory of Communicative Competence', *Inquiry*, 13: 360–75.

Habermas, J. (1972) *Knowledge and Human Interests*. London: Heinemann Educational Books.

Habermas, J. (1976) *Legitimation Crisis*. London: Heinemann Educational Books.

Habermas, J. (1979) *Communication and the Evolution of Society*. London: Heinemann Educational Books.

Habermas, J. (1982) *Philosophical–Political Profiles,* Cambridge, MA: MIT Press.

Habermas, J. (1984) *Reason and the Rationalization of Society*. London: Heinemann Educational Books.

Habermas, J. (1987) *The Philosophical Discourse of Modernity: Twelve Lectures*. Cambridge, MA: MIT Press.

Haggerty, K. and Ericson, R. (2000) 'The Surveillant Assemblage', *British Journal of Sociology*, 51(4): 605–22.

Halimi, S. (2022) 'The Paradox of the War in Ukraine', *Le Monde diplomatique,* March. Available at: https://mondediplo.com/2022/03/03ukraine-paradox, accessed 09.06.22.

Hall, J.A. (1986) *Power and Liberties: The Causes and Consequences of the Rise of the West*. Harmondsworth: Penguin.

Hall, S. (1983) 'The Problem of Ideology: Marxism without Guarantees', in B. Matthews (ed.) *Marx: A Hundred Years On*. London: Lawrence & Wishart. pp. 557–68.

Hamilton, G.G. (1986) 'Patriarchalism in Imperial China and Western Europe: A Revision of Weber's Sociology of Domination', *Theory and Society,* 13(3): 393–425.

Hamilton, G.G. and N.W. Biggart (1984) *Governor Reagan, Governor Brown: A Sociology of Executive Power*. New York: Columbia University Press.

Hamilton, G.G. and N.W. Biggart (1985) 'Why People Obey: Theoretical Observations on Power and Obedience in Complex Organizations', *Sociological Perspectives*, 28(1): 3–28.

Hamilton, J. J. (1978) Hobbes's study and the Hardwick library. *Journal of the History of Philosophy*, 16(4), 445–453.

Hannan, M.T. and J. Freeman (1984) 'Structural Inertia and Organizational Change', *American Sociological Review*, 49(2): 149–64.

Hannan, M.T. and J. Freeman (1977) 'The Population Ecology of Organizations', *American Journal of Sociology*, 82(5): 929–40.

Hardy, C. and Leiba-O'Sullivan, S. (1998) 'The Power Behind Empowerment: Implications for Research and Practice', *Human Relations*, 51(4): 451–83.

Harman, G. (2007) 'The Importance of Bruno Latour for Philosophy', *Cultural Studies Review*, 13(1): 31–49.

Harré, R. (1970) 'Powers', *British Journal for the Philosophy of Science*, 21: 81–101.

Harré, R. (1985) *Varieties of Realism*. Oxford: Blackwell.

Harré, R. and E.H. Madden (1975) *Causal Powers*. Oxford: Blackwell.

Harvey, D. (1982) *The Limits of Capital*. Oxford: Blackwell.

Haugaard, M. (2012) 'Rethinking the Four Dimensions of Power: Domination and Empowerment', *Journal of Political Power*, 5(1): 33–54.

Haugaard, M. (2020a) 'The Faces of Power, Resistance and Justification in a Changing World', *Journal of Political Power*, 13(1): 1–5.

Haugaard, M. (2020b) *The Four Dimensions of Power: Understanding Domination, Empowerment and Democracy*. Manchester: Manchester University Press.

Hayek, F. (1944) *The Road to Serfdom*. London: Routledge & Kegan Paul.

Heath, A. (1981) *Social Mobility*. Glasgow: Fontana.

Henri-Levy, B. (2020) *The Virus in the Age of Madness*. Ithaca, NY: Yale University.

Hesse, M.B. (1960) *Models and Analogies in Science*. Notre Dame, IN: University of Indiana Press.

Heikkurinen, P., Clegg, S., Pinnington, A.H., Nicolopoulou, K. and Alcaraz, J.M. (2021) 'Managing the Anthropocene: Relational Agency and Power to Respect Planetary Boundaries', *Organization & Environment*, 34(2): 267–86.

Hern, A. (2020) 'Shirking from Home? Staff Feel the Heat as Bosses Ramp up Remote Surveillance', *The Observer*, 27 September. Available at: www.theguardian.com/world/2020/sep/27/shirking-from-home-staff-feel-the-heat-as-bosses-ramp-up-remote-surveillance, accessed 10.10.20.

Hickson, D.J., C.R. Hinings, C.A. Lee, R.E. Schneck and J.M. Pennings (1971) 'A Strategic Contingencies Theory of Intra-Organizational Power', *Administrative Science Quarterly*, 16: 216–29.

Higley, J. and L. Field (1976) *Elitism*. London: Routledge & Kegan Paul.

Hill, L. (2001) 'The Hidden Theology of Adam Smith', *European Journal of the History of Economic Thought*, 8(1): 1–29.

Hindess, B. (1982) 'Power, Interests and the Outcomes of Struggles', *Sociology*, 16(4): 498–511.

Hindess, B. (1986) '"Interests" in Political Analysis', in J. Law (ed.), *Power, Action and Belief: A New Sociology of Knowledge?* Sociological Review Monograph 32. London: Routledge & Kegan Paul. pp. 112–31.

Hindess, B. (1987) 'Rationality and the Characterization of Modern Society', in S. Whimster and S. Lash (eds), *Max Weber, Rationality and Modernity.* London: Allen & Unwin. pp. 137–53.

Hindess, B. (1989) 'Classes, Collectivities and Corporate Actors', in S.R. Clegg (ed.), *Organizational Theory and Class Analysis: New Approaches and New Issues,* Berlin: De Gruyter.

Hinings, C.R., D.J. Hickson, J.M. Pennings and R.E. Schneck (1974) 'Structural Conditions of Intra-Organizational Power', *Administrative Science Quarterly,* 9(1): 22–44.

Hintze, O. (1968) 'The Nature of Feudalism', in F.L. Cheyette (ed.), *Lordship and Community in Medieaval Europe.* New York: Holt, Rinehart & Winston. pp. 22–31.

Hirsch, F.R. (1978) *The Social Limits to Growth.* London: Routledge & Kegan Paul.

Hirschman, A.O. (1970) *Exit, Voice and Loyalty.* Princeton, NJ: Princeton University Press.

Hirschman, A.O. (1977) *The Passions and the Interests.* Princeton, NJ: Princeton University Press.

Hirst, P.Q. (1982) 'The Social Theory of Anthony Giddens: A New Syncretism', *Theory, Culture and Society,* 1(2): 72–82.

Hoare, Q., and Nowell-Smith, G. (eds) (1971a) *Selections from the Prison Notebooks of Antonio Gramsci.* Lawrence and Wishart.

Hoare, Q., and Nowell-Smith, G. (1971b), Introduction, *Selections from the Prison Notebooks of Antonio Gramsci*, Hoare, Q., and Smith, G. (eds), London: Lawrence and Wishart, pp. xvii–xcvi.

Hobbes, T. (1839) (ed. Sir William Molesworth) *The English Works of Thomas Hobbes,* Vols 1 and 2. London: J. Bohn.

Hobbes, T. ([1651] 1962) (ed. M. Oakeshott, with an Introduction by R.S. Peters) *Leviathan.* London: Collier-Macmillan.

Hobsbawm, E.J. (1969) *Industry and Empire.* Harmondsworth: Penguin.

Hoffman, A. and Ehrenfeld, J. (2014) 'The Fourth Wave, Management Science and Practice in the Age of the Anthropocene', in E. Lawler, S. Mohrman and J. O'Toole (eds) *Corporate Stewardship: Organizing for Sustainable Effectiveness.* Sheffield: Greenleaf.

Hoffman, A.J. and Jennings, P.D. (2015) 'Institutional Theory and the Natural Environment: Research in (and on) the Anthropocene', *Organization & Environment*, 28(1): 8–31.

Holton, R.J. (1985) *The Transition from Feudalism to Capitalism.* London: Macmillan.

Holton, R.J. (1986) *Cities, Capitalism and Civilization*. London: Allen & Unwin.

Holton, R.J. and B.S. Turner (1986) 'Against Nostalgia: Talcott Parsons and a Sociology for the Modern World', in R.J. Holton and B.S. Turner (eds), *Talcott Parsons on Economy and Society*. London: Routledge & Kegan Paul. pp. 207–34.

Hoy, D.C. (1986) 'Power, Repression, Progress: Foucault, Lukes and the Frankfurt School', in D.C. Hoy (ed.), *Foucault: A Critical Reader*. Oxford: Blackwell. pp. 123–48.

Hume, D. (1902) *An Enquiry Concerning Human Understanding*. Oxford: Clarendon Press.

Hunter, F. (1953) *Community Power Structure*. Chapel Hill, NC: University of North Carolina Press.

Hutchinson, M., Vickers, M.H., Jackson, D. and Wilkes, L. (2010) 'Bullying as Circuits of Power: An Australian Nursing Perspective', *Administrative Theory & Praxis*, 32(1), 25–47.

Ibarra, H. (2020) 'The Pandemic Has Given Businesses a Push to Change', *Financial Times*, 9 June, 17.

Isaac, J.C. (1987) *Power and Marxist Theory*. Ithaca, NY: Cornell University Press.

Jamal, A. (2007) 'Strategies of Minority Struggle for Equality in Ethnic States: Arab Politics in Israel', *Citizenship Studies*, 11(3): 263–82.

Jessop, B. (1982) *The Capitalist State: Marxist Theories and Methods*. Oxford: Martin Robertson.

Jessop, B. (1985) *Nicos Poulanlzas: Marxist Theory and Political Struggle*. London: Macmillan.

Jessop, B. (1987) 'Capitalism, Nation States and Surveillance', mimeo, University of Essex.

Jett, Q.R. and George, J.M. (2003) 'Work Interrupted: A Closer Look at the Role of Interruptions in Organizational Life', *Academy of Management Review*, 28(3): 494–507.

Johnson, T. (1972) *The Professions and Power*. London: Macmillan.

Jones, L. (2022) 'Was Ukraine Betrayed by its Elites?' *UnHerd*, 15 March. Available at: https://unherd.com/2022/03/was-ukraine-betrayed-by-its-own-elites/?=thepostindexfrmemail, accessed 16.03.22.

Jones, T.M., Felps, W. and Bigley, G.A. (2007) 'Ethical Theory and Stakeholder Related Decisions: The Role of Stakeholder Culture', *Academy of Management Review*, 32(1): 137–55.

Judt, T. (2005) *Postwar: A History of Europe Since 1945*. London: Vintage Books.

Julmi, C. (2022). More than just a special case: The value of double bind theory for bringing light into the dark side of organizational paradoxes. *Scandinavian Journal of Management*, 38(2): 101198.

Kamradt-Scott, A. (2020) 'Why "Vaccine Nationalism" Could Doom Plan for Global Access to a COVID-19 Vaccine', *The Conversation*. 8 September. Available at: https://theconversation.com/why-vaccine-nationalism-could-doom-plan-for-global-access-to-a-covid-19-vaccine-145056

Kant, I. (1966) *The Critique of Pure Reason*. New York: Doubleday Anchor.

Katznelson, I. (1973) *Black Men, White Cities*. Oxford: Oxford University Press.

Kavalski, N. and Smith, P.R. (2020) 'Immunity Passports: A "New" Old Idea With Baggage', *Global Policy*. Available at: www.globalpolicyjournal.com/blog/27/04/2020/immunity-passports-new-old-idea-baggage, accessed 30.11.20.

Kenez, P. (2006) *A History of the Soviet Union from the Beginning to the End*. Cambridge: Cambridge University Press.

Ketcham, R. (1987) *Individualism and Public Life: A Modern Dilemma*. Oxford: Blackwell.

Kets de Vries, M.F.R. (2020) *Journeys into Coronavirus Land*. London: KDVI Press.

Kieser, A. (1987) 'From Asceticism to Administration of Wealth: Medieval Monasteries and the Pitfalls of Rationalization', *Organization Studies,* 8(2): 103–24.

King, R. (1986) *The State in Modern Society: New Directions in Political Sociology*. London: Macmillan.

Knights, D. and D. Collinson (1985) 'Redesigning Work on the Shopfloor: A Question of Control or Consent?', in D. Knights, H. Willmott and D. Collinson (eds), *Job Redesign: Critical Perspectives on the Labour Process*. Aldershot: Gower. pp. 197–226.

Knights, D. and H. Willmott (1982) 'Power, Values and Relations: Comment on Benton', *Sociology,* 16(4): 578–85.

Knights, D. and T. Vurdubakis (1994) Foucault, power, resistance and all that. In J. M. Jermier, D. Knights, & W. R. Nord (Eds.), Resistance and Power in Organizations. *Routledge,* London and New York, pp. 167–198.

Kochan, T.A. (2002) 'Addressing the Crisis in Confidence in Corporations: Root Causes, Victims, and Strategies for Reform', *Academy of Management Perspectives*, 16(3), 139–41.

Kornberger, M. (2017) 'The Visible Hand and the Crowd', *Strategic Organization*, 15(2): 174–93.

Korpi, W. (1979) 'Power, Exchange and Inequality', paper presented to the XIth World Congress of the International Political Science Association in Moscow, August.

Korpi, W. (1983) *The Democratic Class Struggle*. London: Routledge & Kegan Paul.

Kostera, M. and Wicha, M. (1996) 'The "Divided Self" of Polish State-owned Enterprises: The Culture of Organizing', *Organization Studies*, 17: 83–105.

Kreckel, R. (1980) 'Unequal Opportunity Structure and Labour Market Segmentation', *Sociology,* 14(4): 525–51.

Kristeva, J. (1984) *Revolution in Poetic Language*. New York: Columbia University Press.

Kristeva, J. (1986) *The Kristeva Reader*. Oxford: Blackwell.

Kroker, A. (1984) 'Modern Power in Reverse Image: The Paradigm Shift of Michel Foucault and Talcott Parsons', in J. Fekete (ed.), *The Structural Allegory*. Minneapolis, MN: University of Minneapolis Press. pp. 74–103.

Kuhn, T.S. (1962) *The Structure of Scientific Revolutions*. Chicago: University of Chicago Press.

Kula, W. (1977) *An Economic Theory of the Feudal System*. London: New Left Books.

Kurnyshova, Y., Shevchenko, T. and Makarychev (2022) 'Paradoxes of Russia's War Against Ukraine: Can Political Science Help?', *CIDOB (Barcelona Centre for International Affairs), Opinion,* April. Available at: www.cidob.org/en/publications/publication_series/opinion/2022/paradoxes_of_russia_s_war_against_ukraine_can_political_sciece_help

Kurzweil, E. (1977) 'Michel Foucault: Ending the Era of Man', *Theory and Society,* 4: 395–420.

Lacan, J. (1977) *Écrits.* London: Tavistock.

Laclau, E. (1975) 'The Specificity of the Political: The Poulantzas-Miliband Debate', *Economy and Society,* 4: 87–110.

Laclau, E. (1980) 'Nonpopulist Rupture and Discourse', *Screen Education,* 34: 87–93.

Laclau, E. (1983a) 'The Impossibility of Society', *Canadian Journal of Political and Social Theory,* 7: 21–4.

Laclau, E. (1983b) '"Socialism", the "People", "Democracy": The Transformation of Hegemonic Logic', *Social Text,* 7: 115–19.

Laclau, E. and C. Mouffe (1985) *Hegemony and Socialist Strategy.* London: Verso.

Laclau, E. and C. Mouffe (1987) 'Post-Marxism without Apologies', *New Left Review,* 166: 77–106.

Landes, S. (1969) *The Unbound Prometheus: Technological Change and Industrial Development in Western Europe from 1750 to the Present.* Cambridge: Cambridge University Press.

Landrum, N.E. (2017) 'Stages of Corporate Sustainability: Integrating the Strong Sustainability Worldview', *Organization & Environment,* 31(4): 287–313

Lane, M. (1970) *Structuralism: A Reader.* London: Jonathan Cape.

Laslett, P. (1965) *The World We Have Lost Further Explored.* London: Methuen.

Laslett, P. (1988) 'The European Family and Early Industrialization', in J. Baechler, J.A. Hall and M. Mann (eds) *Europe and the Rise of Capitalism.* Oxford: Blackwell. pp. 234–42.

Lasswell, H.D. and A. Kaplan (1950) *Power and Society.* New Haven, NJ: Yale University Press.

Latour, B. (1999a) *Pandora's Hope: Essays on the Reality of Science Studies.* Cambridge, MA: Harvard University Press.

Latour, B. (1999b) 'On Recalling ANT', *The Sociological Review,* 47(S1): 15–25.

Latour, B. (2009) *Politics of Nature.* Boston, MA: Harvard University Press.

Latour, B. (2014a) 'Agency at the Time of the Anthropocene', *New Literary History,* 45(1): 1–18.

Latour, B. (2014b) 'Anthropology at the Time of the Anthropocene – A Personal View of What is to be Studied', Distinguished Lecture, *American Association of Anthropologists,* Washington, DC, December (draft for comments): 1–16.

Latour, B. (2014c) 'How Better to Register the Agency of Things', *Tanner Lectures,* Princeton, NJ: Yale University, 26–7 March.

Law, J. (1986a) 'Editor's Introduction: Power/Knowledge and the Dissolution of the Sociology of Knowledge', in J. Law (ed.), *Power, Action and Belief: A New Sociology of Knowledge?* Sociological Review Monograph 32. London: Routledge & Kegan Paul. pp. 1–19.

Law, J. (1986b) 'On the Methods of Long-distance Control: Vessels, Navigation and the Portuguese Route to India', in J. Law (ed.) *Power, Action and Belief: A New Sociology of Knowledge?* Sociological Review Monograph 32. London: Routledge & Kegan Paul. pp. 234–83.

Law, J. and P. Lodge (1984) *Science for Social Scientists.* London: Macmillan.

Lawson, S. (1983) *The Archibald Paradox.* Melbourne: Allen Lane.

Layder, D. (1985) 'Power, Structure and Agency', *Journal for the Theory of Social Behaviour,* 15(2): 131–49.

Layder, D. (1987) 'Key Issues in Structuration Theory: Some Critical Remarks', *Current Perspectives in Social Theory,* 8: 25–46.

Leiff, I.P. (1972) 'Bibliography', *Current Sociology,* 20(2): 57–131.

Leites, N. (1951) *The Operational Code of the Politburo.* New York: McGraw-Hill.

Leites, N. (1953) *A Study of Bolshevism.* New York: Free Press.

Lenzen, M., Moran, D., Kanemoto, K., Foran, B., Lobefaro, L. and Geschke, A. (2012) 'International Trade Drives Biodiversity Threats in Developing Nations', *Nature,* 486 (7401): 109–12.

Littler, C.R. (1982) *The Development of the Labour Process in Capitalist Societies.* London: Heinemann Educational Books.

Liu, H. (2018) 'Re-radicalising Intersectionality in Organisation Studies', *ephemera,* 18(1): 81–101.

Locke, J. (1959) *An Essay Concerning Human Understanding.* New York: Dover Publications.

Lockwood, D. (1964) 'Social Integration and System Integration', in G.K. Zollschan and W. Hirsch (eds) *Explorations in Social Change.* London: Routledge & Kegan Paul. pp. 244–57.

Logue, D. and Clegg, S.R. (2015) *Wikileaks* and *News of the World*: The Political Circuitry of Labeling', *Journal of Management Inquiry,* 24(4): 394–404.

Longden, T., Jotzo, F., Prasad, M. and Andrews, R. (2020) 'Green Hydrogen Production Costs in Australia: Implications of Renewable Energy and Electrolyser Costs', *Centre for Climate & Energy Policy,* CCEP Working Paper 20-07, Canberra, Australia: Australian National University.

Lovell, J. (2011) *The Opium War: Drugs, Dreams, and the Making of Modern China.* Oxford: Picador.

Luhmann, N. (1995) *Social Systems.* Stanford, CA: Stanford University Press.

Lukes, S. (1974) *Power: A Radical View.* London: Macmillan.

Lukes, S. (1976) 'Reply to Bradshaw', *Sociology,* 10: 129–32.

Lukes, S. (1977) *Essays in Social Theory*. London: Macmillan.

Lukes, S. (1982) 'Of Gods and Demons: Habermas and Practical Reason', in J.B. Thompson and D. Held (eds) *Habermas: Critical Debates*. Cambridge, MA: MIT Press. pp. 134–48.

Lukes, S. (ed.) (1986) *Power*. Oxford: Blackwell.

Lukes, S. (2005) *Power: A Radical View* (2nd edn). London: Macmillan.

Macfarlane, A. (1988) 'The Cradle of Capitalism: The Case of England', in J. Baechler, J.A. Hall and M. Mann (eds), *Europe and the Rise of Capitalism*. Oxford: Blackwell. pp. 185–203.

Machiavelli, N. ([1532] 1958) *The Prince*. London: Everyman.

Machiavelli, N. (1970) *The Discourses*. Harmondsworth: Penguin.

Maclntyre, A. (1962) 'A Mistake about Causality in Social Science', in P. Laslett and W.G. Runciman (eds) *Philosophy, Politics and Society* (2nd series). Oxford: Blackwell. pp. 48–70.

MacKenzie, D. (1978) 'Statistical Theory and Social Interests: A Case Study', *Social Studies of Science*, 8: 35–83.

Maclean, M., Harvey, C. and Chia, R. (2010) 'Dominant Corporate Agents and the Power Elite in France and Britain', *Organization Studies*, 31(3): 327–48.

Macpherson, C.B. (1962) *The Political Theory of Possessive Individualism: From Hobbes to Locke*. Oxford: Clarendon Press.

Major, M.J., Conceicao, A. and Clegg, S.R. (2018) 'When Power Relations Fail: The Case of Responsibility Centres in Portuguese Hospitals', *Accounting, Accountability and Auditing Journal*, 31(4): 1199–229.

Malcolm, N. (2002) *Aspects of Hobbes*. Oxford: Clarendon Press.

Malm, A. and Hornborg, A. (2014) 'The Geology of Mankind? A Critique of the Anthropocene Narrative', *The Anthropocene Review*, 1(1): 62–9.

Mann, M. (1980) 'State and Society, 1130–1815: An Analysis of English State Finances', in *Political Power and Social Theory*, 1: 165–208.

Mann, M. (1986) *The Sources of Social Power*, Vol. 1: *A History of Power from the Beginning to A.D. 1760*. Cambridge: Cambridge University Press.

March, J.G. and J.P. Olsen (1976) *Ambiguity and Choice in Organizations*. Bergen: Universitetsforlaget.

Markovits, D. (2019) *The Meritocracy Trap: How America's Foundational Myth Feeds Inequality, Dismantles the Middle Class, and Devours the Elite*. New York: Penguin.

Mann, S., Nolan, J. and Wellman, B. (2003) 'Sousveillance: Inventing and Using Wearable Computing Devices for Data Collection in Surveillance Environments', *Surveillance & Society*, 1(3): 331–55.

Mann, M. (2011) *Power in the 21st century: Conversations with John A. Hall*. Cambridge: Polity Press.

Marcuse, H. (1964) *One-Dimensional Man*. London: Routledge & Kegan Paul.

Marglin, S.A. (1974) 'What do Bosses Do? The Origins and Functions of Hierarchy in Capitalist Production', *Review of Radical Political Economics*, 6(2): 60–112.

Marshall, G. (1982) *In Search of the Spirit of Capitalism: An Essay on Max Weber's Protestant Ethic Thesis*. London: Hutchinson.

Martindale, D. (1960) *The Nature and Types of Sociological Theory*. London: Routledge & Kegan Paul.

Marx, K. (1976) *Capital*, Vol. 1. Harmondsworth: Penguin.

Marx, K. and F. Engels (1970) *The German Ideology*. Moscow: International Publishing Company.

Matheson, C. (1987) 'Weber and the Classification of Forms of Legitimacy', *British Journal of Sociology*, 38(2): 199–215.

Mayer-Schönberger, V. and Cukier, K. (2013) *Big Data: A Revolution That Will Transform How We Live, Work, and Think*. Boston, MA: Houghton Mifflin Harcourt.

Mayo, E. (1975) *The Social Problems of an Industrial Civilization*. London: Routledge & Kegan Paul.

McHoul, A. (1986) *Wittgenstein on Certainty and the Problem of Rule in Social Science*. Toronto: Toronto Semiotic Circle.

McLellan, G. (1984) 'Critical or Positive Theory? A Comment on the Status of Anthony Giddens' Social Theory', *Theory, Culture and Society*, 2(2): 123–9.

Meisel, J.H. (1962) *The Myth of the Ruling Class*. Ann Arbor, MI: Michigan University Press.

Mennell, S. (1996) *All manners of food: eating and taste in England and France from the Middle Ages to the present*. Champaign, Ill: University of Illinois Press.

Meyer, J. and B. Rowan (1977) 'Institutionalized Organizations: Formal Structure as Myth and Ceremony', *American Journal of Sociology*, 83: 340–63.

Meyer, M.W. (1987) 'The Growth of Public and Private Bureaucracies', paper presented to Critical Perspectives on Organizational Theories, ISA-RC 17 Conference, 18–22 July, Wassenaar, the Netherlands.

Michels, R. (1949) *Political Parties*. New York: Free Press.

Milanovic, B. (2019) *Capitalism, Alone: The Future of the System that Rules the World*. Boston, MA: Harvard University Press.

Miliband, R. (1969) *The State in Capitalist Society*. London: Quartet.

Miliband, R. (1970) 'The Capitalist State – Reply to Nicos Poulantzas', *New Left Review*, 59: 53–61.

Mills, C.W. (1940) 'Situated Actions and Vocabularies of Motive', *American Sociological Review*, 5: 904–13.

Mills, C.W. (1956) *The Power Elite*. Oxford: Oxford University Press.

Mills, C.W. (1959) *The Sociological Imagination*. New York: Oxford University Press.

Minson, J. (1986) 'Strategies for Socialists? Foucault's Conception of Power', in M. Gane (ed) *Towards a Critique of Foucault*. London: Routledge & Kegan Paul. pp. 106–48.

Mintzberg, H. (1983) *Power In and Around Organizations.* Englewood Cliffs, NJ: Prentice Hall.

Molotch, H. and D. Boden (1986) 'Talking Social Structure: Discourse Domination and the Watergate Hearings', *American Sociological Review,* 50: 237–86.

Moore, B. (1968) *The Social Origins of Dictatorship and Democracy.* Harmondsworth: Penguin.

Moore, J.W. (2017) 'The Capitalocene, Part I: On the Nature and Origins of Our Ecological Crisis', *The Journal of Peasant Studies,* 44(3): 594–630.

Moriarty, P. (2021) Global nuclear energy: an uncertain future. *AIMS Energy,* 9(5), 1027–1042.

Mosca, G. (1939) *The Ruling Class.* New York: McGraw Hill.

Mouzelis, N. (1988) 'Marxism or Post-Marxism?', *New Left Review,* 167: 107–23.

Muraro, L. (1996) *Partire da sé e non farsi trovare,* in Diotima (ed.) *La sapienza del partire da sè.* Naples: Liguori. pp. 5–21.

Mushtaq, M. (2022) 'Cash-strapped Sri Lanka Looks to Russia to Quench Thirst for Oil', *Nikkei Asia,* 2 June. Available at: https://asia.nikkei.com/Spotlight/Sri-Lanka-crisis/Cash-strapped-Sri-Lanka-looks-to-Russia-to-quench-thirst-for-oil, accessed 03.06.22.

Nagel, E. (1965) *The Structure of Science.* New York: Harcourt Brace Jovanovich.

Nellor, D.C.L. (1984) 'Public Bureau Budgets and Jurisdictional Size', *Public Choice,* 44: 175–83.

Newton, K. (1969) 'A Critique of the Pluralist Model', *Acta Sociologica,* 12: 209–43.

Newton, K. (1975) 'Community Politics and Decision Making: the American Experience and its Lessons', in K. Newton (ed.), *Essays on the Study of Urban Politics.* London: Croom Helm. pp. 1–24.

North, D. (1981) *Structure and Change in Economic History.* New York: Norton.

North, D. and R. Thomas (1973) *The Rise of the Western World.* Cambridge: Cambridge University Press.

O'Brien, P. (1983) 'European Economic Development: The Contribution of the Periphery', *Economic History Review,* 35(1): 1–18.

O'Connor, J. (1972) *The Fiscal Crisis of the State.* New York: St Martins Press.

Oesterich, G.(1982) *Neostoicism and the Early Modern State.* Cambridge: Cambridge University Press.

O'Farrell, C. (1982) 'Foucault and the Foucauldians', *Economy and Society,* 11(4): 449–59.

O'Leary, Stannard, E. and Abdul-Kharim, S. (2017) '1967 Riots: 4 Tense Days That Began "evolution" of Blacks', *New Haven Register,* August 12, www.nhregister.com/new-haven/article/1967-riots-4-tense-days-that-began-11813921.php, accessed 1.12.22.

O'Neill, J. (1987) 'The Disciplinary Society: From Weber to Foucault', *British Journal of Sociology,* 37(1): 42–60.

O'Neill, J. (2022) Will Sanctioning Russia Upend the Monetary System? *Project Syndicate,* March 2, www.project-syndicate.org/commentary/western-sanctions-on-russia-impact-on-monetary-system-by-jim-o-neill-2022-03, accessed 02.12.22.

Offe, C. and H. Wiesenthal (1981) 'Two Logics of Collective Action: Theoretical Notes on Social Class and Organizational Form', *Political Power and Social Theory: A Research Annual,* 1: 67–116.

Oliveira, J. and Clegg, S.R. (2015) 'Paradoxical Puzzles of Control and Circuits of Power', *Qualitative Research in Accounting and Management*, 12(4): 425–51.

Oppenheim, F.E. (1961) *Dimensions of Freedom: An Analysis.* London: Macmillan.

Orsato, R.J. and Clegg, S.R. (1999) 'The Political Ecology of Organizations: Toward a Framework for Analyzing Business-Environment Relationships', *Organization & Environment*, 12(3): 263–79.

Orsato, R.J., Den Hond, F. and Clegg, S.R. (2002) 'The Political Ecology of Automobile Recycling in Europe', *Organization Studies*, 23(4): 639–65.

Orwell, G. (1948) *Animal Farm.* Harmondsworth: Penguin.

Pamphile, V. D. (2022) 'Paradox Peers: A Relational Approach to Navigating a Business-Society Paradox'. *Academy of Management Journal*, 4(65): 1274–302.

Pareto, V. (1935) *The Mind and Society.* New York: Dover.

Parker, M.J. (2000) *Thatcherism and the Fall of Coal.* Oxford: Oxford University Press.

Parkin, F. (1972a) *Class Inequality and Political Order: Social Stratification in Capitalist and Communist Societies.* London: McGibbon & Kee.

Parkin, F. (1972b) 'System Contradiction and Political Transformation: The Comparative Study of Industrial Societies', *European Journal of Sociology,* 13: 45–62.

Parkin, F. (1976) 'System Contradiction and Political Transformation: The Comparative Study of Industrial Societies', in T.R. Burns and W. Buckley (eds), *Power and Control: Social Structures and their Transformation.* London: Sage Publications. pp. 127–46.

Parry, G. and P. Morris (1974) 'When is a Decision not a Decision?', in I. Crewe (ed.), *British Political Sociology Yearbook,* Vol. 1: *Elites in Western Democracy.* London: Croom Helm. pp. 317–37.

Parsons, T. (1937) *The Structure of Social Action.* New York: McGraw Hill.

Parsons, T. (1951) *The Social System.* New York: Free Press.

Parsons, T. (1963) 'On the Concept of Political Power', *Proceedings of the American Philosophical Society*, 107(3): 232–62.

Parsons, T. (1967) *Sociological Theory and Modern Society.* New York: Free Press.

Pateman, C. (1970) *Participation and Democratic Theory.* Cambridge: Cambridge University Press.

Perey, R. (2014) 'Organizing Sustainability and the Problem of Scale: Local, Global or Fractal'. *Organization & Environment*, 27(3): 215–22.

Perrow, C. (2011) *The Next Catastrophe: Reducing Our Vulnerabilities to Natural, Industrial, and Terrorist Disasters*. Princeton, NJ: Princeton University Press.

Peticca-Harris, A., deGama, N. and Ravishankar, M.N. (2020) 'Postcapitalist Precarious Work and Those in the "Drivers'" Seat: Exploring the Motivations and Lived Experiences of Uber Drivers in Canada', *Organization*, 27(1): 36–59.

Pfeffer, J. (1981) *Power in Organizations*. Boston, MA: Pitman.

Pickering, A. (1995) *The Mangle of Practice: Time, Agency and Science*. Chicago: University of Chicago Press.

Pierazzini, M.E., Bertelli, L. and Raviola, E. (2021) 'Working with Words: Italian Feminism and Organization Studies', *Gender, Work & Organization*, 28 (4): 1260–81.

Pierpoint, C. R. (2008) The Florentine, *The New Yorker*, September 8, www.newyorker.com/magazine/2008/09/15/the-florentine, accessed 1.12.22.

Piketty, T. (2018) *Capital and Ideology*. Cambridge, MA: Harvard University Press.

Pine, S. (2022) '"Comme Nostre Frere": Knightly Ritual Brotherhood Reconsidered', *Cultural and Social History*, 1–19. Available at: DOI: 10.1080/14780038.2022.2063044.

Pinnington, A., Macklin, R. and Campbell, T. (eds), (2007) *Human Resource Management: Ethics and Employment*. Oxford: Oxford University Press.

Pogge, T.W. (2001) 'Eradicating Systemic Poverty: Brief for a Global Resources Dividend', *Journal of Human Development*, 2(1): 59–77.

Poggi, G. (1978) *The Development of the Modern State*. London: Hutchinson.

Poggi, G. (1983) *Calvinism and the Capitalist Spirit*. London: Macmillan.

Polsby, N. (1963) *Community Power and Political Theory*. New Haven, NJ: Yale University Press.

Popper, K. (1962) *The Open Society and its Enemies*. London: Routledge & Kegan Paul.

Popper, K. (1965) *Conjectures and Refutations: The Growth of Scientific Knowledge*. New York: Harper Torchbooks.

Porter, D. & Hayes, I. (1968) *I thank you*, Berlin: BMG Rights Management, Universal Music Publishing Group, Warner Chappell Music, Inc.

Poulantzas, N. (1969) 'The Problem of the Capitalist State', *New Left Review*, 58: 67–78.

Poulantzas, N. (1973) *Political Power and Social Classes*. London: New Left Books.

Poulantzas, N. (1976) *State, Power, Socialism*. London: New Left Books.

Prasad, A. (2020) 'The Organization of Ideological Discourse in Times of Unexpected Crisis: Explaining How COVID-19 is Exploited by Populist Leaders', *Leadership*, 16(3): 294–302.

Presthus, R.E. (1964) *Men at the Top*. Oxford: Oxford University Press.

Przeworski, A. (1980) 'Material Bases of Consent: Economics and Politics in a Hegemonic System', *Political Power and Social Theory*, 1: 21–66.

Purtill, J. (2021) 'What is Green Hydrogen, How is it Made and Will it be the Fuel of the Future?' *ABC News*, 23 January, accessed 27.05.22.

Pusey, M. (1987) *Jürgen Habermas*. London: Tavistock.

Rachman, G. (2022) *The Age of The Strongman: How the Cult of the Leader Threatens Democracy Around the World*. New York: Vintage.

Rankin, J. (2022) '"Russia Wins by Losing": Timothy Snyder on Raising Funds for Ukrainian Drone Defence', *The Guardian*, 28 November, www.theguardian.com/world/2022/nov/28/russia-wins-by-losing-timothy-snyder-on-raising-funds-for-ukrainian-drone-defence, accessed 02.12.22.

Rawls, J. (1978) *A Theory of Justice*. Oxford: Oxford University Press.

Reed, M. (2012) 'Masters of the Universe: Power and Elites in Organization Studies', *Organization Studies*, 33: 203–21.

Rex, J. (1964) *Key Problems of Sociological Theory*. London: Routledge & Kegan Paul.

Rhinehart, L. (1972) *The Dice Man*. Frogmore: Panther.

Rockström, J. and Karlberg, L. (2010) 'The Quadruple Squeeze: Defining the Safe Operating Space for Freshwater Use to Achieve a Triply Green Revolution in the Anthropocene', *Ambio*, 39: 257–65.

Rockström, J., Richardson, K., Steffen, W. and Mace, G. (2018) 'Planetary Boundaries: Separating Fact from Fiction: A Response to Montoya et al.', *Trends in Ecology & Evolution*, 33(4): 233–4.

Rockström, J., Steffen, W., Noone, K., Persson, A., Chapin, III, E. Lambin, T. M. Lenton, M. Scheffer, C. Folke, F.S., Schellnhuber, H., Nykvist, B., De Wit, C.A., Hughes, T., van der Leeuw, S., Rodhe, H., Sorlin, S., Snyder, P.K., Costanza, R., Svedin, M. Falkenmark, L. Karlberg, Corell, R.W., Fabry, V.J., Hansen, J., Walker, B., Liverman, D., Richardson, K., Crutzen, P. and Foley, J. (2009) 'Planetary Boundaries: Exploring the Safe Operating Space for Humanity', *Ecology and Society*, 14(2): 32.

Rogers, M. (1977) 'Goffman on Power', *American Sociologist*, 12: 88–95.

Rothschild-Whitt, J. (1979) The collectivist organization: An alternative to rational-bureaucratic models. *American Sociological Review*, 509–527.

Rothschild, J. and Whitt, J.A. (1989) *The Cooperative Workplace: Potentials and Dilemmas of Organisational Democracy and Participation*. Cambridge: CUP Archive.

Rueschemeyer, D. (1986) *Power and the Division of Labour*. Cambridge: Polity Press.

Russell, B. (1938) *Power: A New Social Analysis*. London: Allen & Unwin.

Russell, B. (1986) 'The Forms of Power', in S. Lukes (ed.) *Power*. Oxford: Blackwell. pp. 19–21.

Ryle, G. (1949) *The Concept of Mind*. London: Hutchinson.

Sacks, H. (1972) 'An Initial Investigation of the Usability of Conversational Data for Doing Sociology', in D. Sudnow (ed.) *Studies in Social Interaction*. New York: Free Press. pp. 31–74.

Said, E. (1978) *Orientalism*. New York: Random House.

Salancik, G.R. and Pfeffer, J. (1977) 'Who Gets Power – and How They Hold On To It: A Strategic-Contingency Model of Power', *Organizational Dynamics*, 5(3): 3–21.

Sandel, M. (2012) *What Money Can't Buy: The Moral Limits of Markets*. New York: Allen Lane.

Santos, B.S. (2020) *A Cruel Pedagogia do Vírus*. Coimbra: Almedina.

Sarkar, S. and Clegg, S.R. (2021) 'Resilience in a Time of Contagion: Lessons from Small Businesses During the Corona Virus Pandemic', *Journal of Change Management*, 1(2): 242–67.

Sartre, J.-P. (1959) *L' Existentialisme et les Humanismes*. Paris: Nagel.

Saunders, P. (1979) *Urban Politics*. Harmondsworth: Penguin.

Saussure, F. de (1974) *Course in General Linguistics*. London: Fontana.

Savage, S. (1982) *The Social Theory of Talcott Parsons*. London: Macmillan.

Sayer, D. (1979) *Marx's Method: Ideology, Science and Critique in 'Capital'*. Brighton: Harvester.

Schad, J. and Lewis, M.W., Raisch, S. and Smith, W.K. (2016) 'Paradox Research in Management Science: Looking Back to Move Forward', *Academy of Management Annals*, 10(1): 5–64.

Schattschneider, E.E. (1960) *The Semi-Sovereign People: A Realist's View of Democracy in America*. New York: Holt, Rinehart & Winston.

Scheidel, W. (2018) *The Great Leveller: Violence and the History of Inequality from the Stone Age to the Twenty-first Century*. Princeton, NJ: Princeton University Press.

Schutz, A. (1962) *Collected Papers*, Vol. 1. The Hague: Martinus Nijhoff.

Schutz, A. (1964) *Collected Papers*, Vol. 2. The Hague: Martinus Nijhoff.

Schutz, A. (1967) *The Phenomenology of the Social World*. Evanston, Ill.: Northwestern University Press.

Schutz, A. (1970) 'Concept and Theory Formation in the Social Sciences', in D. Emmet and A. MacIntyre (eds) *Sociological Theory and Philosophical Analysis*. London: Macmillan. pp 1–19.

Sciulli, D. (1987) 'Political Power in Social Theory: Reconsidering Anthony Giddens' Most Systematic Critique of Talcott Parsons', mimeo, Department of Sociology, University of Delaware.

Scott, J. (1985) *Weapons of the Weak*. New Haven, CT: Yale University Press.

Scott, J. (1990) *Domination and the Art of Resistance: Hidden Transcripts*. New Haven, CT: Yale University Press.

Scott, J. (1996) *Stratification and power: Structures of class, status and command*. Cambridge, UK: Cambridge University Press.

Scott, J.C. (1998) *Seeing like a State: How Certain Schemes to Improve the Human Condition Have Failed*. New Haven, NJ: Yale University Press.

Scott, W.R. (1987) 'The Adolescence of Institutional Theory', *Administrative Science Quarterly*, 32(4). 493–511.

Scott, W. R. (2003) *Organization, Rational, Natural and Open Systems* (fifth ed.), New York: Prentice Hall.

Service, R. (2019) *Kremlin Winter: Russia and the Second Coming of Vladimir Putin.* London: Picador.

Servick, K. (2020) 'COVID-19 contact tracing apps are coming to a phone near you. How will we know whether they work?', *Global S&T Development Trend Analysis Platform of Resources and Environment.* Available at: http://resp.llas.ac.cn/C666/handle/2XK7JSWQ/270885

Shah, S.Q.A., Lai, F.W., Shad, M.K. and Jan, A.A. (2022) 'Developing a Green Governance Framework for the Performance Enhancement of the Oil and Gas Industry', *Sustainability,* 14(7): 3735.

Shwayder, D.S. (1965) *The Stratification of Behaviour: A System of Definitions Propounded and Defended.* London: Routledge & Kegan Paul.

Silva, L. and Backhouse, J. (2003) 'The Circuits-of-Power Framework for Studying Power in Institutionalization of Information Systems', *Journal of the Association for Information Systems,* 4(1): 14.

Silverman, D. (1970) *The Theory of Organizations.* London: Heinemann Educational Books.

Simon, H.A. (1952) 'Decision Making and Administrative Organization', in R.K. Merton, A.N. Gray, B. Hockey and H.C. Selvin (eds) *Reader in Bureaucracy.* New York: Free Press. pp. 185–94.

Singh, J.V., R.J. House and D.J. Tucker (1986) 'Organizational Change and Organizational Mortality', *Administrative Science Quarterly,* 31 (4): 587–611.

Skocpol, T. (1979) *States and Revolutions: A Comparative Analysis of France, Russia and China.* Cambridge: Cambridge University Press.

Smart, B. (1985) *Michel Foucault.* London: Tavistock.

Smelser, N. (1959) *Social Change in the Industrial Revolution.* Chicago: University of Chicago Press.

Smith, B. (2022) 'What We Got Wrong about Solzhenitsyn', *UnHerd,* 15 March. Available at: https://unherd.com/2022/03/what-we-get-wrong-about-solzhenitsyn/?=thepostindexfrmemail, accessed 16.03.22.

Smith, D. (1982) '"Put Not Your Trust in Princes" – A Commentary upon Anthony Giddens and the Absolutist State', *Theory, Culture and Society,* 1(2): 93–9.

Smith, S., Winchester, D., Bunker, D. and Jamieson, R. (2010) 'Circuits of Power: A Study of Mandated Compliance to an Information Systems Security "De Jure" Standard in a Government Organization', *MIS Quarterly,* 463–86.

Snyder, T. (2018) *The Road to Unfreedom: Russia, Europe, America.* New York: Tim Duggan Books.

Sohda, S. (2022) Don't be taken in by that £50bn 'fiscal black hole'. It's just a dodgy Tory metaphor, *The Observer,* November 13, www.theguardian.com/commentisfree/2022/nov/13/dont-be-taken-in-by-50bn-fiscal-hole-dodgy-tory-metaphor, accessed 02.12.22.

Soldatov, A. and Borogan, I. (2010) *The New Nobility: The Restoration of Russia's Security State and the Enduring Legacy of the KGB*. New York: Public Affairs.

Soloway, S.M. (1987) 'Elite Cohesion in Dahl's New Haven: Three Centuries of the Private School', in G.W. Domhoff and T.R. Rye (eds) *Power Elites and Organizations*. London: Sage Publications. pp. 96–115.

Spencer, H. (1893) *Principles of Sociology*. London: Williams & Norgate.

Spicer, A. (2023) The work from home revolution is here to stay – if you're rich, white and live in London, *The Guardian*, 14 February, https://www.theguardian.com/commentisfree/2023/feb/14/working-from-home-revolution-hybrid-working-inequalities, accessed 15.02.23.

Spufford, F. (2010) *Red Plenty*. London: Faber & Faber.

Stavrakakis, Y. (2002) *Lacan and the Political*. London: Routledge.

Steffen, W. and Smith, M. (2013) 'Planetary Boundaries, Equity and Global Sustainability: Why Wealthy Countries Could Benefit from More Equity', *Current Opinion in Environmental Sustainability*, 5: 403–8.

Steffen, W., Richardson, K., Rockström, J., Cornell, S.E., Fetzer, I., Bennett, E.M., Biggs, R., Carpenter, S.R., de Vries, W., de Wit, C.A., Folke, C., Gerten, D., Heinke, J., Mace, G.M., Persson, L.M., Ramanathan, V., Reyers, B and Sörlin, S. (2015) 'Planetary Boundaries: Guiding Human Development on a Changing Planet', *Science*, 347: 6223.

Stern, P.M. (1988) *The Best Congress Money Can Buy*. New York: Pantheon.

Stinchcombe, A. (1965) 'Social Structure and Organizations', in J.G. March (ed.), *Handbook of Organizations*. Chicago: Rand McNally. pp. 142–93.

Stone, K. (1974) 'The Origins of Job Structures in the Steel Industry', *Review of Radical Political Economics*, 6: 113–74.

Strauss, A. (1978) *Negotiations: Varieties, Contexts, Processes and Social Order*. London: Jossey-Bass.

Sussex, M. (2022) What legacy will Vladimir Putin leave? *The Conversation*, December 6, https://theconversation.com/what-legacy-will-vladimir-putin-leave-russia-195444, accessed 06.12.22

Taouk, M. (2022) Revenue NSW cancels more than 33,000 COVID-19 fines after Supreme Court hearing, *ABC News*, November 29, www.abc.net.au/news/2022-11-29/revenue-nsw-cancels-33-121-covid-19-fines/101710632, accessed 02.12.22.

Taylor, L. (1972) 'The Significance and Interpretation of Replies to Motivational Questions: The Case of Sex Offenders', *Sociology*, 6(1): 23–40.

Taylor, R. and Rieger, A. (1984) 'Rudolf Virchow on the Typhus Epidemic in Upper Silesia: An Introduction and Translation', *Sociology of Health & Illness*, 6(2): 201–17.

The Economist. (2020a) 'Creating the Coronopticon', 28 March, pp. 17–20.

The Economist. (2020b) 'Protection Racket', 25 April, pp. 48–50.

Therborn, G. (1976) *Science, Class and Society*. London: New Left Books.

Therborn, G. (1977) 'The Rule of Capital and the Rise of Bourgeois Democracy', *New Left Review,* 103(3): 41.

Therborn, G. (1978) *What Does the Ruling Class Do When it Rules? State Apparatuses and State Powers under Feudalism, Capitalism and Socialism.* London: New Left Books.

Therborn, G. (1980) *The Ideology of Power and the Power of Ideology.* London: Verso.

Thomas, J.J.R. (1985) 'Rationalization and the Status of Gender Divisions', *Sociology,* 19(3): 409–20.

Thomas, W.I. and Thomas, D.S. (1928) *The Child in America: Behavior Problems and Programs.* New York: Knopf.

Thompson, E.P. (1967) 'Time, Work, Discipline and Industrial Capitalism', *Past and Present,* 38: 56–97.

Thompson, E.P. (1968) *The Making of the English Working Class.* Harmondsworth: Penguin.

Thompson, J.D. (1956) 'Authority and Power in Identical Organizations', *American Journal of Sociology,* 62: 290–301.

Torfing, J., Ferlie, E., Jukić, T. and Ongaro, E. (2021) 'A Theoretical Framework for Studying the Co-creation of Innovative Solutions and Public Value', *Policy & Politics,* 49 (2): 189–209.

Tourish, D. (2020) 'Introduction to the Special Issue: Why the Coronavirus is also a Crisis of Leadership', *Leadership,* 16(3): 261–72.

Tourish, D.J. and Pinnington, A.H. (2002) 'Transformational Leadership, Corporate Cultism and the Spirituality Paradigm: An Unholy Trinity in the Workplace?' *Human Relations,* 55(2): 147–72.

Tuckermann, H. (2019) 'Visibilizing and Invisibilizing Paradox: A Process Study of Interactions in a Hospital Executive Board', *Organization Studies,* 40(12): 1851–72.

Turnheim, B. and Geels, F.W. (2012) 'Regime Destabilisation as the Flipside of Energy Transitions: Lessons from the History of the British Coal Industry (1913–1997)', *Energy Policy,* 50: 35–49.

Turner, B.S. (1986a) 'Parsons and his Critics: On the Ubiquity of Functionalism', pp. 179–206 in R.J. Holton and B.S. Turner (eds), *Talcott Parsons on Economy and Society.* London: Routledge & Kegan Paul.

Turner, B.S. (1986b) *Citizenship and Capitalism: The Debate over Reformism.* London: Allen & Unwin.

Ulvila, M. and Wilén, K. (2017) 'Engaging with the Plutocene: Moving Towards Degrowth and Post-capitalistic Futures', in P. Heikkurinen (ed.) *Sustainability and Peaceful Coexistence for the Anthropocene.* London and New York: Routledge.

Ure, A. (1835) *The Philosophy of Manufactures.* London: Charles Knight.

Urry, J. (1981) *The Anatomy of Capitalist Society.* London: Macmillan.

Urry, J. (1982) 'Duality of Structure: Some Critical Issues', *Theory, Culture and Society,* 1(2): 100–6.

Vaara, E., Tienari, J., Piekkari, R. and Säntti, R. (2005) 'Language and the Circuits of Power in a Merging Multinational Corporation', *Journal of Management Studies*, 42 (3): 595–623.

Vadén, T. (2014) 'Next Nature and the Curse of Oil', *Next Nature*. Available at: www.nextnature.net/2014/02/next-nature-and-the-curse-of-oil/

Van den Bergh, J.C. and Kallis, G. (2012) 'Growth, A-growth or Degrowth to Stay Within Planetary Boundaries?' *Journal of Economic Issues*, 46(4): 909–20.

Van Dijck, J. (2014) 'Datafication, Dataism and Dataveillance: Big Data between Scientific Paradigm and Ideology', *Surveillance & Society*, 12(2): 197–208.

van Iterson, A., and Clegg, S. R. (2008) 'The politics of gossip and denial in inter-organizational relations', *Human Relations*, 61(8): 1117–1137.

Van Krieken, R. (2018). *Celebrity Society: The Struggle for Attention*. London: Routledge.

Vitali, S., Glattfelder, J.B. and Battiston, S. (2011) 'The Network of Global Corporate Control', *PLoS ONE*, 6(10): e25995.

Waddock, S. (2011) 'We are all Stakeholders of Gaia: A Normative Perspective on Stakeholder Thinking', *Organization & Environment*, 24(2): 192–212.

Walker, S.G. (1990) 'The Evolution of Operational Code Analysis', *Political Psychology* 11(2): 403–18.

Wall, G. (1975) 'The Concept of Interest in Polities', *Politics and Society*, 5: 487–510.

Wall, R., J. Robin and P. Laslett (eds) (1983) *Family Forms in Historic Europe*. Cambridge: Cambridge University Press.

Wallerstein, I. (1974) *The Modern World System: Capitalist Agriculture and the Origins of the European World Economy in the Sixteenth Century*. London: Academic Press.

Watkins, J.N.W. (1965) *Hobbes' System of Ideas*. London: Hutchinson.

Watzlawick, P., Bavelas, J.B. and Jackson, D.D. (1967) *Pragmatics of Human Communication: A Study of Interactional Patterns, Pathologies and Paradoxes*. New York: W.W. Norton & Company.

Wiesner, R., Chadee, D. and Best, P. (2017) 'Managing Change toward Environmental Sustainability: A Conceptual Model in Small and Medium Enterprises', *Organization & Environment*, 31(2): 152–77.

Wearmouth, R.F. (1939) *Methodism and the Working Class Movements of England 1800–1950*. London: Epworth.

Weber, M. (1946) 'Politics as a Vocation', in Gerth, H. H., and Mills, C. W. (Eds) *From Max Weber: Essays in Sociology*, London: Routledge and Kegan Paul, pp. 77–128.

Weber, M. (1947) *The Theory of Social and Economic Organization*. London: Routledge & Kegan Paul.

Weber, M. (1948) *From Max Weber: Essays in Social Theory*. London: Routledge & Kegan Paul.

Weber, M. (1976) *The Protestant Ethic and the Spirit of Capitalism*. London: Allen & Unwin.

Weber, M. (1978) (ed. G. Roth and C. Wittich) *Economy and Society: An Outline of Interpretive Sociology* (2 Vols) Berkeley, CA: University of California Press.

Weber, M. (1986) 'Domination by Economic Power and Authority', in S. Lukes (ed.) *Power*. Oxford: Blackwell. pp. 28–36.

Weedon, C. (1987) *Feminist Practice and Poststructuralist Theory*. Oxford: Blackwell.

Werner, K.F. (1988) 'Political and Social Structures of the West', in J. Baechler, J.A. Hall and M. Mann (eds) *Europe and the Rise of Capitalism*. Oxford: Blackwell. pp. 169–84.

Weick, K. E. (1969) *The Social Psychology of Organizing*. Reading, MA: Addison Wesley Publishing Company.

Weick, K.E. (1995) *Sensemaking in Organizations*. Thousand Oaks, CA: Sage.

Westney, D.E. (1987) *Initiation and Innovation: The Transfer of Western Organizational Pallernslo Meiji Japan*. Cambridge, MA: Harvard University Press.

White, G. (2022) In Putin's Ukraine quagmire, echoes of Soviet failure in Afghanistan, *The Washington Post*, April 2, www.washingtonpost.com/world/2022/04/02/ukraine-afghanistan-russia-parallels-quagmire/, accessed 02.12.22.

Whiteman, G., Walker, B. and Perego, P. (2013) 'Planetary Boundaries: Ecological Foundations for Corporate Sustainability', *Journal of Management Studies*, 50(2): 307–36.

Whitt, J.A. (1979) 'Towards a Class-Dialectical Model of Power: An Empirical Assessment of Three Competing Models of Political Power', *American Sociological Review*, 44: 81–100.

Whitt, J.A. (1982) *Urban Elites and Mass Transportation*. Princeton, NJ: Princeton University Press.

Wickham, G. (1983) 'Power and Power Analysis', *Economy and Society*, 12(4): 468–98.

Wiener, M.J. (1981) *English Culture and the Decline of the Industrial Spirit 1850–1980*. Cambridge: Cambridge University Press.

Williams, K. (1997) *The Prague Spring and its Aftermath: Czechoslovak Politics, 1968–1970*. Cambridge: Cambridge University Press.

Williams, Y. (2001) No haven: From civil rights to Black power in New Haven, Connecticut. *The Black Scholar*, 31(3–4), 54–66.

Williamson, O.E. (1981) 'Transaction Cost Economies: The Governance of Contractual Relations', *Journal of Law and Economics*: 233–61.

Williamson, O.E. (1985) *The Economic Institutions of Capitalism*. New York: Free Press.

Wilson, S. (2020) 'Pandemic Leadership: Lessons from New Zealand's Approach to Covid-19', *Leadership*, 16 (3): 279–93.

Wittgenstein, L. (1968) (trans. G.E.M. Anscombe) *Philosophical Investigations*. Oxford: Blackwell.

Wolfinger, R.E. (1971a) 'Nondecisions and the Study of Local Polities', *American Political Science Review*, 65: 1063–80.

Wolfinger, R.E. (1971b) 'Rejoinder to Frey's "Comment"', *American Political Science Review*, 65: 1102–4.

Wolin, S.S. (1960) *Politics and Vision*. Boston: Little, Brown.

Wood, S. (ed.) (1982) *The Degradation of Work?* London: Hutchinson.

Wood, T. (2020) *Russia without Putin: Money, Power and the Myths of the New Cold War*. London: Verso Books.

Woolgar, S. (1981) 'Interests and Explanation in the Social Study of Science', *Social Studies of Science*, 11: 365–94.

Wright, E.O. (1978) *Class, Crisis and the State*. London: New Left Books.

Wright, E.O. (1985) *Classes*. London: New Left Books.

Wright, C., Nyberg, D. and Bowden, V. (2021) 'Beyond the Discourse of Denial: The Reproduction of Fossil Fuel Hegemony in Australia', *Energy Research & Social Science*, 77: 102094.

Wrong, D. (1979) *Power: Its Forms, Bases and Uses*. Oxford: Blackwell.

Young, R.C. (1988) 'Is Population Ecology a Useful Paradigm for the Study of Organizations?', *American Journal of Sociology*, 94(1): 1–24.

Yukl, G. (2006) *Leadership in Organizations* (6th edn). Englewood Cliffs, NJ: Prentice-Hall.

Zeraffa, M. (1976) *Fictions: The Novel and Social Reality*. Harmondsworth: Penguin.

Zero-Carbon Energy for the Asia-Pacific ZCEAP Working Paper ZCWP03-20, accessed 27.05.22.

Žižek, S. (2020) *Pandemic! COVID-19 Shakes the World*. New York: Polity Press.

Zorina, A., Bélanger, F., Kumar, N. and Clegg, S. (2021) 'Watchers, Watched, and Watching in the Digital Age: Reconceptualization of Information Technology Monitoring as Complex Action Nets', *Organization Science*, 32(6): 1571–96.

Zuboff, S. (2019) *The Age of Surveillance Capitalism: The Fight for a Human Future at the New Frontier of Power*. New York: Profile Books.

Zulfiqar, G.M. (2019) 'Dirt, Foreignness, and Surveillance: The Shifting Relations of Domestic Work in Pakistan', *Organization*, 26(3): 321–36.

INDEX

Abercrombie, N., 170–6
Abrahamsson, B., 274, 276
absolutism, 112, 124, 195, 197, 239, 260, 266,
    269, 270, 272, 274, 275, 277
  ethical, 134
  French, 259, 260, 262
  Marxist, 109, 113
  moral, 168, 213
  new, 259
  princely, 279
  Prussian, 259
  theoretical, 168
action, 10, 40, 78, 84, 90, 92, 94, 111, 198
  accounting-for-action, 191
  alleged effect, 55
  appropriate, 211, 311
  autonomous, 104
  capacities for, 29, 49
  class-based, 119, 121
  climate, 314
  collective, 238
  common, 153
  communicative, 105
  concerted, 60, 71, 147, 230, 231
  consequences of, 191
  constraints on others, 155, 210
  contextualization, 221
  course of, 253
  decision-making, 49, 224
  description, 55, 56
  economic, 258
  effective, 229, 314
  episodic, 77
  extraordinary, 108
  flow of, 223
  freedom of, 6, 133
  future, 19
  individual, 104
  instrumental, 105
  intended, 91, 250
  interests implicit in, 128, 191
  judicial, 293
  moral, 42
  and non-action, 41, 49
  organizational, 207, 211

  political, 13, 122, 213, 266, 319
  principle of, 222
  procedural contexts, 222
  prohibited, 41
  rational, 240, 284
  reasons for, 191
  refraining from, 101
  relational, 67
  responsible, 13, 314
  restraining, 314
  restricting, 154, 210
  scope of one's action, 44, 112, 224, 227
  social, 104, 105, 110, 143, 150, 151, 156,
      204, 220, 290
  sources of, 11
  strategic, 43, 45, 69, 105, 243
  and structure, 139
  sustainability, 313
  temporal contexts, 221
  terrorist, 240
  threshold of, 226
  uncoerced, 146
  urgent, 308
  Weberian theory of, 104
actor network theory, 27, 234, 308, 312–13
Afghanistan, 283
agency
  and choice, 110
  classical liberal conceptions of, 56
  collective, 142, 150, 198
  concept of, 27
  disempowerment of agents, 233, 240, 242,
      244, 247
  individual, 140
  and interaction, 152
  metaphorical continuities between classical
      and modern agency views, 56–7
  metaphysical concerns, 49
  and organizations, 27–8, 203–208
  and power, 6, 11–13, 23–5, 51, 53, 77, 95, 111
  and realism, 135
  social, 188–9
  strategic, 208–212
  and structure, 18, 23–5, 86–94, 157, 168
  see also episodic agency concept of power

Agger, R. E., 67
agnosticism, 213
Akosy, C.G., 242
Alcott, B., 315
Aldrich, H., 216, 243
Alford, R. R., 110
algorithms, 290, 291
Althusser, L., 111, 172–3
Amnesty International, 300–301
analogies, 5, 8, 57, 143
  chess, 219–20
  see also metaphors of/for power
analytical dualism, 281
Anderson, B., 36, 237, 270–2
  publications by, 270
Anderson, P., 11, 162, 169, 173, 182, 242,
    250–4, 260
Anthony, P. D., 209
Anthropocene society, 310–11, 312, 313
anticipated reaction, rule of, 87, 89
Archer, M., 23, 281
architectonics, 10, 44, 45, 202
  architectonic power, 38–9, 167, 321
  and organizations, 27, 319
Arden, J., 299
ascendant class, 174
asceticism, 178, 180
Ashley, D., 149
Assad, T., 200
Assange, J., 292
Astley, W. G., 243–4
atomism, 53, 56
Australia, 220, 275–6, 285, 295, 299, 315, 317
  Asian Renewable Energy Hub, solar and wind
      power produced by, 295
  Australian Labor Party (ALP), 276
  climate crisis, 307
  compulsory voting in, 73
  and COVID-19 pandemic, 305, 306
  democracy, 271
  Federal Government, 236
  Pilbara region, Western Australia, 295–6
  post-war, 237
  social formation, 276
  state formation, 276
  voting in, 73
  'Women who want to be Women' (interest
      group), 123
authority, 22, 90, 91, 100, 178, 180
  of agents, 107
  church, 279
  constraints of, 113
  conventional, 224
  delegation of, 210, 211
  and domination, 223

formal, 200
higher, 209
jurisdictional, 257
legitimate, 144
monarchical, 266
moral, 209
of nature, 136
and power, 144, 147, 199, 211–12
re-structuring, 177
of ruling class, 170
of sovereign, 39
state, 259, 267, 273
structural, 21, 206
sub-types, 84
autonomy, 104, 115, 152, 157, 199, 204
  limits to, 177
  market, 270
  relative, 105, 106, 107, 109, 111, 151, 194,
      266, 297
  state, 117

Bachrach, P., 58, 100, 126, 169, 192, 195
  on agency and structure, 86–94
  and Dahl, 17, 68, 77
  on power
    critique of community power debate, 1, 14,
        15, 17
    and three-dimensional model, 101
    two faces of power, 14–16, 17, 93–4, 97, 99,
        101
  publications by, 15, 90
Baechler, J., 194
Bailey, F. G., 38, 42
Balibar, E., 111
Ball, T., 5, 11, 51, 53–5, 57–8, 93, 94, 100
Banaji, J., 254
Banerjee, S.B., 314
Banfield, E.C., 62
Baratz, M.S., 58, 100, 126, 169, 192, 195
  on agency and structure, 86–94
  and Dahl, 68, 77
  on power
    critique of community power debate, 1, 14,
        15, 17
    three-dimensional model, 101
    two faces of power, 14–16, 17, 93–4, 97, 99,
        101
  publications by, 15, 90
Barbalet, J., 23, 111, 112–13, 140, 152, 153, 157,
    218, 232
Barnes, B., 127, 142, 143, 210, 211, 213, 230
Bauman, Z., 8, 9, 36, 38, 43, 47, 48, 150, 259,
    272, 289, 305, 319–20
  on disciplinary and sovereign power, 163,
      166–7, 177–8, 180, 182

Bearden, M., 283
Beck, U., 297, 307
Behavioural Science (Dahl), 66
behaviouralism, 12, 13, 52, 54, 56, 101, 126, 192
  and intentionality, 77, 78
  modified, 90
  see also Dahl, R.
Belgium, 274
Bennett, J., 313
Bentham, J., 183
Benton, T., 98, 106–109, 124–5, 130, 136, 158,
  197
  critique of Lukes, 17–18
Berger, P. L., 150, 194
Berlin, I., 54
Bernstein, B., 246
Berti, M., 30, 282, 284
Betts, K., 113
Bhaskar, R., 27, 128, 129
bias, mobilization of, 15–16, 87, 89, 153
Biggart, N. W., 200, 221
bio-power, 165–6
Black, M., 57
Black Death, 183, 242, 251, 252, 253
Black Panthers, 16
Blalock, H., 68
Bleicher, J., 116, 149
Bocock, R., 121, 169, 193
Boden, D., 112
Bolsonaro, J.M., 284, 306
Boreham, P., 238
Bourdieu, P., 24, 206
bourgeoisie, 124, 174, 261, 264, 267, 269, 271,
  273
  class, 269, 270
  commercial, 268
  European, 269
  ideology, 171
  national societies, 264, 270
  political claims, 269
  social order, 186
Bradshaw, A., 105, 108, 109
Braverman, H., 178, 241
Brexit, 176
Brenner, R., 268
Bridgman, P., 126
Broström, A., 274, 276
bubonic plague *see* Black Death
Buddhism, 305
Burawoy, M., 205, 232
bureaucracy, 59, 146, 257, 266
  classical model, 263
  dysfunction of, 246
  ideal types, 263, 279
  permanent, 260

public, 264
rule of, 263
Burrell, G., 103
Butler, J., 20

Calás, M., 208
Callinicos, A., 139, 153, 154, 157
Callon, M., 7, 26, 27, 34, 39, 44, 48–9, 212–13,
  214, 215
Campbell, N., 314
Canada, 274
Cantrell, L., 271
capabilities, 134, 135
capacity concept, 20
Capital (Marx), 171, 190, 277
capitalism, 2, 10, 48, 110, 183, 194, 204–205,
  229, 264, 276, 278, 284, 303, 314
  and class power, 115–16
  crisis of, 285
  hypercapitalism, 303
  industrial capitalism, 183, 270, 277, 313
  industrialization, 182, 185, 270–1
  modern, 246
  print, 272
  twentieth-century, 290
  Western, 285, 290
  see also bourgeoisie; working classes
Carchedi, G., 205, 206
Carroll, G., 235
causal powers, 131, 159, 197, 273
Causal Powers (Harré and Madden), 27
causality, 5, 93, 100
  classical conception of, 6, 7, 97
  contemporary approaches, 52–3
  Dahl's model of event causation, 14, 68
  effects and causes, 53
  Hobbes' causal conception of power, 4, 5, 7,
    48, 51–5
  Humean assumptions, 58, 95
  individual, 121
  metaphors, 51, 58
  and realism, 98, 136
  social, 220–1
centralized states, 259–64
Centre de Sociologie de l'Innovation, Paris, 213
Chamberlain, C.W., 10
Chernobyl nuclear reactor meltdown (1986),
  309–310
Child, J., 242
China
  as an autocracy, 298
  Belt and Road strategy, 294
  Communist Party of China (CCP), 30
  and COVID-19 pandemic, 30, 284, 298
  exports, 298

and Global Financial Crisis, 285
ideological hegemony, 290
influence in the Pacific, 293–4
nationalism, 293
as a post-communist capitalist state, 290, 293
potential Taiwan invasion, 293
and Russia, 293, 295–7
sanctions against, 293
Sinopharm vaccine, 284
Tiananmen Square protests (1989), 30
and the US, 205
Chirot, D., 286
Christianity, 108, 174, 178, 179, 250, 291–2, 305
    Church of Rome, 180
    Church tutelage, 278
circuits of power, 26–9, 98, 197–248, 290, 311, 318
    constituting in modernity, 249–80
    and COVID-19 pandemic, 30, 297–8
    and episodic agency concept of power, 27, 28, 29, 320
    facilitative power, 23–4, 28, 241–2
    mechanisms of power, 200–203
    model, 249–50
    power in organizations, 199–200
    and social integration, 27, 29, 232–47
    and system integration, 27, 28, 29, 229, 232–47, 323
    taxation, 254, 256, 257, 259, 262, 277
    see also social integration; system integration
circulatory media, 21, 59, 140, 143, 194, 260
    and Parsons, 143–4
Cistercian monasteries, 179
cities, 73, 93, 119, 284
citizenship, 22, 206, 272, 274–7
civil privatism, 172
civil society, 22, 155, 170, 228, 269, 272, 275
    and centralized states, 263, 264
    institutions of, 169
    life outside, 37, 47–8, 141
    practices, 193–4
    weak, 268
Clawson, D., 185
Clegg, S.R., 2, 15, 22, 115, 155, 187, 199, 200, 208, 279, 286, 294, 303
    on disciplinary and sovereign power, 184, 185
    on episodic agency power, 223, 225
    on organization and agency, 203, 204, 207
    publications by, 1, 3, 4, 19, 27, 95–6, 219
    on social and system integration, 232, 238, 239, 241, 246
clientelism, 262
climate crisis, 281, 282, 284–5, 297, 307–310

anthropocentric change, 307
compulsory national superannuation policies, 317
and COVID-19 pandemic, 316
emissions, 314
flooding, 307
global warming, 308
natural disasters, 312
paradox of, 282, 284
scientists, 308, 312
see also fossil fuels
Clinton, H. 70
clockwork metaphor, 6, 8, 9
Cloward, R.A., 73, 75
coercive elite, 25, 286
coercive power, 22, 296
coercive pressure, 236
coercive state, 170
Cohen, J., 23
Cohen, M.D., 214, 237
Cohen, P., 148
Cold War, 288
Coleman, J., 29, 225
Collinson, D., 145, 157
Communist Party of China (CCP), 30
community
    imagined, 36
    and organicism, 51–2
    political, 16, 42, 47, 51–2
    see also community power debate; community power elite
community power debate, 1, 3, 16, 17, 52, 58
    Atlanta study (1953), 60–1, 62, 64
    power and agency in, 11–13
    reputational methodology, 6–7, 60
community power elite, 60–2
competition, 29, 72, 119, 230, 248, 265, 269, 273
    competitive elites, 246
    interest group, 114
    internal, 270
    market, 244, 289
    military, 267
    pure, 244
The Condition of the Working Class in England (Engels), 171
conflict, 42, 87, 114, 122, 145–7, 294
    class, 115, 117, 275
    conditions of, 275
    of interests, 89
    observable, 101
    overt, 217–18
    and power, 141, 148
    theories, 148
    of values, 90
    zero-sum, 240

Connell, R.W., 3, 173, 175, 276
Connolly, W.E., 35, 37, 103, 125
consensus theory, 145
consistency criterion, 136
constraint(s), 6, 21, 105, 131, 154, 155, 175,
    191, 234, 275, 294
  of authority, 113
  internal, 111
  Marxian, 121
  material, 190
  and motives, 156
  on others, 155, 210
  of power, 110
  structural, 111, 112, 149, 156–7
  technical, 236
  upon human agency, 151
consumption, 47, 113, 173, 176, 253, 257, 315,
    320
contingency theory, strategic, 209
contract(s)/contractual law
  contractual and non-contractual documents,
    1–2, 141
  employment contracts, 85, 205, 208
  Hobbes' framework, 39, 40
  internal contracts, 270
  organizations and agency, contractual
    relation, 203, 204
  and overall labour market structure, 155
  social contract, 39, 43–4
  subcontracting, 181, 202, 305
contradiction, 86, 245, 248
conventionalism, 17, 98, 126, 128–30, 137
  see also positivism; realism
counterfactual, the, 107
Counter-Reformation, the, 279
courtly life, 4, 268
courtly society, 47, 261, 263, 264, 268
Cousins, M., 163
COVID-19 pandemic, 4, 242, 297–307, 316
  and Africa, 306
  and China, 30, 284, 298
  and circuits of power, 30, 297–8
  and dispositional power, 31, 299–301, 303,
    307
  economic policy, 305–306
  exclusion zones, 299
  as exogenous environmental contingency,
    299–300
  hand washing, 302
  lockdowns, 31, 284, 301
  organizing of daily life, 298–9
  paradox of, 282, 284
  and state failure, 306
  as state of exception, 31, 297, 298, 299–300
  vaccines, 281, 284, 302, 306–307

video conferencing, 301
  working from home, 301
  zero-COVID policy, China, 298
creative destruction, 289
Crenson, M.A., 93, 128
Crimean invasion (2014), 282
'Critique of the Pluralist Model, A' (Newton), 71
'Critique of the Ruling Elite Model, A' (Dahl), 71
Cromwell, O., 260, 279
Crozier, M., 244, 246
cultural capital, 206
Cunha, M.P., 22, 30, 282
Cutler, A., 172
Cyert, R., 237
Czechoslovakia
  April 1968 Action Programme, 286
  normalization, 287
  Prague Spring (1968), repression by Red
    Army, 287

Dahl, R., 5, 6, 17, 51, 54, 55, 88, 94, 100, 166, 221
  critique of ruling elite model, 52–3, 62,
    68–71, 75
  event causation model, 14, 68
  methodological challenge to contemporary
    elitism, 11, 62–8
  Modern Political Analysis, 56–7
  positivism of, 97, 98, 125
  on power
    community power debate, 11, 12
    concept/definition, 6–7, 66, 67
    model, 13, 77, 78, 80–1, 99, 101, 110, 135
    New Haven, analysis of power in *see* New
      Haven, Dahl's analysis of power in
    and scientific orthodoxies, 97
    as something which may or may not be
      actualized, 94
    stories, 78, 80, 82
  publications by, 14, 65, 66, 71, 74
  see also episodic agency concept of power
Dallmayr, F., 153
Daudi, P., 165
Davidson, A., 169
Dawe, A., 35
decision-making, 22, 49, 210, 263
  collective, 197
  Dahl's focus on, 6–7
  political, 284
  strategic, 22
  see also non-decision-making
Delacroix, J., 235
democracy, 3, 59, 60, 107, 229, 271, 284, 292
  American, 12, 52, 72, 75, 205
  classical, 31
  deliberative, 23

formal, 172
ideal, 11, 59, 69
liberal, 31, 123, 205, 291, 294, 296
market, 205, 289
paradox in, 284
political, 47, 289
social, 205, 318
Denniss, R., 317
Derrida, J., 160, 161, 187
determinism, 27, 149, 153
  normative, 142
  structural, 109, 112
  'superstructural,' 109
deviance, 174
Dews, P., 163, 218
DiMaggio, P., 186, 234–8, 241
dimensions of power, 97–138
  class-hegemonic *see three-dimensional model below*
  conventionalism, 17, 98, 128–30
  empiricist epistemology, 17
  four-fold schema, 19
  fourth-dimensional model, 19
  hegemony, 18
  and interests, 17
  introduction of 'dimensions' into power analysis, 17
  and language, 20–3
  one-dimensional model, 28, 29, 34, 101, 125, 127, 137, 156, 218
  positivist epistemology, 17
  radical view *see under* Lukes, S.
  realism, 17–18
  three-dimensional model, 3, 16–20, 22, 99–101, 102f, 135, 136
    and episodic power, 110
    evaluating, 113–14
    Gaventa on, 120
    and interests, 101–103, 109, 112
    modification proposal by Benton, 106
    and moral relativism, 97
    problems with, 17, 28
    and social class, 118
    Whitt on, 119–20
  two-dimensional model, 22, 136
  see also Lukes, S.
disciplinary power
  Bauman on, 182, 184
  as a circuit of power, 216
  and dominant ideology, 25–6
  and elitism, 47
  Foucault on, 25, 26, 48, 156, 165, 166, 177, 183, 184–6, 228, 240, 241
  mechanisms, 180
  medieval, 180

new forms, 178, 183, 184, 186, 195, 245
nineteenth-century, 216, 243
practices of, 47, 201, 202, 207, 212
  new, 163, 164, 183
and sovereign power, 176–87, 215–16
stabilized, 187
surveillance, 201
'time-discipline,' 185
Discipline and Punish (Foucault), 3, 163, 176–7
The Discourses (Machiavelli), 42, 45
discrimination, 205
discursive analysis, 26, 189
discursive formulation, 205, 220
discursive framework, 36, 43, 191
discursive power, 85, 162
discursive practices, 9, 22, 161–3, 187, 191
disempowerment, 224, 245, 304
  of agents, 233, 240, 242, 244, 247
disintegration
  and dominant myths, 285–7
  by reform, 287–9
  and resistance, 239–40
dispositional power
  and COVID-19 pandemic, 31, 299–301, 303, 307
  defining, 6
  and episodic power, 17, 94, 95, 99, 100, 219
  and facilitative power, 28, 221, 223, 224, 247
  as 'power to,' 100
  and subordination, 21
  see also circuits of power; episodic agency concept of power; facilitative power; power; state power
distributive justice, 311
Domhoff, W.G., 71
dominant ideology, 137, 168, 169
  categories, 3
  and circuits of power, 28
  collectivist organizations sharing, 21
  conceptual overextension of sovereign power into, 169–76
  and disciplinary power, 25–6
  hegemony problem, 18
  and paradox of emancipation, 108
domination, 2, 3, 30, 34, 84, 94, 114, 115, 124, 173, 206, 223, 225, 228, 240, 244, 246, 247
  class, 114, 115–16, 170, 172, 206
  economic, 205, 207
  loci of, 207–208
  and power, 84, 113, 219
  and rules, 224, 229, 236, 239
  structural properties of, 152, 157
  structure of, 21, 155

and subordination, 152, 208
  Weberian, 94
  see also elites and elitism
Donaldson, L., 200
Dow, G., 239
Doyal, L., 125, 127, 219
Dreyfus, H., 163
duality of structure, 139, 148–57
Duby, G., 181
Dunkerley, D., 155, 187, 199, 200, 207, 279, 303
  on disciplinary and sovereign power, 184, 185
  on organization and agency, 203, 204
  on social and system integration, 232, 241, 246
Durkheim, E., 3, 37, 140, 141, 203, 212, 294, 304
Dyson, D., 262, 275

Eco, U., 179
ecological considerations
  competitive pressures, 216, 240, 250, 279
  destruction, 309
  disasters, 278
  ecological Keyesianism, 307
  ecotax, 315
  futures, 316
  network of planetary processes, 309
  relationality, 308
economic theory, 21, 244
ecotaxation (ecotax), 314, 315, 318
Edwards, R., 185, 241
Ehnmark, A., 45
Eldridge, J.E.T., 186
Elias, N., 47, 261
elites and elitism, 11, 46, 47, 52, 114, 115, 285
  aristocratic elites, 25
  business elites, 88
  circulation of elites, 59
  classical, 52, 58–60
  coercive elites, 25, 286
  community power elite, 60–2
  competitive elites, 246
  contemporary
    and classical elitism, 52, 58
    Dahl's methodological challenge to, 11, 62–8
    and Marxism, 58
    permeability, 25
  courtly elites, 36
  feudal elites, 25
  local elites, 288
  national elites, 25
  old elites, 25
  and pluralism, 53, 65, 86
  putative elites, 64
  ruling elites, 59, 60, 270

Dahl's critique of, 52–3, 62, 68–71, 75
  direct tests of hypothesis, 69, 70
  hypothetical, 70
  identifying, 61
  putative, 70
  stable, 61
  unified, 70
  theory, 58, 59
  see also bourgeoisie; domination
Elitism (Higley and Field), 52
Elliot, G., 173
embodiment, 56, 186, 201, 206, 211, 263
  embodied identities, 206
Emmet, D., 83
Emmison, M., 239
empiricism, 97, 114, 125–8
  classical, 126
  empiricist epistemology, 15, 17
  and positivism, 114, 125, 129
  see also experimental method/experimentalists; science
empowerment, 21–2, 224, 233, 240, 241, 244, 245, 247
enablement, 151, 152, 155, 157, 201
  structural, 156
Engels, F., 170, 171
England, 36, 43, 179, 254, 258–60
  'capitalist revolution,' 194
  civil war, 266, 267
  defeat of landed gentry in, 267
  feudalism *see* feudalism
  as first industrial nation, 266
  landed gentry, defeat of, 267
  occupied, 181
  political development, 266
  seventeenth-century, 174
  textile industry, 265
  see also United Kingdom
English Works (Hobbes), 53
enrolment
  power of, 301
  processes of, 214
  sociology of, 213
  see also translation
episodic agency concept of power, 16, 166, 167, 169, 197, 199, 221–7, 299
  and circuits of power, 27, 28, 29, 320
  and dispositional power, 17, 94, 95, 99, 100, 219
  and organization field, 250
  as 'power over,' 100
  and power *per se*, 100
  and three-dimensional power, 110
  see also circuits of power; dispositional power; facilitative power; power

epistemology
  empiricist, 15, 17
  and interests, 125–30
  positivist conception of, 17, 126
  and radical view of power, 17, 97
  and realism, 98, 136
  relativism, 161
essentialism, 121, 188–9, 193
essentially contested concept, notion of power
  as, 6, 100, 140, 247
ethics, 19, 33, 43, 109, 192, 194, 308, 311, 313
  and dimensions of power, 134, 139
ethnographic research, 43, 213
ethnomethodology, 1, 3, 27, 148
Etzioni, A., 200
eugenics, 164
Eurasian Economic Union, 292
Evans, P.B., 266
event causation model, 14, 68
exhaustiveness criterion, 136
exogenous environmental contingency
  climate change, 318
  and COVID-19 pandemic, 299–300
  responsibilities and power, 314–15
experimental method/experimentalists, 129,
  132, 226
  see also empiricism; science

facilitative power, 23–4, 28, 240, 241–2
  and dispositional power, 28, 221, 223, 224,
    247
  Parsons on, 144, 146
  see also circuits of power; dispositional power;
    episodic agency concept of power; power
fair exchange, 225
false consciousness, 10, 18, 47, 91, 137, 190
Featherstone, M., 149
feminism, 21, 22, 159, 162, 164, 275
Ferraresi, F., 262
feudalism, 163, 174, 180, 181, 182, 183
  agrarian production, 252
  feudal elites, 25
  and peasantry, 253–4, 266
  property relations, 252
  urbanism as a feudal nodal point, 250–9
Field, L., 52
field(s) of force, 28, 29, 77, 99, 164, 169, 217,
  221, 228, 269, 278, 279, 321
  metaphorical continuities, 54, 57
  modern constitutional nation state, 273, 274
  nodal points, 256, 257
  social and system integration, 233–4, 241
  see also organization field
Fleming, P., 19
Florence, Italy, 10, 43–4, 213

Flybvjerg, B., 304
Follett, M. P., 21
Fordism, 186
formal power, 11
fossil fuels, 22, 285, 295, 309, 310
  burning of, 307, 318
  carbon-intensive fossil fuel-based industry, 316
  extraction of, 310
  fossil fuel-based economy, 317
  hegemony, 22
  see also climate crisis
Foucault, M., 9, 11, 20, 34, 156, 168, 184–5,
    191, 192, 193, 218, 247, 259, 277, 300, 301
  on disciplinary power, 25, 26, 48, 156, 165,
    166, 177, 183, 184–6, 228, 240, 241
  and post-structuralism, 4, 26, 160–3
  on power, 3–4
    disciplinary, 25–6, 48
    non-zero-sum conception of power, 23–4
    paradoxes of *see* paradoxes
  publications by, 3, 9, 163, 176–7
  on sexuality, 165
  urban nodal points, 252
Fox, A., 204
Fox-Piven, F., 73, 75
France, 7, 179, 258, 263, 266, 272, 273
  absolutism, 259, 260, 262
  ancien régime, 268
  aristocracy, 268
  Constituent Assembly, 269
  eighteenth-century, 261
  see also absolutism
Frankel, B., 249
Frankfurt School, 171
Frederick William I of Prussia, 263, 279
free association principle, 213
Freeman, J., 234, 235, 243
Freire, P., 120
Frey, F. W., 15, 90, 91–2, 93
Friedland, R., 110
Friedman, A.L., 241
Friedman, M., 244
Friedrich, C.J., 87, 89, 90
Fukushima Daiichi nuclear accident (2011), 310
Fukuyama, F., 289
functionalism, 140, 145, 146, 148, 149
  neo-functionalism, 24
functionaries, 263

Galileo, 53
Gallie, W.B., 100
games, 42, 83–5, 211, 268
  concepts, 14
  language, 49, 161, 219, 289, 311–13
  moves in, 49–50, 83, 84

power, 244
pure, 219
rules of the game, 14, 37, 43, 83, 84, 87, 90,
    92, 204, 210, 219, 220, 230, 253, 274
of skill or chance, 219
social, 86, 219, 220
Gane, M., 149, 163
Garfinkel, H., 1, 21, 191, 204, 211
Garson, D., 120
Gaventa, J.P., 18, 114–25
publications by, 119
Gellner, E., 47, 167, 270
gemeinschaft, 47, 216, 270, 275
gender considerations, 20, 73, 86, 123, 161,
    206–208, 302
feminism, 21, 22, 164
post-feminism, 13
sexual etiquette at cocktail party rule, 13, 85,
    159–60, 220
subjectivity, 162
see also women
generalized symmetry, 213
Geras, N., 189
Gergen, K.J., 31
The German Ideology (Marx and Engels), 170, 171
Germany, 59, 174, 295, 310, 316
of Bismarck, 237
Gerschenkron, N., 267–8
Gibson, Q., 94
Giddens, A., 23, 121, 144, 145–7, 160, 180, 228,
    255, 258, 276, 314
critique of Parsons, 24, 140, 147
duality of structure, 148–57
publications by, 3, 96, 140
Girdwood, J., 202
Global Financial Crisis (GFC), 285, 289, 290
Global Resources Dividend (GRD), 315–16
global warming, 308
Goffman, E., 22, 32n2, 206, 216
Gorbachev, M., 287, 288
governmentality, 249
Gramsci, A., 3, 4, 9, 108, 116, 123, 137, 165,
    168–9, 176, 186
on hegemony, 170–1
organizational outflanking, 228, 229
publications by, 171
and sovereign power, 172, 174
green energy, 295–6, 307
Greenwood, R., 226
Gross, D., 149
Guttman, H., 186

Habermas, J., 24, 98, 123, 124, 140, 154, 172,
    173, 194, 232, 285
critical theory, 108

and ideal speech situation, 104–105
on Parsons, 143–5
publications by, 103
Hall, J. A., 248, 250, 251, 252,
    259, 261
Hall, S., 189–90
Hamilton, C. V., 16
Hamilton, G.G., 200, 221
Hamilton, J. J., 8
Hannan, M.T., 234, 235, 243
Hardy, C., 19, 286
Harré, R., 5, 27, 100, 130, 131, 132, 133–4,
    197, 247
Harris, R., 125, 127, 219
Harvey, D., 204
Haugaard, M., 19–20, 32n1, 318n2
Hayek, F. von, 54
Heath, A., 208
Hegel, G.W.F., 259
hegemony, 3, 10, 18, 22, 28, 115, 137, 168, 170,
    195, 283, 290
class-hegemonic dimension of power
    see dimensions of power
Gramsci on, 169, 170–1
hegemonic order/power, 18, 41
and interests, 114–25
post-structural, 187–91
theory, 175–6
as a war of manoeuvre, 165
see also power, hegemonic
Hegemony and Socialist Strategy (Laclau and
    Mouffe), 26
hermeneutics, 150, 153, 156
Hern, A., 301
Hesse, M.B., 57
heteronomy, 104
Hickson, D.J., 8, 209
Higgins, W., 45
Higley, J., 52
Hindess, B., 110, 121–4, 135, 157, 191, 207,
    218, 224, 239
Hinduism, 305
Hinings, C.R., 8, 209
Hirsch, F., 206
Hirst, P.Q., 149
history of the present, 29–31, 281–318
actants, effects of, 310–13
climate crisis, 307–310
COVID-19 pandemic, 297–307
disintegration
    and dominant myths, 285–7
    by reform, 287–9
integration, consequences of, 289–94
solidarities, 294–7, 302, 307
HIV/AIDS, 242

Hobbes, T., 6, 10, 11, 16, 33–7, 48, 51, 53, 54, 57, 100, 141, 157, 166, 197
  causal conception of power, 4, 5, 7, 48, 51–5, 77
  choice and its conception extension, 39–41
  contrasted with Machiavelli, 5, 7–9, 41–5
  mechanicalism of, 52–4
  metaphors of, 46–8
    clockwork metaphor, 6, 8
  myth, 37–9, 42, 52
  on sovereignty, 36, 39–40, 46, 48
  on state of nature, 38, 39, 83
  see also Leviathan (Hobbes)
Hobsbawm, E.J., 186
Hoffman, A.J., 310–11
Holton, R. J., 24, 146, 182, 233, 250, 257, 258, 264, 265
Hopkins, P., 3
Hoy, D. C., 219
humanism, 56
  Dutch, 258
  radical, 103
  theoretical, 121
Hume, D. I., 5, 51, 53, 55, 57, 58, 95, 130, 156
Hunter, F., 11, 12, 60–2, 68
  criticism of, 64–5
Hussain, A., 163
hypercapitalism, 303
hyper-inflation, 292, 293

Ibarra, H., 304
ideal speech situation, 103–106, 123, 124, 144, 152
  see also Habermas, J.; language
identity, 20, 24, 39, 68, 107, 108, 124, 125, 161, 178, 191, 198, 206, 290, 311
  embodied identities, 206
  female, 208
  fixed and true, 188
  identity politics, 291
  individual, 289–90
  loci of, 270
  markers of, 208, 270
  mistaken, 156
  patriarchal, 291
  personal, 238
  religious, 291
  social, 205, 207, 269, 271, 291, 296
ideology, 18, 133, 171, 172, 290
  dominant see dominant ideology
  and hegemony, 25, 123, 169
  and Marxism, 125, 290
  nature of, 109
  post-structuralist conception of, 125, 157, 188
  traditional conceptions, 125, 157
'Ideology and Ideological State Apparatuses' (Althusser), 173

Imagined Communities (Anderson), 237, 270
imagined community, 36
indexicality, 1, 2, 191, 204, 210–11, 212
individualism, 12, 31, 56, 109, 290
industrial capitalism, 183, 270, 277, 313
industrialization, capitalist, 182, 185, 270–1
instantiation, 142, 144, 153–7, 239
institutional racism, 16
integration
  consequences for West and East, 289–94
  see also social integration; system integration
intentionality
  class, assumption of, 115
  liberal faith in, 54
  mechanical continuities, 56
  and power, 13–14, 77–96
    paradoxes of, 7
    Russell on, 83–4
  and rules, 220–1
interests, 17, 22, 73, 108, 113, 122, 137, 148, 191, 205
  collective, 239
  constellations of, 84
  and epistemology, 125–30
  and hegemony, 114–25
  Marxian conceptions, 114
  objective, 109, 121, 137, 138
  real
    and circuits of power, 28
    and different preferences, 105–106, 107
    and elite, 22
    and possibility of knowledge about, 106
    problems with, 114
    three-dimensional model, 98
  and three-dimensional power, 101–103
interpreters, 210
  legislator/interpreter distinction, 8–11
intersectionality, 3
intrinsic nature/constitution, 132–4
Ireland, 273
Irving, T.H., 276
Isaac, J.C., 57, 136
Islam, 305
isomorphism, 126, 243, 245
  coercive, 267–8
  cultural, 47
  institutional, 29, 186, 216, 234, 235, 237, 241, 267
  mimetic, 261, 267, 279
  mimetic interest, 238
  normative, 237
  rules of practice, 238
  sources, 241
  see also institutionalism

Jamal, A., 22
Japan, 225, 237, 267, 268
Jelinek, M., 208
Jennings, P.D., 310–11
Jessop, B., 110, 249
Johnson, B., 298
Johnson, T., 238

Kant, I., 103, 104
Kantianism, 98, 103, 104, 113
Kaplan, A., 54, 81, 100
Katznelson, I., 54
Ketcham, R., 237
Kieser, A., 178, 185, 200
King, M. L., 15
King, R., 266
kleptocracy, 283, 288
  oligarchic, 291
Knights, D., 125, 139, 145, 157, 241
knowledge, 2, 5, 31, 61, 280
  absence of, 230
  existing, 128, 197
  factual, 43
  hypothetical, 130
  intrinsic, 133
  medical, 162
  objective/true, 36, 37
  origins of, 173
  partial, limited or insufficient, 152, 153
  and power, 8, 15, 44, 45, 162, 163, 202, 211,
      212, 217, 228, 292, 295, 297
  practical, 163
  public, 129
  and realism, 128
  rules of the game, 83, 86
  scientific, 43, 77, 78, 125, 126, 129, 215
  social construction of, 17, 129
  tacit, 78, 82–3
  technical, 201
  theoretical, 128, 129
Knowledge and Human Interests (Habermas), 103
Kornberger, M., 23
Korpi, W., 239
Kostera, M., 286
Kreckel, R., 238
Kristeva, J., 160
Kroker, A., 24, 143
Kuhn, T.S., 37, 126
Kula, W., 254
Kurnyshova, Y., 282, 283
Kurzweil, E., 163

labour markets, 24, 225, 238
labour process debate, 26
Lacan, J., 160, 283

Laclau, E., 9, 11, 111, 187–91, 192–3, 194–5,
    214
  publications by, 26
Landes, D., 185
Landrum, N.E., 315
language, 126, 129, 151, 160, 190, 203, 220,
    296
  centrality of, 198
  of civilized people, 62
  common, 271
  consensus formation in, 145
  dialogues of, 104
  and dimensions of power, 20–3
  diversity of, 270
  games, 49, 161, 219, 289, 310–13
  national, 264, 274
  nationalism, 288
  ordinary, 20, 161, 198
  policy, 292
  and power, 161
  private, 153
  shared community of, 104–105
  and social action, 104
  structuralist theorists, 161
  transparency of, 105, 198
  unified, 274
Laslett, P., 185, 251, 252
Lasswell, H.D., 54, 81, 100
Latour, B., 26, 27, 39, 48–9, 212–13
Law, J., 27, 209, 213, 214, 255, 259
Lawson, S., 271
Layder, D., 23, 111, 112, 139, 140, 149, 150,
    152, 153, 154, 155, 157
legislators, 36, 272
  intellectual, 38
  legislator/interpreter distinction, 8–11
  scientific, 37
legitimation, 38, 118, 124, 144, 299, 319, 320
  competitive bases, 245
  crisis, 172, 297
  institutionalized, 147
  purpose of, 171
Leviathan (Hobbes), 4, 6, 8, 10, 38–9, 52, 167,
    212, 249
liability of newness thesis, 234, 242
liberalism
  agency, classical liberal conceptions of, 56
  classical, 58
  economic, 141, 205
  liberal democracy, 31, 123, 205, 291, 294, 296
  political, 53
Littler, C.R., 185, 241
Locke, J., 51, 53, 55, 56, 57, 83, 166, 219
Lockwood, D., 28, 157, 228, 232, 233, 241,
    281–2

Lodge, P., 213
Louis XIV, King of France (Sun King), 279
Luckmann, T., 150
Luhmann, N., 288
Lukes, S., 4, 6, 13, 15, 23, 41, 93, 108, 137, 139, 147, 150, 157, 166, 168, 175, 176, 192, 193, 195
  Benton's critique of, 17–18
  on different perspectives and real interests, 105–106
  dimensional model *see* dimensions of power
  epistemological position, 97–8
  model of power and structure, 109–114
  publications by, 95
  radical view of power, 10, 17, 18, 28, 41, 48, 97, 98, 101–102, 105, 106, 109, 138, 191
  book on (1974) *see Power: A Radical View* (Lukes)

Macfarlane, A., 194, 259
Machiavelli, N., 164–5, 208, 211, 212, 214
  contrasted with Hobbes, 5, 7–9, 41–5
  and Florence, 10, 43–4, 213
  loss of Chancery position, 8–9
  metaphors of, 46–8
  military analogies of, 8
  publications by, 4, 9, 42, 44–5, 184
  and realism, 42
  on strategies of power, 7, 9
  treatment by the Medici, 8, 10
  unique contributions of, 33
  see also neo-Machiavellians
McHoul, A., 153
MacIntyre, A., 56
MacKenzie, D., 213
McLennan, G., 149
Macpherson, C.B., 38
Madden, E. H., 5, 27, 100, 131, 132, 133–4, 197, 247
Malcolm, N., 9
Mann, M., 29, 180, 194, 223, 227–32, 235, 255, 287
March, J.G., 237
Marcuse, H., 108, 137, 171
Marglin, S., 178, 185, 241, 303
markets, 113, 208, 252, 259, 279, 286, 304, 306, 319
  atypical, 225
  financial, 289, 293
  global capital, 295
  imperfect, 226
  labour, 24, 225, 238
  open, 183
  and states, 264–72
  transformation, 278

marriage, 251
Marshall, G., 186
Martindale, D., 51
Marx, K., 3, 10, 45, 108, 140, 170, 171, 185, 186, 190, 203, 205, 241
  publications by, 170, 171, 190, 277
Marxism, 7, 10, 26, 106, 110, 112, 137, 168, 191, 192, 193
  absolutism of, 109, 113
  classical, 188, 189
  humanist, 108
  neo-Marxian theory, 118, 119
  structural, 128, 138
  Western, 40–1, 297
  see also bourgeoisie
Matheson, C., 200
Mayo, E., 201
mechanics/mechanicalism, 12, 44, 57, 110, 150, 166
  and causality, 100
  classical, 97, 99
  criticisms of mechanicalism, 99–100
  engineering, 54
  Galilean, 53
  of Hobbes, 52–4
  and metaphors, 8, 56, 99, 195, 196
    clockwork, 9, 54
  relation with power, 10, 34, 39, 43, 99, 168, 196
mechanisms of power, 200–203
media, absence of pluralism in, 290
Meisel, J. H., 60, 69
membership categorization devices (MCDs), 215, 234
memorialization, institutional, 30
meritocracy principle, 206, 290
meta-narratives, 36
metaphors of/for power
  causal, 51, 58
  circulatory *see* circulatory media
  clockwork, 6, 8, 9
  continuities, 53–8
    between classical and modern agency views, 56–7
  Hobbes' choice of, 39
  metaphors, 46–8
  and myth, 42
  paradoxes of power, 7
  and symbols, 48
  see also analogies
methodology
  contemporary elitism, Dahl's methodological challenge to, 11, 62–8
  ethnomethodology, 1, 3
  measurement of power, 6, 11, 13, 68
  methodological looseness, 11

methodological protocols, 12
reputational, 6–7, 60
Meyer, J., 216, 234, 235, 246, 285
Meyer, M.W., 246
Michels, R., 59
Miliband, R., 71, 109, 110
  publications by, 173
Mill, J.S., 108
Mills, C.W., 11, 12, 30–1, 60, 67–9, 156
  publications by, 62
mimetic pressure, 236, 237
minority groups, 22
Minson, J., 169, 184, 187
Mintzberg, H., publications by, 199, 200
mobilization of bias, 15–16, 87, 89, 153
The Modern World System (Wallerstein), 265
modernism/modernity, 8, 10, 26, 33, 34, 212
  alternative foundations of modern analysis,
    33–50
  liquid modernity, 290, 305
  metaphors, 46–8
  modern constitutional nation state, 272–8
  and power, 4, 5, 43, 100
    constituting circuits of, 249–80
    paradoxes of, 7–8
    problematic of, 50
Modi, N.D., 284, 298
Molotch, H., 112
monarchy, 38–9, 166–7, 256, 257
monasteries, 178–9, 180, 185
  Cistercian, 179
  mediaeval, 179
  new, 179
money, 16, 74, 193, 194, 262, 292, 305
  discretionary, 237
  and duality of structure, 140, 141, 145
  and Parsons, 143–4
  supply of, 21
  and two faces of power, 88, 89
  and urbanism, 253, 254, 256
Moore, B., 266, 308
moral absolutism, 213
moral philosophy, 103–104
moral relativism, 107, 109, 111–14, 119, 126,
    127, 137, 146, 157, 168, 197, 213
  ideal speech situations, 103–106
  see also relativism
Morgan, G., 103
Morriss, P., 87
Mosca, G., 58–9
Mouffe, C., 9, 11, 187–91, 192–3, 194–5, 214
  publications by, 26
Mouzelis, N., 189
Muraro, L., 22–3
museums, 30

myth
  dominant, 285–7
  functions of, 38
  of Hobbes, 37–9, 42, 52
  of Machiavelli, 41–2
  of order, 9, 10
  of origins, 9
  rational, 285

Nagel, E., 57
nationalism, 237, 288
  anti-Russian, 292
  China, 293
  Hindu, 305
  Russian, 282, 291
  sub-nationalism, 272
  Ukrainian, 282
nationality, 273
NATO, 283
naturalism, 156
Nellor, D.C.L., 246
neo-classical economics, 222
neo-functionalism, 24
neoliberalism, 289, 290, 300, 305
neo-Machiavellians, 11
Netherlands, Dutch humanism, 258
New Haven, Dahl's analysis of power in, 12–16,
    65, 66, 73, 74, 88, 89, 91
New Rules of Sociological Method (Giddens), 3,
    96, 140
New Zealand, 271, 298
Newton, K., 12, 16, 53, 89, 99
  critique of pluralism, 71–5
Nietzsche, F., 165
nodal points, 26, 28, 191, 193–5, 232,
    245, 248, 269, 308
  of discourse, 194, 214
  feudal, urbanism as, 250–9
  limited, 290
  urban, 256
non-decision-making, 13–16, 22, 87, 91, 126,
    166, 169
  abstention form of non-decisions, 91
non-participation, 92
non-zero-sum conception of power, 23–4
normative determinism, 142
norms, 142
North, D., 182
Norway, data protection regulators, 301
nostalgia, 146

obedience, 200, 210
  organizational, 27
obligatory passage points, 26–7, 195, 217, 221,
    247, 249, 250, 257

reformation of power, 214, 215
  social and system integration, 233, 234, 241,
    242, 244, 245
O'Brien, P., 264
Occupy movement, 290
O'Connor, J., 285
Oesterich, G., 258
O'Farrell, C., 162
Offe, C., 238
oligarchy, 47, 59, 68, 227, 295
Olsen, J.P., 237
O'Neill, J., 182, 184–7, 293, 302
ontology
  of agency, 55
  ontological constitution, 19–20
  'ontologically autarchic' entities/individuals,
    11, 12, 54, 56
  social, 25
Oppenheim, F.E., 81
order
  hegemonic, 41
  imagined, 36
  institutional, 232
  myth of, 9, 10
  necessity of, 10
  political, 47
organicism, 51–2
organization field, 209, 229, 234–7, 239,
    249–50, 257, 262, 266, 270–2, 274, 276,
    278, 279
  coherent, 232
  densely populated, 269
  fixed, 267
  new, 259
  stable, 232, 273
  urban, 257
  see also field(s) of force
organization studies, 2, 4, 8
organizational outflanking, 29, 217, 235, 239,
    250, 255, 267, 273, 278, 279
  of resistance, 227–34
organizations
  and agency, 27–8, 203–208
  'cogs, wheels and springs' (clockwork
    metaphor), 6, 8
  collectivist, 21, 29
  and elite theory, 59
  employees, empowering of, 21–2
  empowerment, seeking, 21–2
  formal structure, 202
  impact on earth systems, 309
  learning, 284
  and obedience, 27
  power in, 199–200
  and privilege, 27

resources, 29, 214
sociology of, 27, 212
and strategy, 7
theory, 195, 198, 202, 204, 235, 243
Orwell, G., 64
O'Sullivan, L., 19

Pakistan flooding, 307
Panopticon, 183, 184, 301
paradoxes
  climate crisis, 282, 284
  continuity and discontinuity, 5
  COVID-19 pandemic, 282, 284
  democracy, 284
  of emancipation, 98, 106–109, 160
  of power, 5–8, 19, 22, 211, 283–4
  scholarship, 283
  theory, 282
  Ukraine war, 282, 285
Pareto, V., 11, 59, 60
Parkin, F., 175, 232, 245, 246
Parry, G., 87
Parsons, T., 6, 24, 59, 105, 140–3, 147, 194, 240,
    247
  critique by Giddens, 24, 140, 147
  neo-functionalism of, 24
  and Pareto, 59
  on power, 6, 140–3
    dominant ideology and disciplinary power,
      25–6
    power to, 20–1
  publications by, 141
  socialization theory, 173
Pateman, C., 119–20
patriarchy
  defining, 159–60
  domination, 206
  households, 180
  identity, 291
  patriarchal power, 159–60
  reproduction, 164
  structures, 160
patrimonialism/patrimonial power, 180, 181,
    256–7, 260
Perrow, C., 310
Pfeffer, J., 8, 200
phenomenology, 3, 148, 150, 222
'Phenomenology and Formal Organizations'
    (Clegg), 27
The Philosophy of Manufactures (Ure), 228
Pigouvian taxes, 315
Piketty, T., 285, 290
plague see Black Death
planetary boundary (PB) framework, 308, 309
pluralism, 12, 46, 58, 192

criticisms of elitist studies, 86
and elitism, 53, 65
Newton's critique of, 71–5, 99
and three-dimensional power, 114, 115, 117
Pogge, T.W., 315
Poggi, G., 181–2, 186, 250, 252, 256–62,
    269–72, 274, 276, 278
political community, 16, 42, 47, 51–2, 67
political liberalism, 53
political-military-industrial complex (Mills), 69
Politics and Vision (Wolin), 4
Polsby, N., 65, 67
polyarchy, 12
Popper, K., 57, 111
populism, 285, 306
positional goods, 206
positivism, 1, 17, 126, 156
    of Dahl, 97, 98, 125
    and empiricism, 114
    limits of, 99–100
post-feminism, 13
post-Marxism, 10
postmodernism, 319–21
    power theory, 9, 10
post-structuralism, 10, 11, 26, 133, 158, 160–3,
    191, 193, 214, 232, 248
    circuits of power, 26, 28
    feminist, 198
    ideology, 125, 157
    post-structural hegemony, 187–91
    see also structuralism
Poulantzas, N., 71, 109–111
Powell, W., 186, 234–8, 241
power, 2, 5, 31, 162, 280
    and agency, 6, 11–13, 23–5, 51, 53, 77, 95,
        111
    architectonic, 38–9
    and authority, 144, 147, 199, 211–12
    bio-power, 165–6
    as a capacity, 94
    capillary, 274
    capstone, 259, 279
    causal conception *see* causal conception of
        power; causality; Hobbes, T.
    circuits of *see* circuits of power
    as a circulatory medium, 21, 59
    class, 115
    class-dialectic, 118
    comparison of radical conceptions, 191–3
    dimensions of *see* dimensions of power
    disciplinary *see* disciplinary power
    discursive, 85, 162
    dispositional conception of, 94
    to do something (power to), 20–3, 100, 134
    and domination, 84, 113, 219

economy of, 28
embodiment of, 186
episodic conception of *see* episodic power
essentially contested concept, 6, 100, 140,
    247
facilitative conception of, 23–4, 28, 144, 146,
    240, 241–2
formal, 11, 63
hegemonic, 18
illegitimate, 199
individualist conception of, 12
institutional sources, 163
instrumentality of, 42–3
and intentionality, 13–14, 77–96
    Russell on, 83–4
and knowledge *see* knowledge
latent conflicts, 87
legitimate, 199
measurement of, 6, 11, 13, 68
mechanical conceptions of, 10, 12, 34, 39, 43,
    168, 196
mechanisms of, 200–203
and modernity *see under* modernism/
    modernity
networks of, 180, 261
nodal points of *see* nodal points
obligatory passage points of, 26–7, 195, 214,
    215, 217, 221, 233, 234, 241, 242, 244,
    245, 247, 249, 250, 257
organizational specificity of, 143–4
in organizations, 199–200
organized, 45
over others (power over), 20, 22, 100, 134,
    146, 147, 224
paradoxes *see* paradoxes
Parsons' theory of, 6, 140–3
    dominant ideology and disciplinary power,
        25–6
    power to, 20–1
patriarchal, 159–60
patrimonial, 180, 181, 256–7, 260
per se, 100
practical centre of, 48
primitive notion of, 63
radical view of *see under* Lukes, S.
realist interpretation of, 130, 133–4, 199, 248
recurrent episodes, 286
reformation of, 212–16
relational, 89
representation of, 40, 51, 168, 217, 241,
    248, 319
reputational, 12
reputational approach to, 61, 62, 65
reserve notion of, 40
and resistance, 217–18

and resources, 91, 114, 116
and responsibilities, 313–18
and rules, 219–21
seductive, 192
sharing of (power with), 20–3
and social control, 85
sociology of, 17, 30, 215
soft, 22
sovereign *see* sovereign power; sovereignty
state *see* state power
stories of
   elaborating, 80–3
   example one, 78–9
   example two, 79–80, 82
   example three, 80, 82
strategic conception of, 8, 33, 50
and structure, 138, 197–8, 212
   Lukes' model of, 109–114
   structural face of power, 14–16
and surveillance, 201–203
symbolic, 146
tacit conception of, 5
theory of, 62–3
   and circuits of power, 28
   legislators and interpreters, 8–11
   and Parsons, 6, 140–3
traditional vs newly acquired, 83–4
transformation, 166, 209, 241
'trinitarian' conceptions of, 96
two faces of, 14–16, 17, 93–4, 97, 99, 101
unitary meaning of, 49–50
and wealth, 225
zero-sum conception of, 5, 141
see also hegemony
Power, Rule and Domination (Clegg), 1, 95–6, 219
Power: A Radical View (Lukes), 3, 16–17, 67, 95,
   101, 103
Power and Organizations (Clegg), 19
Power and Poverty (Bachrach and Baratz),
   15, 90
Power and Powerlessness (Gaventa), 119
The Power Elite (Mills), 62
precautionary principle, 306
precision, 11, 15
Presthus, R., 12
The Prince (Machiavelli), 4, 9, 44–5, 184
princely absolutism, 279
print capitalism, 272
probability, 64
problematization, 214
procedural justice, 311
property rights, 143, 183
Prussia, 257, 258, 263, 267, 268
Przeworski, A., 175, 176, 228
'public' law, 260, 263

Pusey, M., 104
Putin, V., 282, 283, 289, 291, 292, 316

quantitative easing, 21

Rabinow, P., 163
racism, institutional, 16
radical humanism, 103
'Radical Revisions' (Clegg), 4
radical view of power *see under* Lukes, S.
ratiocination, 201
rationality, 2, 55, 199, 319, 320
   legal, 223
   legal norms, 19
   limited, 278
   models of organizations, 246
   modes of, 19, 24, 207, 246–7
   organizational, 202
   substantive, 221, 222
Rawls, J., 103–104
Reagan, R., 66, 70
realism, 17–18, 27, 106, 125, 127, 137, 203,
   213, 292
   and agency, 135
   causal mechanisms, 98, 136
   and conventionalism, 98, 128, 129
   epistemologies, 98, 136
   implicit, 98
   and knowledge, 128
   of Machiavelli, 42
   realist interpretation of power, 130, 133–4,
      199, 248
   regularity principle, critique, 197
   in science, 27, 312
reason
   age of, 8
   and agency, 55
   architectonic, 45
   communicative, 105
   intrinsic, 172
   judicial, 104
   moral, 36
   practical, 36
   scientific, 306
reductionism, 28, 121
reform, 269
   agrarian, 268
   disintegration by, 287–9
   educational, 290
   endogenous, 287
   failure to reform organized circuits of power,
      312
   institutional, 287
   political, 267
   radical democratic, 23

Reformation, the, 259, 279
reformation of power, 212–16
regulatory principle, 99, 197
relations of meaning and membership, 216, 224, 228, 232–5, 245, 260, 261, 270–3, 277, 300
   fixing of rules, 28, 233–5, 249
relativism, 127, 161, 162, 187
   see also moral relativism
religious faith, 291–2, 305
Renaissance, 261
renunciation form of non-decisions, 91
representation, 6, 73, 99, 146, 161, 162, 193, 196, 223, 224, 229, 256, 275, 279
   causal, 55
   centres of, 279
   collective, 239
   forms, 168
   of interest, 191, 204, 205, 239, 278
   literal, 202
   means of, 37
   of a natural state, 38
   oversimplified, 38
   pluralist, 65
   of power, 40, 51, 65, 168, 217, 241, 248, 319
   systems of, 190
   technologies of, 309
   territorial, 266
   of women, 275
reproduction, 70, 73, 129, 151, 154, 161–3, 170, 209, 219, 234, 243, 248
   capitalist, 204
   of central principle of organization, 207
   of class structure, 121
   constitutive, 82
   of content, 154
   of economic system, 173
   of a given mode of production, 121
   hegemonic, 249
   of human agency, 124, 149, 244
   ideological, 47
   and innovation, 29
   of labour-power, 173
   of patriarchy, 164
   of power, 28
   social, 281
   of species, 165
   structural, 152, 235
   of substantive rationality, 221
   and transformation, 235, 248
reputational approach to power, 61, 62, 65
reserve powers, 40
resistance, 203
   and circuits of power, 27, 28
   dialectic of, 199
   disintegration attempt through, 239–40

   and obedience, 27
   organizational outflanking, 227–34
   and power, 217–18
resources, 42, 46, 66, 93, 99, 151, 152, 207, 214
   access to, 67, 121, 226
   community, 65
   concept, 67
   of elites, 25
   extrinsic, 134, 135
   mobilizing, 134, 135
   open to exploitation, 63
   organizational, 29, 214
   political, 74
   and power, 91, 114, 116
   private interests, 73
   and rules, 151–3
   sanctioning, 143
   sequestering, 36
   state-building, 36
   unclear, 153
   underlying, 140
   urban, 89
   wealth, 74
responses, 11
revisionism, 189, 190
Rex, J., 148
Rhinehart, L., 151
Ricardo, D., 190
risk society, 307
Rogers, M., 216
Roman Empire, 251, 259, 260
Rothschild-Whitt, J., 21
routines, 91, 211
Rowan, B., 216, 234, 235, 246, 285
Rueschemeyer, D., 185
rule of law, 170, 273, 274
rules, 24, 29, 81, 82, 86, 94, 108, 129, 133, 178, 179, 202, 221
   anticipated reaction, rule of, 87, 89
   democratic, 69
   and domination, 223, 224, 229, 236
   explicit or implicit, 142, 239
   fixing relations of meaning and membership, 28, 233–5, 249
   of the game *see* rules of the game
   informal, 27
   and intentionality, 220–1
   legal bureaucratic, 19
   and power, 219–21
   of practice, 211, 235–8, 244
     fixing, 246, 248
   procedural, 38
   and resources, 151–3
   sexual etiquette at cocktail party, 13, 85, 159–60, 220

social, 85, 220
unclear, 240
rules of the game, 14, 37, 43, 83, 84, 87, 90, 92,
    204, 210, 219, 220, 230, 253, 274
ruling class, 47, 48, 59, 109–110, 170, 173, 192,
    270
    see also elitism
ruling elites, 59, 60, 270
    Dahl's critique of, 52–3, 62, 68–71, 75
    direct tests of hypothesis, 69, 70
    hypothetical, 70
    identifying, 61
    putative, 70
    stable, 61
    unified, 70
Russell, B., 13, 83–4
Russia
    authoritarian kleptocracy, 296
    autocracy, 285, 288, 296, 298, 316
    central bank, 293
    and China, 293, 295–7
    Christianity in, 291–2
    Crimean invasion (2014), 282
    cyber interference by, 282
    cyber-factories, 293
    EU importing of energy resources from, 294
    imperialism, 282, 289
    interregnum, 289
    invading forces, 283
    nationalism, 282, 291
    oligarchs, 283, 288
    Orthodox Church, 297
    poisoning and murder of dissidents, 282
    as a post-communist capitalist state, 290, 293
    sanctions against, 296
    system integration, 295
    and Ukraine war, 19, 281–3, 285, 293, 296, 317
Ryle, G., 94

Sacks, H., 215, 234
sanction of immemorial custom, 84
Santos, B.S., 300, 303, 304, 305
Sartre, J.-P., 111
Saunders, P., 15, 88, 105, 125, 219–20
Saussure, F. de, 161, 203
Sayer, D., 136
Schattschneider, E.E., 3, 15, 87
Schutz, A., 150, 151
science, 9, 37, 57, 59, 77, 126, 127, 129, 130,
    136, 195
    deductive-nomological view of, 57
    natural, 77, 126, 226
    realism in, 27, 312
    on regulatory principle, 99
    scientific orthodoxies, 97

spurious, 125
    see also social sciences
'Science as a Vocation' (Weber), 209
Sciulli, D., 144, 147
Scott, J., 286
Scott, W.R., 25
sensemaking, 27
sex offences, 156
sexual etiquette at cocktail party rule, 13, 85,
    159–60, 220
sexuality, 165
Shah, S.Q.A., 22
Silverman, D., 204, 243
Simon, H. A., 47
Simpson, A.V., 284
Singh, J. V., 235, 241
Skocpol, T., 266, 267, 269
Smart, B., 163
Smelser, N., 185
Smircich, L. 208
Smith, A., 45, 53, 141, 190
Smith, B., 291
Smith, D., 149
Smith, M., 309
Snyder, T., 282, 289
social class
    action, class-based, 119, 121
    ascendant class, 174
    and capitalism, 48, 110
    class consciousness, 121, 122
    class power, 115
    dominant classes, 115–16, 170
    and intentionality, 115
    intra-capitalist class difference, 119
    intra-class conflicts, 117, 118
    reproduction of class structure, 121
    and state power, 109–110
    in the US, 73, 205
    and women, 303
    working classes *see* working classes
    see also bourgeoisie
social democracy, 205, 318
social integration, 28, 157, 216, 232–6, 241,
    242, 244–7
    changes in, 314
    circuits of, 221, 228, 233, 234, 246, 248, 291,
        292, 296–7, 311
    and circuits of power, 27, 29, 232–47
    and climate crisis, 311, 316
    COP meetings, 316
    and COVID-19 pandemic, 306
    defining, 281
    diminished, 285
    dynamic nature, 289
    and faith, 292

forms, 311
 meritocracy principle, 290
 new forms, 295–6
 normative environment of, 317
 obligatory passage points of, 318
 redefining, 288
 social and policy aspects, 285
 and solidarities, 296
 and system integration, 281, 289, 317
 and Ukraine war, 281, 283
 and the USSR, 286–8
 where central, 297
 see also circuits of power; system integration
social sciences, 5, 30, 37, 51, 79, 130, 136, 139, 201
 'normal power' of, 221–7
 see also science
socialism, 21, 92, 193, 277, 287
 state, 246, 278
socialization, 20, 24
 theory, 173
sociology
 British circles, 15
 of enrolment, 213
 founding fathers, 3
 historical materials, 250
 modern, 262
 of organizations, 27, 212
 of power, 17, 30, 215
 radically subjectivist, 150
 of science, 195
 social questions, 277
 of translation, 26, 215
solidarities, 123, 270
 contemporary mechanical and organic,
   294*t*, 296
 history of the present, 294–7, 302, 307
 social integration, new forms, 295–6
Soloway, S. M., 73
solutionism, state-oriented, 313–14
Solzhenitsyn, A., 291
sovereign power, 165, 166, 167, 176, 192
 and disciplinary power, 176–87, 215–16
 dissolution of conception, 176–87
 execution of concept, 195
 over-extension of, 168–9
   conceptual overextension into dominant
     ideology, 169–76
sovereignty, 5, 9, 18, 258
 Communist Party, USSR, 286
 Hobbes on, 36, 39–40, 46, 48
 of power, 165
 Ukraine war seen as an attack on, 281
space
 civic, 292
 conceptual, 247

condensed, 120
 confined, 302
 control-through-space, 182
 free, 182
 individual, 201
 institutional, 24
 management of, 303
 in mass media, 74
 moral, 147
 niche, 216, 250, 255
 operating, 314
 social, 76
 sovereign, 281
 space probe story, 79
 stable, 194
 suburban, 16, 88, 89
 and time, 54, 144, 151, 153, 154, 211, 225,
   227, 250
 time-space distantiation, 180
 urban, 16, 89, 257
Spain, 273
Spencer, H., 8
Spicer, A., 19, 242
Spufford, F., 285, 288
Sri Lanka, 294, 295
St Brieuc Bay, Brest, 27, 215
standing conditions, 58, 93, 94, 130–5, 197
 access to means and resources, 226
 appropriate, 107, 131, 136, 157, 187, 226
 of extrinsic resources, 135
 fixing, 259, 266
 new set of, 245
 organization of, 224, 226
 reconfiguring, 307
Stasi, Democratic Republic, 286
state, the
 authority, 259, 267, 273
 centralized, 259–64
 coercive, 170
 ethnically homogenous, 31
 European system, 273
 and markets, 264–72
 modern constitutional nation state, 272–8
 one party states, 31
 power of *see* state power
 powerlessness of, 31
 running, 263–4
 socialism, 246, 278
 theory, 115
The State in Capitalist Society (Miliband), 71, 173
state of nature, 38, 39, 83
state power, 6, 9, 43, 170, 279, 286
 and class, 109–110
 and draconian powers, 31
 and hegemony, 170

unified, 8, 36
see also dispositional power
Stavrakakis, Y., 283
Steffen, W., 309
Stern, P. M., 74, 75
Stiglitz, J., 285, 290
Stinchcombe, A., 234, 235, 278
Stone, K., 185
strategic agency, 208–212
strategies of power, 7, 9
Strauss, A., 211
structural constraint, 111, 112, 149, 156–7
structural determinism, 109, 112
structural selectivity, 112
structuralism, 111, 148, 149
    Marxist, 128, 187
    super-structuralism, 19, 116
    see also post-structuralism; structural
        constraint; structural determinism;
        structural selectivity; structuration
        theory; structure
structuration theory, 23, 139, 148, 149, 152,
    153, 154, 157
structure
    and agency, 18, 23–5, 86–94, 157, 168
    deep, 2
    duality of, 139, 148–57
    form of life, 2
    and power, 23–5, 138, 197–8, 212
        Lukes' model of, 109–114
        structural face of power, 14–16
    surface, 2
The Structure of Social Action (Parsons), 141
Studies in Ethnomethodology (Garfinkel), 1
subjectivity, 18, 19, 104, 107, 122, 125, 133,
    154, 160, 161, 183, 198, 275, 320
    acts of, 39
    female, 162
    gendered, 162
    individual, 151
    normal, 162
    ruling, 178
    sovereign, 39, 40, 52
    supreme, 48
subordination, 21, 108, 199, 297
    and domination, 152, 208
    peasantry, 267
    strategic, 209
suffragettes, 275
superannuation policies, national, 317
super-structuralism, 19, 116
surveillance, 201
sustainability, 311, 312, 318
    civil, 316
    co-evolutionary, 315

corporate, 314
environmental, 313
regenerative, 315
state-sponsored, 318
weak, 315
Sweden, 205, 257, 276
symbolic legitimacy, 140–1
system integration
    and agency, 314
    changes in, 233, 234
    circuits of, 221, 233, 244, 245–8, 285–6, 290,
        293, 296–7, 311, 312
    and circuits of power, 27, 28, 29, 229, 232–47,
        323
    climate crisis, 312
    contradiction, 245, 297
    and COVID-19 pandemic, 306–307
    defining, 281
    disintegrative effects, 294
    disruption in Europe, 296
    dynamic, 244
    East and West, 294, 295
    and facilitative power, 235–6
    and fields of force, 233
    fragile, 316
    global, 303
    green economy, 317
    liquid modernity, 290
    macro level, 301
    market fictions, 289
    market-led, 297
    and networks, 290, 294, 311
    new models, 317
    obligatory passage points of, 318
    organizational forms, 216
    and organizational outflanking, 229
    policy aspects, 285
    political instability and transformation,
        241–2
    reconfiguring, 296
    redefining, 288
    rupture of, 297
    and Russia/Ukraine, 281, 286, 288, 295, 296, 297
    and social integration, 229, 232, 233, 249,
        281, 285, 291, 297
    sources of resources for power, 248
    subordinate to social, 297
    sustainability, 318
    and techniques of discipline and production,
        232–3, 241, 312
    undermining, 297
    unstable, 241–2, 244
    see also circuits of power; social integration
'System of Politics' (Mintzberg), 199, 200
systematicity, 222

taxation
  circuits of power, 254, 256, 257, 259, 262, 277
  ecotaxation (ecotax), 314, 315, 318
  high, 266
  increase in, 267
  Pigouvian taxes, 315
  public, 260
  revenues, 260
  sites of, 279
Taylor, L., 156, 220
techniques of discipline and production, 28, 246, 255
Tegnell, A., 300
teleology, 289
terrorism, 239
Thatcher, M., 175, 317
The Archaeology of Knowledge (Foucault), 3, 9
theoretical absolutism, 168
theorizing, 1, 2, 24, 50, 137, 167
  academic, 165
  power, 49, 50, 165
  practical, 16, 19
  as a 'twin dialogue,' 128
The Theory of Power and Organization (Clegg), 3
Therborn, G., 125, 187, 229, 267, 277
Thomas, D.S., 283
Thomas, R., 182
Thompson, E. P., 36, 185, 186, 228
Thompson, J.D., 199
Tiananmen Square protests, China (1989), 30
time
  clockwork metaphor, 6, 8, 9
  and space, 53, 54, 144, 151, 153, 154, 211, 225, 227, 250
  temporal contexts of action, 221
  time-space distantiation, 180
TNCs (transnational corporations), 313, 315
Torfing, J., 23
total institutions, 32n2
transaction cost theory, 203
transformation, 129, 161, 190, 219, 229, 231, 239
  balance of power, 278
  capitalist industrialization, 270
  and circuits of power, 318
  dialectical, 284
  field structure, 209
  markets, 278
  modern constitutional nation state, 273
  personal, 22, 108
  political, 22
  power, 166, 209, 241
  and reproduction, 235, 248
  social, 250, 281
  and strain, 29, 241

of war, 255
  see also reproduction
translation, 48–9
  moments in process, 215
  sociology of, 26, 215
  see also enrolment
Treaty of Waitangi, 271, 272
trickle-down economics, 290
Trump, D., 70, 176, 284, 285, 298, 306
'Truth and Power' (Foucault), 176–7
Turner, B.S., 24, 146, 147, 228, 275

Ukraine, war in, 19, 281–3, 285, 293, 295, 296
  and circuits of social integration, 292
  and climate crisis, 317
  gas prices, driving up, 317
  labelled as a 'special military operation,' 281
  paradox of, 282, 285
  and social integration, 281, 283
  and system integration, 281, 286, 288, 295–7
  Ukrainian elites, 283
  Western responses, 283
unintended influence, examples, 85
United Kingdom, 103, 316, 317, 320
  Brexit populism, 285, 306
  working classes, 175
  see also England
United States of America
  administrative entities, 16
  behavioural perspective on politics, 54
  and China, 205
  Christianity in, 291–2
  climate science, 306
  Dahl's challenge to contemporary elitism, 66
  democracy, 12, 52, 72, 75, 205
  federalism, 60–1
  founding fathers, 11
  hegemony, 283
  imperialism, 283
  individuals of colour, 92
  January 6 2021 insurrection, 291
  labour force, trade union membership, 205
  manufacturing firms, 208
  money, importance, 74
  political boundaries, 89
  political debate, 16
  political science community, 15, 52
  public transport, 117
  and social class, 73, 205
  solidarity, 294
  southern, 92
  taxing of profits, 315
  urban transit lobbying, California, 18
  voting in, 65–6, 69, 73, 74
  Watergate hearings, 112

universalism, 194
The Un-politics of Air Pollution (Crenson), 93
urbanism
   administrative areas, 76
   alliances, 257
   assemblies, 257
   centres, 253, 254
   development, 119
   employment, 254
   as a feudal nodal point, 250–9
   forms, 254
   growth, 254
   incomes, 253
   increase in urbanization, 182
   infrastructure, 304
   militia, 257
   nodes/nodal points, 252, 256
   organization field, 257
   political community boundaries, 89
   price commodities, 253
   redevelopment, 65, 89
   renewal, 91
   space, 16, 89, 257
   taxation, 257
   transit, 18, 119
   and war, 256
Ure, A., 228
Urry, J., 149
USSR (Soviet Union)
   Brezhnevite political–economic and
      socio-political orders, 287
   coercive elite, 286
   collapse of, 288, 292
   Communist Party, 285, 286, 288
   glasnost, 287, 288
   Gorbachev's policies, 66, 287
   perestroika, 288
   and social integration, 286–8
   social integration, 288
   state planning/system, 286, 288
   see also Russia

value, 13, 21
   central system of, 142, 174
   common, 174
   consensus, 115
   of control, 225
   defined, 225
   economic, 313
   empirical, 114
   exchange, 238
   heuristic, 202
   interests of, 124
   public, 23
   radical system of, 175

   subordinate system of, 175
   surplus, 303
   transcendent value-standpoint, 124
   ultimate, 240
   unit of, 227
   use, 286
van Iterson, A., 22
Varieties of Realism (Harré), 27
Versailles, 268
vocabulary of motives, 166, 220
voluntarism, 111, 149
voting, 12
   in Australia, 73
   impact of voters, 73–4
   powers of Senators, 65–6, 69, 74
   registration, 73
   in the US, 73
'vulgar economy,' 190
Vurdubakis, T., 241

Wagner Group, Russia, 19
Waitangi, Treaty of, 271, 272
Wall, G., 105
Wall, R., 185
Wall Street, 210
Wallerstein, I., 254, 259, 260, 263,
     264, 266
   publications by, 265
war, 164, 221, 228, 240, 273
   appeasement, 283
   civil, 36, 266, 267, 296
   conditions of, 275
   declaration of, 296
   defeat in, 267
   end to, 40, 167
   First World War, 303
   hegemony as a 'war of manoeuvre,' 165
   inter-war years, 303
   post-war, 12, 229, 237
   preparation for, 255, 282
   prisoner-of-war camps, 231
   purpose of, 282, 283
   siege-based techniques, 255
   transformation of, 255
   in Ukraine, 19, 281–3, 285, 293, 295,
     296, 317
   and urbanism, 256
   waging, 255, 279
   see also warfare
warfare, 194, 229, 251, 254, 256, 265, 267,
     275, 276
   see also war
Watergate hearings, 112
Watkins, J. N. W., 54
Wearmouth, R. F., 3, 186

Weber, M., 13, 26, 83, 105, 140, 163, 178, 185, 186, 199–202, 206, 212, 218, 223, 233, 246, 251, 252, 306, 318
  on domination, 84, 113, 155
  on power and intention, 13, 84, 94
  publications by, 209
  Weberian theory of action, 104
Weedon, C., 159–62, 164, 198
Weick, K.E., 27
welfare state, economic neoliberalism, 290
Werner, K. F., 252
Westney, D. E., 237
Whitt, J. A., 18, 114–25
Who Governs? (Dahl), 14, 65, 74
Wicha, M., 286
Wickham, G., 162, 163
Wiener, M., 173
Wiesenthal, H., 238
Wiesner, R., 313
Williamson, O. E., 203
Willmott, H., 125, 139, 157
Witte, G., 283
Wittgenstein, L., 1, 2, 153, 161, 211, 219
Wolfinger, R. E., 15, 90, 92, 114, 126, 167, 169, 176, 184
Wolin, S., 4, 35, 36, 44, 45
women, 61, 85, 164, 185, 272, 320
  interests, 123, 159, 160
  middle- and upper-classes, 303
  representation of, 275

  social role of, 159
  'Women who want to be Women' (interest group), 123
  working-class, 290, 303
  see also gender considerations
Wood, S., 242
Woolgar, S., 213
working classes, 72, 75, 123, 159, 169, 173, 275, 278, 290
  British, 175
  in capitalist society, 122, 171
  consciousness, 175
  contemporary, 176
  struggle of, 276
  traditional, 184
  in the US, 73
  women, 290, 303
  see also capitalism; social class; socialism
Wright, E. O., 22, 112, 122
Wrong, D. H., 13, 84–6, 90, 94, 99, 100, 159, 160, 217, 227

Xi Jinping, 298, 299

Young, R. C., 243

Žižek, S., 303
Zorina, A., 201
Zuboff, S., 300